# Books by John E. Mack

NIGHTMARES AND HUMAN CONFLICT

BORDERLINE STATES IN PSYCHIATRY
*(Edited by Dr. Mack)*

A PRINCE OF OUR DISORDER:
The Life of T. E. Lawrence

# A PRINCE OF OUR DISORDER

## The Life of T. E. Lawrence

Sketch of Lawrence made in 1919 by Augustus John. Gift of Lawrence
to J. W. Wright, manciple of All Souls College, Oxford, and presented
to the college by Wright's brother. Courtesy of the Warden and
Fellows of All Souls College, Oxford

John E. Mack

# A PRINCE OF
# OUR DISORDER

## The Life of T. E. Lawrence

WITH MAPS AND ILLUSTRATIONS

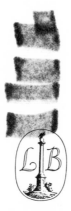

LITTLE, BROWN AND COMPANY
BOSTON – TORONTO

*Fourth Printing*

T 03/76

Acknowledgments of permission to reprint excerpted material appear
on page 538.

LIBRARY OF CONGRESS CATALOGING IN PUBLICATION DATA

Mack, John E      1929–
  A prince of our disorder.

  Bibliography: p.
  Includes index.
  1. Lawrence, Thomas Edward, 1888–1935. I. Title.
D568.4.L45M28   941.083′092′4 [B]   75-22481
ISBN 0-316-54232-6

*Designed by Janis Capone*

*Published simultaneously in Canada
by Little, Brown & Company (Canada) Limited*

PRINTED IN THE UNITED STATES OF AMERICA

To my father, Edward Mack

The reasonable man adapts himself to the world: the unreasonable one persists in trying to adapt the world to himself. Therefore all progress depends on the unreasonable man.

— George Bernard Shaw

If I have restored to the East some self-respect, a goal, ideals: if I have made the standard of rule of white over red more exigent, I have fitted those peoples in a degree for the new commonwealth in which the dominant races will forget their brute achievements, and white and red and yellow and brown and black will stand up together without side-glances in the service of the world.

— T. E. Lawrence

# Acknowledgments

The writing of this book has been a very personal undertaking. I have talked with many people who knew Lawrence and they have become an important part of the book. This is true not only because of information they provided, but also because they helped to re-create for me the times and places in which Lawrence lived. Through them I learned to appreciate the impact his personality could have on other people.

It is not possible to thank all those who have helped me through interviews and letters. Some I have omitted mentioning because I believe they would prefer to remain anonymous. Because of the timing of the writing, many of my informants died after the project began in 1964 and could not see this book. I am sorry they could not have had the latest word about their friend.

I wish to give special thanks to Mrs. Christine Longford and Mrs. Seton Pringle of Dublin, to Miss Lily Montgomery, and to Miss Fitzsimon and other villagers in Delvin, County Westmeath in Ireland. I am also grateful to the villagers of Tremadoc in Wales and the townspeople of Kirkcudbright in Scotland, to members of the Laurie family — Andrew, Molly and Janet — and to Lady Pansy Lamb. I wish also to express my thanks to A. H. G. Kerry, C. F. C. Beeson, Theo and Hilda Chaundy, Elsie Newcombe, Stewart Newcombe, Jr., Sir Basil Blackwell, William Hogarth, E. F. Hall, R. W. Bodey, James Fowle, W. O. Ault, Richard Brinkley, William Sargent, Robert Graves, Basil Liddell Hart, Fareedah El Akle, William Yale, Phillip Knightley, Colin Simpson, Lincoln Kirstein, L. H. Gilman, shaykhs and members of the Howeitat tribe of Jordan, my Bedouin guides R'faifan and Sabah, Lord Rennell of Rodd, Dermot Morrah, E. F. Jacob, Thomas Beaumont, Lowell Thomas, Philip Townshend-Somerville, Henry Williamson and Bertram Rota. I wish to thank especially

Professor Arnold Lawrence and his wife Barbara for their sustained help, understanding and tolerance.

I was particularly fortunate in having excellent consultation and help in the course of the research from Manfred Halpern, P. J. Vatikiotis, Irene Gendzier, Robert Wolff, Gregory Rochlin, Ray Hodgkins and Basil Kohler. Jack Ewalt, former chairman of the Department of Psychiatry at the Harvard Medical School, kept after me until the job was done. Help in Arabic translation has come from Basim Musallam, Wasmaa Chorbaji, Antoine Hallac and Andrawes Barghout. David Pollack was of great assistance in the transliteration of Arabic names. George Vaillant, Bennett Simon, Charles Hofling, and my mother, Ruth Mack, provided valuable critical readings of portions of the manuscript. I feel a particular debt of gratitude to Walter Langsam and L. Carl Brown for page-by-page reading of the manuscript, for their helpful suggestions, and for protecting me from such glaring errors as they were able to spot.

Others not only helped me with their ideas and knowledge, but also offered special friendship and companionship. I would include in this group, among others, Arabella and Charles Rivington, Jeremy Wilson, A. E. ("Jock") Chambers, Edward Nevins, Gladys Page, and many colleagues in the psychiatric and psychoanalytic communities. I am thankful to the staff of the Department of Psychiatry at the Cambridge Hospital and the Cambridge-Somerville Mental Health and Retardation Center, especially to Lee Macht and Robert Reid, for their support and for permitting me leave to complete the book. In a more personal vein I am grateful to my father, Edward Mack, for his ideas about Lawrence as a critic and to my wife, Sally, for her steady encouragement and support at times when the project was foundering.

I have been fortunate in having a great deal of help from directors and staff members of archive collections and libraries. I wish especially to thank Dennis Porter and his staff at the Bodleian Library, Oxford; Sarah Graham-Brown at St. Antony's College, Oxford; Carolyn Jakeman and other members of the staff of Houghton Library, Harvard; June Wilcox at the Huntington Library in Pasadena; and E. F. Jacob at All Souls College, Oxford. Jane Page offered valuable research assistance; Rosanne Kumins and Judith Risch were of great help in preparing the manuscript. I owe special thanks to my assistant, Patricia Carr, for her work on the manuscript and for seeing me through the throes of its preparation, and to Lilith Friedman who selflessly over a period of several years devoted her own time to the realization of this work. Finally, I wish to thank my editors, Llewellyn Howland and Jean Whitnack, for their unusual patience and care in the preparation of the book.

                                                                    J.E.M.

# Contents

Introduction      xvii

### PART ONE: Family Background and Childhood

| | | |
|---|---|---|
| 1 | Chapmans and Lawrences | 3 |
| 2 | Childhood and Adolescence | 18 |
| 3 | Lawrence and His Family: The Burden of Illegitimacy | 26 |

### PART TWO: Youth

| | | |
|---|---|---|
| | Introduction | 37 |
| 4 | Literary Influences | 41 |
| 5 | Crusader Castles | 48 |
| 6 | Lawrence at Jesus College, 1907–1910 | 56 |
| 7 | The First Trip to the Middle East, 1909 | 68 |
| 8 | Lawrence at Carchemish | 76 |
| 9 | The Epic Dream and the Fact of War | 99 |

### PART THREE: The War Years, 1914–1918

| | | |
|---|---|---|
| | Introduction | 111 |
| 10 | The Background of the Arab Revolt | 113 |
| 11 | Two Years in Cairo, 1914–1916 | 130 |
| 12 | The Course of the Arab Revolt | 147 |
| 13 | The Capture of Damascus | 166 |
| 14 | The Achievements of "Aurens" | 175 |
| 15 | The Question of Motivation | 187 |
| 16 | Lawrence the Enabler | 198 |
| 17 | The Conflict of Responsibility | 210 |
| 18 | The Heroic Legend and the Hero | 216 |
| 19 | The Shattering of the Dream | 226 |

PART FOUR: The Political Years, 1918–1922

Introduction     245
20   Arab Self-determination and Arab Unity     248
21   Leaving Damascus Behind     255
22   At the Paris Peace Conference     263
23   Return to England: London and All Souls     274
24   Lawrence and Churchill: The Political Settlements in the
    Middle East     297


PART FIVE: The Years in the Ranks, 1922–1935

25   The Service Years: An Overview     319
26   Ross: The First RAF Enlistment     332
27   The Years in the Tanks     340
28   Cranwell     355
29   India     362
30   Mount Batten     377
31   "Boats, Boats, Boats"     388
32   Retirement and Death     406


PART SIX: Further Dimensions

33   Intimacy, Sexuality and Penance     415
34   Lawrence Assayed     442


Appendix: Twenty-Seven Articles     463
Chapter Notes     471
Bibliography     529
Copyright Acknowledgments     539
Index     543

# Illustrations

Sketch of Lawrence by Augustus John, 1919        frontispiece

Between pages 132 and 133

South Hill

The Lawrence boys: T.E., Bob, Frank and Will

The Lawrence family home at 2 Polstead Road, Oxford

The City of Oxford High School, 1964

Lawrence at the City of Oxford High School

Photograph of Carcassonne by Lawrence

Ned's cottage in the garden

Brass rubbing of a medieval saint by Lawrence and W. O. Ault

Lawrence and his brothers during the Jesus College years

David George Hogarth

Charles Montagu Doughty

Sketch of Sahyun by Lawrence

Entrance to the citadel at Aleppo

Workmen at the Carchemish dig, 1912

The expedition house

Lawrence and Leonard Woolley with a Hittite slab

Dahoum

Lawrence during the desert campaigns

Lawrence with his bodyguards, 1917

Abdullah

Faisal

'Awdah abu-Tayyi

Photograph by Lawrence of children on a beach at Aqaba, 1917

Faisal's camp at Quweira, 1917

Portrait of General Allenby by Eric Kennington

Prisoners defile at Tafila, 1918

Between pages 420 and 421

British forces entering Damascus, 1918

The Damascus Town Hall

McBey portrait of Lawrence, 1918

Statuette of Lawrence by Lady Kennet

Lawrence, Sir Herbert Samuel and Abdullah at Amman, 1921

Queen Mary and Trenchard at St. Omer, 1917

First page of the 1922 (Oxford) edition of *Seven Pillars of Wisdom*

Lawrence's draft preface for Garnett's abridgment of *Seven Pillars of Wisdom*

Clouds Hill

Miranshah, India, 1928

Lawrence at Miranshah

Portrait of Lawrence by Howard Costa

Lawrence with friends in Devonshire

Lawrence at Plymouth, 1930

Inscription by Lawrence on the front page of *Child of the Deep* by Joan Lowell

RAF 200 leaving from Plymouth

The final page of the *Odyssey*

Lawrence and Basil Liddell Hart, 1933

Lawrence at Bridlington, 1934

Bust of Lawrence by Eric Kennington

# Maps

The Middle East at the Outbreak of World War I          left endpaper

The Middle East After the Treaty of Lausanne          right endpaper

Regions of the Middle East in which Lawrence Traveled, 1909–1914      71

The Sykes-Picot Agreement of 1916                                      124

The Battleground of the Desert Campaigns                               149

# Introduction

We have a natural fascination with individuals of extraordinary talent, achievement or power. We are drawn by their glamour and curious about the special abilities that make it permissible, indeed essential, for them to enact upon the public stage the hopes and dreams we all possess but fear or do not choose — or simply have no opportunity — to carry out ourselves.[1]

We follow with great interest the fortunes and decisions of persons in positions of leadership: Our self-regard rises and falls with their successes, vicissitudes or failures, and we second-guess the choices they make. For many of us the identification will continue — for some, more readily than before — if the leader's purpose deteriorates to the expression of personal, often destructive, impulses that are no longer associated with the constructive solution of human problems.

The destructive leader, and the eagerness of a large segment of the population to identify with him, comprise one of the central threats — if not the greatest threat — that faces human society. The power, or potential power, of such leaders in the contemporary world is awesome, and the public is acutely aware of this fact. There is perhaps an increasing unwillingness to entrust our well-being and our lives to individuals whose motives and characters we do not understand and whose ultimate purposes we are ignorant of. There is available in modern depth psychology, if used appropriately in conjunction with other disciplines of the social sciences and the humanities, an approach to the understanding of public figures that may help us to choose more rationally those we would wish to allow to govern us or at least to designate those to whom we would deny this privilege.

This book is the historical and psychological study of a public figure whose decisions and actions have affected, and continue to affect, the lives of millions of people.

It is historical in the sense that I have chosen to examine T. E. Lawrence's actions in the context of the history and politics of the West and the Middle East. As history, the study is limited by the restrictions of biography, which does not attempt, in its focus upon a single person, to provide a balanced or complete view of the events in which the subject played a part, however significant it may have been. Since the analysis must concentrate upon him, it cannot deal fully with all the forces — social, political, economic — that operate simultaneously in the production of historical change.

The study is psychological in the sense that I have chosen to seek an understanding of Lawrence as an individual, to show how one deeply and intensely motivated person affects events of historical importance and how they, in turn, affect him. Yet, though I draw on my training as a psychiatrist in discussing Lawrence, I do not claim a primacy for the psychological determinants of history. Accordingly, I find the term "psycho-historical" unsatisfactory in its implication that the psychological lies outside the historical and acts upon it. On the contrary, individual psychology operates within established, though shifting, historical contexts and becomes one of the many agents of historical change. And historical change depends for its realization upon the joining, through circumstance and chance, of private individual purpose with public or historical opportunity.

I must confess that in the beginning I sought to do a psychological study of Lawrence of the sort more familiar to those engaged in clinical work. I have long been affected by Lawrence's suffering and have found that I could readily identify with the personal elements from which it grew. His conflicts were familiar to me from psychiatry — since they derive from the usual human needs that confront the healthy and the troubled alike — and I attempted to understand them through the skills and methods I had been taught.

But as time went on, I found myself diverted by two dilemmas. First, no matter how fully I was able to "understand Lawrence" through the explication of his personal conflicts, the understanding added little to my appreciation of Lawrence's accomplishments as a man. From the psychological standpoint, although his struggles were interesting and compelling, they differed little from those of many other persons of his or our age and could therefore contribute little to the understanding of human psychology. Second, I found myself becoming steadily more interested in Lawrence's achievements than in his problems; or, stated more precisely, I became fascinated with how he was able to adapt his personal psychology to the historical realities that he came upon, or was able to surmount his personal conflicts in the accomplishment of valuable public services.

When I presented "psychological material" about Lawrence at conferences or meetings, my audience would inevitably offer interpretations about his psychopathology which, however accurate they may have been, left me always feeling that they had not seen Lawrence as I knew him to have been. In reading other psychological studies of historical figures I found myself becoming impatient with the failure of their authors to come to grips with the salient fact of unusual accomplishment, and kept registering the same objection that Lawrence himself had made when he commented upon a biographical essay about a famous British general: that the article "left out of him his greatness — an extraordinary fellow he was."[2]

I do not wish to imply that I do not think that individual purpose and psychology produce historical change. For I believe strongly that history is often the result of individual choice and motive, and of human responsibility, both individual and collective. I agree fully with Sir Isaiah Berlin's warning that "the invocation to historians to suppress even that minimal degree of moral or psychological evaluation which is necessarily involved in viewing human beings as creatures with purposes and motives (not merely as causal factors in the procession of events), seems . . . to rest upon a confusion of the aims and methods of the humane studies with those of natural science. It is one of the greatest and most destructive fallacies of the last 100 years."[3] And I believe with Sir Isaiah that individual human motive and responsibility are among the dominant forces of history and that the evaluation of these determinants is an essential part of the historian's task.

What I *am* stressing is that the personal psychology of a historical figure cannot be studied apart from the familial, social and cultural context in which he developed and functioned. At the same time, his actions and their public impact need to be looked at in terms of a dynamic interplay between his inner drives and purposes and a number of concurrent political, social and historical opportunities and realities. What is happening around him and to him of course plays upon his psychology and affects his actions, a process he may not completely aware of.

I believe that Lawrence's historical reputation has been damaged by the use (or misuse) of psychology to devalue his accomplishments, and by misguided efforts to explain complex decisions and behavior through simplistic explanations or psychological reductionism. Although Richard Aldington's biography, *Lawrence of Arabia: A Biographical Enquiry,* is the most flagrant example of the use of psychology for such denigrating purposes (psychology is not the only instrument of Aldington's devaluation), Lawrence has been the object of an enormous amount of psychologizing, much of it demeaning. Lawrence's candor about his deeper motivations and about the nature and impact of his psychosexual conflicts and traumata, which he offered for the purpose of achieving a fuller understanding of himself and thereby of helping others, has, paradoxically, further served to tarnish his reputation. His historical reputation has been hurt since his death by the vestiges of the same Victorian intolerance from which he suffered throughout his life.

Perhaps every biographer feels to a certain extent that his subject has been incompletely or poorly understood. Otherwise why should there be a need for another biography? I have certainly felt that this was true of Lawrence. Although I have attempted to give as thorough and objective an exposition of the historical evidence as possible in order to achieve a balanced view of the man, and to examine any personal reactions of my own which might lead to distortions of the data, I do not claim to be neutral to my subject. I unabashedly regard him as a great man and an important historical figure, and intend in the pages that follow to show how the evidence led to my opinion. But I have sought to suppress nothing that would lead to a contrary view.

Custom does not require that biographers justify or explain their choice of subject. Ordinarily, the freedom of the biographer to indulge whatever affinity or aversion exists between himself and his subject is taken for granted, and his biases or special intentions may or may not become evident as his book is read. But because this work on Lawrence is not, after all, the kind a psychiatrist usually undertakes, and is one that explores the psychology of a person no longer living, I feel constrained to add a word explaining why I chose to write of Lawrence. The reasons are more ordered in retrospect than they were as they evolved over the years I devoted to the research and writing.

I have long been fascinated by the relationship between the inner life — between dreams, hopes and visions — and action or activity in the "real" world. Perhaps because Freud and the other early psychoanalysts concentrated upon exploring new territories of the mind and the inner mental life of their patients, psychoanalytic research has not formulated a systematic theory of action. Yet the study of action or activity from the standpoint of behavior alone can hardly be adequate: all activity derives from inner drives or impulses, or at least from an interplay between outside influences and internal forces. Direct observations of children; the experience with adults who come to professional attention in the community through their actions; and the influences of the social and community psychiatry movements, which stress the need to obtain knowledge about the environments or "real worlds" in which patients live — all have furnished data about the relation between the inner mental life and action in the outside world. The biographical study of an individual "public" figure who characteristically lives out elements of his inner life in the public arena can, if data about his interior life are obtainable, provide yet another valuable source of information about the psychology of action.

Lawrence has proved to be an extraordinarily rich subject for such a study. Deeply introspective — a trait unusual in men who act forcefully in the outside world — he was driven by painful events he experienced in World War I and in the postwar period to probe his motives and to examine the relation between them and his public actions. Lawrence was highly gifted as a depth psychologist, and although he holds back even as he reveals, he has left in writings and in conversations others have remembered, a record of an intricate pattern of connections among the influences of his personal development, his feelings, his motives, and his actions. His individual psychology and mental life directly relate to the psychology of his followers and his age. The need to know and make known was highly developed in Lawrence and he applied this need to himself as he did to any matter that commanded his attention.

In addition, a particular currency attaches to Lawrence's life and work. Not long before these pages were written, a major war — the fourth in a quarter of a century — led to great loss of life among Arabs and Israelis. Political and economic strife among the peoples of the Middle East continue to threaten the world's peace and stability.

It was out of the defeat of the Ottoman Empire in World War I and the partitioning of it afterward that the present shape of Western Asia took form. Lawrence strongly influenced both the military outcome and the political aftermath. He powerfully and effectively encouraged Arab nationalistic hopes and dreams, and strove to diminish the political dominance of the Western powers in the Middle East before such a change was contemplated in the West. He hoped, too, that the Jewish people would provide leadership in the Middle East by sharing their greater economic and technological sophistication with the Arab people to the advantage of the whole region. It is a hope which, having seemed forlorn for more than twenty-five years, appears less odd or remote at the present time.

But, ultimately, my choice of Lawrence must be seen as a subjective one, deriving from my own predilections and psychological makeup. Lawrence's struggles have been consistently important and moving to me. I have found it easy, though at times disturbing, to identify with his hopes, his actions and his pain. He has enabled me, as he did so many others, to see possibilities that were not dreamed of before.

Several other important associations between individual psychology and public action ("psycho-historical" relationships) are examined in this book. They are less directly related to the *choice* of Lawrence as the subject than those I have already mentioned, but they are sharply illuminated by the example of his life and work. In brief, I am using the example of Lawrence as a paradigm in the discussion of these larger issues. The particular psycho-historical relationships embodied in his life and legend serve as an *approach* to problems which, by their very nature, are interdisciplinary or multidisciplinary. Part of the value of this work will be its applicability to the study of other public figures or historical materials.

There is the general question of the psychology of the individual (applicable to all of us in some degree) who lives out or tries to find solutions for his inner conflicts on the public stage. In addition to the study of the person himself (his family influences, early development and personal motivation), the relationship between his own drive or purpose and historical opportunity becomes of central importance. I have in mind the process whereby a person like Lawrence, with a particular set of personal needs, talents and abilities, finds an appropriate external medium or stage for their fulfillment.

There is an equally tantalizing reciprocal question to be raised: how do governments, peoples, or individuals functioning historically at a particular time find and use a person like Lawrence for their own purposes? The role of chance looms large in human history. Lawrence recognized this fact well in his own case. Near the end of his life he wrote to the poet C. Day Lewis, "As an historian by training I shouldn't like to think that accidental participation in this one war of the infinite series past and to come had made me put it bigly in the foreground of any but its victims."[4]

If one adds the dimension of time or "history," the social system gains further elements. In addition to his immediate relationships with contemporary employers or followers, a public figure may develop over time a lasting significance for another heterogeneous group, one that may be called the "audience of posterity." The life and work of a figure like Lawrence will take on new meaning for future "audiences" depending on what facts about his life, or interpretations of historical materials, are known to the societies or nations for which he has importance and which are themselves undergoing processes of economic, political and ideological change.

Finally, there is the relationship of the subject to his biographers and they to him (and I include in this group the radio and television broadcasters and filmmakers who present public figures, often deliberately distorted, to their audiences). One might call them the representors. The representors discover, rediscover, and even on occasion reinterpret the life and work of a historical figure when he takes on new meaning for them and when they in turn find responsive currents in a public for which the figure has assumed new or renewed meaning.

In the world of mass communication, where trends and fads emerge and disappear in weeks, the importance and meaning of historical figures for their appropriate audiences often shift with great rapidity. One might hypothesize two levels in the reciprocal relationship between a historical figure and his public: a superficial, commercially influenced view or interpretation which is subject to quite fickle contemporary trends; and a more lasting, stable view based on accumulated and accurate scholarship, which will, in the end, come to dominate. I believe, though, that this division will not prove to be entirely valid. It is quite possible that a commercially motivated view of a public figure, distorted but convincing — for example, the popular film *Lawrence of Arabia* — could be the lasting one in the public's mind, however inaccurate it may be from the factual standpoint. A hero may be seen as a scoundrel, and a rogue may be lionized for decades, if not for centuries, and there is no guarantee that, from the public standpoint, "the truth will out."

Beyond these broad considerations of the relation between the public figure and his public, Lawrence's life and example have provided an unusual opportunity to consider the specific psychology of the political leader or military commander and to examine a number of psychosocial issues related to the commander's activity. Lawrence's own epic narrative, *Seven Pillars of Wisdom,* was partly written "to show," as he phrased it, "how unlovely the back of a commander's mind must be."[5] As he assumed what seems to be such exaggerated responsibility for the lives of others, Lawrence invites us to reconsider the very nature of the leader's responsibility to society and to the individuals his actions affect. Because he was so troubled by the moral complexities of his part in the desert campaigns, and in the political settlements that followed the war, and was, to begin with, a man unusually concerned with ethical matters, Lawrence felt compelled to raise a number of questions about the morality of his own actions as a military commander.

They were and still are embarrassing questions, as they concern ultimately the right of one man to endanger other men's lives in a political or military cause. It is of the very nature of warfare that men are encouraged or forced by their leaders to follow political purposes they may not understand, or to take part in wars for whose ends they would not voluntarily have chosen to fight. Such psychosocial questions as the morality and responsibility of leadership are, of course, culturally and historically time-related. A particular leader who examines such questions from a different point of view or who assumes a unique kind of responsibility, may contribute through his personal example to shifting expectations and standards of leadership viewed not only from the political and strategic standpoint, but from the ethical and moral vantage as well.

Related to the issue of leadership or command is the question of heroism. The problem of heroism is in its fullest sense a uniquely psycho-historical matter. It depends upon a series of relationships involving the psychology of an individual (the hero); other individuals or followers who identify with him; the society (or societies) that defines its criteria for the heroic and its expectations for the hero; and, finally, the biographers, historians, journalists, dramatists or other mythmakers who create the narratives and legends from which examples of heroism are drawn. For a biographer who is interested not only in heroism as a psycho-historical problem, but in historical accuracy as well, there is the additional problem in treating a historical figure like Lawrence, around whom legends have developed, of distinguishing actuality from myth and legend. This is not to say that a figure who becomes a hero, even an epic one, cannot in fact have performed great deeds. Rather, the problem is that stories, myths and legends — often of the hero's own telling — surround and embellish the actual deeds, creating a particularly thorny problem for the biographer or historian who tries to tease them apart.

The criteria of heroism, like the expectations of leadership and command, evolve historically, although certain heroic values, such as individual courage and initiative, seem to be the most nearly absolute or the least time-bound. Lawrence is in many ways a transitional hero, standing as he does between the neo-medieval romantic heroes of the nineteenth century and the moral realists of the twentieth. Although there have been few studies of the family history or childhood development of persons who later become heroic figures, Lawrence's family background and early history seems to conform remarkably to what has been hypothesized about the childhood of the hero from the study of myths or the psychoanalysis of the hero fantasies of children who did not become heroes in reality.

And lastly, Lawrence possessed to a unique degree a quality I have called "the capacity of enabling." He enabled others to make use of abilities they had always possessed but, until their acquaintance with him, had failed to realize. The enabling ranged from helping an airman enjoy a day's work to encouraging a people and its leader to achieve a revolution they could not accomplish unaided. Enabling depends upon a unique kind of relationship between the enabler and the enabled. In some ways it resembles the relation between teacher and student, especially that between master and apprentice, which depends heavily on identification. But teaching is, in purpose, didactic: the teacher is often an active giver and the student a more or less passive recipient. Enabling is a more balanced or mutual activity, one in which individuals are helped to realize themselves. Enabling is closer to psychotherapy, but unlike psychotherapy it is not marked by the necessary element of psychopathology or psychological difficulty in the one enabled — only an initial lack of fulfillment or self-realization.

Surely one of the first responsibilities in biography is self-knowledge on the part of the writer. This does not mean that the work can be completely free of bias or distortion. But it does imply that the biographer will find it useful to examine and try to understand the motives that determined his selection of subject, the choice of materials he intends to use and any subjective purposes within himself that might influence the presentation or interpretation of the material. To be sure, some biographical studies are openly denigrating or idolatory; some are written primarily to make money; and others are written principally to advance a political point of view, or even an individual candidacy. But a biographer who sets out to write a historically factual and objective study has the responsibility of trying to identify hidden purposes in himself that might distort the work. I would not offer this caution only to biographers who, like myself, lay great emphasis upon the use of psychological materials. Anyone who explores deeper psychological issues and emphasizes the use of psychological data is brought into a particularly close relationship with his subject. He develops strong feelings toward the subject and in the course of his study personal needs of his own may be aroused that continually tax his powers of analysis.

With regard to sources in this biography, I have made use of the usual written documents upon which biographers and historians must rely: letters, diaries, autobiographical notes, public records, other biographies and essays. In addition I have made extensive use of interviews with persons who knew Lawrence during the various periods of his life. In using the documents, I have, of course, had to consider the relationship between the writer and the recipient, the time and context in which the document was written, and the readers whom the writer might have imagined his words would reach in the future. This is true not only of documents with important psychological significance, although elements of defensive distortion are naturally more likely with such material. The truth of even ostensibly neutral documents, such as military dispatches, is not, as Lawrence well understood, absolute. They often serve for the self-justification or personal aggrandizement of military and political leaders. All accounts of war in particular, he noted, would be unfair in their assignment of credit until "the un-named rank and file" could write the dispatches themselves.[6] Historians, Lawrence wrote in 1927, tend to accept too uncritically the truth of documents. "The documents are liars," he wrote to one historian friend. "No man ever yet tried to write down the entire truth of any action in which he has been engaged."[7]

With interviews the biographer must, as Erik Erikson wrote in *Gandhi's Truth*, assess the information obtained in the light of an understanding of the informant's relationship to the subject — for example, whether the informant is personally attached to him, or seeks (sometimes unconsciously) to seem important to the interviewer or to himself through claiming a special relationship with the great man. Less frequently in my experience — usually when the person being interviewed knew the subject very little — distorted information is provided that discredits the subject. I have found it very valuable in interviewing to make the informant a kind of partner in the work by explaining in detail the nature of

my study and sharing our areas of common interest or empathy in relation
to the subject.

The diagnosis of conventional psychopathological entities is of so little
value or contemporary relevance in the study of public figures that it is
somewhat surprising that it has remained such a popular pursuit. Even
in studying destructive leaders like Stalin and Hitler it does little to
establish that they were paranoid personalities (or whatever), for this will
not distinguish them from other persons who are paranoid. Furthermore,
the judgment of pathological behavior is not absolute. It depends upon
the social context of the behavior and on what is expected of the subject
by those judging him within that context. This is especially true of one
who is a leader of some sort. Judging the appropriateness of his behavior
is difficult without full knowledge of the forces and stresses constraining
him, and it is subject to bias that derives from political preferences. The
person who seeks in his expectations of himself to reach beyond what
ordinary men are willing or able to undertake draws upon extraordinary
means of adaptation and also exposes himself to great failure and disappointment. He is especially vulnerable to the development of pathological symptoms and unusual behavioral responses.

With Lawrence, the more acquainted I became with the social context
in which his public actions took place, and the public demands with
which he had to contend, the more understandable I found his troubled
personal responses to be. This by no means implies that an understanding
of the emotional elements in Lawrence or in any leader is irrelevant to a
study such as this. Rather, these internal elements, deriving from the
leader's own psychology, must be seen as operating within a constant field
of forces making up the elements of the social and political world. Conventional psychiatric diagnosis, with its emphasis on a given moment in
time and upon behavioral outcomes looked upon in their own right, fails
often to consider this fuller context.

More important than the leader's pathology is how he was able to reach
positions of power and through his actions affect the course of history. An
understanding of his personal psychopathology will be of value in this
connection only if it sheds light on how he was able to achieve positions
of leadership, maintain power, or draw other men into destructive courses
through living out his madness in the public domain.

The development of psychoanalysis at the turn of the twentieth century
provided a new method for the understanding and treatment of the
psychoneuroses. Its students became interested in the armchair analysis
of the works of writers and artists like Shakespeare and Leonardo. In
fragments of their writing examples were sought of repressed sexuality
and other childhood conflicts that had been found to play a part in the
etiology of the neuroses and in the formation of dreams. Similar uses —

not by the psychoanalysts themselves usually — were made of the concepts of psychoanalysis in biographical studies of public figures ("pathographies"). Such studies were common in the early decades of the twentieth century and often were used for debunking purposes.[8]

In studying the life of a person of great accomplishment, we are interested in how the influences of parental figures, other family members, nannies, teachers, colleagues and friends fostered through love, or promoted through a variety of relationships and examples for identification, the development of the special qualities that enabled him to achieve what he set out to do or become. We are particularly interested in how areas of conflict worked together with special abilities and shaped the direction of later accomplishments or intensified the motive for achievement. Even if the events or traumata of adult life play upon the vulnerabilities incurred in the earlier years and lead to emotional difficulties (like those Lawrence suffered from in the war), or even produce grossly psychopathological reactions, our interest nevertheless remains focused upon the person's creative efforts to surmount the disorder, rather than upon the psychopathology as such.

A biographical study of a figure no longer living, which seeks to examine and interpret psychological data, suffers from the absence of the kind of psychological information that direct interviews with the subject himself can give. But it may have certain advantages. For one, it may be more balanced. From written documentation and interviews knowledge can be gained of every phase of the subject's life and a fuller, richer picture of his character emerges, one less weighted in the direction of psychopathology, a picture more equable in its view of strength and weakness, love and hate, bitterness and humor. This is fortunate for the biographer's purposes. He is interested in his subject, not as a figure alone with his suffering, or allied with a therapist in order to resolve his personal dilemmas, but rather as one who lives and acts in the context of a series of relationships with others, whose lives he influences and whose needs and demands move his own life in directions not always of his choosing.

This book is divided into six parts. The first deals with Lawrence's family background, childhood and adolescence up to the time of his admission to Oxford in the fall of 1907, with the exception of two summer trips to France that seem related more to the years that followed and thus are included subsequently. Part Two deals with the period of Lawrence's youth from the age of nineteen, when he went up to Oxford, to the beginning of World War I when he was twenty-five. It includes his undergraduate years; his trips to France in 1906, 1907, and 1908; his first trip to the Middle East; and the three years spent at Carchemish working as an archeologist. Part Three describes the critical years of

World War I, out of which Lawrence's principal fame as a historical figure derives. Part Four is concerned with the four years of Lawrence's participation in the political struggles over the postwar fate of the Middle East. These are also the years in which Lawrence wrote *Seven Pillars of Wisdom*. Part Five deals with Lawrence as an enlisted man in the ranks of the RAF and Tank Corps from 1922 to his death at forty-six, two months after his retirement in 1935. Finally, Part Six contains discussions of aspects of Lawrence's intimate life and personality that spanned his thirteen years in the ranks.

Because the emphasis of this book is upon the relations between Lawrence's inner life — the psychological forces that shaped and moved him — and the actions and events that grew out of them or through which they were played out, more space has been devoted to the social and political-historical aspects of his life than to his importance as a literary figure. His writings are used as source materials, to bring out aspects of his psychology or to help in the understanding of the development of his historical reputation and legend. Likewise, I have not concerned myself with Lawrence as a literary critic, although his letters are full of literary criticism. I have taken great pains to develop as complete a picture of Lawrence the human being as I could, even including seemingly small details that illuminate particular aspects of his personality. For I believe that his fundamental importance for human history, and his lasting ability to influence the lives of others, derives as much from the example of what he was as from what he did.

# ONE

# FAMILY BACKGROUND AND CHILDHOOD

# 1

# Chapmans and Lawrences

Many, but by no means all, the significant facts regarding T. E. Lawrence's ancestry are now known, especially since the publication in 1955 of Richard Aldington's *Lawrence of Arabia: A Biographical Enquiry.* Yet despite a good deal of speculative psychologizing, we still lack a full understanding of Lawrence's family background and the meaning of his childhood experiences for his personal development, later life experiences and historical place.

In giving information about his forebears, Lawrence provided a characteristically provocative and puzzling assortment of bits and pieces from his own incomplete knowledge. He both revealed and concealed in what he told his biographers, in part to protect family members still living, but also because such hide-and-seek behavior was an element in his personality. When he wrote to Basil Liddell Hart, for instance, he prefaced the information he gave (which was, in fact, quite extensive) by saying: "There are (as I hinted at Hindhead) things not quite desirable in this. Without wanting to censor I suggest alternatives — written with the allusiveness that hints at knowledge refusing to betray itself between the lines."[1]

Lawrence's psychological uncertainties regarding his own identity correspond nicely with the ambiguities of his ancestral background, which, naturally, constituted one of the underlying causes of his later psychological confusion. In the 1927 manuscript of Robert Graves's biography (corrected by Lawrence, who had already supplied the basic data), appeared exotically: "He was born in 1888 in North Wales, of mixed blood, none of it Welsh; it is Irish, Spanish, ~~Isle of Skye~~ [*Hebridean*], Dutch and ~~Swedish~~ [*Norse*]."[2] He tried to put off further inquiry from Graves by declaring that sources of information regarding his family background and childhood were "nil."[3] Later, Lawrence answered Liddell Hart's questions about his origins with: "Father Anglo-Irish, with ¼ Dutch. Mother Anglo-Scotch with a dash of Scandinavian."[4]

Lawrence's fullest account of his paternal family background is contained in a letter to John Buchan: "'Lawrence', like 'Shaw' [he had by that time changed his name to Shaw], was an assumption. My father's people were merchants in the Middle Ages: then squires in Leicestershire. In Tudor times they had promoted themselves to soldiering, and had married with a Devon family: by favour of one of these cousins (Sir Walter Raleigh) they got a huge grant of County Meath in Ireland, from Queen Elizabeth: and they lived till the Irish Land Acts did away with most of the estate. My father had other troubles too, which made him change his name, and live abroad, in Wales and England, the latter half of his life. So there weren't any Lawrence ancestors or relations: but it's not my line to say so, since the fiction is less trouble than the truth."[5]

Lawrence's father, Thomas Robert Tighe Chapman, was born in 1846 and inherited his father's estate in 1870, when his older brother died. In 1914, after the death of his cousin Benjamin James, he became the seventh and last Chapman baronet, but he lived only five years after succeeding to the title. Little is known of his life or personality when he was in Ireland. He married a cousin, Edith Sarah Hamilton, in 1873 and by her had four daughters between 1874 and 1882. Edith Chapman was described by my informants as having been a most severe, sour and religiously strict person who was known locally as "the Vinegar Queen."[6]

The Chapman family settled on an estate at Killua in County Westmeath northwest of Dublin, and in 1782 a Chapman baronetage was established.[7] The Chapman manor house, Killua Castle, now in ruins, was formerly a preceptory of the medieval religious order of the Knights Hospitalers. The branch of the family from which Lawrence was descended acquired in due course a large manor house called South Hill, near the village of Delvin. Like the other members of the displaced Protestant gentry of English origins, the Chapmans looked to England for help, married into their own group, mingled little if at all with the surrounding Irish Catholic peasantry (who regarded them with suspicion and resentment), and satisfied their sense of social responsibility by doing good works of the Lady Bountiful variety in the local community. As one Irish schoolteacher of Delvin told me, the "planters" were "not Irish," did not look after their tenants who worked the farms, "grabbed" land from the people, and gave little in return.[8]

Lawrence was quite conscious of the family connection with Sir Walter Raleigh, which served the fantasy of his derivation from a heroic past. He would like, he wrote in 1927 to Charlotte Shaw, George Bernard Shaw's wife, to buy some acres of land in the Irish county from which his father had come, in order "to keep some of Walter Raleigh's gift in the family of which I have the honour of being not the least active member!"[9] To another friend he pointed out his father's resemblance to Sir Walter, but disclaimed a direct lineage: "Raleigh isn't an ancestor, only the son of one. My father, middle-aged, was his walking image. I'm not like that side of the family though."[10] Lawrence related his later actions to his ancestry, but not specifically to the heroic aspects. "My matter of fact ancestry compels me to carry my impulses into action," he wrote to Charlotte Shaw in 1926.[11]

According to a family companion with whom I spoke, Thomas Chapman was described by his daughters as having been a somewhat morose and not very effective man in Ireland, one rather uninterested in the usual country pursuits of hunting, shooting and fishing.[12] He drank a good deal then, and one daughter recalled that he had to hide liquor from his intolerant wife. Lady Chapman also disapproved of the things he did well and tried to deprive him of any enjoyment in them. An old gardener remembered that the Chapmans held frequent prayer meetings.[13]

Sometime between 1878 and 1880 — the exact date is unknown — the father brought from Scotland to South Hill a young girl to be a companion and governess for his children. Sarah, as she called herself, was attractive, strong-willed and highly capable. The daughters grew very fond of her, and the father likewise. One of them recalled that whenever their father came into the room and the governess was present his ordinarily dour manner changed: his face brightened noticeably and he became "all gay."[14] Efficient and energetic, Sarah was soon managing the house in a businesslike way.

Eventually, at an undetermined date, she left the family's employ, and soon thereafter Chapman took lodgings in or near Dublin, where the two lived together as Mr. and Mrs. Chapman when he was in the city. In this period, according to one story of doubtful authenticity, he joined the Salvation Army and went about Dublin wearing a blue Army jersey with the name across the front.[15] Their first child, Montague Robert, was born in Dublin on December 27, 1885. On his birth certificate, they gave their address as 33 York Street. According to a Chapman cousin, they were ultimately found out by the Chapman butler, who overheard Sarah in a grocery store giving her name to the grocer as "Mrs. Chapman" and followed her home. Shortly after the inevitable row at South Hill, Thomas and Sarah with their child left Ireland for North Wales.[16] They settled in the village of Tremadoc, where in due course their second child, Thomas Edward, was born — on August 16, 1888.

The embittered Lady Chapman's refusal to permit a divorce prevented Thomas and Sarah from ever marrying. Soon after Robert's birth, they assumed the name of Lawrence ("privately, not by deed poll or other instrument," T.E. told a friend many years later).[17] On the birth certificate of their third son, William George, they stated that they had been married in St. Peter's Church, Dublin,[18] but no record of the ceremony exists in the church's registers.

The Lawrences stayed in Tremadoc for a little more than a year, then moved to Kirkcudbright, Scotland, where it was less damp. They rented a large comfortable house on the edge of town, one that had formerly belonged to the provost (mayor). Here William George was born on December 10, 1889. From Scotland the family moved to the resort of Dinard on the Brittany coast, and then to the Isle of Wight and the New Forest in Hampshire. The fourth son, Frank Helier, was born in St. Helier, Jersey, in 1893. The family settled finally in Oxford in 1896. Mrs. Lawrence told a woman friend in Oxford that between 1893 and 1900 she gave birth to three other sons; two of them were born dead, and the other lived for only a few hours.[19] In 1900 the last son, Arnold Walter, was born.

Before settling in Oxford, the family chose to live in places on the seacoast, where they could make friends with English people not of their class (and thus less likely to identify them or be suspicious of the relationship). The seacoast also facilitated communication with Ireland and enabled the family to enjoy sailing.

Because Thomas Lawrence was less dominant and overwhelming than Sarah, his effect on T.E.'s development and character has been slighted by biographers. And because he died forty years earlier than Sarah (in 1919, at seventy-two), we have fewer firsthand recollections of him and fewer documents concerning his life. The picture of Thomas Robert Tighe Chapman that emerges has, as with T.E. himself, elements that are difficult to reconcile. Many of them found later expression in T.E.'s personality.

There is to my knowledge nothing written about Thomas Chapman by anyone who knew him before he left South Hill in the mid-1880's, when he was in his late thirties. The Debrett and Burke baronetages of the period states that he was a justice of the peace for County Westmeath. His dourness, which Sarah's presence dissipated, was due, one assumes, to his unhappy marriage.

Little is known of his early life or family relationships. According to T.E., his father had no interest in the land, but was a fine snipe and pheasant shooter and a yachtsman.[20] T.E. pictures him rather romantically as "on the large scale, tolerant, experienced, grand, rash, humoursome, skilled to speak, and naturally lord-like. He had been 35 years in the large life, and a spend-thrift, a sportsman, and a hard rider and drinker."[21] This swashbuckling image of Chapman in Ireland is superseded in T.E.'s accounts by that of the domesticated Thomas Robert Tighe Chapman Lawrence in England, "remodeled" by Sarah. He never attained a stature in his son's eyes comparable to that of the revered military and political chiefs under whom T.E. was to serve. Lawrence once wrote to his friend Hugh Trenchard, marshal of the RAF and the third and last of the leaders he idolized: "If my father had been as big as you, the world would not have had spare ears for my freakish doings."[22] A kind of uncomplaining riches-to-rags image adds to the picture of Mr. Lawrence. T.E. wrote later, "It was my father who was wonderful in throwing up all his comforts to go away with her: and I never remember his being sorry at having so little, as we grew bigger."[23]

The picture of the grand lord of the manor, carried off and transformed by a powerful woman, is, though accurate in certain respects, probably exaggerated at both its Irish and English poles. It is difficult, for example, to explain altogether satisfactorily how such a strong, heroic and religious man could be induced in his prime to give up his name, estates and entire status in life for love, living thereafter a quiet life as a displaced country gentleman, no matter how comely or compelling the woman. Except for the notation in the baronetages that Thomas Chapman heard cases as a J.P. in County Westmeath, we have no concrete evidence to support our suspicions that Thomas Robert Chapman was less grand a figure in Ireland than T.E. liked to believe. But there is evidence that he was somewhat more of a personage in England than the accepted biographical accounts might suggest.

The earliest description of Thomas Lawrence I have been able to obtain came from members of the Laurie family, who were neighbors and friends of the Lawrences in the New Forest (1894–1896) and maintained ties with them at Oxford. They pictured him as a slender man whose clothes fitted loosely, "like a scarecrow," gentle and kind, but diffident, shy and unsure of himself, seeming to feel terribly out of place in the genteel English surroundings of Oxford.[24] He had become a teetotaler, and the sometimes sad countenance, which had been observed in Ireland, was in evidence once more. A photograph of him taken about 1900 shows a man with a long face, a large Roman nose and narrow shoulders. He was not, according to his oldest son, physically strong.[25] Another member of the Laurie family, a boy named Andrew, who lived for brief periods in the Lawrence home (because he suffered from asthma attacks in his own house but not in theirs), described the father as thoroughly domesticated and extremely kind. Andrew recalled the father's judicious intercession in a playful scrap with six-year-old T.E., who was generally "lively and mischievous": "I was in bed and Ned [T.E.] came in and took hold of the bedclothes and yanked them off. I ran after him and slapped his head. His father said, 'Andrew, Andrew, he's a smaller boy than you.' "[26]

Mr. Lawrence enjoyed spending time with the boys, playing word-guessing games or going through boys' magazines with them. In England he was an enthusiastic sportsman, with a license to shoot in the New Forest, one who retained the manners of a gentleman. Although T.E. and his older brother, Bob, did not hunt with him — "Our sympathies were with the game," Bob said — Mr. Lawrence would frequently come home at the end of the day with a "couple of snipe."[27] Mr. Lawrence's other interests, which he shared with his sons, included photography, the architecture of medieval castles and cathedrals, and bicycling, of which he was one of the earliest enthusiasts. He had considerable skill as a carpenter (T.E. himself was extremely skillful in building and making repairs around the house or at a campsite) and once, at Mrs. Lawrence's request, built a meat safe in which recently killed game was stored.[28]

In his later years at Oxford, Mr. Lawrence is remembered by family friends as a gentle soul, tall, sensitive and quiet, dominated absolutely by Mrs. Lawrence, "the drum major."[29] A neighbor offered this description of him: "[The] Father was a tall, slender man, very distinguished looking, looking rather like Bernard Shaw, I should say.[30] He had a red beard and whiskers, and he always went about in a Norfolk jacket and breeches, and was always waving when we passed him — very friendly looking." He was "stately, courtly and friendly, an obvious aristocrat in hiding."[31] Others recall him at home as anxious, smoking a great deal, retiring to the smoking room to calm himself; or as "a country G.B.S." in tweed knickers.[32] T.E.'s teacher at the City of Oxford High School and at Oxford University, L. Cecil Jane, wrote in a letter to Robert Graves that Thomas Lawrence was "one of the most charming men I have known — very shy, very kind."[33]

According to his youngest son, Arnold, Thomas Lawrence was a rather unworldly, impractical man. He could, however, on occasion be sound in business matters. At one time he had holdings in an Irish railroad that was in financial difficulty. He was effective through his personal intervention in making it solvent again. He was dissuaded by Mrs. Lawrence from investing in the first pneumatic tire company on the grounds that he would be throwing his money away. The company made such a fortune that the family could have been millionaires. (Arnold Lawrence, reflecting upon this fact, remarked that he was glad for his own offspring that his father had not made this investment: "children who are born rich are nervous about it.")[34]

When Thomas Chapman broke away from Ireland and became Thomas Lawrence, he had to leave his estates and most of his money to his wife. It then became necessary for him to receive support from the family estate in Ireland. He would make trips there, perhaps twice a year, in connection with the management of his affairs and to see old friends and hunting cronies, and would be gone as much as a fortnight. Although Chapman-Lawrence was able to find a group of hunting companions in Oxford, his move naturally brought about a considerable fall in social standing.

Sarah Lawrence was a remarkable woman, possessing unusual energy, great charm and prodigious will and determination. She was short of stature, like T.E., and had similar piercing china-blue eyes, a fair complexion and a firm chin. In her strong character she maintained as many contradictions as her famous son did in his. The story of her life is fragmentary and has, aside from a few published sources, been pieced together from the accounts of those who knew her personally and in whom she confided.[35]

Her stoicism was legendary. In her nineties, when she broke her leg and was confined to a wheelchair, she insisted on getting in and out of the chair by herself, without help. "It's good for me!" she asserted.[36] A fine firsthand account of Mrs. Lawrence at ninety is provided by Victoria O'Campo in her book *338171 T. E.: Lawrence of Arabia.*

Lawrence told his biographer Liddell Hart that his mother was, like himself, illegitimate.[37] She was born "Sarah Junner" on August 31, 1861, near Sunderland in County Durham in the north of England. Her father was John Junner, a "shipwright journeyman," and her mother, Elizabeth Junner, whose maiden name is also given as Junner, may have been a relative of his.[38] In the Chapman household, however, she used the surname Lawrence, and on Robert's birth certificate in Dublin she is registered as Sarah Chapman, "formerly Laurence" (sic). On T.E.'s birth certificate she gave her maiden name as Maden, but on Will's certificate, she appears with the surname of Jenner.

In her earliest years, Sarah was taken to Scotland, where she spent the remainder of her childhood, although it is not known at what age she moved there from County Durham. She told T.E. that her mother died of alcoholism, and according to Arnold Lawrence, T.E. believed she never knew who her father was.[39] Convinced that there was a predilection for alcohol on both sides of the boys' family — she believed, perhaps even more than other Victorian parents did, that alcoholism was hereditary — she warned the children sharply against its evils, and apparently tried with the power of her own will to overcome the influence of heredity on her husband.[40]

In Scotland, according to her friend Elsie Newcombe, Sarah spent some years of her early childhood on a farm owned by one of her grandfathers in Perthshire. She told an Oxford friend that she had had to walk six miles back and forth each day to school in Blairgourie near Perth. By this time her grandmother had died, and she was looked after by an aunt who was married to the rector of an Evangelical (low-church) parish. She recalled her aunt and uncle as strict but "just" and described a rather forlorn childhood. Sometime during her adolescence she moved to the Isle of Skye where, when she was about eighteen, it was arranged by a Mr. Andrew Balfour, agent for the Chapman estate, that she be sent to Ireland as a nursery-governess for the Chapman daughters.[41]

In the New Forest, when she was in her early thirties, she was described as "hardheaded" but kind, speaking with a soft Scottish burr and occasionally mispronouncing words.[42] A photograph of her from about this period shows a handsome, attractive woman with a full, strong face, good complexion and a pert, straight, rather sharp nose.

At Oxford, Mrs. Lawrence was remembered as very straitlaced by the boys' friends. She did not approve of dancing or the theatre (Shakespeare was the exception). Once during Lawrence's undergraduate years he, Will and Frank wanted to go with a young girl to a light musical comedy they knew Mrs. Lawrence would disapprove of. They told her they were going to see Shakespeare so as to forestall her objections. Another time Ned or Will mentioned Oscar Wilde, and Mrs. Lawrence told the boy not to say that name, especially in front of a girl.[43]

Despite her puritanical severity Mrs. Lawrence was described with deep affection, and at times with awe, by her Oxford friends and acquaintances. Mrs. Thomas Hardy once called her "a heroine, and a very sweet one."[44] She was on the one hand hospitable and generous, and devoted to her friends ("her friends were her friends for life once she liked someone"), while on the other extremely definite in her opinions — "clear as a brook," according to Elsie Newcombe.[45] Mrs. Newcombe, whose son was about to leave to join the armed services in World War I, remembers her also as an emotional person who sat knitting a Balaklava helmet for him while tears streamed down her face.[46] She was "fearfully keen on walking," even in her eighties and nineties, and martyrlike, forced herself to hobble about soon after she had broken her leg.[47] Despite her strict religiosity she confessed shortly before her death that she doubted the existence of an afterlife.

Those who knew her agreed that she seemed at times to suck or draw the vitality out of people. David Garnett called her "a terror," a person who devoured people "like a lion." He felt that it was necessary to handle her as one would a lion: "If you know what to say it won't eat you up. Better to step out of the way."[48] Others — especially people who did not know her well — found Mrs. Lawrence overpowering and terrifying. Although not intellectual, she possessed an extraordinary memory, read a good deal, especially botanical books, and in her nineties could remember the names of a great variety of plants.[49]

Arnold Lawrence felt that his mother tried to redeem herself vicariously through all her sons, to whom she transmitted her sense of sin. She wanted each of them to become a missionary and to devote his life to God and Christianity. In this ambition she succeeded only with Robert. It also seemed to Arnold that his mother tried to swallow, absorb, or smother her sons.[50]

In 1955, with the publication of his biography of Lawrence, Richard Aldington disclosed publicly that the Lawrences had never married. The fact was well known by then in Oxford and had been indicated earlier in less widely circulated books, but had not been acknowledged in Mrs. Lawrence's presence by her friends. They wished to spare her the knowledge that the fact had been made public, and so one day when it was learned that there would be a discussion of the Aldington book on the BBC, they tried to keep Mrs. Lawrence, now ninety-five, from the radio. But Robert, who had denied the facts even to himself, led her straight to the room where the program was on the air.[51] Mrs. Lawrence sat through it stoically, without moving or speaking out. At the end she got up and walked stiffly out of the room without comment.[52] At the end of her life she admitted — the confession gave her visible relief — that she had had a responsible part in T.E.'s "nervousness." During a febrile illness late in her life, she was heard murmuring, "God hates the sin but loves the sinner," and "God loves the sinner but he hates the sin."[53]

Mrs. Lawrence survived her husband by forty years. As an old woman she was well accepted and had many good friends. For her ninety-fourth birthday one of them had a party in her honor to which many of the leading scholars and citizens of Oxford were invited.[54] She died in 1959 at ninety-eight.

One of the most difficult tasks in my research concerning the Lawrence family has been attempting to understand the motivations of the parents and the manner in which they were able to reconcile the discrepancies between their avowed principles and the reality of the situation in which they were living. I must stress that we are not dealing with the world of the 1970's (in which it is still difficult socially and psychologically for a middle-class couple to live and rear children out of wedlock) but with late Victorian England. As Arnold Lawrence stated the matter: "In that day someone who did that was odd — it just wasn't done."[55]

How was Mrs. Lawrence, reared according to strict fundamentalist codes, and later to become a devoted mother herself, able to take a man from his wife and children forever and live with him thereafter "in sin"? Her friends in Oxford have speculated from their knowledge of her that she believed she was giving up her own soul to save from worse sins the soul of a somewhat morally lackadaisical Irish country gentleman who drank too much, and it is true that except for an occasional glass of claret he stopped drinking. Or perhaps she believed — easy to speculate after what ensued — that she would be serving God if she were to bear sons to a man who had served the Lord less than well in having only daughters. One of Mrs. Lawrence's Oxford friends, knowing her interest in biblical teachings, is of the opinion that Mrs. Lawrence justified her actions, at least in part, through the example in Genesis 16, where Sarah, unable to bear Abraham children, suggested that he have a child by Hagar instead (the Chapman daughters, in Mrs. Lawrence's view, presumably did not count).[56] Always conscious of her unmarried state, and insisting upon a scrupulous literal truthfulness, Mrs. Lawrence referred to Mr. Lawrence as "Tom" or "the boys' father" — never as "my husband."

One may suspect, in view of her own illegitimacy and severe upbringing, that she was living out elements in her personal psychology derived from early childhood and her own birth out of wedlock. But a suspicion is not always a fact. What can be well documented, however, is the impact her conflicts had upon the lives and characters of her sons, conflicts she could not help imposing on them.

Although the change in Mr. Lawrence's social status is well established, there is no material that reveals what it was like for him to live with his decision, or what the radical change in his life, whereby he gave up so much, meant for him personally. Our richest source is T.E. himself, but his view of his parents' relationship is deeply colored by its effect upon his own psychology. From India in 1927 and 1928 he wrote long passages about his mother in letters to Charlotte Shaw, who had become, T.E.'s denials notwithstanding, a kind of mother-confessor for him. "My mother [was] brought up as a child of sin in the Island of Skye by a bible-thinking Presbyterian,"[57] he wrote Mrs. Shaw in 1927 (a year later he phrased it "brought up as a charity child in the Island of Skye"),[58] "then [she became] a nurse maid, then 'guilty' (in her judgment) of taking my father from his wife. . . . To justify herself, she remodeled my father, making him a teetotaler, a domestic man, a careful spender of pence. They had us five children, and never more than £400 a year: and such pride against gain, and such pride in saving, as you cannot imagine. Father had, to keep with mother, to drop all his old life and all his friends. She by dint of will raised herself to be his companion: social things meant much to him: but they never went calling, or on visits, together. They thought always that they were living in sin, and that we would some day find out."[59] Later he wrote: "Mother was always caring (to my mind) too much about such essentials as food and clothes. Life itself doesn't seem to me to matter, in comparison with thought and desire. That was how my father acted. Our pinched life was very hard on him: — or would have been if he had pinched with [sic] only he didn't. He was pinched, instead, and that's a mere trifle."[60]

The social isolation to which Lawrence refers was confirmed by others who knew the family in Oxford. The isolation was partly self-imposed; for the fact that the Lawrences were unmarried was not known in Oxford while Mr. Lawrence was living (in London it was gossiped about from the time the couple left Ireland).[61] To one of his biographers Lawrence wrote: "The mother kept to herself, and kept her children jealously from meeting or knowing their neighbours."[62] The self-consciousness of the parents meant that the family members were thrown upon themselves more than would be usual and may account in part for Robert Lawrence's reflection: "Our parents were always with us."[63] Sir Basil Blackwell, a classmate of T.E.'s at Oxford, stated bluntly that the family was ostracized. Blackwell and the other undergraduates knew "something was odd" in the Lawrence family. "Oxford was very correct in those days," Sir Basil said; yet even by Oxford standards "they were so punctilious, churchgoing and water-drinking."[64]

One direct result of the father's descent in the social scale, and the restriction in his outside contacts, was that he was forced to accommodate himself more to the mother's way of life. For example, the mother, who had limited formal education, was quite comfortable and friendly with the men who did construction around the house, with other working people, and with the local solicitor, but less so with the gentry. However congenial she found these men, they were not persons of the same social level as her husband. Nevertheless, Mr. Lawrence made considerable concessions to Mrs. Lawrence's choices and became friendly with these men to please her.[65]

The union was, according to T.E., "a real love match,"[66] and all my sources, which include several of his childhood playmates, agree that the Lawrence home was a warm and loving one, a household that other children liked to visit.[67] The parents were affectionate with each other and devoted to their children (though not physically demonstrative towards them), and they made other children feel welcome.[68]

Arnold Lawrence feels that his father's role in the family has been distorted by those writers who have depicted Mr. Lawrence as weak in relation to Sarah. Although Mr. Lawrence tended to be gentle, quiet and reserved, and reluctant to show his feelings, he could be very firm when necessary. At times of family crisis he was the one who stepped in and made the basic decisions. Arnold Lawrence also feels that his father was an understanding person who had a considerable capacity to make peace: he could often find the right words to ease family tensions. Also, through his knowledge of people and skill in handling social situations, he was able to make others feel better, an ability T.E. grew up to possess as well. Although most of the time he left the handling of the children and the household to Sarah, on occasion he would raise his voice to intervene when he felt that she was being unduly harsh, and she would subside. His gentleness was such, however, that it was she, as we shall see later, who administered the physical discipline in the family.[69]

Arnold Lawrence was impressed with his father's quiet authority. He recalls an incident from his own childhood when a carter was beating a horse. Mr. Lawrence went up to the young man and spoke to him softly and the beating stopped. On another occasion Arnold was surprised how firmly and effectively his father dealt with a group of Oxford undergraduates who were acting obstreperously.

The family belonged to the Evangelical congregation that worshipped at St. Aldates Church, where the Reverend Alfred M. W. Christopher, a leader of the nineteenth-century Evangelical revival, was rector. Canon Christopher and others of his congregation believed literally in the Bible.

An Evangelical atmosphere filled the Lawrence household, with the mother practicing her religion as a matter of course and expecting her sons to follow suit. For Thomas Lawrence religion was a less concrete or ritualistic matter and more a question of emotional experience.[70] The family attended St. Aldates Church regularly, contributed financially to it,[71] and held Bible readings in their home every Sunday and in the morning before the children went to school. Thomas would lead the readings as the children drew around him. He would also kneel, according to Bob, and lead prayer sessions. I have seen the well-thumbed and extensively annotated and underlined Bibles from which the parents read to their children.[72]

The five Lawrence boys were "a most happy band of brothers," Mrs. Lawrence wrote after T.E.'s death, and to a major extent this seems to have been true.[73] A group of sons may form close ties in a family in any circumstances, but the Lawrences' self-imposed isolation when their children were growing up in Oxford may have fostered a still closer attachment among them. This close comradeship within the family may have contributed to Lawrence's predilection throughout his life for the companionship of a society of men. Lawrence made the connection himself, rather grimly in sentences he wrote for Liddell Hart: "The five brothers . . . were brought up to be self-sufficient, and were sufficient till the war struck away two and left in their sequence gaps in age that were overwide for sympathy to cross. Then their loneliness seemed to rankle, sometimes. To friends who wondered aloud how he could endure the company of the barrack-room and its bareness T.E. might retort, almost fiercely, that he had gone back to his boyhood class and was at home."[74]

Although he was the second son, Lawrence was clearly the leader among the children, and played the role of oldest brother oftener than Bob did. Bob studied medicine under the famous British physician Sir William Osler, and served with great courage as a doctor on the front lines in France during World War I.[75] Later he became a medical missionary in China, where he was joined by Mrs. Lawrence. But aside from these achievements, Bob was so overprotected and stifled by her, and absorbed so literally by the exaggerated climate of religiosity through which she sought to justify herself, that he was unable to deal directly with any of the emotional issues that arose within the family. He remained attached inseparably to his mother until her death. Lawrence wrote to Mrs. Shaw in 1928: "The chickens are beyond her cluck, you see: all except the elder brother and he's queer company. You will not persuade him of anything, if you do see him. He is illuminated from inside, not from out. His face, very often, shines like a lamp. Such an odd family."[76]

In 1964 and 1965, when I visited with Dr. Lawrence, he was living in a vicarage and was vigorous, alert and kind. He had retained fundamentalist religious beliefs and considered beauties of nature, such as a recent ice storm that had turned the small branches of trees in the churchyard into gleaming ropes of ice, to be evidence that the second coming of the Lord was not far off. He died in 1971 at eighty-six.[77]

T.E.'s preeminence among his brothers had several aspects. He was the most inventive and imaginative of the boys and thus their leader in family games and activities. He also had a strong maternal side, derived from his identification with his mother, which manifested itself quite early in a readiness to help her take care of the younger children, and in a lively capacity for empathy — a quality often associated more with women than with men. "Mrs. Lawrence once gave my wife and myself a tin travelling bath for our children," Robert Graves wrote. In a note accompanying the gift she had written: "I used to bathe Ned in it, and Ned later bathed Arnie. He was a very good nursemaid." Later, when T.E. saw this bathtub in Graves's home, he remarked that it gave him a "violent revulsion to recall such physical dependency."[78]

T.E.'s extensive knowledge and early travel experience added to his natural inclination to assume the role of teacher with his younger brothers, and in his letters to them he delighted in sharing experiences he thought they would enjoy or information he believed they might profit from. At times he could sound rather pedantic. When he was eighteen, he replied to a letter from Will, who was a budding archeologist: "Your letter bristles with inconsistencies." He then proceeded to lecture Will on the differences among Roman, Celtic, Saxon, British and Danish structures and artifacts.[79] Finally, when he came to recognize his mother's smothering qualities, he offered to help his younger brothers, especially Arnold, achieve physical and even emotional distance from her.

The most important relationship among his brothers for Lawrence during childhood and youth was with Will, only sixteen months younger than himself. From all descriptions Will was an attractive boy, tall, handsome, finely built, graceful and intelligent. He was thought by some to have been the mother's favorite. One of his friends said of him, "He was really an Adonis to look at, beautiful in body, and I think in many ways he might have been as great a man as Ned."[80]

Will was a fine athlete and won the City of Oxford High School gymnastic cup two years in succession. He won a history exhibition (a type of scholarship), as T.E. had done, to St. John's, and after graduation from Oxford became a teacher of history at a college in Delhi, where he had unusual success in gaining the trust and affection of the Indian students.[81] Will had a deep religious faith that complemented his intellectual abilities, and an affectionate and generous nature. His friend E. F. Hall tells the story that he came upon Will practicing high dives from Brighton pier one day during a vacation. He was surprised to see this — diving was not a skill or interest Will was known to possess — and asked him why he was doing it. Will replied that he was standing in for another young man who was in a diving contest but had broken his leg. "He's got a large family to support and I'll do the high diving for him and give him the money if I win," he explained to Hall. "That kind of thing," Hall added, "came from the mother."[82]

Though T.E. and Will were deeply devoted to one another and close companions throughout childhood, Will's greater success in athletics, his tall stature and striking good looks, and the possibility that Sarah favored him, may all have contributed to T.E.'s avoidance of conventional athletic achievement and competition, and to his intense need to prove himself through overwhelming physical adversities. Although he never spoke or wrote of jealous feelings toward Will, it would have been only natural for him to have had them. Hall said to me, "I've often wondered whether Ned's tiny stature may have in some way or other made him a little bit inhibited in relation to his rather beautiful brother."[83] When the young woman to whom Ned proposed marriage preferred, and then became betrothed, to Will his feelings toward Will became further complicated. After Will was killed in France in World War I, Lawrence found that he could no longer "go on living peacefully in Cairo" and sought out a more active role in the war.

The next brother, Frank, was the least unusual of the group, but an able person in his own way. He was the only one of the boys to go in for team sports, which earned him some disdain from T.E. Like T.E. he went to Jesus College, and one of his contemporaries has offered this picture of him: "He was a born leader, was Captain of Football for two years, 1911–13, and also of cricket. Very quiet in speech and manner, he was the embodiment of school loyalty and keenness in everything. He was an excellent shot and Captain of the School Miniature Rifle Club when it did so well in the Oxford League and later, as an undergraduate, he was Captain of the Oxford Twenty."[84] Like Will, Frank was killed in World War I.

The youngest brother, Arnold, twelve years younger than T.E., was the only one of the five to marry and become a parent. Lawrence's affection for this "child-of-the-old-age of my two extraordinary parents" comes through clearly in his many letters to "Arnie." As an interested big brother T.E. served as an inspiration as well as a buffer against their mother's dominating influence. Although he helped Arnold carve a separate life for himself, told him about their illegitimacy, and advised him to leave home as soon as he could manage it, Lawrence could never quite reconcile himself to his brother's marriage. "Prostitution is marriage à la carte," he told Arnold jokingly in a letter when he learned of his plans. "I always thought we wouldn't go in for it in our family."[85]

Arnold, like T.E., became an archeologist, but unlike his older brother had the opportunity to pursue an academic career in his chosen field. However (also like T.E.), Arnold did not follow the path of conventional scholarship. He went to Ghana to start a new national museum and found that he got along better with the illiterate tribesmen in the bush than with the officials.[86] T.E. wrote of him in 1927: "He gets enthusiastic never, except in denunciation."[87] Elsie Newcombe, a friend of both brothers, told me that she could share jokes and plain fun more openly with Arnold than with T.E.

Fundamentally kind behind his reserve and critical wit, Arnold has borne the burden of having to live two lives. For forty years he has conducted the job of being his famous brother's posthumous keeper with rare skill, fairness and, most of the time, patience, while living simultaneously his own private life.

# 2

# Childhood and Adolescence

T. E. Lawrence was born in a cottage called Gorphwyspha ("place of rest") at the edge of Tremadoc village. As was then the usual practice, he was delivered by a midwife. Although according to his birth record in Portmadoc Lawrence was born on August 15, 1888, his mother said that he was born in the "early hours" of August 16, the date Lawrence used as his birthdate.[1]

The principal available sources of information about the earliest years, before the family moved to Langley in the New Forest, are the published accounts written by his mother and older brother (the latter was still living during much of the time the research for this book was undertaken).[2] T.E.'s own accounts are probably based primarily on information supplied to him by his parents.[3] I have no reason to question his mother's reports on matters of neutral fact, although she might, in her pride over the accomplishments of an extraordinary son, have exaggerated somewhat his precocity. Her assertions of complete harmony within the family may be questioned, and of course her omission of any reference to the family's situation or to Lawrence's conflicts is not unexpected. Robert Lawrence, even more than the mother, expunged from his own mind, not to mention the printed record, any material suggesting that family life was anything but idyllic ("We had a very happy childhood which was never marred by a single quarrel between any of us"),[4] or that T.E.'s childhood was other than completely virtuous. However, I believe that he too in matters of neutral family history has been a reliable reporter.

The family moved when Lawrence was thirteen months old to Kirkcudbright, a port in the southern part of Scotland, where Will was born. For three years, between the time T.E. was three and six, the Lawrences lived in Dinard, a French port and resort on the Brittany coast, a popular watering place, where many English people lived or vacationed. The fourth son, Frank, was born during the Dinard years at St. Helier in Jersey when Lawrence was four and a half. Because any boy born in France was due to serve as a conscript in the French army, the parents arranged to have Frank's birth take place in the Channel Islands in order to assure the child of English citizenry. (A photograph of Ned at the age of five shows a boy with piercing eyes dressed in a dark outfit with richly embroidered lace about the neck, and black velvet stockings.)[5]

At Dinard the boys had lessons from an English governess, and went briefly to the Frères school near where they lived. Lawrence attended private gymnastic classes with other English boys in the larger port city of Saint-Malo, near Dinard. The Lawrences evidently kept in touch with several French families in Dinard, as there were many tidings conveyed by Lawrence to his parents from French people he visited there during his 1906, 1907 and 1908 trips in France, and he stayed for considerable periods of time with one of these families in Dinard, the Chaignons, during his travels.

Although Mrs. Lawrence regularly employed "nannies" to help her in bringing up her children, the first four were breast-fed by their mother for at least a year.[6] Mrs. Lawrence stated that T.E. was big as a child and from infancy was particularly active and energetic, "constantly on the move," exploring and mastering his environment.[7] Once he followed his father up a ladder into a loft, and on another occasion early in his second year he had to be rescued by his mother from a high window ledge, which he had reached by climbing over a sewing machine.[8] Before he was nine, he had become the leader of the brothers in inventing games for them to play. These were usually war games and were marked by both humor and imagination. A favorite was the assault by virtuous and noble, but very aggressive, dolls or animal figures upon a tower, which had to be entered in order to rescue it from enemies ("fourscore of men") within.[9]

The nannies played a significant role in the boys' upbringing as they did in so many English families of the period. One of them, Kate Vickery, lived with the family for several years, until she had to leave abruptly when T.E. was six or seven to be with a sister in Canada. T.E., who called her "Kattie," was distinctly her favorite. After her departure she was never seen again by the boys except for one reunion several years later.[10] Miss Vickery was succeeded by Florence Messham, with whom Lawrence later corresponded.[11]

Lawrence's precocity as a child has been a matter of great interest to some of his biographers. Aldington, especially, has taken considerable pains to challenge T.E.'s claims to exceptional childhood accomplishments, particularly intellectual ones.[12] Aldington quibbled over the accuracy of Lawrence's claim to an early ability to read and write. He challenges Mrs. Lawrence's statements that T.E. learned the alphabet before he was three through hearing Robert taught and he also questions Robert's recollection that T.E. was able to read a newspaper upside down at about five.[13] Lawrence himself wrote that he was "reading (chiefly police news) at four"[14] and "could read and write before I was four."[15]

Although it is possible that both he and members of the family exaggerated the facts or distorted them through faulty memory, their statements are quite consistent with the exceptional intellectual abilities Lawrence demonstrated throughout his life. Such early milestones are familiar among very gifted children. They are also consistent with the statements that he had a child's fluency in French by the age of six (or "as a boy")[16] — not so remarkable considering that by six he had lived in France for two and a half years — and began learning Latin at five.[17]

In the spring of 1894 before Lawrence was six, the family moved from Dinard to the Isle of Wight and then to Langley on the edge of the New Forest, where they remained for two years in a red-brick villa called Langley Lodge. According to his mother, Ned was already able to read English books "at a glance" and remember their content. Strong and big as a young child, he was able to climb trees without falling. Soon after coming to Langley, he impressed his family by proving that distant rumblings were the guns of the fleet, not thunder. He had observed the smoke from a high perch in a tree.[18] He also learned to swim and ride a pony at this time. As Langley Lodge was near the Solent and Southampton Water, and the fleet was at Spithead, there were many opportunities to see ships of all kinds — oceangoing steamers, naval vessels and yachts. According to Robert, T.E. demonstrated a precocious ability to identify fossils on the beach near Langley, anticipating his later skill in identifying archeological findings. Robert Lawrence showed me several specimens that Ned had found, which contained imprints of sea urchins and other fossil remains.[19]

The first observation of Ned by someone outside of the family comes during this period. The Lawrence boys were friendly with several children of the agent of a nearby estate in the New Forest. One of them, Janet Laurie, recalled the first time she met Ned. Her parents had wanted another son and so kept her hair short and dressed her like a boy. She was in church, and behind her were two or three Lawrence brothers with their nanny, Florence Messham. She heard one of the boys, who proved to be Ned, say to Miss Messham, "What a naughty little boy to keep his hat on in church." She turned around and put out her tongue and said, "I'm not a boy, I'm a girl." She overheard Miss Messham ("I took a great dislike to her") say, "Well, she may not be a little boy, but she's a very rude little girl." Thus the friendship began.[20] On another occasion, Ned refused to come down out of a tree to have tea with her. "I'm not going to have tea with any girl," he protested. He climbed like a monkey and seemed to have no fears. The children had a donkey and cart at their disposal, and enjoyed chasing the donkey and riding about in the cart. Even at six, she said, he could be "frightfully bossy; he used to order us about, but in a very nice way." He exerted "a quiet authority."

Like Mrs. Lawrence and Bob, Janet had lively recollections of T.E.'s humor and sense of fun, and spoke of the generally happy atmosphere in the Lawrence home. But she observed that "there was always something he was not satisfied with, even as a small child," something sad, "a secret something of unhappiness," which inspired the feeling that she ought to take care of him or protect him. These qualities seemed to grow stronger as he grew older. He was always outside the ring of children, had odd eating habits (he ate chiefly porridge and bananas), and was not good at group games, such as cricket, which he later came to disdain proudly.[21]

In 1896, when T.E. was eight years old, the family settled in Oxford in order, according to Bob, to obtain a proper education for the children.[22] They lived in a red-brick Victorian house at 2 Polstead Road in a middle-class neighborhood on the outskirts of town. We are fortunate in having detailed, published descriptions of Lawrence's boyhood by those who knew him in Oxford. Allowing for the glow that tends to bathe in a golden light the memory of a great figure, the picture is nevertheless of a child who was remarkable in many ways.

Even as a boy of eight or nine Lawrence demonstrated extraordinary energy, curiosity, powers of observation and invention. What is also remarkable — the significance of this I will discuss later — is that there was no discernible transition from early childhood to adolescence, as we understand adolescence, with its frequent rebellious storms and the development of sexual interests. Lawrence had, in my opinion, no real adolescence at all, his energies remaining in many respects those of a lively and lively-minded schoolboy. "His great abilities and interests," as George Bernard Shaw wrote, "were those of a highly gifted boy."[23]

Lawrence's insatiable curiosity about the past and its evidences in the present dominated his childhood interests. His rummagings and excavations about Oxford, beginning when he was eight or nine, for pieces of old pottery, stone and glass, or his tearing away at the pews of churches in and around Oxford to find brasses of medieval knights to rub (he perfected the technique), are well documented. Indeed, so intense was Lawrence's perseverance in the levering up of pews and furniture to get at old brasses that an article once appeared in a local paper complaining of vandalism.[24] On another occasion, when he was fifteen or sixteen he pulled a whole roof, or a large piece of one, that interested him, off a collapsing old house on a main Oxford street. This interest was no ordinary childhood exploration but, as one of his friends, C. F. C. Beeson, described it, "a passionate absorption beside which my urge was more akin to the curiosity of a magpie in a Baghdad Bazaar."[25]

Lawrence also avidly sought information about other structures and artifacts of earlier times, especially of the Middle Ages — castles, armor, costumes, heraldry, crypts (possessing human bones), illuminated manuscripts, leatherwork, and old coins. The earliest account of Lawrence's archeological explorations occur in an essay he wrote himself — his first "published" writing — entitled "An Antiquarian and a Geologist in Hants [Hampshire]," which appeared in the City of Oxford High School magazine when he was fifteen.[26] The article, signed "L.ii," describes a family cycling tour in Hampshire ("it was unanimously decided, by the votes of the family council . . ."). Included in it are descriptions of a thirteenth-century abbey and depictions of the countryside and wildlife that demonstrate Lawrence's intense powers of observation. Of this quality in Lawrence Sidney Webb would one day remark, "This fellow describes every blade of grass and foot of gravel he walked over."[27] The article concludes with a description mingled with an awkward and childish effort at humor: "We crossed over to Whiteparish, in which all things ought to be white, yet we saw a big black horse, a chimney sweep, some dirty ducks, and a drove of brown cows, with one black one."

Lawrence's adventures as a boy, especially his travels by boat with his friends on the Trill Mill Stream have often been told. What struck me most in talking over these times with his friends from childhood, who remembered them with great delight, is the unselfconscious way in which Lawrence would lead them on escapades they would never have thought to undertake themselves.[28] These were not ordinary childhood pranks or adventures. To carry out the Trill Mill Stream voyages (the Thames divides near Oxford and one of its streams passes under the city and emerges at Folly Bridge) Lawrence had to know when the level of the water was lowest (in summer), how to smash the lock on the iron gates which blocked the exit at Folly Bridge, the right kind of punt to use, and an effective method of illumination.

What also needs to be emphasized is the excitement, humor, and sense of delightful mischief he inspired in his companions, raising their usual existence to a special level. One passenger, the only girl to my knowledge to pass under the city of Oxford in a punt with Lawrence, described how thrilling the adventure was but also her fear that passage would be made stormy by the rush of someone's bathwater emptying into the stream. Other examples of the mischievous, affectionate and adventurous aspects of Lawrence's boyhood nature are provided in the early contributions to *T. E. Lawrence by His Friends.*

Lawrence attended the City of Oxford High School from the time of his arrival in Oxford in 1896 to his graduation and entrance into Jesus College, Oxford, in 1907. The high school was opened in the nineteenth century, when the dons were allowed to marry and thus sought a school to which they could afford to send their children.[29] It was not a public school in the English sense, but more like an American public school, with an independent board of governors drawn from the city and the university.[30]

The Lawrence boys, dressed by Mrs. Lawrence in their blue-and-white striped jerseys, were thought somewhat sissyish at first, but became popular when they were better known.[31] One school friend has described how T.E., with a characteristic "mask" or "grin," would stand silently on the edge of groups playing cricket or football.[32] "At school they used to stick me into football or cricket teams," he wrote Mrs. Shaw, "and always I would trickle away from the field before the match ended."[33] Although he avoided these group and contact sports, preferring to play chess with a pocket set, he enjoyed cross-country paper chases and inventing games of mock warfare with his playmates.[34]

Lawrence's second essay in the school magazine is a satirical piece written in pseudo-technical style about how to put together an improvised game of playground cricket. The short article reveals Lawrence's cynicism toward this "folly" and concludes, "The balls go, some into the side windows of the school, some through those of [a] factory, others again attach themselves to the windows opposite."[35] A third essay, written when he was eighteen, is also a satirical piece directed principally at himself, on how to "annex a vacant emolument" (that is, obtain a scholarship) in history by showing an interest in antiquities and admiring the right books. Lawrence expressed contempt in later years for his early education,[36] but the contempt seems in part to have been the result of later embitterment; it is not discernible in documents or data from the time itself.

As a schoolboy Lawrence read voraciously and widely but not necessarily deeply. At this time he became interested in the Middle Ages and its feudal, romantic and chivalric traditions and myths, and clearly enjoyed his private reading more than the formal lessons. From the age of about sixteen, he told Liddell Hart, he studied war because he was filled with the idea of freeing a people — from what he did not say.[37]

He also told Liddell Hart that "the long school hours and the plague of homework cut into the pursuit of archeology that was already the child's passion,"[38] and to another friend he complained that these school years were "miserable sweated years of unwilling work . . . nor do I think the miseries of grown-up feelings are as bad as those of boys."[39] In a passage in *The Mint*, Lawrence's account of his RAF initiation, he revealed that he suffered during his school years from a constant fear of being punished by his teachers, although there is no evidence that he actually elicited much disciplinary action. "Hazardously suspended penalty," he wrote, "made my life from eight to eighteen miserable, and Oxford, after it, so noble a freedom."[40]

A contemporary record dispels any notion that Lawrence neglected his studies in favor of his other interests. One of his teachers wrote the following report when Lawrence was thirteen years and nine months old: "I have every confidence in stating that Thomas Edward Lawrence is a very persevering boy and works well at his lessons and is exceedingly well-behaved. I have attended the prize givings at the Oxford High School for Boys and can therefore speak with some authority. I also notice he has been successful in gaining prizes on several occasions and is well up in his form."[41] One of his prizes at school was for an essay on Tennyson, whom he had selected for special study.

Lawrence did, however, sometimes find that his studies afforded him an opportunity to make gentle fun of his teachers. When he was in the fifth form, there were two tutors, one named Binney, the other Tubbie. In translating a passage on ancient games from the *Aeneid*, Lawrence reported that some object was brought in tubs. His tutor asked if he couldn't think of another word. "In bins," he suggested.[42]

His efforts to inure himself, as if for some important future hardship, danger or important task, first became evident during his early teens: "Right from a boy he was preparing himself for some big thing that fate had in store."[43] Lawrence delighted in teasing a friend who was born on August fourteenth by pointing out that he was less fortunate than Lawrence, who was born on the fifteenth — like Napoleon. In his home he had a coffin-shaped box almost six feet long, two feet high and two feet wide. His mother complained, "That boy of mine's sleeping there every night now."[44] Overhead were brass rubbings — "the room was hideous with them," another friend recalled[45] — one of which depicted a corpse being eaten by worms. Every night when he went to bed "he'd think of this chap dying, eaten by worms."[46]

Lawrence told Liddell Hart in 1929 that he had enlisted in the artillery "about 1906" and "did eight months before being brought out."[47] When he was going over the passage concerning this episode in the manuscript of Liddell Hart's biography, Lawrence wrote: "This is hush-hush. I should not have told you. I ran away from home . . . and served six months. No trouble with discipline, I have always been easy; but the other fellows fought all Friday and Saturday nights and frightened me with their roughness."[48] There is also a veiled reference to this episode in *The Mint* (written in 1922) in connection with a discussion of the violence and bullying of enlisted men in the barracks: "Twenty years ago — or seventeen years, my limit of direct experience — they [the troops] were indeed brutal. Then every incident ended in dispute and every dispute either in the ordeal of fists (a forgotten art, today) or in a barrack-court-martial whose sentences were too often mass-bullying of anyone unlike the mass."[49] I have been unable, however, to unearth any confirming evidence of these six or eight months of military service between 1904 and 1907 before he went up to Oxford at the age of nineteen in October 1907.[50]

Granted, his mother states that Lawrence was "out of school for a term" when he broke his leg rescuing a smaller boy from a bully, but the time was spent convalescing, not bicycling off to the army. She states that he did not grow much after the accident (she is mistaken in implying that his growth was halted as a result of the injury), which would indicate that it occurred quite late — when he was seventeen or eighteen.[51] I have been unable to obtain school or army records that shed any light on the matter. Several of Lawrence's childhood friends, including C. F. C. Beeson, who attended the City of Oxford High School, recall no period of absence, such as Lawrence described to Liddell Hart, and doubt that the six months could have been "fitted in." Bob Lawrence once told Arnold that it was not possible that T.E. was away from home for six to eight months.[52] The most likely explanation is that the episode was the elaboration of something real but smaller, perhaps a period of a week or two, which Lawrence needed later in his life to embellish into something greater when writing as a military expert to a well-known military historian.

During the adolescent years Lawrence showed no interest in girls, according to C. F. C. Beeson, a close companion at this time.[53] Whereas Beeson would go to St. Giles Fair (a traveling fair still held on the widest street in Oxford each September, at which teen-agers have an excellent opportunity to be together) to meet girls "for roistering and philandering," as he put it, Lawrence had no interest and stayed away. Beeson would also go to dances and parties at Christmastime and found them "exhilarating," while Lawrence avoided them altogether. Similarly, Lawrence would avoid the "Eights Week" festivities, a kind of annual springtime regatta on the Thames, with dances, picnics and entertainment and "every possible chance for flirtations."[54]

# 3

# Lawrence and His Family: The Burden of Illegitimacy

Lawrence's illegitimacy, and its meaning for him throughout his life, cannot be separated from his relationships with his parents, from his conscious and unconscious views of them, their personalities, their lives and relationship with one another, and above all, from his identification with them. The evidence regarding the great significance of Lawrence's illegitimacy for him is beyond dispute. However, it is not the mere fact of illegitimacy, with its social consequences, but rather the complex interplay of psychological and psychosexual developmental forces and social realities that gave the illegitimacy its weight in the formation of Lawrence's character and the emergence after the war of his psychological and sexual conflicts. Lawrence's offhand, sometimes humorous dismissals of the matter not only show his attempt to reject its importance, but reflect also a kind of enlightened social viewpoint, above the battle.[1] A more tolerant social climate might have eased somewhat the burden of Lawrence's conflict over his illegitimacy, but it could not have relieved him completely of the deeper psychological problems it occasioned.

It is not possible to establish a precise time when Lawrence "learned" that his father had another family and that his parents were not married. A childhood friend recalls hearing Lawrence say, "My father told me I was a bastard when I was eleven"; yet in his only written statement on the subject (the only one, that is, of which I am aware) Lawrence denies flatly that his parents told him.[2]

In view of the intense and precocious curiosity of his young mind, what probably happened is that he pieced together the reality from his own observations. Arnold Lawrence told me that Lawrence wrote either to his friend Lionel Curtis or his mentor David Hogarth that when he was four and a half he began to discover what the situation was from trying to understand a discussion his father was having with a solicitor about managing the estate in Ireland. In the years after that, Lawrence told his brother, he "worked it out for himself."[3] Although this is psychologically possible, and even likely, I have not found the letter in which the statement occurs. Arnold Lawrence is convinced his brother understood the fact of their illegitimacy by the time he was nine or ten years old.[4] I disagree emphatically with Aldington's statement that Lawrence's claim to have known before he was ten was "very likely a rhetorical expression deriving from Lawrence's vagueness over numbers."[5]

Whether or not a solicitor was discussing the situation within earshot of the four-and-a-half-year-old Ned, it is true that as a child Lawrence had other opportunities to overhear discussions between his parents. No matter how scrupulously discreet they may have been, they could well have underestimated what a lively-minded and intensely curious child like Ned might pick up and piece together from bits of conversation. In addition, the father sometimes made trips to Ireland and visited with former Irish friends in London, and the mother kept up correspondence with relatives in Scotland, all of which provided puzzling, incongruous clues for Lawrence to work out. Land agents were in fact coming from Ireland to meet with the father at least once a year to discuss arrangements with the tenants and other matters.[6]

The fact that T.E.'s parents never told him directly of their situation but left him to figure it out for himself only served to underscore the deception and intensify his resentment of them for it. The paragraph that follows the passage in which Lawrence tells Mrs. Shaw that he discovered his illegitimacy as a child demonstrates clearly his resentment and conflict, together with the self-hatred thus engendered. Written in 1927 at a time when there was considerable strain between Lawrence and his mother, the letter reveals as well how inextricably intertwined were his feelings about his parents (especially his mother) and their relationship, his illegitimacy, and his views of marriage and parenthood as they applied to himself. "They thought always that they were living in sin," he wrote, "and that we would some day find out. Whereas I knew it before I was ten, and they never told me; till after my father's death something I said showed mother that I knew, and didn't care a straw.

"One of the real reasons (there are three or four) why I am in the service is so that I may live by myself. She has given me a terror of families and inquisitions. And yet you'll understand she is my mother, and an extraordinary person. Knowledge of her will prevent my ever making any woman a mother, and the cause of children. I think she suspects this: but she does not know that the inner conflict, which makes me a standing civil war, is the inevitable issue of the discordant natures of herself and my father, and the inflammation of strength and weakness which followed the uprooting of their lives and principles. They should not have borne children."[7]

It is the conflict described in this letter, deriving from the discrepancy between his parents' avowed Christian values and their position as pillars of their church in Oxford society and the actualities of their unmarried state, that was the most disturbing aspect of the illegitimacy for Lawrence and had the greatest influence upon his later development. It would not have been so difficult had his parents not felt forced to maintain the deception with the children. A person's inner sense of worth derives from an identification with valued parents, but Lawrence's parents were on the one hand persons of high ideals and standards while at the same time their actual lives violated fundamentally what they purported to represent. His identification with them includes both elements. He is identified with their ideals, which he accepts, but also with their failure to live up to them. They are, furthermore, deceivers, and he has been made a part of the deception.

To make matters still more difficult his mother required of him that he *redeem* her fallen state by his own special achievements, by being a person of unusual value who accomplishes great deeds, preferably religious and ideally on an heroic scale. Lawrence did his best to fulfill heroic ideals. But he was plagued, especially after the events of the war activated his inner conflicts, by a deep sense of failure. Having been deceived as a child he was later to feel that he himself was a deceiver — that he had deceived the Arabs — although, as we shall see, his conviction about this far outweighed the reality.

I do not mean to imply that the influence of the illegitimacy on Lawrence's development was altogether negative. Part of his creativity and originality lies in his "irregularity," in his capacity to remain outside conventional ways of thinking, a tendency which I believe derives, at least in part, from his illegitimacy. Lawrence's capacity for invention and his ability to see unusual or humorous relationships in familiar situations come also, I believe, from his illegitimacy. He was not limited to established or "legitimate" solutions or ways of doing things, and thus his mind was open to a wider range of possibilities and opportunities.

In addition to its psychological meaning, Lawrence's illegitimacy had important social consequences and placed limitations upon him, which rankled him deeply and preyed on his mind. Certain schools and social opportunities were not available; he was excluded from some social groups and may have been considered a liability for a number of professional posts, especially in governmental circles.[8] At times he felt socially isolated when erstwhile friends shunned him upon learning of his background.[9] Lawrence's delight in making fun of regular officers and other segments of "regular" society (however well deserved the mockery) derived, one suspects, at least in part from his inner view of his own irregular situation. His fickleness about names for himself is directly related, of course, to his view of his parents and to his identification with them. As far as I have been able to discern, Lawrence did not share with his childhood friends or with schoolmates at Jesus College the facts of his illegitimacy, for none of those I interviewed who knew him during that period were aware of it.

According to Elsie Newcombe, the wife of Colonel Stewart F. Newcombe, an officer and good friend with whom Lawrence served during the war, Lawrence told her husband in 1914 that his parents were not married and he "had no right" to the name Lawrence.[10] What induced Lawrence to start telling his friends at this time in his life is not known. Perhaps it was because the matter was becoming known in Oxford anyway, or he had lived away from home so long his views of it had changed. During the decades that followed he told a number of his friends about it and wrote hints and bits to others. (Copies of these letters are among the Lawrence papers in the Bodleian Library.)

Lawrence's bitterness, pain and anxiety lest the matter come out publicly are evident behind the humor and the tone of inconsequence with which he sometimes dismissed it. In giving his address to Lord Winterton in 1923 he wrote casually, "My constant address (as Lawrence — did you know that wasn't my real name?) is at 14 Barton Street, Westminster."[11] To Lionel Curtis in 1926: "Your remark about ancestry, for which you apologized, I've entirely forgotten! So what can it have been? Bars Sinister [the heraldic sign erroneously believed to be the sign of illegitimacy] are rather jolly ornaments. You feel so like a flea in the legitimate prince's bed!"[12] Or to A. E. "Jock" Chambers, whom he wrote in 1924: "This address is my safest one: it may be any name. 'Shaw' I call myself, but some write Ross and others Lawrence. Hippocleides doesn't care!"[13] He signed this last letter: *

TES.
or J.H.R.
or TEL
or EC.

More seriously he wrote to Sir Fred Kenyon, who was cataloguing the *Seven Pillars of Wisdom* in 1927: "My 'Lawrence' label (an invention for his own reasons, of my father's late in life) is worn out."[14] To the American publisher F. N. Doubleday: "So you see the name 'Lawrence' bars itself. It is worth a lot of money, because of Arabia: whereas my father chose it because it meant nothing, to his family."[15] And again to Curtis, who was preparing an entry for *Who's Who* about him: "Of

* From the Bodleian Library, Oxford.

course write anything you please; so long as you don't give away (i.) my original family (ii.) my present address."[16]

In trying to understand Lawrence's relationship with his parents, one should not presume that the documents, especially the letters to Mrs. Shaw, which disclose his deeply ambivalent attitude toward them, depict the family relationships as they actually existed when he was a child. (Lawrence's relationship with Charlotte Shaw will be explored in Part Five.) The letters to Mrs. Shaw, written in the loneliness of India, are introspective. They follow a decade of experiences that had destroyed the relative inner harmony that T.E. had achieved in childhood and young adulthood. They disclose thoughts and feelings Lawrence might never have become conscious of, or at least ones he might not have dwelled upon, had his life and character not become so severely dislocated. They represent an effort on his part to understand himself, a kind of self-analysis directed toward a mother-figure who evoked his inner attitudes toward his mother but with less experience of pain. (In her letters to him Mrs. Shaw spoke of similar conflicts with her own parents.) Lawrence's letters reveal his inner mental representations of his parents — not literally the parents themselves.

This is not to say that these ambivalent attitudes toward his parents did not begin to form in Lawrence's childhood. Rather, the words of his letters reflect the impact of the complete life experience which followed childhood, the insights and conflicts established thereafter, and the strained relations between Lawrence and his mother, which resulted from his insistence upon remaining beneath his station in the ranks.

Lawrence's father and mother, even by the high standards of the day, were in many ways very good parents. Their religious and moral strictness did not prevent them from giving their sons wide freedom to learn, to explore their environment, and to travel, opportunities which Ned and Will in particular took advantage of. And they provided a secure, loving home and rich educational opportunities.

Lawrence's father from all accounts was devoted to his sons and their welfare, and as mentioned previously, he enjoyed many activities with them.[17] Lawrence's letters contain a number of references to these mutual interests, especially photography ("he taught me before I was four years old") and bicycling. They went together on summer bicycle tours in England from as early as 1903 and in France in 1907. Lawrence acknowledges his father's kindness to him, and Arnold states that the elder Lawrence was very fond of his second son.[18]

T.E. wrote to Liddell Hart that his father's family seemed unaware that the five sons existed, "even when after [my father's] death, recognition of their achievement might have done honour to the name."[19] But it is not clear to whom this statement referred. Lawrence's difficulty with his father was quite different. It lay in the defeat of his masculinity, and of his view of himself as a strong and effective person — the result of being identified with the elder Lawrence as his son. For in Lawrence's eyes his father was a devalued person, transformed and reduced by his mother. Whereas once Thomas Lawrence had been "on the large scale," "grand," "naturally lord-like," "a hard rider and drinker" and a "spend-thrift," in the mother's hands he had been "remodeled" into "a teetotaler" and "a domestic man." We have seen that in reality the father was some-what less heroic in his former life than Lawrence imagined, and a good deal more of a person in the home in Oxford than the letters to Charlotte Shaw would suggest. But for reasons of his own psychology, Lawrence viewed him in the way that he did.

Much of Lawrence's resentment of his mother, which had a number of causes, was related to her role, in his view, in reducing Thomas Lawrence. Not only did Lawrence accuse his mother of carrying off his father and cutting him down, but in a passage which has something of the tone of a jealous son, he also accuses her of devoting herself too fully to keeping him that way. The following passage also reveals the dominant element in Lawrence's relationship with his mother, the deeply ambiva-lent love-hate attachment by which he was both drawn to her and yet repelled: "Mother is rather wonderful: but very exciting," he wrote. "She is so set, so assured in mind. I think she 'set' many years ago: perhaps before I was born. I have a terror of her knowing anything about my feelings, or convictions, or way of life. If she knew they would be damaged: violated: no longer mine. You see, she would not hesitate to understand them: and I do not understand them, and do not want to. Nor has she seen any of us growing: because I think she has not grown since we began. She was wholly wrapped up in my father, whom she had carried away jealously from his former life and country, against great odds: and whom she kept as her trophy of power. Also, she was a fanati-cal housewife,[20] who would rather do her own housework than not, to the total neglect of herself."[21] The letter also reveals Lawrence's intense struggle to grow as a separate person despite his mother's overpowering personality.

The terror of closeness with his mother lest she destroy his inner self (a conflict most sons resolve, at least in part, in childhood and adolescence) is further revealed in another letter to Mrs. Shaw a year later. "I wonder how you will like her," Lawrence wrote (a meeting between Mrs. Shaw and Mrs. Lawrence was anticipated); "she is monumental really! and so unlike you. Probably she is exactly like me; otherwise we wouldn't so hanker after one another, whenever we are wise enough to keep apart. Her letters are things I dread, and she always asks for more of mine (I try and write monthly: but we haven't a subject we dare be intimate upon: so they are spavined things) and hates them when they come, as they do, ever so rarely. I think I'm afraid of letting her get, ever so little inside the circle of my integrity: and she is always hammering and sapping to come in. A very dominant person: only old now, and, so my brother says, very much less than she has been. She has so lived in her children, and in my father, that she cannot relieve herself, upon herself, at all. And it isn't right to cry out to your children for love. They are prevented, by the walls of time and function, from loving their parents."[22]

Again, three months later he wrote: "I've not written any letters of this sort to anyone else, since I was born. No trust ever existed between my mother and myself. Each of us jealously guarded his or her own individuality, whenever we came together. I always felt that she was laying siege to me, and would conquer, if I left a chink unguarded."[23]

Lawrence's relationship with his mother, deeper, more complex and more troubled than that with the father, played a central role in his personal development, the direction of his life, and the formation of his character. He was probably not her favorite in the conventional sense of receiving the most affection, and she seems not to have been especially demonstrative toward him physically (although the nannies were more so).[24] However, all my informants agree that Lawrence was adored by his mother, who was deeply devoted to his welfare, and that he was the child in whom both parents had the most important emotional investment. He was treated differently, as if he were special, and it was expected from childhood that it would be Ned of all the sons who would do something important with his life.[25]

Mrs. Lawrence's original hope that her sons would provide her personal redemption by becoming Christian missionaries was fulfilled only by Robert. Frank and Will were killed in the war, and Arnold resisted intensely ("I just didn't pay any attention to her") and ceased in his own estimation to be a Christian.[26] As for T.E., in Oxford he took part in the family Bible readings, attended faithfully Canon Christopher's sermons at St. Aldates, and even taught Sunday School classes, although according to one of his friends Lawrence lost a Sunday School post for reading the class a beautiful story of Oscar Wilde's (Wilde was then in disgrace).[27] Mrs. Lawrence saw in T.E.'s reverent 1908 letter describing Chartres Cathedral an indication of his love of God and she had copies of it made and distributed to her friends.[28] But a careful reading of the emotion-filled letter indicates that Lawrence's response was largely aesthetic, and that his appreciation was not of God Himself but of the cathedral as "a place truly in which to worship God."[29] A year later, when he went to Syria, his mother believed that he was on a special mission of some kind, one with religious significance.

But the direction of Lawrence's later life, ascetic though it may have become, was secular in the extreme. When Bob went out to China as a medical missionary, accompanied by the mother (perhaps it would be more accurate to say that he accompanied her), T.E. disparaged their missionary activity in a number of letters.[30]

Lawrence's closeness to his mother, his need to please her, his sensitivity, and his intense identification with her and with her conflicts made it almost inevitable that the imposition of her ambitions, emotional needs, guilt and demands upon him would ultimately have a devastating effect upon his personality. His psychological vulnerabilities may be traced in large part to their relationship. "The strongest impression I have," his younger brother Arnold once wrote, "is that his [T.E.'s] life has been injured by his mother."[31] Lawrence struggled to resist her smothering and absorbing influence, to become completely separate and distant from her. Even his puckish rebellion against every form of authority and his conspicuous pursuit of "nonsuccess" may be seen in part as a defiance of her authority.

Lawrence's resemblance to his mother, which extended beyond their physical similarities to include basic personality characteristics, was obvious to his friends. One, a woman, remarked to me: "T.E. got his firm chin and the piercing blue eyes from his mother, his strength of character and ability to martyr himself in the desert. She had those martyr qualities. . . . She forced herself. Nothing would get him down either."[32] And his resemblance to his mother was well recognized by Lawrence himself, although he seemed pleased when Charlotte Shaw wrote to him after meeting Mrs. Lawrence that she did not see the resemblance. Lawrence replied: "It interested me very much that you found no likeness between us. I had taken it for granted (not knowing myself at all) that we're so like that we clashed. You'd suggest it is because we are unlike: or rather, if you are right, it is unlikeness which is a possible cause of our clashing so, when we meet: for we do rub each other up the wrong way."[33]

Lawrence's resistance as a child to his parents' authority often took familiar forms of naughtiness. Discipline, according to Arnold, was administered in the form of severe whippings on the buttocks and was delivered by his mother because his father was "too gentle, too imaginative — couldn't bring himself to."[34] Arnold remembered receiving only one such beating himself. His mother once told him, "I never had to do it to Bob, once to Frank and frequently to T.E." The beatings seem to have been brought on by nothing more than routine childhood misbehavior, such as T.E.'s resistance to learning to play the piano. In any case, what was unique about them, Arnold felt, was that they seemed to be given for the purpose of breaking T.E.'s will.[35] Never losing her faith in such punishments, Mrs. Lawrence once remarked in her later years that the reason Lord Astor's horses never won was because he wouldn't whip them.[36]

In actuality T.E. was a dutiful and devoted son. Robert Lawrence stressed to me T.E.'s sensitivity to their parents' feelings and his affectionate ways in the family. He wrote long, devoted letters home when he was away, especially before the war, describing in great detail what he was seeing and doing. The letters, which were directed principally to his mother, must have pleased his parents immensely. They do not contain much in the way of personal disclosure of feeling toward his parents, but such reticence was common among young Englishmen of the time. Lawrence wanted very much to please his parents and often felt he was disappointing them or would eventually do so.

In 1911, when Lawrence was doing archeological field work near Carchemish, in Turkey, he wrote home: "Poor Father! his sons are not going to support his years by the gain of their professions and trades. One a missionary: one an artist of sorts and a wanderer after sensations; one thinking of lay education work: one in the army, and one too small to think. None of us can ever afford to keep a wife: still the product of fairly healthy brains and tolerable bodies will not be all worthless in this world. One of us must surely get something of the unattainable we are all feeling after. That's a comfort: and we are all going for the same thing under different shapes: Do you know we illustrate the verse about heart, soul, mind, body? Will Arnie prove the strength that will make it all perfect and effective?"[37]

In another letter the following month Lawrence emphasized further the antimaterialistic idealism of the Lawrence brothers: "I fear father is right about us and our careers: but this idealistic disregard for the good things of the world has its bright side. And to say that he had 5 sons, none making money, would be a glorious boast — from my point of view at least."[38]

# TWO

# YOUTH

# Introduction

After the war, when Lawrence looked back over a decade of involvement in what he came to regard as an alien cause, he warned of "the dreamers of the day."[1] He called them dangerous men, "for they may act their dream with open eyes to make it possible." His own dreaming of the day, his preoccupation with a personal crusade, with the liberation of a people in bondage, began during his schoolboy days. "I had dreamed, at the City School in Oxford, of hustling into form, while I lived, the new Asia which time was inexorably bringing upon us," he says in the epilogue to *Seven Pillars of Wisdom*, his epic account of the events of the Arab Revolt.[2] Later, after a series of interviews with him, Basil Liddell Hart wrote: "The idea of a crusade, the idea underlying it, revolved in his mind, giving rise to a dream crusade, which implied a leader with whom in a sense he identified himself yet remained as . . . a sympathetic observer. Naturally, it would be a crusade in the modern form — the freeing of a race from bondage. Where, however, was he to find a race in need of release and at the same time of *sufficient* appeal to him? The Arabs seemed the only suitable one left, and they fitted in with the trend of his interests."[3] Lawrence, given this passage by Liddell Hart for critical review, changed only the word "*sufficient*" to "historical." Schoolboys who dream of performing heroic deeds, even perhaps of leading an oppressed people out of bondage, are not unusual. What is unusual and perhaps unique in Lawrence's case is the particular confluence of personal history, psychological need, extraordinary capabilities, and historical opportunity that made it possible for these dreams to be enacted in reality.

As we have seen, Lawrence began in early childhood to lead expeditions, to study soldiery and to read of warfare. At nine and a half he was making his first brass rubbings of knights in armor,[4] and at fifteen he was reading treatises on techniques of warfare and military castle building.

During the years in which he was an Oxford undergraduate, he prepared himself further for the major acts and events of his life. He traveled in France, and studied its castles and military architecture. He became imbued with the military, psychological and philosophical themes of the Crusades, and above all with the romantic literature of medieval France.

This literature supplied the Crusaders with an ideology that could ennoble, if not the deeds themselves, at least what motivated them, and could help to rationalize the excesses of their behavior. These works were the principal literary sustenance of Lawrence's youth. E. M. Forster's comments, in an unpublished passage that was to introduce an edition of Lawrence's letters, provide an appropriate introduction to this period, in which a romantic quest begins to take shape:

> From eighteen onwards he extended his holiday range to France — circled there more and more widely until, at Aigues-Mortes, he was stopped by the Mediterranean. By the time he was twenty he had picked up medieval military architecture, and seen every twelfth century castle of importance in England, Wales, France. The notion of a Crusade, of a body of men leaving one country to do noble deeds in another, possessed him, and I think never left him, though the locality of the country varied: at one time it was Arabia, later it was the air. Had he been a Christian, his medieval equipment would have been complete and thought-proof: he would have possessed a positive faith and been happier: he would have been the "parfait gentil knight," the defender of orthodoxy, instead of the troubled and troublous genius who fascinated his generation and failed to fit into it. He would have been much smaller. In the Aigues-Mortes letter the imperfections of his armour already appear. He longs to set sail, like St. Louis; but for where? And he longs, like Wordsworth, to be at peace.[5]

Complementing his absorption with the Crusades, in both their military and romantic aspects, Lawrence's personal preparations for the deeds he believed he would someday be called upon to accomplish were thorough and extensive during these years. He applied his intellectual powers to learning all he could about military strategy and began to become acquainted with the Arab lands and people during his first trip to the East in 1909. He applied also his manual dexterity and physical endurance to testing his short but sturdy frame for the ordeals that lay ahead. He undertook extraordinary feats of climbing and walking in France and Syria under conditions of personal privation.

The time he spent at Jesus College may also be looked upon as a period of intellectual, physical and emotional preparation, unusual for an undergraduate in its singleminded concentration upon the study of medieval society, architecture, warfare and literature. Oxford was a time of greater freedom for Lawrence than his schoolboy days, but the work of inuring himself for some great task ahead continued unabated. While at Oxford he came to know David Hogarth, the archeologist and traveler to the East, whose fatherly interest was to be decisive for Lawrence's career. It was also during these years that Lawrence made what was, to my knowledge, the only serious attempt to become close to a young woman. His reaction to the rejection he received seems to have had a lasting effect upon the direction of his emotional attachments.

Soon after Lawrence's graduation from Oxford, Hogarth arranged for him to join Hogarth's British Museum archeological explorations at the site of the ancient Hittite city of Carchemish in Asia Minor. Strategically located at a crossing that commanded the upper Euphrates, it appeared as a great mound rising a steep one hundred feet out of the river, a ruin set in a windswept treeless land. The village of Jerablus, some forty houses built on rising ground, was about half a mile away. "Very magnificent must Carchemish have been," his archeological companion, Leonard Woolley wrote, "when its sculptures were gay with colour, when the sunlight glistened on its enamelled walls, and its sombre brick was overlaid with panels of cedar and plates of bronze; when the plumed horses rattled their chariots along its streets, and the great lords, with long embroidered robes and girdles of black and gold, passed in and out of the carved gates of its palaces; but even now, when it lies deserted and in heaps, it has perhaps in the melancholy of its ruin found a subtler charm to offset the glory of its prime."[6]

The three years at Carchemish afforded Lawrence, then in his early twenties, an excellent opportunity to live and travel in the Middle East and to study its people and cultures under conditions of relative personal and political stability.

These years were, for the most part, full and happy ones for Lawrence. A psychoanalyst presented only with the history of Lawrence's life during this period of his youth would find little that would lead him to anticipate the tortured and tormented soul that emerged from the campaigns of World War I. It is true that Lawrence turned away from civilized bourgeois English society to a world of fellowship among men in a foreign culture. But many Englishmen, many men of other civilized nations, have left a conventional course to find another life truer to the demands of their own natures, and Lawrence's archeological interests took him naturally to the Carchemish site when the opportunity arose.

Indeed, there was nothing in Lawrence's behavior or writings to indicate conflict about his choice. "Till the war swallowed up everything," he commented on the manuscript of Graves's biography, "I wanted nothing better than Carchemish, which was a perfect life."[7] Half the letters Lawrence ever wrote to his family, at least of those that have been preserved, were written in this period of less than four years. They are full, rich accounts, eagerly drafted, of a life that seemed satisfying in every respect. We get from them a picture of an unusually gifted young man, learning and mastering a hundred skills, pursuing what his friend Ernest Altounyan called "the exquisite realization of self."[8]

It was as if Lawrence were converting himself into an instrument of achievement, in dedication to an abstract conception of self. He seems to have given little thought to the ends that he would later strive to attain. For while he remained in many ways boyish and emotionally immature, Lawrence was becoming increasingly perceptive about other people, sensitive to their psychology and personal needs, and paradoxically mature beyond his years in the experience of life and the handling of men. His own emotional involvements remained selective and highly controlled, and account for the intense sense of loneliness so many of his friends observed.

The most significant skill Lawrence developed during these years was his capacity to use his knowledge of other peoples to move out of his own cultural framework. The exploration of the consequences for Lawrence of this identification with the Arab peoples is a major theme of later chapters of this book.

# 4

# Literary Influences

Too little attention, it seems to me, has been paid to the literary influences on Lawrence during his youth. In these years reading may provide much stimulation for the growth of ideas and dreams, and, ultimately, the impetus for action and the form the action takes. Its effect is often lasting.

Although Lawrence read widely, his reading was dominated by medieval romantic works, especially French, and the ideas of medieval romanticism came to fill his consciousness.[1] Arnold Lawrence is of the opinion that his brother's medieval researches were "a dream way of escape from Bourgeois England," and that neither medieval history nor archeology continued to hold his attention when he ceased to need them for the benefit of his own personality.[2] Earlier, Lawrence had shown an interest in epic tales, such as the *Kalevala* of Finland; *Huon de Bordeaux*, the French fairy-tale epic of the early thirteenth century; and Lucian's *True History*, a satire on the *Odyssey*. He told Robert Graves that although at Jesus College he "read history, officially," he "actually spent nearly three years reading Provençal poetry, and mediaeval French chansons de geste. When time came for degree wasn't prepared for exam."[3] Later, to Liddell Hart, he wrote that in addition to "the usual school boy stuff. . . . I also read nearly every manual of chivalry. Remember that my period was the Middle Ages, always."[4]

The intensity of Lawrence's interest in medieval epic poetry and the depth of his identification with the world it depicted is conveyed in the recollection of a college friend: "I remember a rare occasion when he came to a meeting of the College Literary Society: a paper was read on the *Chanson de Roland*. When it was over Lawrence spoke for about twenty minutes in his clear, quiet voice, ranging serenely about the epic poetry of several languages. It was all first hand: *you felt that he had 'been there.'* "[5] (Italics added.)

At twenty-two Lawrence wrote his mother that he was reading with pleasure *Le Petit Jehan de Saintré,* a fifteenth-century manual of chivalric manners, which describes the education and tutelage from early childhood, chiefly at the hands of women of the court, of a budding knight.[6] The romance of Tristan and Iseult and thirteenth-century *fabliaux* (droll stories concerned with adultery, wantonness, and the corruption of the clergy) are other readings that Lawrence mentions specifically.[7]

The romantic revivals in epic form of Norse, Icelandic, Arthurian, and other legends and tales of heroism by the nineteenth-century English medievalist William Morris were always favorites of Lawrence. He also read with pleasure the works of other romantic Victorians, among them Christina Rossetti, Maurice Hewlett and Tennyson. Lawrence's interest in the revival of handicrafts and in printing was inspired by medieval influences, especially by Morris, who had elaborately printed Chaucer and other medieval works at his Kelmscott Press. In addition, Lawrence read Froissart and other chroniclers of the world of the Middle Ages,[8] and had in his collection at home such modern works as the Everyman's Library *Medieval Stories and Romances,* which contained a popular exposition of chivalry, including "what Sir Guy says to Saladin about the Rule of Chivalry."[9]

Lawrence's devotion to Sir Thomas Malory and the Arthurian legends which, like himself, were born in Wales and developed in France, epitomized his medievalism. At eighteen, as he sat gazing out over the sea off Brittany, he quoted rapturously to his mother, in a manner which would embarrass a youth of today, Tennyson's *Idylls of the King* (in which Queen Victoria's poet laureate popularized and chastened for his sovereign's readers the lusty legends of King Arthur's Court).[10] Malory's *Morte d'Arthur* was one of three books Lawrence carried with him throughout the Arabian campaign.

The original *chansons de geste* were poetic, sometimes epic narratives, composed by the trouvères of eleventh-century France to commemorate the deeds of Charlemagne and other legendary heroes. The *Chanson de Roland,* an epic, is the most famous. The *chansons de geste* set down in verse the heroic values of feudal society. Noble deeds are performed by knights and barons, whose special qualities and virtues appear in their early childhood, against less worthy enemies and rivals. Actual historical events are related, though distorted by legend. Manly virtues of sacrifice, bravery, and loyalty to the king and country are depicted. The most important human relationship in these epic tales of adventure is that between men (Oliver and Roland, for instance) and is characterized by close Christian comradeship and love; little is said of romantic love between men and women.

By the end of the eleventh century the Muslims had taken possession of the Holy Land and the Church summoned the nobility of Western Europe to the rescue. The *chansons de geste* which arose before the Crusades, would, in their original form, have had little to offer the Crusaders. Their rough heroes were concerned chiefly with local and largely nonreligious wars, whose limited purposes did not contain much to inspire the Crusaders. But several developments in the latter part of the eleventh century served to create a literature that became intimately associated with the Crusades and furnished in poetic form their inspiration and rationale. There arose in the warmer atmosphere of Provence the poetry of the troubadours, who, as servitors of their feudal lords, sang the praises of the ladies of the court in poems and lyrics of romantic love. Within the Church the idealization of the Virgin Mary, which eventually became a cult, contributed richly to the new image of women as beings to be worshipped. Furthermore, the castles built in Europe in the twelfth century provided courts and a more settled society, in which romantic interests could flourish, refinements of life could develop, and the value of women might be appreciated. The position of women of the upper class improved as "the castle became a court where feminine graces might shine, and the Virgin, the Mother of God and the Queen of Heaven, took powerful hold on human hearts."[11]

Late in the twelfth century in France there arose a new literary form, the *romans d'aventure*, attributable to a specific author. These tales added another dimension to the knightly ideal: the cult of courtly love. New materials, less tied to the actualities of local French wars than the *chansons de geste*, were found in the "Matière de Bretagne" (derived from the Arthurian romances brought into Brittany from Wales in the twelfth century), and in Ovidian and other classical themes of love which were brought from the south. In the court of Eleanor of Aquitaine, mother of Richard I, the writers of *romans d'aventure*, the most famous of whom was Chrétien de Troyes, told of Tristan and Iseult, of Lancelot, Arthur and Guinevere, of Percivale, Galahad and the quest for the Holy Grail.

Following the inspiration of the trouvères of northern France, the troubadours of Provence and the *romans d'aventure*, the ideal of courtly love developed. Whereas before the twelfth century women had been subjugated and seen as inferior, or as instruments of the devil to tempt men into evil, now the knight's lady was placed on a pedestal. He went off to reclaim the Holy Land from the infidels, not for God alone (the Church had an ambivalent attitude toward this diversion of the knight's energies from his holy struggle), but for love of his lady, and his valorous deeds were performed for her as acts of worship.[12] Romantic gallantry combined with the older elements of chivalry contained in the *chansons de geste* brought to flower the ideals of the medieval chivalric code, which was to evolve ultimately into our rituals and stereotypes of gentlemanly behavior. "Whatever may have been his true reason for fighting, his only avowed motive was the love of his lady, which was the formula which usually accompanied the challenge to combat. All the heroes of the age have a mistress in the background, who uplifts them to acts of valour."[13] Usually this relationship was outside marriage, for marriage was considered incompatible with love, but any other lady, any other man's wife, would do.[14]

What is most striking about the chivalric ideal, as it developed in twelfth-century France, is the contrast it presented to the actualities of medieval court life and the Crusades themselves. Henry Adams pointed out that at the social level "while the Virgin was miraculously using the power of spiritual love to elevate and purify the people, Eleanor [of Aquitaine] and her daughters were using the power of earthly love to discipline and refine the courts. Side by side with the crude realities about them, they insisted on teaching and enforcing an ideal that contradicted the realities, and had no value for them or for us except in the contradiction."[15] Similarly, the elevation of women in the chivalric ideal did little to raise the position of women in medieval society.[16] From the social standpoint it was a veneer, furnishing the men of the period with a psychologically useful ideology. Similar contrasts existed among the ideals of courtly love themselves. On the one hand they are curiously platonic and virtuous, while in some of the tales, especially those derived from Arthurian legends, the knights are heavily engaged in romantic liaisons that are filled with lust, adultery, incest, and the murder of rivals, and that result in the birth of illegitimate children, King Arthur himself being a prime example.

But these social and emotional contradictions pale in significance when compared with the extraordinary discrepancies between the lofty faith and heroic idealism of the Crusaders and their actual performance. As Steven Runciman put it: "There was so much courage and so little honour, so much devotion and so little understanding. High ideals were besmirched by cruelty and greed, enterprise and endurance by a blind and narrow self-righteousness; and the Holy War itself was nothing more than a long act of intolerance in the name of God, which is the sin against the Holy Ghost."[17]

I myself cannot help but believe that the inspiration for the chivalric ideal, and the strong investment in an ideal of romantic love, came in part from the awareness in the courts of Europe of the acts of cruelty, aggression and hatred in which the knights of Europe were engaged. For the chevalier of twelfth-century Europe, the illusions of ideal love and epic heroism offset in secular terms his actual behavior just as the Church's concept of a Holy War counterbalanced the crimes against religious faith in which Christendom was engaged. The literature of the nobility drew its materials not principally from the Crusades themselves, but from the nobler legends of the continent and the magical stories of the Knights of the Round Table.

These discrepancies, as we shall see, have striking parallels with the contrasts in Lawrence's psychology, and with the gulf which came to separate his own romantic ideals, much influenced by the medieval concepts that inspired his actions, from the realities which he encountered in their execution. But there is little evidence that he paid much attention to the seamy side of the Crusades, despite the fact that he read widely in medieval history, had medieval history scholars as tutors, and wrote his thesis after making several trips to France and Syria for the purpose of studying Crusader castles. In fact, in his stress on the military, technical, strategic and tactical aspects of the Crusader castles he seemed to avoid considering in detail the purposes to which these structures were put or the real purposes of the Crusaders in the East. In the thesis he wrote at Oxford based on these researches, he does discuss the differences between the military orders of knighthood, the Templars and Hospitalers, and the different sorts of castles they built, but says little about the range of their activities.[18]

Lawrence wrote his mother of his admiration for Richard I after visiting Richard's castle, Château-Gaillard: "The whole construction bears the unmistakeable stamp of genius. Richard I must have been a far greater man than we usually consider him: he must have been a great strategist and a great engineer, as well as a great man-at-arms. I hope Mr. Jane [one of Lawrence's tutors] will emphasize this in his book. It is time Richard had justice done to his talents."[19]

Yet in his admiration for Richard as a military strategist, Lawrence seems to overlook the cruelties of this Crusader, of which he must have been aware (for one, Richard butchered more than two thousand Saracen prisoners at Acre when his negotiations with Saladin hit a snag).[20] In one passage only, in a letter to his mother during his travels, does Lawrence indicate his awareness of the excesses of the Crusaders, and this concerned a "civil" campaign, the Albigensian Crusade against the heretics of southern France. "The town had been taken, and the Crusaders wanted to kill the heretics," Lawrence wrote his mother, "but there were many Catholics in the town as well. 'What shall we do?' they asked the Legate, Peter of Castelnau. 'Kill them all,' said he. 'God will recognize his own,' and some 8000 were butchered in cold blood. Pleasant people those 13th Century Crusaders."[21] Much later, Lawrence wrote Liddell Hart that he had no general interest in the Crusades as a religious enterprise, and evidently told him that his sympathies were more with the Crusaders' opponents than with them.[22]

Lawrence's apparent unconcern with the true behavior of the Crusaders does not, in my opinion, reflect cruelty or unconcern with suffering on his part, but rather, his need to isolate the technical aspect of a problem from its meaning and to sustain an ideal conception even when certain facts would otherwise challenge it. Lawrence's medieval reading helped him to build a myth of the absolute contest of the forces of good against evil. When the actual events of the Arab campaigns made it impossible for him to maintain this myth he became deeply troubled.

Lawrence's attraction to medieval romanticism has other, more personal psychological determinants. He was beginning to develop within himself a heroic ego ideal which he could counterpose to the threat to his self-regard that the childhood discoveries concerning his parents' situation had brought about. The medieval romances suited him ideally. The world they depicted was one in which men of noble birth acted as proper heroes, were not drawn down in station by their ladies, and engaged in noble deeds on an epic scale, having been, like himself, chosen for this purpose in childhood. Although the romances of the court were an exciting diversion, and the images of romantic love inspiring, the business of war and the close comradeship among men loyal to one another was perhaps more important.

Women in this literature represent many of the ambiguities with which Lawrence wrestled in his perceptions of his mother. Beautiful, sublime and sexual on the one hand, they were worshipped in an idealized, ritualized and platonic fashion on the other. True to their true lovers, they frequently betrayed their husbands, while the husbands themselves regularly betrayed their wives. Although the medieval noblewoman dominated her knight through the demands she made for worshipful devotion and the accomplishment of extraordinary tasks, she also inspired in him the sense of her own value. To please her he strove to bring back to her accounts of great deeds she could admire. In the rollicking Arthurian romances women are consistently adulterous, though some are remarkably steadfast in their loyalty to the object of their infidelity. Yet simultaneously the chaste figure of the Virgin, the Mother of God, accompanies the warrior, and in some medieval tales substitutes for the knight in tournaments when he is delayed because of devotion to her.[23] For Lawrence the redemption of the fallen woman, whose value is inextricably bound to his own worth, was a compelling need. Unable to sustain an idealized view of women, he ultimately abandoned the effort, and his view of women in their sexual functioning became, as we shall see, debased in his later years.

It is difficult to see how this medieval literature, had it not served strong personal needs in Lawrence's psychology, could have compelled so fully the attention of someone of his critical ability. For no matter how fine the style, beautiful the poetry, or lyrical the imagery, it is essentially a literature of fantasy, of make-believe. The *chansons de geste*, the *romans d'aventure* and the Arthurian romances and myths are fairy stories, often lovely ones, that appeal to the childlike and unrealistic mind, a mind that needs to be nourished on a glorious and idealistic conception of the world that is not bound by the limitations of actuality. That Lawrence could for three years and more be so preoccupied with this literature that he claimed he was unprepared for his examinations supports the view that major aspects of his personal development were arrested during the years of childhood. Yet it is a testimony to his genius that he was able later to adapt heroic fantasies, that seemed to draw upon the myths of these youthful readings, effectively in the pursuit of positive historical objectives.

Lawrence's literary medievalism bears an indirect connection with his later attraction to Arab culture. The poetry of the troubadours and the literature of medieval courtly love contain many of the themes to be found in the popular Arab poetry that reached Spain and France after the Arab conquests in the eighth century. As E. Lévi-Provençal has pointed out, the figures of the lovers, the situations in which they find themselves, and the impediments to their fulfillment are similar in both literatures.[24] The degree of Lawrence's exposure to Arab literature is not known, although his mentor Charles Doughty, the traveler in Arabia, encouraged him to read early Bedouin poetry.[25] It does, however, seem likely that he found in the Arab world romantic aspects that appealed to the same needs in his personality as had the romantic literature of medieval Europe, which so dominated the readings of his youth. In any event, once Lawrence became immersed in Arab society, whose tribal structure resembled in many ways the feudal society of medieval Europe, his interest in the world of the Middle Ages and its literature subsided.[26]

# 5

# Crusader Castles

At thirteen Lawrence began to go on bicycle trips in England to visit medieval castles and churches. Often he went alone, but sometimes he would be accompanied by his father and other family members, or by his friend C. F. C. Beeson. According to Beeson, Lawrence was interested in the design of military buildings as early as 1905. Toward the end of that year the two friends had exhausted the accessible examples in England, and they read during the winter of 1905–1906 in the Radcliffe and Ashmolean libraries in preparation for the investigation of the ruins and restorations of France.[1]

The Lawrence family had kept in touch with French friends in Dinard, especially with a family named Chaignon. Lawrence spoke competent though not elegant French. The Chaignons' home seemed often to have served as a kind of base for Lawrence's travels during his summer trips. In all, six trips to France are documented during the years 1906–1910 in the *Letters*, although Lawrence wrote Graves that he made eight such tours during his school and university vacations.[2] According to Beeson, Lawrence was in France during a summer before 1906, but he did not know any details. Mrs. Lawrence was aware of her adventurous son's tendency to take somewhat reckless chances and to be accident-prone, so she was eager for Beeson to accompany Ned in France in order to watch out for him.

The trips to France that concern us here are the bicycle tours Lawrence made during the summer holidays of 1906, 1907 and 1908 when he was eighteen, nineteen and twenty. On the 1906 trip, which lasted four weeks, he was accompanied by Beeson. In April 1907, during his Easter holiday, he visited the medieval castles of North Wales, not far from his birth-place.[3] In August 1907, Lawrence traveled with his father for part of the month, and their shared interest in photography stimulated Lawrence's picture-taking. On the 1908 trip, which lasted six weeks, he was alone.

Lawrence traveled on the latest model of high-speed bicycle, with dropped handles and an unusually high top-gear ratio, specially built to his order in a shop in Oxford.[4] During 1906 Lawrence and Beeson ("Scroggs") confined themselves to the parts of Brittany near Dinard, Saint-Malo and the Channel coast. In 1907 Lawrence reached the Loire. In 1908 he traveled the length and breadth of France, reaching Champagne, the Mediterranean, the Pyrenees and the western part of the country. The plan to undertake eventually a detailed study of the military architecture of the Crusades may have begun to take shape during the 1906 and 1907 trips, both made before Lawrence began his studies at Jesus College, but only the 1908 tour was specifically devoted to this purpose.

The published accounts do not bring out the extent to which these travels, like so many of the ventures of Lawrence's youth, were a personal preparation, a testing of his body and his spirit for future trials. Beeson noted how his friend, whom he had known for about two years before their trip to France, "had to prove himself." Lawrence was "always making himself tough, always climbing, always testing the limits of his powers."[5] Beeson also felt strongly Lawrence's leadership qualities. Once in Brittany they visited a castle ruin with a moat that was crossed by a bridge. According to Beeson, Lawrence had to jump the moat instead of using the bridge. Lawrence seemed to the more cautious man to take unusual, even reckless, chances when climbing about old walls with loose stones. An image has stayed in Beeson's mind of Lawrence atop some rocks in France with his foot trembling as he tried to find a footing. Beeson warned, "You'll fall," and offered to help. But Lawrence would not let him.[6] Beeson was also impressed with his friend's resourcefulness. On one occasion when his tire was punctured, he became quite troubled about the possible delay in the trip. But Lawrence was not frustrated or irritated. He knew someone "around the corner" who could fix it. Lawrence frequently repaired his own tires.

Beraud Villars, a Frenchman who has written a good biography of Lawrence, has criticized him, correctly I think, for failing in his travels in France to understand the "soul" of the country.[7] But Villars did not realize Lawrence's determination and singlemindedness of purpose, this preparation of himself, of his mental and physical equipment, for a great task.

Lawrence's letters home, especially on the first (1906) trip, contain several proud statements of how fit and strong he was becoming, with a fine physique, which he attributed to not eating too much, certainly not as much as his hosts: "The Chaignons told me yesterday that the English ate all too much. I was rather amused and told them that they ate too much for strength: I said that Mr. Chaignon might possibly be nearly as strong as I was if he ate as little as I did: it wasn't a bit too personal, they talk very freely about each other and myself. It rather surprised Mr. Chaignon — was a new idea for him. He had just acknowledged that I was the stronger of the two. I told them that Bob was weaker than I because he ate too much; they think I am très original; they don't know if I'm in earnest or not."[8] A few days earlier he had written that Mme Chaignon "got a shock when she saw my 'biceps' while bathing. She thinks I am Hercules."[9]

On his trips Lawrence wrote proudly home of how lightly he could travel, how little he could get by with eating, and how cheaply he could live in the most meager of surroundings. His letters contain long accounts of his thrift. For instance, in 1906: "My silk shirt was a blessing. It took up no space, and every day I used to roll it tightly around my other articles, and it used to hold them all in place. Thus my luggage was never larger or longer than my carrier. Father will be very interested to learn this, for the carrier is a small one. It went through the trip excellently and gave absolutely no trouble. I carried two pairs of socks and wore a third. Next time I would only carry one pair and would not trouble to bring a sponge. A spare pair of trousers is useful and in fact necessary: also a spare shirt. A coat is quite useless if a cape is carried: by this means the weight can be reduced to practically nil."[10]

According to Beeson, his friend was not fastidious about food and would eat most of what was available in the countryside. When they went to a farmhouse for a meal, T.E. would be greeted as a familiar friend (which suggests that he had made at least one previous visit to Brittany since his early childhood years in Dinard). When the food in France was really unfamiliar or bad, Lawrence could complain colorfully. He once described the food of the Tarn district of the south: "Their food is weird and wonderful (*omelette aux pommes de terre* yesterday and other articles unspecified and indescribable), the bread tastes like . . . can you imagine leather soaked in brine, and then boiled till soft: with an iron crust, and a flavour like a brandy-snap? It takes me considerable mental and physical effort to 'degust' a mouthful: milk has not been heard of lately, butter has a smell like cream cheese, but a taste like Gruyère (thank goodness for the Roquefort, 'tis the district, and its strength would make palatable (or indiscoverable) a cesspool), and in fact a dinner for me is like an expedition into Spain, Naples, the North and Antarctic regions, Central Australia, Japan, etc."[11]

Lawrence's letters from France, though pedantic with detail at times (especially the long descriptions of churches and castles), are suffused with the excitement and pleasure of discovery. They show an enormous range of interests, from the position of the grandmother in the French family ("she is all powerful . . . an affront to her usually causes a 'conseil de famille' ") to tipping (or not tipping) castle guides. Lawrence begins here to show the descriptive powers that were later to characterize his literary work. Little of the cynicism that embittered his spirit after the war is evident in these enthusiastic, sometimes joyous and frequently poetic accounts. He found "a special joy" in Carcassonne: "One does not need a guide with one, all is free and open except some of the towers: there are guides, but no fees."[12] His ecstatic reverence for the beauties of Chartres gave his mother special pleasure, although she misinterpreted his aesthetic raptures. George Bernard Shaw appreciated Lawrence's description of Chartres, which Lord Carlow had privately printed in an elaborate edition after Lawrence's death. But Shaw chided Lawrence for omitting the stained-glass windows, and characteristically goes him one better in his own account:

> In this example of the first attempts of the late Lord Carlow to rival Jenson, Caxton, Morris, Ashendene Acland, and Count Kessler as an artist-printer, we find E. T. [sic] Lawrence, Quondam Prince of Damascus, a boy writing to his mother, already showing symptoms of the itch for description which at the end of his life developed into a mania, and broke through every convention. . . .
> . . . Lawrence describes it all indiscriminately with one amazing exception. He does not mention its transcendant glory: the stained glass windows. True, they are indescribable. But why did he not say so? [13]

Suspecting that Robert Lawrence, who edited *The Home Letters of T. E. Lawrence and His Brothers,* might, with his need to deny any discord or problem within the family, have omitted passages that in his view would blemish its image, I decided to read the original letters, which are preserved in the Bodleian Library.[14] I discovered that indeed Dr. Lawrence had omitted numerous passages, particularly from the earliest letters, which show the most youthful exuberance and irreverence on the part of his younger, less inhibited and less restrained brother. The omitted passages, which give the letters considerably more humanity and make them less pedantic, are those which express anything critical or insulting about other persons or places, negative or discordant comments, some complaints, boyish accounts of politics, and various small kindnesses or expressions of concern or affection toward other members of the family that Dr. Lawrence thought too trivial to print. In his way, Dr. Lawrence seemed to be attempting to maintain his own version of a family myth, one of sanctity and purity.

The omitted passages contain in particular long descriptions of the crudeness of the lives and habits of the people of Brittany, which contrasted sharply with the Arthurian "Matière de Bretagne" and other romantic French medieval literature in which Lawrence was simultaneously steeping himself. He was disparaging of the drunkenness, poor manners, overeating and ignorance of the Bretons, although he showed an understanding and fondness for particular individuals. "A child is always the person to ask for directions as to the road, or distances; they know better than their elders here," he wrote in irritation.[15]

Lawrence grew extremely impatient with the Chaignons' timidity, conventionality and exaggerated concern for his safety. They seem to have been acting *in loco parentis,* especially during the earlier trips. "At seven at night," he wrote, "no one of them except Madame Chaignon will go a step beyond the door without some sort of cap; it is quite a fetish with them and the other French: they used to cry out all manner of extraordinary things as I rode past: one would think they were badly off for a sensation. They ask where you lost your hat! The best reply I think is that one has just swum across the channel, and had lost the hat half way."[16] There are also several youthful discussions of politics, including Lawrence's first disparagement of traditional military generals, whom he here called (just after the Boer War) "of the Winston Churchill type."[17]

Although these letters do not reveal much of Lawrence's inmost feelings, they are filled with conscientious and affectionate concern for each member of the family, and inquiries about Oxford neighbors. He shares a great deal about his interests with his family and considerately selects particular topics that he knows will match the interests of each one. For his mother, in addition to the poetic sharing of lines of Tennyson and the raptures over Chartres Cathedral, Lawrence seems to go to endless pains to find a petticoat of the type she has asked for. To his father, to whom only two letters are specifically addressed, he writes of politics, of cycling (a beach for doing "a little speed work on the sands"), of false teeth and medieval architecture. Will, who was starting out in archeology at the Ashmolean Museum in Oxford, receives gently reproving words about his archeological errors and advice on how to proceed. Finally, with Arnie, who was six to eight years old during this period, he shares his delight in small things: "Tell Arnie I saw a brown squirrel run up the wall, and he went right up the keep to where Scroggs was sketching: when Scroggs moved he jumped to the main well. He was a very good jumper. The squirrels about here are very large and carry their tails like the foxes do theirs, straight out behind."[18] Or later: "Accept my best worms Arnie and have all ready to hug me on Tuesday."[19] To his friend Beeson, in addition to providing details about medieval towns and architecture, Lawrence compared the women of Arles ("glorious") and Tarascon ("hideous, exactly like grey horses").[20]

Lawrence took advantage of a new university regulation that allowed him to submit a thesis as an additional part of his final examinations for his degree.[21] He chose as his topic the influence of the Crusades on European military architecture to the end of the twelfth century, not an unexpected choice. We have seen already how extensively Lawrence traveled in England, Wales and France from 1905 to 1908 visiting the important castles. He felt that it was essential to examine and photograph their architectural features at first hand in order to establish the influence of one form of building upon another, to determine by comparisons the periods in which particular developments occurred, and to fix the dates of various transitions. He now needed to study the castles of Syria and Palestine "from their own evidence" and accordingly visited the Middle East for the first time in the summer of 1909.[22] But his keen desire to go there had been awakened the previous summer when he reached the Mediterranean and wrote to his mother in excitement: "I felt that at last I had reached the way to the South, and all the glorious East. Greece, Carthage, Egypt, Tyre, Syria, Italy, Spain, Sicily, Crete . . . they were all there, and all within reach . . . of me. I fancy I know now better than Keats what Cortes felt like, 'silent upon a peak in Darien.' Oh I must go down here, — farther out — again! Really this getting to the sea has almost overturned my mental balance: I would accept a passage for Greece tomorrow."[23]

Lawrence's travels gradually made him doubt the traditional view, propounded particularly by the nineteenth-century authorities C. W. C. Oman and E. G. Rey, that the Crusaders drew their excellence in castle building from the East, and that Syrian workmen were imported even to build Château-Gaillard, the masterpiece of Richard I.[24] Particularly "in treating of Latin Fortresses in Syria itself," Lawrence insisted that "documentary evidence of building is absolutely valueless. Medieval fortresses must in every case be dated from their own evidence."[25]

In the limited time available to him he scrambled over endless fortifications, steps, towers and ruins making notes and plans and taking photographs for his thesis. Mosquitoes, indigestible food, snakes and assault by suspicious natives were among the obstacles he encountered. In the course of his personal examinations of castles and cathedrals (his need was always, as his friend E. F. Hall phrased it, "to see for himself"),[26] Lawrence would delight in finding errors in the guidebooks ("Mondoubleau which the guidebooks called ix cent. Really it was an enormous keep of the latest xii").[27] And he gave way to a boyish delight in the discovery of a "beautiful" latrine at a castle in Brittany during one of the earlier explorations, and chided his prudish older brother for not appreciating it when he visited there: "By the way, did not Bob, (many thanks for the post card) go and see the castle? What could he have been thinking about not to mention these most attractive domestic conveniences?"[28]

The excitement of discovery comes through vividly in Lawrence's letters, as his suspicions regarding the castle builders of Southern Europe are confirmed by his own findings. " 'Eureka,' " he wrote Beeson, from France in 1908, "I've got it at last for the thesis: the transition from the square keep form:* really it's too great for words."[29]

* A traditional Norman tower structure.

The need to come to startling conclusions — what he called "my rather knight-errant style of tilting against all comers in the subject,"[30] — or, more importantly, to overturn the position of the "regulars," Oman and Rey, led Lawrence to overstate somewhat the implications of his findings. "There is no evidence," he wrote, "that Richard* borrowed anything great or small, from any fortress which he saw in the Holy Land: it is not likely that he would do so, since he would find better examples of everything in the South of France, which he knew so well. There is not a trace of anything Byzantine in the ordinary French castle, or in an English one: while there are evident signs that all that was good in Crusading architecture hailed from France and Italy. A summing up of the whole matter would be the statement that 'the Crusading architects were for many years copyists of the Western builders.'"[31]

Yet Lawrence himself acknowledges the possibility of mutual influence, "the transfer of trifling detail," because East-West interchange among the upper classes was constant.[32]

The actual writing of the thesis was done in the winter of 1909–1910 and completed by the end of March. Despite its somewhat overly sweeping conclusion, his tutor was so impressed with the work that he gave a dinner for the examiners to celebrate it.[33]

According to Lawrence he refused to have his thesis printed because it was only a preliminary study, "not good enough to publish."[34] In 1929 he wrote of it: "An elementary performance, and I think it has been destroyed or left behind somewhere, in the course of my life. At any rate, I haven't a notion where it is — but a strong memory that it was worthless."[35] This self-disparaging view of the work, so characteristic of Lawrence, was directly contradicted by the statement of Professor Ernest Barker, one of Lawrence's medieval history teachers, who had studied and written about various aspects of the Crusades himself. Barker read the thesis when Lawrence submitted it and concluded: "It proved conclusively, so far as I could judge, that the old theory of the influence of the castles of Palestine on western military architecture must be abandoned, and that instead of the East affecting the West, it was the West that had affected the East."[36]

Lawrence's fundamental point, that the early Crusaders from Southern Europe took a lot of knowledge about military castle building with them when they went to the East, and did not learn the art from Byzantine examples, has been largely sustained by subsequent writers. These writers also agree that there was more interchange and mutual influence between East and West than Lawrence acknowledges, that there is much that is not known about who influenced whom, and that more firsthand comparisons, based on direct examinations of the evidence from the castles

---

* Lawrence does not mention the French or other European Crusaders.

themselves, is needed to achieve accurate dating and to learn fully the history of military castle building.[37]

A letter to his parents of January 24, 1911, indicates that Lawrence was then contemplating writing a "monumental work on the Crusades." If he had done such a book, it would have included further considerations of these questions, and he wrote later to his biographers that his "basic intention in exploring Syria" during his youth "was always to write a strategic study of the Crusades" or to write a history of the Crusades.[38]

One unhappy byproduct of these years of exploration was malaria. Lawrence was subject to recurrent bouts of it through most of his life. He probably contracted the disease in 1908 in the south of France when he was nearly twenty. "I have however forgotten what a mosquito bites like, since I left the marshes of the coast. Aigues-Mortes is celebrated for the ague in winter," he wrote home from there in August of 1908.[39] Lawrence's statement to Graves, "I got malaria in France, when I was sixteen," is almost surely an exaggeration "youthwards."[40]

# 6

# Lawrence at Jesus College, 1907–1910

Oxford was still a place of the hansom cab and the horse-drawn carriage in the first decade of the twentieth century, and life at Jesus College was not atypical of the university community as a whole:

> Freshmen were photographed with the distraction of a shower of lumps of sugar thrown by their seniors. Terms were kept by attending chapel at 8 A.M. or by "keeping a roller," i.e. putting a mark against one's name on a sheet at 7:40 A.M. in Hall. A short "choir practice" on Sundays, attended by most men living in college, counted as a "roller" or chapel if one subsequently went to chapel on Sunday evening. Thus with careful management it was possible to score three out of the required seven appearances in a single day.
>
> Breakfast, taken in one's room, might be a considerable meal and it was not uncommon to give breakfast parties. Luncheon on the other hand, was usually frugal. Before going out to play games it might be bread and cheese, Cooper's marmalade, and college ale. Tea was also taken in one's rooms or ordered perhaps from the stores and brought up by the "boy." Dinner, always well attended, was the only meal in the hall.[1]

The prizes and distinctions Lawrence received as a schoolboy in ancient history, English language and literature, and scriptures enabled him to receive in January 1907 a Meyricke Exhibition in Modern History to Jesus College, which provided £40 toward his tuition.[2] He failed to receive a history "scholarship" at St. John's College, which would have brought him £100. He told one biographer that he had studied too much mathematics before he switched to a concentration in history in his last year at the Oxford City High School.[3] He entered Jesus College in October 1907, when he was nineteen. He was nearly twenty-two when he completed his studies.[4]

His interest in medieval history and antiquities provided a unifying force to Lawrence's college years. He was observed by many of his friends to be odd in certain ways, "utterly unlike anyone else," but in no way did he seem more unusual to his classmates than in the degree to which he "knew what he wanted"[5] and devoted his time to the intense pursuit of knowledge of "medieval poetry and buildings, and of a multitude of strange places."[6]

Lawrence lived in the college for only one term (the summer of 1908). His parents had a well-equipped, sturdy two-room bungalow built for him at the back of the garden behind their house in order that he might pursue his studies in privacy and quiet.[7] One friend has described his visits with Lawrence there, and the atmosphere in this little house. Lawrence maintained the rooms in the austere and simple fashion that best expressed his personality; the walls were draped with a green workshop cloth to keep out the noise. "It was the most silent place I have ever been in. The silence was almost palpable and as we lay on cushions, or rather I lay uncomfortably and he squatted, we agreed that only in silence can the soul hear its own accents, and that only a withdrawal from the world can ensure a man the honesty and integrity of his purpose — and we went on to consider what we could do in life."[8]

Even though Lawrence lived at home rather than at the college and rarely, if ever ("never," Lawrence insisted), appeared in the dining hall, he made an intense impact upon those classmates who came to know him. One classmate, T. P. Fielden, wrote that he and a friend of his, A. T. P. Williams, would "raid" Lawrence at times in his room, and would usually find him on the floor with three or four books, reading them concurrently, page by page.[9] Williams (a history scholar who later became head of Winchester and then dean of Christ Church) wrote of Lawrence:

> I have never since felt anything like the extraordinary fascination which Lawrence's curious penetrating knowledge of medieval poetry and building, and of a multitude of strange places, had for me. Even then, when he was only nineteen or twenty, he had wandered all over France on his bicycle, living on milk and apples; there and elsewhere he had explored, and seemed to remember everything. Probably he talked much more freely then than later, but it was not merely or mainly what he said, endlessly interesting as it was, that made him a wonderful companion: there was a sureness and completeness about his whole being which matched the depth and steadiness of his eyes.[10]

Lawrence's mother confirmed his assertion that during this period he was a vegetarian. "For about three years," she wrote, "he gave up eating meat, and lived on a vegetable, milk and egg diet. For breakfast he always had porridge and milk, never touched tea or coffee; sometimes if he was going for a long ride he would ask us to have porridge ready for him on his return. Cakes and fruits he liked."[11]

Although Lawrence had no interest in group athletics, he was a keen participant in the Oxford Officers' Training Corps, "the territorials," and was a member of the signal detachment. His pleasure in this may have stemmed from the fact that this group functioned as a bicycle corps, military style.[12] Sometimes the signal corps slept out in tents. Lawrence, according to Sir Basil Blackwell (a fellow signal-corps member) was "quirky" and would never, despite his living later as an Arab in the Middle East, stick his head out of the tent during the night. Another friend and classmate, E. F. Hall, attributes this to a literal following of the orders forbidding "sleeping out": Lawrence "kept the letter of the law by sleeping with his legs inside the tent, and his head among the guyropes; and if I remember rightly it was a copy of the *Odyssey* carried inside his tunic pocket that was his constant companion."[13]

Hall observed, as Beeson had, the intensity with which Lawrence seemed to be preparing himself for some future role. Lawrence had known Hall (later to become an archdeacon in Devon) since the fourth form at the City of Oxford High School and frequently came into his rooms in college. Hall noticed there were times when his young friend's eyes "appeared to burn with the intensity of a soul in pain — they could be positively terrifying after overstrain of work."[14] On one such occasion Lawrence surprised Hall by firing a revolver out of the window of a house on an Oxford street (the cartridges, to Hall's relief, proved to be blanks). "One glance at his eyes left no doubt at all that he told the truth when he said that he had been working for forty-five hours at a stretch without food, to test his powers of endurance. I did not realize that he was, in his own later words, 'hardening for a great endeavor.' . . . I thought it was that other side of him — the consuming power of the 'desire to know' — in this case, how much the human frame could stand."[15]

Another student remembered thinking that Lawrence "had the mind of a medieval monk: his values were quite different than ours, the games of the average undergraduate meant little to him and of ambition or dreams in the usual worldly sense he had none. To be self-sufficient in the Platonic or perhaps the Stoic sense was his ideal."[16]

The most important adult figure for Lawrence in Oxford from 1908 on, and the person who helped him to focus his archeological interest, was David Hogarth. In 1908 Hogarth succeeded Sir Arthur Evans, the pioneer discoverer of the Minoan civilization, as keeper of the Ashmolean Museum, and it was at this time that he took an interest in Lawrence, whom he discovered helping the assistant keeper arrange the medieval pottery at the museum. He soon gave Lawrence a part-time job sorting the pottery fragments.[17]

The son of a country clergyman, Hogarth had traveled widely in Greece, Asia Minor, Syria, and the Levant before settling in Oxford. He remained a man of the world, knowledgeable in its ways and places, deft and sensitive in the handling of men. He was an excellent scholar of the Middle East, and a careful, creative archeologist, who could have been a great one had he possessed the patience for its endless details and had had less protean interests and capabilities.[18] Several of his books on travel in the Middle East inspired a generation of travelers and were classics of their time. In his writings and conversation Hogarth made the Middle East seem alive and real to Lawrence, and its attraction for him, stimulated by the older man (they were separated in age by twenty-six years), soon became irresistible. By the time Lawrence made his first trip to Syria and Palestine in 1909, although he had known Hogarth for only a year (Lawrence tends to overstate how young he was when they met), he had already come to depend upon Hogarth's kindness, understanding and gentle strength. Hogarth was, Lawrence wrote to Mrs. Shaw in 1924, "a very kind, very wise, very loveable man, now in failing health. I'd put him high among the really estimable human beings. All my opportunities, all those I've wasted, came directly or indirectly, out of his trust in me."[19]

The most insightful picture of the relationship between Hogarth and Lawrence was provided by Hogarth's only son, William, in an interview. William, who until his death was head of the Athlone Press in London, remembered with pleasure the familiar figure of Lawrence in the household. Lawrence took a great interest in William, who was a young boy then, and taught him to paddle a canoe and to shoot. The elder Hogarth, according to William, represented the academic and worldly life of Oxford more than T.E.'s own father could. David Hogarth was also the first of Lawrence's friends who belonged to the intellectual world, and was in full standing in that world.[20]

Hogarth was affected by Lawrence's brilliance and charm, and came to treat him somewhat like an adopted son. Lawrence in turn became his disciple. Hogarth, in William's view, was a calm, unexcitable, though tolerant person — "if he had a fault he was too unemotional" — who provided shape and stability to Lawrence's life. He understood his young friend and could deal firmly with Lawrence's psychological extravagances, telling him directly when he thought he was being silly or when "his behavior was a bloody nuisance" (as it was when Lawrence created problems for himself later in the writing of *Seven Pillars of Wisdom*).[21]

Hogarth was, Lawrence wrote after his death, "the parent I could trust, without qualification, to understand what bothered me," and "the only person to whom I had never to explain the 'why' of what I was doing."[22] He came to represent what Lawrence valued most in Oxford. Several months after Hogarth's death Lawrence wrote to an artist friend: "Hogarth *shone* in Oxford, because he was humane, and knew the length and breadth of human nature, and understood always, without judging. Oxford seems to me a quite ordinary fire-less town, now he is gone. He was like a great tree, a main part of the background of my life: and till he fell I hadn't known how much he had served to harbour me."[23] As a friend wrote to Lawrence, Hogarth had been "a tower of strength standing between you and the hateful outer world."[24]

Vivyan W. Richards, a Welsh-American "metaphysician" who was at Jesus College with Lawrence and who was perhaps his closest contemporary friend during those years, has provided an account of their relationship and of Lawrence's activities at that time.[25] Richards's description (like those of so many of Lawrence's friends) is colored by the intensity of his enchantment with Lawrence and his affection which, in Richards's case, was a worshipful devotion. Knightley and Simpson, in their recent book, have elaborated upon Richards's love of Lawrence. The authors imply that Richards would have desired a physical intimacy with Lawrence, but that he received from him only affection and respect of a spiritual sort.[26]

Richards shared with Lawrence a passion and a nostalgia for a medieval, heroic, chivalric world before the advent of gunpowder and printing, a world free of the materialism of contemporary life. Together they were attracted to the medieval cult of William Morris, with his emphasis on personal craftsmanship. They made a pilgrimage to the Cotswold town in which Morris had lived and worked, and planned printing schemes that were inspired by Morris's printed replications of illuminated manuscripts.

Richards described Lawrence's personal habits during these years, especially his enjoyment of hot baths (one of the few pleasures Lawrence never denied himself), and how little he ate and slept. Together, Richards wrote, they explored Oxford at night, and once Lawrence took a dip through a gap in the ice of a frozen river (a feat not confirmed by anyone else).[27] Richards recorded in some detail the many books Lawrence read, especially the works of the Romantic poets, and observed him debating details and dates of medieval history and architecture with other undergraduates. Richards also noted Lawrence's efforts at brass rubbing (especially when the armor interested him), wood carving and photo developing. But Lawrence saw a narrowness in Richards's outlook and interests, which may have discouraged him from committing himself too deeply to any of their projects.

Above all, "it was the intoxication of his dear companionship that I could never resist,"[28] Richards wrote, and he repeatedly referred to himself as Lawrence's pupil, one who was enchanted and inspired by his friend's endlessly fascinating interests, schemes, adventures and knowledge as they sought out the cultural feast that Oxford and its environs could furnish to two sensitive undergraduates. Richards stressed Lawrence's humor and fondness of jokes, and he emphasized the subtle, spontaneous and individual nature of his pranks. Lawrence had no interest, according to Richards, in "crowd fooling," of the kind perpetrated during the Fairs or the Eights Week regatta.

For me the most valuable picture of Lawrence as an Oxford under-graduate came from interviews I had with an American historian, W. O. Ault. Ault came up to Jesus College in 1907 as a Rhodes Scholar from Kansas. His account is of particular value because like Lawrence he was greatly interested in the Middle Ages (he eventually became an eminent medieval historian at Boston University), and he was the only other member of their class to study medieval history with the same tutor as Lawrence, Reginald Lane Poole. For the latter reason alone, Ault came into frequent contact with Lawrence, and they often met with their tutor together throughout the three-year course.

Ault recalls Lawrence as small, with an "insignificant" physique, the head too large for the body, a long face, tow hair and a very quiet manner. His voice was low-pitched and soft, but not effeminate. Ault did not notice the giggle that has been described by some. He confirms that Lawrence took no part in the life of the college, did not eat in the dining halls, lived at home much of the time (somewhat unusual even for local students), and did not turn up for the college photograph of his class. He did not take part in organized athletics, which was, according to Ault, quite rare.

Ault was deeply appreciative of Lawrence's kindness to him: "Lawrence seemed to put himself out. He was very understanding of me as someone from another country. The English young men at Oxford tended to treat the Americans rather contemptuously — like schoolboys — but Lawrence was decidedly a friend and helped me to feel more at home. No other person took the trouble he did to be kind."[29]

Lawrence shared his many hobbies and interests with the midwesterner, taking him on bicycle rides through the countryside surrounding Oxford (Ault was to write his thesis on medieval farming) to visit various churches and discover new brasses. Lawrence introduced Ault to the art of brass rubbing, and Ault still treasures, and has hanging in his home in Newton, Massachusetts, several rubbings they did together. Lawrence showed him that sometimes the brasses in the church floors had different, older, reliefs on the opposite side. He would bring along a screwdriver, and while Ault stood guard at the gate, he would unscrew a brass and turn it over. The assurance that they were doing something sacrilegious lent additional excitement to the discovery.

Lawrence also shared his particular interest in medieval armor with Ault, and several times they visited the shop of a smith who was the local authority on how suits of armor had been made. From his young companion and the smith Ault learned how the suits were fashioned to be thick enough to withstand arrows, and assembled so as to present a glancing surface, yet not so heavy that a knight could not get around.

In their work together with Poole, Ault developed a great respect for Lawrence's intelligence and intellectual inventiveness as well as for his sense of humor. He recalls Poole, a fellow of Magdalen and an eminent historian, as rather stuffy, a view Lawrence shared. "Smoke always came out of the *center* of his mouth," Ault recalled, "and his hands were well manicured. He looked as if he had descended from a long line of maiden aunts." Lawrence confessed to Ault one day that he had decided to stir Poole up by submitting an essay in a colloquial style. During their tutorial, Poole turned to Lawrence and said, "Your essay is good enough but your style is that of a tuppenny-ha'penny newspaper."[30]

In summary, Ault felt Lawrence to be an exceptionally fine, sensitive and perceptive young man. And he thought Lawrence, with his brilliance and humor, would have made an exceptional don had his career not taken a different direction.

Lawrence drew from his relationships with his tutors at Oxford a great deal of the intellectual sustenance upon which his later career as a scholar-leader was based. He admired Poole despite Poole's correctness — "my most unpontifical official tutor at Oxford" — whom he credited with having "read every book, and remembered the best ones."[31] But he respected most and was influenced most strongly by his unofficial tutor or "crammer," the historian L. Cecil Jane.

A tense, spare, rather ascetic person, with a long loping stride, Jane had begun teaching Lawrence privately in history when Lawrence decided to switch from mathematics to history during his last year at the City of Oxford High School.[32] Lawrence continued to be coached by Jane until he took his finals in June 1910, and according to his mother, they arranged during the last year for Lawrence always to be Jane's last pupil so he would have extra time.[33]

Lawrence valued Jane as a thorough historian and was stimulated by his ideas. To Robert Graves he wrote that he would go to Jane nearly every day "and discuss nearly every point of all history." He described Jane admiringly as a "fully-charged personality,"[34] but also as "quite abnormal." In a letter home, Lawrence indicated that Jane could become "morbid" at times and suffered from a "harmless form of insanity" (probably a form of depression).[35] He wrote a fuller view of his former teacher in recommending him as a coach to his brother Will, who was thinking of writing a thesis: "Mr. Jane's tuition would be great joy to you: it is not filling, but intensely stimulating. He will give you the minimum of pertinent facts, and leave you to mould them to your purposes. Don't hesitate to argue with him. He does not know till it is challenged, half the reasons which make up his mind."[36]

Jane's view of his special student is contained in a letter written in 1927 to Robert Graves, which Graves published in part in *Lawrence and the Arabs.*[37] Here is the complete text of Jane's letter, including passages omitted by Graves:

> I coached him in his last year at the Oxford City School and saw a great deal of him all through his time at Oxford. He would never read the obvious books. I found out in the first week or two that the thing was to suggest rather out-of-the-way books. He could be relied upon to get more out of a suggestive sentence in a book than an ordinary man would get from a volume. His work was always on his own lines, even to the hours when he came to me. Shortly after midnight to 4 A.M. was a favorite time (living at home he had not to bother about College regulations: it was enough for his mother to report that he was "home by twelve"). He had the most diverse interests historically, though they were mainly medieval. For a long time I could not get him to take any interest in late European History — was very startled to find that he was absorbed by R. M. Johnston's *French Revolution*. His special subject for the history school was the crusades, and I have copies of the books which he used, with some very typical notes in the margin — and they are interesting for the passages which he underlined. While he was at school still I used to be amused [not "surprised" as Graves has it] by his fondness for analyzing character: it was a little habit of his to put questions to me in order to watch my expression: he would make no comment on my answer but I could see that he thought the more. In many ways he resembled his father very much, quite one of the most charming men I have known — very shy, very kind. Lawrence was not a bookworm, though he read very fast and a great deal. I should not call him a scholar by temperament and the main characteristic of his work was always that it was unusual without the effort to be unusual. He loved [not "liked" as in Graves] anything in the nature of satire; guilty of having . . . [several words illegible] beyond me to finish a book which was hanging fire by coming to my rooms to read in MS and enjoying it — especially the more frivolous parts in it; that is why he appreciated Gibbon's notes so much. He was very diffident about his own work; he never published his really admirable (but small) degree thesis which he wrote on the military architecture of the crusades: illustrated by photographs and plans made on the spot. His first visit to the East was for . . . [several words illegible] of that work.
>
> He took a most brilliant first class, so much so that Mr. R. L. Poole (his tutor at Jesus) gave a dinner to the examiners to celebrate it. He was very silent [not "robust" as in Graves], a little difficult to know — and always unexpected. His study (at home in his garden built by himself) [no, for him, by his parents] was typical, slightly oriental in character. When he did talk it was always very refreshing and very original with a quiet vein of satire in it.[38]

Lawrence responded to Jane's special interest in him with small attentions — he sent Jane photographs of French castles — and with a concern for Jane's welfare that continued long after Lawrence graduated from Oxford. The concern was expressed in several letters sent to his family from the Middle East. In one of these he wrote: "It would be a distinct kindness if Will went down to see him [Mr. Jane] occasionally, on pretexts such as Green's [an Oxford friend] request might afford, or even a letter from me. He lives so much alone, and is so short of money (not his own debts either, but other people's) that he gets very much despondent, and visitors who talk decently encourage him. And he is too interesting for it to be an ordeal."[39] Lawrence visited Jane himself as late as the spring of 1921 at Aberystwyth College in Wales to which his former teacher had transferred for reasons of health in the previous year.[40]

It was during the undergraduate years that Lawrence made his most important effort to establish a serious relationship with a woman. The young woman was Janet Laurie Hallsmith. When I first interviewed Robert Lawrence regarding the details of his younger brother's childhood he referred me to several members of the Laurie family for further information — two sisters and a brother, with whom he had remained in touch. These were the children whose father was the agent of an estate in the New Forest near Langley Lodge, where the Lawrences lived from 1894 to 1896. Lawrence's childhood friendship with Janet and the other Laurie children has already been described. The account that follows was supplied to me in interviews by Mrs. Hallsmith herself. She seemed to me utterly candid within the limits of memory, and I sensed no conscious interest on her part in embellishing her story in order to claim an important association with a famous man.

In 1899 Janet was sent to Oxford to boarding school and to be near the Lawrences. Two years later, her father drowned in Southampton Water and she returned home to be with her mother. She continued to visit the Lawrences in Oxford and sometimes stayed with them. She and T.E. saw each other frequently through his undergraduate years. "I always spent Sunday afternoon at tea with him," she said, "and sort of watched him grow up." Later she visited "Ned" on occasion in the detached bungalow. Although women were not officially allowed in the undergraduate rooms, Lawrence served Janet and her sister breakfast in his room on at least one occasion.

The relationship between Ned and Janet from childhood on was one of ragging and teasing. He would chide the rather tomboyish girl for not being a boy or tease her for not being capable of doing things as well as he could. The teasing, she said, had a tender quality and she never felt hurt by it. At an Oxford breakfast party, she recalled, T.E. dared her to throw a lump of sugar across a court into an open window. She took the challenge and after two misses the third shot went in and hit the occupant. T.E. had ducked out of sight, and there she was, embarrassed to find herself spotted in the window by the irritated don across the way. This childlike, playful quality characterized their relationship. They never discussed their feelings about each other, especially as he seemed unable to, and she had never thought of him seriously as a suitor or mate. On the contrary, he maintained an emotional distance. Once when he was about nineteen she remarked to him, "Ned, you never look me in the eye." He replied, "It gives me a painful sensation to look into your eyes."

Janet was therefore surprised when Lawrence's interest in her took a more serious turn. She had always felt toward him as an older sister toward a clever brother, and he also inspired in her a feeling that he needed to be taken care of. Besides, he was more than two years younger and too short — he was the same height if not shorter than she was. Mrs. Lawrence had wanted her to marry Bob, who was nearer her age. But Bob was "so terribly good," and he once had corrected her for using the word "pub" ("Pub is not a nice word," he had said). Janet's heart was turning to Will despite the more than three years' difference in their ages. He was the tallest and handsomest of the Lawrence boys and in her view the most "dashing."[41]

When T.E. asked her to marry him, she was understandably taken aback. He was about twenty-one at the time, still an undergraduate, when he proposed. She had come to the Lawrences' for dinner, and she and Ned had stayed at the table after the meal was over. He bolted the door so the parlormaid could not come in. "We were joking about his brothers when he suddenly proposed." There had been no warning, no preliminaries, such as a kiss or a revelation of feelings. Though she felt that the proposal was a serious one, in her astonishment she laughed at him. He seemed hurt, but merely said, "Oh, I see," or "All right," and spoke no more about it.

Despite Mrs. Lawrence's objections Janet and Will had hoped to marry, but he was killed in the war in 1915. In 1919 Janet married Guthrie Hallsmith, a war hero who later failed as an artist. Because her father was dead she asked Lawrence to give her away. At first he agreed, but just before the wedding he sent her a note saying he could not go through with it, offering as his reason that he was too short and would look silly walking down the aisle with her. But the two remained friends. He occasionally visited the Hallsmiths at their home in Newquay in Cornwall and was godfather of their first child.

Mrs. Hallsmith was a woman of warmth and charm, and like both T.E. and his mother, a person of indomitable will. At eighty-six, having suffered several bouts of heart failure, she continued to relish her life and the people and things around her.

Nine months after first speaking with Janet Hallsmith of her relationship with Lawrence, I visited Lawrence's childhood friend the Reverend E. F. ("Midge") Hall and his wife on Dartmoor in Devonshire. We were talking of Lawrence's shyness when one of the Halls offered spontaneously, "There was one girl he loved." They seemed reluctant to reveal her identity until I told them I thought I knew, having spoken with Janet Hallsmith several months before. "Oh, you know then," Hall said. "I have never mentioned it to anybody." And went on to tell me that Lawrence as a youth had spoken with him of his love for Janet Laurie.[42]

Once during his undergraduate days, Hall told me, Lawrence arranged for himself, Janet and "Midge" Hall to go boating on the Thames. But instead of taking Janet with him, he fixed it so that Midge and Janet went in a punt and he followed fifty yards behind in a canoe. Afterwards Hall asked Lawrence "what on earth" he had done that for. Lawrence replied that he was "observing" his friend and Janet from afar. He then added, as if to himself, "I'm getting over the disappointment of letting the other man speak for the girl I adore. I don't know." Hall said that he did not think Janet ever really reciprocated Lawrence's love for her.

When he saw Janet Hallsmith at a later time, Hall said to her, "You know Ned Lawrence adored you," and she replied that she had known but could not consider him seriously as a suitor. As if to sum up his memory of the relationship of his two friends, Hall remarked, "She was a lovely girl, a lovely girl. She was a dear. He worshipped from afar."

It is difficult to weigh the importance of Lawrence's relationship with Janet Laurie and the disappointment it contained, for he never wrote about it, and except for Midge Hall, never spoke of it to his friends. There are only sparse references to Janet and the Lauries in the *Home Letters*. Because the relationship had begun in childhood he was able to accept her as a good friend and could allow her to penetrate to a degree his already strong reserve. They had fun and played games together. Yet strong feelings of attraction and love built up in the boy, perhaps without his realizing their intensity. But he was unable to share his emotions, to communicate these feelings to the girl, or to change the relationship to an adult one. Janet was therefore naturally surprised when T.E. proposed so abruptly and did not intend to hurt him when she reacted with anxious laughter. Perhaps she sensed that his conflicts, his essential immaturity, prevented his courting a woman successfully, at least at this time. As the incidents Hall described showed so clearly, Lawrence had to be the observer — to worship from afar.

The Greek ΟΥ ΦΡΟΝΤΙΣ (Does Not Care), which he chose to place over the entrance of his cottage, Clouds Hill, after the war, applies to many aspects of Lawrence's life and character, but is particularly appropriate to the way Lawrence handled his feelings of disappointment over the failure with Janet. The expression derives from the story in Herodotus of Hippocleides, who was the successful suitor of the princess Agarista, but drank too much wine and began dancing on a table. He disgraced himself by standing on his head and beating time in the air with his legs (the Greeks wore short skirts). When Agarista's father cried, "You have danced away your wife," Hippocleides replied cheerfully, "I don't care."

We will never know in what way Lawrence's disappointment in love affected his decision to leave England and live in the Middle East, in its predominantly male society, for the better part of the next five years.

Probably it was one factor among several that determined his life plan, a plan not established by a single decision, but by a series of smaller steps that depended always on a variety of personal interests and external circumstances.

Yet I am of the impression that this disappointment played a significant part in Lawrence's turning to Syria and to Carchemish, where a congenial life among men, the archeologist's world of the dig, the camp and the campfire, without the need to relate seriously to women, provided what Lawrence claims were the pleasantest years of his life. Although I am in substantial agreement with Janet Hallsmith and other women who have maintained that it is nonsense to say that Lawrence hated women — he had, after all, a number of social relationships with them that were mutually gratifying — because of his deeply ambivalent attitude toward women as sexual beings, and the intense sexual inhibitions related to this attitude, he never, to my knowledge, ever again attempted to form a serious love bond with a woman. Throughout his life he chose voluntarily the worlds of men — the dig and the military — where the demands of women would be minimized. He remained, according to his brother Arnold, a virgin until his death.

At the end of their college years British students underwent six days of final examinations. The examination essays determined then, as now, graduation, class standing and the possibility of honors, and were circulated among members of a committee that included professors to whom the student had not previously been exposed, possibly from Cambridge University as well as from the various Oxford colleges. The students were then quizzed orally on what they had written. The mark they received on their essays might be raised but not lowered as a result of the oral examination.

Lawrence, as a result of his travels and reading in French poetry, claimed he was unprepared for these examinations and was advised to submit a special thesis (his study of Crusader castles), to supplement the other papers. He received a First Class Honors degree in modern history.

There are five memorials to Lawrence at Jesus College. A bronze tablet greets the visitor at the main entrance. A copy of a portrait by Augustus John (the original is in the Tate Gallery) hangs in the hall. James McBey's pencil sketch of Lawrence, drawn at Damascus in 1918, hangs in the Senior Common Room. More recently a replica of the bust by Eric Kennington (the original is in the crypt of St. Paul's Cathedral) was placed in the chapel by Robert Lawrence. Finally, the Lawrence family established the Lawrence Brothers Memorial Scholarship in memory of T.E., Will and Frank. As J. N. L. Baker has written: "In the long history of the College no member has attracted so much comment and controversy as Lawrence; none has merited greater appreciation."[43]

# 7

# The First Trip to
# the Middle East, 1909

Lawrence began his first journey to the Middle East in mid-June 1909 aboard the Pacific and Orient steamship *Mongolia,* which took him by Gibraltar through the Mediterranean to Port Said, Jaffa and Beirut. By the time he returned to Oxford in October his travels, mostly on foot, had taken him through much of northern Palestine, along the Lebanese coast to parts of western Syria, and eastward to the Euphrates region of southern Asia Minor, where he was later to spend three important years working at the site of the ancient Hittite city of Carchemish.

The explicit reason for the trip was his desire to study at first hand the castles of Syria and Palestine as part of the research for his thesis on the military architecture of the Crusades. But his longing to explore the lands of the Middle East, the places where Western civilizations originated, went much deeper. His friend Richards said that the lectures of the Egyptologist Flinders Petrie at Oxford had stimulated it. But Lawrence's letter to his mother on first reaching the Mediterranean the year before reveals a deeper passion. And his developing attachment to David Hogarth influenced his desire to go there himself.

On this trip Lawrence became exposed for the first time to a radically different culture, and began the process of absorption in its way of life out of which his later triumphs and personal torments were to grow. He wrote lightly to his mother that he felt "most inclined to build a tent on Tell el Kadi [one of the mounds in Palestine] and be a hedonistic hermit."[1] Neither his writings on this journey nor those of the Carchemish period reveal evidence of conflict, or of the struggle with personal identity that was to lead him later to warn against the submergence of oneself in an alien culture.

On this first trip Lawrence already shows, however, a remarkable ability to adapt to the ways of life of the Arab cultures, to live, even then, "as an Arab with the Arabs."[2] He was always attracted more to the Bedouins and their renunciation of civilization than to the town Arabs, whose settled lives resembled too much what he wished to reject in bourgeois English society. "The two selves [the Bedouin and the overcivilized European], you see, are mutually destructive," he wrote in 1927 on a typescript of Graves's biography. "So I fall between them into the nihilism which cannot find, in being, even a false God in which to believe."[3]

At Hogarth's suggestion Lawrence wrote early in 1909 to Charles M. Doughty, the famous explorer, to get his "opinion on a walking tour in Northern Syria." Doughty, who had not traveled north of Damascus, discouraged Lawrence from such a journey in summer, calling it "wearisome, hazardous to health and even disappointing," and warned him of the heat, squalor and long distances. "Long daily marches on foot a prudent man who knows the country would I think consider out of the question," Doughty wrote. "The population only knows their own wretched life and look upon any European wandering in their country with at best a veiled ill will. You would have nothing to draw upon but the slight margin of strength which you bring with you from Europe."[4] Lawrence, obviously not dissuaded, answered wryly, "My little pleasure trip appears to be more interesting than I had bargained for: I have fortunately a few months to think about it in."[5] More than two decades later he would write: "Upon each return from the East I would repair to Doughty, a looming giant, white with eighty years, headed and bearded like some renaissance Isaiah."[6]

During those months he consulted C. H. C. Pirie-Gordon, a young archeologist who had recently visited some of the Crusader castles. Pirie-Gordon asserted (in contradiction to Aldington's statements to the contrary nearly fifty years later) that "the guide books were less helpful than at present when dealing with places off the main routes frequented by pilgrims and tourists." He lent Lawrence an annotated map of his own earlier journey to Syria and copies of photographs he had taken of various castles.[7] According to Lawrence's mother, whose memory was admirable, he took with him in addition only a light-weight suit with many pockets in which he carried "all his things": two shirts of thin material, a spare pair of socks, and a camera with many packets of film. A month after his travels began, his *iradehs* arrived. These were official letters of introduction from the Ottoman cabinet to the governors in Syria, which had been obtained for Lawrence by Lord Curzon (then chancellor of Oxford University). They provided him with privileges, protection and assistance while traveling in the Ottoman Empire, "a piquant passport for a tramp to carry," as Lawrence put it.[8] The *iradehs* declared that Lawrence, then not yet twenty-one, was "Professor of University and Artist."[9]

Toward the end of the trip, which he said covered eleven hundred miles, the "noble stockings" had proved to be the weakest link and had "succumbed at last; three holes lately: but I have only the one pair with me (economy!), and they have now done 450 miles: not bad, because they are thin wool. Boots are worn out, but will perhaps last me through. I don't want to have them soled."[10] This was unfortunate or foolish, for two weeks later the boots were walked "to bits" and his feet were covered with "cuts and chafes and blisters," which had rubbed up into sores.[11]

Lawrence's first view of the Middle East in early July at Port Said (then a squalid but rapidly growing seaport teeming with peoples of diverse ethnic groups from all over the earth) was clearly disappointing. The lovely harbor of Beirut, which he reached on the sixth, was an improvement. Leaving Beirut shortly thereafter, Lawrence walked south to Sidon, then southeast to Banias and Safed, and south to the Sea of Galilee. He followed the western shore to Tiberias, took the road west to Nazareth and crossed Carmel to the coast. Turning north he walked up the coast through Haifa, Acre, and Tyre and returned to Beirut at the beginning of August. In August he walked up the coast into northern Syria through Tripoli, Latakia and Antioch, arriving in Aleppo in early September. From Aleppo he went by car to Urfa, and possibly to Harran on the edge of Mesopotamia. He returned to Beirut on September 30 and was at sea on the way home in early October. In a letter home he stated his intention to spend three days in Damascus, and he wrote Liddell Hart more than twenty years later that he did so ("I was also at Damascus, and I forgot how I got there"),[12] but there is no contemporary or later account of this visit. During these wanderings he wrote that he visited thirty-seven of the fifty or so Crusader castles.[13]

In preparation for his trip Lawrence learned some conversational Arabic from a Syrian Protestant clergyman living in Oxford.[14] He probably knew a little more than the eighty words he acknowledged to Graves[15] because he was able to make himself understood even upon arriving in Port Said.[16]

During his wanderings Lawrence often stayed with Syrian families, especially poorer ones, and sometimes he slept in the open air. He was clearly moved by the hospitality of the native people, which contrasted so sharply with the warnings he had received. "This is a glorious country for wandering in," he wrote his father, "for hospitality is something more than a name: setting aside the American and English missionaries, who take care of me in the most fatherly (or motherly) way: — they have all so far [August 15 from Tripoli] been as good as they can be — there are the common people, each one ready to receive one for a night, and allow me to share in their meals: and without a thought of payment from a traveller on foot. It is so pleasant, for they have a very attractive kind of native dignity."[17]

The accounts of Lawrence's travels in Palestine and Syria on this first

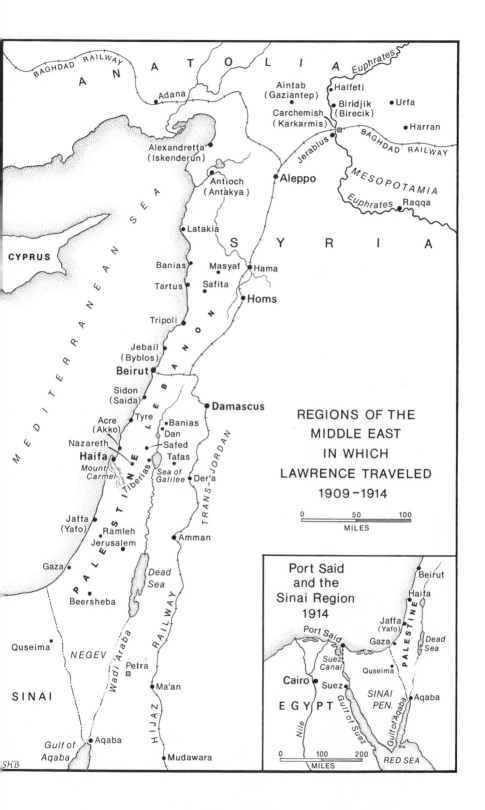

BAGHDAD RAILWAY

A  N  A  T  O  L  I  A

*Euphrates*

Adana

Aintab
(Gaziantep)
Halfeti
Biridjik
(Birecik)
Urfa
Carchemish
(Karkarmis)
Harran

Jerablus

BAGHDAD RAILWAY

Alexandretta
(Iskenderun)

Antioch
(Antakya)
Aleppo

M  E  S  O  P  O  T  A  M  I  A

Euphrates

Raqqa

Latakia

S  Y  R  I  A

CYPRUS

Banias
Masyaf
Hama
Tartus
Safita
Homs

Tripoli

L
E
B
A
N
O
N

M  E  D  I  T  E  R  R  A  N  E  A  N    S  E  A

Jebail
(Byblos)
Beirut

Sidon
(Saida)
Tyre
Damascus

Acre
(Akko)
Banias
Dan
Nazareth
Safed
Haifa
Tafas
Mount
Carmel
Sea of
Galilee
Der'a

P
A
L
E
S
T
I
N
E

T
R
A
N
S
-
J
O
R
D
A
N

REGIONS OF THE
MIDDLE EAST
IN WHICH
LAWRENCE TRAVELED
1909–1914

Tiberias

Jaffa
(Yafo)
Ramleh
Jerusalem

Amman

Gaza

Dead
Sea

0          50          100
MILES

Beersheba

H
I
J
A
Z

R
A
I
L
W
A
Y

Quseima
NEGEV

W
a
d
i

'
A
r
a
b
a

Petra

SINAI

Ma'an

Gulf of
Aqaba
Aqaba
Mudawara

SHB

Port Said
and the
Sinai Region
1914

Beirut

Haifa

Jaffa
(Yafo)
Port Said
Gaza
Dead
Sea

Suez
Canal

Cairo
Suez
Quseima

P
A
L
E
S
T
I
N
E

SINAI
PEN.

Aqaba

E  G  Y  P  T

Nile

Gulf
of
Suez

Gulf
of
Aqaba

0       100       200
MILES

RED SEA

trip are contained principally in a dozen or so letters he wrote home, in a few fragments he related to Robert Graves and Basil Liddell Hart, in the bits and pieces told by his family and friends, and in brief accounts written to Sir John Rhys, his principal at Jesus College, and to Doughty. One very rich and detailed letter to his mother, which fills a dozen book pages even without the minor bowdlerizations of his older brother, provides a full account of the first month of his travels in Palestine. The letters covering the later part of the trip, especially after Lawrence left Aleppo, are less frequent and far less complete. During this time, however, he suffered from malaria and was robbed and almost murdered.

These letters provide only sparse, subdued indications of Lawrence's emotional responses to the many new experiences he was undergoing. But they are filled with illuminating, meticulous descriptions of the sights and geography and of the attitudes of the people in the lands he was discovering. They demonstrate, as had the letters from France, Lawrence's capacity to observe each aspect of the unfamiliar world surrounding him with such exquisite care that it seems to become his own, and he, as a consequence, to belong to it. The climate, houses, foods, the way the foods were cooked and served, the process of hospitality, the beds and the bedding, are all recorded in great detail. The flora and fauna, friendly and hostile, are all accounted for down to the fleas, sometimes with good humor. "The Arabs say that the king of the fleas lives in Tiberias," he wrote, "but I can guarantee he has summer residences elsewhere as well."[18]

Although this journey, much of it in settled regions, took Lawrence among Arabs, he had little opportunity to grasp the tribal relationships, knowledge of which proved so vital later. He did, though, gain a thorough introduction to many of the habits, mores, fears, superstitions and other characteristics of the Arab peoples. He lamented the deterioration of Palestine and the Palestinians, which had occurred since Roman times,[19] and the poverty of the Bedouins, remarking prophetically of the thistle-covered lands around Galilee: "The sooner the Jews farm it all the better: their colonies are bright spots in a desert."[20]

Lawrence's traveling on foot and alone aroused great curiosity among the Arabs, which was intensified by his camera on its odd-looking tripod: "Such a curiosity has never been seen and all the village is summoned to look at it."[21] Peculiarities of the Ottoman currency and the aggravating postal system he reserved for his little brother, then nine, who evidently had a special interest in such matters. Lawrence had particular scorn for the Baedeker descriptions of castles, his area of expertise: " 'Buildings resembling towers'," wrote Baedeker, "(which are towers)," wrote Lawrence; " 'small arched apertures resembling loopholes' (and which are loopholes) and other inanities much worse but too long and childish to quote."[22]

Lawrence was enthusiastic at this time about the educational and reforming efforts of the American mission in the Levant and the college in Beirut. At Jebail north of Beirut he was given warm hospitality by Miss Holmes, the American missionary, and met Fareedah el Akle, the Syrian schoolmistress who was to become his Arabic teacher and good friend. In a passage that his zealously Christian older brother omitted from the *Home Letters* he noted the dangers for Muslims of Christian conversion: "It would be equivalent to signing their death sentence, the few converts there have been have all had to go abroad, but there are many secret adherents."[23] Despite the richness of the region in biblical and other ancient lore, Lawrence made, except for occasional references to Scriptures that seem aimed at pleasing his mother, few historical references of any kind in these letters. His interest seemed to be absorbed by observations of the life of the present.

During the last weeks of his trip Lawrence had several troublesome and dangerous adventures, which he related to his family as humorously, innocently or incompletely as possible in order not to alarm them. Because of his editing and the further distortions provided by the secondhand dramatizations of others (to which Lawrence may have contributed), it is difficult to piece together exactly what happened.

First, Lawrence reveals that late in August at Safita north of Tripoli he had a pistol and was persuaded by a group of Arabs to keep watch with it against "thieves," who turned out to be their landlords after the rent.[24] It appears that he was attacked on two other occasions. At Masyaf, also north of Tripoli, he was shot at from two hundred yards by "an ass with an old gun." Lawrence returned the fire and thinks he may have grazed the horse, which bolted "about half a mile" with its rider.[25]

This is probably the incident described (most likely with a number of distortions) by Fareedah el Akle in an essay she wrote on Lawrence after his death.[26] Here the "ass" has become "a huge cruel-looking Turk," and the grazed horse, a grazed little finger on the Turk, which Lawrence bandages, the two ending up as friends like "David and Goliath." How much of this romanticization is from Lawrence's yarn-telling and how much the embellishments of his admirers is beyond my capacity to determine.

The more serious attack was not described to his family at all. On September 24 he wrote to Sir John Rhys to thank him for his help in obtaining the *iradehs* and said only that the previous week he had been "robbed and rather smashed up" and was not yet "fit for walking again."[27] A fuller account, with Lawrence's editorial corrections, is supplied by Graves.[28] According to this passage, in a village near the Euphrates a Turkoman was led to believe by the villagers that a ten-franc copper watch Lawrence was carrying was gold. He stalked his victim, knocked him down, took his revolver, and tried to shoot him with it, but did not understand the safety latch. He then hit Lawrence with stones, robbed him, and left him hurt. Fortunately, Lawrence's injuries were not so grave that he was unable to make it five miles to the next village. The local authorities and the village elders gave up the thief and returned Lawrence's stolen property, which included the watch, his money, his revolver and Hittite antiquities (including thirty seals which Hogarth had asked him to bring back).[29] To Rhys he wrote: "Lord Curzon's Iradés were invaluable in the matter: they stirred up the local authorities to a semblance of energy, so that the man was caught in 48 hours. Before this I employed them innumerable times: in fact without them there would have been several times unpleasantness."[30]

To his parents he wrote on September 22: "I find an absurd canard in the Aleppo paper of a week ago: my murder near Aintab (where I didn't go). I hope it has not been copied."[31] This may be a reference to the robbery and beating. Pirie-Gordon's account of the incident in *T. E. Lawrence by His Friends* is at some variance with the above; it seems to be based on stories told to him by third parties and should probably be discounted.[32] Lawrence did, however, send him back the map he had borrowed, apologizing for the bloodstains on it.

On his way back from Urfa, Lawrence wrote his parents that his camera had been stolen from his carriage "while the coachman I left on watch was asleep."[33] David Garnett, who edited the *Collected Letters of T. E. Lawrence,* challenges this account on the grounds that Lawrence wrote Sir John Rhys that the camera was stolen when he was robbed and beaten. I can, however, find no reference to the camera in the letter to Sir John. In any event he returned successfully with the photographs and other material for his thesis.

"The stories of his adventures and the hardships he endured on that trip, as he related them to us later, would make the most thrilling reading," wrote Fareedah el Akle, a quarter of a century afterwards. "They would sound like the Arabian Nights. Yet Lawrence made very light of all his sufferings and would joke over them. Many were his narrow escapes from death at the hands of cruel Kurds and Turks."[34] This is a revealing passage, for it conveys the sense of excitement, drama and romance that Lawrence could inspire even in an ordinarily sensible Syrian schoolteacher. It was part of his character to do so, and furnishes the biographer — who attempts to distinguish those distortions of fact which are Lawrence's responsibility from the luxurious myth-making of his audiences — with a challenging assignment. In 1909, when he was just twenty-one, Lawrence was already creating in the substance of his life and his vivid accounts of it material for legends about his adventures and exploits, activities which were, *in reality,* extraordinary.

Toward the end of his trip Lawrence wrote home, "It is remarkable that all these 3 months on most unaccustomed and most changing food and water my stomach has never been upset."[35] But, as we have seen, much else was. In addition to being beaten and robbed, and enduring footsores, cuts and blisters, Lawrence also had four attacks of malaria.[36] Yet he wished to extend his trip, claiming that Sir John Rhys "won't care if I am early or late." Only lack of money or, more significantly, his poor physical condition required that he return. When he did go back to college in October, Sir Ernest Barker, a family friend who was then of St. John's College, described his face as "thinned to the bone by privation."[37] In spite of all his hardships Lawrence succeeded in bringing back with him from Syria jars of Tyrian purple dye for a printing scheme to be carried out with one of his friends.[38]

Midway in this first journey to the Middle East, Lawrence wrote his mother, "I will have such difficulty in becoming English again, here I am Arab in habits and slip in talking from English to French and Arabic unnoticing."[39] Thus, on this first trip of his youth to the Middle East, Lawrence had already started to go beyond the ordinary gathering of knowledge. He had begun to identify himself with Arab ways and Arab life, and to move away from his Anglo-Irish self. It was his knowledge of the Arab world, combined with a deepening of this identification to the point where he could grasp and share with the Bedouin tribesmen their own often dimly appreciated hopes and dreams of change, that enabled him to accomplish his role in the Arab Revolt.

After his return to England, Lawrence wrote to Doughty in November that his tour "has ended happily (I reached Urfa my goal) and the Crusading Fortresses I found are so intensely interesting that I hope to return to the East for some little time."[40] A meeting (their first) followed which, according to Hogarth, "diminished in no way the disciple's fervour."[41]

# 8

# Lawrence at Carchemish

In a letter of May 18, 1911, Gertrude Bell, by that date already an experienced desert explorer, wrote to her stepmother that she had "found . . . a young man called Lawrence," and added parenthetically, "he is going to make a traveller."[1] In fact, during the three and a half years from December 1910, when Lawrence left England bound for Athens, Constantinople and Beirut, to June 1914, when he came back shortly before the outbreak of World War I, he visited England only three times for periods totaling about six months. He spent the bulk of his time during these years in the region of Carchemish, in what is now south-central Turkey, and in northern Syria, but his travels took him into northwestern portions of Mesopotamia and as far south as Aqaba and the Sinai Peninsula. Through comparing his letters, including a large unpublished correspondence with E. T. Leeds of the Ashmolean Museum, it is possible to follow his whereabouts with some accuracy.

A tracing of Lawrence's journeys on a map of the Near East shows his travels to be predominantly in its western and northern regions, among the towns and cities of Syria, Lebanon and southern Anatolia. His contacts were thus as much with the settled Arabs of the towns as with the nomads, and with Circassians, Kurds, Turkomans, Armenians and other peoples of the north as well as with the Bedouin tribesmen.

Following his graduation from Oxford in June 1910, Lawrence had made three trips to France in the summer and fall, visiting churches and cathedrals, and studying the origins and history of medieval pottery in England ("looking at Medieval Pots") for the Ashmolean Museum in Oxford.[2] Meanwhile, the British Museum decided, on the recommendation of David Hogarth, to reopen its excavations at Carchemish. Because of political tensions in the region the Ottoman authorities delayed granting permission until the spring of 1910.³ Then Hogarth obtained for Lawrence a Magdalen demyship, or four-year travĕling scholarship, which enabled him to take part in the project.

In November Lawrence wrote to Leeds: "Mr. Hogarth is going digging: and I am going out to Syria in a fortnight to make plain the valleys and level the mountains for his feet: — also to learn Arabic. The two occupations fit into one another splendidly."⁴ He hoped also to continue his studies of the castles and history of the Crusades, to be published as "The Seven Pillars of Wisdom" or "my monumental work on the Crusades"⁵ (not to be confused with the *Seven Pillars of Wisdom* which he eventually published).

Lawrence left England in early December and arrived in Beirut three weeks later, having visited en route Athens and Constantinople for the first time. He described these visits to his family meticulously and lyrically. There is indeed a tone of awe and reverence in his letter about Athens, and at the Acropolis he was so moved that "[I] walked through the doorway of the Parthenon, and on into the inner part of it, without really remembering who or where I was. A heaviness in the air made my eyes swim, and wrapped up my senses: I only knew that I, a stranger, was walking on the floor of the place I had most desired to see, the greatest temple of Athene, the palace of art, and that I was counting her columns and finding there what I already knew. The building was familiar, not cold as in the drawings, but complex, irregular, alive with curve and subtlety, and perfectly preserved. Every line of the moldings, every minutest refinement in the sculptures were evident in that light, and inevitable in their place."⁶ His descriptions of the bustling Constantinople, which he thought "may well stand for life and activity," are even more thorough.

On board ship Lawrence enjoyed himself arguing about "the infallibility and general excellence of Popes" with three French-Canadian priests on their way to Jerusalem, and also was applauded for his tactful handling in French of a strident debate among them and a French-Egyptian lawyer about French politics.⁷

Lawrence arrived in Beirut shortly before Christmas of 1910 and soon left for the mission school at Jebail (ancient Byblos), a few miles up the Mediterranean coast, where he studied Arabic for the next two months and enjoyed the hospitality and companionship of Miss Holmes, the school's director; Mrs. Rieder, one of the French teachers; and Miss Fareedah el Akle, his Arabic teacher.

Miss Akle, who had first met Lawrence briefly on his 1909 journey, wrote to me her recollections of his visits and of her relationship with him. The minor inaccuracies the letter contains are allowable perhaps when one considers that sixty years had intervened.

Long ago on Christmas Eve, 1909 [actually 1910],[8] I met T.E. for the
first time at an American mission school in Jebail . . . where I was teaching.
Lawrence had come there as a young man of 21-years [9] to study Arabic, as
he had been appointed to work on the excavation of a Hittite city in Jerablus,
Carchemish, near the Euphrates, and he needed Arabic to work there.

It was a great pleasure to be chosen to teach him Arabic — which is
reckoned to be the second hardest language in the world — but Lawrence
picked it up very easily and in a short time he could speak and write a little
as he was extremely intelligent and a good linguist. The time I spent as
Lawrence's teacher was very pleasant. Every day we would study for an
hour on a red sofa in the large hall, Lawrence holding the cat on his lap. T.E.
had a nice sense of humor, and the time seemed to pass very quickly. Teaching him gave me the opportunity of understanding him, although sometimes
he was difficult to understand. I remember his saying something to me once
and I looked puzzled. He said, "Let me explain." After he told me what he
meant I thought, "Why didn't I see that straight away." I think that T.E. if
he were here, would say to people, "Let me explain!" and we would see
clearly what he meant when quite often biographers do not see what he
meant at all.

Besides [my] being T.E.'s teacher, we both had common interests: books
and authors, archeology and the Arabs. (I felt as keenly as he did about the
Arab nation and their history.) All of this helped me to understand Lawrence
well. — I don't mean to give a history of T.E. but I should like to speak about
what struck me most about him — the spiritual side of his character.

Lawrence did not speak of religion much, but he lived a religious life. He
was a man of the spirit and lived rather in the spirit than in the body. I
always wondered what was the thing which helped Lawrence lead this
wonderful life of service. He did his utmost to use all his gifts, great or small,
in the best possible way. Once I remember, he bought an old book from a
monastery so old, torn, and worm eaten that no one would have bought it.
He wanted to give it to Miss Holmes as a present — she was the president
of the American mission school — and he said he must do his best to fix
it as no other book was available. He worked on it hours and hours and,
when he had finished, I could not believe it was the same book. All his
work — great or small — he undertook to do well throughout his life.

Once, talking to Lawrence about an important matter, I asked him a
question and he said, "Help comes from within, not from without." This
seemed to me to reveal the secret of his inner life. He seemed to be a man
guided by a dynamic power in him: the power of the spirit.[10]

I should add that Miss Akle was critical of my view of Lawrence's
conflicts, as expressed in an article I had sent her, and wrote to a friend
of hers, "Lawrence seems to me to be like an oyster which has, through
pain and suffering all through life developed into a pearl which the world
is trying to evaluate, taking it to pieces layer by layer, without realizing
the true value of the whole."[11]

In February 1911, before beginning work on the dig, Lawrence accompanied Hogarth and Gregori, the Cypriot headman at the site, on a

tour by rail and sea — not on foot this time — of cities and sights of northern Palestine. They journeyed to Jerablus via Der'a, Damascus and Aleppo. In March they arrived in Carchemish and the archeological work was begun.

In choosing to work and live at Carchemish and in Syria during these important years of his young manhood, Lawrence removed himself from the burdens of a structured academic life and the confinements of English society. He chose instead an entirely new and self-contained world, one in which he became an important personage, known by everyone throughout the region, and fondly by all but those who crossed him. It was a free world, lived out of doors for the most part. Although women travelers and friends sometimes visited the site, Carchemish was largely a masculine society, free of the burdens of sexual jealousies and commitments.

When away from the dig Lawrence missed "the delicious free intimacy of the men of Carchemish."[12] To his childhood nurse he wrote toward the end of the first spring, "We are having a splendid time out here: not that we are finding very much, but the place is splendid, and the workmen, and the climate."[13] Later he called Carchemish "the jolliest place I've ever seen. A marvelous, unreal, pictured pageant of a life."[14]

He worked first under Hogarth directly and then with R. Campbell-Thompson. "Mr. Hogarth does the writing up of the results," he wrote his family soon after his arrival. "I do the squeezing and drawing the inscriptions and sculptures, and (with the great Gregori of the *Accidents of an Antiquary's Life* [one of Hogarth's books]) direct the men."[15] And a few weeks later: "The most pleasing part of the day is when breakfast hour gets near. From all the villages below us on the plain there come long lines of red and blue women and children, carrying bread in red-check handkerchiefs, and wooden measures full of leben [sour goat's milk] on their heads. The men are not tired then, and the heat is just pleasant, and they chatter about and jest and sing in very delightful style. A few of the men bring shepherd's pipes, and make music of their sort. As a rule, they are not talkative: they will sit for minutes together at the house-door without a word: often coming out in the morning we have found 100 men grouped outside, wanting work, and have not heard a sound through the open window just above! The only time they get talkative is when they are about half-a-mile apart. A little companionable chat across the Euphrates is a job — except to one's ears near by, for sound carries tremendously in this region, and they bawl with their raucous voices."[16]

The digging during the day was arduous labor for the workmen, who earned about eight piastres or fourteen pence a day. The early digging often involved moving large stones and the remains of buried walls and houses. Lawrence wrote of the stones: "Some of them weigh tons, and we have no blasting powder or stone hammers with us. As a result they have to be hauled, prehistoric fashion, by brute force of men on ropes, helped to a small extent by crowbars. At this moment something over 60 men are tugging away above, each man yelling Yallah as he pulls: the row is tremendous, but the stones usually come away. Two men out of three presume to direct operations, and no one listens to any of them, they just obey Gregori's orders, and their shouting is only to employ their spare breath. Now they are raising the 'talul,' the curiously vibrant, resonant wail of the Bedawi [Bedouin]. It is a very penetrating, and very distinct cry; you feel in it some kinship with desert-life, with ghazzus and camel stampedes. (Meanwhile the stone has slipped and fallen back into the trench, and Gregori's Turkish is deserting him.) Whenever he is excited he slips back into Greek in a high falsetto voice, that convulses our hoarse-throated men."[17]

The evenings were "filled up with odd jobs that might have been done in the day, squeezing and copying inscriptions, writing up pottery and object lists, journals, etc. Also it gets cold after sunset, and we go to bed early (about 10 or 11 as a rule), to avoid it. In the matter of food all goes quite easily, except for the Haj's* quite inadvertently emptying a curry tin into a pilaff! It was like eating peppered flames, and the other two are now crying aloud about their livers!"[18]

At night, when it was not too cold and windy, Lawrence often slept out on top of the mound. He enjoyed bathing in the Euphrates, and later brought from Oxford a Canadian canoe for excursions on the river. The canoe was fitted with an outboard motor and Lawrence took great pleasure with the engine, anticipating his gratification in mechanical work with air-sea rescue boats in the RAF many years later.

The digging ceased after some four months, and in July Lawrence began a one-month walking journey of the Euphrates region around Carchemish to study several castles in the area, notably at Harran, "Rum Kalaat" and Aintab (Gaziantep), and to search for engraved Hittite seal stones because, as his brother suggested, "it would lead to strange people and places."[19] He contracted dysentery and had more bouts of malaria, from the last of which he had not yet fully recovered when he returned to England in August. He visited Doughty during that time, and returned to Port Said and Beirut in early December. He spent the next few weeks in and around Jerablus, where the archeologists were engaged in struggles with Salim Tumah, "the local magnate," over the ownership of the site, and with German railroad personnel about the course of the Baghdad Railway, then under construction in the area. The archeologists were also preparing for the new season. Even though embroiled in these activities, Lawrence found time for trips to Aleppo and Damascus. In January 1912 he was sent for a month to Egypt, to excavate a tomb with

---

* Hajj Wahid was the chief guardian of the site. "Hajj" is a title meaning that its bearer has been on a pilgrimage to Mecca.

the famed Egyptologist Flinders Petrie at Kafr Ammar, forty miles south of Cairo. Then he returned to Jerablus, and in March Leonard Woolley, who replaced Campbell-Thompson, arrived.

After more lawsuits related to the struggles over the site (Lawrence was actually imprisoned for a short time, charged with trespassing, "restraint, conveyance and unlawful possession")[20] they were able to resume digging on March 17.

A year had now passed since Lawrence's arrival in Carchemish, and despite the vicissitudes, he was able to write home happily and romantically: "We are all well, very well, and as yet cordial: we have books, and pistachios, and six kinds of soap — if not seven. We eat a lot, and sleep a lot, and talk a lot, and I have for the second time, assimilated [Francis] Thompson's *Mistress of Vision*. It is very good. We sleep by the ropes of the camp, and we rise with the dawn and we tramp with the sun and the moon for our lamp, and the spray of the wind in our hair."[21]

Ernest Altounyan, the son of an Armenian surgeon in Aleppo whose company and hospitality Lawrence frequently enjoyed, recalled Lawrence at Carchemish in 1911 as a "frail, pallid, silent youth," one who was impersonal and curiously isolated from others. His speech was soft and reluctant. "By fall," Altounyan wrote, "he had spun his cocoon, but had not yet the assurance that enables the full-grown man to leave it when required."[22]

Winifred Fontana, the wife of the British consul in Aleppo, with whom Lawrence developed a friendship based on shared literary and aesthetic interests, describes him as looking "about eighteen" in the spring of 1911 and noted that he had cast off "much of his absorbed and discomforting aloofness with his visiting clothes and clad in shorts and a buttonless shirt held together with a gaudy Kurdish belt, looked what he was: a young man of rare power and considerable physical beauty. The belt was fastened on the left hip with a huge bunch of many-coloured tassels, symbol, plain to all Arabs that he was seeking a wife."[23] Woolley confirmed that Lawrence had his tassels made bigger than anyone else's, but observed, more accurately, that they did not necessarily signal that he was looking for a wife, but only that he was yet a bachelor.[24] Woolley also observed that although Lawrence could live and work with the poorest tribesmen under conditions of utmost simplicity, he also "quite appreciated comfort," an appreciation his older colleague seems to have shared.

Seven weeks after Woolley's arrival, Lawrence wrote E. T. Leeds: "We are building a great house, with mosaic floors and beaten copper fittings, Damascus tiles on the walls (including yours!) and much stone carvings. The little relief of doves over our bathroom door is charming and Woolley fancies himself in the bathroom: a gleaming mosaic floor reflecting his shining body against the contrast of the red-stuccoed walls: and the repoussé copper bath to put new tints into the water. Our fireplace is fine — a good deal of Hittite base and column work, and basalt mould-ings. We are putting in a burnished copper hood, and polished over mantel. The whole effect will (I hope) be chaste and yet rich. We really have no complaint of the way the museum is doing us — or we doing the museum."[25] In addition Lawrence provided the room with fine rugs, arm-chairs of black wood and white leather that he had had made in Aleppo, antique pots, and a piece of Morris tapestry.[26]

As the months went by, Lawrence became better and better known in the region, and not only because of the notoriety created by the doings connected with the dig. His growing knowledge of Arabic, his readiness to involve himself with Arabs and others from all strata of society, his concern for the people, and his colorful style of handling problems made him a popular figure. This fact, or phenomenon, was attested to by many observers who visited the site. "All Syria has heard of me: — and of us," he wrote home exuberantly, two months after the digging began.[27] By June he was writing, "Today I cured a man of compound scorpion-bite by a few drops of ammonia: for that I have a fame above Thompson's as a hakim [doctor] and as a magician who can conjure devils into water, from my mixing a seidlitz powder for the Haj in the kitchen before visitors."[28]

Lawrence's characteristically ambivalent attitude toward this fame, which soon extended into the markets of Aleppo, where he had many dealings in various kinds of antiquities, is reflected in a letter to his family in June of 1912, written after he had shown a duly impressed Englishman about the town. The Englishman asked: " 'I was wondering how many times you have been to Aleppo, and I was wondering how many times you have been in the bazaar, and I was wondering how many purchases you have made, and how many people spoke to you:' and when I had satisfied him on all those points he said: 'When I was trying to buy that embroidery in the silk bazaar, and wanted all your attention, nine old acquaintances greeted you with all signs of returning gladness, and six new ones were presented.' And just as he said so one of the dervishes [they were watching five dancing dervishes] got up and said: 'Did you not travel with me in the train last year?' and a muleteer and carriage-driver called out together 'Salaamat, effendi!' and Haj Wahid's sister, passing, asked me of the health of his wife. I have not seen that English-man since, for the consular dragoman [interpreter] drove up just then, and begged me to come to the government with him. And yet I think not six people in Aleppo know my name! Baron the hotel keeper told me laughing at lunch time that nine people had called to see me with antikas up till then: It is now evening, and I have not seen him to ask for more modern figures. Such is fame and a famous servant, and the power to know things in Aleppo."[29]

Lawrence was excited by Aleppo, a great trading center of Western

Asia and one of the "Seven Pillar" cities of his proposed book: "Aleppo is all compact of colour, and sense of line; you inhale Orient in lung-loads, and glut your appetite with silks and dyed fantasies of clothes. Today there came in through the busiest vault in the bazaar a long caravan of 100 mules of Baghdad, marching in line rhythmically to the boom of two huge iron bells swaying under the belly of the foremost. Bells nearly two feet high, with wooden clappers, introducing 100 mule-loads of the woven shawls and wine-coloured carpets of Bokhara! Such wealth is intoxicating: and intoxicated I went and bought the bells."[30]

Digging continued into June of 1912, at which time Lawrence made a short trip to the port of Alexandretta to see to the shipment of pottery for the Ashmolean. In June also, with the aid of advice and medicine from his family physician in Oxford, Lawrence struggled to help the local physicians and authorities fight a cholera epidemic in the Aleppo region, where ninety to ninety-five percent of cases were proving fatal. In July he returned to the site, still functioning as a "house physician," got "an attack of fever" himself, and returned to Jebail in August for a visit and to study more Arabic. He seems to have begun wearing Arab dress about this time.

Digging was resumed at Carchemish in September, with somewhat disappointing results, which were compounded by shortages of money from the British Museum, further attacks of fever and two broken ribs for Lawrence himself, and more difficulties with the Germans who were constructing the Baghdad Railway. In mid-November he set off for England, where he remained about six weeks, and returned to Beirut in mid-January of 1913. He found northern Syria snowbound.

There were many serious difficulties, including the disputes over the ownership of the site, during the years at Carchemish, with considerable personal danger at times to Lawrence, Woolley and the others. Woolley seemed willing to resort to strong-arm tactics when the work was impeded by the Ottoman authorities, and more than once threatened the local governor and other officials with a revolver, including a judge in his own courtroom. Woolley's intimidation of the authorities, which seemed at times the only effective way to enable the work to go on, caused such notoriety as to bring about a less than cordial reception for him later from the British ambassador in Constantinople.[31] A body of laws called Capitulations, by the terms of which foreigners in the Ottoman Empire were left to be judged on many important matters by their own courts, encouraged Lawrence and Woolley in an attitude of taking matters into their own hands. "You must be ignorant of our privileges here," Lawrence wrote home in June 1912. "If I murder Haj Wahid in our courtyard before the eyes of all the police of Biridjik [Birecik], no one can legally interfere; they might but I could sue them for it. If I was in a Turkish prison I would get out (of its ruins) double quick."[32] He did not, of course, tell his parents that he had recently spent some time in such a prison.

Lawrence's reports of "incidents" at Carchemish — his letters are filled with them — convey the sense that he was involved in a great adventure, a romantic game in which he played many different parts, an unending lark, a romp. Even the digs were "like a great sport with tangible results at the end of things."[33] Yet at the same time he was teaching classes to Arab adolescents and treating poisonous insect bites, cholera, malaria and other diseases. Mrs. Fontana recalled "the dark-eyed, richly coloured Arabs who came to exhibit their finds on the 'Dig' or to beg quinine for their fevered children (Lawrence seemed to know all by name and their children's names too)" and who "watched him with fascinated affection."[34] He was able in a letter to his brother Arnold, twelve at the time, to make an angry battle between two hundred invading Kurds and as many Arabs sound like comic opera: "Wasn't that a lovely battle? Absolutely no one hurt."[35] The year before, with Fareedah el Akle's help, he had found a jackal's skin for Arnie.

Gunrunning at Beirut was equally amusing. "At Aleppo I stayed five days more than I needed," he wrote early in 1913, "entertaining two naval officers, who became partners in my iniquity of gun-running at Beirut. The consular need of rifles involved myself, the consul-general at Beyrout, Flecker, the Admiral at Malta, our Ambassador at Stanbul, two captains and two lieutenants, besides innumerable cavasses [consular guards], in one common law-breaking. However Fontana [the consul in Aleppo, embattled presumably by Kurds, for whom the gunrunning was being done] got his stuff, and as he was too ill to entertain the porters, I had to trot them over to Aleppo."[36]

By the time Will Lawrence visited the site in September of 1913, Lawrence had become a major local personage, a hakim, "a great Lord in this place."[37] "Ned is known by everyone," Will wrote, "and their enthusiasm over him is quite amusing." He reassured their parents that they "must not think of Ned as leading an uncivilized existence. When I saw him last as the train left the station he was wearing white flannels, socks, and red slippers, with a white Magdalen blazer, and was talking to the Governor of Biridjik in lordly fashion."[38] Lawrence's evening garb, according to Woolley, was even finer. Over his white shirt he would put on "a white and gold embroidered Arab waistcoat and a magnificent cloak of gold and silver thread, a sixty-pound garment which he had picked up cheaply from a thief in the Aleppo market; in the evening too his hair was very carefully brushed: sitting in front of the winter fire reading — generally Homer, or Doughty's poems, or Blake — he would look with his sleek head and air of luxury extraordinarily unlike the Lawrence of the day time."[39]

Luther Fowle, an American missionary who was working at Aintab (Gaziantep) near Carchemish, stayed with the English archeologists late in 1913 and has provided a valuable description of his visit. By the time he arrived, Lawrence and Woolley's house had become as richly appointed as any professor's home in England: "In the center was the delightful living-room with open fireplace, built-in bookcases filled with the well-worn leather-bound volumes of the classics with which a British scholar would naturally surround himself, and a long table covered with the current British papers as well as the archeological journals of all the world." Fowle stressed the good faith and friendship which existed between Lawrence and Woolley and the native people. "They insisted that they were safer on the banks of the Euphrates than if they had been in Piccadilly. The leaders of the two most feared bands of brigands in the region, Kurdish and Arab, were faithful employees of the excavators, one as night watchman, the other in a similar position of trust. Of course there was no stealing and no danger. Had not these men eaten of the Englishmen's salt?"[40]

Woolley, who found Lawrence lovable and unusually able, was sensitive to the "feeling of essential immaturity," the persistent gifted-schoolboy in Lawrence. He teased Woolley with practical jokes, some of which Woolley found quite annoying, and made elaborate preparations for one of Hogarth's visits by decorating Hogarth's normally simple mud-walled room with pink satin curtains trimmed with lace and adorned with big pink bows. A pink cushion, hairpins, cheap scents and other reminders of domestic life were distributed about the room to make Hogarth feel "at home." Hogarth not unexpectedly flew into something of a rage when he discovered the joke, but Lawrence, according to Woolley, grinned over the jest for days.[41] Yet (also according to Woolley) Lawrence was himself unusually sensitive to ridicule and could not tolerate jokes made at his own expense.

In the actual work of the dig Woolley found Lawrence "curiously erratic," and whether he would work steadily or not depended on how much the particular task sustained his interest. Lawrence had responsibility for photography, sculpture and pottery. He could take careful notes but often was impatient with the written record. His memory for the fit of a particular Hittite fragment was extraordinary, and he could describe from memory the stratum and associations of a particular potsherd that had been excavated in a previous season, whether by Woolley or himself.[42] He "would make brilliant suggestions but would seldom argue in support of them," Woolley observed. "They were based on sound enough argument, but he expected you to see these for yourself, and if you did not agree he would relapse into silence and smile."[43]

His valuable contributions to the work at Carchemish notwithstanding, it is doubtful that Lawrence would ever have had the discipline, or the desire, to concentrate with sufficient singlemindedness on a particular academic project to become a professional archeologist. A passage in a letter home makes this clear. "At least," Lawrence wrote, after expressing concern whether he would ever accomplish his printing project with Richards, "I am not going to put all my energies into rubbish like writing history, or becoming an archeologist. I would much rather write a novel even, or become a newspaper correspondent."[44]

In the Carchemish period it becomes evident that Lawrence's central interest was in the *self*, not in himself in the sense of mere selfishness or egotism, for his remarkable generosity and kindness to the Arabs and to his friends, and the pains he undertook on behalf of almost anyone to whom he could be of service, have been testified to repeatedly. Rather, it was in perfecting and preparing himself through mastery. I believe this was as much an end in itself for Lawrence as it was a deliberate preparation for some great future task. Whether he was repairing the flue in the house chimney or perfecting his ability to shoot, or enduring the pain of broken ribs and the discomfort of dysentery, Lawrence was concentrating on making himself a perfected and refined instrument.

Ernest Altounyan is the only one of Lawrence's friends from this time who seems to have understood this quality. "Students of his life," Altounyan wrote, "cannot but be impressed by his persistence as a learner. Nothing could master him, but he proved a brilliant pupil in each successive school; until once more driven to tyranny by his unique sense of proportion. This quality has seldom met with its due regard in human history." Altounyan went on to say that Lawrence's "insistence on equality, running all up and down the human scale, is his finest flower," and that "taken in conjunction with an exquisite realization of self, it could hardly fail to be effective and place great power in the hands of the user."[45]

It was to E. T. Leeds, assistant keeper of antiquities at the Ashmolean, younger and less venerable than Hogarth (although venerable enough for Lawrence to address him frequently as "O Leeds") that Lawrence was able to express a Rabelaisian, bawdy side of his personality and his refusal to take things too seriously. This quality was not evident to the same degree in other letters written in these years — certainly not in those to his straitlaced mother. These letters, because of restrictions Leeds imposed on David Garnett, have not been published. Lawrence sent to Leeds a continuing stream of tiles, seals, pots, statues, sculptures and other antiquities with a running commentary to match. Of a homely statue of a Hittite woman Lawrence wrote, sending a drawing of her stolid form: "Only those like ourselves, who worship the silentness of beauty wrapped in darkness, can taste the full joy of her when she shows us her form stripped of the conventions that garb her in from public gaze. I had a half-hour of pure contemplation in ecstasy."[46] Later in the same vein he wrote: "I send you a lady, who is not steatopygous, stopping short modestly thereof. She is flint-age, from Jebail, in polished clay, and hideously ugly . . . but she will make a bust in your portrait gallery of Eve's more immediate descendants."[47] Another lady was "a goddess of the Hittites — Hittite — a creation O Leeds of a brick-maker I think. She is shaped like a whiskey-bottle, only rougher, with mighty breasts . . . a divinity indeed."[48] When a lion on a slab was damaged he wrote: "You ask us what would have been the effect on a lion of castrating it. . . . Well we didn't know exactly, so have tried on one of ours: all its mane dropped out, and it mews like a cat. The men say this becomes hereditary."[49]

Of the food shortage on a survey expedition Lawrence made equally light: "Our menu is a broad one, we eat bread and eggs: and Turkish delight. Only yesterday we finished the eggs, and nearest hens are three days' journey to the N. if only a camel would start laying we would be in Paradise tomorrow.

We have evolved rather a sporting dinner: Wooley you know likes a many storied edifice.

*Hors d'oeuvre*

The waiter (Dahoum) brings in on the lid of a petrol box half a dozen squares of Turkish delight,

*Soup.*
*Bread soup.*

Then

*Turkish delight on toast*

Then until yesterday

*Eggs*

Then, sweet . . .

*Turkish delight*
*Dessert*
*Turkish delight*

Of course bread is ad lib."[50]

When Lawrence heard that C. F. Bell, curator of art at the Ashmolean, was to be operated on for appendicitis, he wrote gently in an archeological motif: "If C. F. B. is really a son of Anak [a stalwart race that lived in Palestine before its conquest by the Israelites] he will be worth digging up. Let me know what they found inside: seriously, I hope all is well: 3 months is a long convalescence."[51]

By the beginning of March 1913, Lawrence's most exciting season of "furious" digging had begun, and he entertained himself and his friends with windy canoeing on the Euphrates. Archaeologically, this spring — the whole year in fact — proved to be very rewarding, with the excavation of many fine slabs and sculptures, "the richest British Museum digs since Layard's,"[52] but it also saw, sadly, the collapse of the mission school in Jebail.

In late June, Lawrence's archeological researches took him into new country down the Euphrates around Rakka in Mesopotamia, and in July he returned to England, bringing with him his two Arab friends from Carchemish: Dahoum, the donkey boy, and Hamoudi, the local foreman at the site. He housed them in his bungalow on Polstead Road. The visit was the cause of some difficulties and humor.[53]

One day when his mother and Janet Laurie were present, Lawrence pointed at Janet and asked Hamoudi, "How much is she worth?"

"No good, no good, no worth," came the forthright answer. ("I was a scrawny and miserable-looking thing," Janet explained to me).

Then, pointing to his mother, Lawrence asked, "How much is Mother worth?"

"Oh, a cow," answered Hamoudi. (In contrast to Janet, Mrs. Lawrence apparently looked better fed and more prosperous.)[54]

Upon their return to Jerablus in August Lawrence wrote home that "the Hoja [Hamoudi] and Dahoum entertain large houses nightly with tales of snakes as long as houses, underground railways, elephants, flying machines, and cold in July. I have not yet had the chance of hearing anything ludicrous. You know these two are too sophisticated to be comic in their relation: — they usually say the just — if unilluminative thing."[55]

In the fall the digging was resumed, the house was expanded and partitioned into twenty-two rooms, and Lawrence received a gift of a leopard from a government official in Aleppo.

If the first Syrian trip introduced Lawrence to the Arab world, it was in the Carchemish years that he learned about the Arab peoples. He became thoroughly conversant with the intricacies of their tribal and family jealousies, rivalries and taboos, their loves and hates, and their strengths and weaknesses. It was this carefully gathered knowledge, together with his remarkable ability to identify with the feelings and personal priorities of individual Arabs, to know the emotions and concerns upon which their self-esteem, security, power and prestige were based, that enabled Lawrence to win the confidence and acceptance of the Arab peoples, both during the Carchemish years and afterwards during the war.

The pages of his correspondence are filled with instances of his handling with tact, subtlety and strength countless disputes among the local Arab workmen, between the local people and various authorities, and of course between the Englishmen themselves and the local Arab and Turkish officials. If anything, Lawrence downplays his personal role in his description of events. Troubles seem to get settled magically since he fails to provide the evidence that would show precisely how he, or anyone else, manipulated people and events.

Shaykh Hamoudi, the chief local foreman at Carchemish, who was to go on to work with Woolley at Ur for more than two decades, was interviewed by Ernest Altounyan at the time of Lawrence's death. Hamoudi said that Lawrence's endurance seemed so great to the local people at Jerablus that they could not believe in his death, for "he could outride, outwalk, outshoot and outlast the best of them."[56]

Lawrence's ability to articulate for the Arabs their purposes and aims better than they could for themselves is attested to by Hamoudi: "While we would twist and turn with our object far away, almost out of sight, he would smile and point out to us what we were after, and make us laugh, ashamed."[57] Hamoudi's devotion to Lawrence was deep and intense, and depended in part upon his young friend's ability to empathize with the Arabs' thoughts and feelings. "Once," said Hamoudi, "he fell sick in my house and when it appeared that he would be very ill, the neighbors came around and advised me to put him out, lest he should die and his family should suspect me and the government put me in prison. I refused to listen; but before he lost consciousness he called me and said, 'Don't be afraid, Hamoudi. See, here on this paper I have written to my father to say that if I die you are not the cause.' So I fed him with milk and nursed him till he was well."[58]

This incident illustrates also how dangerously ill Lawrence was, probably during the 1911 walking journey across the Euphrates. Hamoudi said he grieved for him more than for a son he had lost. Passionately, with biblical phrases, Hamoudi declared to Altounyan ("pacing up and down the Aleppo stone paved hall"): "Tell them in England what I say. Of manhood the man, in freedom free; a mind without equal; I can see no flaw in him."[59]

Woolley and others have attested to Lawrence's rapport with the Arab men (his fluency in Arabic was an important ingredient in his success), but Woolley also says that Lawrence had no great liking for many individual Arabs (Dahoum and Hamoudi were among the exceptions).[60] Woolley observed astutely that Lawrence's ability to get along with the men hinged on a similarity between him and them, a childlike enjoyment in turning "the whole work into a game," the "fun of the thing" appealing to him as much as the scientific interest. In addition Lawrence's "uncanny knowledge of their family history gave Lawrence a peculiar prestige." It was Lawrence, again according to Woolley, who invented the system of saluting a discovery with revolver shots, proportioned to the importance of the discovery.

A streak of nihilism was present in Lawrence, even then. When Woolley would find Lawrence sitting with the men discussing a point of village custom or a question of local dialect and would object that no work was being done, Lawrence would grin and ask what anything mattered.[61]

The archeologists' cultivation of personal relationships with the Arabs and their attention to the individuality of the workmen and their families contrasted sharply with the autocratic way the German engineers handled the groups of Arab workers they employed to build the railroad. To the Germans a particular workman was usually just a number in a gang. This difference in treatment naturally worked to the advantage of the Englishmen in dealing with all sorts of local problems, and resulted for the Germans in endless delays in construction. According to Hubert Young, a young British officer who visited the camp in 1913, Lawrence "by his mere personality . . . had converted the excavation into a miniature British Consulate. His rough native workmen would have done anything for him."[62] Another visitor, Luther Fowle, reported that because "the Teuton could not see why the Arab should not and would not accept his regime of discipline and punishment" the Germans were always needing more laborers, "while the Englishmen a few hundred yards away, were overwhelmed with them."[63]

One practice the Englishmen developed that helped to foster loyalty among the workmen was the custom of giving extra piasters on payday for discoveries that the men brought to their employers. The archeologists would examine the item — a fragment of pottery, for example — and give a bonus according to its value, sometimes paying a small amount for a virtually valueless object in order to encourage the finder. This practice also had the advantage of assuring that the workmen took unusual care of what they found and did not lose, steal or break fragments of pottery and other articles.[64]

Most striking was Lawrence's ability to deal with a situation by applying his knowledge of the psychology of the individuals involved, and the local customs or beliefs to which they subscribed. On one occasion a local shaykh threatened to "ensorcel" Lawrence and his associates Campbell-Thompson and Hajj Wahid when they dismissed the shaykh's son from the dig. Force was recommended, but instead Lawrence suggested fighting local fire with local fire. The English should threaten to make a wax image of the old shaykh, which would be stuck with a pin through its heart at midnight. The ritual involved pulling out one of the last hairs from the shaykh's head. The threat of black magic worked and peace was restored.[65] Lawrence described to Hogarth another example of the use of sorcery, in this case to quell the bullying of a local gendarme.[66]

Lawrence was evidently quite capable of using force or direct intimidation when he thought it necessary. "He had," Woolley wrote, "a cool indomitable courage which showed itself clearly in such troubles as we had with Turks and Germans, its earnestness nearly always disguised by an imprudent enjoyment of the humor of the situation; he did not mind the risk, and the bluff appealed to him immensely."[67] Once Lawrence was stoned by several Kurdish tribesmen when he tried to stop them from dynamiting fish. By threatening to have the local police inspector removed for incompetence, he browbeat the man into agreeing to punish them.[68]

In an account written during World War I, Woolley describes Lawrence's angry response to the flogging one of the German engineers gave the Englishmen's houseboy for a minor offense. When Lawrence accosted the director of the railway operation and accused the engineer of assault, the following exchange took place:

"Herr X never assaulted the man at all; he merely had him flogged."

"Well, don't you call that an assault?"

"Certainly not. You can't use these natives without flogging them. We have men thrashed every day — it's the only method."

"We've been here longer than you have and have never beaten one of our men yet, and we don't intend to let you start on them."[69]

By threatening to flog the German engineer in front of the whole village, Lawrence was able to force a public apology from him, to the great amusement of the villagers.

Lawrence's knowledge of family relationships within the tribes helped him to prevent bloodshed from the vengeance of blood feuds. "Our people are very curious and very simple," he wrote his family three months after reaching Carchemish, "and yet with a fund of directness and child-humor about them that is very fine. I see much of this, for I sleep on the mound and start the work every day at sunrise, and the choosing of new men so falls to my lot. I take great care in the selection, utterly refusing all such as are solemn or over-polite, and yet we are continually bothered by blood feuds, by getting into the same trench men who have killed each other's kin or run off with their wives. They at once prepare to settle up the score in kind, and we have to come down amid great shouting, and send one to another pit. There is no desire to kill, and public opinion does not insist on vengeance, if there is 50 feet of earth between the offender and the offended."[70] Two years later one such feud broke out among the workmen from two great families, and "the digs for six days were two armed camps, not eating together, or speaking, walking the same path, or labouring in the same gang."[71]

Because of his knowledge Lawrence took increasing responsibility for arbitrating local disputes, a role he was to execute skillfully and painfully during the war. Once with fifteen horsemen he retrieved a Kurdish girl who had been abducted by one of the wealthy local Turks.[72] According to Lawrence's brother Will, "The Kurds apply to him continually as arbitrator in tribal difficulties,"[73] and Fowle reported that "the even-handed justice of the two Englishmen was so well known and respected that they had come to be the judges of various issues of all sorts between rival villages or in personal disagreement."[74]

Lawrence stressed his poverty, and enjoyed, especially on his tramps in Syria, living more roughly than most Westerners could or would consent to do. But this Spartan attitude was assumed more for self-training and because it was a realistic and effective way to live in that region than because of actual poverty, for money was available to him from the demyship and usually from the British Museum and from his family. "In 1914 I was a pocket Hercules," Lawrence wrote later, "as muscularly strong as people twice my size, and more enduring than most."[75] We have seen how comfortably Woolley and Lawrence lived, and how opulently Lawrence sometimes dressed. So it is more accurate to say that it was Lawrence's ability to take on the coloration of the people he was among, to live *as if he were* a poor native, which enabled him to enter the life of the local tribes and come to be so fully accepted.

As early as 1911 he was writing home of his preference for the Arab as compared to the European, and the destructive effect of the latter upon the former: "The perfectly hopeless vulgarity of the half-Europeanized Arab is appalling. Better a thousand times the Arab untouched. The foreigners come out here always to teach, whereas they had much better learn, for in everything but wits and knowledge the Arab is generally the better man of the two."[76] In 1914 his preference for things Arab had not yet extended to riding horses and camels, for according to Stewart Newcombe, "Lawrence at that time hated riding horses and had no love for a camel, preferring to walk."[77] By April 1914, Lawrence's involvement in the Middle East was such that he could write home: "I don't think that I will ever travel in the West again: one cannot tell of course, but this part out here is worth a million of the rest. The Arabs are so different from ourselves."[78]

Prominent in Lawrence during these years was a sense of fun, a joy in life, which, though childlike — or perhaps because it was childlike — his companions found infectious. Accompanied usually by his Arab friends, he thoroughly, and quite innocently, enjoyed himself, canoeing on the Euphrates and "sailing down the Syrian coast, bathing, harvesting, and sight-seeing in the towns. Certainly no hermitry!"[79] Winifred Fontana was referring, I believe, to this quality of innocence, violated and destroyed during the war, when she wrote to Robert Graves, upon reading his biography of Lawrence in 1927: "I am glad you passed on my memory of his youthful beauty and colour. Surely there were others who observed it? It is odd how vividly and how often I remembered that bright hair — all through the war when one wondered if it had been trampled into mud yet — and after, as if it were something significant in itself."[80]

From among the seemingly endless stream of visitors to the site, especially in the last year, from his wanderings, and from visits to Beirut, Smyrna, Jebail, Aleppo, Damascus and Cairo, Lawrence developed many friendships and acquaintances that enriched his life and also were of use to him later during the Revolt. The strength and importance of certain of Lawrence's friendships with other men ("comparable in intensity to sexual love, for which he made them a substitute," his brother Arnold wrote) became apparent during this period.[81]

With his increasing knowledge of the world Lawrence took on more and more the role of mentor to his younger brothers, and his letters were filled with somewhat pedantic advice and information about their schooling, facts of history, books, and the like. Although he was reserved in the expression of intimate feelings to his brothers, he addressed himself to their individuality, supported their right to choose their own course, and did not urge them to be like himself. "Frank, I suppose goes up [to Jesus College, Oxford] in October," he wrote in 1913, "and there will be the usual heartburning as to whether he is to live in or not. As a social being he would probably prefer to, and if so he may like a Phoenician bronze bowl as an ashtray . . . for accept my prophecy as sure that he will begin to smoke soon. It is an imitative vice, like short hair, which insinuates itself. In case he lives at home, he must have my little house: — it is for the reverse reason . . . I had it that I might be quiet: Frank that he may be noisy . . . and it speaks many things for the catholicity of the place, that it is equally adapted for each."[82] Arnold — twelve by this time — Lawrence entertained with accounts of battles and animated descriptions of adventures with Dahoum (who was only fifteen at the time), and of crocodiles, hippopotami, spiders, scorpions, snakes and sepulchers.

Lawrence found R. Campbell-Thompson, the other archeologist who was at Carchemish during the early months at the dig, to be "good fun" and pleasant, but was troubled by his jingoism and his excessive love of guns. "I think Thompson is a little cracked," he wrote home with some concern. "He has brought out two rifles with about 200 cartridges, and some revolvers with hundreds of cartridges, and sabres and fencing masks (stolen at Haifa fortunately) and hundreds of useless stuffs."[83]

Lawrence found much more in common with Woolley, whom he had known at Oxford, and admired, at least at first, his aggressive way of handling difficulties. "You should have seen Woolley," he wrote Leeds. "When the police tried to hold up his donkeys, he charged down upon them, drawing his revolver from his sash with the 126 tassels, and shouting mixed Greek, Arab, Italian, English and Turkish. Arrived at the spot he shouldered aside the Corporal and the guard, and pulled the donkey-line himself. The beast, like all donkeys, wouldn't go without being dragged. However, Woolley dragged him."[84]

But they were not personally close, and although they served together in Cairo during the war, seem not to have corresponded thereafter. Woolley found Lawrence "the best of companions," but also very reserved and detached in spite of their many long talks. Lawrence would undo

with ridicule any "sentiment" he expressed. After Lawrence's death
Woolley wrote:

> I do not remember his ever admitting to any affection for anybody though
> I knew perfectly well that in the case of certain people the affection was
> there and deeply felt; in all matters of the emotions he seemed to have a
> peculiar distrust of himself. Similarly he never discussed religion, at least in
> its personal aspects, but he gave to Hamoudi an Arabic version of the
> synoptic gospels and was very pleased to find that it impressed him; but he
> hated missionary activities and was vitriolic in his abuse of missions, though
> one of his best friends in Syria was Miss Holmes of the American mission at
> Jebail. He was fond of talking to the men about the Moslem faith, but had
> no admiration for it except for its insistence on the virtue of charity.[85]

Hogarth remained the strongest guiding force in Lawrence's life during
these years, although Charles Doughty seemed to have been a kind of
spiritual forebear. Hogarth stayed at Carchemish only for two months
(March and April) in 1911, supervising the digging thereafter from
England. Lawrence's attitude toward his mentor was one of boyish awe.
"Mr. Hogarth is a most splendid man," he wrote home in March 1911,
and "has read, and still reads most things, and likes talking about them
and the people who write."[86]

By the spring of 1914 the awe was no less, though it could be tinged
with humor: "A breathless hush of expectation — and the scratching of
this pen — relieve the usual clatter of our house," Lawrence wrote Leeds.
"This is Sunday, and we are all dressed in our best, sitting in our empty,
swept, and garnished rooms, awaiting the coming of the CHIEF. He is
expected today: and is coming heavy with importance: Woolley is
nervous, and I myself can only exist in scribbling to you."[87]

In November 1911, before returning to the East, Lawrence arranged to
see Doughty once again in order to discuss his travels. He wrote beforehand, "I have been a twelve-month in Northern Syria [actually only
eight months unless the four months in 1909 are included, but Lawrence
had already written Doughty about his first trip], some four months of
which I spent with Mr. Hogarth digging up what was left of the Hittites
in the ruins of Carchemish on the Euphrates" (actually only two months
were spent digging with Hogarth). Soon after returning, Lawrence took
a letter from Doughty to one al-Bassam, a former friend of Doughty's who
lived in Damascus. Lawrence discovered that memories of Doughty from
thirty-five years back remained alive among the Arabs of Syria, and faithfully reported the gratifying fact to the old traveler.[88]

Doughty remained for Lawrence throughout these years and afterwards
the inspiration for his travels in Arab countries, and provided him with an
outstanding example of how to learn about Arab peoples through living

among them. "I am not trying to rival Doughty," Lawrence wrote his family in May of 1912. "You remember that passage that he who has once seen palm-trees and the goat-hair tents is never the same as he had been: that I feel very strongly, and I feel also that Doughty's two years wandering in untainted places made him the man he is, more than all his careful preparation before and since."[89]

It was in the Carchemish period that Lawrence began to cultivate a widening circle of friends who complemented the multiple facets of his personality. Each seemed to lay claim to knowledge of some piece of him, the more uncritical insisting upon the congruence between a shifting part and the whole. Yet his brother Arnold, who knew him well, acknowledged that T.E. "when he had just been with someone or was just going to see someone . . . tended to take on the characteristics of that person,"[90] with the result that each could find an aspect of himself or herself in Lawrence. Sometimes common acquaintanceship with Lawrence brought his friends into new relationships with each other, but more often he kept his relationships isolated — "separated by bulkheads" was the phrase Graves used to describe this quality.[91]

Lawrence began to look among artists and writers for his friends, valuing them often too highly as he valued himself too little. They in turn found in Lawrence, of whom they seemed to have been universally fond, an object of imagination or beauty for their work. Ernest Altounyan, in whose father's Aleppo home Lawrence spent many enjoyable hours, devoted a small book of poetry to Lawrence (to my knowledge Altounyan's only published poetry), and Winifred Fontana, the wife of the Aleppo consul, was moved upon seeing Lawrence at Carchemish — "his fine eyes lost in thought about Doughty's *Arabia Deserta,* open across his knees" — to pull out her sketch pad and start drawing him. Even his brother Will was inspired several months after his visit to Carchemish to write a poem ("To T.E.L.") predicting his potential greatness. Lawrence in turn would sometimes find aspects of himself in the personalities and work of his friends.

Lawrence's friend James Elroy Flecker, who served as the British vice consul in Beirut in 1911 and 1912, died in a sanatorium in Switzerland early in 1915. Lawrence thought highly of Flecker's poetry and called him "the sweetest singer of the war generation." He drafted an essay on Flecker in 1925, and described him as "always embroidering, curling, powdering, painting, his loves and ideals, demonstrative, showy, self advertising, happy."[92]

When Lawrence was fond of someone, he was wont to take unusual pains on their behalf. He provided great support to Fareedah el Akle in her struggles with her employer, the strict Miss Holmes, and wrote to her at length, offering advice and help for which she was very grateful.[93] Lawrence seemed always ready to fulfill requests one might have thought irritating, such as the call for an iron dog collar that interested a lady in England who had four Arab dogs. For his ailing friend Flecker, Lawrence wrote in June 1914, simply to entertain him, a long, satirical account of a "battle" between the Circassians guarding the German railway activities and the Kurdish and Arab railway workmen.[94] When he was unable to keep an appointment he had made with a lady in August 1912, Lawrence wrote on the same day two slightly different letters of apology, sending one by rail and one by post lest one of them fail to reach her in time.[95] Mrs. Fontana has described the extraordinary consideration that Lawrence showed to her and her children when they visited the site. He made sure they had a dry place to sleep, enticed a band of Kurdish musicians to play and sing for them, took her canoeing on the "swirling" Euphrates and then to an island to gather wildflowers, and paddled "the difficult and dangerous return journey against the current with a coolness and skill that fired my imagination."[96] That he could be deliberately inconsiderate and rude like a naughty schoolboy when someone annoyed him, or was acting pompously, is also well known.

Clearly the most valued relationship of all for Lawrence at Carchemish was with Dahoum, the waterboy or donkey boy at Jerablus. He was only fourteen when Lawrence first met him in the spring of 1911. According to Woolley he was nicknamed Dahoum by his mother at birth because he was a very black baby (Dahoum is a form of *tehoum*, which means "the darkness that was on the face of the waters before creation").[97] Other of Lawrence's biographers say he was called Sheikh Ahmed, though Lawrence provides no direct confirmation of this. Thomas Beaumont, who served with Lawrence in the desert but never met Dahoum, said his name was Salim Ahmed, but no substantiating evidence for the "Salim" exists.[98] By Lawrence's description Dahoum was "mixed Hittite and Arab," and Woolley states that his family lived on the *qal'a* (the mound, which had formerly been a fortress or citadel), and thus traced his lineage from the original inhabitants of the area. Woolley saw a resemblance between Dahoum's face and "those rather heavy and fleshy captains who head the sculptured procession at the portal of our Hittite Palace."[99] Lawrence found Dahoum an immensely appealing boy, more intelligent than most of the local Arab and Kurdish inhabitants, and taught him photography and other skills that were useful in the work. On Lawrence's many trips away from the site, Dahoum was his frequent companion. They swam together often, and talked a great deal to each other and shared many hours of silence. Lawrence admired the way Dahoum spoke Arabic and wrote Miss Fareedah, "If I could talk it like Dahoum . . . you would never be tired of listening to me."[100] When Lawrence became dangerously ill with dysentery during the journey across the Euphrates in the summer of 1911, Dahoum visited Lawrence daily at Hamoudi's home, and Lawrence in turn tended Dahoum the following year when the latter became ill with a malignant form of malaria and nearly died.

The subject of further education for Dahoum, who talked of going to school in Aleppo, came up frequently. But for Lawrence Dahoum represented the pure and natural simplicity of the Arab unspoiled by Western influences, and he was hostile toward the idea of formal education for him. Dahoum's personality supplied, as Arnold Lawrence indicated in a note in the 1911 diary, "the largest element to the figure of S.A.," to whom Lawrence dedicated *Seven Pillars of Wisdom.*[101]

In addition to the close companionship between them, Dahoum represented for Lawrence an aspect of an ideal he sought: the pure descendant of an ancient Eastern race uncorrupted by Western influences. Lawrence called him still in 1912 a savage "who wrestled beautifully."[102] Woolley wrote that Dahoum was "beautifully built and remarkably handsome" and that the village was scandalized by the intimacy of the friendship, especially when Lawrence had Dahoum pose for a naked figure he carved in the soft local limestone and set up on the edge of the house roof. But Woolley denies firmly that there was any sexual relationship between Dahoum and Lawrence, and stresses Lawrence's puritanical nature.[103]

Dahoum's personality was to a great degree "created" by Lawrence to serve as a kind of ideal self stripped of its Western complexities, a self Lawrence sought to achieve. Arnold Lawrence, who was thirteen and a half when T.E. brought Dahoum and Hamoudi to Oxford, observed how like a son Dahoum was to his brother, "made into what he was by the older man." The family became fond of Dahoum, sixteen by this time, and Mrs. Lawrence tried, to her sons' amusement, to break through the language barrier by speaking to him in French during his visit to Oxford.[104]

When Lawrence left Carchemish and returned to England in June 1914, Hajj Wahid and Dahoum were left to dispose of what was left behind at the site. During the war Dahoum was appointed guardian of the site by the Turks and thus exempted from service in the Turkish army,[105] but he died of typhus before the war ended.[106] Lawrence's grief over this loss was strong and deep and probably inspired the dedicatory poem in *Seven Pillars of Wisdom* ("To S.A."), as Dahoum came to embody the joy and innocence which Lawrence lost in the war and felt he had once had at Carchemish. Later, at a time of unhappiness in the Tank Corps, Lawrence wrote to a young friend, with whom he had been able to share in the RAF ranks a companionship somewhat similar to the one he had known with Dahoum: "You and me, we're very unmatched and it took some process as slow and kindly and persistent as the barrack room to weld us comfortably together. People aren't friends till they have said all they can say, and are able to sit together, at work or rest, hour long without speaking. We never got quite to that, but we're nearer it daily . . .

and since S.A. died I haven't experienced any risk of that's happening."[107] In 1919 when he was working on *Seven Pillars of Wisdom*, Lawrence wrote on the back flyleaf of a book of poetry the following note, obviously concerned with his feelings for Dahoum: "A (?) I wrought for him freedom to lighten his sad eyes: but he had died waiting for me. So I threw my gift away and now not anywhere will I find rest and peace."[108]

# 9

## The Epic Dream
## and the Fact of War

In September 1910, three months before Lawrence set off for the Middle East and for Carchemish, he wrote his mother a letter containing the following passage: "It is lovely after you have been wandering in the forest with Percivale or Sagramors le desirous, to open the door, and from the Cherwell to look at the sun glowering through the valley-mists. Why does one not like things if there are other people about? Why cannot one make one's books live except in the night, after hours of straining? and you know they have to be your own books too, and you have to read them more than once. I think they take in something of your personality, and your environment also — you know a second hand book sometimes is so much more flesh and blood than a new one — and it is almost terrible to think that your ideas, yourself in your books may be giving life to generations of readers after you are forgotten. It is that specially which makes one need good books: books that will be worthy of what you are going to put into them. What would you think of a great sculptor who flung away his gifts on modelling clay or sand? Imagination should be put into the most precious caskets, and that is why one can only live in the future or the past, in Utopia, or the Wood Beyond the World. Father won't know all this — but if you can get the right book at the right time you taste joys — not only bodily, physical, but spiritual also, which pass one out above and beyond one's miserable self, as it were through a huge air, following the light of another man's thoughts. And you can never be quite the old self again. You have forgotten a little bit: or rather pushed it out with a little of the inspiration of what is immortal in someone who has gone before you."[1]

The letter is one of the more revealing that Lawrence wrote. It discloses his view that it is his mother with whom he can share the deeper, spiritual side of himself, that "Father won't know all this." It explains his interest in printing in order to give great books — whether someone else's or his own — a form worthy of the quality of their content. Above all it reveals the degree to which this twentieth-century Percivale, this modern grail-seeker, lived in the imagination, especially in the imagination of others. Even at twenty-two he could write of the need to pass out beyond his "miserable self" and to follow "the light of another man's thought" — finding "the right book at the right time" — especially by someone he could regard as immortal. The present would not do, though he would always live in the present and master its requirements. Lawrence felt he could "only live in the future or the past, in Utopia." He tried to achieve this in two ways in the years that followed — through trying to transform a baser reality into a lofty ideal in a war, and through his own subsequent effort at writing an epic. For Lawrence present life was measured always against an ideal of the imagination, particularly a medieval ideal, and his most important actions, especially during the war years, may be seen as efforts to impose upon grimmer circumstances, to which he had also to adapt, his utopian imaginings.

Lawrence recognized that this idealistic questing was to some extent a family problem shared with his brothers. In a letter to his family, written soon after arriving at Carchemish, he referred to himself as "an artist of sorts and a wanderer after sensations," and reassured his parents that "one of us must surely get something of the unattainable we are all feeling after."[2] Fareedah el Akle, with whom he found so much in common, seems to have possessed a feminine counterpart to Lawrence's hero fantasies. She once wrote to him: "I never told you that my great desire was (when young) to be an Arab princess. I mean to say to have been born among them as an Arab princess."[3]

Lawrence's writings during the Carchemish years, so filled with accounts of his learning, of mastery and of the details of his daily life and adventures, give little evidence of the workings of the epic dream as they were expressed in his writings after the experiences of the war years. At Carchemish life itself, celibate, intense and full, was experienced as ideal, an existence in which the biblical past, freed of the degradations of the modern world could, with a minimum of stretching of the imagination, be experienced as a perfection in the present.

It would be fascinating to know the degree to which Lawrence actually lived out his daily experiences in terms of the imaginative vistas created for him by the authors he was reading. Unless we know this, it is mere speculation to attribute significance to the choice of books at a given time. Yet this choice, probably more than a matter of taste, may have psychological meaning, especially if a pattern can be perceived. At Carchemish Lawrence's predilection for medieval epic works is still evident, especially early in these years, although he began to show an interest in more modern French and English literature. Doughty's works, epic in style themselves, continued to be important to him.

On his walking trip in northern Syria in search of castles, seals and "strange people and places," Lawrence had with him "my Rabelais, Holy Grail, Rossetti and Roland."[4] But it is the works of William Morris, especially his Victorian-Icelandic-Anglo-Saxon-German epic poem *Sigurd the Volsung*, that moves and inspires Lawrence most at this time. Over and over he urges this book on his parents and friends with repeated demands to know their opinion of it. He called it "the best poem I know" and was delighted as the members of the family, upon his urging, revealed that they were reading it. He was especially pleased when he learned his mother was reading it, and he related it to his life among the Arab peoples. "So mother reads Sigurd!" he enthused. "I want to know whether it is the most beautiful book any of you have ever seen: and what she thinks of the telling of the tale: remember the tale itself is Norse, and it is perhaps the most near to us of all the Norse tales — the one we can best assimilate and enjoy — better of course, if one knows a simple people, as I happen to know the Arabs."[5]

How one reacts to the "telling" of such a tale is, I suppose, a matter of cultural perspective and literary taste as well as of personal psychology. To a reader of the present age, at least to this reader, the poem seems terribly dated, disjointed — in fact, silly. The Icelandic versions (Morris had traveled in Iceland) of Anglo-Saxon and Teutonic myths of several generations and tribes of barbarian peoples were purified in Morris's Victorian poetry. His *Sigurd* is filled with the familiar medieval glorification of certain loves, lusts, murders, wars and vendettas, and the disparagement of others. What is interesting from the standpoint of Lawrence's psychology in this transparently Oedipal tale is the degree to which the story is dominated, and the action of the male heroes determined, by the loves and wills of passionate beautiful women and demigoddesses, from whom all important knowledge and power derive. Morris depicts a world of jealousy and conflicting loyalties on the part of both men and women, a world in which treachery, betrayal and vengeance abound, and in which powerful women use the instrumentality of love to manipulate their sons, husbands and lovers, and to inspire them to perform deeds of heroism on their behalf and to their greater glory.

Another favorite book of Lawrence's in this period was Maurice Hewlett's *Richard Yea and Nay* ("Read *Richard Yea and Nay* in Egypt for the ninth time. It is a masterpiece"),[6] a turn-of-the-century novel which tells how Richard I's indecisiveness cost him the love of his sweetheart. Perhaps this story recalled for Lawrence the consequences of his own hesitations with Janet Laurie.

It is difficult to appreciate in the 1970's the gulf that separates us — a gulf that Lawrence helped to create — from the pre-World War I generation of educated Englishmen, many of whom could view the approach of war with exhilaration. In April 1915, Churchill could still find in Rupert Brooke's death something glorious and exciting, the embodiment of the "spirit of 1914," a voice "more true, more thrilling, more able to do justice to the nobility of our youth in arms engaged in this present war, than any other — more able to express their thoughts of self-surrender, and with a power to carry comfort to those who watched them so intently from afar."[7] Apart from Lawrence's personal psychology, in his devotion to the heroic romance he was part of this spirit of 1914, for in these tales, as in the idealism of the prewar generation, war appears to have little objectionable reality, and its murder, bloodshed, grief, inanity, cruelty and pain all glow in a hazy light of greatness, of glory and of nobility.

The idea that Lawrence, while at Carchemish, was employed by the British government to spy on the Germans on the railway and to engage in other espionage activity under the guidance of David Hogarth has been stressed recently by Knightley and Simpson.[8] "There can be no doubt," they say, "that the dig had a dual purpose" of espionage and archeology. They assert Lawrence's connection, through a tenuous series of links via Hogarth and Lionel Curtis (whom he did not meet until after the war), to the precepts of the Round Table, an organization of politically minded British intellectuals who were not themselves involved with spy activities.[9]

In 1965 I had the opportunity to discuss this question with Hogarth's son, William. He could, of course, have been incompletely informed about his father's activities, but seemed confident that David Hogarth had been candid with him: there was military intelligence but no official secret service in 1912, and many British subjects, especially consuls and officers working overseas, were spies in an informal sense, that is, subject to being asked by Foreign Office officials upon their return from sensitive areas what they might have seen or heard. In the Ottoman Empire, Hogarth said, every British official was a spy, but that "neither my father nor Lawrence were officially employed as spies." Hogarth and Sir Edward Grey, who was Foreign Secretary from 1905 to 1916, had been to public school together at Winchester and were in frequent contact before the war, and through such informal channels Hogarth kept the Foreign Office informed, to the extent of his knowledge, regarding the activities of the Turks and Germans in Syria, and naturally enlisted the help of Lawrence, who was constantly on the scene at Carchemish, in this service.[10]

Remarks of Lawrence's in his letters have been quoted by Villars and by Knightley and Simpson as evidence of spying; for example, "the strongly-dialectical Arabic of the villagers would be as good as a disguise to me";[11] and, "for some reason Mr. Hogarth is very anxious to make me learn Arabic."[12] These comments suggest that if Lawrence was involved in espionage he was unevenly informed of his leader's purposes.

Lawrence certainly made efforts to keep Hogarth informed about the progress of the Baghdad Railway and was naturally pleased with delays the Germans incurred in its construction. "Can you tell D.G.H.," he wrote Leeds in February 1913, "on the authority of Mr. Contzen [the railway manager] here, that station construction E. of Harran is suspended at least temporarily, and the men sent home? And that yesterday I walked over the wooden bridge and entered Mesopotamia dry-shod? and that they are knocking in the iron piers of the permanent thing? He always asks after the Baghdad railway."[13]

Lawrence hardly behaved like the model secret service agent. According to Hubert Young, Lawrence told him that one of the German engineers suspected him of spying on the railway and causing difficulties with the local labor. However, wrote Young, "he [Lawrence] did not go out of his way to remove this impression," but on the contrary, took a mischievous delight in rousing the German engineer's suspicions: "He even told us that he had gone so far as to drag some large pipes up to the top of the mound, whereupon the German had reported in a frantic telegram, which somehow fell into his hands, that the mad Englishman was mounting guns to command the railway-bridge over the Euphrates."[14] By the summer of 1913 Lawrence had apparently succeeded in rousing the suspicions of the Ottoman authorities, for he wrote, probably to Hogarth: "The old government has life in it yet . . . it is beginning to keep watch on where I go: at least the ombashi came to me this afternoon, grinning, with orders to go down to Abu Galgal [in northwestern Mesopotamia] with me to protect me . . . as he said 'praise God you are already back, I can perform my duty without ceasing.' "[15] Colonel Stewart Newcombe, who was based in Cairo at the time, wrote Ronald Storrs in 1953 that "to suggest that either man [Woolley or Lawrence] was secretly working for M.I. [Military Intelligence] before that date is, to me, ridiculous."[16]

The matter would seem to have been laid to rest by a letter written in 1969 by R. D. Barnett, keeper of Western antiquities at the British Museum, to *The Times Literary Supplement* after reading a review there of Knightley and Simpson's book. Barnett summarized the archeological interest in Carchemish since at least 1876 and wrote, "There is not the least evidence of ulterior motives in the choice of the site." He reviewed the private (that is, nongovernmental) funding of the work, pointed out that the British Museum was the natural body for administering it, and concluded emphatically: "No suggestion, therefore, of political or sinister purpose whatever can be seen by us to attach to this phase of Lawrence's and Hogarth's career as far as we are aware."[17]

What is more striking from my own point of view than serious intelligence activity is the curious innocence of the archeologists of Carchemish, the lack of serious concern (like most of their generation) about the clouds of war which they could see gathering in the West and in the Middle East from 1912 to 1914, as the Ottoman Empire began to crumble under the attacks of Italy and the Balkan League. Even in 1913 and 1914 seemingly endless streams of visitors of many nationalities came to Carchemish, while the great powers were arming and the preliminary bouts of World War I were being fought. In Lawrence's letters to his family during the 1909 trip to Syria he indicated his awareness of secret native Christian societies in Beirut and Damascus, but the leaders of the political secret societies out of which the Arab nationalist movement grew were drawn from privileged Muslim families.[18] There is no evidence that Lawrence was in touch with these societies.

Lawrence's concerns about Germany and the Germans seem entirely parochial, and he felt that the skirmishes and battles involving the British archeologists and the German railroad managers reflected little more than the working conditions of the railway workers and the route of the railroad bed. Lawrence was aware in the beginning of 1912 of "great rumors of wars and annexations." These were "not to be believed yet, but such a smash is coming out here."[19] Eight weeks later he wrote to Leeds, "Haldane,* according to consul, is negotiating an entente with Germany." But, added Lawrence innocently, "I have anticipated him, in arranging one with the Teutons here. There is nothing but supping and giving to sup. Haj Wahid looks worried, as though in coming to Jerablus he had not anticipated dinner-parties. However, D.G.H. said: 'be very pleasant to the Railway' and we walk about with our arms round each other's necks."[20]

By November Bulgaria had broken with Turkey after a short war and Lawrence observed that she "has every possibility of finishing off Turkey (if the powers let her) because the Turks are such helpless stupids," but they (the archeologists) "will sit out here and look on at what is going to come of Turkey,"[21] despite the fact that Turkey was already frantically levying "every able-bodied man as soldier," thereby causing a problem in finding workers at the site. The following March Lawrence wrote home irritatedly, "Germany is going in for armaments, England for insurances, and all of them for nonsense . . . consider the suffragettes."[22] But despite all of this, 1913 proved to be Lawrence's best year archeologically speaking, and the pleasures of canoeing on the Euphrates continued.

There is little in Lawrence's letters of this period that indicates much enthusiasm for the potentialities for Arab freedom that the destruction of the Ottoman Empire might mean, probably in part because he was aware of the importance of retaining a show of neutrality while working within the Ottoman Empire, and the danger to his position that might result should a politically pro-Arab letter be read by the Turkish authorities. He did, however, write cautiously on April 5, 1913, during the first Balkan War: "As for Turkey, down with the Turks! But I am afraid there is, not life, but stickiness in them yet. Their disappearance would mean a chance

---

* Richard Haldane, the lord chancellor, had been sent by the British cabinet on an official peace mission to Germany early in 1912.

for the Arabs, who were at any rate once not incapable of good government."[23]

In January 1914, Lawrence and Woolley were called on a two months' survey of the eastern Sinai (the region known in the Bible as the Wilderness of Zin) and the region of Wadi 'Araba from Aqaba to Petra, under the sponsorship of the Palestine Exploration Fund. In this expedition, which was initiated by Lord Kitchener and supervised by Stewart Newcombe, an archeological "cover" concealed a political and strategic purpose. During the expedition Lawrence became familiar with the region, especially around Aqaba, knowledge of which was to prove especially valuable during the campaigns of 1917. He was aware of the political nature of the expedition and wrote home that "we are obviously only meant as red herrings, to give an archeological colour to a political job."[24] The purpose of the survey was to complete the mapping of this area, which was of particular importance because it constituted the border region between Egypt and the Ottoman Empire. Nonetheless, Turkey gave permission to survey north of Aqaba, but not around Aqaba itself, which probably accounted for the resistance to mapping, photography and archeologizing Lawrence encountered from the governor there.

It was during this time that Lawrence first met William Yale, a young American who was surveying in the Negev for a road to be built by the Standard Oil Company. Yale recalls coming across Lawrence, Woolley and Newcombe at Beersheba in January 1914. Yale was annoyed because he felt Lawrence "played me for a sucker," revealing nothing of what he was doing in the desert, pretending to be sight-seeing, and asking Yale and his party if they had seen Petra and this or that ruins. Lawrence later told Yale that he had received a telegram from London ordering him to get in touch with Yale's party and find out what "some American oil men" were up to in the desert.[25]

Lawrence's excitement at being "alone in Arabia" (that is, at Aqaba) with no Western companion, and visiting the beautiful ruins of Petra, alternates with arrogant accounts of his struggles with the Ottoman authorities. The Turkish government was understandably "sore" to discover that their permission given to survey for purposes of archeological and biblical research, however foolishly granted, was turned into part of what Lawrence called "a military game." Lawrence returned to the dig in March for a last season, closed the site in June, and returned to England. He then worked on writing up the archeological findings, and the report of the survey was elaborately published by the British Museum early in 1915 with the title *The Wilderness of Zin*, a kind of archeological whitewash. A shorter report was published by Woolley in the 1914 statement of the Palestine Exploration Fund.[26]

By the time he returned to England, Lawrence had become highly skilled and resourceful, with an extraordinary capacity to adapt himself to a great range of situations and challenges. Though not yet twenty-six he had demonstrated his abilities as a leader of other men through his capacity to do most things better than they could; by his courage and his willingness to do almost anything first before he expected someone else to do it; by his readiness to take responsibility even for matters that were only his concern because he made them so; and above all through his capacity to understand a problem as it was perceived by other people. He was especially effective in leading Arab peoples, whose language he spoke, and they were awed by his knowledge of their ways and by his apparent fearlessness. He could also be as boyish or seemingly innocent as they, and this permitted him to get close to them. When it came to getting the natives in and around Carchemish to be vaccinated against cholera, of which one might think they would be suspicious, he had no difficulty. "I can get that done most easily," he wrote his family doctor, "for the Arabs do as I want most charmingly."[27]

We have seen also that he was well on his way to rejecting his British, his Western, identity and to assuming a new one among the Arabs. At the same time he rejected particularly the Ireland of his origins. "Why go to such a place," he wrote home upon hearing that his father was in Ireland.[28] A few months later he advised his parents, "Don't go to Ireland, even to play golf. I think the whole place repulsive historically: they should not like English people, and we certainly cannot like them."[29]

Lawrence's romantic and somewhat ambivalent asceticism, his longing for a simple life of poverty and renunciation while at the same time enjoying many creature comforts, relates to this same dilemma. His attitudes are beautifully reflected in a short essay he wrote for his college magazine in 1912, which appeared in the 1912–1913 issue. The essay is a description of a trip that Lawrence and Dahoum were taken on by a poor old Arab man and a boy to the ruins of a great palace in the desert between Aleppo and Hama. They passed through a succession of rooms, courts and arcades filled with the rich scents of jasmine and of tropical blossoms until they came to a great hall. Here, "the mingled scents of all the palace . . . combined to slay each other, and all that one felt was the desert sharpness of the air as it swept off the huge uncontaminated plains. 'Among us,' said Dahoum, 'we call this room the sweetest of them all,' therein half-consciously sounding the ideal of the Arab creed, for generations stripping itself of all furniture in the working out of a gospel of simplicity."[30] The piece is signed anonymously "C.J.G."

During the early months at Carchemish Lawrence had planned to build a house on property he owned in Epping Forest and to print on a hand press with his friend Richards fine illuminated works, following the lead of William Morris and his Kelmscott Press. His letters home are full of discussions with and instructions to his father regarding the business aspects of this scheme, much of which has been gratuitously omitted from the published *Home Letters*. Gradually, however, Lawrence came to question Richards's business sense and his own suitability for the project. Finally, recognizing his increasing involvement in the Arab world he backed out uncomfortably in December 1913, writing his friend in conclusion: "Carchemish will not be finished for another four or five years: and I'm afraid that after that I'll probably go after another and another nice thing: it is rather a miserable come down. I haven't any money; can I offer you a carpet? They are about the only things remaining out here that are any good: Arabs have no handicrafts."[31]

His brother Will evidently had confidence that the "another and another nice thing" would include something worthwhile, for two months later he dedicated "To T.E.L." the following lines:

> *I've talked with counsellors and lords*
> *Whose words were as no blunted swords,*
> *Watched two Emperors and five Kings*
> *And three who had men's worshippings,*
> *Ridden with horsemen of the East*
> *And sat with scholars at their feast,*
> *Known some the masters of their hours,*
> *Some to whom years were as pressed flowers:*
> *Still as I go this thought endures*
> *No place too great to be made yours.*[32]

# THREE

# THE WAR YEARS, 1914–1918

# Introduction

Lawrence's five years of travel, study, and work as an archeologist in Syria, Palestine and Anatolia made it natural that he would find his way into the British military service as an intelligence officer at British head-quarters in Cairo. He was exceptionally suited for this work. It was perhaps less predictable that in less than two years he would find himself in the role of a leader of a modern guerrilla war in the Arabian desert. For by the end of 1916 he was in the process of galvanizing the flagging Arab Revolt (restricted at that time to the Bedouin of the Hijaz) into a campaign which would carry ultimately to Damascus and beyond.

From the standpoint of both the historian and the psychologist the war years, especially 1917 and 1918 — the two years of his participation in the Revolt — were the most critical of Lawrence's life. Although his public contributions continued after the war, his historical importance grew out of his activities and accomplishments during those two years. Whatever his subsequent opinions of his wartime achievements, without them there would have been no Lawrence of Arabia as a figure of actuality or of legend.

From the personal or psychological standpoint the years of the Revolt were a watershed for Lawrence. Until the war he was an unusual, versatile and reasonably well-balanced genius with a somewhat undisciplined passion for archeology, a long-standing interest in medieval military architecture and literature, and a great capacity for friendship with all sorts of people. The application of his varied gifts in the service of the Arab Revolt, while they resulted in extraordinary accomplishments and furnished the ingredients of a peculiarly contemporary heroic example and legend, included for Lawrence personally a series of shattering experiences, the psychological impact of which he was forced to contend with for most of the remaining years of his life. These psychological changes, and the unusual insights Lawrence brought to bear in trying to understand and deal with his suffering, have provided the psychologically minded biographer with an unusual opportunity to learn something about a person (and to a varying degree we all share some of his characteristics) who is compelled to live out the demands of his inner life in the public domain.

# 10

# The Background of
# the Arab Revolt

The revolt of the sharif of Mecca, Husayn Ibn Ali, and his sons against the Ottoman authority in June 1916 provided Lawrence with a unique opportunity to exercise his diverse talents. These abilities, the most important of which was his capacity to enable the fragmented Arab tribesmen of the Hijaz and portions of Syria to translate their passion to be free of Turkish rule into an effective military operation, had to be exercised in the context of British war policy in the Middle Eastern theatre. This dual purpose — of motivating and guiding the Arab Revolt, while at the same time, as a British officer, serving his country's military and political policies — was inescapable, having been built into his situation from the outset. It renders to a large degree futile the arguments, however carefully based on his own dispatches to higher British authorities, that he was really serving British imperial policy rather than the cause of Arab independence. He was, by the very definition of his situation — he played, to be sure, a major part in *choosing* to enact his special role among the Arabs — attempting to do both.

The history of Lawrence's actions and writings during the war years needs to be seen in terms of his struggle to reconcile these two purposes, which at times were in substantial conflict. Although his position in serving two masters was not his only source of torment, it was nevertheless very real. In order to understand his position during the war, it is necessary to explore the background of the situation in which he found himself in Cairo when he arrived there in December 1914 and to review the development of British policy in the Middle East up to the onset of the Arab Revolt.

To the Arab peoples, the conquest by the Ottoman Turks in the early years of the sixteenth century of territories that included what is now

Egypt, Syria, Lebanon, Israel, Iraq, Jordan and the lands of the Arabian Peninsula along the east coast of the Red Sea, represented the substitution of rule by one sultan for rule by another. Not since the tenth century, when the Muslim Empire of the Prophet Muhammad began to disintegrate, had the Arab peoples known any semblance of political unity, and they had never, of course, experienced national unity in our modern sense. From that time until the present day the political history of the Arab world has been marked by political fragmentation and division, and for most of the period, rule by foreign powers. The dream of national political independence, with which Lawrence intoxicated his British and Arab adherents and also, to a degree, himself, represents an ideal which, for most of the previous thousand years, had had little currency among the political realities of the Arab world.

As recently as 1970, P. J. Vatikiotis, an authority on Arab culture, politics and history, could write with justification:

> What, then, can one say about Arab Nationalism as a force for political development in the Arab world today? Without doubt literate, articulate Arabs (especially those in towns and cities) share a sentiment, a feeling of belonging to an entity they call the Arab Nation (al-umma al-'arabiyya). This is the meaning of al-qawmiyya al-'arabiyya, Arab Nationalism, or Arab solidarity. But is this sentiment a determinant of political action and organization? So far, it has not proved to be so. Arab Nationalism has not achieved its goal of making the Arab Nation co-extensive with one Arab State. For the moment, Arabs are at least legally citizens, or subjects, of several sovereign states exhibiting various forms of political organization, different political structures, and disparate levels of economic development. These states exhibit varying degrees of ethnic, religious and communal heterogeneity. The one thing they have in common, with one exception, is that their populations are overwhelmingly Muslim, and all are Arabic-speaking. In one way or another, they also shared a common experience of foreign domination, rule, or tutelage not too long ago. Moreover, most of them had been, at one time or another, in the period of 1517–1918, part of the Ottoman Empire.[1]

I am using the word Arab, not in its original sense of denoting a member of the nomad tribes of the Arabian Peninsula, but with the more modern connotation provided by George Antonius, a Christian Arab. In his definition, "Arab" has come to mean "a citizen of that extensive Arab world — not any inhabitant of it, but that great majority whose racial descent, even when it was not of pure Arab lineage, had become submerged in the tide of arabisation; whose manners and traditions had been shaped in an Arab mould; and most decisive of all, whose mother tongue is Arabic. The term applies to Christians as well as Moslems, and to offshoots of each of these creeds, the criterion being not islamisation but the degree of arabisation."[2]

By this definition Antonius was certainly correct when he wrote that there has been a "lack of anything approaching national solidarity in the Arab world." Although written in 1938, his explanation for this remains current today:

> The unifying force generated by the genius of the Prophet Muhammad had remained a force so long as Arab power had remained supreme. As that power waned, its cohesive influence weakened; and the diverse people it had welded together into a cultural whole fell gradually asunder to form separate entities, regional and sectarian, according to the district, clan or creed to which they belonged. Side by side with that disintegration, a process of religious evolution was going on, which had led not only to the birth of new confessions, among both Moslems and Christians, but also to an increased emphasis on sectarian differences and to the growth of confessional loyalty as a substitute for cultural solidarity.[3]

Recently, Manfred Halpern has formulated this tendency toward "confessional loyalty" in socio-psychological terms. He has seen the political fragmentation as deriving from fundamental aspects of Arab psychology and ways of engaging in human relationships. Halpern has emphasized the tendency of persons reared in Muslim cultures to yield to authority ("subjection"), and to submerge individual identity, essential for mature political self-consciousness, with that of a protective overwhelming authority ("emanation").[4]

It is against this background that one should view Lawrence's actions and writings during the years of World War I and thereafter. "I meant to make a new nation," he wrote in an introduction to *Seven Pillars of Wisdom*, "to restore a lost influence, to give twenty millions of Semites the foundation on which to build an inspired dream-palace of their national thoughts."[5] These lofty aims, whose overreaching grandness Lawrence came to recognize, not only flew directly in the face of the real politik of the Western powers, of which he came increasingly to complain, but also disregarded what George Kirk has called "the fatal Arab tendency to political separatism."[6] The disappointment of Lawrence's unrealistic aims was inevitable. The consequences for history of his having pursued them so passionately and effectively are still unfolding and still being debated.

Until the nineteenth century there was little national consciousness among the Arab peoples in the Ottoman Empire. Local, internal authority in Arab lands tended to be left in the hands of feudal amirs and local Arab chiefs.[7] Largely in response to pressures from the Western European states, the Ottoman Empire made a number of efforts to modernize the imperial administrative and judicial organization. But these reforms, whether successful or inadequate from the administrative standpoint, failed to prevent the emergence of movements for autonomy in various parts of the empire. Contact with the West influenced these movements strongly but in varying ways. For instance, in the Wahhabi movement in the Arabian Peninsula in the eighteenth and nineteenth centuries, the anti-Turkish agitation was an entirely Muslim movement and, in addition, anti-Western. In contrast, the drive of Muhammad Ali and Ibrahim Pasha to unite the Arab lands under their rule in the early decades of the nineteenth century was both motivated by personal ambition and strongly inspired by Western, especially French, nationalistic, political and cultural influences. During the occupation of Syria between 1831 and 1840 by Ibrahim Pasha, European and American missionary activity was encouraged, especially in Lebanon, which became the gateway for the entry of Western influences into the Asiatic provinces of the Ottoman Empire.

Some scholars, especially Zeine N. Zeine and George Kirk, have questioned whether these missionary activities, which were concerned predominately with religious education and conversion, with teaching the population to read and write, and with developing largely nonpolitical curricula in the missionary colleges, were important in the fomenting of the nationalistic movements which grew up in the empire in the decades before World War I.

Although the political repression under the regime of the sultan Abdul Hamid II (1876-1909) intensified the Arabs' desire for independence, it would appear that Arab nationalists feared British, French and Russian colonial expansion, against which the Ottoman government seemed to offer some protection, more than they did the familiar tyrannies of the empire. In 1882 Egypt fell under direct British occupation, and Muslim leaders, in Zeine's words, "were not blind to the ambitions and interests of the Great Powers in the Ottoman Empire and feared lest any further weakening of the Empire should lead to the occupation of the Arab lands in the Near East by one or more of those powers."[8]

Many leading Arab Muslims sought greater political freedom, an extension of civil liberties, and an end to misgovernment, but remained loyal to the Ottoman government. But their desires were shared by Turkish liberals, the most successful of whom were a group called the Young Turks, which had grown up among Turkish expatriates in Europe and was therefore strongly imbued with Western concepts of parliamentary government and constitutional reform. In July 1908 they came to power in a bloodless revolution in Constantinople accompanied by the rejoicing of the populace.

The Young Turks, however, and their ruling Committee of Union and Progress (CUP), were soon engaged in a tyranny of their own which, unlike the rule of Abdul Hamid II, attempted to control not only the political life of the Arab peoples at a local level, but even their religion and education. Promulgating a chauvinistic Turkish nationalism called

Pan-Turanianism, they attempted to "Turkify" the Arab lands. Despite these efforts to exploit Pan-Islamism, the CUP was in many respects anti-Islamic, and sought, against Arab opposition, to translate the Koran into Turkish and to make a sentimental cult of such pagan Turanian conquerors as Genghis Khan.[9] As I wrote some years ago:

> The young Turks attempted to force unity through Turkifying everything, without regard to local customs or differences in race. They imposed the Turkish language on everyone, and even went so far as to forbid the teaching of Albanian in Albanian schools and Arabic in Arabian schools. Compulsory service in the Ottoman army was imposed on Christians and Moslems alike. To a greater extent than under Abdul Hamid the central government interfered with every detail of local administration. Hundreds of local Abdul Hamids appeared all over the Empire and served to encourage racial hatreds. The revived electoral system became the channel of unexampled corruption, violence and murder. In the elections the opposition was not only kept from the polls, but was often shot down in cold blood.[10]

These repressive national and racial policies of the Young Turks fanned the flames of Arab political nationalism, and a number of Arab societies and political parties (the most famous of which was the ultra-secret al-Fatat, created in Paris in 1909) were formed to defend the Arab cause and protect Arab rights. Members of these societies dreamed of a united Arab Empire, which took precedence in their thinking over allegiance to any single Arab or Muslim country.[11] Recent massacres of the Armenians indicated to the Arab leaders what might be in store for them and helped to stimulate Arab political activity. However, despite the intensification of underground political activity by these secret societies between 1909 and 1914 (many of them functioned in Europe), most of the Arabic-speaking Muslims remained loyal to the Ottoman Empire, even during the war. The secret societies, though strongly nationalistic, feared European designs on Arab lands and remained on the side of the empire out of fear of the Western powers. Al-Fatat, for example, was not prepared to support Britain against Turkey.

In contrast to their policy in Egypt, until 1914 the British favored the maintenance of the Ottoman Empire intact, despite its weakened and corrupt state. British economic and political interests had been expanding in the Middle East throughout the nineteenth century, and political tranquillity in the regions of Suez, the Red Sea and the Persian Gulf had a high priority. Britain's prewar aim was to preserve a stable but politically docile Ottoman Empire, which would maintain the favored conditions of the "capitulations," whereby non-Muslims and foreigners within the Empire were exempt from its jurisdiction, and which could also serve as a buffer against Russian expansion.

Until the rise of Germany after 1870, Russia and France were Britain's chief competitors in the Middle East. Various struggles to achieve a balance of power in the region resulted in an understanding between Britain and France in 1904 whereby France agreed to give Britain a free hand in Egypt in return for a free hand in Morocco. The Russian show of might on the steppes of Asia in the latter part of the nineteenth century pressured Britain into an agreement in 1907 that divided Persia into British and Russian spheres of influence. Although Germany had sent a military mission to Turkey as early as 1883 to modernize the Ottoman army, British policy in relation to Germany revealed far greater concern about its power in Europe than in the Middle East. As late as 1913–1914 Britain entered into an agreement with Germany in which it consented to the construction of the Baghdad Railway to Basra in Mesopotamia in return for having two directors on the board of the railway and German recognition of the exclusive rights of the Anglo-Iranian Oil Company to extract oil in the region of the Persian Gulf.[12] In 1904, however, Britain also entered into an entente with France that was aimed at controlling German power in Europe. Russia joined the entente in 1907.

The humiliating Ottoman defeats at the hands of Italy in 1911, and twice at the hands of the Balkan powers in 1912 and 1913, resulted in the loss of Libya and almost all European Turkey. The political instability and hastening disintegration of the Ottoman Empire made the nineteenth century British policy of favoring its reform rather than partition seem increasingly less viable. But as late as July 1913, Sir Edward Grey, the British secretary for foreign affairs, could write, "The only policy to which we can become a party is one directed to avoid collapse and partition of Asiatic Turkey."[13]

On the Ottoman side these defeats led only to a more violently nationalistic and anti-Arab policy, and the further penetration of Pan-Turanian ideas into the Ottoman army. This resulted in a deep antipathy toward the Unionist government among the army officers, many of whom were Arab.[14]

In 1911 Lord Kitchener, who had a long history of distinguished service to Great Britain in Egypt and the Sudan, became British agent and consul general in Egypt. Although he would not act against Turkey when Britain was not at war with her, he did order the survey of the Sinai that Lawrence and Woolley took part in and he became sympathetic to the advice of those in Cairo who advocated a policy of stimulating Arab nationalism and "detaching the Arabs from the Turks."[15] "The liberation of subject races in the Ottoman Empire is a traditional occupation of the British public," David Hogarth wrote shortly after World War I, and "no ministry, forced into hostilities with the Turks, would have been suffered to abstain long from the declaration of a pro-Arab policy, and from measures to enforce it. . . . Kitchener's responsibility [prior to the declaration of war against Turkey, was] not for the adoption of such a policy, but only for the initial measures taken to declare it and put it in action."[16]

There were various movements toward national independence among the Arab peoples during the months preceding the outbreak of World War I. Uprisings occurred in Cyrenaica, Yemen, Iraq and Arabia during 1913 and 1914. But it was the revolutionary activities of the sharif of Mecca and his sons in the Hijaz (the regions of the Arabia Peninsula along the Red Sea) that became in 1914 the focus of British military and political policies, and that ultimately furnished Lawrence with the opportunity to exercise his initiatives.

Husayn Ibn Ali was appointed sharif and amir of Mecca in the summer of 1908 by the Ottoman sultan and the Turkish grand vizier, the appointment having become entangled with the rivalry between the "Old" and the "Young" Turks, the latter favoring the representative of a different Meccan clan.[17] The sharifs of Mecca, all of whom were of the Hashemite family and claimed direct descent from the prophet Muhammad through his daughter Fatimah, had ruled Mecca and the Hijaz since the tenth century, gaining considerable political autonomy from the Ottoman central government. These sharifs, each of whom bore the title "Protector of the Two Holy Cities," had the responsibility of protecting Mecca and Medina and overseeing the annual pilgrimages. Because of their special position and their claim to descent from the Prophet, the Meccan sharifs enjoyed great privilege and prestige throughout the empire. Husayn himself had been brought to Constantinople with his three sons in 1898 because of a disagreement with his uncle, then the reigning amir of Mecca.

The Hashemite family's long association with the old Ottoman regime undoubtedly played a significant part in the struggles between Husayn and the Young Turks, who were attempting to bring him under their authority. Despite powerful Unionist (Young Turk) pressure, however, Husayn remained loyal to the sultan, did not respond to the call of the Arab deputies in Constantinople to lead an Arab national movement, and even assisted the Turks in putting down an uprising of al-Idrisi, a territorial ruler in Yemen. This action earned Husayn the enmity of the Arab nationalists, and until 1914 he was regarded by them as a supporter of the Ottoman state. The Arabs of the Hijaz, especially the Bedouin, opposed the extension of the Hijaz railroad beyond Medina to Mecca: they feared a further loss in the tolls they could levy during the annual pilgrimage. The Ottoman regime's attempt to extend the railroad by military force was opposed by the local Bedouin, and Wahib, the local *vali* (Ottoman representative) in Mecca, advised that Husayn be deposed.

Husayn's second son, Abdullah, negotiated with the Unionist government an agreement, under which, in exchange for permission to construct the railroad, the sharif would receive one third of its revenues and the amirate would be Husayn's for life and then hereditary in his family. But these agreements did not allay his anxiety, and he looked to Great Britain for support. In February of 1914, Abdullah went to Cairo to see Lord Kitchener (they had met a year or two before) and through him to enlist Britain's aid in his family's struggle against the Ottoman government. But Kitchener would give him no definite assurance because Britain was not at war with the Ottoman Empire. Similarly Ronald Storrs, who was sent by Kitchener in April 1914 to visit Abdullah, declined to supply even "a dozen, or even a half-dozen machine guns" on the same grounds.[18] But despite the lack of direct assurance, Abdullah seems to have been convinced that Britain would support Husayn against the Turks, particularly when she intervened in April to have the Arab revolutionist 'Aziz Ali al-Misri released from a Turkish prison, where he had been held since his arrest in February.

On September 24, Kitchener, now secretary of state for war, wrote the famous message to Cairo in which he asked that Storrs send a "secret and carefully chosen messenger" to Abdullah to ascertain whether "he and his father and Arabs of Hejaz would be with us or against us" in the event of German-Turkish aggression against Great Britain.[19] Abdullah and Storrs had become friendly during Storrs's visit in April: Abdullah was impressed with the Englishman's ability to quote the Koran and had enjoyed quoting pre-Islamic poetry himself. When Storrs's messenger turned up, Abdullah arranged for a meeting with his father that resulted in a favorable reply.

The messenger gave a verbal report to Storrs on October 30, the day that Britain declared war on Turkey, and according to Storrs, quoted Husayn and described his behavior as follows:

> "The Ottoman Empire has rights over us and we have rights upon her. She has made war upon our rights, and I am not responsible before God if she has made war upon our rights; nor am I responsible before God if we have therefore made war upon hers." He gesticulated with his arms as he spoke, and threw back the long sleeve of his garments, saying "my heart is open to Storrs even as this, and with a gesture, stretch forth to us a helping hand and we shall never at all help these oppressors. On the contrary we shall help those who do good. This is the Commandment of God upon us: Do good to Islam and Moslems — Nor do we fear nor respect any save God. Give him my greeting, fitted to him and to his country."[20]

Kitchener, learning of this recondite but otherwise positive response to his telegram, cabled Abdullah on October 31 that Britain was now at war with Turkey and "if Arab nation assist England in this war England will guarantee that no intervention takes place in Arabia and will give Arabs every assistance against external foreign aggression."[21]

Thus the evolving alliance between Great Britain and the Hashemite sharif of Mecca grew out of the political and military needs of each. Britain sought an ally in Arabia against Turkey, while Husayn and his family sought to enlist British aid in their internal struggle against an Ottoman regime which was attempting to subvert the traditional authority and autonomy of the Meccan sharif.

"Feisul [Husayn's third son] talked to me something about the genesis of the Arab rising," Lawrence wrote during the war. "It was first imagined by his brother, Abdullah, who reckoned that the Hejaz was capable of withstanding Turkey with the aid of the Syrian and Mesopotamian armies, and our diplomatic help. He approached Lord Kitchener to this end, and obtained satisfactory assurances, but the scheme was put off on Feisul's representing that Turkey was too strong for them."[22] Kitchener's cable of October 31, which was received by Abdullah in mid-November, "caused him the liveliest satisfaction," strengthened his argument for revolt with his father, and conveyed to Husayn "an unmistakeable invitation to foment a revolt of all the Arabs."[23] A second messenger was sent to Cairo to Husayn in December, but the sharif was not yet ready to rebel.[24]

The entrance of Turkey into the war against the Allied powers placed the sharif in a difficult position. While Abdullah was encouraging revolution with the evidence of probable British support, the Unionist regime in Constantinople was pressing him for a show of loyalty, and inviting him to join Turkey in a *jihad* or Muslim Holy War, against the Allied infidels — a war which was in fact declared in mid-November. Husayn stalled, feeling "that the Holy War was doctrinally incompatible with an agressive war, and absurd with a Christian ally: Germany."[25] The failure of Turkish attacks upon the Suez Canal early in 1915 brought new demands for loyalty and for the sending of Arab "volunteers" to aid the Unionist cause.

In the last week of January 1915, Husayn received an emissary from al-Fatat, the Arab nationalist secret society, now centered in Damascus, who said that senior Arab officers in the Ottoman army favored revolt to gain independence and asked if the sharif would collaborate and act in concert with them. But the sharif was cautious in his reply and responded by sending his third son, Faisal, to Damascus. Faisal arrived on March 26 and made contact with members of the secret societies al-Fatat and al-'Ahd.[26] In the four weeks he stayed there, he was sworn into both societies and became imbued with their doctrines of militant Arab nationalism.[27] But the designs of the European powers in the Middle East had become clearer by this time, and the secret societies, which contained among their members many Arab officers in the Ottoman army, were reluctant to rebel against the Ottoman Empire lest they merely end in substituting one form of foreign domination for another.

According to Lawrence, "To most of them the word was never given; for those societies were pro-Arab only, willing to fight for nothing but Arab independence; and they could see no advantage in supporting the Allies rather than the Turks, since they did not believe our assurances that we would leave them free. Indeed, many of them preferred an Arabia united by Turkey in miserable subjection, to an Arabia divided up and slothful under easier control of several European powers in spheres of influence."[28] Nevertheless, many Syrians and Iraqis found their way into the Arab forces and served with distinction during the campaigns.[29]

In May Faisal was in Constantinople, where he professed his loyalty to the Ottoman officials and the sultan. He then returned to Damascus, where he received a protocol drawn up by al-Fatat and al-'Ahd to be brought to the sharif. The protocol explained the conditions of independence under which they would cooperate with Britain against Turkey in a revolt to be proclaimed by the sharif of Mecca. Large parts of the Arab world were to be granted independence and the exceptional privileges granted to foreigners under the Capitulations were to be abolished.[30] But a year of negotiations and struggles on Husayn's part with the Ottoman government and rival Arab tribes was to pass before he was ready to proclaim his rebellion, and by this time the repressive measures of Jemal Pasha had destroyed the possibility of an effective revolt in Syria. The failure of the Syrian Arab leaders to rebel at a time when a revolt might have been successful weakened greatly the Arab negotiating position after the war when the political future of Syria was being decided.[31]

Messages sent or inspired by Kitchener to Sharif Husayn in the closing months of 1914 had encouraged an Arab rebellion against the Ottoman authority and implied that British support for this and for eventual Arab independence would be forthcoming. But by the spring of 1915 the "Arab question" had receded from any position of high priority in practical British military and political policy.[32] The overriding importance of the war in Europe and of maintaining cooperative relationships with Britain's two major allies on the continent, France and Russia, was determining British policy. The Allies on the Western Front were stalemated, but with enormous loss of life, while the Russians were pressed in the Caucasus and sought a diversion against Turkey.[33] Sir John Maxwell, the commander-in-chief in Egypt, favored a landing at Alexandretta and urged it upon Kitchener, who seems to have favored it in principle. But the needs of the Western Front led to the decision in London to launch an attack on the Dardanelles and force a landing at Gallipoli in order to capture Constantinople and defeat Turkey in Europe. After the defeat of the British at Gallipoli in the summer of 1915, a landing was again considered at Alexandretta, but French objections to a British invasion so near to their area of interest in the Levant, and their preference for a landing at Salonika, caused the British to abandon their Alexandretta plan.

Meanwhile on the diplomatic front the first half of 1915 was character-ized by the slow evolution of interest in the partition of the Ottoman Empire among the Great Powers in the event of its defeat (a policy which, needless to say, contained potential incompatibilities with the approach being simultaneously evolved of encouraging alliances with Arab leaders in return for postwar independence for their lands).[34] In the event of its fall Constantinople and the Dardanelles were to be ceded to Russia, by an Anglo-Soviet agreement of March 1915. At the same time "the maze of Arabian politics," as Zeine described it, included a variety of assurances and agreements by the Allies with a number of Arab rulers in the Arabian Peninsula, other than Sharif Husayn.

In reviewing the history of this period, one is struck by the juxta-position of philosophies, representing two historical eras, each trying to adapt itself to the fast-changing realities within the Ottoman Empire in 1915 and 1916. The old colonialism of the nineteenth century, represented by Curzon and Cromer, which looked upon Asia and Africa as regions to be manipulated or carved up in accord with the commercial territorial policies of the European empires, and which regarded Asiatics and Africans as largely incapable of self-government, was being challenged by the liberal strain in British politics, represented by men like Hogarth and Storrs, and eventually Lawrence, who dreamed of Arab indepen-dence and unity under British guidance. It was into the center of this clash of policies, philosophy and politics that Lawrence would insert himself so actively in the coming years.

Faisal returned from Damascus to Mecca on June 20, 1915, with reports of Turkish atrocities in Syria. Though a convert to revolution he still urged delay. Abdullah, however, continued to press his father for action, while Sir Reginald Wingate, the sirdar of the Sudan in Khartoum, con-ferred with Sir Gilbert Clayton, the director of civil and military intelli-gence in Cairo. Wingate and Clayton, acting together, conferred in turn with Arab leaders in Cairo and encouraged the Arab rebellion. At this point Abdullah seems, at least to a degree, to have had his way, for on July 14 Husayn sent a note to Henry McMahon, the British high commis-sioner in Cairo, offering the possibility of "joint action" in the war in return for British recognition of the independence of "the entire Arab nation."[35] With the receipt of Husayn's letter in Cairo British and Hashemite policy became joined.

It is beyond the scope of this discussion to analyze fully the political influences that underlay the Husayn-McMahon correspondence and the Sykes-Picot Agreement of 1916, or to attempt to sort out completely the alleged discrepancies and similarities between them. Yet certain points are pertinent and need special mention. The two sets of negotiations — the Husayn-McMahon understandings and the Sykes-Picot Agreement — re-flect very different priorities of policy, priorities which were to a degree

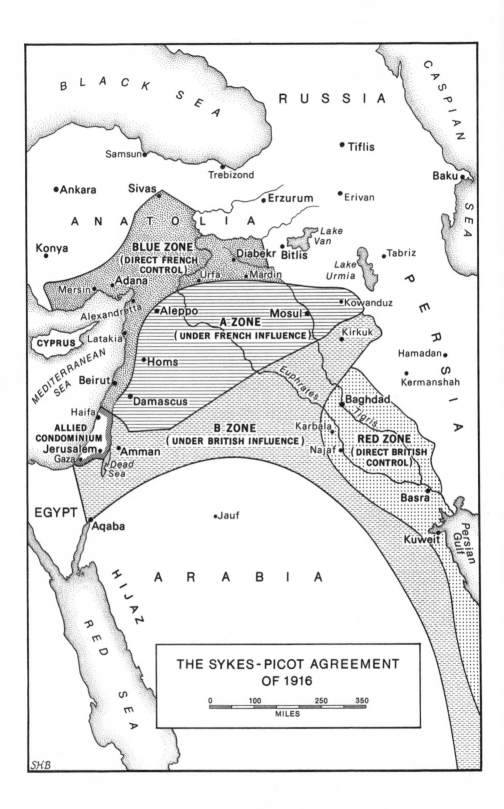

THE SYKES-PICOT AGREEMENT
OF 1916

0    100    250    350
MILES

mutually incompatible. (It is surprising in view of this fact that the agreements dovetailed on as many points as they did.) The important McMahon letters, which were sent to Husayn from October 1915 to March 1916, were formulated under the influence of the "Arabophiles" in Cairo and a nationalistic Arab officer al-Faruqi (a member of al-'Ahd who had defected in October 1915 from the Ottoman army). They were directed primarily toward securing the alliance of the sharif,[36] and were meant "to persuade him, by offers of assistance and guarantees of his future autonomy and independence, to throw off the Turkish supremacy and to keep open the pilgrimage for the Muslim subjects of the Allies."[37] The Sykes-Picot negotiations, which were taking place virtually simultaneously between Britain, France and Russia, were initiated in London, Paris and Petrograd, and represented a typical colonialist approach to anticipated changes wrought by war — the designation of spheres of influence among the Great Powers, and the partition of the territories of a defeated adversary.

Both agreements spoke of the independence of the Arab peoples, but differed on the conditions of this independence and the regions to be included. Both assumed Arab independence in the Arabian Peninsula. Both allowed for French control of a long coastal region on the Mediterranean (now part of Syria and Lebanon) and British control in southern Mesopotamia. McMahon led Husayn to believe that the interior of Syria would be independent, while the Sykes-Picot Agreement divided this large and important region into British and French "zones of influence." McMahon was vague about Palestine, perhaps permitting the Arab view "that Palestine did fall within the area of promised Arab independence."[38] The Sykes-Picot Agreement specified that Palestine would be under international control, except for a small British enclave containing the ports of Haifa and Acre.

The McMahon-Husayn and Sykes-Picot negotiations have taken on great symbolic significance beyond the specific terms that they contain, being the first approaches to the political future of the Arab peoples formerly living within the vast territories of the Ottoman Empire. Although they formed the initial basis for the approach to the problem of the Ottoman lands during the war, events soon made their stipulations largely obsolete. Arab leaders and spokesmen have naturally resented deeply the failure of the British to fulfill the promises of the McMahon letters (Antonius called the Sykes-Picot Agreement "a shocking document"), while British apologists have asserted that no promises were made or binding agreements concluded, that "horse-trading was going on on all sides in the international market," and that, after all, the British did help the Arabs get the Turks out of Arabia and Syria.[39] In balance, truth and justice probably lie somewhere between these positions.

During the same months that he was corresponding with McMahon,

Husayn was simultaneously trying to negotiate his sovereignty with the Ottoman government in return for neutrality, or even alliance with the Ottoman cause.[40] Furthermore, there was really no basis upon which Husayn, despite his selection by the British as the most likely ally in Arabia or Syria to oppose the Turks, could negotiate as a spokesman for *all* of "the Arabs" in the Ottoman Empire, especially when the Syrian Arab nationalists had forfeited their initiative (and therefore their bargaining strength) by their failure to rebel against Turkey during 1914–1916. Even the sharif himself had not yet revolted in May 1916, when the Sykes-Picot Agreement was signed, and as Hogarth wrote in 1920, as late as April 1916 "the prospect of Arabs taking part in their own liberation was nebulous."[41] There seems little question, however, that the enticements and offers to Husayn and his family that were made in the course of his negotiations with Kitchener and McMahon did much to stimulate the hopes and ambitions of the Hashemite family for political hegemony in Arabia and Syria.

On the other hand the Sykes-Picot Agreement, which divided the Arab lands among the Great Powers, was negotiated without the knowledge of the sharif, or any of the other Arab leaders, who did not know of its contents until May 1917 at the earliest. Although Mark Sykes, Britain's choice to work out the treaty with France and Russia, knew that letters were being exchanged between Cairo and Mecca, it is not clear that *his* negotiations were known in Cairo before 1917. When Liddell Hart asked Lawrence after the war, "When did McMahon know of [the] Sykes-Picot Treaty?" Lawrence answered, "Not until Sykes told him [that is, in 1917], Sykes saying casually, 'Haven't you heard of my Treaty?' Others nearly threw up."[42]

As Elizabeth Monroe has written (overstating the case to make her point), 1916 was the last year of the "old familiar world of intact empires," the last year in which there could be "secret agreements secretly arrived at, and treatment of whole populations as chattels. It was also the last year of freedom from criticism by anti-imperialist allies."[43] Lawrence's role in hastening the end of that familiar world is the subject of the chapters that follow. In 1915 and 1916 he was only beginning to grasp fully the ambiguities of the situation in which he would soon find himself as he moved into his place at the crossroads of British policy and Arab dreams.

In letters of December 1915 and January and February 1916, McMahon and Husayn agreed essentially to disagree on the matter of Syria, leaving the question to be disputed, settled, or otherwise pursued after the war. McMahon reiterated "the interests of our ally France" and Husayn protested that "any concession to give France or any other power possession of a single square foot of territory in those parts is quite out of the question."[44] The British translation of this last passage is less emphatic: "It is impossible to allow any derogation that gives France or any other power a span of land in those regions."[45] The impracticality of an Arab uprising in Syria, which was altogether ruled out with the arrest by Jemal Pasha of the Arab nationalist leaders and the transfer of Arab military units, made Husayn the only logical choice as an ally for Great Britain in the Arab lands, despite great reluctance in Cairo "to take our main action upon . . . one of the most barbarous Arab provinces [the Hijaz] instead of that obviously best fitted to lead in nation-making [Syria]."[46] Husayn's reluctance to respond to the call for a Holy War; the wide prestige of the sharif of Mecca among the Muslim Arabs; the strategic location of his lands along the Red Sea and flanked by the Hijaz railroad; and the unsuitability (because of their primarily local interests, lack of fighting potential or too great distance) of other tribes in Yemen or the interior of the Arabian Peninsula — all made him the best choice available as an ally in Arabia. But by the beginning of 1916 he still had not rebelled.

In January 1916, Husayn sent Faisal to Damascus once again in order to allay Turkish suspicions. There Faisal stayed in Jemal's headquarters, where they discussed raising volunteers from the Hijaz for the war against the Allies. He was taken by his host to see his Syrian friends hanged, along with various Arab notables, and was shown scenes in films depicting atrocities presumably committed by Australian troops against Egyptian men and women.[47]

From January to May, with Faisal still in Damascus, Husayn continued to negotiate with Jemal for general amnesty for Arab political prisoners and the recognition of the traditional status and privileges of the amirate of Mecca. Throughout this time Faisal was asserting his loyalty to the Ottoman Empire, which naturally caused Jemal considerable bitterness when he discovered that he had been betrayed.[48] As Jemal refused the sharif's terms and as his tone became increasingly menacing, Faisal, who had been in secret correspondence with his father throughout this period, determined to leave Damascus and to support the break from Constantinople.[49] In mid-May he set out for Medina and Mecca in order to help in the final preparations for the Revolt. He asked permission of Jemal, who was by now quite suspicious, to go to Medina to accompany a contingent of Arab "volunteers," led by his older brother Ali, to Jerusalem.[50] To Faisal's dismay Jemal replied that Enver Pasha, one of the Ottoman leaders, was on his way and that they would go to Medina together and inspect the troops. Faisal had planned to raise his father's crimson banner as soon as he arrived in Medina and take the Turks unawares, and here he was to be saddled with "two uninvited Turkish guests to whom, by the Arab law of hospitality, he could do no harm, and who would probably delay his action so long that the whole secret of the revolt would be in jeopardy."[51]

"The irony of the review was terrible," Lawrence wrote later. "Enver, Jemal and Feisal watched the troops wheeling and turning in the dusty plain outside the city gate, rushing up and down in mimic camel-battle, or spurring their horses in the javelin game after the immemorial Arab fashion. 'And are all these volunteers for the Holy War?' asked Enver at last, turning to Feisal. 'Yes,' said Feisal. 'Willing to fight to the death against the enemies of the faithful?' 'Yes,' said Feisal again; and then the Arab chiefs came up to be presented, and Sherif Ali ibn el Hussein, of Modhig, drew him aside whispering, 'My Lord, shall we kill them now?' and Feisal said, 'No, they are our guests.' "[52]

Faisal soon found Medina full of Ottoman troops, for Jemal had decided to reinforce the Medina garrison. Husayn ordered Faisal to Mecca in order that the rebellion could begin. Although Faisal again recommended delay — until August — Husayn feared that his correspondence with the British had become known and that the troops had been sent to deal with him. The visit of a German mission under Baron von Stotzingen along the Hijaz railroad and then to Yenbo on the Red Sea caused additional alarm. The news that the Turks had massacred thousands of Armenians and had abducted Armenian women may also have troubled the sharif.[53]

Word from Syria of a further crop of political executions finally convinced even the reluctant Faisal, and on May 23 a message was telegraphed to McMahon in Cairo (who had continued to correspond with the sharif regarding additional money, supplies and equipment that would be forthcoming from Britain in the event the rebellion was raised): "Sherif's son Abdullah urgently requires Storrs to come to Arabian coast to meet him. Movement will begin as soon as Feisal arrives at Mecca."[54]

In the first days of June, a mission composed of Storrs, Hogarth and Captain Kinahan Cornwallis, among others, met on an Arabian beach with Zayd, the sharif's youngest son, to consider final details of the rebellion.[55] On June 4 Storrs received this message from the high commissioner, who was reporting the Indian government's concern about the threat of hostilities in Arabia: "India asks whether situation necessitates stoppage of the Haj [annual pilgrimage to Mecca] from India. India is unwilling to offend Moslem feeling by notification of stoppage. Please discuss this with Abdullah."[56] But the next day Faisal and Ali proclaimed the independence of the Arabs from Ottoman rule, and on June 10, 1916, the Revolt began in Mecca, which was wrested from its small Turkish garrison after three days of fierce fighting.[57]

In a flowery proclamation issued at the end of June, Sharif Husayn recounted the executions and other atrocities, treachery and crimes perpetrated against Islam by the Young Turk leaders and declared:

> We can leave the judgment [of Turkish misdeeds] to the Moslem world, but we may not leave our religion, and our existence as a people to be the plaything of the Unionists. God (blessed be He) has made open for us the

attainment of freedom and independence, and has shown us a way of victory, to cut off the hand of the oppressors, and to cast out their garrison from our midst. We have attained independence, an independence of the rest of the Ottoman Empire, which is still groaning under the tyranny of our enemy. Our independence is complete, absolute, not to be laid hands on by any foreign influence or aggression, and our aim is the preservation of Islam, and the uplifting of its standard in the world.[58]

At the time the rebellion began, Gallipoli had been evacuated and the British garrison in Mesopotamia had surrendered. Great Britain was grateful to have this new ally on the Arabian Peninsula. As Zeine has pointed out, the invitation to rebel which Britain had offered and agreed to support, was extended to Sharif Husayn and limited to the Arabs of the Hijaz region of Arabia. In no way had Great Britain envisaged or planned to support "with men and arms a great Arab Revolt from one end of the Asiatic possessions of the Ottoman Empire to the other."[59] In this shift of policy Lawrence's role was to prove critical. As Hogarth wrote of the Revolt a year or two after the end of the war: "It would not have been begun but for Kitchener's invitation in the first instance, and assurance of British support in the second; it could not have been sustained without the money, food-stuffs, and munitions of war which Great Britain provided; it might never have spread beyond the Hedjaz but for the long sight and audacious action of Lawrence; and it won through to Damascus only as a flying right wing of [General] Allenby's last drive."[60]

Although Arab nationalism played a relatively minor role as we have seen in the inception of the Revolt (Husayn having turned its precepts to his local advantage), the extraordinary success of the rebellion provided a powerful stimulus to Arab nationalistic aspirations, which have had as great if not a greater impact upon the modern world as the immediate military and political results of the campaigns themselves.

# 11

# Two Years in Cairo, 1914–1916

Lawrence was in Oxford when the First World War began in August 1914. The war seemed at first to provide an exciting, even romantic, opportunity for the small stratum of educated young Englishmen. "The whole world was their oyster and seemed sure to go on being so till the end of time," Arnold Lawrence wrote me, and went on to say that "Rupert Brooke's 'Now, God be thanked Who has matched us with His hour'[1] expressed the general relief of [my brother] Frank's friends at having something big enough to do, when the war started."[2]* And T. E. Lawrence wrote Flecker in December, "Not many dons have taken commissions — but 95% of the undergraduates have taken or applied for them."[3]

Lawrence wrote that he tried to enlist himself but the War Office "was then glutted with men, and [they] were only taking six-footers."[4] According to Lawrence, Hogarth made an appointment for him to see Colonel Coote Hedley, head of the Geographical Section of the General Staff (Intelligence) of the War Office. But Hedley states that he had not heard from Hogarth before Lawrence came to see him. In fact, Hedley wrote to Liddell Hart, "I well remember the pleasure and *surprise* with which I saw Lawrence, for I knew all about Lawrence and did not need a recommendation from anyone."[5] Hedley recalls Lawrence in gray flannels, hatless and looking "about 18." He obtained a commission for him as a second lieutenant, and Lawrence then worked for about three months in London finishing the Sinai maps from the Palestine survey and making other maps of Belgium and France. Hedley knew that intelligence officers would be needed in Egypt and he told the Division of

* Frank, the fourth Lawrence boy, was an undergraduate at Jesus College when the war broke out.

Military Intelligence that he had "the ideal officer for that work in my office."[6] Because of his effective work with Hedley, and his knowledge of the regions of the Middle East in which Great Britain was becoming engaged with Turkey and Germany, Lawrence was transferred to a rudimentary intelligence section that was being formed in Cairo.

During the less than two years in Cairo, from December 1914 to October 1916, when Lawrence began to take a more active role in the operations of the Arab Revolt, he performed a variety of intelligence functions. But beyond these assigned tasks he began to involve himself in what he was able to do best of all, the influencing of others. This capacity was not, of course, new, but for the first time he became acquainted with important military and political figures who were concerned with formulating British policy — at least at the local level — in the regions of the Egyptian theatre. His ambition was to influence policy beyond the opportunities of his station as a second lieutenant or later as a staff captain. The frustration imposed by his junior status may have caused him to react in ways that only accentuated his immaturity — refusing to look, dress, or carry himself as a good regular military officer was expected to do.

In Cairo Lawrence served at first with Woolley, George Lloyd, and Aubrey Herbert under Stewart Newcombe. The group reported to Sir Gilbert Clayton, who was director of intelligence for the Egyptian army. Lawrence continued to piece together maps of the region, but also put to use his detailed knowledge of the several districts and peoples of Syria and Palestine, and of the various strata of Turkish society, in eliciting information about Turkish prisoners ("I always knew their districts, and asked about my friends in them. Then they told me everything").[7] Because of his knowledge of the region, Lawrence was the logical person to receive information about the size and movements of the Ottoman army, and various spies and other agents of the Allies in the field funneled information through him to his superiors. He also produced and supported the printing of a handbook on the Ottoman army, gathered information about seditious movements in Egypt, and was sent on intelligence missions to the Western Desert in North Africa and to Greece.

'Abd al-Rahman Shahbandar, a Syrian nationalist and physician who had recently escaped from a Turkish prison in Damascus, talked with Lawrence in Cairo early in March 1916 concerning the Arab movement and the political situation in Syria. His account of his visit gives a perceptive description of Lawrence at this time from the point of view of an Arab nationalist leader. Already, it seems, Lawrence held a position of considerable leadership in the British intelligence effort. Shahbandar was impressed that Lawrence knew the names of the secret societies and much about them. "It appears to me that this man is different from the rest of the Englishmen whom we have seen so far, that he listens attentively to the political organization of the Arabs and that his questions show a depth in the subject which is not present except with one who has in it a pleasure and a passion." Among the British intelligence officers in Cairo whom Shahbandar had met, "Lawrence was at the center of their orbit of movements and the instrument of their execution, although his appearance among the other people was the least."[8]

In addition to these duties and activities Lawrence was the liaison officer to the Survey of Egypt, a civil department of the Egyptian government whose scientific activities, especially geographic and geological, were brought during the war into close collaboration with the activities of military intelligence in Cairo. Ernest Dowson, who was director-general of the Survey, has written of his first impression of Lawrence in Egypt:

> At the outset must be pictured the extremely youthful and, to our unseeing eyes, insignificant figure with well-ruffled light hair, solitary pip on sleeve, minus belt and with peaked cap askew, who in these days and throughout his closest connection with the Survey used to be continuously at Giza [the location of the Survey offices on the west bank of the Nile in Cairo], riding his motorcycle Boanerges with a care which was remarked both there and also later when he visited the Government Press at Bulaq.[9]

Colonel Pierce Joyce, Lawrence's superior officer in the Hijaz, also remembers Lawrence's scruffy, unmilitary appearance in the Cairo years:

> My first and very brief meeting with him was at Port Sudan in 1916 when he accompanied Admiral Wemyss to Khartoum to discuss Arabian affairs with Sir Reginald Wingate. I confess the memory of this meeting merely recalls the intense desire on my part to tell him to get his hair cut and that his uniform and dirty buttons sadly needed the attention of his batman. I should most certainly have done so had he not been surrounded by such distinguished people.[10]

Storrs corroborates Joyce that Lawrence was "utterly careless of his dress" during this period. He has given this description:

> His forehead was high; his face upright and, in proportion to the depth of the head, long. His yellow hair was naturally-growing pre-War hair; that is parted and brushed sideways; not worn immensely long and plastered backwards under a pall of grease. He had a straight nose, piercing gentian-blue eyes, a firm and very full mouth, a strong square chin and fine, careful, and accomplished hands. His Sam-Browne belt was as often as not buckled loose over his unbuttoned shoulder strap, or he would forget to put it on at all. Once at least I had to send my servant Ismain running with it after him into the street. . . . Save for official purposes he hated fixed times and seasons. I would come upon him in my flat, reading always Latin and Greek, with

South Hill, home of Thomas Robert Tighe Chapman in Delvin, County Westmeath, Ireland. Courtesy of the Sisters of Charity of Jesus and Mary, the Belgian Order of nuns occupying the house in 1965

The Lawrence boys, taken when T. E. Lawrence was seven or eight.
Left to right: T.E., Bob, Frank, and Will. Arnold was not yet
born. Courtesy of Arnold Lawrence

2 Polstead Road, Oxford, home of
the Lawrence family from the
time T. E. Lawrence was eight
until after World War I.
Photograph by the author

The City of Oxford High School
in 1964, shortly before it was
closed. Photograph by the author

Lawrence at the City of Oxford
High School. Courtesy of the
Principal and Fellows of Jesus
College, Oxford, and the Head-
master of the Oxford School

Photograph of Carcassonne by
Lawrence from *Crusader Castles
II: The Letters.* Courtesy of the
Harvard College Library

The cottage built for Ned Lawrence
in the garden behind the house at
2 Polstead Road. Photograph by
the author

Lawrence and his brothers during the Jesus College years. Left to right: T.E., Frank, Arnold, Bob and Will. Courtesy of Arnold Lawrence

Brass rubbing of Thomas Cranley, Archbishop of Dublin (1477–1517) by Lawrence and W. O. Ault. Courtesy of Professor Ault; photograph by the author

David George Hogarth,
about 1910. Courtesy of
Mrs. Caroline Barron

Portrait of Charles Montagu
Doughty by Eric Kennington,
1921. From the National
Portrait Gallery, London

Pen-and-ink sketch of
Sahyun by Lawrence,
in *Crusader Castles I:
The Thesis.* Courtesy
of the Harvard
College Library

SAHYUN     The South - East Corner.

The tower of entrance is the furthest to the left.     The great moat runs along before
the round tower on the right.

Entrance to the citadel at Aleppo, in *Crusader Castles, II: The Letters.*
Courtesy of the Harvard College Library

Workmen at the Carchemish dig, spring of 1912. Lawrence is second
from left in the front row and Woolley is beside him in the safari
hat. Courtesy of the Trustees of the British Museum

Exterior and living room of the expedition house at Carchemish.
Lawrence and Woolley had it constructed in the spring of 1913 for
the use of the archeologists. Courtesy of the Trustees of the
British Museum

Lawrence and Woolley at Carchemish with a Hittite slab. From the Imperial War Museum, London

Dahoum at Carchemish. From the Bodleian Library, Oxford

Lawrence during the desert campaigns.
From the Imperial War Museum, London

Lawrence with his bodyguards, March 1917.
From the Imperial War Museum, London

Abdullah. From the Bodleian
Library, Oxford

Faisal (French official
photo). From the Bodleian
Library, Oxford

'Awdah abu-Tayyi. From the Bodleian
Library, Oxford

Photograph by Lawrence of children sitting on a beach at Aqaba, 1917. Courtesy of the Harvard College Library

Faisal's camp at Quweira, 1917.
From the Bodleian Library, Oxford

Portrait of General Allenby by Eric Kennington.
From the National Portrait Gallery, London

Prisoners defile at Tafila, 1918.
From the Bodleian Library, Oxford

corresponding gaps in my shelves. But he put back in their places the books
he did not take away; of those he took he left a list, and never failed to return
them reasonably soon, in perfect condition.[11]

Storrs recalls that "as a colleague his quickness and instantaneous grasp
of essentials was astonishing. 'What does he want?' he would ask as we
examined an Arab, or an Arabic document. For what he wanted usually
proved to be something very different from the demand expressed."[12]
Storrs recalled that Lawrence seemed to "gulp down all I could shed for
him of Arabic knowledge, then bounded for him by the western bank of
the Suez Canal; yet never by the 'pumping' of crude cross-examination. I
told him things sometimes for the mere interest of his commentary. He
was eager and unfatigued in bazaar-walking and mosque-hunting. I
found him from the beginning an arresting and an intentionally provocative talker, liking nonsense to be treated as nonsense, and not civilly or
dully accepted or dismissed. He could flame into sudden anger at a story
of pettiness, particularly official pettiness or injustice."[13]

The most complete picture of Lawrence in his professional role during
these years is provided by Dowson.[14] I offer it in some detail, for the
qualities he displayed in this description "foreshadowed," as Dowson
noted, "those displayed in the wider and more exacting arena of Arabia
later." Dowson has captured better than anyone else the qualities of
Lawrence's personality, his determination to deflate pomposity, expose
inefficiency, and explode pretension. Naturally this irritated at times those
who were the objects of his challenges or who found him threatening to
their established postures or positions.

Dowson has described how Lawrence criticized severely the system of
transliteration of Arabic place names into Roman characters that was
being followed by two map officers, considerably older than himself, who
had spent many months studying the subject. They naturally resented
"having to take orders from such a boy, and felt that the War Office had
acted in accordance with the ineptitude traditionally pertaining to it in
burlesque in putting such a youngster in charge of anything."

In situations like the Survey, where there was a tradition of efficiency,
Lawrence's insistence upon performance of high quality was appreciated
and respected, and no one was perturbed, but other officers who
were less sure of themselves resented Lawrence's effrontery. Although
Lawrence had access to all the offices of the Survey and its craftsmen,
Dowson "never received a grouse about him: and I never heard of an
instance of misunderstanding or friction being created by him either
through faulty human contact."

Dowson attributed "the elasticity of response to military requirements"
that his office achieved to "a remarkable combination of qualities in
Lawrence." These included "a rare capacity to regard an operation of any

sort objectively, and in the process to get inside the skin of the participants," the concentration of his vast ambition upon "achievement (large
or small) rather than for approbation of his personal performance"; the
capacity to leave men "to the utmost extent possible to do their own
work"; and the ability to avoid any belittlement of the work of others.
"His tremendous keenness," Dowson noted, "about anything to do with
the work was remarkable and infectious, with the consequence that his
frequent walks round the various offices and workshops had a most
stimulating effect on the men."

Dowson was impressed also with Lawrence's "extraordinary capacity to
get his own way quietly," working with or around the apparatuses of
government and administration "when this seemed of critical importance
to a necessary end," and recalled also his "extraordinary resourcefulness
and his versatile competence." Dowson describes a small crisis in which
there was an urgent need for a particular intricate spare part which
existed only under seal at the depot of a hostile firm. GHQ could do
nothing without referring the matter to London, which might produce no
results, or at best an intolerable delay. When Lawrence was told of the
problem he asked for an exact description of the article and the precise
location of the premises. The following morning he brought the article
along, saying without explanation that there had been "no difficulty."

Dowson noted that "the diversity of Lawrence's capacity was so remarkable that one only slowly and skeptically accepted its genuineness.
It sprang, I think, from unusual clarity of mind working on an unusual
catholicity of knowledge. This enabled him to seize and apply essentials
even in technical processes with which he was quite unfamiliar." Having
in mind the uses to which he would put this ability later, Dowson
stressed Lawrence's "visualization and photographic memory of topo-
graphical features of any ground which he had traversed" that he drew
upon in the compilation of new territories, which he could then integrate
with pieces of information about a locale he was receiving from other
sources. Finally, Dowson noted as many others have, Lawrence's puckish
humor, "his irrepressible fooling," which, more than his abilities or
achievements, "[we] keep in our hearts and memories."

The weeks in London after the war started, particularly after Turkey's
entry at the end of October 1914, seemed to drag for Lawrence. Once he
knew he was to be transferred to Egypt he looked forward to it eagerly
and resented official delays. Shortly before embarking with Newcombe
from Marseilles on December 9, he sent Leeds a small piece of red tape
affixed to War Office notepaper with the notation, "a sample of official
red tape."[15] Soon after arriving in Cairo, he wrote Leeds, "Today we got
the Office, and we all have the Intelligence: it is only a simple process of
combining the two. Newcombe is Director . . . a magnificent but unpaid

position . . . the Gods alone know what our pay is to be . . . for me I'm broke already, so have only a lack-lustre interest in the thing. Woolley looks after personnel . . . is sweet to callers in many tongues, and keeps lists of persons useful or objectionable. One Lloyd who is an M.P. [member of Parliament] of sorts and otherwise not bad looks after Mesopotamia . . . and Aubrey Herbert who is a quaint person looks after Turkish politics: between them in their spare time they locate the Turkish army, which is a job calling for magnifiers. . . . And I am bottle-washer and office boy pencil-sharpener and pen wiper . . . and I think I have more to do than others of the faculty. If we can get somebody to grapple with the telephone (which burbles continuously) I will be as happy and lazy as I want to be. Perhaps someday there will be work to do . . . but Carchemish seems a most doleful way away."[16]

Lawrence had written Hogarth after arriving, "It promises to be good fun," but soon began to be bored with the map-making, geographical reports and interviewing agents. He turned his attention to Middle Eastern politics — Syria was his greatest interest — and itched for a more active role in the war.

His famous resentment of French colonialism was expressed as early as February 15, 1915, in a letter to his family: "So far as Syria is concerned it is France and not Turkey that is the enemy . . . but I wish I could give it to Germany in some way, for the shameless way in which she dragged Turkey into the war. I don't think any nation has ever done in high politics anything quite so ———— [word illegible]."[17]

In March Lawrence pressed on Hogarth his views of the advantages of a landing at Alexandretta on the North Syrian coast, and as early as March 22 was demonstrating his knowledge of the politics of the various tribes of the Arabian Peninsula, and his desire to "pull them all together, and roll up Syria by way of the Hedjaz in the name of the Sherif."[18] His hopes for a landing at Alexandretta were disappointed in April when a British expeditionary force was sent to Gallipoli "beastly ill-prepared, with no knowledge of where it was going, or what it would meet, or what it was going to do."[19]

Lawrence's exasperation with tracking the movements of a Turkish army that he was taking no more active part in defeating was expressed to Leeds: "There are 40 divisions in the Turkish Army, in peace time, and that is doubled now that it is war, and the only one really settled, the one we 'defeat' from time to time on the canal, is located in the Caucasus by the Russians, at Pardirma by the Athens people, in Adrianople by Bulgaria, at Midia by Roumania, and in Baghdad by India. The locations of the other 39 regular, and 40 reserve divisions are less certain."[20] He also expressed to Leeds his exasperation with the influence of the conservative British Indian government on policy in the Arab areas. "Out upon all this show! I'm fed up, and fed up, and fed up: — and yet we have to go on doing it, and indeed we take on new jobs every day, because the W.O. [War Office] handed over this Med-force to our mercies,* with a side-request to keep India (Augean stable) and Basra [in Mesopotamia] up to date. The only branch I want, Arabian politics, they won't give us, but leave in the hands of a juggins in Delhi, whose efforts are to maintain the Aden Hinterland — a cesspit — in its status quo. Pouf —."21

In May, Lawrence's brother Frank was killed in France, and Lawrence wrote to his family that they should put a brave face on their loss. He found intolerable his mother's giving way to her grief in a letter to him and replied: "Poor Dear Mother, I got your letter this morning, and it has grieved me very much. You *will* never understand any of us after we are grown up a little. *Don't* you ever feel that we love you without our telling you so? — I feel such a contemptible worm for having to write this way about things. If you only knew that if one thinks deeply about anything one would rather die than say anything about it. You know men do nearly all die laughing, because they know death is very terrible, and a thing to be forgotten till after it has come.

"There, put that aside, and bear a brave face to the world about Frank. In a time of such fearful stress in our country it is one's duty to watch very carefully lest one of the weaker ones be offended: and you know we were always the stronger, and if they see you broken down they will all grow fearful about their ones at the front."22

As the Dardanelles campaign dragged on toward its ultimate collapse Lawrence continued to press without success for a landing at Alexandretta. Although he remained disappointed with the incompetence and failure of British policy and operations in the Near East, he saw in this failure an opportunity for the point of view that he shared with others in the Intelligence Office in Cairo. "I am pleased on the whole with things," he wrote home in October. "They have gone against us so far that our government has become more reasonable, and the final settlement out here, though it will take long, will I think be very satisfactory. We have to thank our failures for that: and to me, they are worth it."23

In September Lawrence's brother Will was shot down in France. His death was not known officially until the following May, but Lawrence took it for granted. He had been close to Will and was much troubled by his death. He wrote of his feelings to Leeds in an understated way: "I have not written to you for ever so long . . . I think really because there was nothing I had to say. It is partly being so busy here, that one's thoughts are all on the jobs one is doing, and one grudges doing anything

---

* The Intelligence Office in Cairo, of which Lawrence was a member, was assigned the responsibility of being the "intelligence base" for the Mediterranean Expeditionary Force being sent to Gallipoli and Salonika, and he was therefore in telegraphic communication with Gallipoli, Greece, Russia and London.

else, and has no other interests, and partly because I'm rather low because first one and now another of my brothers has been killed. Of course, I've been away a lot from them, and so it doesn't come on like a shock at all . . . but I rather dread Oxford and what it may be like if one comes back. Also they were both younger than I am, and *it doesn't seem right, somehow, that I should go on living peacefully in Cairo*" [italics added].[24]

Thereafter, Lawrence became increasingly impatient to enter more actively into the military effort.

At Christmas Lawrence wrote home rather awkwardly and sternly, "I'm afraid that for you it will be no very happy day; however, you have still Bob and Arnie at home [later Robert Lawrence was to serve with distinction as a doctor in France] which is far more than many people have. Look forward all the time."[25] Lawrence's letters to his family seemed to pick up in tone, principally, it would appear, because the policy of supporting Arab efforts on the Arabian Peninsula that he and his associates were pressing for was becoming accepted by the British government, and he was able to devote his own efforts to studying Arabia.

But as the weeks of 1916 passed without a more active role for him, Lawrence became increasingly impatient. "We do nothing here except sit and think out harassing schemes of Arabian policy. My hair is getting very thin and grey. . . . I'm going to be in Cairo till I die," he wrote.[26]

Those in Cairo, like Lawrence, who sought to advance the British war effort by capitalizing on Arab independence movements in various parts of the Ottoman Empire, had hoped that an uprising could be promoted in Mesopotamia, and that it might be possible to win the Ottoman Mesopotamian forces to the Allied side. Sayyid Talib, whom Lawrence described as "vigorous but unscrupulous," was the leader of the movement in Mesopotamia, and 'Aziz Ali al-Misri, the founder of the secret society al-'Ahd, was idolized by the Arab army officers there. But the British military and political authority for Mesopotamia was the Indian government, which was hostile to the aspirations for independence of the Mesopotamian people. Early successes in this theatre by General Charles Townshend, who defeated with British troops the Turkish forces at the first battle of Kut-el-Amara in September 1915, could only have confirmed the Indian government's belief in the correctness of their policies.

A dispatch sent from General Staff (Intelligence) at Kut to the Indian Foreign Office on November 8, six weeks after this victory, demonstrates the characteristic British attitude in the Mesopotamian theatre toward the Arabs and their strivings for independence:

The formation of an autonomous state in Iraq [Mesopotamia] appears to be impossible and unnecessary. Here in Iraq there is no sign of the slightest am-

bition of the kind among the people, who expect and seem to be quite ready
to accept our administration. Other ideas may grow in the course of years as
they have in India, but we are of the opinion that from the point of view of
Iraq it is highly inexpedient and unnecessary to put into the hands of the
backward people of the country what seem to us the visionary and premature
notions of the creation of an Arab State, notions which will only tend to
make endless difficulties for *Great Britain* [italics added] here and serve no
present purpose but to stimulate a small section of ambitious men to turn
their activities to *a direction from which it is highly desireable to keep them
for many years to come* [italics added]. Moreover, so far as we know, there
is no personality who could be called upon to assume the high position of
Ruler of an Independent Arab State.[27]

Later in November, Townshend's Indian and British forces ran into
stiff Turkish resistance at Ctesiphon on the way to Baghdad and retreated
back to Kut, where a five-month siege began early in December. In March
1916, Lawrence was sent by the high commissioner in Egypt, Henry
McMahon, on a mission to negotiate with the Turkish commander and
"try to ransom from him, on grounds of humanity or interest, those of the
garrison of Kut whose health had suffered by the siege, and whom captiv-
ity would kill."[28] An additional purpose of his mission was to negotiate
"with Arab elements in Turkish army with a view to detaching them from
Turks and making afterwards side with Arab movement."[29] McMahon
wrote Sir Percy Cox, the chief political officer in Iraq (who, in his report
of Lawrence's activities, said of the mission, "I cannot as a political officer
of the Government of India afford to be identified with it")[30] that he was
sending Lawrence because "he is one of the best of our very able intelligence staff here and has a thorough knowledge of the Arab question in
all its bearings."[31] Lawrence, however, has given the additional reason
that he was selected because "I had put the Grand Duke Nicholas in
touch with certain disaffected Arab officers in Erzurum [a Turkish city on
the Caucasian Front which had fallen to the Russians in February]. Did
it through the War Office and our Military Attaché in Russia. So the
War Office thought I could do the same thing over Mespot."[32]

Both aspects of Lawrence's mission were unsuccessful. The ransom
offer (which had reached the sum of £2,000,000 by April 28, the day
before the garrison surrendered)[33] failed because the Ottoman commander would not agree to it, and the effort to promote an Arab mutiny
was hopeless because no groundwork had been done by local British
authorities in Iraq. There had been insufficient planning and time to permit Lawrence's contacts with potential Arab rebels in the area to produce
useful results. Furthermore, as Suleiman Mousa, a Jordanian biographer
of Lawrence, has suggested, enmity toward the Ottoman Empire among
Arabs in Iraq was not on a par with the hatred felt by the Bedouin and
Arab nationalists in the Hijaz and Syria.[34]

Some sense of the depth and extent of blundering that went into this campaign — which Lawrence called "a British disgrace, end to end"[35] — is conveyed rather poignantly in one of Townshend's last dispatches to his headquarters two days before he surrendered. He wrote of the great strain he had been under, that he was ill in mind and body, and that he had been given "all responsibility with entire conduct of all operations without a single order having been given me and with not a word of praise or reward."[36] A detailed account of the horror of disease, starvation and death that was Kut in April 1916, and the negotiations for the surrender of Townshend's force (in which Lawrence took part), is contained in the (then) anonymous diary of Aubrey Herbert, a British intelligence officer from Cairo who was present during this period.[37]

Upon his return to Cairo in May, Lawrence wrote a scathing report, criticizing every aspect of the campaign. According to one of Lawrence's fellow officers, it was bowdlerized by the staff in Cairo to protect the commander-in-chief, General Sir Archibald Murray,[38] and seems not to have survived. The dispatches and reports submitted by Lawrence that did survive concern the political tensions and lack of information among the several British commands, and accounts of the surrender terms (and their betrayal) by the Ottoman commander.[39] The first of these goes to the heart of the problem. Lawrence and Cox (whom Lawrence respected but considered "ignorant of Arab societies and Turkish politics," though "very open" to the views of Lawrence and his group)[40] had discussed the situation and had agreed upon the necessity of reconciling the differing views of Egypt, Mesopotamia and India; they recommended that a "round table conference under the presidency of a statesman, who would carry sufficient weight with all three elements," be convened.[41]

The chief significance of the Mesopotamian episode in Lawrence's development as a political and military leader lay in the lesson it contained: the futility, and ultimately the terrible danger, for *all* the population involved, of a Western power's pursuing its national policies on foreign soil with utter disregard for the nature and political aspirations of the local population. Although Townshend's army contained, according to Herbert, five thousand Arabs — half his force — the Mesopotamian and Indian governments had done little work with Arab leaders in the area. Much too late, and after the fact, Lawrence, the Arab expert, was sent to Mesopotamia with orders from Egypt to "promise to do all we can to help Arab Independence."[42] As Lawrence wrote in one of his accounts, the Arabs in the Kut region "had shown themselves, in the main, friendly to us, but had not been asked to take any active part in operations."[43] No effort had been made to work with Arab goodwill, to cultivate it in the pursuit of mutually advantageous policies.

This failure was a classic demonstration of the arrogance or ignorance (or both) that Western "great" powers often display when they work with weaker, local governments of differing cultures. Even from a narrowly military point of view, unless the armies or the weaponry are of overwhelming superiority, as they were in Allenby's campaign in Palestine in 1918, it is unusual for an effective result to be achieved by an alien force in a foreign land. This is especially true if there is a hostile, politically well-organized segment of the population that has the sympathy of the local people. None of these actualities of guerrilla warfare was lost on Lawrence, who was decades ahead of his time and his government in grasping their reality. It is a testimony to his persuasiveness that he was able to convince his superiors in the government to allow him a free hand in working with and through native leaders and populations in the pursuit of British national goals during the years of the Arab Revolt.

At the time of the Mesopotamian campaigns Lawrence was evidently tactless in communicating to local British regular army officers his disdain for traditional approaches. Hubert Young has described "the passion of contempt for the regular army" which Lawrence seems not to have suppressed during his mission in Mesopotamia, and claims that the antagonism between Lawrence and the Mesopotamian military authorities was to have "serious [adverse] effects on British policy in the Middle East."[44] I have not found evidence to support this assertion. In any event Lawrence seems to have learned to control his hostility and to pursue his aims more subtly thereafter.

Aboard ship returning to Cairo in mid-May of 1916, Lawrence wrote a voluminous, descriptive letter to his family, giving many details of what he had observed of the lands and peoples of Mesopotamia, but omitting most of his political involvement and his feelings about the Kut disaster. He revealed his preference for the regions of the upper Euphrates, where he had spent more contented years, over the Mesopotamia he had just visited, and revealed in tales and reminiscences his longing for Carchemish.[45] "Hereafter I will again be nailed within that office at Cairo — the most interesting place until the Near East settles down," he wrote, as if he had no inkling of the direction his life would take in but a few months.

Just a few weeks after Lawrence returned from Mesopotamia to Cairo late in May, news came of the revolt of Sharif Husayn and his sons against the Turks. "The Reuter telegram on the revolt of the Sherif of Mecca I hope interested you," Lawrence wrote home cautiously, three weeks after learning of the Revolt. "It has taken a year and a half to do, but now is going very well. It is so good to have helped a bit in making a new nation — and I hate the Turks so much that to see their own people turning on them is very grateful. I hope the movement increases, as it promises to do. You will understand how impossible it is for me to tell you what the work we do really consists of, for it is all this sort of thing.

This revolt, if it succeeds will be the biggest thing in the Near East since 1550" (he is referring, presumably to the conquests by Suleiman the Magnificent).[46] Lawrence seems so often, as in this instance, to write of momentous matters in a boyish and personal way.

At the time the Revolt began, Lawrence suggested supplementing the official bulletins of the Cairo Intelligence Office with summaries of news and other information from the various theatres of war in the Near East. These summaries, which together constitute a collection of documents filling three volumes, were known as *The Arab Bulletin*, of which twenty-six copies were issued under the editorship of Hogarth.[47] Lawrence contributed a number of items.

The *Bulletin* is a valuable source of information concerning the disposition of the various tribes throughout the Middle East toward the Ottoman government and the Allies; the progress of the campaigns; the fortifications, troop strengths and movements, and other information about the Ottoman army; the political situation within the Ottoman central and local governments; and the activities of their German allies. The *Bulletin* also contains much data about the personalities and relationships of leaders throughout the Arab world. The early issues convey from intelligence reports and journalistic excerpts from North Africa and the Middle East the complex mixture of reactions which greeted the news of the Revolt of the sharif of Mecca against the Ottoman authority.[48]

The Revolt itself proceeded hesitantly during the early months. After the fall of Mecca attacks on the Turkish garrison at Medina failed, and although there were some local successes, Lawrence wrote home in mid-September, "Things in Arabia are not going too well."[49] In August Sir Reginald Wingate, the sirdar of the Sudan (under whose command the military operations in the Hijaz fell at this time), sent Colonel C. E. Wilson to take residence in Jidda (the port for Mecca on the Red Sea), and at the end of the month Faisal complained to Wilson of the lack of military support from Great Britain, which had yet to acclaim the Revolt publicly.[50] Wilson considered the situation of the sharifian forces to be desperate and the Arab movement in danger of collapse. He recommended that a brigade of troops be sent to Rabegh on the Red Sea coast to support Faisal.[51] But the War Office in London, influenced by the India Office's opposition to supporting the Arab movement, considered that such an effort would be futile and wired to Cairo, "Gallipoli and Mesopotamia should have given quite sufficient proof of such futility."[52]

The indifferent success of the Revolt at this time was also due to the reluctance of some of the local tribes in the Hijaz to become allied with a losing cause and thereby risk Turkish reprisal. The absence of proper liaison for the Arab forces in the field, and of military information for the sharif and his sons, were additional factors. All this was compounded by a confusion among the various British authorities in Cairo and the Sudan on how to proceed, to which were added the intrigues of a French mission which reached Jidda in September. "The Arab Revolt became discredited; and Staff Officers in Egypt gleefully prophesied to us its near failure and the stretching of Sherif Hussein's neck on a Turkish scaffold," Lawrence wrote afterwards.[53]

In the meantime, if one were to go by Lawrence's letters to his family, he seems to have had nothing better to do over the summer of 1916 than to design new Hijaz postage stamps for Sharif Husayn, which were to replace the Turkish issues then in use. "I'm going to have flavoured gum on the back," Lawrence wrote in late July, "so that one may lick without unpleasantness."[54] (The red ones were flavored with strawberry essence and the green ones with pineapple, Lawrence told a friend many years later, but the Arabs liked the taste so well that they sucked it all away so that the stamps fell off in the post.)[55] His personal position became more difficult in the summer of 1916, when Sir Gilbert Clayton, who had been a sympathetic and flexible supporter of Lawrence's irregular ways and strong advocacy of the Arab Revolt, was replaced by Thomas Holdich as director of the intelligence section in which Lawrence was serving.[56] Holdich, whom Lawrence described as "excellent in O. [Operations] and fatal in I. [Intelligence],"[57] took his orders from Sir Archibald Murray, the general in charge in Egypt, who had little interest in supporting the Arab uprising. Lawrence found his enthusiasm for, and efforts to help, the fledgling Arab Revolt increasingly stifled by unsympathetic superiors.

Having determined that Holdich was "keeping me away from the Arab affair," Lawrence states in *Seven Pillars*, "I decided that I must escape at once, if ever. A straight request was refused; so I took to stratagems. I became, on the telephone (G.H.Q. were at Ismailia, and I in Cairo) quite intolerable to the Staff on the Canal. I took every opportunity to rub into them their comparative ignorance and inefficiency in the department of intelligence (not difficult!) and irritated them yet further by literary airs, correcting Shavian split infinitives and tautologies in their reports."[58]

One may question whether Lawrence's insubordination was really as tactless as this sounds, as he hardly would have avoided disciplinary action if it had been. In any event, in October he succeeded in wangling leave to accompany Storrs, whom Abdullah had been urgently begging to come to Jidda for consultation regarding a crisis with the Turks on the Red Sea coast.[59] Lawrence states that officials were only too glad to get rid of him; Storrs reports more soberly that he applied for Lawrence because of "gratitude for his assistance in the Hedjaz stamp issue and in other matters, the high value I attached to his judgment on any question, and his admirable company."[60]

At about this time Lawrence applied for a transfer to the Arab Bureau and joined the group in November. The Arab Bureau, formed in February

1916, consisted of a small group of Arab experts, most notably Hogarth and Clayton, who were particularly concerned with political intelligence and the sharifian cause, and from the time of its formation acted as a staff and intelligence office for the Arab campaign. In contrast, the intelligence section that Lawrence was then serving in was under the War Office and more preoccupied with conventional military operations in the Sinai and Palestine. With his departure for Jidda on October 13, 1916, Lawrence embarked upon the two-year period of his life from which his principal fame and notoriety have derived.

It is very difficult to assess Lawrence's role during his two years in Cairo, or to gauge his influence during this period upon the development of British military and political policies and strategies in relation to the Arab peoples. His letters demonstrate his impatience, his intense frustration at policies and decisions of which he disapproved, and his frustration at not having a more active part. To Leeds early in 1916 he described himself as "a miserable grain of faith trying to move mountains."[61] Gertrude Bell provides a contemporary glimpse of the enormity of his youthful ambitions for achievement in a letter written after she had visited with Lawrence during his mission to Mesopotamia. "This week has been greatly enlivened by the appearance of Mr. Lawrence sent out as liaison officer from Egypt," Miss Bell wrote. "We have had great talks and made vast schemes for the government of the universe."[62]

Yet if he was as insolent as he claims he was (which I doubt), or consistently as "thoroughly spoilt and posing" as Young found him to be in Mesopotamia,[63] it is doubtful that he would have got very far in influencing anyone. The contemporary evidence of McMahon, Storrs, Dowson and Hogarth attest to the high regard in which Lawrence was held at this time and the extraordinary depth and range of his abilities. Hogarth wrote in 1920 of Lawrence's "singular persuasiveness" and that when he "was still a second lieutenant in the Cairo military intelligence, but with a purpose more clearly foreseen than perhaps that of any one else, he was already pulling the wires."[64] To pull these wires Lawrence as a second lieutenant or staff captain worked largely through men like Hogarth, Clayton and Storrs, who had closer access than he did to those who actually formulated policy.

But in what direction was he trying to pull? Lawrence's antagonism toward French colonial ambitions in Syria is well known, and his 1915 letters to Hogarth arguing for Arab revolts in order to "biff the French out of all hope of Syria" are also well known and often quoted.[65] In 1915, Lawrence's hopes for an Arab uprising lay at first with al-Idrisi in Yemen[66] rather than with Husayn (although he recognized the sharif's prestige in Syria), and it is possible that he was unaware during 1915 of the negotiations his government was then carrying on with the sharif.

In two reports found in the Public Record Office written by Lawrence early in 1916 he set forth his views concerning the anticipated partition of the Ottoman Empire. They are written in a tone of British chauvinism and hard political realism of which any old colonial hand might be proud. In one of these essays he advocated the British conquest of all Syria on strategic grounds, or, should that prove economically, politically and militarily impractical, an agreement and a division of "our spoils with France." (Lawrence would probably have had at that time no knowledge of the McMahon-Husayn correspondence or the Sykes-Picot negotiations which were then in progress.) After the reduction of the Ottoman Empire to holdings in Anatolia, "the most probable claimant — barring the Sultan — to the Khalifate would be the Sherif of Mecca, who has been active in the last few years in Arabia and Syria, asserting himself as an arbiter of morals. He is held down by Turkish money — which we, via Egypt or India could replace with interest — and by a Turkish Army Corps."[67]

Lawrence advocated cutting the Hijaz railroad (as he would later lead the Bedouin in doing), in order to prevent supplies from reaching the Turkish garrisons, and to disrupt local Ottoman administrations by severing their communications with the central Ottoman government. With the Ottoman army in the Hijaz divided into "an assembly of fearful Syrian peasants and incompetent alien officers," the Arab chiefs in the Hijaz "would make their own hay: and for our pilgrims sake one can only hope quickly." This approach, Lawrence predicted, would render the Ottoman government helpless in the Hijaz, and would enlist the help of the Bedouin because the railroad had reduced their annual tolls during the pilgrimages.[68]

In the other paper, written in January 1916, Lawrence wrote that Husayn's activity would be useful to the British government in disrupting and defeating the Ottoman Empire, and also because "the states he would set up to succeed the Turks would be as harmless to ourselves as Turkey was before she became a tool in German hands." He feared colonization by another European power and wrote that "if properly handled [the Arabs] would remain in a state of political mosaic, a tissue of small jealous principalities incapable of cohesion, and yet always ready to combine against an outside force." Husayn, Lawrence wrote further, had "a mind some day to taking the place of the Turkish Government in the Hedjaz himself. If we can only arrange that this political change shall be a violent one, we will have abolished the threat of Islam, by dividing it against itself, in its very heart. There will then be a Khalifa in Turkey and a Khalifa in Arabia, in theological warfare, and Islam will be as little formidable as the Papacy when the Popes lived in Avignon."[69]

These are cynical, coldly written documents. Although they anticipate policies that Lawrence would personally implement, they indicate no sympathy with or interest in Arab freedom, independence or nationalism. On the contrary they advocate using attitudes and ambitions of the Arabs

and their leaders in the pursuit of British military and political policies —
policies of conquest and occupation at that. He seems to have written in
this hard tone with youthful relish, as if to show he was "one of the boys."
Yet it is difficult to interpret Lawrence's personal motives in writing these
papers. We do not know for whom in particular they were intended, or
even to whom they were immediately addressed. "The Politics of Mecca"
found its way to the high commissioner and to Sir Edward Grey, the
foreign secretary in London, and Lawrence may well have been trying to
present the kinds of arguments which could influence or change the views
of superiors who were fundamentally hostile to or at least unsympathetic
to supporting the Bedouin and Husayn on the grounds of traditional
English imperialistic policies and opinions. Most of these officials would
not have wished to hear arguments favoring the formation of cohesive,
free, independent and potentially anti-British Arab states. Lawrence may
have thought that once his government had begun to pursue a policy of
supporting the sharif and the Arabs of the Hijaz, he could, with his
knowledge of the Arab world, then influence policy in his own direction.
Finally, it must be kept in mind that these papers were written in the
beginning of 1916, when Lawrence was not yet twenty-eight, at a time
when the destructive consequences of manipulating other peoples' minds
and lives were not yet fully evident to him. They need to be seen from
the perspective of his subsequent personal and political development.

Looking back to these years after the war Lawrence had some tendency
to exaggerate his role and importance in specific policy decisions. In 1915,
for example, in his letters to Hogarth (and possibly in other papers and
reports that have not survived) he urged strenuously a landing at Alexandretta as the strategic "key of the whole place" (Syria), and provided
extensive justifications for his position. It is not known what Hogarth did
with this information: whether he in turn argued for the Alexandretta
scheme with higher British authorities on the basis of Lawrence's justifications. In 1929 Lawrence wrote to Liddell Hart, "I am unrepentant about
the Alexandretta scheme which was, from beginning to end, my invention,
put forward necessarily through my chiefs. (I was a 2nd Lieutenant of
3 months seniority!) Actually K. [Kitchener] accepted it, and ordered it,
for the Australian and N.Z. forces: and then was met by a French
ultimatum."[70] But there apparently were extensive high-level discussions
of the possibility of a landing at Alexandretta, "which Kitchener had more
than once discussed with Maxwell before the War, and to which he
steadily adhered,"[71] and it is unlikely that Lawrence could have exerted
more than a minor influence, however agilely he could skip through or
leap over channels. In any event the scheme, which might have shortened
the war in the Middle East, was repeatedly rejected.

Lawrence seems also to have been less than completely accurate in
what he told his biographers about the role of Cairo Intelligence in the

Russian capture of Erzurum in Anatolia in February 1916, although this is more difficult to substantiate. It will be recalled that Lawrence told Liddell Hart that the reason he was selected for the Mesopotamian mission the following month was that he had put the Grand Duke Nicholas, who was in charge of the Russian forces in the Caucasus, in touch with disaffected Arab officers in Erzurum. But to Graves he had written in 1927 that the capture of Erzurum had been "arranged."[72] Now it is true that Lawrence, who had had an important intelligence hand in the Dardanelles operations and the evacuation of Gallipoli in January, may have supplied useful information to the Russians on the whereabouts of Turkish troops that were being removed from the Gallipoli campaign; and it is also true that the Arab Bureau may have influenced the results of the battle at Erzurum through the propaganda activity. But all this is quite different from an "arranged" capture, and the available evidence indicates that Erzurum fell only after severe fighting.

These apparent distortions seem to have been made by Lawrence "off-hand" and only when his involvement was relatively minor. And he made them long after the fact. They apparently relate to problems of self-esteem, which came to the surface after his war experiences. He seems never to have made similarly distorted statements regarding his influence in bringing about the Arab Revolt, or in persuading British officials to encourage and support the sharifian rebellion during late 1915 and early 1916, although his influence in these events seems to have been of considerable importance. Hogarth, in fact, called Lawrence "a moving spirit in the negotiations leading to an Arab Revolt and organizing the Arab Bureau."[73]

# 12

# The Course of
# the Arab Revolt

I am going off tomorrow for a few days. I hope to be back in about a fortnight or less," Lawrence wrote on October 12, 1916.[1] With these casual words Lawrence announced his first trip to Arabia, a trip which would begin his active involvement in the desert campaigns.* When Lawrence went with Ronald Storrs to Jidda in response to Abdullah's distress call, the Arab forces under Husayn's four sons had captured most of the towns in the vicinity of Mecca, but were unable to capture Medina, which was held by a strong Turkish garrison. Until the Arab forces were strengthened, they were in danger of losing from Turkish counterattacks what they had gained during the summer, and the Turkish army would continue to be able to move supplies freely down the Hijaz railroad from Damascus.[2]

Lawrence soon left Storrs and went by sea to Rabegh, up the coast from Jidda. He then journeyed inland by camel and met on October 23 with Amir Faisal for the first time. "I felt at first glance that this was the man I had come to Arabia to seek — the leader who would bring the Arab Revolt to full glory," Lawrence wrote dramatically of this meeting.[3] He learned from Faisal what the Arabs needed, and persuaded British officials in Cairo to provide sufficient supplies, ammunition, modern weapons and money to enable Faisal to develop an effective fighting

---

* This chapter is written as much as possible from contemporary sources in order to avoid the transformations of later hindsights. I will not attempt here to provide a detailed narrative of the *military* operations of the Arab Revolt or of the Palestine campaigns. These have been described many times in writings by Lawrence himself; by Liddell Hart, Young, Antonius, Birdwood, Stirling, and Mousa; in the British official history of the war; and in many other works by officers and officials who took a personal part in one or another aspect of the operations. Rather, this chapter will summarize the general course of the Arab campaigns and Lawrence's part in them.

force. These materials soon began arriving through the coastal base at Yenbo.

Lawrence was successful in discouraging the plan favored by Colonel Edouard Brémond, head of the French mission in the Hijaz, and others of sending large numbers of British, French, Egyptian or Indian troops into battle: the Bedouins would not have tolerated this kind of direct intervention "and would certainly scatter to their tents again as soon as they heard of the landing of foreigners in force."[4] In any event, as Lord Hankey wrote, at this stage of the war "the question that arose about Egypt was not one of sending reinforcements, but solely of how many divisions could be drawn from there to France."[5] Even so, in November Hogarth was able to write with some optimism to his sister: "All round, however, the coast is clearing and my own particular little war is going quite well in its own strange way. It is 'the Asian Mystery that it has lived till now'! December will make six months and I hardly dared to give it three."[6]

The strategy that Lawrence and other officers evolved — of working through the Arab forces in the Hijaz while utilizing a small number of British officers, such as Newcombe, Garland, Joyce, Hornby and Davenport, in an advisory and planning capacity — suited well the relatively weakened state of the Allied forces in the Middle Eastern theatre at that time. It also kept British casualties to a minimum, an important objective for Lawrence. He became the principal intermediary between the British and French commands and Faisal's forces in Arabia, and also to a degree among the Arab tribes ("I see myself as primarily Intelligence Officer, or liaison with Feisal," he wrote in a dispatch to Cairo in December).[7] But he was or became, as we will see, much more than a liaison officer. By his powerful influence on Faisal (and on Faisal's brothers and father as well), and through Faisal's dependence upon him for weaponry, supplies, money, advice and technological help, Lawrence placed himself in a position to have a correspondingly strong influence upon the course of British-Arab relations in the years to come.

Lawrence recognized that a direct assault upon the railroad head of Medina, with its strong garrison (eleven thousand men according to the estimate he made in September 1916 from his interviews of Turkish prisoners),[8] would, to be successful, require more numerous forces than were available to the Arabs and would also cause many casualties, which might discourage the Arab effort altogether.

He evolved instead, during a ten-day period of illness in Abdullah's camp in March, a strategy that he summarized concisely in an essay called "Evolution of a Revolt," which he wrote after the war.[9] His plan was to use the mobile Arab forces, familiar with the desert terrain, to break up the communications of the more conventional, static Turkish forces. The large garrisons, especially Medina, would not be assaulted

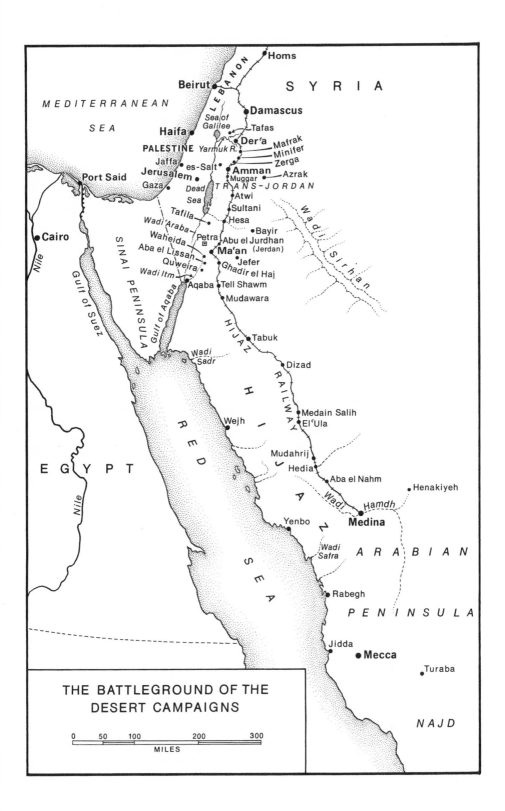

HOMS

SYRIA

BEIRUT

MEDITERRANEAN SEA

LEBANON

Damascus

Sea of Galilee

Haifa

Tafas

PALESTINE

Der'a

Yarmuk R.

Mafrak

Minifer

Zerga

Jaffa

es-Salt

Jerusalem

Amman

Azrak

Gaza

Muggar

Dead Sea

TRANS-JORDAN

Wadi Sirhan

Atwi

Sultani

Tafila

Hesa

Port Said

Wadi Araba

Bayir

Cairo

Wah'eida

Abu el Jurdhan (Jerdan)

SINAI PENINSULA

Aba el Lissan

Petra

Ma'an

Quweira

Jefer

Wadi Itm

Ghadir el Haj

Nile

Gulf of Suez

Aqaba

Tell Shawm

Gulf of Aqaba

Mudawara

Wadi Sadr

Tabuk

HIJAZ RAILWAY

Dizad

RED SEA

Wejh

Medain Salih

El'Ula

EGYPT

Nile

Mudahrij

Hedia

Aba el Nahm

Henakiyeh

HIJAZ

Yenbo

Wadi Hamdh

Medina

ARABIAN

Wadi Safra

Rabegh

PENINSULA

Jidda

Mecca

Turaba

THE BATTLEGROUND OF THE
DESERT CAMPAIGNS

NAJD

0    50    100        200        300

MILES

directly, for the Arab forces were not numerous or powerful enough to capture and hold them. The Hijaz railroad, the principal artery of communication and supply, would be kept working, "but only just," with a maximum of loss and discomfort for the enemy.[10]

Lawrence was concerned more with what the tribesmen thought than what they did, for his strategy was founded on the advantages inherent in a sympathetic local population. He has expounded clearly in his writings (*Seven Pillars of Wisdom* and "Evolution of a Revolt") the now-familiar principle that success in guerrilla warfare can be had by a small number of active, committed rebels in an otherwise passive but supportive population. In the Hijaz, Trans-Jordan and Syria, the various tribes, brought psychologically into sympathy with the aims of the Revolt, would form a ladder to Damascus.

Turkish traffic was indeed interrupted by demolishing the railroad at strategic points; the Arab forces under the tutelage of Lawrence and his fellow officers began to fight effectively as guerrillas, and the valuable port of Wejh was captured in January of 1917 by a British naval force acting in collaboration with the Arab forces. Seeing these successes, the tribes in the Hijaz that had hesitated to declare their loyalty to the sharifian cause began to join Faisal's army. The Arab forces enjoyed, in Lawrence's phrase, "the constant affluence of newcomers."[11]

As the success of the Revolt took hold in the desert, it also gained favor in Cairo. "Sir Archibald Murray [the British commander]," Lawrence wrote, "realized with a sudden shock that more Turkish troops were fighting the Arabs than were fighting him, and began to remember how he had always favoured the Arab revolt."[12] Others, like Wingate and Admiral Wemyss, who had supported the Revolt from the start, took pride in its success. In his dispatches Lawrence revealed the gratification he felt at Faisal's pride over the achievements of the tribes acting together in their own behalf. In a report sent to headquarters just after the capture of Wejh Lawrence wrote: " 'Yes, we [Faisal is speaking] are no longer Arabs, but a nation.' He was proud, for the advance on Wejh of the Juheina [tribe] was the biggest moral achievement of the new Hedjaz government. For the first time the entire manhood of a tribe, complete with its transport and food for a 200 mile march, has left its own diva [sic], and proceeded (without the hope of plunder or the stimulus of inter-tribal feuds) into the territory of another tribe with a detached military aim."[13]

A week before the capture of Wejh, Lawrence wrote to Stewart Newcombe a letter which conveys his exhilaration with the early successes of the Revolt and the schoolboy spirit he maintained at that time. The letter also contains a clear expression of his view that the British would do best to work through the Arabs, leaving them the primary responsibility for their own destinies.

"This show is splendid: you cannot imagine greater fun for us, greater vexation and fury for the Turks. We win hands down if we keep the Arabs simple . . . to add to them heavy luxuries will only wreck this show, and guerrilla does it. It's a sort of guerre de course, with the courses all reversed. But the life and fun and movement of it are extreme. . . .

"After all it's an Arab war, and we are only contributing materials — and the Arabs have the right to go their own way and run things as they please. We are only guests."[14]

Two weeks later Lawrence wrote to his family: "The job I have is a rather responsible one, and sometimes it is a little heavy to see which way one ought to act. I am getting rather old with it all, I think! However it is very nice to be out of the office, with some field work in hand, and the position I have is such a queer one — I do not suppose that any Englishman before ever had such a place."[15]

As the tribes of the Hijaz came forth to join Faisal, Lawrence wrote to his family enthusiastically in mid-February, "The Arabs of the Hedjaz are all for the Sherif, some keenly enough to volunteer, others less keen, but all well wishers." He continued: "The Arab Movement is a curious thing. It is really very small and weak in its beginning, and anybody who had command of the sea could put an end to it in three or four days. It has, however, capacity for expansion — in some degree — over a very wide area. It is as though you imagine a nation or agitation that may be very wide, but never very deep, since all the Arab countries are agricultural or pastoral, and all poor today, as a result of Turkish efforts in the past.

"On the other hand the Arab movement is shallow, not because the Arabs do not care, but because they are few — and in their smallness of number (which is imposed by their poverty of country) lies a good deal of their strength, for they are perhaps the most elusive enemy an army ever had, and inhabit one of the most trying countries in the world for civilized warfare. So that on the whole you may write me down a reasonable optimist. I hope that the show may go as we wish, and that the Turkish flag may disappear from Arabia. It is indiscreet only to ask what Arabia is. It has an East and a West and a South border — *but where or what it is on the top no man knoweth. I fancy myself it is up to the Arabs to find out!*"[16] (Italics added)

Lawrence's determination to leave open-ended the question of where the northern border of Arabia was, and his plan of helping "the Arabs to find out," was to bring him into constant struggles with Colonel Edouard Brémond. Brémond had the responsibility not only of helping in the military struggle against Turkey but also of representing the French government, which may have been just as unsure about where the top of Arabia was but certain that far enough north there should be a French lid in Syria on Arab national expansion.[17]

Although Lawrence was becoming, as he put it, "a monomaniac about the job at hand," he managed to find time to send his younger brother, now nearly seventeen, some stamps newly printed for the Hijaz, and to ask him what other kinds he wished.[18]

In February 1917, from his base at Wejh, Faisal made contact with the Howeitat and other nomadic tribes of what is now Jordan and northern Saudi Arabia, and obtained their assurances of loyalty. In a dispatch in mid-February Lawrence wrote: "Feisal swore the Abu Tayi Sheikhs* on the Koran to wait while he waited, march when he marched, to show mercy to no Turks, but to everyone who spoke Arabic, whether Baghdadi, Aleppine, or Syrian, and to put the needs of Arab Independence above their lives, their goods or their families. He also began to confront them with their tribal enemies, and force them to swear internal peace for the duration of the war."[19]

In March Lawrence met 'Awdah abu-Tayyi, "the greatest fighting man in northern Arabia," whose support would be necessary for the advance on Aqaba and for "swinging" the tribes north as far as Ma'an.[20] In the spring of 1917, in the tents of the Bedouin leaders and in consultation with Clayton, Wingate and other British officers in Egypt, the plan to take Aqaba by land was developed. Lawrence, 'Awdah and Nasir (the sharif of Medina) set off early in May from Wejh toward the Wadi Sirhan, a famous roadway, camping ground and chain of wells in the desert northeast of Aqaba, with the plan of cutting back to the southwest and taking the important port by land from the rear.

At the beginning of June, Lawrence started from the Sirhan with two men on a secret and dangerous mission to Baalbek (now in Lebanon) and Damascus to confer with Arab nationalists in Syria and to seek out the opportunities for an uprising there.[21] The value of this mission is described in a letter found among General Wingate's personal papers: "Lawrence's exploit in the Syrian Hinterland was really splendid and I hope you will have an opportunity of putting in a word that will help him to get the V.C., which in my opinion he has so thoroughly earned. Clayton and G.H.Q. are now digesting the information he has collected with a view to working out a scheme of cooperation from Sinai, Baghdad and the Hedjaz. There are at any rate the makings of a useful diversion against the railway line north of Maan."[22]

After returning to the Wadi Sirhan, Lawrence, 'Awdah, and several hundred Bedouin from various tribes of the region moved back in a south-westerly direction, taking the Turkish forces by surprise. They moved through Bayr, Al-Jafr, Aba el Lissan, Quweira, and down the narrow and rugged defile in the Wadi Itm to Aqaba, where the Turkish garrison surrendered on July 6.

---

* The Abu Tayi was a branch of the Howeitat tribe of southern Jordan.

With the capture of Aqaba — it was taken almost without casualties — the war in the Hijaz ended. Faisal could move his base there from Wejh, Sinai was secure, and the British were provided with a vital seaport for supplying their armies in Palestine for operations to the north. "After the capture of Akaba," Lawrence wrote a decade later, "things in the field changed so much that I was no longer a witness of the Revolt, but a protagonist in the Revolt."[23]

A contemporary example of how Lawrence's exploits during the previous month were regarded by other British officers is provided in the diary (not accurate in all its details) of an intelligence officer in Cairo, Captain Orlo Williams, who wrote four days after the capture of Aqaba: "Lawrence of I [the corps to which he was attached] has just returned, dressed as an Arab, from a most gallant adventurous sojourn in Arabia. He went up from Maan along the railway to near Tadmor and thence to Damascus, destroying several bridges on the way, thence back down Palestine seeing Arab and Druse chiefs, whom he found politically favourable to the Sherif. Then on July 2nd he set the Arabs about Maan onto the Turks, with the result that a whole Turkish battalion was wiped out and the Arabs now hold the coast."[24]

The following month George Lloyd wrote to Wingate: "[Lawrence] has done wonderfully good work and will some day be able to write a unique book. Generally the kind of men capable of these adventures lack the pen and the wit to record them, adequately. Luckily Lawrence is specially gifted with both."[25]

Lawrence returned to Cairo from Aqaba and was pleased to learn that Edmund Allenby had replaced Archibald Murray as commander-in-chief of Allied forces in Egypt. A relationship of great mutual trust and respect grew between them, and Lawrence persuaded Allenby that Faisal's Arab forces, based now at Aqaba, could, under his (Lawrence's) guidance, be a valuable adjunct on the right or eastern flank of Allenby's armies advancing through Palestine. In order to forestall opposition from "King" Husayn (the sharif had proclaimed himself king early in November), who might see in the transfer some loss of authority, Lawrence visited him in Jidda. The king accepted the transfer of Faisal "from the area of King Hussein to become an army commander of the Allied expedition under Allenby."[26] After the meeting Lawrence described the old man, whom he had not met before, as "pitifully unfit for the rough and tumble of forming a new administration out of the ruins of the Turkish system."[27]

In August, Faisal's army — and Lawrence as his principal liaison — was transferred from Wingate's command to the Egyptian Expeditionary Force under General Allenby, which meant that Lawrence's work was more clearly under Allenby's jurisdiction. Allenby wrote of their working relationship: "After acquainting him with my strategical plan, I gave him a free hand."[28] As we shall see, this "free hand," which was used to encourage Faisal toward dreams of an Arab empire in Syria, was to have increasing political significance as the theatre of war moved northward into territories where the political interests of the Great Powers were to come into conflict.[29]

Ten years later Lawrence wrote to Charlotte Shaw of his relationship with Allenby: "All he required of us was a turnover of native opinion from the Turk to the British: and I took advantage of that need of his, to make him the stepfather of the Arab National Movement — a movement which he did not understand and for whose success his instinct had little sympathy. He is a very large, downright and splendid person, and the being publicly yoked with a counter-jumping opportunist like me must often gall him deeply. You and G.B.S. live so much with poets and politicians and artists that human oddness attracts you, almost as much as it repels. Whereas with the senior officers of the British Army conduct is a very grave matter."[30] To another officer who had also served under Allenby, Lawrence observed: "I love him as Petrie loves a pyramid — not madly, but in proportion."[31]

Over the next three months Lawrence was engaged in moving back and forth between Cairo and Aqaba, arranging for the countless needs of the forces based there, planning and participating in train-wrecking and other raids along the railroad south of the Turkish base at Ma'an (described in detail in *Seven Pillars of Wisdom*), encouraging Faisal (who at times lost heart), and attending to endless organizational problems and details that related to his liaison work with the Arab and British forces. In late August he wrote to his family that the campaign was "for the moment . . . heavy and slow, weary work, with no peace for the unfortunate begetter of it anywhere."[32]

No detail seemed too small to escape Lawrence's attention. When he returned to Aqaba in mid-August he wrote home: "My milk camel has run dry: a nuisance this, because it will take me time to find another. I have too much to do, little patience to do it with, and things are going tolerably well. It is much more facile doing daily work as a cog of a machine, than it is running a campaign by yourself."[33]

In his letters Lawrence reflected different attitudes, according to whom he was writing. To a fellow officer (W. F. Stirling), for example, he wrote in a schoolboy tone: "The last stunt was the hold up of a train. It had two locomotives, and we gutted one with an electric mine. This rather jumbled up the trucks, which were full of Turks shooting at us. We had a Lewis, and flung bullets through the sides. So they hopped out and took cover behind the embankment, and shot at us between the wheels, at 50 yards. Then we tried a Stokes gun, and two beautiful shots dropped right in the middle of them. They couldn't stand that (12 died on the spot) and bolted away to the East across a 100 yard belt of open sand into some scrub. Unfortunately for them the Lewis covered the open stretch. The whole job took ten minutes, and they lost 70 killed, 30 wounded, 80 prisoners and about 25 got away. Of my hundred Howeitat and two British NCO's there was one (Arab) killed, and four (Arabs) wounded.

"The Turks nearly cut us off as we looted the train, and I lost some baggage, and nearly myself. My loot is a superfine red Baluch prayer-rug.

"I hope this sounds the fun it is. The only pity is the sweat to work them up and the wild scramble while it lasts. It's the most amateurish, Buffalo-Billy sort of performance, and the only people who do it well are the Bedouin. Only you will think it heaven, because there aren't any returns, or orders, or superiors, or inferiors; no doctors, no accounts, no meals, and no drinks."[34]

But to E. T. Leeds, perhaps because he was not a military man, Lawrence wrote of the same episodes more candidly, telling more of his troubled feelings, experience of danger and sense of horror. He described the raid more briefly, mentioned getting "a good Baluch prayer-rug," but added, "[I] lost all my kit, and nearly my little self." Lawrence then went on to say: "I'm not going to last out this game much longer: nerves going and temper wearing thin, and one wants an unlimited amount of both . . . on a show so narrow and voracious as this one loses one's past and one's balance and becomes hopelessly self-centered. I don't think I ever think except about shop, and I'm quite certain I never do anything else. That must be my excuse for dropping everyone, and I hope when the nightmare ends that I will wake up and become alive again. This killing and killing of Turks is horrible. When you charge in at the finish and find them all over the place in bits, and still alive many of them, and you know that you have done hundreds in the same way before and must do hundreds more if you can . . ."[35]

Finally, to his family he wrote in a breezy tone, conveying nothing of his true feelings: "I'm now back in Akaba, after having had a little trip up country to the Railway, for the last fortnight. We met all sorts of difficulties, mostly political, but in the end bagged two locomotives and blew them up, after driving out the troops behind them. It was the usual Arab show, done at no cost to us, expensive for the Turks, but not decisive in any way, as it is a raid and not a sustained operation. There are few people alive who have damaged railways as much as I have at any rate. Father may add this to the qualifications that I will possess for employment after the war!"[36]

In October 1917, Lawrence wrote home of his efforts to find a job in Cairo for his younger brother Arnie, who was reaching the age when he was in some danger of being sent to the Western Front. At about the same time, Hogarth wrote to his wife from Cairo:

> He [Lawrence] is going out of reach again now for a spell and they [his family] must not expect letters from him; but whenever I have news of him I'll let them know the facts whether through you or direct. But the intervals

will be long. Tell his mother he has now five decorations including the C.B. (to qualify for which he had to be promoted to major) and despises and ignores the lot. Says he does not mind what they give him so long as he has not to wear them! He is in this [word not legible] but very hard and his reputation has become overpowering.[37]

Not all the efforts in which Lawrence was involved were so successful. General Allenby's forces had advanced through Palestine and captured Beersheba at the end of October.[38] Lawrence and a group of raiders left Aqaba late in October in order to assist Allenby's armies by cutting the vital railroad that linked Damascus and Der'a with Jerusalem, Gaza and the Mediterranean coast. Lawrence and one party aimed to destroy a vital bridge across the Yarmuk River west of Der'a, but the Howeitat tribesmen were now operating in cultivated and settled lands outside their native areas. The bridge was reached, but the raiders were spotted by the Turkish sentries before they could lay their charge of explosives, and although other less vital bridges south of Der'a were destroyed, the mission ended in failure.[39]

Something of the danger for Lawrence of these missions is conveyed in Hogarth's letters to his wife. "He . . . is away now on a very risky venture, and I'll be more than glad to see him out of it." And a few days later: "I only hope and trust TEL will get back safe. He is out and up against it at this moment. If he comes through it is a V.C. — if not — well, I don't care to think about it! But, of course not a word to his mother." And two weeks after this: "I have been on tenterhooks, as he was on a very dangerous venture, which failed as I feared it must, but without involving him in the worst fate. So far as I know he is unwounded and he says he is very well and cheerful [as of November 14, the date of Lawrence's last communication with Hogarth]. But he is still far away, and has dangerous things to do — is, in fact doing them every day (this last not for Mrs. Lawrence)."[40]

Following these missions Allenby instructed Lawrence to reconnoiter in the vicinity of Der'a. In mid-November Lawrence set out "in this wintry weather to explore the country lying about Deraa"[41] accompanied by Talal, a shaykh of Tafas, a village northwest of the town. (The traumatic attack at the hands of the Turks that awaited him there and its significance for his future is discussed in Chapter 19.) After escaping from Der'a, Lawrence reached Azraq, a palm-shaded oasis west of Amman, on or about November 22 and returned to Aqaba on the twenty-sixth.[42]

On the twenty-ninth, Hogarth wrote his wife that Lawrence had been awarded the Croix de Guerre with palms by the French, "their equivalent of the V.C. . . . Tell his mother, for he won't!"[43] Lawrence's response to this award indicated his attitude toward medals and honors and also the support for his credo of renunciation that he assumed his parents would give him. "The French Government has stuck another medal on to me," he wrote home, "a croix de guerre this time. I wish they would not bother, but they never consult one before doing these things. At least I have never expected one, and will never wear one or allow one to be conferred on me openly. One cannot do more, for these notices are published in the Press first thing, and to counter-announce that one refused it, would create more publicity than the award itself. I am afraid you will be rather disgusted, but it is not my fault, and by lying low and simply not taking the things when given me, I avoid ever really getting them."[44]

On December 9 Jerusalem fell to General Allenby's advancing forces. Hogarth described the capture as "a great, but a very thorny acquisition."[45] Lawrence was among the official group entering the city because Allenby "was good enough, although I had done nothing for the success, to let Clayton take me along as his staff officer for the day."[46] Of the capture Lawrence wrote his family: "It was impressive in its way — no show, but an accompaniment of machine gun and anti-aircraft fire, with aeroplanes circling over us continually. Jerusalem has not been taken for so long; nor has it ever fallen so tamely before. These modern wars of large armies and long-range weapons are quite unfitted for the historic battlefields."[47]

Lawrence was moved by this historic occasion to lecture his seventeen-year-old brother, who was struggling with exams, about his views of history: "I see Arnie is getting slowly up the obstacles of many exams. They are silly things, terrible to the conscientious, but profitable to the one who can display his goods to effect, without leaving holes visible. As real tests they are illusory. So long as you can read good books in the languages they effect, that's enough for education: but it adds greatly to your pleasure if you have memory enough to remember the why and wherefore of the waxing and waning of peoples, and to trace the slow washing up and down of event upon event. In that way I think history is the only knowledge of the easy man. It seems to me that is enough of didactic."[48]

Lawrence also wrote to Leeds after the entry into Jerusalem and described the enormous amount of captured Turkish booty. He wrote then of his concern that he was "getting terribly bound up in Eastern politics, and must keep free," and, prophetically, "I've never been labelled yet, and yet I fear that they are going to call me Arabian now. As soon as war ends I'm going to build a railway in South America, or dig up a South African gold-field, to emancipate myself. Carchemish will either be hostile (Turks will never let me in again) or friendly (Arab), and after being a sort of king-maker one will not be allowed to go digging quietly again."[49]

Hogarth has provided illuminating glimpses of Lawrence at this time to his son, William: "T.E.L. was with me at Gaza [on December 10 or

11] and is now here [Cairo] for a day or two, looking much fitter and better than when I saw him last. He still looks absurdly boyish for 28!"[50] And to his wife a week later: "It was a refreshing contrast to have T.E.L. about for a week. He anyhow only lives for one thing. They put him up at the Residency this time and made much of him. He went about happily in a second lieutenant's tunic and badges somewhere between a lieutenant and a captain, and no decorations and no belt. When he went to Jerusalem with Allenby he is reported to have borrowed from one person and another a regular staff outfit with proper badges and even decorations. I only hope he appears in the cinema pictures taken on that occasion, because, otherwise, an unknown aspect of him will be lost."[51]

The remainder of December was taken up with operations against the Hijaz railroad and the stations east of Aqaba — Ramleh, Tell Shahm and Mudawara. These raids are significant in that Lawrence was accompanied by other British officers, among them Alan Dawnay and Captain L. H. Gilman, who could confirm through firsthand experience his accounts of the operations.[52]

In January 1918, the well-known battle of Tafila, an important center in the region southeast of the Dead Sea, was fought using Arab "regulars," a force under the command of Ja'far Pasha al-'Askari that was composed largely of Turkish prisoners of war who had elected to secure their release by joining the Revolt.[53] The battle, which was actually a defensive engagement that turned into an offensive rout, was described in the official history of the war as "a brilliant feat of arms."[54] Lawrence was awarded the D.S.O. (Distinguished Service Order) for his leadership at Tafila, which was evacuated and then reoccupied by the Arab forces in March. Of the D.S.O. Lawrence wrote his family in his characteristic tone, disavowing pleasure in his awards and recognition: "It's a pity all this good stuff is not sent to someone who would use it! Also I'm apparently a colonel of sorts [he had been recently promoted to lieutenant-colonel]."[55]

In February of 1918, Lawrence evidently became quite despondent, especially following a serious misunderstanding with Zayd, Faisal's youngest brother, who was unable to account satisfactorily for the absence of some funds that Lawrence had been counting on to pay the forty thousand men now on Faisal's payroll. He wished to quit and confessed to Hogarth that he "had made a mess of things: and had come to Allenby to find me some smaller part elsewhere."[56]

An entry by Hogarth in *The Arab Bulletin*, written in February 1918, reveals a similar discouragement with aspects of the progress of the Revolt. The Arab regular forces were often unreliable and inefficient, while the Bedouin demonstrated "the nomad's acute distaste for sustained action and winter campaigning." The enemy's line of communication was not permanently cut, although the Hijaz railroad had ceased to be of practical service to the Turks. "Nowhere as yet," Hogarth wrote, "have the Arabs held on for more than three days, at the outside, to any station or other point captured on the line, nor have they wrecked any of the larger bridges. . . . Emir Zeid, who is in command of Feisal's advance force, hesitates to advance, deterred partly by the continued cold, partly by nervousness about operating in a new country under conditions unlike those of Arabia proper, but most of all by the natural inertia and weakness of purpose which he shares with some of his brothers."[57] Lawrence's despondency seems to have lifted somewhat when he discovered in Cairo the extent to which the War Cabinet was relying upon Allenby to move to Damascus and, if possible, Aleppo. He decided then that "there was no escape for me."[58]

But at the very time he was feeling despondent and wanting to give up his role in the campaigns, he was becoming increasingly like an amir himself in his dress and prestige in the desert. He wrote his family early in March: "Three of my camels have had babies in the last few weeks. That makes me about thirty riding camels of my own, but then my body-guard of servants is about 25, so there are not so many to spare."[59] Late in February Hogarth had written his son:

> Major Lawrence is over here at present in full Sheikh's costume, and is sharing my living tent. The first day he was held up twice by the military police and his servant, an old ageyli [an Arab tribesman] from Qasim, definitely arrested, being in possession of a revolver and cartridges and quite unable to explain himself. He took it quite calmly, however, and was soon released. Lawrence's dagger is very pretty — a sherifial present; his *agal* [band for the head garment] is a good gold one and his *aba* [robe] (from Hasa) fair, but not as good as my sherifial one. He wears a long white silk shirt to his ankles underneath, and the sleeves trail on the ground showing below the aba like some undergarment got loose.[60]

William Yale, who was based in the American Diplomatic Agency in Cairo during the war, provides a firsthand picture of Lawrence's work among the Arabs during this period, in his reports to the State Department in February and March of 1918. Yale interviewed Lawrence and read his secret dispatches. The reports are based on information Lawrence gave him regarding the political situation in Syria, tribal attitudes toward the Allies, and the resentment of Palestinian and other Arabs toward the vigorous Zionist effort to reconstruct the Jewish colonies at this time. Yale wrote of Lawrence in his March 11 report: "He has a knowledge of the sentiments and feelings of the Arab tribes that probably no other Westerner has. His knowledge of the true condition of affairs existing, at the present time, among the Arabs should be more accurate than that of any other person." The report continued: "Major Lawrence said that everything had been prepared, and that he and his

Bedouins were ready, when they should receive word from General Allenby, to cut the Hedjaz R.R. North of Ma'an and establish relations with the British right flank."[61]

In the spring of 1918 the Arab forces were able to cut the Hijaz railroad for good between Ma'an and Mudawara to the south, thus isolating the large Turkish garrison at Medina, estimated then at twelve thousand men.[62] Although the Arabs did not have sufficient forces or "staying power" (tending to loot and take booty following raids and then retire to their tents) to seize and hold the major rail points like Ma'an, Abu el Jurdhan [Jerdun], and Mudawara, the large numbers of Turkish troops they killed, wounded, captured or "contained" at Medina and other isolated Turkish garrisons was of great aid to Allenby in preparing his decisive summer offensive.

In June Lawrence began his preparations for the participation of Faisal's armies in Allenby's final drive. Allenby had agreed to transfer the forces of Sharif Ali and Abdullah to the northern army under Faisal's command, but King Husayn would not allow it. Lawrence went to Jidda and talked with Husayn on the telephone, but the king was obstinate and sheltered himself "behind the incompetence of the operators in the Mecca exchange."[63]

The close collaboration of British and Arab forces along the narrowing Northern Front had become a more complex matter. Greater numbers of British officers were working closely with Arab regular and Bedouin forces (including a British-commanded camel corps), which had swelled in numbers. Negotiations with the large Ruwallah tribes and their legendary chief, Nuri Sha'lan, and with the Bani Sakhr and other northern tribes, whose loyalty to the sharifian cause was less clear, added to the difficulties. Misplaced confidence in the willingness of the Bani Sakhr tribesmen to move actively against the Turks may have played a part in the failure of the operations around es-Salt in the spring of 1918, "the Bani Sakhr tribe remaining quiescent at the critical moment."[64] Furthermore, as the Bedouin followers of the Revolt moved northward, they came increasingly to require the collaboration of settled Arabs of the towns of Syria, whose concepts of Arab nationalism and independence were not identical with the rebellion of the sharif of Mecca and his family against the Turkish government, and were not always willing to fight on the side of Faisal and his brothers against the Ottoman forces, which contained many Arab troops.

An additional difficulty for the British command and for Lawrence arose during the summer of 1918, when he discovered that Faisal, in response to an overture of Jemal Pasha early in June, had been negotiating a possible separate settlement of the Revolt.[65] Faisal appears to have been influenced in this direction by Syrian officers in his army, by recent failures of Bedouin raids, and by his concern, natural under the circumstances, that Arab gains in Syrian territory, which the tide of war had by then reached, would be negated by British commitments to the French. The British felt obliged to provide him with fresh assurances that the Arabs would be permitted to hold any territory they themselves liberated (which would later complicate the postwar political situation), and Lawrence apparently influenced Faisal to continue the struggle by letting him know subtly that he was aware of his activities.[66] Further, Hogarth, in a secret report to Storrs in August, indicated clearly his awareness that educated Syrians would oppose a sharifian administration in their territory, and he, Hogarth, even considered a separate peace with Turkey.[67] But Hogarth ended by urging continuing reliance on the sharifian Revolt as the "chief instrument" of British policy, while trying to bring the Revolt increasingly under the control of British officers working with the sharifian forces.[68] This appears to have been the policy that was followed for the remainder of the war.

Lawrence's letters during the summer of 1918 convey the frenetic pace at which he rushed from Cairo to Wejh to Jidda to Aqaba as he prepared for the offensive that was soon to come. Colonel Pierce Joyce, who was commander of the British section of the Arab northern army, has recalled:

> It was during these desert trips that I first realized Lawrence's joy in motion and craze for speed. One memorable day Lawrence rode in from a visit to G.H.Q. all smiles while we were at lunch in our improved mess at Guweira [north of Aqaba]. He could scarcely eat for eagerness and yet his conversation was about a herd of wild ostriches which had crossed his path on the way over, and describing how his Bedouin escort had fled after them in a vain endeavor to make a capture. It was only afterwards, in Feisal's tent that he announced the glad tidings of the gift of 2,000 camels from G.H.Q., the essential link to the goal of his ambition, the Arab drive north and the capture of Damascus. He was like a boy released from school that day and his energy dynamic.[69]

By the summer of 1918 the Turks were offering a stiff reward for Lawrence's capture. One officer wrote in his contemporary notes: "Though a price of £15,000 has been put on his head by the Turks no Arab has, as yet, attempted to betray him. The Sherif of Mecca (King of the Hedjaz) has given him the status of one of his sons, and he is just the finely tempered steel that supports the whole stunt structure of our influence in Arabia. He is a very inspiring gentleman adventurer."[70] The English press received orders from the censor's office "not to publish any photograph of Lieutenant-Colonel T. E. Lawrence, C.B., D.S.O., for this officer is not known by sight to the Turks, who have put a price on his head, and any photograph or personal description of him may endanger his safety."[71]

Lawrence chose to forgo the possibility of disguising himself to the enemy in order to be readily known by Arabs who could be expected to be friendly. "In the desert I shaved daily," he wrote to Liddell Hart. "My burnt red face, clean shaven and startling with my blue eyes against white headcloth and robes, became notorious in the desert. Tribesmen or peasants who had never set eyes on me before would instantly know me, by the report. So my Arab disguise was actually an advertisement. It gave me away instantly, as myself, to all the desert: and to be instantly known was safety, in 99 cases out of the 100.

"The hundredth case was always the eventuality to be feared. If I saw it coming, I would get into a soldier's cap, shirt and shorts, and get away with it, or draw my headcloth over my face, like a visor, and brazen it out. No easterner could ever have taken me for an Arab, for a moment."[72]

An illuminating and amusing account of the extraordinary tactical problems encountered in coordinating the activities of the Arab regular and irregular forces with the British, French, Gurkha and Egyptian units of Allenby's armies is provided by Hubert Young, who had responsibility for transport and supply. At one time, for example, Ja'far, commander of the Arab "regular army," and his officers resigned temporarily because they took offense at a proclamation of King Husayn's in which he insulted the officers and "told Jaafar Pasha that he was not entitled to command the Arab army which acknowledged only Allah as its leader and [that he] was also extremely rude to the Emir Feisal."[73] Even Lawrence himself contributed to the difficulties of planning effective strategy. According to Hubert Young (a regular officer himself), Lawrence was unrealistic about the problems involved in transporting equipment and supplies for conventional troops because his own experience had been chiefly with mobile Bedouin raiders, who traveled light and lived off the land. When it came to planning the attack on Der'a, Lawrence's "first idea" was "that he would mount a thousand Arab regulars on five hundred camels, two men riding each animal, and send them swooping across the three hundred miles which separate Waheida from Deraa with their supplies and ammunition tied on with bits of string, and a roll of apricot paste, or *qamr-ud-din,* as the Turks call their staple ration, snugly stowed in each of the thousand haversacks. How long he thought the ride would take was never quite clear. He probably calculated on about eighty miles a day, a distance which his Bedouin irregulars could easily manage. Say four days for the trip to Deraa, one day for demolitions, and three days to race back in if General Allenby's big push was unsuccessful."[74]

Lawrence's quality of "doing it himself" when something needed doing or when an operation had failed is well illustrated by Young. In mid-September, in preparing for Allenby's offensive, which was to begin a few days later, an Arab force was to cut the line south of Der'a. But at the appointed time the column was still twenty miles away and "not even a body-guard could now move fast enough to cut [it]."[75] Lawrence decided to do it himself:

> Let him have a tender and a machine-gun and he would run down the line and do in a bridge. There was quite a good one at kilometre so-and-so, with a covered approach down the Wadi which the car could manage. There was only a small post on the bridge, and with luck he ought to be able to do the job before the Turks realized what was happening. It would be rather amusing. To one at least of his hearers it did not sound at all amusing, it sounded quite mad. But this was again the Lawrence whose madness had taken Akaba, and his madness on this occasion cut the Deraa-Amman line. Escorted by two armoured cars, and accompanied by Joyce and another officer, Winterton, he drove off that afternoon in the open tender, crammed to the gunwale with gun-cotton and detonators. While the machine-guns of the escort scattered the small Turkish post, the tender was driven right down to the bridge, where Lawrence laid and fired his charge. Then the small gay figure bumped airily away, perched high on the deadly boxes which any chance shot might blow into a thousand pieces.[76]

During the days immediately preceding and following Allenby's attack, which began on September 19, Lawrence and other British officers were engaged in the final destruction of the rail lines around Der'a and in operations against the Turkish forces south of Damascus. These operations successfully isolated Der'a and cut communications between Damascus and the south. They also contributed to the strategy of leading the Turks to believe that the main thrust of Allenby's attack would come in this vicinity. But Allenby attacked instead against the Turkish west wing along the coast and with such force that the enemy troops were soon retreating in disorder.

"Lawrence," said Young, "was of course his own master. I found out afterwards that he thought we were all under his orders, but I did not know this at the time, and still regarded him more as Feisal's liaison officer with General Allenby than as a real Colonel in the army, a position which he gave the impression of holding in great contempt. I had never been taken into his confidence, and knew nothing about his political schemes."[77]

Until this stage of the war the Arab tribes around Der'a and towards Damascus had not come out openly in support of the Revolt. They were "seated on the fence waiting to see which way the cat was going to jump," fearing a slaughter at the hands of the Turks.[78] However, when Allenby's offensive proved victorious in the closing days of September, the Arab tribes and villages south of Damascus rose against the retreating enemy forces.[79] In reprisal, a column of Ottoman troops committed atrocities against the village of Tafas, three miles northwest of Der'a. (The atrocities led to a loss of control on Lawrence's part that was of considerable personal significance and will be discussed in Chapter 19.)

At dawn on the following day, September 28, Lawrence entered Der'a alone.[80] Later in the morning the regular Arab forces under Nuri al-Sa'id, Ruwallah tribesmen seeking revenge for Turkish atrocities, and General George Barrow in command of the Fourth British Cavalry Division converged upon the town. (General Barrow states he arrived at 9:30 A.M.)[81]

Alec Kirkbride, a young British officer who accompanied Lawrence during a great number of his activities in the closing days of the campaign before Lawrence left Damascus, also entered Der'a the morning of the twenty-eighth. In his memoirs he wrote: "We [Kirkbride and Lawrence] reached our destination before the cavalry came in sight and we hoisted the flag of the Hedjaz. The place [Der'a] was a shambles. Dead and wounded Turks, with a few Germans, lay in the shade of the station buildings; while others unhurt, sat or wandered aimlessly about waiting for something to happen. . . . The townspeople of Deraa were looting furniture and stores which had escaped destruction by fires, which still smouldered here and there."[82]

Lord Birdwood's description in his biography of Nuri al-Sa'id is similar, and he states that by the time General Barrow arrived the Ottoman soldiers had left the town "in filth" and that "wild tribesmen were racing around the streets on their ponies in complete disregard of their own safety and that of everyone else."[83]

General Barrow has left his own account of what happened. He describes Arab atrocities against an ambulance train full of sick and wounded Turks that was drawn up in the station. "In the cab of the engine was the dead driver and a mortally wounded fireman. The Arab soldiers were going through the train, tearing off the clothing of the groaning and stricken Turks, regardless of gaping wounds and broken limbs, and cutting their victims' throats. The atrocities which the Turks are said to have inflicted on the Arab people gave cause for vengeance. But it was a sight that no average civilized human being could bear unmoved."[84] Barrow states he asked Lawrence to get the Arabs out of the station area, but Lawrence said he could not because it was "their idea of war." Barrow then told Lawrence he would take the responsibility for doing so and ordered his men to clear the station, which was done, and the station then was picketed by British sentries.

Nuri's version of the meeting, according to Birdwood, was that Barrow attempted to make him withdraw his forces, "whereupon Lawrence produced written instructions from Allenby to the effect that Arabs should be allowed to take over local administration wherever they entered through their own exertions."[85] Lawrence "managed to ease the situation by arranging for the general's immediate material requirements,"[86] but he was troubled over Barrow's performance. In his view the general had delayed unnecessarily in watering the cavalry's horses en route to the town. Also, Barrow had come without orders "as to the status of the Arabs" and, Lawrence believed, thought of them "as a conquered people."[87] Both charges Barrow hotly denied. He accused Lawrence of "being inebriated by the exuberance of his own imagination."[88]

Young, who arrived shortly after Barrow — at "about ten o'clock" — takes a conciliatory approach:

> Until the Sherifian detachment arrived, there was no sign of any organized Arab force, and he [Barrow] naturally hesitated to leave at the mercy of what he regarded as a pack of ragamuffins a town which had been evacuated by the Turks as a result of his own advance. Lawrence had adopted toward him what I am told was his usual attitude towards British Generals, a mixture of schoolboy cheek with an assumption of omniscience and of being in General Allenby's confidence which Barrow found extremely trying. Even when our comparatively orderly force appeared, he was inclined to be a little contemptuous at first, and I have no doubt that we presented an odd spectacle to eyes accustomed to British and Indian units. This passed off, though, and he and his staff were hospitality itself to the rather dishevelled group of British officers.[89]

Thus at Der'a, just hours before the capture of Damascus, the regular and the irregular were merged. The tensions that arose between Lawrence and Barrow represented only the first brush, a minor curtain raiser to the brewing political struggle between East and West, between the Great Powers and their Arab allies, that was to be joined at Damascus.

# 13

# The Capture of Damascus

The capture of Damascus represented the climax of the Palestinian and desert campaigns and of Lawrence's personal role in the Revolt. As the Ottoman armies retreated from the city, there converged upon it in the opening days of October 1918 the military forces of the Western powers — British, Australian and French — the sharifian forces of King Husayn, and the various Syrian factions for whom Damascus was the spiritual center. For each group the city had political importance, but for the Arabs it had great spiritual significance as one of the historic centers of the Muslim world. For them it was the "capital" of the desert, and the first capital of the caliphs outside the Hijaz. "Damascus," as Gertrude Bell wrote in 1907, "holds and remembers the greatest Arab traditions."[1] W. T. Massey, an official correspondent of the London newspapers with the Egyptian Expeditionary Forces (Allenby's armies), understood this when he wrote with alarm of the fires that the retreating Turkish soldiers and Germans had set: "For four thousand years Damascus had been coveted by martial kings and the tide of battle had often surged round her, but so fair a jewel was the city that barbarian rulers and their hordes had never destroyed her. She was the oldest living city in the world, and when watching the fires we wondered if we were going to witness her first destruction."[2]

There are scores of accounts of the capture of Damascus and the early, confused days of its occupation by the various Allied forces. Many of them are from firsthand witnesses of part if not all the events of those days. These reports, including the official ones, seem to be particularly prone to the subjectivity and attendant distortions that, perhaps inevitably, often accompany accounts of emotionally charged events. Lawrence's descriptions in *Seven Pillars of Wisdom* are not exempt from this criticism. In particular, one would think in reading them that Damascus was captured by Arab armies almost unaided, whereas the Arab entry into Damascus was made possible by the hard-won victories of Allenby's armies. Lawrence's official reports to headquarters and for *The Arab Bulletin* are more objective and less emotional in tone.[3]

The sharifian forces in the closing weeks of the war were operating in the belief that the British government would abide by the "Declaration to the Seven" issued in July 1918, an agreement made in response to the entreaties of seven Syrians in Cairo the previous month.[4] By this declaration Britain, in contradiction to the terms of the Sykes-Picot Agreement, would support the independence of all areas emancipated by the Arabs themselves during the war. The question of "who got to Damascus first" thus took on an additional significance. There is evidence to indicate that British forces were given orders to avoid entering Damacus, when they might have captured the city hours or days earlier than they did, in order to enable the Arab forces to claim that they, not the British armies, liberated the city.[5] And Allenby's readiness to recognize an Arab provisional government immediately following the capture of the city suggests that this was in fact British policy.

According to Lawrence's report to headquarters of October 1, an Arab force left Der'a on September 29 under Sharif Nasir of Medina and Nuri al-Sa'id, "following up on the 4th Cavalry Division on the right flank." After meeting some Turkish resistance and taking six hundred prisoners on the thirtieth, "the Sherif sent a mounted force forward to get contact with his followers in the gardens East of Damascus, to find that his local committee had hoisted the Arab flag and proclaimed the Emirate of Hussein of Mecca at 2:30 P.M."[6] Lawrence states that he himself entered the city at 9 A.M. on October 1 "amid scenes of extraordinary enthusiasm on the part of the local people. The streets were nearly impassable with the crowds, who yelled themselves hoarse, danced, cut themselves with swords and daggers and fired volleys into the air. Nasir, Nuri Shaalan, Auda Abu Tayi and myself were cheered by name, covered with flowers, kissed indefinitely, and splashed with attar of roses from the house-tops."[7]

But in *Seven Pillars* he wrote that there was an initial period in which the crowds were mostly silent and "looked and looked, joy shining in their eyes,"[8] while to his fellow officer W. F. Stirling he wrote in 1924: "My memory of the entry into Damascus was of a quietness and emptiness of street, and of myself crying like a baby with eventual thankfulness, in the Blue Mist [a Rolls-Royce armored car] by your side. It seemed to me that the frenzy of welcome came later, when we drove up and down in inspection."[9]

Elie Kedourie, a Middle East scholar whose hostility toward Lawrence is often transparent, makes much of the fact that in *Seven Pillars of Wisdom* Lawrence does not mention that an Australian light horse brigade entered the city in the early morning hours of October 1 and "it is to them that Damascus may be said to have formally surrendered."[10] Yet later in the same article Kedourie acknowledges that "it seems clear that a number of Sherifial irregulars were in the city by midnight on the 30th September."[11]

It is difficult to understand what is meant by Damascus being formally surrendered. According to the Australian General Henry Chauvel, the commander in the area, the Ottoman governor and Jemal Pasha had fled the city the day before. In a critique of *Seven Pillars of Wisdom* that Chauvel wrote in 1936, he says that the city was surrendered to "Emir Said Abd-el-Kader ['Abd al Qadir al-Jaza'iri], who, having assumed control of Damascus on the departure of Djemal Pasha on the afternoon of the 30th September, surrendered the City to Major Olden of the 10th Light Horse at 6:30 A.M. on the 1st October, 1918."[12] This is hardly impressive authority, since 'Abd al-Qadir was removed by Sharif Nasir and Lawrence in favor of other local leadership on the same day. Another version of these events is provided in the British official history, which observed rather understatedly as early as 1930: "There has been some controversy as to which troops were the first to enter Damascus."[13] In any event Allenby was prepared to recognize a sharifian government in Damascus as long as the sharifians were present in the city at approximately the time of its capture.

A firsthand Arab view of the events in Damascus and Lawrence's part in securing the authority of the Arab provisional government has been provided by Dr. Ahmad Qadri, a Syrian nationalist who was present with Lawrence in the city on October 1. When Qadri entered the town hall he was surprised to see that "the good-hearted" Shukri al-Ayyubi seemed to be accepting the authority of the Algerian Jaza'iri brothers, 'Abd al-Qadir and Muhammad Sa'id. This surprised Qadri because these two had not been among the nationalists who had worked with Faisal. Rather, they had worked with the Ottoman government and had ties to France. Qadri has written:

> We could not endure this situation after the great victories we had achieved and Lawrence desired to remove them from intervention in the affairs of government. I agreed with him about that, so we entered the hall of the big Serai [town hall] to discuss the situation with Sherif Nasir [leader of the Arab forces until Faisal's arrival on October 3]. There was arguing going on among the Arab leaders and Emir Said invited Sherif Nasir to come to his house. Wise men convinced him not to leave. Nasir told Said that he must stay. Lawrence said to Emir Said, "This is the opinion of those in whose hands the power is — that you must return to your home. If you do not accept this, Sherif Nasir will order the forces under his power to arrest you. And you must know that the British forces are ready to help the Arab forces to secure calmness and law in the city."

Sa'id, according to Qadri, left in anger.[14]

Lawrence was able to persuade Chauvel to recognize Shukri al-Ayyubi, a Damascene who had been a high-ranking officer in the Ottoman army, as the head of the local administration of the city in the name of the sharif of Mecca. Chauvel later regretted that he had done this because he learned that Shukri al-Ayyubi had not, as Chauvel said Lawrence had claimed, been elected by the majority of the inhabitants.[15] The point is hard to credit since it is difficult to conceive how a general election of the citizenry of a just-conquered city of 300,000 in turmoil could have been brought off in just a day.

There does seem to have been an extraordinary release of control in Damascus on the day of its liberation, with outbursts of joy on the part of the populace in welcoming the Australian, British and Arab liberators in the morning, followed by rioting and looting and violent settling of old scores in the afternoon.[16]

The confusion surrounding the question of who quelled the riots and disorder in Damascus on the day of its capture is typical of the controversy that surrounds those days. Lawrence minimizes the degree of looting, rioting, murder and other violence in the town on the part of the Arabs. He implies that disorder was caused largely by the counterrevolutionary activities of the Algerian brothers 'Abd al-Qadir and Muhammad Sa'id and their followers. In his report for *The Arab Bulletin* Lawrence wrote: "We called out the Arab troops, put Hotchkiss [a type of gun] round the central square, and imposed peace in three hours, after inflicting about twenty casualties."[17] But it seems clear from the accounts of Massey, Chauvel and Kirkbride (who used his own strong-arm methods, including shooting troublemakers with his pistol) that the Arab soldiers had great difficulty maintaining order.[18] Kedourie has written indignantly that the reader of *Seven Pillars* "gathers the impression that Damascus was placed out of bounds to the Australian soldiers because they might meet with disagreeable incidents from which Allenby designed the Northern Arab Army to shield them. In view of the exertions of the Australians to restore order in Damascus which the Sherifians could not preserve, Lawrence's account seems an offensive travesty of the facts."[19] But Chauvel also wrote in 1936: "The Hedjaz supporters were out to make as little as possible of the British and were endeavouring to make the populace think that it was the Arabs who had driven out the Turk. That was quite evidently why I had been asked [by whom, Allenby?] to keep my men out of the city and why I had not yet been asked for any police, though Shukri Pasha [al-Ayyubi] knew that I had a whole regiment of Australians standing by for the purpose in the grounds of the Turkish barracks."[20]

Chauvel acknowledges that it was not until the next day (October 2) that he sent a large force through the city (which he says Lawrence opposed) to bring order. "The effect was electrical," he wrote; "the bazaars were opened and the city went about its normal business." Allenby wrote his wife the following day (October 3): "The town is quiet now, but there was a little pillaging and shooting the day before yesterday, quickly repressed by Lawrence."[21] Chauvel makes no mention of Lawrence's restoration of order, which seems to have impressed Allenby more than the efforts of Chauvel and his troops.

Lawrence has written vividly in *Seven Pillars* of his efforts to cope with the enormous problems he faced during his few days in Damascus, problems which included sanitation, fire, starvation and disease. It is difficult at this date to evaluate his role accurately, but it was a crucial one according to eyewitness accounts by such officers as Kirkbride and Stirling. "A thousand and one things had to be thought of, but never once was Lawrence at a loss," Stirling wrote.[22]

General Wavell, one of Allenby's biographers, has written, perhaps with justification, that "Lawrence's story of the events in Damascus after the entry and of his dealings with Chauvel is not the whole truth, and is unjust to Chauvel."[23] The events surrounding the capture of Damascus followed a period of intense emotional strain for Lawrence. Furthermore, as Allenby's letter to his wife suggests, much of the responsibility for maintaining order in the city fell on Lawrence's shoulders. It is not unexpected, therefore, that he would express resentment toward those whom he felt did less than they could, especially those in positions of authority. Lawrence virtually ridicules Chauvel, making him out to be an insensitive army general, more concerned with observing protocol than tending to the suffering around him. The degree to which the imputation is justified is not an issue that I can settle. There is no question that Lawrence was in a deeply wrought-up state during those days in Damascus and his pen (which could be most sharp in criticism of those with whom he differed) may well have been unfairly caustic in letting out his anger as he recalled those gruesome events. Yet it is clear that Lawrence worked intensively and effectively to bring order to Damascus and some rudiment of needed services to the city and its people in these first few days of its liberation, and that in his view Chauvel, who was officially in charge, acted too slowly and did not do enough.

A well-known episode involving the Turkish military hospital seems to have been a matter of particular controversy between Lawrence and Chauvel, although only Lawrence has described it in detail. The two men agreed in their reports that the fleeing Turks had left the hospital in desperate condition and that Turkish prisoners cleaned it up and buried the dead. Chauvel wrote, in contesting Lawrence's account in *Seven Pillars*, that the hospital was "discovered by Lieutenant-Colonel Bouchier of the 4th Light Horse (vide British) Brigade," but Lawrence's complaint was just that: the British and Australians discovered it, but no one did anything about it.

Lawrence's account, similar but less lurid and dramatic than the one in *Seven Pillars,* comes from an unpublished portion of a letter written in 1929 to William Yale, who was in Damascus during the first days of October 1918:

"About the hospital. Some American* (not you, I think: someone Red Cross or Medical at lunch in the hotel on the 2nd day) asked me to improve the hospital. I had not heard of a Turk hospital, but went to the old barracks after lunch, and was refused admittance by the sentry. I was in Arab kit, and the barracks ground occupied by Australians. I surmounted this difficulty, and looked at the charnel house inside, and went to the town hall for help. Nuri lent me one of the four (?) Arab army doctors, and I took Kirkbride, one of my officers. We pressed a working party from the Turkish prisoners at the gate (poor wretches, they should themselves have been in hospital) for the Australians wouldn't help and turned the Turkish doctors, who were skulking in their quarters, back to work. I am very relieved to hear from you they were Armenians. They spoke Turkish, so I took them for that, and was disgusted at their callous neglect. Before night we had buried all the dead, fed all the possible living, and had posted orderlies to serve water etc.: also got lamps in each ward. I rang up the British general [Chauvel] and asked him to take it over, as it was utterly beyond my resources. He would not.

"Next day [October 3] we cleared about six wards, and got the food better. There were no medical stores with the Arabs, and Damascus could supply little. The English would supply none. By evening the place looked good — relatively to what it had been on the day before. I dare say it was all wrong still: but we were making bricks without either straw or clay, almost, and our progress pleased me.

"Next day Allenby arrived and gave Chauvel orders to relieve the Arabs of the hospital. That I expect, ended the difficulty. I had done my utmost to improve it as soon as I knew of its state. The British guard over it for the first two days had prevented the Arab authorities from hearing of it. They did their best to prevent our entering it, when we did hear of it."[24]

Chauvel claims that the cleanup of the hospital and burial of the dead by the Turkish prisoners was done "under the supervision of the Corps Medical Staff,"[25] but Kirkbride, who stayed on after Lawrence had left to make sure the job was completed, disputes this. Kirkbride gives a detailed account of these events in his memoirs but makes no mention of the presence of any helping or supervising British or Australian medical personnel.[26] In fact, the only mention of British or Australians follows his account of the digging of a trench for the corpses by the prisoners: "These proceedings were observed with interest by some Australian troopers whose regiment occupied the adjacent barracks, but they did not offer to help."[27]

* "An Australian doctor" in *Seven Pillars.*

I interviewed Yale in 1966 and we discussed the hospital. He said "an Australian officer" asked him, about October 3, "Have you seen the Turkish barracks?" (that is, the hospital), and they went there together. Yale said he found the conditions at the hospital as bad as Lawrence had described and felt sorry that he had not done more to help. He was told by the Turkish (or Armenian) doctors that just before his arrival the hospital had been sacked by Arabs, and he criticized Lawrence for failing to report the fact. Yale complained to the British authorities as an officer representing the United States Army but was told to mind his own business as he was not a soldier. Yale confirmed Lawrence's assertion that the British were under orders not to do anything about the hospital. He said that the Australian officer who brought him there told him that he (the Australian) would be court-martialed if Yale told his superiors that he brought him there, as he had *previously been told not to do anything about the hospital.*[28]

Chauvel does not comment on Lawrence's specific assertion that he refused to take over the hospital. He says only that the hospital was handed over to the Arab administration, and "Lawrence wanted me to hand over all the hospitals in Damascus to the Arab administration." He continued: "I could not agree as regards the European hospitals, particularly as we would want them ourselves, but I did hand over the Turkish and Syrian hospitals. Incidentally, we had to take over the big military hospital [the one in question] again some four days later. It was in nearly as bad a condition as when first discovered."[29] Whomever Lawrence may have wished to have "administer" the hospital, it is hard to believe that help from the British authorities for the improvement of its state was not desired and requested. It is not clear what the "again" in Chauvel's assertion "we had to take over again four days later" refers to since British medical personnel seem to have provided little help in these first terrible days.

On October 3 Allenby and Faisal both arrived in Damascus and a meeting between them was arranged at the Victoria Hotel in the afternoon with Lawrence acting as interpreter and other British and Arab officers present.[30] Allenby told Faisal that he would recognize an Arab military administration of occupied territory east of the Jordan from Damascus to Ma'an, but that he would remain in supreme command as long as military operations continued. Allenby also informed Faisal of the terms of the Sykes-Picot Agreement, by which the French were to have the protectorate over the coastal regions of Syria, and the Arab administration would be excluded from Palestine.

Chauvel described the drama that occurred after Faisal received this news:

Feisal objected very strongly. He said that he knew nothing of France in the matter; that he was prepared to have British assistance; that he understood from the Advisor that Sir Edmund Allenby had sent him [Lawrence presumably]; that the Arabs were to have the whole of Syria including the Lebanon but excluding Palestine; that a country without a port was no good to him; and that he declined to have a French Liaison Officer or to recognize French guidance in any way.

The Chief turned to Lawrence and said: "But did you not tell him that the French were to have the Protectorate over Syria?" Lawrence said: "No Sir, I know nothing about it." The Chief said: "But you knew definitely that he, Feisal, was to have nothing to do with the Lebanon." Lawrence said: "No Sir, I did not."

After some discussion the Chief told Feisal that he, Sir Edmund Allenby, was Commander-in-Chief and that he, Feisal, was at that moment a Lieutenant-General under his command and that he would have to obey orders. That he must accept the situation as it was and that *the whole matter would be settled at the conclusion of the war* [italics added]. Feisal accepted this decision and left with his entourage (less Lawrence) and went out of the City again to take on his triumphal entry which I am afraid fell flat as the greater bulk of the people had seen him come in and out already!

After Feisal had gone, Lawrence told the Chief that he would not work with a French Liaison Officer and that he was due for leave and thought he had better take it now and go off to England. The Chief said: "Yes. I think you had!" and Lawrence left the room.[31]

Chauvel wrote that he thought Allenby "had been a little hard on Lawrence and told him so." Allenby then said, according to Chauvel: "Very well, send him down to my Headquarters and tell him I will write to Clive Wigram [assistant private secretary of George V] about him, asking him to arrange for an audience with the King. I will also give him a letter to the Foreign Office in order that he might explain the Arab point of view.' General Allenby then left by car for Tiberias. Lawrence left Damascus next day in one of my cars for GHQ, having handed over to Cornwallis."[32]

Although Lawrence was ending his direct military involvement in the Revolt, and did in fact leave Damascus on October 4, he had already played a part in setting in motion the several-sided political struggle that would follow the war. For as Chauvel continues in his 1929 account of the events of October 3, 1918, "Neither my Chief of Staff nor I knew at that time that Feisal had already taken steps to proclaim the Hedjaz authority in the Lebanon and, I presume with Lawrence's knowledge, had already despatched Shukri Pasha [al-Ayyubi] to Beirut to take over the administration thereof."[33] Chauvel recalled with some annoyance that "the fat was in the fire" when Shukri unfurled the Hijaz flag in Beirut, as one of his (Chauvel's) staff was present and "the whole thing was reported at once to the French."[34] Yale wrote in 1929: "Many of us at the time were convinced that it was part of the British scheme to make the French position in Beirut untenable. We thought T.E.L. advised the Arabs to seize Beirut."[35] Lawrence denied to Yale that he had had anything to do with encouraging Shukri to go to Beirut.[36]

There are many reasons why Lawrence left Damascus when he did. He was emotionally and physically spent (he looked thin and wasted).[37] He was disillusioned with the behavior of the Arabs, which had not conformed with the lofty outlines of his dream. Stirling describes Lawrence as "depressed" on the eve of the entrance into Damascus, and when he asked him about it, Lawrence replied, "Ever since we took Deraa the end has been inevitable. Now the zest is gone, and the interest."[38] In his own official report of October 1, the day Damascus was taken, Lawrence wrote, "I would like to return to Palestine as I feel that if I remain here longer, it will be very difficult for my successor."[39] As he later wrote Basil Liddell Hart about his departure, "Never outstay a climax."[40] Learning that he would have to work through a French liaison officer if he were to stay on was certainly a disappointment and probably hastened Lawrence's departure, but it would hardly have come as a surprise.

Finally, I suspect that he recognized that with the fall of Damascus the important struggle in the Middle East would soon become a political one, to be fought in the centers of power in Egypt, England and France rather than in the deserts and towns of Arabia and Syria, and that he wished to pursue his purposes in this new arena. Although the obvious interpretation of Lawrence's closing words of *Seven Pillars,* describing how he felt after Allenby gave him permission to leave ("and then at once I knew how much I was sorry") is that they refer to his sorrow about the whole Arab affair, they also suggest a more immediate regret at leaving Damascus before the job was done.

# 14

# The Achievements of
# "Aurens"

No psychologist can account for the appearance in a particular human being of a given set of talents. No historian who chooses to study how a particular person effects historical change can avoid altogether dealing with the proposition: "It was so-and-so's unique ability to do such-and-such that permitted $x$ to happen." In trying to define and describe the "unique ability," one can be tempted into oversimplification, especially if, as was so strikingly true of Lawrence, the subject can undertake a vast array of personal transactions (some simple, some complex) in a fashion that seems easy or even effortless (that is, easy or effortless if the expenditure of energy and the personal toll involved are not examined too closely). In this chapter I am especially concerned with exploring how Lawrence accomplished what he did in the Arab Revolt, what the gifts were that he brought to bear upon it, and how he applied these gifts to the social, military and political realities that obtained in Arabia, Palestine, Trans-Jordan (both Palestine and Jordan were then part of Syria) and Syria during the campaigns.

There has been considerable controversy in both the Western and Arab worlds regarding Lawrence's achievements in the Revolt, and even regarding the importance of the Revolt itself. I have no expectation that my contribution will settle these issues. On the one hand there are the denigrators, the most extreme of whom have been Richard Aldington and the writer Malcolm Muggeridge in England, to whom Lawrence is simply a fraud. Almost as troubling, especially to the Lawrence family, are the blind idolators whose idealization of Lawrence is not open to rational criticism.

As for the importance of the Revolt itself, from the military standpoint it is generally recognized that the Arab operations on the eastern flank of the British armies in the Sinai, Palestine and Syria, which were commanded by Murray and later by Allenby, constituted a front of secondary importance. But secondary does not mean trivial. Allenby called the Arab effort "invaluable," and Field-Marshal Wavell concurred.[1] In the opinion of J. B. Glubb ("Glubb Pasha," who was later to command the Arab Legion in Trans-Jordan), "the Arabs made a valuable contribution to victory . . . the whole Arab campaign provides a remarkable illustration of the extraordinary results which can be achieved by mobile guerrilla tactics. For the Arabs detained tens of thousands of regular Turkish troops with a force scarcely capable of engaging a brigade of infantry in a pitched battle."[2]

Basil Liddell Hart, basing his statements on figures from the British official history of the war, has summarized the impact of the Revolt and Lawrence's achievement:

> On the eve of Allenby's offensive in September, 1918 his troops totalled 250,000 and the Turks had an equal number in that theatre of war. But he was able to attack with a five to one superiority of force because close on 50,000 Turks were pinned down by the Arab force of 3,000 east of the Jordan, operating under Lawrence's immediate direction, while a further 150,000 Turks were spread over the rest of the region in a vain effort to stem the tide of the Arab Revolt so that little more than 50,000 were left to meet Allenby's assault. If it is unlikely that the Arab forces could ever have overcome the Turks without the punch provided by Allenby's forces, the figures make it much clearer that Allenby could not have defeated the Turks without Lawrence.[3]

The official history also concludes: "Prior to the final offensive with its many thousands of prisoners, the Arab campaign killed, wounded, captured or contained well over 25,000 troops. Like the Spanish guerrillas in the Peninsular War, the Arabs gave the British invaluable aid, while largely dependent upon them for their opportunities."[4]

From the political standpoint, the encouragement of the Arab Revolt by the British, followed by its gathering success during the last two years of the war, provided a powerful stimulus to Arab nationalistic aspirations. In the postwar period the forces of Arab nationalism, which had grown in strength during the war, and the drive of the Arabs toward freedom and independence played an important part in the decline of traditional colonialism.

What of Lawrence himself and his role in the Revolt? In recent decades interest has become so focused upon the legendary or sensational aspects of Lawrence's career, especially with the publication of books by Richard Aldington and by Knightley and Simpson, and the film extravaganza *Lawrence of Arabia*, that sober appreciation of his accomplishments has been difficult. Inaccuracies in Lawrence's full narrative of the Revolt, *Seven Pillars of Wisdom,* have been sought so diligently by his critics that the impression has grown that it is full, if not of lies, at least of marked distortions of truth.

There are, of course, distortions and partial truths in *Seven Pillars,* but these have less to do with the facts of Lawrence's accomplishments than with embellishments of their details for dramatic purposes or with the protection of other people. In writing to his biographers Lawrence tried to be explicit about those points where his writing is less than fully accurate. Concerning the passages dealing with the capture of Damascus Lawrence wrote, "I was on thin ice when I wrote the Damascus chapter and anyone who copies me will be through it, if he is not careful. S.P. is full of half-truth: here."[5]

The subscribers' edition of *Seven Pillars,* of which about two hundred copies were printed in 1926, was sent to thirty officers who served in the Revolt, including such men as Allenby, Joyce, Newcombe, Young, Peake, Stirling, and Winterton. Copies were widely circulated and read by many others who had firsthand knowledge of the events of the Revolt. Some of the officers later wrote their own reminiscences or versions of the campaigns in books and articles, most of which are referred to in this book. Stirling, for one, who worked closely with Lawrence in the later months of the campaign, says in *Safety Last* that Lawrence "sent the book to me to review as to fact."[6]

Neither Stirling nor any other of these men ever questioned the veracity of Lawrence's account. Concerning the attack and seizure of Aqaba by land, for example — the single exploit of the campaigns for which Lawrence is best known — he has been accused of undeservedly claiming credit for its strategy. Suleiman Mousa in particular states that "the plan for capturing Aqaba was devised by Faisal and Auda in Wejh."[7] But Colonel Edouard Brémond, the leader of the French mission (who resented Lawrence), confirms that the plan was discussed in conference before 'Awdah abu-Tayyi joined in the Revolt, and Jean Beraud Villars, a French biographer of Lawrence, who spoke with Colonel Stewart Newcombe about it, has stated: "Colonel Newcombe has confirmed that the Aqaba exploit was entirely conceived by Lawrence who was its real leader and animating spirit, although for reasons of diplomacy that are understandable the official command was left in the hands of the Arab chieftains."[8] Theodora Duncan of California has corresponded with scores of men who were involved in the campaigns, many peripherally, but none has challenged Lawrence's account of his role in them.[9]

Allenby, Lawrence's commander through the greater part of the campaigns wrote that Lawrence was "the mainspring of the Arab movement."[10] W. T. Massey, who was a correspondent with Allenby's army, wrote in the closing weeks of the war, before Lawrence had written

*Seven Pillars* and before the ballyhooing of Lowell Thomas: "The story of the Arab army has not been written, and I doubt if anyone could write it except Colonel Lawrence. Certainly no other British officer knows so much about it, and probably a great deal will remain secret, but if he would tell the world something of the Arab army's operations, and could be persuaded not to efface himself, we should have one of the most fascinating books on the war. I hope we shall see it."[11] Field-Marshal Wavell, who served in Egypt from 1917 to 1920, expressed a view similar to Allenby's: "The quickening of Sherif Hussein's family revolt into the movement that poured into Damascus [was] something that no one else could have achieved, even with unlimited gold: it was a spiritual even more than a physical exploit, the value of which to the Allied cause was great."[12]

When Aldington attacked Lawrence as a charlatan and a fraud he aroused most intensely the ire of Lawrence's fellow officers. The angry reaction of Captain L. H. Gilman, who commanded an armored-car battery in close association with Lawrence until near the end of the campaign, is typical:

> Aldington makes what is tantamount to an insinuation of the basest treachery on the part of Lawrence. He would have us believe that Lawrence was guilty of perpetrating one of the biggest hoaxes in history; of the deception of all his friends and former brother officers; of allocating to himself the honour and glory of exploits which belonged to others. . . .
>
> All this and more we, who knew and trusted him, are invited to believe. Those of us who are still alive will not easily be taken in by Aldington's glib and costive pen. Our faith in Lawrence is too great to be thus shaken, and we will not rest until the stigma of this foul indictment has been wiped from the slate.
>
> Aldington's book is so cleverly and plausibly contrived that many who had no first hand knowledge of Lawrence may give credence to a great deal that has been written.[13]

Gilman then proceeds to refute Aldington on specific matters of which he had firsthand knowledge, such as Lawrence's presence and courage in operations against the Hijaz railroad that Aldington had denied.

Gilman wrote me of his association with Lawrence: "It is the duty of a soldier to be courageous, or appear to be so, and Lawrence certainly had a super-abundance of that commodity! . . . I do not believe there was a man alive, at the time of the Arabian campaign, who could have taken on the job Lawrence so successfully and steadfastly accomplished. His knowledge of the country, the people, and their language had fully equipped him. He had no military training but seemed to be a natural exponent of guerrilla warfare, in which the Arabs excelled." Gilman concluded his letter with saying that he would never again read a book that would "sling mud at the honour and memory of one of the most gallant men in military history."[14]

Finally, there are the favorable assessments of C. S. Jarvis and St. John Philby. Though Jarvis did not serve in the Arab campaigns, he worked on the borders of the Hijaz for fourteen years as an Arab administrator, knew the Arabs of the desert well, studied the Arab Revolt, and has written a biography of his friend F. G. Peake ("Peake Pasha"), who served with Lawrence during the campaigns and was later head of the Arab Legion in Trans-Jordan. Jarvis has provided a detailed analysis of Lawrence's accomplishments in the Revolt.[15]

St. John Philby, an outstanding Arabist who spent forty years in Mesopotamia and Arabia, and was to disagree with Lawrence and struggle with him on several political fronts after the war, defended him eloquently from the attacks of his detractors and understood his central role in the campaigns.[16]

A German view of Lawrence has been provided by Franz von Papen. "The British can indeed count themselves fortunate," he wrote, "to have had the services of a man with such understanding and affection for the Islamic world. From the military point of view his activities were probably not of great importance, but politically and economically they were of priceless value."[17] During World War II the Germans attempted to follow Lawrence's tactics, including paying the tribesmen, in efforts to infiltrate the lands along the east coast of the Red Sea. But they were unsuccessful in securing the loyalty of the local population.[18]

The evaluation of Arab assessments of Lawrence, especially by one unfamiliar with the language and with many of the political and cultural forces involved, presents a number of problems. There is clearly no one "Arab view" of Lawrence. Rather, there are many Arab views, and to be fairly assessed each needs to be examined with an eye to the religion, nationality, political background and political beliefs of the Arab writer, exactly when he wrote his book or article, and the sources he used. It is especially important to find out whether he actually witnessed the events he describes (although an eyewitness account by no means guarantees an absence of distortion), and to determine any other influences on his objectivity or point of view. The same may be said about the assessment of Western views of Lawrence, although the directions of distortion and the reasons for it are easier for one trained in the same culture to determine.

Worthy of particular mention here is the understandable reluctance of committed Arab nationalists to credit a foreigner with the leadership of their own war of liberation — and with a leadership both heroic and successful at that. Their attitude came across clearly to me in my talks with residents in Amman and with the Bedouin of the Jordanian desert.[19] Even

King Abdullah of Trans-Jordan, though he acknowledges in his memoirs
Lawrence's influence among the Arabs of the desert tribes, is at the same
time resentful of it.[20] One young resident of Amman (not a Bedouin) told
me after an interview I had had with a Bedouin shaykh: "Shaykh
Muhammad [who had been too young at the time to take part in the
campaigns] said to me after [your] talk [with him]: 'Why would I want
any British foreigner like Lawrence leading me. I am an Arab. You are
an Arab. You would not want a foreigner leading you.' " My young companion did not tell me how he had answered Shaykh Muhammad, but
he told me his own view: "I would say yes, he helped me. I would never
say he was the leader. I would say I was."[21]

One must assume that Lawrence understood this aspect of Arab psychology in choosing to work through Faisal and the other Arab leaders.
The assumption was well substantiated in my interviews with the Bedouin
shaykhs. One Howeitat shakyh said to me: "Lawrence was like a servant
to our master Faisal. He used to teach us plans, but the war was carried
on by the brave Bedouins." Another said: "He was not a leader but a
guide (*dalil*)." From a third: "He was a servant of the Ashraf [the
sharifs]."[22] Another Howeitat shaykh, who did take an active part in the
Revolt, told me that he talks about the events of the Revolt and about
Lawrence with his children, but he does not tell them to be courageous
like Lawrence. Rather he says to them, "You should be like I was, strong
and courageous before Lawrence."[23]

From the political standpoint, Arab writers who are or might otherwise
be appreciative of Lawrence's service to the Arab peoples, deeply resent
his singleminded espousal of the sharifian cause, whereby Hashemite
governments were imposed on other Arabs, especially the Syrians. On
three occasions the sons of King Husayn were installed as rulers of other
Arab groups.

Anis Sayigh, a well-known Arab nationalist and journalist, is representative of these writers. He has described in his book on the Hashemite
leadership in the Arab Revolt the problems for Arab political unity that
have derived from Faisal's preponderance as a military leader during the
Revolt and from Faisal's willingness to rely on Lawrence for political
liaison among the Allies, while at the same time becoming the instrument
of Lawrence's personal dreams for the Arab peoples.[24]

'Abd al-Rahman Shahbandar, a Syrian nationalist who was assassinated
in 1940, wrote a series of articles in 1931, in which he attempted to evaluate Lawrence's role among the Arabs. Shahbandar met Lawrence in Cairo
in 1916 and was one of the "Syrian Seven" who approached British
authorities there in 1918. He warned against assessments of Lawrence
that merely served political propaganda purposes. "If you ask a hundred
of those who have struggled in the Arab Revolt and saw Lawrence on
the battleground 99% will say that he is only loyal to his nation," Shahbandar wrote in his first article of his series. "But the information I will

publish in my coming articles will cause most of my readers to think differently, because history is one thing and political propaganda which the newspapers compete in publishing is another thing."[25]

Most difficult to assess are the various Arab accounts of events that Lawrence has written of himself, especially in *Seven Pillars of Wisdom*. Suleiman Mousa, a Jordanian working in the Press and Information Department of Amman, published in 1966 the only full-length biography of Lawrence by an Arab writer. His book has been translated into English.[26] A strong supporter of Arab and other Muslim political positions, Mousa has set out to show that the Arab Revolt was predominantly an Arab affair and that Lawrence exaggerated his own part in it, which was a minor one, and gave insufficient credit to the Arab leaders and fighters. Mousa supports his theses by relating interviews with surviving participants of the Revolt who dispute Lawrence's statements regarding his services in planning the strategy, and even contest his claim to have been present in various journeys, battles and raids.

The most controversial of these journeys is the one into Syria of June 1917, which Lawrence reported in his letter to Clayton of July 10, 1917.[27] Mousa, on the basis of his investigations, has concluded that the story of the trip was entirely fabricated and that the journey never took place.[28] He has based much of his argument on the recollections forty years later of Nasib al-Bakri, a Syrian nationalist whom Lawrence described in his letter to Clayton as "volatile and shortsighted." Bakri claimed that Lawrence never left the base where they both were at the time the journey began. Arnold Lawrence has rebutted Mousa's account and has referred to independent confirmation by Antonius, who had details in his own account other than those of Lawrence's report. But Mousa asserts that Antonius must have relied on accounts by Lawrence, Robert Graves and Basil Liddell Hart.[29] Subhi al-'Umari, a young Syrian officer who joined the Arab armies in October 1917 (four months after the events in question), considers the trip impossible, that Lawrence could not have moved about so freely in the lands in question or reached the points he claimed he did because they were full of Ottoman forces. According to al-'Umari, only a foreigner with minimal knowledge of the country would believe Lawrence's story.[30] On the other hand, Anis Sayigh, a Palestinian, accepts the fact of the trip but turns its purposes against Lawrence. According to Sayigh, Lawrence traveled to Damascus and met its mayor, Ali Ridah al-Riqabi, in a suburb, but his purpose was to prevent an uprising of Syrian nationalists and thereby to delay an Arab victory.[31] His letter-report to Clayton indicates that the purpose of the journey was to determine the loyalties of various Syrians and tribal groups. After seeing it, Hogarth wrote Clayton: "The W.O. [War Office] is optimistic about Arabia and Syria, however, and much bucked by T.E.L.'s report and scheme"[32] — hardly what one would write about a plan of delay.

Lawrence's own war diaries, one of which contains a contemporary draft of the Clayton report, tend to support his account of the trip. The diaries are written in pencil, upside down, and are very difficult to decipher, but two colleagues of mine were able to make out the following words, using special lighting and magnification: "Clayton. I've decided to go off alone to Damascus, hoping to get killed on the way: for all sakes try and clear this show up before it goes further. We are calling them to fight for us on a lie, and I can't stand it."[33] Later in the account, according to Knightley and Simpson, Lawrence wrote, " '[I] learnt that Hachim was NE of Ragga [Rakka?] and Ibn Murshid in prison in Damascus and my plan thus failure. . . . I was able to get satisfactory assurances . . . in El Gabbu [Gaboun] . . . has been entrusted by the Turks with the defense of Damascus!' "[34] Lawrence has himself compounded the question of what ("if anything") occurred on this journey by his own incomplete treatment of it.

I find myself unable to reach any conclusion as to what actually happened, and am not sure that even with investigation by an impartial scholar familiar with the country and peoples in question could the matter be resolved. It should be noted, however, that for the accounts of the trip to have been fabricated, as Mousa and al-'Umari claim they were, Lawrence would have had to falsify not only detailed official reports but his penciled diaries as well, and have persuaded Clayton, Hogarth and Wingate of their truth (Wingate recommended Lawrence for the Victoria Cross on the basis of this journey). Furthermore, since the information in the report was evidently used by British intelligence afterwards in the campaigns, without disclosure of errors or misleading data in it, Lawrence certainly made the journey unless he was able to obtain a great deal of quite specific information from some other source.

My own Bedouin informants, who were active in the engagements along the Hijaz railroad and from Aqaba northward, attribute a major responsibility to Lawrence in planning, supplying and coordinating (not leading) the campaigns in contrast to the statements of al-'Umari and Mousa, which repeatedly disparage his role. Al-'Umari even dismisses Lawrence's function in teaching the use of explosives for demolition purposes. According to al-'Umari, demolition was an easy thing to do, readily mastered by the Arabs, which Lawrence purposely made sound difficult in his reports in order to claim credit for himself and make himself a hero. This contrasts sharply with what my Bedouin informants told me. One Howeitat tribesman, who fought in the campaigns along the railroad, told me spontaneously (I did not ask him about the demolitions): "He was the only one in charge of the explosions. He was the only one who knew the explosives and he used to go from one place to another and try to explode the trains and railways . . . he was an expert on trains, on mines. He used to plant the explosives, and then the Arabs used to shoot and kill the Turks."[35] Another tribesman told me, "He used to put in the dynamite himself because they were ignorant about this and did not know how to place it themselves."[36]

James D. Lunt, a British officer who served in the Jordanian desert, dined with a Howeitat shaykh at Bayir. This shaykh recalled, as had the Bedouin whom I had interviewed, that Lawrence was as tough as the toughest Bedouin, among the finest of camelmen, lived like a Bedouin, had an uncanny knowledge of the scandal of the desert which he used to good effect, and seemed to know all the wadis, wells and hills from Azraq to Aqaba.[37] At the conclusion of the evening Lunt's Bedouin host said to him of Lawrence, "Of all the men I have ever met he was the greatest Prince," and the Arab audience present signified their assent.[38] Ja'far al-'Askari, an Iraqi who commanded the Arab regular army and engaged in many activities during the campaign with Lawrence, spoke of him as the bravest man he had known.[39]

W. M. M. Hurley, an RAF officer with whom Lawrence later served, had had occasion in 1928 to travel in Trans-Jordan and meet Arabs there who had taken part in the campaigns. "I saw the places he had wrecked on the railway," Hurley wrote, "the areas where he had maintained his camps, and, above all, the people whom he had inspired to victory. On every side his name was still a legend: 'Aurens Bey' whom the older Sheikhs spoke about in awe and veneration, and whom the younger generation of the Bedouin accepted in their tradition as akin to deity."[40] Carl R. Raswan, who journeyed extensively among the Bedouin, wrote in 1935, "I have met many of his [Lawrence's] old companions and also enemies, and whether they loved or feared him, they all agree that 'Aurens' was the most sincere friend that ever came from Europe to take up the Arab cause, though most of them regretted that he did not have a chance to side with Ibn Saud."[41]

Sometimes the Arab accounts, even when more than one reporter was an eyewitness of the events being described, contradict one another. The events around Tafas in the last days before the capture of Damascus provide a case in point. Al-'Umari describes the atrocities at Tafas committed by the retreating Turks against the villagers and his own desire to take revenge against the Turkish prisoners, but he says that Nuri al-Sa'id and Ali Jawdat (who was in charge of the Arab forces) calmed him and no vengeance was taken.[42] Ali Jawdat, on the other hand, states in his own memoirs that he tried without success to control his soldiers and officers from avenging themselves for the massacre upon the Turkish prisoners.[43] Mousa cites a report from a former Ottoman officer denying that any killing of women and children took place at all.[44] For a Western writer such as myself to extract the truth from the self-serving distortions in all this is a difficult task indeed.

Nuri al Sa'id, one of the ablest of the Arab officers, an Iraqi who later served his country with distinction until his assassination in 1958, was warm in his praise of Lawrence and generous in his estimate of Lawrence's value to the Arab cause.[45] When Lawrence's abridged version of *Revolt in the Desert* appeared in 1927, Nuri reviewed it for the Baghdad *Times*. In his review he wrote: "It was possible for Lawrence to understand the Arabs at the first instance better than any other Britisher who worked for the Arab cause; and perhaps even now he surpasses all others in this knowledge. Without exception I remember Lawrence whenever we now encounter any difficulty, and ask myself whether we shall be again so fortunate as to have another friend of Lawrence's type." With regard to the accuracy of the book Nuri wrote, "Lawrence is thoroughly candid in his book, which is throughout accurate. If the book is lacking in any way, it is information to which the author had no opportunity of access."[46]

George Antonius was not a participant in the campaigns, but in his important history of the Revolt, looked at from an Arab perspective, he consulted Faisal, other members of the ruling family, and officers who took part in the war. He questions the accuracy of some of the statements of fact and interpretation in *Seven Pillars of Wisdom*, citing barriers of culture, language and temperament from which Lawrence suffered, but he is unequivocal in his acknowledgment of Lawrence's value in the service of the Arabs. "On more than one occasion in the years that followed the war," Antonius wrote, "have I heard the late King Faisal declare that, with the exception of Lawrence whose genius entitled him to a place of his own, the claims of Colonel S. F. Newcombe or of Major Joyce to Arab gratitude were not less strong than those of any other Englishman."[47]

Shahbandar has also written of Lawrence's value to the cause of Arab nationalism, and understood the limitations placed upon him, and the ambiguity of his position that resulted from the secret Anglo-French agreements. "Lawrence spent all possible energy to establish the strongest foothold for the Arabs to have full independence under their own flag," Shahbandar concluded in the fourth and last article of his series, "but what use was there when the British had understandings with their allies, the French, which tore apart any possibility of full independence."[48]

In summary, there remains a need for an objective analysis by a scholar familiar with both the Western and Arab cultures of Lawrence's part in the Arab Revolt from both the military and political standpoint. My own view — which I in no way claim to hold in freedom from the cultural biases that have been described — is that Lawrence's role in the Arab Revolt was an extraordinary one. Although there may have been distortions and exaggerations in Lawrence's accounts of the Revolt, especially the romanticization in *Seven Pillars of Wisdom*, these are not so great as some Western and Arab denigrators have claimed. His basic description of the development, leadership and course of the Revolt, and of his own participation in it, are much as he described. My assessment of the evidence largely bears up the prediction Lawrence made to Robert Graves in 1927: "All the documents of the Arab Revolt are in the archives of the Foreign Office, and will soon be available to students [not for almost forty years] who will be able to cross-check my yarns. I expect them to find small errors, and to agree generally with the main current of my narrative."[49]

Without in any way reducing the value of what other Allied officers, British and French, accomplished in the Revolt, or detracting from the heroic efforts of the Arabs in their own behalf, the evidence, taken all together, supports the view that Lawrence was predominant in organizing, coordinating and shaping the Revolt, in conceiving its possibilities, in obtaining effective British support for it, and in transforming the raw energies of Arab frustration and idealism into an effective guerrilla movement of national liberation.

Nor is the charge that he claimed credit for himself while denying the important role of his British and Arab colleagues accurate, although he could be biting in his criticism of those who disappointed or betrayed him. In the introductory paragraphs of *Seven Pillars of Wisdom* Lawrence tried to explain why the book takes on such a self-centered cast. With his characteristic false modesty (false not because it was not genuine but because it gave a false picture of reality) Lawrence downplayed his own role and elevated that of others: "Then there is the question of my British colleagues. This isolated picture throwing the main light upon myself, is unfair to them. Especially I am most sorry that I have not told what the non-commissioned with us did. They were inarticulate, but wonderful, although without the motive, the imaginative vision of the end, which sustained their officers. Unfortunately my concern was limited to this end, and the book just a designed procession of Arab freedom from Mecca to Damascus. It was intended to rationalize the campaign, that everyone might see how natural the success was, and how inevitable, how little dependent on direction or brain, how much less on the outside assistance of the few British. *It was an Arab war, waged and led by Arabs, for an Arab aim, in Arabia* [italics added].

"My proper share was a minor one, but because of a fluent pen, a free speech, and a certain adroitness of brain, I took upon myself, as I describe it, a mock primacy. By the accidental judgment of a publicist who visited us in the field, this mock primacy was published abroad as truth. In reality I held a subordinate official place. I never held any office among the Arabs; was never in charge of the British mission with them."[50]

As will be discussed later, the most serious limitation of Lawrence's effort grew out of his fantasy of the shape of the Arab world, a conception that derived as much from the need to fulfill a dream of his own as it did from the political and national actualities he found in Arabia and Syria.

This romantic fantasy of a pure race of Bedouin — God's original children living closer to Him than other human beings, closer surely than the overcivilized English — whom he would enable amirs of Mecca to lead to a new tomorrow began to take shape in the early years of the war.

The dream grew, as we shall see, out of deep personal roots. Because of the power of his drive and the scope of his talents, he was able to impose it for a time upon the Allies and the Arabs alike. From his standpoint it was shattered with deeply disturbing consequences by the events of the war. The results of his capacity to live it out still persist in the Middle East, but some of the most important constructive forces for change in that troubled region are linked to Lawrence's dream if, indeed, they do not grow out of it.

# 15

# The Question of Motivation

A decade after the desert campaigns were over, Lawrence wrote Robert Graves: "During the Revolt I had a motive, within me, for activity, and therefore became capable of imposing my will on others. The very accident that normally I am empty of motive, helped make the rare motive, when it finally came, overpowering."[1] With this statement Lawrence draws our attention from the activity itself to the motive behind it.

A discussion of someone's motivation in relation to events in which he has taken some vital part implies the possibility of choice: that he was not simply performing actions required by a situation he had no part in creating, or to which he was drawn by circumstances beyond his control. The more effectively a person like Lawrence can impose his will upon events, shape their course or influence their outcome, the stronger our fascination with the psychology of his motivation becomes — even stronger if these events have a sufficiently sharp impact and continue to affect our own lives. For we recognize then among the determinants affecting the course of history — and ourselves with it — the internal drives and purposes of an unusual person. We wish to understand him, to learn why he chose the directions he did.

On the other hand, no person's life conforms to a grand design. It is a popular pastime for readers as well as biographers to discern in the childhood or adolescence of a great man the antecedents of his later choices and actions, especially since Freudian psychology has called so forcefully to our attention the early motivational roots of so much later behavior. A great man himself is no less guilty of this retrospective harmonizing of the past and the present than the rest of us, as he looks back upon his life and tries to make intelligible to his followers and to himself the turns he took and the choices he made.

But the reality is more complex. Personal drive and need are influenced throughout the course of one's life by the shifting actualities of the human and nonhuman environment, and their outlet and expression must conform with or be adapted to a great variety of what, for lack of a better expression, is called historical circumstances. In fact, the "historical figure" may be defined as one who is uniquely able to adapt his internal drives, capabilities and personal conflicts to historical situations and to the opportunities he discerns, or with which he is confronted. To the extent to which he uses these characteristics to fulfill the political or other purposes of a government or a people — as Lawrence did with Whitehall and the Arab leaders — the historical figure or leader is himself "chosen" by his times.

Finally, when one considers motivation one must recognize its multiple dimensions and levels. On the surface, motivation is usually highly practical and relates simply to influencing or conforming to an immediate set of circumstances or realities. Motivation of this kind, dictated as it is by the exigencies of day-to-day reality, is readily discerned by the observer, who does not require that the subject let him in on his purposes. Between this level and the deepest or "ultimate" levels of motive and need in the dark recesses of the soul are various strata of motivation deriving from different psychological levels of consciousness and periods of development, which find outward expression in the multiple confluences of private purpose and public opportunity.

Lawrence's importance as a historical figure derives from his ability to impose his will not only through actions and decisions of his own, but through his unusual capacity to influence his superiors — men like Allenby and later Churchill — to act in directions of his choice. "Allenby, Winston, Trenchard. I have a fine taste in chiefs," Lawrence wrote to another British officer many years later.[2]

But beyond his work through such men as these Lawrence gains importance as a historical figure by virtue of his introspective nature and gifts of psychological perceptiveness regarding the motivation of himself and others. He teaches us what "a person like Lawrence" is like, insofar as it is possible to generalize from his psychological characteristics to those of others who live out their inner fantasies and conflicts in the public domain. The extraordinary consciousness of self that is most evident in *Seven Pillars of Wisdom,* in letters to Charlotte Shaw, Lionel Curtis and others, and in *The Mint* (his book about his experiences in the RAF) was not so evident before the war.

Lawrence was particularly aware of the multiple levels of his motivation, and taught us to expect to find a number of motivational levels in any leader, rather than to conclude that he or anyone else is likely to be motivated by one purpose alone. I believe the efforts of Lawrence's biographers to find *the* definitive motive for important periods of his life, such as the years of his participation in the Arab Revolt, to be in error.

Lawrence retained, as is well known, the child's pleasure in teasing and in making riddles — for example, in the merry chase he has led his biographers regarding the identity of "S.A.," the object of his dedicatory poem in *Seven Pillars of Wisdom*. Like Rumpelstiltskin he provoked interest in his own identity and piqued his audience with clues, but at the same time he seemed to dread their really "finding" him. Yet his psychological torment and his need to live out private conflict in public action or, after abandoning action, in writings that would find their way to public scrutiny, have made it possible for us to learn about the internal sources of his actions.

There are two summary statements by Lawrence, both written during 1919, of his motivation in pursuing what he called "the Arab affair." The first is a letter to a British Foreign Office staff member, written probably in November 1919; the second appears in the epilogue to *Seven Pillars of Wisdom*. In both expositions Lawrence refers to motives of personal caring, patriotism, curiosity and ambition, ranged in that order. This ranking reflects more accurately, in my opinion, Lawrence's estimate of the worthiness of these motives, or their relative freedom from conflict, than it does their actual order of strength or depth. The Foreign Office letter (I) and the epilogue (II) are reproduced here for comparison:

I

Dear ——,

You asked me "Why" today, and I'm going to tell you exactly what my motives in the Arab affair were, in order of strength: —

(i). Personal. I liked a particular Arab very much, and I thought that freedom for the race would be an acceptable present.

(ii.) Patriotic. I wanted to help win the war, and Arab help reduced Allenby's losses by thousands.

(iii). Intellectual curiosity. I wanted to feel what it was like to be the mainspring of a national movement, and to have some millions of people expressing themselves through me: and being a half-poet, I don't value material things much. Sensation and mind seem to me much greater, and the ideal, such a thing as the impulse that took us into Damascus, the only thing worth doing.

(iv). Ambition. You know how Lionel Curtis has made his conception of the Empire — a Commonwealth of free peoples — generally accepted. I wanted to widen that idea beyond the Anglo-Saxon shape, and to form a new nation of thinking people, all acclaiming our freedom, and demanding admittance into our Empire. There is, to my eyes, no other road for Egypt and India in the end, and I would have made their path easier, by creating an Arab Dominion in the Empire.

I don't think there are any other reasons. You are sufficiently Scotch to understand my analysing my own mind so formally. The process intended was to take Damascus, and run it (as anyone fully knowing the East and West could run it), as an independent ally of G.-B. Then to turn on Hejaz and conquer it: then to project the semi-educated Syrians on Yemen, and build that up quickly (without Yemen there is no re-birth for the Arabs) and finally to receive Mesopotamia into the block so made: all this could be done in thirty years directed effort, and without impairing British holdings. It is only the substitution of a 999 years' lease for a complete sale.

Now look what happened when we took Damascus: —

Motive (i). I found had died some weeks before: so my gift was wasted, and my future doings indifferent on that account.

Motive (ii). This was achieved, for Turkey was broken, and the central powers were so united that to break one broke all.

Motive (iii). This was romantic mainly, and one never repeats a sensation. When I rode into Damascus the whole country-side was on fire with enthusiasm, and in the town a hundred thousand people shouted my name. Success always kills hope by surfeit.

Motive (iv). This remained, but it was not strong enough to make me stay. I asked Allenby for leave, and when he gave it me, came straight home. It's the dying remains of this weakest of all my reasons which made me put up a half-fight for Feisal in Paris and elsewhere, and which occasionally drives me into your room to jest about what might be done.

If you want to make me work again you would have to recreate motives ii and iii. As you are not God, Motive i is beyond your power.

I'm not conscious of having done a crooked thing to anyone since I began to push the Arab movement, though I prostituted myself in Arab Service. For an Englishman to put himself at the disposal of a red race is to sell himself to a brute, like Swift's Houhynyms. However my body and soul were my own, and no one can reproach me for what I do to them: and to all the rest of you I'm clean.

When you have got as far as this, please burn it all. I've never told anyone before, and may not again, because it isn't nice to open oneself out. I laugh at myself because my giving up has made me look so futile.[3]

## II

Needless to say, when the Arab thrust northward from Hejaz began, Damascus was not my ultimate end: but by the time it was taken most of my springs of action were exhausted, and so I withdrew myself. Throughout my strongest motive had been a personal one, omitted from the body of the book, but not absent, I think, from my mind, waking or sleeping, for an hour in all those years. Active pains and joys flung themselves up during my days, like towers: but always, refluent as air, this persisting, hidden urge re-formed and became a very element of life: till near the end. It was dead before we reached the town.

Next in order had been the superficial, but powerful, motive, of a wish to win the war, with the conviction that we must have Arab help if we were to win the Eastern war, at a price we could afford. Throughout I tried to make the hurt of so exploiting the blood and hope of another people as small in degree as it seemed necessary in kind. When Damascus fell the Turkish war, and probably the German, was decided: and so this motive also died.

Then I was moved by intellectual curiosity, by the desire to feel myself the inspiration of a national movement, thrilling with the ideals and efforts of all a race. From this cup I drank as deeply as any man should do, when we took Damascus: and was sated with it. More would have set in me the vice of authority and smirched my hope, clean as I felt it, to create some lively thing of black marks on white paper. For three days I was arbitrary: and by use that motive died.

There was left to me ambition, the wish to quicken history in the East, as the great adventurers of old had done. I fancied to sum up in my own life that new Asia which inexorable time was slowly bringing upon us. The Arabs made a *chivalrous* [italics added] appeal to my young instinct, and when still at the High School in Oxford already I thought to remake them into a nation, client and fellow of the British Empire.

The necessary Turkish elements to re-shape Anatolia were ready to my hand, could be grasped before the allies saw the hollowness of their victory while they were still made generous by the German army in Flanders. A strong Syria might dominate Mecca, Yemen was not difficult, and then the centre of gravity would have shifted eastward, and Bagdad been ceded to me gracefully.

However, this remained a dream, because of the insubstantiality of abstract ambition by itself as a sole motive: and is here written only for men to call fantastic. It was a fantasy, to believe that an illiterate spirit of nationality, without authority, without a city, or a ship, or a rifle, or a leader of its own could meet Turkey in arms and wrest away its old capital. They gave me the orts and objects of our fighting materials for my share. I studied them to the best of my ability, and used them as far as I could make them go, in a fashion neither dull nor negligent. After such training, with material resources to reinforce the spiritual, the little rest of my ambition might have been not difficult.[4]

The "personal" motive, the "particular Arab" almost certainly refers to Dahoum, whose personality, as was previously mentioned, furnished the most important component for the "S.A." poem. It was Dahoum for whose freedom Lawrence struggled during the war — "To earn you Freedom, the seven pillared worthy house, that your eyes might be shining for me when we came," he wrote in the dedicatory poem.[5] But Dahoum, as we have seen, died of typhus in 1918 before the war ended.[6] That Dahoum was an inspiration to Lawrence during the war, and is included in the dedication of his postwar narrative, is understandable. It is, however, characteristic of Lawrence that he creates a puzzle and invites his potential audience to try to solve it, thus making public once again a matter of private feeling. It is likely that the intensity of feelings expressed in relation to Dahoum is displaced in part from Will, of whom Lawrence was very fond. There is hardly a mention of Will in Lawrence's writings and letters after Will's death in 1915.

Concerning Lawrence's patriotism there is very little to add. He devoted himself wholeheartedly to the Allied cause, utilizing Arab help, and, as Arnold Lawrence has written, "anaesthetized his emotions and turned himself into an instrument of victory."[7] Lawrence has been seen by some of his detractors as working solely for British interests and motivated principally by British imperialism. It is a view I do not share and find difficult to understand.

The motives of "intellectual curiosity" and "ambition" are so closely related that I shall treat them together. The distinction he seems to be making here is between taking himself, and the extent and limits of his capabilities, as the object to be explored ("intellectual curiosity") and working toward the evolution of a political design for the Middle East ("ambition"). But these aims are so intertwined, and derive from sources of energy within Lawrence that are so closely interrelated, as not to admit of separate treatment.

We have seen in earlier chapters that Lawrence's choice of the Arabs as the national movement he would choose to "hustle into form" was to some degree fortuitous, even though his dream of "freeing" them dated back to his childhood (by "freeing" he seems to have meant inclusion in the British Empire).[8] Through the preparations of his earlier years in the Middle East, his maneuvering himself into Cairo at the appropriate time at the beginning of World War I, and the initiatives he took there in 1916 to bring himself from Egypt into Arabia, he turned a historical opportunity into an actuality.

In the early chapters of *Seven Pillars of Wisdom* Lawrence reveals a fantasy of himself as a kind of contemporary armed prophet, the most recent in the history of prophets, inspired in the desert, who had been spiritual and military leaders of the Semitic peoples since the beginning of recorded history. The Arabs of the desert, he writes, were "incorrigibly children of the idea" and "could be swung on an idea as on a cord; for the unpledged allegiance of their minds" (and by implication their susceptibility to the development of an allegiance with one, such as Lawrence, who would choose and be able to lead them and to "arrange their minds") made them "obedient servants."⁹ The awesome scope and form of this prophet fantasy does not seem to have become fully apparent to Lawrence until after the campaigns were over and he turned to writing his narrative. However, the shape of his continuing ambition, the quickening "root of authority," and his power to convert fantasy into reality clearly evoked fear in Lawrence and played a part in his personal retreat after the war.

In the introductory chapter of the 1922 (Oxford) edition of *Seven Pillars of Wisdom* Lawrence made the most definitive statement of his historical dream and his anxiety about it:

"This, therefore, is a faded dream of the time when I went down into the dust and noise of the Eastern market-place, and with my brain and muscles, with sweat and constant thinking, made others see my visions coming true. Those who dream by night in the dusty recesses of their minds wake in the day to find that all was vanity; but the dreamers of the day are dangerous men, for they may act their dream with open eyes, and make it possible. This I did. I meant to make a new nation, to restore to the world a lost influence, to give twenty millions of Semites the foundation on which to build an inspired dream-palace of their national thoughts. So high an aim called out the inherent nobility of their minds, and made them play a generous part in events; but when we won, it was charged against me that the British petrol royalties in Mesopotamia were becoming dubious, and French policy ruined in the Levant. I am afraid that I hope so. We pay for these things too much in honour and innocent lives."¹⁰

Lawrence wrote in *Seven Pillars of Wisdom* that as he approached his thirtieth birthday (August 15, 1918) he looked back upon medieval-Napoleonic fantasies of glory and achievement that he had previously entertained: "It came to me queerly how, four years ago, I had meant to be a general and knighted, when thirty." But his intensely self-critical nature rejected what he called "crude ambition" and his "detached self" eyed "the performance in the wings in criticism." The favorable opinion he was receiving of his successes made Lawrence anxious and he sought to dissect and examine his motives, to be truthful with himself. "Here were the Arabs believing me, Allenby and Clayton trusting me, my bodyguard dying for me," Lawrence observed, and felt that the good reputation was due to his acting, to a "craving for good repute among men," and to fraud. He asked himself whether "all good reputations were founded, like mine, on fraud." He observed how his "self-distrusting shyness held a mask, often a mask of indifference or flippancy, before my face, and puzzled me.¹¹

But Lawrence recognized behind this a powerful, egoistic, aggressive drive for fame and ambition (he called it his "egoistic curiosity"), whose proportions frightened him and which he ultimately rejected. He knew that his studied indifference "was only a mask; because despite my trying never to dwell on what was interesting, there were moments too strong for control when my appetite burst out and frightened me."[12] A few paragraphs later he wrote: "Self-seeking ambitions visited me, but not to stay, since my critical self would make me fastidiously reject their fruits. Always I grew to dominate those things into which I had drifted, but in none of them did I voluntarily engage. Indeed, I saw myself a danger to ordinary men, with such capacity yawing rudderless at their disposal."[13]

For Lawrence there seemed to be some conflict over all strong passions, as if he distrusted powerful feelings of any kind. His insight into this quality in himself was unusual. "I was very conscious of the bundled powers and entities within me," he wrote; "it was their character which hid. There was my craving to be liked — so strong and nervous that never could I open myself friendly to another. The terror of failure in an effort so important made me shrink from trying; besides, there was the standard; for intimacy seemed shameful unless the other could make the perfect reply, in the same language, after the same method, for the same reasons.

"There was a craving to be famous; and a horror of being known to like being known. Contempt for my passion for distinction made me refuse every offered honour."[14]

Anis Sayigh, a Lebanese of Palestinian origins and a well-known Arab nationalist writer, has written a perceptive analysis in Arabic of Lawrence's prophet fantasy and role among the Arab peoples.[15] Sayigh sees Lawrence as being in the tradition of Englishmen who had for three centuries exercised in the Middle East "a prophethood directed toward humanitarian aims." But Lawrence's prophethood, according to Sayigh, was not a religious one, for he was not religious and his age was more complex. The call to prophethood of previous ages would not have been appropriate in the early part of the twentieth century. Lawrence's mission, as Sayigh understands it, was one of reconciling the aims of Arab nationalism, which he supported, with the mission of Britain in the Middle East, as he tried to influence it, and each had responsibilities to the other. Lawrence "wished to save the Arab world from Turkish occupation and the greed of the French, Germans and Russians and to give the Arabs a place in the family of liberated nations."[16] Lawrence, in Sayigh's view, saw Britain as having a special mission or responsibility in the underdeveloped world, and he in turn had the responsibility for defining Britain's mission, fixing its boundaries, and supervising it.

Sayigh stresses also Lawrence's belief that in return the Arabs would, in the psychological sense, liberate the Western mind. "His mission was to protect the alliance between the British and the Arabs, so the British would liberate the Arabs through better arms and international power, from the Turks and the Europeans," Sayigh wrote, while "the Arab psyche of absolute individualism would liberate British mentality from the precipitates of the Victorian age." Lawrence, Sayigh concluded, "gave Britain the right of trusteeship over the East as he gave himself the trusteeship over the two."[17]

Sayigh, in my opinion, answers effectively the question of whether Lawrence's "real" motive was to serve the British or the Arabs during the campaigns. Clearly, in this Arab view he was trying to reconcile the complex and often conflicting aims of both. His intolerant conscience occasioned him much suffering over the limitations of the success of his efforts. Writings about Lawrence abound with discussions of whether he "really cared" about the Arabs. It is clear that the Arab peoples played a part in the fulfillment of vast dreams and historical fantasies on Lawrence's part and in this sense he "used" them. On the other hand there is no inherent contradiction between this larger purpose of personal ambition and caring at a personal level. It is the kind of discourse which often fails to be effectively joined because it is carried on at different levels.

Lawrence's older brother spoke with me about Lawrence's affection for individual Arabs and of his distress over the deaths of his young friends Da'ud and Farraj, and the pain he experienced over the atrocities, other deaths and various hardships suffered by the Arabs in the desert.[18] In most of his writings on the campaigns, Lawrence does not dwell on this "sentimental" aspect of himself (although I believe his feelings are only too apparent in *Seven Pillars*), but stressed instead his interests in and views of strategy and the international politics of the Middle East.

In his letter to the Foreign Office staff member, Lawrence wrote, "I don't think there are any other reasons," and he would perhaps have been irritated at efforts to look beyond the "reasons" to which he has given direct testimony. But the highly personal nature of his endeavor in the Middle East, its seeming emergence out of the intense energies of a private purpose, invite our search for some motive in Lawrence's character and personal development that lay outside British policy and Arab need, some driving force within himself. Elie Kedourie recognized this and noted that "the violently personal terms" in which Lawrence would speak "of the public and far-reaching events in which he had been involved" could not be accounted for by "the events in which he happened, quite by chance [not quite] to be mixed up."[19] Rather, wrote Kedourie, "the answer must be sought in his agitated and forceful personality." Kedourie does not inquire further what this answer might be.

A biographer needs to exercise special caution as he approaches the question of deeper personal motives, those inner drives which the subject tries to mold to the opportunities and requirements of external reality.

This is no less true of Lawrence. For even though his introspective nature, his need to wash his mental linen in writings that would inevitably become public, gives us more opportunity than is usually available when studying historical figures to gain insight into the psychological roots of significant actions, direct evidence for interpretations, even in his case, is nevertheless limited. Only inferences that are no more than likelihoods can be drawn.

The pivotal concept linking Lawrence's passionate pursuit of his "mission" in the Arab cause with his background and personal development lies, in my opinion, in the idea of redemption. Arnold Lawrence understood well his mother's hope that her sons would redeem her guilt. With the deaths during the war of Frank and Will, the burden fell upon T.E., and we have seen how urgently he felt the need to become more active in the campaigns after they died. His reference in *Seven Pillars of Wisdom* to the Germans in Syria as "the enemy who had killed my brothers" suggests this personal element.[20]

The language of renunciation and redemption pervades *Seven Pillars of Wisdom*. Lawrence saw the Arabs of the desert as exemplifying the ideal of renouncing the desires of the world, and his identification with this element he saw (or wished to see) in them played an important part in the structure of the private fantasy by which he was propelled during the campaigns. "The common base of all the Semitic creeds, winners or losers, was the ever present ideal of world-worthlessness," Lawrence wrote in *Seven Pillars*. "Their profound reaction from matter led them to preach bareness, renunciation, poverty; and the atmosphere of this invention stifled the minds of the desert pitilessly."[21] Or: "The desert Arab found no joy like the joy of voluntarily holding back. He found luxury in abnegation, renunciation, self-restraint. . . . His desert was made a spiritual ice-house, in which was preserved intact but unimproved for all ages a vision of the unity of God."[22]

The Arabs were idealized as his own ancestors were devalued. He wrote of the "fine-drawn Arabs whom generations of in-breeding had sharpened to a radiance ages older than the primitive, blotched, honest Englishmen."[23] But the Arabs were a subject people, held in bondage by the Turks, fallen from the former prosperous state of their civilization. In fitting his image of the Arab condition to the outlines of his personal dream, Lawrence condensed time and smoothed out the irregularities of historical fact and detail. "With the coming of the Turks," he wrote "[Arab] happiness became a dream. By stages the Semites of Asia passed under their yoke, and found it a slow death. Their goods were stripped from them; and their spirits shrivelled in the numbing breath of a military Government."[24]

The struggle to create and redeem runs throughout *Seven Pillars of Wisdom*, and Lawrence's personal identification with the Arabs is striking. His redemption and theirs are so intertwined as to be indistinguishable, and he became fully aware that he had attempted to achieve the former through the latter. He would sacrifice himself on behalf of the Arabs and redeem thereby the lowly state (as he perceived it) of both. But the profound egoist root of this self-sacrifice could not escape his ruthless self-examination. It confirmed his belief in his deceitfulness, his illegitimacy, and deepened the sense of sin and guilt, lowering his self-regard still further. "To endure for another in simplicity gave a sense of greatness," Lawrence wrote. "There was nothing loftier than a cross, from which to contemplate the world. The pride and exhilaration of it were beyond conceit. Yet each cross, occupied, robbed the late-comers of all but the poor part of copying: and the meanest of things were those done by example. The virtue of sacrifice lay within the victim's soul.

"Honest redemption must have been free and child-minded. When the expiator was conscious of the under-motives and the after-glory of his act, both were wasted on him. So the introspective altruist appropriated a share worthless, indeed harmful, to himself, for had he remained passive, his cross might have been granted to an innocent. To rescue simple ones from such evil by paying for them his complicated self would be avaricious in the modern man. . . . Complex men who knew how self-sacrifice uplifted the redeemer and cast down the bought, and who held back in his knowledge, might so let a foolish brother take the place of false nobility and its later awakened due of heavier sentence. There seemed no straight walking for us leaders in this crooked lane of conduct, ring within ring of unknown, shamefaced motives cancelling or double-charging their precedents."[25]

To the political deceit of the Revolt was added for Lawrence what he considered the psychological deceit of using another people's need vicariously for personal redemption. No external success or approval as judged in the eyes of the world could affect the inner condemnation of this crime. "The hearing other people praised made me despair jealously of myself, for I took it at its face value; whereas, had they spoken ten times as well of me, I would have discounted it to nothing. I was a standing court martial on myself, inevitably, because to me the inner springs of action were bare with the knowledge of exploited chance."[26]

# 16

# Lawrence the Enabler

All my experience of the Arabs was of the God-father role," Lawrence wrote to Mrs. Shaw. "My object . . . was always to make them stand on their own feet."[1]

To enable another to do for himself what he cannot do without your help presents not only practical and psychological difficulties but raises inevitably a number of moral questions as well. This "enabling" is an essential aspect of such diverse human pursuits as child-rearing, psychotherapy and organizational leadership. It becomes the central dimension of action should a person attempt, as Lawrence did, to reach across cultures to help another people achieve a revolution that it could not accomplish without an outsider's help. No matter how much the helper attempts to identify with the ideals and purposes of another group or people, and works in the service of *its* values and needs, it is doubtful whether he can keep completely separate his own idea of what the others ought to have, or ought to want, or avoid influencing them to dream his dreams. Thus, depending upon the effectiveness of his influence or the scope of his powers, the helper inevitably becomes a kind of aggressor, imposing upon the recipients of his aid his own ideas and needs. When one nation helps another, the imposition is largely political or economic, the serving of national interest in concert with or at the expense of another's. When one person who, because of exceptional abilities brought to focus on an unusual historical situation, has a chance to assume a powerful personal role, the opportunities for him to live out his personal needs and impulses in the service of those he is helping are very great indeed.

Lawrence understood this dilemma profoundly. It lay at the heart of his conflicts regarding what he considered his exploitative role among the Arabs, the mutual prostitution he felt he had been a part of. He tried desperately to exploit no one, to serve the Arabs in the terms of *their* needs, the Allies in terms of *theirs,* and to fulfill at the same time a progressive and humanitarian vision of the progress of history. I believe that within the constraints of the situation he succeeded as well as anyone could have. But Lawrence was also serving his own psychological needs and trying to resolve profound personal conflicts. Ultimately, the shadow of these conflicts, aggravated by the actualities and traumata of the war experience, especially the conflicts that grew out of his need to identify so deeply and thoroughly with the people he was helping, came to dominate his view of himself as the Arabs' leader.

His judgment of what he had accomplished among the Arabs, accurate in a personal psychological sense, often excluded from his feelings any balancing appreciation of the good he had accomplished in the service of Arab ideals and freedom. "A man who gives himself to be a possession of aliens," he wrote early in *Seven Pillars of Wisdom,* "leads a Yahoo life, having bartered his soul to a brute-master. He is not of them. He may stand against them, persuade himself of a mission, batter and twist them into something which they, of their own accord, would not have been. Then he is exploiting his old environment to press them out of theirs. Or, after my model, he may imitate them so well that they spuriously imitate him back again. Then he is giving away his own environment: pretending to theirs; and pretences are hollow, worthless things."[2] The very uncertainty or instability that characterized Lawrence's sense of his own identity operated as an asset in relation to his work with the Arabs. It furnished him with a flexibility that enabled him to shift back and forth between an identification with the Arab world and Arab ways and his role as a British officer (although a rather scruffy one).

It could be argued with justification that no one asked Lawrence to get so involved in the Arab Revolt and assume such thorough responsibility for its conduct and progress that he would have to "barter his soul." But once having taken the responsibility upon himself he did not have the benefit of the personal distance from the agonies of death and mutilation that is the prerogative of most commanders and strategists in modern warfare. Lawrence was simultaneously a commanding strategist of the Revolt, and in the thick of its bloody encounters. In a letter to his friend Richards, written during the last year of the war, he suggests the admixture of pain and pleasure his unique role brought him: "My bodyguard of fifty Arab tribesmen, picked riders from the young men of the deserts, are more splendid than a tulip garden, and we ride like lunatics and with our Bedouins pounce on unsuspecting Turks and destroy them in heaps: and it is all very gory and nasty after we close grips. I love the preparation, and the journey, and loathe the physical fighting."[3]

Lawrence possessed an impressive array of talents and qualifications which suited him well for his work in the Revolt. These included a remarkable memory, intellectual brilliance, flexibility and vision, unusual physical stamina, and great personal courage. In addition he was well schooled during his previous years at Carchemish, and his travels in Syria, in the characteristics of the lands and peoples with whom he would have to deal, and he had read extensively about the history and science of war. But his most important qualities were psychological, the capacity, above all, to identify with the feelings, hopes, fears, ideals and way of life of another people so different from himself, and to draw them, in turn, into an identification with him.

Lawrence the scholar was very much in evidence when he was planning the tactics of the campaigns. "I was not an instinctive soldier, automatic with intuitions and happy ideas," he wrote Liddell Hart, "and when I took a decision, or adopted an alternative, it was after studying (doing my best to study) every relevant — and many an irrelevant — factor. Geography, tribal structure, religion, social customs, language, appetites, standards — all were at my finger-ends. The enemy I knew almost like my own side.[4] I risked myself among them a hundred times, to learn."[5] On reading the typescript of this passage, which Liddell Hart wished to use in his biography, Lawrence thought it might sound boastful. He made the substitution I have put in parentheses and deleted the word "all." But beyond all this, the integration of a successful Arab guerrilla campaign — combining operations of raids on camelback, in armored cars, and eventually in airplanes, with more traditional movements of regular forces — was an art, which the British recognized in giving Lawrence so much latitude.

Lieutenant-Colonel W. F. Stirling, who was with Lawrence during much of 1918, has provided a valuable firsthand picture of the courage, endurance and psychological gifts which enabled Lawrence to work successfully with the Arabs. The following paragraphs are from an article written by Stirling and published before Lawrence's death:

> What was it that enabled Lawrence to seize and hold the imagination of the Arabs? . . . The answer may partly be that he represented the heart of the Arab movement for freedom, and the Arabs realized that he had vitalized their cause; that he could do everything and endure everything just a little better than the Arabs themselves. . . . The Emir Feisal treated him as a brother, as an equal. . . . But chiefly, I think we must look for the answer in Lawrence's uncanny ability to sense the feelings of any group of men in whose company he found himself; his power to probe behind their minds and to uncover the well springs of their actions.
>
> His powers of endurance, too, were phenomenal. Few of even the most hard-bitten Arabs would ride with him from choice.* He never tired. Hunger, thirst and lack of sleep appeared to have little effect on him. He had broken

---

* Apparently this was not true of the more competitive shaykhs. See paragraph 3 of Joyce's remarks quoted below.

all the records of the dispatch riders of the Caliph Haroun al Raschid which had been sung for centuries in the tribal sagas. On one occasion he rode his camel three hundred miles in three consecutive days [no one ever seems to comment on the camel's endurance]. I once rode with mine fifty miles at a stretch, and that was enough for me. . . . His spiritual equipment overrode the ordinary needs of flesh and blood.[6]

The most valuable eyewitness view of Lawrence during the campaigns and at work among the Arabs has been provided by Colonel Pierce Joyce, an Irishman and Lawrence's immediate superior during most of the Revolt. Unlike many of the officers who served in the campaigns, Joyce has never published his memoirs or written an essay about the war or about Lawrence. His accounts are contained in the unpublished transcripts of two BBC broadcasts he made in April 1939 and July 1941 respectively. He spoke as follows:

On a matter of principle Lawrence never trusted Regular officers in general. He considered them limited in imagination, and insufficiently elastic to withstand the shocks of Arab strategy and tactics. . . . On my part I was suspicious of a Lieutenant with no executive command but with a definite political significance and therefore from my point of view entirely to be mistrusted.

Happily this initial setback eventually turned into a great personal friendship which survived many subsequent differences of opinion of how Regular troops should be utilised. The almost impossible tasks initiated in his fertile brain would have shocked the leaders of a Spanish Inquisition, and we had only quite ordinary and unimaginative personnel with which to carry them out. "It is all such sport," he used to say, and certainly his enthusiasm must have been infectious, for the hours of sport were few and the days and months of dust and sun were long and weary. On this occasion his appearance was such a contrast to the untidy Lieutenant I had met at Port Sudan that one suddenly became aware of contact with a very unusual personality. . . . At this, as at dozens of other conferences we attended together, Lawrence rarely spoke. He merely studied the men around him and when the arguments ended as they usually did, in smoke, he then dictated his plan of action which was usually adopted and everyone went away satisfied. It was not, as is often supposed, by his individual leadership of hordes of Bedouins that he achieved success in his daring ventures, but by the wise selection of tribal leaders and by providing the essential grist to the mill in the shape of golden rewards for work well done.

His individual bravery and endurance captured their imagination. Initial successes made "Orance," as the Arabs called him, a byword in the desert and there was always competition among the sheiks to ride with him on a foray. Like the rest of us he had many disappointments, but nothing could shake his determination to win through, or his restless energy in initiating alternative plans when things went wrong. . . . Lawrence and I used to do many desert trips on reconnaissance work, in the famous Rolls Royce Tender

which he christened "The Blue Mist." The desert leagues became furlongs.
. . . Lawrence invariably sat beside the driver indicating the direction with
his hand and with an open throttle we tore across sand dunes and ridges under his almost uncanny guidance [a number of the men who accompanied
Lawrence in the desert have remarked upon his ability to recall the location
of a bush, a rise or a rock after he had once seen it]. . . .

It was during these desert rips [sic] that I first realized Lawrence's joy in
motion and craze for speed.[7]

"My habit of always hiding behind a Sherif was to avoid measuring
myself against the pitiless Arab standard, with its no-mercy for foreigners
who wore its clothes, and aped its manners," Lawrence wrote of what
Joyce had referred to as his "wise selection of tribal leaders."

In the earlier broadcast (April 1939), Joyce emphasized Lawrence's
shrewd judgment in the selection of Arab personnel and his ability to
appeal to the imagination of the Arab leaders:

> Feisal was, of course, his outstanding success. Here was the man Lawrence
> had come to Arabia to find and who would bring the Arab Revolt to full
> glory. Sherif Nasir, Ali Ibn el Hussein, Auda Abu Tayi were all instruments
> of successful ventures. Hosts of others appeared and as quickly disappeared
> when they had carried out their task and earned their reward. It is difficult
> to keep Arab irregulars any length of time in the field and so it was ever
> changing personnel on whom Lawrence had to rely for support. . . . His
> disregard for conventions in uniforms is well known — while in Arab dress
> he outrivalled the splendour of Descendants of the Prophet. This again was
> not merely personal vanity. Arabs have a respect for fine raimant, which they
> associate with riches and power. It made him an outstanding figure among
> them, excited their curiosity, and therefore increased his authority when
> dealing with them.[8]

Lawrence's selection of the regal-looking Faisal to be the principal
military leader of the Revolt in preference to his more politically minded
and steadfastly anti-Ottoman older brother, Abdullah, has been frequently written about. Their first meeting at Hamra is dramatically described in *Seven Pillars of Wisdom* and the passage gives the impression
that Lawrence's decision was made spontaneously on the spot ("I felt at
first glance that this was the man I had come to Arabia to seek").[9]
Actually, there were rather detailed intelligence files in Cairo on the
sharif's sons, and the decision by Lawrence to work principally through
Faisal's leadership was a practical one, based in part on these intelligence
reports. In the first issue of *The Arab Bulletin*, which was published early
in June 1916, Faisal was reported to be "a good leader" — with "immense
authority" with the tribes.[10] His assets in these accounts included an
attractive appearance and personal qualities, an imposing manner, natural
ability as a soldier, popularity among the Bedouin, efficiency, lack of

prejudice against Christians, and years of experience living in Syria and Constantinople. Liabilities included his readiness to become discouraged, a streak of unreasonableness and narrow-mindedness, a hot temper, and a tendency to be impulsive and rash.[11] In a letter to Newcombe written in January 1917, Lawrence's enthusiasm for Faisal was unrestrained and he called him "an absolute ripper."[12]

Lawrence's relationship with Faisal was many-faceted, and statements of his about the amir, when taken out of context, seem to contradict other comments.[13] When writing to the British authorities, for example, Lawrence would stress Faisal's strength, while in private correspondence and conversation he stated that Faisal was not brave.[14] Lawrence distinguished, however, between spiritual and physical courage. If Lawrence's view of Faisal is taken in its totality, it provides an internally consistent though complex picture of the relationship from Lawrence's standpoint.[15] Records of Faisal's observations about Lawrence are far more fragmentary.

After his first meeting with Faisal at Hamra on October 23, 1916, Lawrence wrote only that he had been "arguing with Feisal (who was most unreasonable) for hours and hours." The next day they had another "hot discussion" which lasted all morning and "ended amicably."[16] After these meetings Lawrence wrote the following detailed description of Faisal for *The Arab Bulletin*: "Sidi Feisal. — Is tall, graceful, vigorous, almost regal in appearance. Aged thirty-one. Very quick and restless in movement. Far more imposing personally than any of his brothers, knows it and trades on it. Is as clear-skinned as a pure Circassian, with dark hair, vivid black eyes set a little sloping in his face, strong nose, short chin. Looks like a European, and very like the monument of Richard I, at Fontevraud [Lawrence's medieval hero again]. He is hot-tempered, proud, and impatient, sometimes unreasonable, and runs off easily at tangents. Possesses far more personal magnetism and life than his brothers, but less prudence. Obviously very clever, perhaps not overscrupulous. Rather narrow-minded, and rash when he acts on impulse, but usually with enough strength to reflect, and then exact in judgment. Had he been brought up the wrong way might have become a barrackyard officer. A popular idol, and ambitious; full of dreams, and the capacity to realize them, with keen personal insight, and a very efficient man of business."[17]

Having found his Arab fellow-dreamer in the desert, Lawrence proceeded to pull the strings of the Revolt far more through Faisal, who clearly trusted him, than through any other Arab leader. But Faisal used Lawrence as well to fulfill his own personal ambitions. Sir Reginald Wingate considered it improbable that a man like Faisal, who "had been dancing for years" on the tightrope of Arab-Turkish affairs, who was familiar with European questions and manners, and sophisticated politically in his own right, "would have been used by a young man so inexperienced in politics and world affairs as Lawrence."[18] In my opinion Lawrence was experienced politically ahead of his years and the using, as in most mutually advantageous relationships that contain an element of exploitation, went in both directions.

Lawrence appears to have identified in many ways with Faisal, so much so that in writing of him he often seemed to be writing about himself, or perhaps, about what he had helped Faisal to become. "One never asked if he were scrupulous," Lawrence wrote in *Seven Pillars of Wisdom*, "but later he showed that he could return trust for trust, suspicion for suspicion. He was fuller of wit than of humor. . . . .

"Meanwhile, here, as it seemed, was offered to our hand, which had only to be big enough to take it, a *prophet* [my italics] who, if veiled, would give cogent form to the idea behind the activity of the Arab revolt."[19] In the conversations in the tent Faisal "kept command of the conversation even at its hottest, and it was fine to watch him do it. He showed full mastery of tact, with a real power of disposing men's feelings to his wish."[20]

Clearly, despite assertions to the contrary, Lawrence did like Faisal. Three months after their first meeting he wrote his family: "Sherif Feisal (3rd son of Sherif of Mecca), to whom I am attached, is about 31, tall, slight, lively, well-educated. He is charming towards me, and we get on perfectly together."[21] A decade later this feeling had not changed despite Lawrence's disappointment in some of Faisal's limitations.

I have not been able to examine whatever memoirs Faisal may have written. Clearly he valued his relationship with Lawrence. Even Abdullah, who did write his memoirs and resented Lawrence's "influence among the tribes," acknowledged that Lawrence was successful in his work with Faisal's army and "was regarded as the moving spirit in the Revolt."[22] Ronald Storrs wrote in his memoirs that Faisal spoke to him of Lawrence "with a good-humored tolerance which I should have resented more if I had ever imagined that kings could like king-makers."[23] Lawrence wrote Faisal in November 1932, and Faisal in his reply thanked him "for the interest you have had of our affairs despite your being at far distant from us. As a sincere friend of us who has ever been our valuable support, I wish you pleasant long life."[24]

In interviewing Faisal some years later, Mrs. Stuart Erskine found him evasive when she asked him about Lawrence.

"Lawrence?" she quotes the king as saying. "He said many things about me which are not a bit true and I should probably say things about him which would not be true either. He was a genius, of course, but not for this age."

"For a past age," she suggested.

"On the contrary, for the future. A hundred years hence, perhaps two hundred years hence, he might be understood; but not today."[25]

Lawrence's dispatches for *The Arab Bulletin,* and those of his other Arab-minded colleagues, were filled with the fruits of their studies. Lawrence's reports in particular covered a broad range of subject matter, which included diaries of his journeys and raids; analyses of the geography, tribal structure, personalities, rivalries and religious tenets of the Arab leaders; and discussions of the political problems and history of the area.

From a psychosocial standpoint his "Twenty-seven Articles," on the handling of Arab tribesmen, which was written early in August 1917, not long after the capture of Aqaba, is the most important and most remarkable. The articles reveal, above all, the results of Lawrence's unremitting study of the Bedouin, his understanding of their psychology (and of other men's as well), and his extreme sensitivity to the self-regard of others lest through injuring the self-esteem of another person the bond might be broken or a potential alliance be prevented. The articles stress objectivity, self-control and discipline, and the holding of oneself emotionally and physically aloof. He explains the importance of working through the tribal leaders and describes the political rewards for the Arabs and the Allies of respecting the "conception of the Sherif." Doing too much for the Arabs is to be avoided because "it is their war." (When Lawrence wrote to King Husayn in June 1918, he referred to "your small Northern army,"[26] although to Robert Graves he wrote rather cynically of Husayn: "We had to pretend that he led.")[27] He discusses the value, difficulties and dangers for a foreigner of wearing Arab dress, while at the same time retaining British identity ("They make no special allowances for you when you dress like them . . . you will be like an actor in a foreign theatre") and stresses the need to do it "the whole way" if Arab things are worn. "This road should not be chosen without serious thought," he warns. There is much else on discussing religion with Bedouin (their faith is so intimate and intense a part of their daily lives "as to be unconscious"), using Bedouin raiding skills and tactics in warfare, the problems of mixing town and desert Arabs, pitfalls of talking about women ("avoid too free talk"), the selection of servants, and the need to look for inner motives behind the proffered explanations. Lawrence concludes with the advice to "bury yourself in Arab circles," for "your success will be just proportional to the amount of mental effort you devote to it." The complete text of the "Twenty-seven Articles" is provided in the Appendix, pp. 463–467.

Many British officers observed at first hand the steadfastness with which Lawrence personally adhered to the tenets of his twenty-seven points, worked, in fact, *through* and *with* the Arab leaders, and retained his patience with them and the tribesmen despite extraordinary frustrations. G. F. Peake wrote, for example: "He was always very conscious of the fact that he was a European and a Christian and also that the desert tribesmen were proud people, jealous of their freedom and fanatical as regards their religion. . . . His strong personality and knowledge of the Arabs of the desert no doubt enabled him unobtrusively to get his plans adopted, without rousing the latent antipathy to all who are not of their race and religion."[28] A. F. Nayton, the military governor of Beersheba, wrote long after the war to Arnold Lawrence of "the infinite patience with which . . . Lawrence handled the Arabs, notwithstanding many disappointments and the innumerable times he was 'let down' by them."[29]

Several of the Howeitat shaykhs* whom I interviewed in Jordan in April of 1967 remembered Lawrence vividly. None of them, they said, had ever been interviewed. Their memories of battles and raids, of places and names, were surprisingly detailed and apparently accurate (except for dates), considering that the events had taken place a half century before. Perhaps this is due to the absence of literacy, and the dependence on recollections through sight and sound, when communication is achieved orally. "Their very illiteracy has trained them to a longer memory and a closer hearing of the news," Lawrence once wrote.[31] These men had ranged in age from fifteen to twenty-eight at the time of the Revolt. The interviews were tape-recorded and except for one of them were translated into English on the spot. Later they were gone over by a second translator to check for accuracy and fill in omissions.

What was most striking to me in these interviews was the way in which they presented a kind of mirror image of the "Twenty-seven Articles," a confirmation of the effectiveness of this treatise on Arab social psychology seen from the Bedouin point of view. All of these men found dignity and personal pride in their role in the Arab Revolt, which remained for some of them the most important period of their lives, the time when they set aside their traditional quarrels and worked together toward the common goal of getting rid of the Turkish oppressor and obtaining freedom for their lands and people. The leadership in their eyes was provided by their own tribal shaykhs through an understanding with Faisal and the Ashraf (the sharif's family). They took great pride in the fact that the victory was an Arab victory achieved by Arabs. Lawrence's role (he was the only Englishman any of the men I interviewed remembered in any detail, and the only one who dressed and lived as an Arab among them) was deeply valued, but he was seen as a planner (including the attack on Aqaba and the battle of Tafila),[32] the encourager and coordinator of the Revolt, the one who obtained supplies, guns and ammunition. But he worked through Faisal and the other Arab leaders. "Because Faisal trusted Lawrence we all trusted him," one shaykh told me. "He was a servant of our master, Faisal, among the Bedouin."[33]

My informants stated clearly that their acceptance and trust of

---

* Lawrence once commented in one of his dispatches, "A feature of the Howeitat is that every fourth or fifth man is a sheikh." [30]

Lawrence grew out of his willingness to live among them, speak their language, wear their clothing, and eat their food. One said, "He was a friend, an Arab . . . he was a faithful man . . . he was an Englishman, but he was a pure friend to the Arabs . . . we suspect those who do not eat with us."[34] (Compare this with Lawrence's "they taught me that no man could be their leader except he ate the ranks' food, wore their clothes, lived with them, and yet appeared better in himself.")[35] Although there were educated Arabs in the campaigns, Lawrence used, according to these tribesmen, "to walk with the Bedouin."

The detailed and careful way in which Lawrence would look after the needs of the tribes was stressed by several men. One told me:

> You know he had learned Arabic. He used to come to a shaykh and say, "We are going to work for a month or two. How many are your people and how much money do you need so that they will not suffer hunger while you are away with your men at war?" He used to think of everything. Now this is what we loved. Because before we went on any expedition he used to know which tribes the expedition was going to consist of. He used to have a big statement — a detailed statement of every member of that family that was going to go on this expedition and knew full well how many members of this expedition would stay behind, and he used to give them enough money to buy food, rice, fat and everything that would keep them going for four months or how long he thought the expedition would last.[36]

The Bedouin valued Lawrence also as a teacher. He was the one who showed them the use of explosives and other means of winning, but he did not just do it for them. They won their own battles. The men who worked most closely with Lawrence felt that he had cared about them personally and they returned the feeling. They would bring him accounts of raids or of prisoners captured, and Lawrence would be lavish in his appreciation and encouragement. Lawrence often did not carry a gun or take part in hand-to-hand combat, but he would risk his life laying the mines by the railroad. The Bedouin were impressed with his bravery, especially as he seemed to risk his life frequently in blowing up the trains. One shaykh told me, "He was very brave with the Arabs . . . whenever he found an injured person he would go into battle and get him away and take him to the camp."

Sometimes Lawrence would summon the shaykhs to his tent — "Majlis Lawrence" — and they would have a big meal of rice and lamb and discuss tactics and share the small talk of tribal life. One shaykh recalled Lawrence bringing out some money after he found out that one of the shaykhs sitting at the table had three wives. "You give this money to your first one and this to the second and this to the third," Lawrence said, "but don't tell one that you gave the other one any so she might think she is special."[37]

Considerable mutual respect and love seem to have developed during the many months that the shaykhs and tribesmen fought with Lawrence. They were saddened when the parting came at Damascus. Shaykh 'Ayd told me, "Some of the shaykhs were crying because he left. . . . He told them he was leaving and they shook hands and said: 'Have I done anything wrong towards you?' and he said, 'No, on the contrary . . .' and he saw they had tears in their eyes and he said good-bye and they knew he was going."[38]

A Lebanese colleague of mine recently listed three types of Western "innocents" who have traditionally been drawn to the Middle East: the missionaries; those with an ethnocentric bias who wish to modernize the area; and the romantics who idealize the Arabs of the desert.[39] The most consistent criticism of Lawrence, and one which is certainly valid from our contemporary perspective, is that he falls into the third, the romantic, category. Lawrence idealized the Bedouin life, its freedom from civilization, and feared the effect of contact with the West: "The poverty of Arabia made them simple, continent, enduring. If forced into civilized life they would have succumbed like any savage race to its diseases, meanness, luxury, cruelty, crooked dealing, artifice; and, like savages, they would have suffered them exaggeratedly for lack of inoculation."[40]

Lawrence longed to be part of this society, but knew he could not be. "You guessed rightly that the Arab appealed to my imagination," he wrote during the war to his friend Richards. "It is the old, old civilisation, which has refined itself clear of household go[o]ds, and half the trappings which ours hastens to assume. The gospel of bareness in materials is a good one, and it involves apparently a sort of moral bareness too. They think for the moment, and endeavour to slip through life without turning corners or climbing hills. In part it is a mental and moral fatigue, a race trained out, and to avoid difficulties they have to jettison so much that we think honourable and grave: and yet without in any way sharing their point of view, I think I can understand it enough to look at myself and other foreigners from their direction, and without condemning it. I know I'm a stranger to them, and always will be: but I cannot believe them worse, any more than I could change their ways."[41]

Anis Sayigh has discussed the consequences of Lawrence's hostility to the "trappings" of civilization for the Arab world. Lawrence, he says, wished to impose his fantasy of the way of life of the desert Arabs on all Arabs, a way of life many modern Arabs understandably think of as backward. Lawrence longed for the world of the tribal chiefs, with no formal government, which imprisons, and no factories, modern armies, police or schools, which mold men's minds. He was critical of the settled life of Egypt and Lebanon, which is why he would not cooperate with the Arab nationalists of the cities and insisted upon imposing Hashemite rulers of Bedouin origin upon the Arab peoples of the cities as well as the desert. Sayigh goes on to say that not only did Lawrence try to impose his preferences upon the Arab world, but he was able to influence British leaders after the war of his views. He would have served the modern Arab world better, Sayigh believes, had he sought a new Arab civilization that would digest all classes in a society in which the Bedouin would have become a stable part of the totality.[42]

How realistic or feasible this would have been for Lawrence in 1918 is a difficult question. Sayigh's argument remains, however, one of the most telling criticisms of Lawrence's influence upon the modern Arab world and of his role as an enabler of change and growth for the Arab peoples with whom he worked and lived.

# 17

# The Conflict of Responsibility

Lawrence had no power to appoint anybody to be Governor of Damascus," General Chauvel wrote with obvious irritation in 1929,[1] and, in fact, no official authorization has been discovered for Lawrence's assumption of authority during the Revolt, either in this instance or in many others. But whether one considers that Lawrence took authority legitimately or usurped it, he did assume *personal responsibility* for the course and conduct of the Arab Revolt in the field and for the political assurances made to the Arab leaders during the course of the war. After the capture of Aqaba he wrote his family as if the Revolt were a personal charge that he dared not neglect: "It is more restful in Arabia, because one feels so nervous of what may happen if one goes away. I cannot ask for leave, as I know there is so much to do down there, and no one to do it."[2] At times he felt he "had a reserve of confidence to carry the whole thing, if need be, on my shoulders."[3]

This exaggerated sense of responsibility finds its fullest and most vivid expression in *Seven Pillars of Wisdom* and contributes greatly to the egoistic tone of the book. Whether or not he was officially limited to serving as an intelligence officer in a liaison capacity to Amir Faisal, Lawrence makes clear in passage after passage that he considered himself responsible for the direction and conduct of the Arab campaigns, an attitude he undoubtedly maintained during the war itself, although it is less evident in the official dispatches. "My personal duty was command," he wrote in *Seven Pillars*, "and the commander, like the master architect, was responsible for all."[4] "All" included not only the strategy, organization and coordination of the Revolt but the lives and well-being of virtually every participant in the Allied effort, English and Arab, and to some degree of the enemy as well.

In conceiving and implementing the strategies of the desert campaigns Lawrence concerned himself both with the use of materials and the planning of tactics and with the psychological dimension of warfare — with the influencing of men's minds. The psychological element of command, he wrote, "considers the capacity for mood of our men, their complexities and mutability, and the cultivation of what in them profits the intention. We had to arrange their minds in order of battle, just as carefully and as formally as other officers arranged their bodies: and not only our own men's minds, though them first: the minds of the enemy, so far as we could reach them: and thirdly, the mind of the nation supporting us behind the firing-line, and the mind of the hostile nation waiting the verdict, and the neutrals looking on."[5] Lawrence's inner sense of responsibility, especially for individual human lives, corresponded in intensity with the scope and intensity of his ambitions and contributed greatly to the increasing anguish he experienced as the months of the Revolt passed, the horrors mounted, and he realized he could not possibly fulfill its exacting and (by the judgments of most people) unrealistic terms.

The futility and unnecessary slaughter of Kut-el-Amara had impressed Lawrence deeply, for in the introductory chapter to the 1922 (Oxford) edition of *Seven Pillars* he drew upon it to exemplify his contempt for what he called "murder" war. "I went up the Tigris," he wrote, "with one hundred Devon Territorials, young, clean, delightful fellows, full of the power of happiness, and of making women and children glad. By them one saw vividly how great it was to be their kin, and English. And we were casting them by thousands into the fire, to the worst of deaths, not to win the war, but that the corn and rice and oil of Mesopotamia might be ours. The only need was to defeat our enemies (Turkey among them), and this was at last done in the wisdom of Allenby with less than four hundred killed, by turning to our uses the hands of the oppressed in Turkey. I am proudest of my thirty fights in that I did not have any of our blood shed. All the subject provinces of the Empire to me were not worth one dead English boy. If I have restored to the East some self-respect, a goal; ideals: if I have made the standard of rule of white over red more exigent, I have fitted those people in a degree for the new commonwealth in which the dominant races will forget their brute achievements, and white and red and yellow and brown and black will stand up together without side-glances in the service of the world."[6]

But Lawrence did not limit his injunction against killing to English boys and men: "To me an unnecessary action, shot, or casualty, was not only waste but sin. I was unable to take the professional view that all successful actions were gains. Our rebels were not materials, like soldiers, but friends of ours, trusting our leadership."[7] Or: "In the pursuit of the ideal conditions we might kill Turks, because we disliked them very much; but the killing was a pure luxury. If they would go quietly the war would end. If not, we would urge them, or try to drive them out. In the last resort, we should be compelled to the desperate course of blood and the maxims of 'murder war,' but as cheaply as could be for ourselves, since the Arabs fought for freedom, and that was a pleasure to be tasted only by a man alive."[8] And, finally: "To man-rationale, wars of nationality were as much a cheat as religious wars, and nothing was worth fighting for: nor could fighting, the act of fighting, hold any need of intrinsic virtue. Life was so deliberately private that no circumstances could justify one man in laying violent hands on another's: though a man's own death was his last free will, a saving grace and measure of intolerable pain."[9]

In passage after passage of *Seven Pillars,* Lawrence describes his personal intervention in disputes and other tribal matters, of which one may justly ask what affair it was of his to become involved. But he held steadfastly to the view that jealousies and feuds could easily have disrupted what unity the Revolt possessed, and his ability to identify with Arab psychology, his detailed knowledge of the tribes, and his position *outside* any one of them make his justification for interfering plausible. His long trek back through the burning desert to retrieve the straggler Gasim ("a gap-toothed, grumbling fellow, skrimshank in all our marches, bad-tempered, suspicious, brutal, a man whose engagement I regretted"), is well known. Lawrence did it, he wrote, because "Gasim was my man: and upon me lay the responsibility of him," and because he needed to avoid being excused on the grounds that he was a foreigner ("that was precisely the plea I did not dare set up, while I yet presumed to help these Arabs in their own revolt").[10]

Later he felt obliged to end the life with his own pistol of his mortally wounded, loyal servant Farraj.[11] Of this merciful killing another British officer wrote:

> His dilemma was whether to abandon him alive for the Turkish soldiers to wreck their vengeance on, or to end his life before leaving him. Lawrence chose the latter course. It will, of course, be asked why he did not order one of the Arabs to perform this tragic task. The answer is a simple one. No Arab tribesman would have obeyed such an order. It would have started a blood feud in which many innocent men would have lost their lives. Moreover, he knew that the German and Turkish governments had done everything possible to rouse the religious and patriotic feelings of the Turkish soldiers. They especially emphasized that the Arabs were not only in rebellion against the Sultan but worse still were apostates, fighting under the orders of Europeans and Christians. In short, no Arab could expect any mercy from the Turks. It must be remembered that Lawrence had no doctors nor even a medical orderly with pain relieving drugs. He therefore took the only course available to end the suffering of a man he could not help.[12]

"In one six days' raid there came to a head and were settled," Lawrence wrote, "twelve cases of assault with weapons, four camel-liftings, one marriage, two thefts, a divorce, fourteen feuds, two evil eyes, a bewitchment."[13] He described the blood enmities that existed among the many tribes, who he asserted but "for my hand over them would have murdered in the ranks each day. Their feuds prevented them combining against me; while their unlikeness gave me sponsors and spies wherever I went or sent, between Akaba and Damascus, between Beersheba and Bagdad."[14] On one occasion, in order to prevent a feud from growing, he executed a man who had killed a man from another tribe.[15] "A highly sensitive and imaginative man cannot do such things as if he were doing no more than putting on his boots," George Bernard Shaw wrote after Lawrence's death. "I once asked him whether he felt badly about such horrible exploits. He said, of course he did, very badly indeed."[16]

Lawrence found his role in the Revolt increasingly odious and disturbing to him personally, and felt his position in it to be false in fundamental ways. An important source of his shame derived from his gradual recognition that in manipulating and inspiring the Arabs to pursue the aims of the Revolt with such energy he was fulfilling an essentially egoistic aim, which derived from the nature of his own ambitions. Lawrence recognized with some alarm the power of his influence upon the Arab leaders, and came more and more to question the morality of exploiting their highest ideals and desire for freedom, not only as "one more tool to help England win,"[17] which has been most stressed in analyses of Lawrence's conflict, but in the service also of his own inner drives and needs.

The most obvious dilemma deriving from Lawrence's self-assumption of responsibility grew out of his position as intermediary between Faisal and Allenby. The dilemma became especially acute after he became aware of the terms of the McMahon pledges and the Sykes-Picot Agreement (probably before his trip into Syria in June of 1917).[18] "I was Feisal's adviser," Lawrence wrote, "and Feisal relied upon the honesty and competence of my advice so far as often to take it without argument. Yet I could not explain to Allenby the whole Arab situation, nor disclose the full British plan to Feisal."[19] Although Lawrence wrote that he had "early betrayed the treaty's [the Sykes-Picot Agreement] existence to Feisal," and Picot and Sykes had met King Husayn at Jidda concerning its terms in June 1917, Lawrence clearly did not feel that the Arab leaders understood its implications or that his own responsibility was mitigated by any such revelations or confessions on his part. Repeatedly in *Seven Pillars of Wisdom* he wrote of his continual bitter shame at what he considered to be the false pretenses under which he was urging the Arabs on in the Revolt, using them as an instrument of British policy, while he knew that they would likely lose in the postwar diplomatic maneuverings of the Great Powers much of what they had gained in liberating their lands from the Ottoman Empire during the campaigns. On his trip into Syria in June 1917, Lawrence wrote on army message forms, "We are calling them to fight for us on a lie and I can't stand it."[20]

But one may ask with Elie Kedourie, what "had Lawrence to do with the bargain" the British had made with the French, the Russians and the Arabs, "and why should he feel dishonoured if the bargain were not kept? He was not the British Government after all, nor the keeper of its conscience. Neither did the British Government authorize him to make bargains or distribute promises. What business, then, had he to 'endorse' promises, especially if, as he says, he 'had no previous or inner knowledge of the McMahon pledges or the Sykes-Picot Treaty?' "[21] Were not the Arabs rebelling against Turkey by their own choice, and was not Lawrence's wholehearted assistance helping them to become free of the tyrannical Ottoman authority? Even if Britain had made a secret deal with the French (and just how secret it was for King Husayn and his sons remains an unsettled question — it was in no way secret after November 1917, when the Bolsheviks published the terms of the Sykes-Picot Agreement in their newspapers), the Arabs could only be better off in their postwar negotiations with the British and French if they were militarily successful in liberating their own lands during the campaigns, as Lawrence was trying to help them do.

But Lawrence was not guided by these conventional and logical considerations alone. He knew that "Arabs believe in persons, not in institutions," and he was the person who represented to them the purposes and commitments of the British government. He was, therefore, in the terms of *his* morality, responsible. He felt that his entire position was false and that *he* was responsible for misleading the Arabs into pursuing their revolution, as if it were being fought entirely on the basis of British (and therefore his) promises.

In actuality the Arabs may have been better off anyway to have fought, with Allied help, as they did, and then to navigate after the war, as they had during it, among the not-unfamiliar shoals of Anglo-French rivalry. But Lawrence was too caught up in his personal turmoil to consider the matter in this light. "I could see that if we won the war the promises to the Arabs were dead paper. Had I been an honourable adviser I would have sent my men home, and not let them risk their lives for such stuff,"[22] he wrote, and "in revenge I vowed to make the Arab Revolt the engine of its own success . . . and vowed to lead it so madly in the final victory that expediency should counsel to the Powers a fair settlement of the Arabs' moral claims. . . . Clearly I had no shadow of leave to engage the Arabs, unknowing, in a gamble of life and death. Inevitably and justly we should reap bitterness, a sorry fruit of heroic endeavor."[23] He continued: "Before me lay a vista of responsibility and command, which disgusted my thought-ridden nature."[24] Further British assurances to the Arabs in

1918 only added to Lawrence's personal distress, which he treated with irony, answering the Arab leaders, when they would ask him which agreement to believe, "the last in date."[25]

But driven by what he variously called his inner "beast" or "demon," Lawrence claimed for himself, and for his own conscience, the responsibility for the Revolt and for its military, political and human consequences. Yet in so doing he provided an example of leadership to the Arabs that did much to enable them to achieve what they did in their rebellion. Lawrence recognized the egoism of this assumption of responsibility, especially the aspect which involved his identifying with another people's need and suffering, and it clearly troubled him deeply. "A reef on which many came to a shipwreck of estimation," Lawrence wrote, in a passage which, though it employs the literary "our" or "we," clearly applies to himself, "was the vanity that our endurance might win redemption, perhaps for all a race. Such false investiture bred a hot though transient satisfaction, in that we felt we had assumed another's pain or experience, his personality. It was triumph, and a mood of enlargement; we had avoided our sultry selves, conquered our geometrical completeness, snatched a momentary 'change of mind.'

"Yet in reality we had borne the vicarious for our own sakes, or at least because it was pointed for our benefit: and could escape from this knowledge only by a make-belief in sense as well as in motive.

"The self-immolated victim took for his own the rare gift of sacrifice; and no pride and few pleasures in the world were so joyful, so rich as this choosing voluntarily another's evil to perfect the self. There was a hidden selfishness in it, as in all perfections."[26]

This kind of personal assumption of responsibility is, I believe, unusual among military commanders, who seem, more often, to regard themselves as subservient to other leaders or to larger political purposes. Usually they are able to justify the killing over which they preside as necessary in view of the larger military or political effort. Lawrence's self-centered scrupulosity appears to be unrealistic, even grandiose. Yet perhaps only through such exaggerated personal assumption of responsibility by those in positions of leadership can men find ways other than war to settle their disputes.

# 18

# The Heroic Legend
# and the Hero

Men need heroes in order to transcend the limitations and disappointments they experience in their everyday lives. Heroes embody ideals and values shared in the culture, ready examples with whom the rest of us may identify. But the *creation* of heroes depends upon the compliance of history, the coming together of special events and situations with unusual men or women who take hold of these circumstances, force upon them their own actions and personalities, and transform them along the lines of their own dreams.

The concept of heroism embraces a series of psychosocial interrelationships and tensions among various individuals and groups. These include the hero himself; the people (or peoples) among whom he lives and acts; his followers (who may vary in size as a group from a small band to a nation or nations); his chroniclers and biographers; contemporary propaganda; and, finally, the audience of posterity, whose view of the hero will shift according to cultural need and the materials about him made available by those who choose to examine the oral traditions and the writings (and now the audio-visual materials of the mass media) that concern the hero's performance and reputation. Although man is known to have created heroes as far back as the days when he painted the actions he admired on cave walls, the concept of the hero evolves or shifts according to what a given people or a historical age values or can tolerate.

Heroic ideals must be consistent with the realities of a particular society's circumstances. The admired hero of one age or people could well be seen as the immoral enemy and destroyer in another or vice versa. During his lifetime the hero has some, though often limited, control over what he would wish to represent. After his death he becomes public property and his meaning for history is determined by those of his works which endure and by the interpretations of his historical audience and his various biographers.

There are probably heroic qualities which are not bound by time or epoch, but anyone who tries to name them is in danger of reflecting the narrower perspective of his own values or the values of his age. E. M. Forster, whose empathy for and appreciation of Lawrence was perhaps the most profound of all of Lawrence's friends, called courage, generosity and compassion, all of which he felt T.E. possessed, "the three heroic virtues" that qualified his friend as a hero. But I am not sure that generosity and compassion have always been so valued, and I suspect that figures like Lawrence, and interpreters of his life such as Forster, have helped make them become so.

James Notopoulos in his article "The Tragic and the Epic in T. E. Lawrence," has written that ours is an age in which hero and heroic acts are anachronisms and that the hero is "out of joint" with our pragmatic world.[1] Notopoulos is certainly correct as regards the Homeric heroes or the romantic heroes of the Age of Chivalry, whose acts of valor are committed and admired quite unselfconsciously, with little regard for their political consequences or toll in personal suffering. But for the contemporary leader to be heroic he must fulfill different requirements. The horrors and atrocities of war have become so much the personal experience of humanity, and the dangers of mass destruction so acute, that the traditional elevation of courageous generals or other winners of battles and wars to the status of heroes seems to be becoming — at least for the present — a thing of the past, especially as the political wars of our computer age leave less to the initiative of individuals in the field.

The capacity for *individual* mastery, initiative and achievement is probably an essential requirement for all heroes. Heroic values, bred as they are of necessity, must include in our dangerous age much that is not romantic, qualities such as restraint and renunciation. Our heroes must, in an age when survival of the race is endangered, display examples of conduct that will offer protection (probably always an essential quality of heroism, although variously achieved in different eras), and such protection may be offered perhaps more by self-consciousness and restraint than by the decisive actions of traditional heroes.

Lawrence is a transitional figure in the history of heroism. Imbued with the epic tradition, and raised on a heavy diet of medieval romanticism and its Victorian revival, he brought to his role in the Revolt traditional concepts of chivalric heroism combined with the goal of leading an oppressed people out of bondage in the biblical sense. He tried through self-improvement to embody the ideal of courage, stamina and skill that both Arabs and Britons could look up to and emulate.

The generosity and compassion of which Forster wrote have been less stressed, but they stand out in *Seven Pillars* and shine forth when one speaks of Lawrence with friends who remember him. One little-known member of the Arab Bureau said of Lawrence, "What he hid, I believe, and still believe, was a tender reverence for human life which his duty as a soldier compelled him to violate, and so he was always stressed by an inner conflict."[2] But it is this conflict about human life, the inability to justify killing, the self-consciousness, guilt and exaggerated responsibility-taking that make Lawrence a valued example for the twelfth century, a contemporary hero.

In his essay "T. E. Lawrence: The Problem of Heroism," Irving Howe has written: "The hero as he appears in the tangle of modern life is a man struggling with a vision he can neither realize nor abandon, 'a man with a load on his mind.' "[3] Howe also points out: "What finally draws one to Lawrence, making him seem not merely an exceptional figure, but a representative man of our century, is his courage and vulnerability in bearing the burden of consciousness."[4] Lawrence is, in Howe's phrase, "a prince of our disorder"[5] (which will recall the words of Lunt's Bedouin host: "Of all the men I have ever met he was the greatest Prince").

The precise assessment of Lawrence's instrumentality in the shifting concepts of heroism is very difficult. He is part of the process of shift and the determination of his individual role within it is virtually impossible. He seems to have understood that he represented a new sort of heroism, and was prepared to challenge those who would criticize him through invidious comparison with static or more traditional concepts.

One reviewer of the subscribers' edition of *Seven Pillars*, Herbert Read, wrote in 1927:

> The story fails to reach epic quality because Colonel Lawrence, however brave and courageous he may have been, is not heroic. About the epic hero there is an essential undoubting directness: his aim is single and unswerving; *he questions neither himself, his aims, nor his destiny* [italics added]. He may share his glory with his chosen band, his *comitatus*, but essentially he is self-possessed, self-reliant, arrogant and unintelligent. Colonel Lawrence was none of these things; in all these things he was at the contrary pole — full of doubts and dissemblings, uncertain of his aim, his pride eaten into by humility and remorse, his conduct actuated by intellectual and idealistic motives. It is no disparagement to say that out of such stuff no hero is made.[6]

When Lawrence read Read's review he wrote to Edward Garnett: "I do not like his categorical specification of a hero . . . who in God's name laid this down? Is the hero to be a changeless thing, in the world? And why make Aeneas your archetype? I can't think of any other character in fiction who fits his definition. . . . Isn't he slightly ridiculous in seeking to measure my day-to-day chronicle by the epic standard? I never called it an epic, or thought of it as an epic, nor did anyone else, to my knowledge. The thing follows an exact diary sequence, and is literally true, throughout. Whence was I to import his lay-figure hero? Leaders of movements have to be intelligent, as was Feisal, to instance my chief character. Read talks as though I had been making a book, and not a flesh-and-blood revolt."[7]

The contemporary hero, the "man with a load on his mind," seems to be a kind of political-spiritual figure, such as Mohandas Gandhi, Martin Luther King, or Dag Hammarskjöld, whose examples are of peace, non-violence and renunciation. Lawrence, though a soldier and a hero of war, is also a hero of nonwar. By the assumption of exaggerated personal responsibility for what war really is, he has demonstrated war's unsuitability as material for heroism according to the twentieth-century consciousness he helped to create. His conflict is the product of war and his self-consciousness grows out of it. But this self-consciousness in turn alters the qualities of heroism, so that the shift in the direction that heroism has taken seems to pivot around Lawrence's personal change and experience in the war itself. As Lawrence was changed by his war experience, his self-conscious shift in values becomes our property and his evolving ideals affect our own. He asks us to expect more of our heroes as he expected more of himself, and we are influenced thereby to be more self-critical and to demand more of our leaders.

Although we may know a fair amount about what to value in our heroes, we know very little about the psychology or personal development of the person who is himself destined to become a heroic figure. It would seem important to understand more about this. A vital ingredient in hero-valuing or hero-making is the resonance that the follower or worshipper finds between conflicts and aspirations of his own and those he perceives in the person he chooses to idealize. The worshipper (or, less dramatically, the one-who-does-the-valuing) needs to be able to find that unfulfilled, ideal aspects of himself are fulfilled by and through the hero, even though the worshipper does not recognize the fulfillment consciously. The hero needs to appear to have mastered his struggle to achieve his ideals in such a way that an identification with him seems to offer the possibility of similar mastery to the follower. Thus, psychological conflict and mastery, the overcoming of deep inner dissatisfaction through reaching out toward an ideal, would seem to be an essential aspect of the psychology of the hero. At the same time the process the hero undergoes, in reaching for what he values, and the idealized solution he actually achieves for himself, must be sufficiently recognizable or familiarly human to allow for empathy and identification by the follower. Finally, the hero's solutions of his conflicts, his efforts to achieve an ideal, must be creative. He must strive for new solutions, new values and new directions (even if some of these, in reality, may be old — and merely revived), and they must be for a larger group or for mankind, not just for a few individuals.

The psychological development of the hero originates, as it does for us all, in his cultural background, the circumstances of his ancestry and family, and in his early life. There is a set of ideas, quite common in childhood, that might be called the hero fantasy. It derives from the limitations of being a child, subject to the power and authority of one's parents. They appear to the child to be the cause of the frustration of all his wishes. The fantasy enables him to transcend these limitations. In it, he finds out that the parents with whom he is living are imposters who are deceiving him after having usurped the place of his real parents. These impostors do not fully appreciate his value, as his real parents would (they are usually of royal or noble birth and so, of course, is he). The child imagines that he will embark on a heroic quest in which he will perform great deeds and will also restore his real parents to their rightful place, eject the impostors, and be reunited in greatness with his true forebears, who will recognize and appreciate fully his deserving qualities. A variation on this fantasy is that the parents are reduced from former greatness and need to be restored by the child's heroic efforts.[8]

For most children the romantic notions of the hero fantasy are corrected by the inescapable reality of the actual family situation, and by other encounters with situations and persons in the outside world that confront the child daily with the reality of his limitations. By late adolescence he usually has abandoned the fantasy and seeks other solutions for the painful conflicts that recognition of his limitations has imposed.

It is a unique aspect of Lawrence's psychological development that he did not give up his fantasy but sought *his* solutions to earlier conflicts through the kind of heroic activity out of which new myths could be created. I believe the reason for this direction of Lawrence's development may be found in the actualities of his family background, which conformed *in reality* to so many of the elements of the hero-fantasy. His real (former) father was, if not of royal, at least of more noble birth, than the displaced country gentleman Ned Lawrence lived with in Oxford, "kept" as his mother's "trophy of power." Lawrence's actual father *had been*, if not a different person, *in fact* of higher status, and therefore Lawrence himself was or should have been, as well. The guilt of the parents *had* led them to deceive the child regarding his origins, which were kept by them shrouded in mystery and uncertainty. As regards Lawrence's personal development, far from being encouraged to give up his fantasies of restoring his family to its rightful status, his parents, especially his mother, sought *their* redemption and liberation from guilt through the heroic acts he would some day perform. He would justify their transgressions by his ennobling accomplishments, achievements his mother very much approved of.[9]

Unusual gifts of mind and body, which Lawrence appeared quite early to possess, seemed to make possible for parents and child alike the overcoming of ordinary limitations, and Lawrence's childhood friends experienced the sense that almost anything was possible on an adventure with Ned Lawrence. The disturbance of self-esteem resulting from the identification with his parents' sin produced an inner tension, out of which grew the drive to live out the heroic fantasy. It is this tension (the "standing civil war" of which he wrote to Mrs. Shaw), this conflict of self-esteem, which drove Lawrence to seek some public stage upon which he could live out its demands. He strove to silence once and for all through noble and heroic deeds, and through living up to an ideal of personal conduct, the inner voice that reminded him of the fallen aspect of himself. It will be recalled that Lawrence's intensive reading during his youth of medieval chivalric and romantic writings lent additional richness, breadth and variety to the forms of his heroic fantasies and dreams.

As we shall see, far from permanently resolving the conflict, Lawrence's participation in the Arab Revolt only intensified it and brought it more to the surface. The Revolt provided the stage on which he could live out the heroic fantasy of his inner life. Through his achievements in the Revolt, and his sharing in his writings the inner terms of the ambivalent struggle for heroic achievement, Lawrence offered himself as a hero to others who were struggling with conflicts similar to his own. Through his example, Lawrence has helped others to achieve what he could not achieve for himself, and what they might not have been able to achieve without him.[10]

The Lawrence legend grew, I believe, directly out of the elements of his personal psychology that I have just described. It was the product of Lawrence's psychology and personality, operating through his writings and his contacts with others, which found a receptive audience in England and America, and to a lesser extent in other European countries, after the ravages of World War I had begun to destroy the illusion that modern war is romantic. Lowell Thomas's illustrated lectures, films and writings undoubtedly hastened the creation and popularizing of the Lawrence legend, although it was already taking shape in military, diplomatic and academic circles before Thomas began his performances in New York and London.[11] Lawrence's accomplishments were, however, in actuality so remarkable, and the "fit" between the elements of his psychology that contributed to the tendency of legends to grow up around him and the need of his potential historical audience for a new type of heroic figure was so natural, that the creation of a "Lawrence-of-Arabia" was, in my opinion, inevitable.

"The limelight of history," Shaw wrote in an essay on Lawrence, "follows the authentic hero as the theatre limelight follows the *prima ballerina assoluta.*"[12] Furthermore, many of the activities that contributed to the Lawrence legend took place some time *after* Lowell Thomas's performances in London — Lawrence's contributions, for example, to the political solutions in the Middle East, his retreat to the RAF, and the circulation of *Seven Pillars of Wisdom* among an increasing number of people during the 1920's. Finally, there is no way that the *lasting* appeal of the Lawrence legend, his endurance as a contemporary historical and legendary figure, can be explained on the basis of the publicity he received during the immediate postwar period.

Much has been written of Lawrence's need to dramatize himself, to seek publicity while simultaneously eschewing it, to "back into the limelight." But he was critical of that aspect of himself which, in spite of himself, gave in, often unconsciously, to self-dramatizing. He was aware of his inclination to mislead in his writings: he wrote, for example, to Mrs. Shaw, in 1927: "The reviewers [of *Revolt in the Desert*, his abridgment of *Seven Pillars of Wisdom*] have none of them given me credit for being a bag of tricks — too rich and full a bag for them to control."[13]

But I believe that this insight was to some extent the rationalization of the tendency to dramatize, which seemed to be outside Lawrence's control and which was spawned by psychological needs of which he was unaware. This tendency reached its fullest expression in *Seven Pillars of Wisdom*. One of Lawrence's purposes in writing the book was to invite his public to create with him a new and different self, a mythological Lawrence, larger than life, a self that would be immune to or beyond personal pain and conflict, and one that would replace the self he felt he had debased. The new self would be ideal in its honesty and integrity, a participant in epic events described in the epic mode, committing great deeds in war and yet responsible for war and rejecting it as no commander before had been or done, a Lawrence that was to be merciless if not all-seeing in his self-scrutiny.

The irony is that, objectively, the real Lawrence corresponded in so many ways to the ideal one he sought to create through his dramatizing and embroidering. But from his inner psychological perspective the real self was debased by the war and his experiences in it, and fell far short of the ideal self he had to invent, with the help of others, through legend-making.

The dramatic richness of *Seven Pillars of Wisdom* is widely acknowledged. Its value as a contemporary epic derives in part from its power to lift everyday events and personal struggles to a higher plane. Some of these events contained an intrinsic drama. In other instances Lawrence brought, through his passionate literary descriptions, drama and beauty to events of the Revolt — even the arrangement of corpses — that would otherwise have been merely horrible, painful or ordinary. Lawrence understood that legend-making often reduced the drama or humanity of actual events, but he was compelled by other forces. He wrote, for example, that "since Egypt kept us alive by stinting herself, we must reduce impolitic truth to keep her confident and ourselves a legend. The crowd wanted book-heroes, and would not understand how more human Auda ['Awdah abu-Tayyi] was because, after battle and murder, his heart yearned towards the defeated enemy now subject, at his free choice, to be spared or killed: and therefore never so lovely."[14]

Lawrence's consciously critical mind rejected the idea of himself as a hero. He felt his kinship with the vulnerability and humanity of other men — knew, for example, that his bowels sometimes gave way when he was frightened. "Strong praise and strong blame," he once wrote, "are results of half-knowledge; to know the real motive or mood of heroism is often to make it accidental or involuntary or instinctive. You cannot admire the stars, since they are only fire and mud in nature."[15]

Among the more familiar of the dramatically embellished passages of *Seven Pillars of Wisdom* is the one in which Lawrence describes his first meeting with Faisal ("I felt at first glance that this was the man I had come to Arabia to seek — the leader who would bring the Arab Revolt to full glory"), which is in sharp contrast to his matter-of-fact official dispatch. The passage continues with a colorful, high-keyed description of Faisal among his followers. "'And do you like our place here in Wadi Safra?'" Faisal asks. "'Well; but it is far from Damascus,'" Lawrence replies. "The word had fallen like a sword in their midst," he continues. "There was a quiver. Then everybody present stiffened where he sat, and held his breath for a silent minute. Some perhaps were dreaming of far off success: others may have thought it a reflection of their late defeat. Faisal at length lifted his eyes, smiling at me, and said, 'Praise be to God, there are Turks nearer us than that.' We all smiled with him; and I rose and excused myself for the moment."[16]

The meeting with Allenby is similarly raised to the level of high drama. Vividly self-effacing here, Lawrence writes: "He was hardly prepared for anything so odd as myself — a little barefooted silk-skirted man offering to hobble the enemy by his preaching if given stores and arms and a fund of two hundred thousand sovereigns to convince and control his converts."[17]

In passage after passage of *Seven Pillars of Wisdom* Lawrence provides accounts which throw the spotlight on himself and credit him with a central place in actions whose grandeur is raised to epic proportions. Yet this self-elevation (unnecessary from a purely objective standpoint in view of his actual accomplishments) is invariably matched with countervailing passages of self-disparagement, and proclamations of the baseness of his position and of his deceit, which become a kind of litany. Similarly, events in which Lawrence focuses credit upon himself, such as the capture of Aqaba ("Akaba had been taken on my plan by my effort. The cost of it had fallen on my brains and nerves"),[18] seem always to be matched by accounts, such as his description of his role at Tafas, that exaggerate negative, even almost criminal, activity. Grand success and spectacular failure seem to alternate throughout the book. In the passages of horror — and there are many — even brutality, cruelty and gore are made somehow glorious; and tortures are stretched in intensity beyond belief. It is as if there is operating in Lawrence in writing this book — and I am treating it here as a psychological document rather than as a literary work — a balance scale controlling the economy of his self-esteem. The glorification of himself, and of the great events of the Arab Revolt in which he took part, seems to serve to overcome his low self-regard. But some internal monitor, or busy conscience under the control of a low self-estimate, seems always to swing the pendulum of judgment back in the direction of self-disparagement.

*Seven Pillars of Wisdom* has been criticized as a work of history because of alleged distortions of fact. The historian L. B. Namier, who considered Lawrence "a man of genius, a great artist," wrote gently of him that "he seemed to dislike the precision of dates."[19] There are distortions in the book, but they come not, in my opinion, from a simple alteration of facts — it is remarkable how much valuable historical information the book does contain when its psychological and literary purposes are considered. Rather, the distortions and inaccuracy result from Lawrence's need, deriving from the conflicts and his self-regard, to elevate the tale to epic proportions and to make of himself a contemporary legendary figure.

The legend-making did not of course end with *Seven Pillars of Wisdom*. The Lawrence of myth continued to grow and be enriched by the tales he told his friends (from which, once they are retold, it is impossible to distinguish the embellishment and embroidering that is Lawrence's from that of his friends and biographers) and especially from the accounts he supplied his biographers. Sometimes Lawrence seemed unable to resist writing as if the whole Middle Eastern campaign, even the capture of Damascus, were related to his personal wishes, motives and accomplishments. For example, after teasing Liddell Hart with a cryptic note about the relationship between his dedicatory poem ("To S.A."), and his sadness at the end of the campaigns over the death of Dahoum (he never just comes out and says he felt grieved about the loss of Dahoum), Lawrence wrote: "The unhappy 'event' happened long before we got to Damascus. *I only took D.* (so far as that motive was concerned) for historical reasons."[20] [Italics added]

Richard Goodwin, writing of another modern guerrilla leader, noted: "Still there was always a remoteness — a knowledge that no matter how close you came the man was withholding something. It is a quality useful to leadership and essential to heroic myth."[21] A classic example of such mystification occurs in the exchanges that took place between Lawrence and Robert Graves — at this time Graves was preparing his biography of Lawrence — concerning Lawrence's June 1917 journey behind Turkish lines into Syria. Graves's struggle to obtain the truth, and Lawrence's evasive, teasing, half-revealing-half-concealing replies (he seemed especially to enjoy teasing Graves), which raise as many questions as they answer, occupy six of the 180 pages of *T. E. Lawrence to His Biographer, Robert Graves.* At the conclusion of the merry chase Lawrence wrote Graves: "~~Once during this~~ [Lawrence's deletion].* You may say that 'the more picturesque incidents reported of this journey are demonstrably untrue: but that L's (failure or) refusal to provide accurate details throws upon him responsibility for such fictions as are current.'[22]

"You may make public if you like the fact that my reticence upon this northward raid is deliberate, and based on private reasons, and record your opinion that I have found mystification, and perhaps statements deliberately misleading or contradictory, the best way to hide the truth of what really occurred, if anything did occur." And then in a postscript: *"The lighter you can touch on it the better I'll be served.* Sorry: on these points I can't afford to help you."[23] During the war there was reason to keep the details of the journey secret, especially to protect Syrian nationalists who had taken risks to see Lawrence. If such reasons still existed, Lawrence could have indicated as much without so much tantalization. The preponderant effect of the passage, if not its motive, seems to be mystification. It is the stuff out of which legend is created.

Lawrence emerged from World War I a public figure. From then on, the private Lawrence, Lawrence as a real person, and the mythological Lawrence of legendary heroism begin their complex relationship with one another. At times they seem to coincide, while at other times they diverge widely. During his lifetime the actual Lawrence was forever the critic of the heroic one, especially of the *mythic* heroic character he could not help creating. His insight into his own limitations, his awareness of the distortions of truth the legend he helped to create contained, and his profound intellectual awareness of the impure mixture of creditable and discreditable characteristics that define all men, made the idealized versions of his life that were growing up about him especially distasteful.

Yet the myth continued and he continued to furnish much of its substance. Even in his postwar renunciations and self-effacement, Lawrence continued to provide valuable and precocious ethical examples.

* The deletion was made legibly (by design?) — as if he were "on the point of making a confession," says Graves.

# 19

# The Shattering of
# the Dream

Psychic trauma is a violation, the penetration or shattering of the inner defenses by events whose impact is overwhelming, and whose continuing aftereffects cannot readily be integrated by the functioning personality. Trauma occurs at the border between the individual and the external world, between the self and an environment which breaches it. The potential for traumatization lies within the personality, in the childhood development, psychological defenses, ambitions and sexual predilections that create areas of particular vulnerability. The person's feeling of worth, because of injuries in his early development, may be an important area of potential vulnerability.

Although the experience of traumatization is essentially one of pain, traumata frequently occur in connection with pleasure for several fundamental reasons. First, whether consciously or not, the person seeks out or tends to place himself "in the way of" pleasurable experiences. As he becomes emotionally involved, as the "self" becomes invested, he becomes especially vulnerable or exposed to traumatization. Second, pleasures, especially sexual ones, are often associated with aggression and violence, which, in their admixture with pain, are categorized as "sado-masochism." These experiences, because of their unique emotional intensity, are particularly likely to breach psychic defenses and thus become traumatic. Finally, judgments of conscience, of internal disapproval, may be particularly harsh in matters of pleasure, especially for persons who have been subjected to strict or guilt-ridden child-rearing, and this self-disapproval provides in itself an important element of trauma.

The struggle to deal with the continuing effects of a traumatic experience goes on long after its occurrence, sometimes for the rest of a person's life. Depending upon the range of psychological strengths and skills available to him this struggle may take differing forms: shifts in the direction of his way of life (abandonment of a profession, withdrawal from society); the development of symptoms of mental illness; and various efforts to integrate the experience through creative activity or other forms of communication that give evidence of the continuing inner conflict. Those who witness such struggles — for example a person in the throes of a vital decision who vacillates between alternatives — may find them confusing and contradictory, as the oscillations of the elements of the struggle seem to swing now one way and now the other, much as a boat on a stormy sea rolls and pitches as it seeks to maintain its equilibrium. If the person places himself in situations of unusual jeopardy, either out of a need to master fear, to test himself, or to assume unusual responsibility (all of these are applicable in Lawrence's case), he will naturally expose himself more frequently to trauma. Its actual occurrence, however, even in an environmental "field" in which its likelihood is quite great, depends to a large extent on circumstances and on chance. It is a frequent, paradoxical characteristic of trauma that its repetition, often in a particularly painful form, is sought in later years because of the unconscious wish to repeat the pleasurable elements of the experience; the desire to master or erase its traumatic nature; and, finally, the need to seek in the repetition punishment for the unacceptable elements of pleasure that both the original and the subsequent repetitions of the experience contained.

Had the discrepancies between the grand, prophetic, private and public purposes that the events of the war were meant to fulfill for Lawrence, and the actualities of the campaigns, been limited to disappointments with the rapacious behavior of the Arabs or with Britain's failure to live up to its various promises to them, Lawrence would have been understandably disappointed, or even disillusioned, but he would not have suffered a painful and irrevocable psychic injury. The shattering of his defenses resulted from much more specific physical and emotional experiences related to the daily horrors of the war itself.

The assault Lawrence endured at the hands of the Turks at Derʿa in November of 1917, and the loss of control he suffered a few miles away at Tafas ten months later, were the severest traumatic experiences he underwent during the course of the campaigns. Both experiences in different ways represented personal violations, an overwhelming of psychological defenses, and the shattering of the integrity of the self. There is some evidence that they were psychologically linked. The depravity and horror of Derʿa and Tafas stood for Lawrence in the boldest possible contrast to his noble prophetic dream, for which the capture of Damascus was to be the culmination. So bitter was the pain attached to the achievements of the campaigns that it filled their triumphs with bitter irony, as the subtitle of *Seven Pillars of Wisdom* ("A Triumph") conveys.

It was a fundamental aspect of Lawrence's psychology — or, more accurately, of the elements of his psyche that he brought to bear in dealing with troubling experiences — to bring the public into his personal struggles, to make (even though with reluctance) private suffering a matter of public record. He was aware, of course, of the introspective quality of *Seven Pillars of Wisdom,* and his reluctance to bring it to public attention is related more to its self-revelations, its links to his personal conflicts, than to such practical reasons as passages that are critical of other people. *The Mint* and many of Lawrence's letters similarly reveal his continuing struggle to overcome the destructive experience of the war, whose persisting effects he sought to surmount through creative writing. His writings are filled with the swings of self-esteem from heights of egoism and confidence to depths of despair and self-contempt, and with other paradoxes of feeling, contradictions of attitudes, and contrasts of emotion that are the characteristic substance of inner conflict. The wish to make himself known stands for Lawrence alongside the desire to hide or deceive; unusual candor and factual honesty exist side by side with secrecy and distortion; and a desire to evoke sympathy appears to war with unusual stoicism.

These puzzling contradictory qualities are what have made Lawrence seem mysterious to many people, fascinating to others, and exasperating, irritating or even boring to still others. George Bernard Shaw was undoubtedly right when he wrote that by contrast to other public figures, such as David Lloyd George or Ramsay MacDonald, Lawrence was very well known indeed. "Well, I defy you to tell me about either of them one tenth of what everybody knows about Lawrence," wrote Shaw.[1]

This struggle to "work out" in introspective psychological activity the continuing effects of traumatic experiences is familiar to the psychoanalyst or psychiatrist who attempts in the privacy of his office to help a suffering patient. Together they examine the patient's personality and look at what he wishes to see and yet not see, to understand yet to obscure, to resolve but still to avoid. It is puzzling and somewhat unfamiliar to find similar psychic activity in writings that are destined to reach the public (writings, that is, that are not fiction). It is as if Lawrence's readers and biographers (myself included, I hasten to add) were invited to function as posthumous psychiatrists for a man who never chose to be a patient during his lifetime. Although Lawrence would probably be alternately amused and irritated at the way his psychic bones have been endlessly picked over since his death, he would be glad, I am sure, if his public self-exposure could contribute to human understanding and to the relief of suffering. He would, I am quite certain, want others to benefit from any knowledge or insights gained from studying and analyzing the struggles he could not resolve altogether for himself.

There are three written accounts by Lawrence of what happened at Der'a. The first (in point of time), quite brief, is in a report on the activities of the Jaza'iri brothers, Muhammad Sa'id and 'Abd-al-Qadir, to the deputy chief political officer at British headquarters in Cairo, dated June 28, 1919.[2] The second, far more detailed, is in the 1922 (Oxford) edition of *Seven Pillars of Wisdom* (a key paragraph and one less critical passage were eliminated from the 1926 [subscribers'] edition). The third account, also quite brief, occurs in a letter to Mrs. Shaw written in 1924. These passages, although each stresses a different aspect of what happened, are generally consistent except on one point, namely, whether Lawrence was positively identified by the Turkish bey. In the Cairo report Lawrence claims he was identified, but in *Seven Pillars of Wisdom* he suggests that the bey did not really know who he was. There is no evidence in the letter to Mrs. Shaw to substantiate Aldington's and Knightley and Simpson's assertions that Lawrence admitted to her that he gave in specifically to the *bey's* pederasty. He does suggest that he had not written in "the book" everything that had occurred and indicates that he will now tell her the missing facts. However, the letter, although candid enough, adds nothing that is not in the 1922 *Seven Pillars* version, although he tells more in the letter about how he felt and the relationship between this experience and his retreat into the ranks after the war was over.

Though Lawrence rarely talked about the Der'a incident to his friends, the reports of what he did say have only compounded the confusion. For example, George Bernard Shaw wrote in the flyleaf of his wife's copy of the subscribers' edition of *Seven Pillars*: "one of his chapters (LXXXI) tells of a revolting sequel to his capture by the Turks and his attraction for a Turkish officer. He told me that his account of the affair is not true. I forebore to ask him what actually happened."[3] Considering the highly private and intimate nature of what occurred, Lawrence's candor is quite exceptional. The distortions in his accounts, the doing and undoing, and the inability, as Lawrence wrote to Mrs. Shaw, "to put it plain" completely, are hardly more than one would expect in the recollection and retelling of any severely traumatic experience, all the more so if the teller is aware that his tale will become more or less public property. We, the public, may wish to know more, but it is doubtful whether Lawrence could have been more accurate or more explicit in recalling precisely what happened to him. Experiences so acutely painful and disturbing, both physically and emotionally, are especially prey to distortions of recollection, which the mind imposes upon memories that are, from the standpoint of the self-regard, intolerable and unacceptable.

On or about the night of November 20, 1917, Lawrence set out with an elderly Arab companion on a reconnaissance mission which required that he enter the railroad junction of Der'a south of Damascus. In his 1919 report to general headquarters in Cairo he wrote: "I went into Deraa disguised to spy out the defenses, was caught and identified by Hajim Bey, the governor, by virtue of Abd el Kadir's description of me. (I learned all about his treachery from Hajim's conversation, and from my guards.) Hajim was an ardent paederast and took a fancy to me. So he kept me under guard till night, and then tried to have me. I was unwilling, and prevailed after some difficulty. Hajim sent me to the hospital, and I escaped before dawn, being not as hurt as he thought. He was so ashamed at the muddle he had made that he hushed the whole thing up and never reported my capture and escape. I got back to Azrak very annoyed with Abd el Kadir, and rode down to Akaba."[4]

In *Seven Pillars of Wisdom* (in very tiny handwriting in the original manuscript)[5] Lawrence describes his capture by a Turkish sergeant near Der'a station, his unsuccessful effort to pass himself off as a Circassian (and therefore exempt from military service and not a deserter subject to Turkish imprisonment), and the bey's "fawning" attempt to seduce him. "Incidents like this," he wrote, "made the thought of military service in the Turkish army a living death for wholesome Arab peasants, and the consequences pursued the miserable victims all their after life, in revolting forms of sexual disease."[6] When the bey tried force, Lawrence resisted and kneed him in the groin. Then, according to Lawrence's vividly detailed and lurid account, the bey retaliated by hitting, biting and kissing him, and by forcing a bayonet through a fold in the flesh over Lawrence's ribs and turning the blade. Lawrence quotes the bey as saying, "You must understand that I know:* and it will be easier if you do as I wish," but then Lawrence adds, "It was evidently a chance shot, by which he himself did not, or would not mean what I feared."[7] Lawrence still refused the bey's advances and the latter "half whispered to the corporal to take me out and teach me everything."[8] There follows a still more vivid account of his being whipped, beaten, kicked, and otherwise tortured horribly by the soldiers and of his fear, sensations and struggles to handle the severe pain and to dissociate himself from what was happening.

The account of the torture contains two references to sexual molestation mingled with the assaults ('they would squabble for the next turn, ease themselves, and play unspeakably with me"; and, "I was being dragged about by two men, each disputing over a leg as though to split me apart: while a third man rode me astride").[9] The sequence of events during this part of the account is rather hard to follow. The brutality seems so severe that it appears virtually incompatible with survival, much less a return to activity within a few days.

After a bruising and lacerating kick by the corporal, which damaged a rib, "I remembered smiling idly at him, for a delicious warmth, probably sexual, was swelling through me: and then that he flung up his arms and

* Presumably, who Lawrence was.

hacked with the full length of his whip into my groin. This doubled me half-over, screaming, or, rather, trying impotently to scream, only shuddering through my mouth. One giggled with amusement. A voice cried, 'Shame, you've killed him.' Another slash followed. A roaring, and my eyes went black: while within me the core of life seemed to heave slowly up through the rending nerves, expelled from its body by this last indescribable pang."[10]

After this, Lawrence's beaten body was returned to the bey, who rejected him "as a thing too torn and bloody for his bed." Lawrence states that he was then taken to a wooden shed, where he was washed and bandaged by an Armenian dresser and then allowed, unguarded, to obtain some "shoddy clothes" and corrosive sublimate (poison) to "safeguard against recapture."[11] He describes his unopposed escape, his observations at the time of how the town might be captured, and his return to his two Arab companions, to whom he told "a merry tale of bribery and trickery, which they promised to keep to themselves, laughing aloud at the simplicity of the Turks."[12] He indicates again that he did not believe, at the time at least, that he had been identified — "Halim [one of his companions] had been up to Deraa in the night, and knew by the lack of rumour that the truth had not been discovered."[13]

"During the night," Lawrence's account concludes, "I managed to see the great stone bridge by Nisib. Not that my maimed will now cared a hoot about the Arab Revolt (or about anything but mending itself): yet, since the war had been a hobby of mine, for custom's sake I would force myself to push it through. Afterwards we took horse, and rode gently and carefully towards Azrak, without incident,[14] except that a raiding party of Wuld Ali let us and our horses go unplundered when they heard who we were. This was an unexpected generosity, the Wuld Ali being not yet of our fellowship. Their consideration (rendered at once, as if we had deserved men's homage) momently stayed me to carry the burden, whose certainty the passing days confirmed: how in Deraa that night the citadel of my integrity had been irrevocably lost.

"I was feeling very ill, as though some part of me had gone dead that night in Deraa, leaving me maimed, imperfect, only half myself. It could not have been the defilement, for no one ever held the body in less honour than I did myself. Probably it had been the breaking of the spirit by that frenzied nerve-shattering pain which had degraded me to beast level when it made me grovel to it, and which had [sic] journeyed with me since, fascination and terror and morbid desire, lascivious and vicious perhaps, but like the striving of a moth towards its flame."[15]

This account of Lawrence's experience at Der'a, the only one that is detailed, leaves several unanswered questions. These include, for example, how even a man of his toughness could have been so badly tortured and yet return to action so soon without evidence of permanent injury; why, even if he were not identified with certainty, he was permitted to escape; and just what is meant by the "core of life" heaving up and being expelled from its body by pain, that is, whether this was Lawrence's way of describing orgasm, or loss of consciousness, or what.

Arnold Lawrence, who never questioned the factual nature of his brother's account of the Der'a experience, wrote me several years ago that "outside evidence of the Deraa episode is scarcely to be expected," a statement which, despite various efforts on my part and others to substantiate or refute Lawrence's accounts, still remains essentially valid.[16] The *Sunday Times* authors, Knightley and Simpson, sought out information about Hajim Bey himself, who was the governor of the region and based at Der'a at the time of this episode. Their informants, who included the bey's son (the bey himself having died in 1965), insisted that the bey was an aggressive heterosexual — he kept diaries which detailed his activities with girls and a case of gonorrhea — and they doubted that he was homosexual. The bey's son told Knightley and Simpson that his father never mentioned having met Lawrence (not surprising considering the circumstances under which they apparently met). It is, of course, not unlikely that despite his heterosexuality, which seems to have had a compulsive quality, the bey may have been bisexual and kept his homosexual activities secret. Or, as the *Sunday Times* authors suggest, the "paederast" in question may have been someone else.

If the bey's homosexuality cannot be established, his brutality is well substantiated. There are, in King's College, London, among Colonel Joyce's papers, notes made by an Arab soldier which document atrocities committed by Hajim Bey and his soldiers at es-Salt. The Arab soldier, Ibn al-Najdawi, wrote that Hajim Bey, the district officer of Hauran, accompanied by three hundred volunteers, attacked es-Salt, decapitated and otherwise mutilated Arab and Kurdish children and their families, killing in all seven hundred people and burning their homes.[17]

Some of Lawrence's biographers have been skeptical about the occurrence of the Der'a episode, and a prominent American historian has recently found the story "most implausible."[18] Richard Meinertzhagen, with whom Lawrence served in the Middle East and in the Colonial Office, claimed in his memoirs that Lawrence told him he was "sodomized by the Governor of Deraa, followed by similar treatment by the Governor's servants," but that he could not publish the account of the incident because it was too degrading and " 'had penetrated his innermost nature.' "[19] This statement appears in a diary entry of July 20, 1919, and seems an authentic contemporary statement. However, many of Meinertzhagen's "on-the-spot" diary entries, none of which were published until 1959, when the author was in his late seventies, seem to be amalgams of contemporary notes, later recollections, and Lawrence's own writings.

Liddell Hart once told me that during the period in which he was preparing his biography of Lawrence, he talked with several Allied participants in the campaign who told him that Lawrence arrived back in Aqaba after the Der'a incident badly shaken, pale and obviously distraught.[20] I also wrote to Captain L. H. Gilman for any information he might have concerning the authenticity of the episode, and Gilman replied:

> As regards Deraa, I am afraid I cannot help you very much as only Lawrence knew what happened. We knew that he had been through some distressing experience, but Lawrence never alluded to it not even when, subsequently, I was alone with him. I really only learned the details of his experience from his own account in *Seven Pillars of Wisdom*. The whole affair must have been a horrible nightmare, and you, of all men, must know how difficult it is to describe a nightmare.[21] Neither I, nor any of the other British officers who served in Arabia, had any doubt that he did suffer this indignity, and Lawrence was far too gallant and honourable a man to invent this experience: there would have been no point in it.[22]

There the matter must rest, at least for me. I have little doubt that Lawrence underwent a painful, humiliating assault at Der'a at the hands of the Turkish commander and his soldiers, and the element of sexual pleasure he experienced in the midst of such indignity, pain and degradation was particularly intolerable and shameful to him. A passage in a letter to Mrs. Shaw refers unquestionably to a sexual surrender of some sort: "For fear of being hurt, or rather to earn five minutes respite from a pain which drove me mad, I gave away the only possession we are born with — our bodily integrity."[23] But there is no way of telling from this letter to whom the surrender was made or the form it took, only that the surrender itself was an abomination to him ("It's an unforgivable matter, an irrecoverable position: and it's that which has made me foreswear decent living, and the exercise of my not-contemptible wits and talents").[24]

Ten years afterwards Lawrence wrote Robert Graves that the incident at Der'a "apparently did permanent damage" to his nerve, "coming as it did after the grave disappointments of the bridge and the train failures" and the exhaustion of the preceding few months.[25] His friend Eric Kennington believed that in an effort to redeem his fallen "sublime standard" Lawrence "made the rest of his life an intermittent struggle to reclaim or re-create his soul, by altruistic labour, self-denial and penance."[26]

From 1919 to 1925, Lawrence wrote and rewrote the passage dealing with the episode in *Seven Pillars of Wisdom* — nine times he told Mrs. Shaw. He relived its agonies, but he also seems to have been able to achieve to some extent a therapeutic working-through of its influence.[27] "That is the 'bad' book," he wrote to Mrs. Shaw, "with the Deraa Chapter. Working on it always makes me sick. The two impulses fight so upon it. Self-respect would close it: self-expression seeks to open it. It's a case in which you can't let yourself write as well as you could."[28] He had written also to Edward Garnett of his shame over including the incident in the original version of the book, and his conflict about the passage accounted in part for his reluctance for several years to publish even a limited version of the complete book. "For weeks I wanted to burn it in the manuscript," he wrote Garnett, "because I could not tell the story face to face with anyone, and I think I'll feel sorry, when I next meet you, that you know it. The sort of man I have always mixed with doesn't so give himself away."[29]

In the subscribers' edition, published in 1926, Lawrence called the incident "the earned wages of rebellion,"[30] as if it were a punishment warranted by his improper role in the Revolt as a whole. Despite various efforts to come to terms with the experience through his writing and acts of penance, Lawrence continued, at least until 1930, to relive in terrible nightmares the horrors of Der'a and other war experiences.[31] The Der'a episode also contributed to Lawrence's need for repeated acts of penance, which included severe whippings by a tough Scotsman named John Bruce (see Chapter 33).

The episode at Der'a, and the part Lawrence played in the events that took place ten months later at the Syrian village of Tafas three miles northwest of Der'a, appear to be connected by the motive of vengeance. He told a service comrade that he had wished to do back "ten fold" to the Turks what they had done to him at Der'a. Lawrence did not specifically speak of Tafas in this context, nor do I wish to imply that he deliberately took revenge at Tafas for the violation at Der'a. I am suggesting only that his apparent loss of control at Tafas was linked to and perhaps made possible by the humiliation he had experienced ten months before, and the desire for revenge it left within him. Of the link between the Der'a assault and Lawrence's later flagellation problem there is little doubt.

In contrast to the episode at Der'a there were several witnesses of the events around Tafas other than Lawrence himself, and one would think it would be simpler therefore to determine accurately what occurred. Unfortunately, as in many historical events, especially those which are emotionally charged or cast credit or blame upon their participants, exactly who saw or did what is not so easy to determine. The film *Lawrence of Arabia* shows the six-footer Peter O'Toole as Lawrence, his arms covered with blood, having enthusiastically entered into the slaughter of Turkish prisoners. After the film came out, a former British soldier in Allenby's army, George Staples, who claimed he knew Lawrence "in Arabia," is reported in an interview in a Canadian newspaper to have said of the film's depiction of the episode: "It was just like I remembered it."[32] But the interview, solicited evidently to promote the film, contains internal inconsistencies which cast doubt upon its historical value. For one, Staples could not have been an eyewitness because he was in a regiment of the Middlesex Yeomanry, which was over thirty miles from Tafas when the massacre took place.[33]

There are two written accounts by Lawrence of these events. The first, his official report for headquarters,[34] was written hurriedly, probably in Damascus. According to this report, a Turkish column of about two thousand men retreating to the northeast passed through Tafas and "allowed themselves to rape all the women they could catch." The report continues: "We attacked them with all arms as they marched out later and bent the head of their column back towards Tel Arar. When Sherif Bey, the Turkish Commander of the Lancer rearguard in the village, saw this he ordered that the inhabitants be killed. These included some twenty small children (killed with lances and rifles), and about forty women. I noticed particularly one pregnant woman, who had been forced down on a saw-bayonet. Unfortunately, Talal, the Sheikh of Tafas, who as mentioned, had been a tower of strength to us from the beginning, and who was one of the coolest and boldest horsemen I have ever met, was in front with Auda abu Tayi and myself when we saw these sights. He gave a horrible cry, wrapped his headcloth about his face, put spurs to his horse, and rocking in the saddle, galloped at full speed into the midst of the retiring column, and fell, himself and his mare, riddled with machine gun bullets, among their lance points.

"With Auda's help we were able to cut the enemy column into three. The third section, with German machine-gunners resisted magnificently, and got off, not cheaply, with Jemal Pasha in his car in their midst. The second and leading portions after a bitter struggle, we wiped out completely. We ordered 'no prisoners' and the men obeyed, except that the reserve company took two hundred and fifty men (including many German A.S.C.) alive. Later, however, they found one of our men with a fractured thigh who had been afterwards pinned to the ground by two mortal thrusts with German bayonets. Then we turned our Hotchkiss on the prisoners and made an end of them, they saying nothing. The common delusion that the Turk is a clean and merciful fighter led some of the British troops to criticize Arab methods a little later — but they had not entered Turaa or Tafas, or watched the Turks swing their wounded by the hands and feet into a burning railway truck, as had been the lot of the Arab army at Jerdun. As for the villagers, they and their ancestors have been for five hundred years ground down by the tyranny of these Turks."[35]

The continuing Arab attack upon the retreating Turkish Fourth Army resulted in its destruction. The account of this slaughter concludes: "Old

Auda, tired of slaughter, took the last six hundred prisoners. In all we killed nearly five thousand of them, captured about eight thousand (as we took them, we stripped them, and sent them to the nearest village, where they were put to work on the land till further notice) and counted spoils of about one hundred and fifty machine guns and from twenty-five to thirty guns."[36]

The account in *Seven Pillars of Wisdom* is more detailed, more dramatically vivid and realistic. The grotesque horror of the slaughter of pregnant women and children at Tafas is described relentlessly. The death of a mortally wounded child and the desperate suicidal charge of Talal are richly described. Lawrence quotes himself as saying to the men around him, "The best of you brings me the most Turkish dead."[37] The vengeful assault by the Arabs was led by 'Awdah "while the flame of cruelty and revenge which was burning in their bodies so twisted them, that their hands could hardly shoot. By my orders we took no prisoners, for the only time in our war.[38] . . . By nightfall the rich plain was scattered over with dead men and animals. In a madness born of the horror of Tafas we killed and killed, even blowing in the heads of the fallen animals; as though their death and running blood could slake our agony."[39]

One group of Arabs had not heard the "no prisoners" order and captured about two hundred Turkish prisoners. "I had gone up to learn why it was," Lawrence wrote, "not unwilling that this remnant be let live as witnesses of Talal's price; but a man on the ground behind them screamed something to the Arabs, who with pale faces led me across to see. It was one of us — his thigh shattered. The blood had rushed out over the red soil, and left him dying; but even so he had not been spared. In the fashion of to-day's battle he had been further tormented by bayonets hammered through his shoulder and other leg into the ground, pinning him out like a collected insect.

"He was fully conscious. When we said, 'Hassan, who did it?' he drooped his eyes towards the prisoners, huddling together so hopelessly broken. They said nothing in the moments before we opened fire. At last their heap ceased moving; and Hassan was dead; and we mounted again and rode home slowly (home was my carpet three or four hours from us at Sheikh Saad) in the gloom, which felt so chill now that the sun had gone down."[40]

General Allenby wrote to his wife a few days afterwards: "My cavalry had some sharpish fighting outside the town (Damascus) and a good many dead Turks are still lying about. . . . The number of prisoners is appalling. . . . Barrow (commanding 4th. Cavalry Division) had to leave 2000 behind as they could not keep up. He put them in villages and told the inhabitants to take care of them. Very likely their throats are cut by now. Lawrence tells me that his Arabs found one village where 40 women and 20 or 30 children had been bayoneted by the Turks, in pure wantonness. After that very few, if any, prisoners were taken by them."[41]

The young Arab soldier Subhi al-'Umari wrote confidently that, although Lawrence's description of the Turkish massacre at Tafas was accurate, it must have been based on hearsay because he (Lawrence) was not there at all.[42]

Suleiman Mousa seems to credit the word of an Ottoman officer that no massacre of women and children occurred at Tafas,[43] but all other observers who have written of this event, including Subhi al-'Umari, agree that it did. For example, Lord Winterton, a British officer attached to the Arab forces, wrote in an early article published before Lawrence's accounts appeared: "Tafas is a village inhabited by Arab fellaheen, and the Turks, on the pleas that some of the inhabitants sympathized with General Nuri's force, committed some abominable atrocities, even bayoneting children in arms, before the village was taken."[44] Similar descriptions of the atrocities are provided by F. G. Peake, Ali Jawdat (one of the Arab leaders), General Chauvel, Hubert Young and Lord Birdwood (Nuri al-Sa'id's biographer).

The question of Lawrence's personal role is more complex. No British officer arrived in Tafas with Lawrence, Allenby's cavalry having bypassed the villages and towns, and none of the Arab accounts written by participants in the campaign (including Ali Jawdat's memoirs) refer specifically to Lawrence's actions at Tafas. Hubert Young, who was nearby at the time, wrote: "Ali Jaudat told me that he and Lawrence had tried vainly to save a batch of prisoners from being massacred by Bedouin, whose latent savagery had been aroused by the sight of butchered women and children."[45]

The most detailed accounts have been provided by Peake (who arrived in Tafas shortly after Lawrence) in notes prepared in 1963 (after the film *Lawrence of Arabia* had been released) and in 1965.[46] In the second paper Peake wrote:

> It is complete nonsense to say that the Turks killed no Arabs in Tafas. I arrived in Tafas some time after Lawrence, as my heavily loaded camels could not keep up with him. When I arrived in Tafas I saw that T.E.L.'s Bedouin were entirely out of control. They, infuriated by the dead men, women and children, lying in and around the village (which I myself saw) were rushing about shouting and seeking out any Turks who might be alive. Lawrence came running to me and ordered me to restore order as soon as possible. This I was able to do by dismounting 100 of my men and marching with bayonets fixed on the village. The sight of this disciplined body of soldiers was enough. The tumult and the shouting died and the Bedouin rode off northwards in the hope of catching up with the Turks who had already retreated. I was told later that they might have killed a straggler or two, but when they came up with the main body they found them ready to resist. Gradually during the afternoon they drifted back to their leader, T.E.L. I was ordered by Lawrence to collect and guard all Turks as they arrived from the battlefield in Palestine. As their numbers increased, I had

to employ a number of Turkish prisoners to help my Egyptian soldiers. This, I think, is sufficient to prove that there never was any No Prisoners order.

In the earlier account Peake wrote that he regarded Lawrence's use of "we" in his writings as indicating the assumption of responsibility for actions of the Arabs he had helped to bring about. In Peake's view Lawrence had stated that "by my orders we took no prisoners" because "he obviously wished to assume the responsibility for an occurrence which neither he nor anyone else could at that time have prevented. He knew that, in future, it would be severely criticized but as he had originally stirred the Arabs to rebel against the Turks [not really so], it was only just that he should be blamed and not the Arabs."[47] Lawrence's subsequent activity and orders to Peake convinced Peake "that when Lawrence had the power to control the Arabs he used it effectively. Previous to my arrival he could only try to influence the Sheikhs to stop their followers killing the Turkish soldiers, but such was their fury that they had no mind to listen to him." Of the view of Lawrence at Tafas shown in the film Peake wrote, "It is to be regretted that a film showing Lawrence of Arabia should give the impression that he was a callous person or rather enjoyed seeing such horrible scenes. It would have been no less interesting and far more truthful had he been shown rushing about on foot trying to persuade the Sheikhs to call back their men."[48]

Even if there was no specific "no prisoners" order, there remain questions of Lawrence's role in the death of the two hundred captured Turks who had pinned down Hassan and what is meant by the statement in *Seven Pillars* "we killed and killed." Did Lawrence personally take a hand in the slaughter? Arnold Lawrence has shed some light on the first question. After the film *Lawrence of Arabia* appeared, which demonstrated that Lawrence enjoyed killing and which showed him as a hysterical sadist, Arnold Lawrence wrote for a London weekly: "My brother expressly states that he himself ordered that no prisoners be taken* — 'The best of you brings me the most Turkish dead' — but makes plain, I should have thought, that he did so because he shared the ungovernable fury of every Arab. Unquestionably he afterwards suffered deeply over his loss of control; I suspect that largely accounts for his insistence, throughout the rest of his life, that no Englishman could so serve an alien race without prostituting his own self."[49] In notes Arnold Lawrence prepared on the Tafas episode after receiving Peake's material he wrote, "In conversation with me, T.E.L. gave me clearly to understand that he had himself given the order to execute the 200 captured Turks who had pinned down Hassan;† that he had then regarded it as an execution was unmistakeable."[50]

---

* Arnold Lawrence wrote this before receiving Peake's accounts of Tafas.
† On my manuscript he wrote, "I wonder now whether he did even this."

As regards Lawrence's taking a personal hand in the killing, there is no direct outside evidence. Kirkbride, who was not nearby during the Tafas action, describes the killing of a group of Turkish prisoners by the Tafas villagers, "who were beside themselves with fury, and by the Bedouin, whose blood lust was now aroused,"[51] but he does not mention Lawrence.

In another context, before the film was made, Kirkbride wrote of Lawrence: "His tastes were anything but bloodthirsty, and he appeared to be genuinely shocked by the free use which I made of my revolver during the evening after we entered Damascus, when he would insist on rescuing Turkish stragglers from being murdered by the local populace." And: "Occasionally, someone turned nasty in Damascus and I shot them at once before the trouble could spread. Lawrence got quite cross and said, 'For God's sake stop being so bloody-minded!'"[52] After the film appeared, Kirkbride wrote to Liddell Hart:

> It is complete nonsense to describe him [Lawrence] as having been either sadistic or fond of killing. (These are not always the same thing.) He once told me that his ideal of waging war was based on the professional condottieri of medieval Italy. That is to say, to gain one's objectives with a minimum of casualties *on both sides*. . . . T.E.L. had a horror of bloodshed and it is because of that that he tends to pile on the agony in the passages of *Seven Pillars of Wisdom* dealing with death and wounds — not because he liked seeing others suffer.[53]

But Kirkbride's opinions are not evidence on Lawrence's conduct after the Turkish massacre at Tafas. My own opinion, which is based on the available evidence and what is known of Lawrence's character, is that Lawrence did lose control to the extent of ordering the execution of the two hundred prisoners. Seeing Hassan pinned down was the last straw after all Lawrence had seen and been through. I believe it to be highly doubtful that he personally took part in the killing, and I also believe that he did make an effort, as Peake describes, to control the excesses of the Arabs. I agree with Peake that the "we" regarding the "no prisoners" order and the other events around Tafas is a commander's "we" and derives from Lawrence's wish to assume full responsibility for the wild excesses of 'Awdah and the other Bedouin, to cover up for them.

But I believe, too, that this "we" reflects how intense Lawrence's identification with the Bedouin had become: he could feel their desire for revenge as if it were his own.[54] This identification with the Arabs *in revenge* connected with his own desire for revenge for what had been done to him by the Turks at Der'a ten months before and, combined with the other stresses of the campaigns he had undergone, accounts for his loss of control.

Arnold Lawrence had firsthand knowledge that his brother suffered deeply and felt considerable guilt over the loss of control at Tafas. No matter what the provocation, Lawrence could not reconcile his conduct with his own standards as a military officer or with his personal ideals regarding the value of human life. His brother has pointed out that because Allenby's cavalry bypassed the villages and towns they may not have seen the slaughtered villagers at Tafas. In consequence, the shock with which the British reacted to the Arabs' revenge was not mitigated by an understanding of the circumstances and "added greatly to T.E.'s difficulty till he left for England, if not afterwards."[55] The episode illustrates how dangerous it is for a sensitive person to become too personally absorbed in the daily activity of a military campaign for which he has, at the same time, a more general responsibility.

Peake is obviously correct in his observation that Lawrence knew he would in the future be severely criticized for this episode, but the point may in fact be extended further. I would suggest that Lawrence allowed ambiguities regarding his role at Tafas to stand and that he permitted criticism thereby. This interpretation is consistent with the guilt that Lawrence felt over the episode, and his need to court criticism and seek penance following the campaigns.[56]

I have dwelt at length upon the Tafas episode, and have taken particular pains to try to establish Lawrence's role in it, because it not only, I believe, is pertinent to the evaluation of his character, but raises at the same time issues pertinent to assessing the actions and personality of any public figure. A man who, with little provocation, orders, takes part in, and even enjoys killing helpless prisoners, while experiencing no guilt, is a sadist who invites little sympathy or interest. The film *Lawrence of Arabia* would lead us to believe this true of Lawrence. On the other hand, a man who, after observing extreme atrocities committed against people with whose lives and suffering he has become overly identified, gives way to the impulse to order a retaliatory execution by the victims of these atrocities is a different, more complex person, who may be deserving of our compassion and understanding as well as our criticism.

Damascus, the lodestar, was to have been the fulfillment of Lawrence's prophet dream. Its capture was to have been the glorious culmination of triumphant leadership, whereby a deserving people were sparked into liberating themselves from bondage. In a personal psychological sense its capture was meant to symbolize a final redemption, and the success of the Arab Revolt should have gained Lawrence peace from the criticism of an exacting self-regard that had demanded heroic achievement as the price of relief from an unconscious sense of worthlessness, of being the illegitimate result of sin and deception. Lawrence wrote later that he wept upon entering Damascus "for the triumphant thing achieved at last."[57] But the dream ended there for Lawrence and "its capture disclosed the exhaustion of my springs of action."[58] The treachery of 'Abd al-Qadir, whom Lawrence was instrumental in deposing after entering Damascus, came to represent the painful contrasts and paradoxes of his experience in the Arab Revolt. Whether al-Qadir deserved it or not (and there is evidence that he did, at least in part), he became the object of Lawrence's intense hatred. His betrayals are elevated to major importance in *Seven Pillars of Wisdom* and in a subsequent official report (issued months after his death). The report was devoted exclusively to his actions and those of his brother, although it is doubtful that al-Qadir played as significant a role as the one Lawrence assigned to him. It appears that he had offered his help at first to the sharifian cause but subsequently betrayed it.

In a scene in *Seven Pillars of Wisdom*, Lawrence conveyed the extreme bitterness, irony and sense of degradation he felt on the day before he left Damascus. A medical major, thinking Lawrence was responsible for the still-terrible conditions of the hospital, burst out at him, " 'Scandalous, disgraceful, outrageous, ought to be shot.' " The powerful passage continues: "At this onslaught I cackled out like a chicken with the wild laughter of strain; it did feel extraordinarily funny to be so cursed just as I had been pluming myself on having bettered the apparently hopeless.

"The major had not entered the charnel house of yesterday, nor smelt it, nor seen us burying those bodies of ultimate degradation, whose memory had started me up in bed, sweating and trembling, a few hours since. He glared at me, muttering 'Bloody brute.' I hooted out again, and he smacked me over the face and stalked off, leaving me more ashamed than angry, for in my heart I felt he was right, and that anyone who pushed through to success a rebellion of the weak against their masters must come out of it so stained in estimation that afterward nothing in the world would make him feel clean. However, it was nearly over."[59]

Lawrence was twenty-eight when he first took an active, personal part in the Arab Revolt. Although he had seemed thus far to his friends and acquaintances an unusual, even odd, sort of genius, he had not given evidence of being deeply troubled, or even especially introspective. But his experiences in the Revolt, however his part in it is assessed, were personally shattering. The horrors he observed and took part in during 1917 and 1918 following the deaths of his two brothers; the political conflict; the disillusionment with the behavior of the Arabs; the multiple bouts of febrile illness;[60] the death of Dahoum; and, above all, the traumatic assault at Der'a and the loss of control at Tafas, brought about profound changes in Lawrence's mental state and personality.

The Der'a and Tafas experiences are, in my opinion, of special importance because of their link with the substance of unconscious conflicts and with areas of psychic vulnerability which, until these events occurred, had remained merely potential areas of emotional disorder (all men, I believe, harbor such areas) without overt indication of unusual distress).

But Der'a and Tafas touched off in Lawrence — there seem to be no right words — or brought into his consciousness in an abrupt and devastating way, forbidden or unacceptable sexual, aggressive and vengeful impulses. Until this time, what he had felt as merely a strong attraction to renunciation and self-denial, a kind of idealistic puritanism not without its normal place in the England of his day, became exaggerated into a powerful need for penance through degradation and humiliation, a need that was accompanied by a permanently lowered self-regard. In addition, he was left with a compulsive wish to be whipped, attributable directly to the Der'a experience, which was the source of much later misery and which I will be discussing later in this book.

The other result of the traumatic experiences was a marked increase in introspection. Before the war Lawrence rarely took himself as the object of his curiosity, but after 1918 he turned to studying himself intensively. It is usual for persons who have undergone severe psychic traumata or who suffer from various forms of emotional distress to try to understand themselves through introspection: self-understanding is a time-honored path to the relief of emotional pain. But it is perhaps unusual to find such introspection in a public figure, especially one who has been a military leader.

Long after the war's end Lawrence wrote to Herbert Samuel, the former high commissioner of Palestine, a letter that captures his perception of his war experiences: "I'm glad [Hogarth] sent you the last copy of my Seven Pillars, though I am sorry too, for you will look down on me, as a human being, after you have read it. Yet, when other people judge me as harshly as I judge myself, I find myself pleading that I was in a horrible position in Arabia, throughout, with the choice of no more than evils before me: and that I tried always to do the least harmful of them, and to do it so that the fewest small people were harmed by it. However, all these things are finished."[61]

# FOUR

# THE POLITICAL YEARS
## 1918–1922

# Introduction

During the four years following the end of World War I and before his enlistment in the RAF in 1922 Lawrence's work and personality became known in the Western world. These were the years in which he struggled to fulfill in the political realm what he felt to be the responsibilities he had undertaken in the campaigns of the war in the Middle East. During this time "Lawrence of Arabia" was created by the public, and for Lawrence himself a gulf began to grow between his inner self as he felt it to be and the unfolding legendary figure he was both drawn to and loathed. These were years in which Lawrence expanded enormously his range of personal relationships and came to know many of the important public figures, writers and artists of the Great Britain of his day. Archeology was cut off to him as a profession, even had he chosen to pursue it, because he could not enter the countries of the Middle East except under political surveillance.[1]

This was a time in which the leadership of the Western powers could still move men and countries around like pawns and bargained and dealt in states and whole populations. As Arnold Toynbee, who was a British delegate to the Paris Peace Conference, wrote, Lawrence and the other advocates for the Middle Eastern peoples "sank deeper in the mire till they were as deeply bogged down as the rest of us."[2] In this period the disappointments in the postwar political arena merged psychologically for Lawrence with the painful effects of his war experiences and led, finally, to a major change in the course of his life.

Hannah Arendt recognized the extraordinary intensity of the conviction that underlay Lawrence's pursuit of his postwar aims. "Never again was the experiment of secret politics made more purely by a more decent man," she wrote. She felt that the imperialists destroyed Lawrence, reducing him until "nothing was left of him but some inexplicable decency."[3] This view is too strong, I believe. The political struggle did not destroy Lawrence, although it contributed greatly to his disillusionment. He accomplished much during these years and was able ultimately, with Winston Churchill, to impose his convictions to a large extent upon the final postwar settlements for the Arab regions. But "politically the thing was so dirty that I grew to hate it all before it came out more or less honestly in the end," he wrote to a friend many years later.[4]

Even his denigrators acknowledge that Lawrence was able to an extraordinary extent to impose his will upon the region's future. "On the threshold of the contemporary Middle East," Elie Kedourie wrote in 1956, "stands the figure of T. E. Lawrence, an object at once of awe and pity. He is a portent, a symbol of the power of chance over human affairs, and of the constant irruption into history of the uncontrollable force of a demonic will exerting itself to the limit of endurance. The consequences of his actions have touched numberless lives, and yet their motives were strictly personal, to be sought only in his intimate restlessness and private torment."[5]

These were also the years in which Lawrence first wrote and rewrote *Seven Pillars of Wisdom,* in which he attempted — he was probably the first military commander to do so — to fuse a narrative of battle with the examination of the meaning that making war had for a responsible leader, to connect the motive for making war with the impact of its horror upon the individual. He also wrote articles about Middle Eastern politics, guerrilla strategy, and dynamiting, and about the Arab lands and peoples.

The saga of the writing of *Seven Pillars of Wisdom,* which began in 1919, continues through most of this period. The burden and excitement of writing it reflect the conflict which resulted from reliving his wartime experiences over and over again. On the other hand, the constant and repeated reworking of the memories and materials of the war served a therapeutic role for Lawrence and helped to integrate them and modify their devastating impact.

He entered the RAF three months after he had completed the third and final basic text of the book, although he would continue to rework, criticize and abridge the material for five more years. The writing of *Seven Pillars of Wisdom* was curiously related to his friendship with his much-valued predecessor Charles Doughty, whose classic work, *Travels in Arabia Deserta,* Lawrence brought once more before the public, while he hid his own narrative from public view.

A definitive analysis of the postwar political settlements in the Middle East, or even of the significance of Lawrence's part in them, is beyond my competence or intention. Rather, I will attempt to describe carefully these political questions in order to show how they are related to the personal struggles and suffering Lawrence was undergoing during this time. The emphasis in this section will be, as it has been throughout the book, upon the relationship between inner psychology and creative action, between the private man and his public impact.

# 20

# Arab Self-determination and Arab Unity

As Lawrence, without official position or orders, assumed personal command of the desert war, he took, with even less well-defined authority, similar personal responsibility for the postwar political negotiations that would determine the political future of the Arab lands that had been wrested from the Ottoman Empire during and after the war's course. It was a natural extension of the "godfather" role he began to assume for himself in 1916.[1] The Arabs, he knew, believed in individuals, not in institutions, and he had been the individual who had represented Great Britain's capabilities, inspiration and assurances to them.[2]

As he had taken it upon himself to represent Britain's plans and promises to the Arabs, so he would try to see to it that these promises were honored. "I salved myself," Lawrence wrote not long after the war, "with the hope that, by leading these Arabs madly in the final victory I would establish them, with arms in their hands, in a position so assured (if not dominant) that expediency would counsel to the Great Powers a fair settlement of their claims. In other words, I presumed (seeing no other leader with the will and power) that I would survive the campaigns, and be able to defeat not merely the Turks on the battlefield, but my own country and its allies in the council chamber. It was an immodest presumption: it is not yet clear if I succeeded: but it is clear that I had no shadow of leave to engage the Arabs, unknowing, in such hazard."[3]

Between 1918 and 1922, in London, Paris, Oxford, Cairo and Amman, Lawrence fought to fulfill what he considered to be his responsibilities to the Arab peoples he had led or influenced during the war. To achieve his ends he used the persuasive powers of his intellect as well as the full range of talents at the disposal of his flexible and winning personality. He waged a war of words in personal negotiations and in public and private papers and letters, even "becoming an Arab" again, at the risk of looking ridiculous, when he thought it would serve a useful purpose. Irving Howe has observed that Lawrence's loyalty to the Arabs during the immediate postwar period, "this stubbornness — let us call it by its true name: this absolute unwillingness to sell out — began to strike his British colleagues as unreasonable, an embarrassment to their diplomacy."[4]

Lawrence's experiences between 1915 and 1920, and his personal associations at All Souls College in Oxford, especially with Lionel Curtis, brought about a marked increase in his political sophistication. The practical amalgam he hoped to make in 1916 of Arab nationalistic aspirations and British national interests had been replaced by a more farseeing vision of change for the Arab world and for Asia. He conceived that the Arab regions from North Africa to the Indian Ocean would become the first African or Asiatic countries to achieve dominion status within the British Empire, "our first brown dominion."[5] His conception of dominion status for these lands ran counter to the more traditional imperialism that still influenced the postwar peace conferences, as the victors prepared to divide the spoils of war. Lawrence's effect upon the direction of British imperialist interest in the years after the war has yet to be evaluated objectively.

Lawrence saw in 1920 that the example of the Bolshevik Revolution along the northern frontiers of Arab Asia would have a powerful influence in strengthening and encouraging indigenous political nationalism in Western Asia.[6] "The Bolshevist success," he wrote, "has been a potent example to the East of the overthrow of an ancient government, depending on a kind of divine right, and weighing on Asia with all the force of an immense military establishment."[7] Lawrence called his conceptions of Asiatic dominions within the British Empire "the new Imperialism," perhaps in part to reduce the threatening character of his arguments for his British readers. His notions were not imperialistic by the standards of the period, or even of our own, although a kind of chauvinism in Lawrence seems to have been quite genuine. He envisioned a system of alliances between the Arab Asiatic countries whereby they would join the British Empire for military protection and security, but remain politically autonomous within it. "I think there's a great future for the British Empire as a voluntary association," he wrote in 1928.[8] To achieve this end the British government would have to encourage the assumption of political responsibility among these countries and to pull back from a governing role to an advisory one.

Lawrence's most concise expression of his view of this change was set forth in an anonymous article which appeared in September 1920 in the political monthly the *Round Table*. The writing seems to have been inspired by striking current examples of traditional imperialism in the British administration of Iraq and the French take-over in Syria. We are continuing to see the realization of some of the prophecies contained in this article in the passing decades of the twentieth century:

"This new condition, of a conscious and logical nationalism, now the dominant factor of every indigenous movement in Western Asia, is too universal to be extinguished, too widespread to be temporary. We must prepare ourselves for its continuance, and for a continuance of the unrest produced by it in every contested district, until such time as it has succeeded and passed into a more advanced phase. It is so radical a change in the former complexion of Western Asia as to demand from us a revision of the principles of our policy in the Middle East, and an effort to adjust ourselves, that the advantage of its constructive elements may be on our side.

"This new Imperialism is not just withdrawal and neglect on our part. It involves an active side of imposing responsibility on the local peoples. It is what they clamour for, but an unpopular gift when given. . . . We can only teach them how by forcing them to try, while we stand by and give advice. This is not for us less honourable than administration: indeed, it is more exacting for it is simple to give orders, but difficult to persuade another to take advice, and it is the more difficult which is most pleasant doing. We must be prepared to see them doing things by methods quite unlike our own, and less well: but on principle it is better that they half-do it than that we do it perfectly for them. In pursuing such courses, *we will find our best helpers not in our former most obedient subjects, but among those now most active in agitating against us* [italics added], for it will be the intellectual leaders of the people who will serve the purpose, and these are not the philosophers nor the rich, but the demagogues and the politicians. . . . Egypt, Persia and Mesopotamia, if assured of eventual dominion status, and present internal autonomy, would be delighted to affiliate with us, and would then cost us no more in men and money than Canada or Australia. The alternative is to hold on to them with ever-lessening force, till the anarchy is too expensive, and we let go."[9]

The history of the changing relations between the Great Powers and their former colonies since World War I may be looked at in terms of contrasting examples — instances in which prepared withdrawal has been followed by peaceful affiliation as contrasted with efforts at continued colonial control resulting in bloodshed and suppression.

Political nationalism as we are familiar with it in the twentieth century is a product of European history. Its growth among the Arab countries of Western Asia has been promoted in large part by contact with the European Great Powers, although its ideas were actively taken up in the Middle East, especially in Syria, in the later years of the nineteenth century and the first decades of the twentieth. World War I, with its use of propaganda and the need of the Allies for partners in the East against

Turkey and Germany, brought an enormous increase in contact between the Western powers and the Arab countries, and thus a marked growth in Arab nationalistic ambitions. "The astonished peoples of Western Asia," Lawrence wrote in 1920, "could not choose but hear us, and began, willingly or unwillingly, to see what we were like, and comprehend our least notions. They did not always like them, but they learned a lot. In particular they learned what each of us was fighting for (they heard it from all our mouths, and we all said much the same thing), and a thing sworn to by so many witnesses must surely be true. This liberty, this humanity, this culture, this self-determination, must be very valuable."[10]

From the time of his first dispatches in 1916 Lawrence distinguished between Arab nationalistic feeling — the drive toward self-determination — and political unity or the formation of a single Arab national state or confederation. He was always a strong advocate of self-determination, but never seems to have believed deeply in the concept of Arab political unity. He doubted that the Arab countries would voluntarily surrender their autonomy to become part of a nation. There is often a suggestion in Lawrence's political writings, especially during the war, that his doubts about Arab unity relate not only to its feasibility but also to the threat to British national interests that a strong Arab nation might present. "When people talk of Arab Confederation or Empires they talk fantastically," he wrote in 1928; "it will be generations, I expect — unless the vital tempo of the East is much accelerated — before any two Arab states join voluntarily. I agree that their only future hope is that they should join; but it must be natural growing together. Forced unions are pernicious, and politics, in such things, should come after geography and economics. Communications and trade must be improved before provinces can join."[11] To Mrs. George Bernard Shaw he wrote even more bluntly: "I'd as soon unite the English-speaking races as the Arabic-speaking. Some amalgamations there may be, must be, if their show progresses well: but not any general union or confederation, in my time, I hope. The tremendous value, and the delight of the Arab areas lie in their concentrated localization."[12]

Six years later (1928) in a starkly realistic, negative mood he wrote on the manuscript of Liddell Hart's biography: "Arab unity is a madman's notion — for this century or next, probably. English-speaking unity is a fair parallel. I am sure, I never dreamed of uniting even Hedjaz and Syria. My conception was of a number of smaller states."[13]

But in 1920 he had been neither so sure nor so cynical. He conceived then of "the Arab movement" as developing in stages, born in the desert as he felt all ideas were originally, moving to Damascus with Faisal the father (and perhaps Lawrence the godfather), and reaching its final realization under the leadership of Baghdad. Mesopotamia, Lawrence believed, would (because of its natural resources, potential wealth and strategic geography) ultimately "be the master of the Middle East, and the power controlling its destinies."[14] He concluded: "The question of a unity of the Arabic peoples in Asia is yet clouded. In the past it has never been a successful experiment, and the least reflection will show that there are large areas, especially of Arabia, which it would be unprofitable ever to administer. The deserts will probably remain, in the future as in the past, the preserves of inarticulate philosophers. The cultivated districts, Mesopotamia and Syria, have, however, language, race and interests in common. Till today they have always been too vast to form a single country: they are divided, except for a narrow gangway in the north, by an irredeemable waste of flint and gravel: but petrol makes light of deserts, and space is shrinking today, when we travel one hundred miles an hour instead of five. The effect of railways, air-ways and telegraph will be to draw these two provinces together, and teach them how like they are: and the needs of Mesopotamian trade will fix attention on the Mediterranean ports. The Arabs are a Mediterranean people, whom no force of circumstances will constrain to the Indian Ocean: further, when Mesopotamia has done her duty by the rivers, there will remain no part for water transport in her life — and the way by rail from Mosul or Baghdad to Alexandretta or Tripoli is more advantageous than the way to Basra. It may well be that Arab unity will come of an overwhelming conviction of the Mesopotamians that their national prosperity demands it."[15]

Lawrence hoped that the Zionist movement would have the result of bringing the Jews into a position of technological leadership in the Arab regions of Asia and North Africa and that they would help to raise the material level of their Arab neighbors. "The Jewish experiment," he wrote in 1920, "is a conscious effort, on the part of the least European people in Europe, to make head against the drift of the ages, and return once more to the Orient from which they came. The colonists will take back with them to the land which they occupied for some centuries before the Christian era samples of all the knowledge and technique of Europe. They propose to settle down amongst the existing Arabic-speaking population of the country, a people of kindred origin, but far different social condition. They hope to adjust their mode of life to the climate of Palestine, and by the exercise of their skill and capital to make it as highly organised as a European state. The success of their scheme will involve inevitably the raising of the present Arab population to their own material level, only a little after themselves in point of time, and the consequences might be of the highest importance for the future of the Arab world. It might well prove a source of technical supply rendering them independent of industrial Europe, and in that case the new con-federation might become a formidable element of world power. However, such a contingency will not be for the first or even for the second generation, but it must be borne in mind in any laying out of foundations of empire in Western Asia. These to a very large extent must stand or fall by the course of the Zionist effort, and by the course of events in Russia."[16]

There is no evidence that Lawrence anticipated the intransigence and hostility that would develop between Arabs and Jews. But as the war drew to a close he was faced with much more practical political problems. As the Arab Revolt advanced northward successfully under his and Faisal's leadership it produced a rebirth of nationalistic aspirations in Syria that had been crushed by the Young Turks in 1915.[17] "Syrians of Syria are enlisting by thousands in the ranks of his [Faisal's] armies," Lawrence wrote in 1918, two months after the armistice.[18] Syria was nationalistic in sentiment from south to north and there were many Iraqi officers in Faisal's army who soon carried the wave of Arab nationalistic feeling to their own homeland.[19] An Anglo-French declaration of November 7, 1918, born in part out of the exhilaration and good will that attended the winding up of the war, seemed to favor the upsurge of nationalism. The British and French leaders would, they promised, work toward "definite freedom of the peoples so long oppressed by the Turks," "encourage and assist in the establishment of native governments in Syria and Mesopotamia," "ensure equal and impartial justice for all," and "aid the economic development of the country by inspiring and encouraging local initiative."[20] But the co-signers soon reverted to prewar imperialist patterns and were confronted, therefore, during the next few years with native rebellions in Egypt, Iraq and Syria.

Lawrence has been criticized by modern Arab nationalist writers for failing to believe in or support Arab unity. They resent his recommending the division of Greater Syria — what is now Syria, Lebanon, Jordan and Israel — into separate countries (Greater Syria had been, according to Suleiman Mousa, "the moving spirit of the Arab countries" for centuries).[21] They also resent his backing Faisal and the Hashemite family and neglecting other, especially Syrian, nationalist leaders.[22] Anis Sayigh, for example, has noted that Husayn, with his Bedouin background, had too narrow an outlook to represent Arab nationalist interests in Europe, and that Faisal, because of Lawrence's influence, gave up many nationalist demands in Paris and London. Mousa and Sayigh take particular exception to Lawrence's imposing Hashemite rulers on several Arab states.

But these are arguments based on the vantage point of this decade. In 1918 at the close of the war there seemed, apart from Faisal, no Arab nationalist leader with sufficient authority to represent all the Arab peoples, one who was above the factionalism of the fragmentary nationalistic movements that existed after the war and who possessed enough prestige to speak for the Arab peoples at the Paris Peace Conference.

The political situation had not changed greatly from Lawrence's description of it in 1917: "The largest indigenous political entity in settled Syria is only the village under its sheikh, and in patriarchal Syria the tribe under its chief."[23] Furthermore, there was no viable conception of nationhood among the Arabs of Greater Syria in 1919, let alone of Greater Syria and Iraq combined.

The history of the Arab-speaking regions since 1945, when the last colonial reins were released, testifies to the difficulty that these countries have encountered in developing the unity that some Arab nationalist leaders have sought. 'Abd al-Rahman Shahbandar, the Syrian nationalist leader (he was one of the Seven Syrians who extracted the promise of postwar independence from the British high command in Cairo in June 1918) wrote from the perspective of 1931: "Lawrence spent all possible energy to establish the strongest foothold in order for the Arabs to have full independence under their own flags. But what use was there when the British had understandings with their allies, the French, which tore apart and dispersed this full independence."[24] Indeed, soon after the start of the Peace Conference, which opened in Paris in January 1919, it became evident that France, far from observing the spirit of the Anglo-French declaration issued just two months before the conference began, was determined to compensate for her suffering in World War I with the acquisition of a new colony in Syria. She justified this colonization, which amounted virtually to a conquest, on the grounds of her long-standing commercial interests in the Levant, her protective role in relation to the Maronite Christian Sect in Syria and Lebanon (the hostility of the Muslim majority in Syria was ignored or misunderstood), and the Sykes-Picot Agreement of 1916, which recognized French interests in the area.

Lawrence has been criticized repeatedly for his intractable "hostility" toward the French.[25] But the simple fact is that French colonial policies (over which he could have no liberalizing influence) ran in direct opposition to his political and humanistic beliefs and to the personal commitments, however wisely or unwisely made, that he had undertaken. The meaning of these commitments to Lawrence, the depth of his disappointment over their frustration, and the recognition of the limitations of his power to fulfill them is a principal theme in the pages that follow.

# 21

# Leaving Damascus Behind

Although Lawrence left "the silky coolness of the Damascus dust"[1] on October 4, 1918, the Allied forces continued to move northward through Syria during the rest of the month. By the twenty-sixth, Beirut, Homs, Hama and Aleppo were in Anglo-Arab hands, and the Turks had been driven back within the borders of Asia Minor. At the time of the signing of the Turkish armistice on October 31, the Allied forces, dominated by the British and their Arab companions, were in possession of virtually all Syria and Mesopotamia.[2] Particularly embarrassing from the standpoint of future Anglo-French relations was the fact that in Beirut, the Levantine center of French interest, an Arab government had been declared and Arab flags hoisted, though temporarily, with Allenby's permission (also temporary) and Lawrence's possible connivance (later denied by him).[3] The stage was set for the Anglo-French struggle over Syria that was to occupy the peacemakers for the next two years.

Despondent that his extraordinary efforts during the campaigns had seemed to come to so little, Lawrence returned to Cairo. There he wrote, "I feel like a man who has suddenly dropped a heavy load — one's back hurts when one tries to walk straight."[4] Lawrence met Wingate on October 14 and gave early notice of his opposition to French claims in Syria and of his intention to struggle in England to hold his government to their commitments to self-determination for their Arab allies.[5] He returned to England through Italy by train, and later told Graves and Liddell Hart that he was promoted temporarily to full colonel at his own request in order to get a berth on an express staff train to Le Havre, to which this higher rank would entitle him.

Lawrence's ambivalent attitude toward his military rank is reflected in this and in other stories of the period in which he both ridicules and capitalizes on the fact of his colonelcy. The stories follow the pattern of the myth of the hero: Lawrence, appearing at his scruffiest, is mistaken for a nobody by an officer of lower rank and less deserving than he, who demands a salute or other show of respect (in one case an officer was even accompanied by a lady, "probably not his wife!").[6] Lawrence then reveals his true identity, delivers a bit of a moral lecture, and the chastened officer goes away red-faced with embarrassment, to the delight of Lawrence and whatever ordinary folk of humble station happen to witness the scene.[7]

Lawrence arrived in England on or about October 24, after stopping in Rome on the way back long enough to learn from Georges Picot that the French intended to impose French advisors on Faisal.[8] Robert Lawrence told me that he appeared wasted and weighed only seventy to eighty pounds instead of his usual 112 pounds or more.[9] Although this weight loss seems virtually inconceivable, a portrait done by James McBey during this period shows Lawrence's gaunt appearance.[10]

Emaciated or not, in less than a week after arriving in England and before the armistice with Turkey was signed, Lawrence was putting forward his ideas for the Near East at a meeting of the Eastern Committee of the War Cabinet. The chairman was the foreign secretary, Lord Curzon, for whom, it has been said, the British Empire was the successor of the Roman and "the instrument of divine will" as well.[11] In welcoming Lawrence at the meeting, Curzon said that "His Majesty's Government had for some time watched with interest and admiration the great work which Colonel Lawrence had been doing in Arabia, and felt proud that an officer had done so much to promote successful progress of the British and Arab arms."[12]

Lawrence was asked to furnish the cabinet with a memorandum in which he set forth his views in more detail.[13] He emphasized British interests in Western Asia, calling the area between Egypt, Persia and Anatolia "our Monroe area," and tactfully reminded his readers of the reason for the selection of the sharif of Mecca and his sons as the leaders for Britain to back in the Revolt and of their noble sacrifices in the Allied cause. He lauded their loyalty and achievements in battle (as General Allenby's "handmaid," of course) and pressed for an autonomous Syria under Faisal's rule ("sovereign in his own dominions with complete liberty to choose any foreign advisers he wants of any nationality he pleases"). Neither France nor the French were mentioned.

In this memorandum, as in his statement to the Eastern Committee the previous week, Lawrence said that the Arabs could accept Jewish "infiltration" in Palestine, and Zionist advice and assistance, as long as it was under a British "façade" and an independent Jewish state was not established. He followed this memorandum with a more detailed proposal for the Arab administration of Iraq.[14]

In the meantime, on October 30, Lawrence had an audience with King George V, a famous episode in which the king wished formally to bestow upon him the C.B. (Companion of the Bath) for Aqaba and the D.S.O. (Distinguished Service Order), honors for which he had already been gazetted (that is, the recommendation of the honors had already been published in a British official gazette).

A meeting with the king himself would naturally be an incident about which myths and stories would proliferate (some of which, as Arnold Lawrence has pointed out, "caused more harm to T.E.L.'s reputation than he can have anticipated")[15] and I shall not attempt in this instance to distinguish fully the actuality from the legend since no recorders of the event, except perhaps the king's secretary, seem to have been exempt altogether from leaving distortions. What is certain is that Lawrence declined to accept the decorations and explained to the king that his reasons for doing so concerned his wish to dramatize and uphold the Arab cause, to accept no official honors for what he regarded as his ignoble role in it, and to impel the British government through the force of his own moral example to honor its responsibilities to its Arab allies.

Whether the audience was public or private (certainly it was private: Lawrence would not have wished to cause the king public embarrassment), whether Lawrence was insulting or courteous, whether the king was insulted or understanding, whether Lawrence did or did not threaten to fight the British, the French or anyone else if Britain let the Arabs down are questions that have been debated by Lawrence's critics, friendly and hostile. The most reliable account of the meeting is in the actual record of the Court:

> During the conversation, Colonel Lawrence said that he had pledged his word to Feisal, and that now the British Government were about to let down the Arabs over the Sykes-Picot Agreement. He was an Emir among the Arabs and intended to stick to them through thick and thin and, if necessary, fight against the French [not the British] for the recovery of Syria.
>
> Colonel Lawrence said that he did not know that he had been gazetted or what the etiquette was in such matters, but he hoped that the King would forgive any want of courtesy on his part in not taking these decorations.[16]

Arnold Lawrence pointed out that the gesture was effective in attracting attention to the Arab cause, and had a particular impact upon Winston Churchill, who was instrumental more than two years later in rectifying Arab grievances — to the extent it lay within his and Britain's power to do so.[17]

On November 8 Lawrence began his sponsorship of Faisal as representative of the Arabs at the Peace Conference. "I believe there will be conversations in Paris in fifteen days time between the Allies about the question of the Arabs," he telegraphed King Husayn with Foreign Office approval, and urged him to have his son prepared to leave Syria for France and to telegraph "the Governments of Great Britain, France, the United States and Italy telling them that your son is proceeding at once to Paris as your representative."[18] On November 21, at another meeting of the Eastern Committee of the War Cabinet, Lawrence was delegated to meet Faisal at Marseilles and to offer at least the possibility of sharifian government in Iraq. In this meeting Lawrence reiterated his conviction that "there would be no difficulty in reconciling Zionists and the Arabs in Palestine and Syria, provided that the administration at Palestine remained in British hands."[19] After some delay Husayn telegraphed the necessary confirmation, Faisal sailed for France (on an English ship), and Lawrence duly met him in Marseilles as arranged. Accompanied by a small party, Faisal was to tour France, meet the French president, and then travel to England.

Ahmad Qadri, who was a member of Faisal's party, states that despite their courtesy the French made a point of regarding Faisal as an Arab shaykh from the Hijaz rather than as a leader who had played an important role in the Allied victories in the desert.[20] Together the party traveled to Lyons, where they were met by Colonel Brémond. Brémond subsequently wrote that he had been given certain instructions concerning Lawrence: "With Lawrence you must be very clear and show him he is on the wrong track. If he comes as a British colonel, in an English uniform, we will welcome him. But we will not accept him as an Arab, and if he comes disguised he has nothing to do with us."[21] According to Brémond, Lawrence was indeed dressed "en costume oriental," although Lawrence denied that he had met Faisal in Arab dress.[22] In any event Nuri al-Sa'id, who was also a member of the Arab party, noted "some coldness between Lawrence and the French."[23] Lawrence was asked to return to England, which he promptly did, but not, according to Qadri, before explaining to Faisal that the French were plotting to keep him away from the Peace Conference.[24] Faisal and his companions were then given red-carpet treatment and escorted ceremoniously about France. Commenting on the incident after being informed by Liddell Hart in 1933 of Brémond's account, Lawrence wrote: "Feisal was guest of the French Government, whose duty (and pleasure) it was to do the entertaining. So a foreign hanger-on was out of place. He [Brémond] was quite nice and (I thought) quite right about it. He gave me no idea that his instructions were as you report."[25]

Just at this time (November 26, 27 and 28, 1918) there appeared in The Times three articles written anonymously by "a correspondent who was in close touch with the Arabs throughout their campaign against the Turks after the revolt of the Sherif of Mecca."[26] Lord Winterton, who was well connected in official circles, had put Lawrence "in touch with the right people in Fleet Street so that the Arab point-of-view might have a 'good press!' "[27] And one of Winterton's friends, Evelyn Wrench, introduced Lawrence to "various newspaper friends." The articles are clearly propaganda pieces written in support of the Arab cause and the leadership of Faisal. They are written in the first person, although the author's personal role is minimized. The campaigns are made to sound like cleanly fought adventures by a worthy and effective ally of a British nation that had the diplomatic wisdom to recognize its value, and Faisal is made the undisputed hero of the piece.[28]

One of the newspapermen with whom Lawrence was put in touch after the armistice was Geoffrey Dawson, editor of *The Times*. In the letter to Dawson that accompanied the articles Lawrence championed the Arab cause: "The points that strike me are that the Arabs came into the war without making a previous treaty with us, and have consistently refused to listen to the temptations of other powers. They never had a press agent, or tried to make themselves out a case, but fought as hard as they could (I'll swear to that) and suffered hardships in their three campaigns and losses that would break up seasoned troops. They fought with ropes around their necks (Feisal had 20,000 alive and 10,000 dead on him. I the same: Nasir 10,000 alive, and Ali el Harith 8,000) and did it without, I believe, any other very strong motive than a desire to see the Arabs free. It was rather an ordeal for as very venerable a person as Hussein to rebel for he was at once most violently abused by the Moslem press in India and Turkey, on religious grounds."[29] Lawrence reviewed the value received by Britain from the Arabs in the Revolt, debated the value of an alliance with the Arabs, and credited McMahon, the high commissioner in Egypt, with bringing about the sharif's entry into the war, as advised by Storrs, Clayton and Lawrence himself. Lawrence followed this with his sharifian solution for the Near East and concluded, rather unrealistically: "The old Sherif wants to be prayed for in Mosques on Friday. He is, already, in Syria, and in parts of Mesopotamia, and will be generally if we leave things alone."[30]

On December 9, Faisal was finally ready — or, perhaps more accurately, was allowed — to leave France for England,[31] and Lawrence met him in Boulogne. According to Brémond's description Lawrence was dressed in white and under the dark sky gave the effect of "a Catholic choir boy." Lawrence with pointed politeness invited Brémond to accompany them to London, but Brémond declined regretfully because his mission was over and he had not been given "the latitude to accept."[32]

In England one of the first things Lawrence did was to arrange a meeting between Faisal and Chaim Weizmann, the Zionist leader (none other than Arthur Balfour, the foreign secretary, had advised Weizmann to seek an agreement with Faisal).[33]* At the meeting Faisal and Weiz-

* In the Balfour Declaration of November 2, 1917, the British government had gone on record as favoring "the establishment in Palestine of a national home for the Jewish people."

mann discussed the possibility of reconciling Zionist hopes in Palestine with Arab ambitions in Syria.

At this time the hope of Jewish-Arab collaboration in the Middle East was very much alive. Lawrence and Weizmann had met during the desert campaigns and Weizmann and Faisal had had a meeting in June 1918, at Aqaba. Less well known was the fact that both Lawrence and Weizmann had met in Palestine with Palestinian Arab leaders who, even early in 1918, were suspicious of the extent of British collaboration with the Hashemite family to the exclusion of other Arab groups.[34] But in the first months after the war's end Arab-Jewish cooperation under British auspices did not seem so difficult, and Lawrence strove to use his friendships with both Faisal and Weizmann to achieve these purposes. He even hoped that Zionist wealth could be used to support Faisal's government in Syria and to block French interests thereby. The vital distinctions between a Jewish homeland (or the possibility of unlimited Jewish immigration into Palestine) and the establishment of a sovereign Jewish state seem not to have been considered at this time.

On December 13 Faisal is quoted as having told a Reuter's correspondent: "The two main branches of the Semitic family, Arabs and Jews, understand one another, and I hope that as a result of interchange of ideas at the Peace Conference, which will be guided by ideals of self-determination and nationality, each nation will make definite progress towards the realization of its aspirations. Arabs are not jealous of Zionist Jews, and intend to give them fair play, and the Zionist Jews have assured the nationalist Arabs of their intention to see that they, too, have fair play in their respective areas." He looked toward "mutual understanding of the aims of Arabs and Jews," and the clearing away of former bitterness, "which indeed had practically disappeared even before the war."[35] The *Jewish Chronicle* wrote of the Weizmann-Faisal meeting that "a complete understanding between the Emir and Dr. Weizmann was arrived at on all points."[36] Later in the month Lord Rothschild gave a dinner in Faisal's honor at which the amir again "emphasized the kinship between the Jews and the Arabs, and the harmony between the Jewish nationalist and the Arab nationalist aspirations."[37]

On January 3, 1919, an agreement between Faisal and Weizmann was drawn up by Lawrence,[38] and signed in this spirit in anticipation of the Peace Conference. By the terms of the agreement, Jewish immigration was to be encouraged and the rights of Arab peasants and farmers were to be protected in exchange for Zionist economic and political support of an Arab state, whose boundaries with Palestine were to be established at the conference.[39] The parties agreed to act "in accord and harmony at the Peace Conference." Faisal left himself an escape clause (whose tone Lawrence tried to soften in his English translation) in which the amir stated categorically that if Britain did not live up to its promise of Arab independence he "would not be bound by a single word of the Agreement."[40] As it turned out, the agreement never acquired validity because this last condition was never fulfilled. But it does demonstrate the hopes existing at that time, and toward which Lawrence and British leaders such as Sykes and Ormsby-Gore strove: that Zionist and Arab interests could be brought together for the progressive political and economic development of the Middle East.[41] None of those involved in the agreement seem to have anticipated either the hostility that soon would arise in Palestine and in other parts of the Arab world to the establishing of a Jewish homeland in Palestine, or the mishandling on all sides of the problems of Arab-Jewish relations.[42]

During the approximately three weeks they spent together in England in December of 1918, Lawrence hardly left Faisal's side, and took great pains in his behalf. He attempted to fulfill all the amir's various needs, and dressed in Arab garb accompanied him to an audience with King George (Lawrence's second meeting with the king). And Lawrence was indeed effective in securing British backing for Faisal at the Peace Conference, which soon took place.[43]

Soon after returning to England Lawrence picked up the strands once more of his friendship with Charles Doughty. Doughty opened the correspondence, and in replying, Lawrence brushed lightly over the tops of his experience in the Arab Revolt: "It's been a wonderful experience and I've got quite a lot to tell. I'm afraid it is not likely to be written for publication, since some of it would give offence to people alive (including myself!)."[44]

After the new year Lawrence went to a party in Arab dress, "for fun," he wrote many years later.[45] But at the time he embarrassed himself by having done so and wrote apologetically: "I behaved like a lunatic yesterday. But I have been trying for three years to think like an Arab, and when I come back with a bump to British conventions, it is rather painful, and I keep deciding to put an end to it. However, nothing ever happens."[46] Lawrence also discussed his views about Asia and the Arabs with the American publisher F. N. Doubleday and with Rudyard Kipling, both of whom he met at dinner parties in London shortly before leaving for the Peace Conference. Kipling, who had lived for many years in the United States and was on friendly terms with many American politicians, was impressed by Lawrence's ideas and urged him to approach the Republicans, led by Henry Cabot Lodge, since Wilson, in his opinion, was "on the wane" and inclined "to give lofty advice and return to his national fireside."[47]

Lawrence approached the Paris Conference optimistically. "I'm off to Paris, ('peace work,' they call it)," he wrote to a fellow officer of the Hijaz campaign. "In the Hedjaz there is nothing, for Jidda isn't a white man's country! In Syria everything depends on the conference. We may find ourselves shut out, or let in, on the same ground as the rest of the earth. And till the end of the conference I cannot tell you."[48]

By the end of the conference Lawrence was deeply frustrated, disillusioned and troubled.

# 22

# At the Paris
# Peace Conference

The rulers of the world have sat here with the problem of human living before them, laid out on their table by the tragedy of war," the American journalist and reformer Lincoln Steffens wrote Allen H. Siggett on April 13, 1919. "That should have opened their minds and hearts too and led them to tackle the job in some new, big way. They wanted to. There was good-will here. But their old habits of mind, their fixed attention upon things they do not really want, their age, their education, — these have made it impossible for them to do their work. . . .

"So they have failed. They have the appearance of success, but, — they have failed. And it does not matter. The problem will be solved. Other, newer men, with a fresher culture, — the men I have seen lately, — they will have their turn now."[1]

Despite the idealism of Woodrow Wilson and his Fourteen Points (Point 12 proclaimed that the non-Turkish nationalities of the Ottoman Empire should "be given an opportunity for autonomous development"), the echoes of nineteenth- and early twentieth-century European nationalism could be heard at the Peace Conference. As Jon Kimche has written, "the whole history of the Middle East in the half century between 1919 and 1969 is a history of the undoing of the work of the Paris Peace Conference of 1919 and the settlements made after the First World War."[2]

Even Lloyd George, who did make an effort at the conference to support a self-governing Syria as had been promised in the agreements made during the war, had little grasp of the meaning of Arab nationalistic aspirations. Deals were made between leaders concerning other peoples, regions and countries without regard to the interests of those peoples. "When Clemenceau came to London after the war," Lloyd George wrote in his memoirs, "I drove with him to the French Embassy through cheering crowds who acclaimed him with enthusiasm. After we reached the Embassy he asked me what it was I specially wanted from the French. I instantly replied that I wanted Mosul attached to Irak, and Palestine from Dan to Beersheba under British control.* Without any hesitation he agreed. Although that agreement was not reduced to writing he adhered to it honestly in subsequent negotiations."[3]

Lawrence arrived in Paris in the second week in January and attended the conference officially as a technical advisor to the British delegation. During the next three months he identified himself with Faisal and the Arabs (Faisal represented and defined the Arab cause because he led the Arab delegation). Lawrence frequently interpreted and translated for Faisal, and wore an Arab headcloth when he believed it would strengthen the Arab position. He also took pains, as revealed in the Foreign Office files, to see that members of the Arab delegation were afforded by the Great Powers the diplomatic courtesies and access to the telegraphic facilities they needed.[4] Lawrence operated in Paris — though unsuccessfully for his cause at the conference — at the pinnacle of power, taking part in meetings with Clemenceau, Lloyd George, Wilson and other world leaders. A decade later he would write to a British politician: "Anyone who had gone up so fast as I went (remember that I was almost entirely self-made: my father had five sons, and only £300 a year) and had seen so much of the inside of the top of the world might lose his aspirations, and get weary of the ordinary motives of action, which had moved him till he reached the top. I wasn't a King or Prime Minister, but I made 'em, or played with them, and after that there wasn't much more, in that direction, for me to do."[5]

Lawrence was, as Gertrude Bell wrote her family at the time, "the most picturesque" figure at the conference,[6] and his legend grew whether or not he believed it to be his conscious wish that it should. Lawrence spent a lot of time with members of the American delegation and with American newsmen. He hoped for a time that the Americans would take responsibility for the administration of Syria — they would, he believed, care more about the interests of its people than the French would.[7] As a result of the earlier cooperation of Faisal with the Zionists, the British Zionists were able to introduce Faisal to the leaders of the American delegation in Paris and help get the Arab cause before the Peace Conference.[8] But the effort was not successful. As Churchill wrote: "The idea that France, bled white in the trenches of Flanders, should emerge from the Great War without her share of conquered territories was insupportable to [Clemenceau] and would never have been tolerated by his countrymen."[9] Syria was to be part of the French booty of World War I.

---

* Did he know where these places were? They do not delimit the boundaries of any country. Perhaps Lloyd George used the expression purely symbolically, but symbolizing what? Mosul was in the sphere of French influence in the Sykes-Picot Agreement, which was thus undone casually in a conversation between two world leaders carving up the spoils of war.

As early as January 11, 1919, just a few days after arriving in Paris, Lawrence attended a dinner with Lionel Curtis, William Bullitt and others in which "the discussion was about Poland and Colonel Lawrence's expedition and experiences."[10] One of the guests, David Hunter Miller, a legal advisor to the American delegation, wrote of the discussion in his diary: Lawrence expressed the hope that the United States could administer Syria; his attitude was "distinctly anti-French." Miller found Lawrence's conversation "remarkable," and it seems to have been from his diary that the story arose of Faisal's reading the Koran while Lawrence, seeming to interpret his "speech," gave a talk about whatever he chose. In Miller's contemporary version, the setting of the speech had been Glasgow in December 1918, not Paris as in a later rendition of the story.[11] Faisal, according to Lawrence as reported by Miller, "leaned over to Colonel Lawrence and said to him in Arabic, 'Instead of making a speech I'm going to get up and recite a chapter from the Koran [the chapter of the Cow, according to Arnold Toynbee] and as your interpretation you can say anything that you damn please!' "[12]

Even in the first days of the Peace Conference, two months before Lowell Thomas began his talk and film show in New York, Lawrence had already become a legendary figure. James Shotwell, an American history professor on leave from Columbia University, also kept a contemporary diary of the Peace Conference. He describes Lawrence as "that younger successor of Mohammed, Colonel Lawrence, the twenty-eight-year-old conqueror of Damascus, with his boyish face and almost constant smile — the most winning figure, so every one says, at the whole Peace Conference."[13] Shotwell goes on to describe Lawrence joking with Faisal and translating for him at informal gatherings of American officials where they pleaded their case:

> Lawrence came in the uniform of a British Colonel, but wore his Arab headdress to keep his friend company (they wore them through the meal and all evening). His veil over his explorer's helmet was of green silk and hung down over his shoulder with a tassel or two of deep red. Around his head was a similar double strand of big, colored braid, as in the case of Feisal's, about three-quarters of an inch in diameter and looking much like a crown. He has been described as the most interesting Briton alive, a student of medieval history at Magdalen College, where he used to sleep by day and work by night and take his recreation in the deer park at four in the morning — a Shelly-like person, and yet too virile to be a poet. He is a rather short, strongly built man of not over twenty-eight [actually thirty] years, with sandy complexion, a typical English face, bronzed by the desert, remarkable blue eyes and a smile around the mouth that responded swiftly to that on the face of his friend. The two men were obviously very fond of each other. I have seldom seen such mutual affection between grown men as in this instance. Lawrence would catch the drift of Feisal's humor and pass the joke along to us while Feisal was exploding with his idea; but all

the same it was funny to see how Feisal spoke with the oratorical feeling of the South and Lawrence translated in the lowest and quietest of English voices, in very simple and direct phrases, with only here and there a touch of Oriental poetry breaking through.[14]

One cannot help wondering what happened to Faisal's humor and arguments in Lawrence's free translations. William Yale told me that some of the Americans felt that Lawrence and Faisal's joking was at their expense and were offended. But Yale was somewhat embittered toward Lawrence over several encounters in which he felt that Lawrence made him look foolish.[15]

Lawrence kept his own diary for a short time during January and the few notes he made are optimistic in tone. He had reason to believe then that the Americans or the British would taken responsibility for Syria and for promoting an independent state under Faisal, and that French control could be prevented. "The campaign in favour of America cooperating in the East, to secure the practice of her ideals, goes well. . . . I want to frighten America with the size of the responsibility, and then that she should run us for it instead. The Americans are rather fed up with France."[16]

Three days after the dinner that Shotwell described, Lawrence and Faisal had an opportunity to meet with Wilson himself, and this meeting, together with the help of Howard S. Bliss, president of the American University at Beirut (whom the United States had invited to bring evidence on the Syrian question), contributed to Wilson's appointment of a committee of inquiry for Syria.[17] "About work — it is going on well," Lawrence wrote to his family. "I have seen 10 American newspaper men, and given them all interviews, which went a long way. Also, President Wilson, and the other people who have influence. The affair is nearly over, I suspect. Another fortnight, perhaps. Everybody seems to be here, and of course it is a busy time. I have had, personally, one meal in my hotel since I got to Paris! That was with Newcombe, who turned up unexpectedly."[18]

Because Faisal was at the head of the only Arab delegation at the Peace Conference, the "Arab position" was to all intents and purposes his position.[19] Probably with Lawrence's help, he wrote for the conference several memoranda, in which he set forth his wishes for the independence of the Arab lands liberated from the Ottoman Empire during the war. In these memoranda he wrote of the dream of unity of the Arabs of Asia, but did not discuss the political organization of the regions, the form of government to be secured, or who was to rule.[20] Faisal referred repeatedly to the principles of national freedom and autonomy set forth by Wilson and expressed his confidence that "the powers will attach more importance to the bodies and souls of the Arabic-speaking peoples than to their own material interests."[21]

On February 6, Faisal, accompanied by Lawrence, presented his case to the Peace Conference. Lawrence was dressed "in flowing robes of dazzling white," according to Lloyd George; "in Arab dress," according to Arnold Toynbee; and in "Arab headcloth, with Khaki uniform and British badges," according to Lawrence.[22]

Toynbee has provided a firsthand account of Lawrence and Faisal's appearance before the Council of Ten (the leaders of the Allied governments). The French had heard how Lawrence had "put the Arabs' current political case in a telling speech in English" while Faisal read from the Koran, thus saving themselves the trouble of drafting an identical speech in two languages. The French had a Moroccan employee present to verify that Lawrence was actually translating Faisal's speech accurately. Having advance intelligence of this move by the French, Lawrence had written an Arabic version of his speech for Faisal to deliver and an English version for later delivery by himself.

"When the moment arrived," Toynbee wrote, "Faisal recited Lawrence's speech in Arabic and Lawrence followed him with a recitation of it in English, but then there was a hitch. Clemenceau understood English and also spoke it (an accomplishment that gave him a valuable advantage over his Anglo-Saxon and Italian colleagues); but the Italians were as ignorant of English as all the Ten were of Arabic. The only foreign language that the Italians understood was French. President Wilson then made a suggestion. 'Colonel Lawrence,' he said, 'could you put the Amir Faysal's statement into French now for us?' After a moment's hesitation, Lawrence started off and did it; and, when he came to the end of this unprepared piece of translation, the Ten clapped. What had happened was amazing. Lawrence's spell had made the Ten forget, for a moment, who they were and what they were supposed to be doing. They had started the session as conscious arbiters of the destinies of mankind; they were ending it as captive audience of a minor suppliant's interpreter."[23]

Over the next three months the question of Syria at the Peace Conference became embroiled in the struggles between Great Britain and France, especially between Lloyd George and Clemenceau.[24] The attitude of the French bureaucrats — Clemenceau, himself, as Lloyd George acknowledged, "was not annexationist by inclination or political training"[25] — was that the sacrifices of war entitled them to Syria, and they resented British and American efforts to forestall the annexation. As Elizabeth Monroe wrote, "Lloyd George's retreat before Clemenceau over Syria took place by stages in 1919."[26]

During February and March Lawrence seems to have been engaged in endless luncheons and other meetings with little productive result — "the lines of resentment hardening around his boyish lips."[27] Alexander Michailovitj, a prominent Russian nobleman and political figure in the Czarist regime, provided the following colored picture of Lawrence in Paris during these weeks:

None of the all-knowing newspaper correspondents could be bothered to recapitulate the peace-makers' antecedent promises. It became the lot of Col. T. E. Lawrence to mutter well-chosen damnations at the mere sight of these glorious diplomats. The youthful hero from Arabia, in his flowing romantic beduin-cape, understood from the very first moment, that the big four were all set to break the promises he had given the desert chiefs in 1915–1916, in return for their much-needed help against the Turks. As the living personification of eternal opposition, poor Lawrence wandered among Versailles' well-cut hedges, casting hateful glances at Arthur Balfour's aristocratic features and baggy clothes. I sympathized with him. We both spoke of the past to people who only recognized the present. We both had come with reminders of "done duties" to statesmen known for never paying back their debts. We both tried to appeal to the honour of those, to whom "honour" is but a word which in the dictionary stands under the letter H.[28]

At some time during this period he gave an interview to Lincoln Steffens. Although the interview was sought by Steffens, Lawrence used the opportunity to try to influence the Americans through Steffens to take responsibility for the Armenian mandate. Lawrence probably knew Steffens's reputation as a reformer and his intolerance of commercial or other exploitation. The interview, which was not published for twelve years, is filled with irony on Lawrence's part as he tries, with tongue in cheek, to prevail upon the noted "idealism" of the Americans and to get them to take responsibility for a people he called "the perfection of the true commercial spirit." Lawrence led Steffens to offer suggestion after suggestion. He even lured him into suggesting that the Americans handle the Armenians as they had handled the American Indians (by massacring them). "He reminded me," Steffens wrote, "that we were so idealistic and enjoyed such repute for philanthropy that we seemed to be able to do anything within reason without losing either our idealism or our good name."[29]

The question of Armenia was an important one. William Westermann, one of the American delegates, wrote that "the liberation of Armenia was the one outstanding result expected from the Near Eastern negotiations at the Peace Conference," and held the American isolationism responsible for the failure to pursue and protect the independence of Armenia. He went on to say that the United States might have saved thousands of people from starvation there during the postwar period had she accepted responsibility for the mandate. "The mandate for Armenia was offered us," Westermann observed, "and we refused to accept its obligations and the undoubted troubles which their acceptance would have entailed. We feared foreign entanglements."[30]

On February 27 the Zionist representatives presented their case before the Council of Ten at Paris.[31] In line with the Balfour Declaration of 1917, Chaim Weizmann asked for the creation of a Jewish national home, with immigration of seventy thousand to eighty thousand Jews annually, and permission to build Jewish schools where Hebrew could be taught. He denied that this meant the establishment of an autonomous Jewish government.[32] Nevertheless the Zionists were troubled when Faisal a day or two later gave an interview to a French paper which contained remarks unfriendly to the idea of a sovereign Jewish state.[33] A meeting was arranged between Felix Frankfurter, then a Harvard Law School professor, who was representing the Zionists, and Faisal, with Lawrence present to summarize in English Faisal's position. Lawrence drafted a letter setting forth Faisal's views, which expressed sympathy for the Zionist movement, spoke of "working together for a reformed and revived Near East" ("our two movements complete one another"), wished "the Jews a most hearty welcome home," and asserted that "there is room in Syria for both of us." It was published on March 5 in the New York *Times*.[34]

On March 20, President Wilson proposed sending an inter-Allied commission to Syria "to elucidate the state of opinion and the soil to be worked on by any mandatory."[35] In a meeting on March 29 with Colonel Edward House and with Lawrence acting as interpreter, Faisal expressed his delight with the idea of an inter-Allied commission, but the French refused to send a representative — they realized that any investigation of Arab opinion in Syria would work against their colonial interests there. But in the meantime, on March 25, a meeting had taken place at the Paris apartment of Wickham Steed, now editor of *The Times*, in which French and British Arab "experts" met with a number of French journalists to discuss the sending of a commission. According to Steed, Lawrence agreed on the unsettling effect sending a commission might have on Syria and offered to urge Faisal to stay in Paris to negotiate directly with the French.[36] A letter of Gertrude Bell's describing the meeting indicated that Lawrence had "outlined the programme of a possible agreement (between Feisal and the French) without the delay which is the chief defect of the proposal for sending a Commission."[37]

Faisal met with Clemenceau on April 13, and "the Tiger" reportedly told him: "I would agree with everything you want. But the French nation cannot agree that there shall be no sign of her in Syria to indicate her presence there. If France is not represented in Syria by its flag and by its soldiers, the French nation will consider it as a national humiliation, as the desertion of a soldier from the battlefield. . . . However, we do not want to send a large force but only a few men . . . and there will be no objection to have your flag side by side with ours."[38]

Presumably, they reached some sort of verbal agreement that permitted a French mandate in Syria, with the Syrians to elect their own prince and to retain some degree of autonomy. Letters to this effect were actually exchanged in mid-April between Clemenceau and Faisal. But neither Lawrence nor Faisal seems to have been willing to accept the French terms or trust French intentions in Syria, and Lawrence advised Faisal against an agreement to a French mandate.[39] Faisal seems to have been at this point strongly opposed to any French penetration in Syria and wished to have an inter-Allied commission sent immediately. On April 20 he wrote to Clemenceau, thanked him for his kindness and "disinterested friendliness" and "for having been the first to suggest the dispatch of the Inter-Allied Commission which is to leave shortly for the East to ascertain the wishes of the local peoples as to the future organization of their country. I am sure that the people of Syria will know how to show you their gratitude."[40] This statement, which seems to be filled with irony, strongly suggests the thoughts of Lawrence. Three days later Faisal left France for Syria, no agreement having been reached.

On April 7 Lawrence received a telegram that his father had developed influenza complicated by pneumonia and that he should come home if possible. He returned quickly to England, but was distressed to discover that he was too late to see his father alive.[41] There is to my knowledge no written statement of Lawrence's about his father's death, nor any information on how he reacted to it. This would appear to be a prominent example of a characteristic of Lawrence's that his younger brother Arnold has stressed: exercising extreme self-control to avoid showing troubled emotions. The more despairing and troubled Lawrence might feel, the more reserved and guarded he would become about his feelings.[42]

After returning to Paris from his visit home Lawrence stayed long enough to advise Faisal not to make a deal with the French. Then about April 23, at the time Faisal returned to Syria, Lawrence flew off to Cairo in one of a squadron of Handley-Page airplanes (his luggage consisted of a haversack and two books) to pick up some belongings and his wartime papers and reports. Unfortunately, the plane crashed near Rome and the two pilots were killed. Lawrence escaped with a cracked shoulder blade and some other minor injuries, to which he paid no attention while he busied himself with helping the victims of the crash.[43]

David Garnett in *The Letters of T. E. Lawrence* wrote that he regarded this accident as "a turning point in Lawrence's life" and one that contributed to Lawrence's later emotional difficulties.[44] I was skeptical about this and on the advice of Arnold Lawrence wrote to Francis Lord Rennell of Rodd, son of the British ambassador to Italy, at whose embassy quarters Lawrence stayed after the accident. Lord Rennell replied to my inquiry:

> I was serving in the British Embassy in 1919 during the closing months of my father's 11 year Ambassadorship there . . . when I received a message from the Italian Authorities that a British plane had made a crash landing and that one of the occupants was Lawrence who had been admitted to hospital in Rome with some not serious injuries. I immediately went up to

the hospital to see him but found him so little injured or shocked that I was able to bring him down in a day or two to stay in the British Embassy where I was living with my father and mother until he was fit enough to go on to the East in another plane shortly afterwards. During those days he was in the house he was perfectly normal psychologically and seemed in no way different to when I had known him in Egypt and elsewhere during the war.[45]

The ambassador and his wife were able to persuade Lawrence to stay only a few days in Rome, but while he was there they talked about "Arabian affairs." Rodd senior observed that he could well understand how "Lawrence must have been a difficult problem to the authorities."[46]

As Lord Rennell mentioned, Lawrence resumed his journey to Cairo in another aircraft. The trip was marked by an almost unbelievable sequence of delays for aircraft malfunctioning, damage and repairs, and took him to Taranto, Valona in Albania (where he led a glowworm-catching competition), Athens (where he showed the squadron commander, Captain T. Henderson, around the places of archeological interest), Crete and Libya. He reached Cairo late in June. Captain Henderson later wrote: "After the accident at Rome we greatly admired his pluck in deciding to fly on with us, especially as he was incapacitated by his arm, and we had the Mediterranean to cross — the first time for a squadron not fitted for landing on water. During the crossing, when all signs of land and shipping had disappeared, T.E. pushed a note in my hand, 'Won't it be fun if we come down?' I didn't think so!"[47]

Lawrence clearly enjoyed his three months with the Handley-Page squadron. The series of flights influenced his decision to join the RAF. The irony of his remark to Henderson is evident and the unnecessary danger to which pilots and their crews were exposed when flying over water may have played a part in Lawrence's eventual interest in developing air-sea rescue boats.

Lawrence managed to find time during the trip to write portions of the narrative of his war experience, which was by this time taking shape. Chapter 2, he states, was written between Paris and Lyons in the Handley-Page: "Its rhythm is unlike the rest. I liken it to the munch, munch, munch of the synchronised Rolls-Royce engines!"[48] The introduction was begun while they were heading down the Rhone Valley toward Marseilles and completed "on my way out to Egypt."[49]

In June 1919, when the peace treaty had been signed at Versailles and Wilson had returned to the United States, Lawrence wrote the following passage for the introduction to *Seven Pillars of Wisdom*. Although he subsequently suppressed it, it stands as one of the most beautiful things he ever wrote:

"In these pages the history is not of the Arab movement, but of me in it. It is a narrative of daily life, mean happenings, little people. Here are no lessons for the world, no disclosures to shock peoples [sic]. It is filled with trivial things, partly that no one mistake for history the bones from which some day a man may make history, and partly for the pleasure it gave me to recall the fellowship of the revolt. We were fond together, because of the sweep of the open places, the taste of wide winds, the sunlight, and the hopes in which we worked. The morning freshness of the world-to-be intoxicated us. We were wrought up with ideas inexpressible and vaporous, but to be fought for. We lived many lives in those swirling campaigns, never sparing ourselves: yet when we achieved and the new world dawned, the old men came out again and took our victory to remake in the likeness of the former world they knew. Youth would win, but had not learned to keep: and was pitiably weak against age. We stammered that we had worked for a new heaven and a new earth, and they thanked us kindly and made their peace."[50]

In Crete Lawrence met for the first time the great Arabist H. St. John Philby, later to become the only Western advisor close to Ibn Saud. Philby was on the plane that picked up Lawrence in Crete. They evidently got on well and Philby was impressed by Lawrence's "easy manners and friendly approach."[51] They flew together to Cairo, where, Philby wrote, "we . . . championed diametrically opposite causes in the hospitable atmosphere of Allenby's home on the banks of the Nile."[52]

If Philby was arguing then the cause of Ibn Saud and Lawrence that of the Hashemite family, the Saudi champion had reason to be getting the better of the argument. In May, while Lawrence was somewhere between Italy and Crete, Ibn Saud and his Wahhabi tribesmen had invaded the Hijaz. An opposing force sent by King Husayn and led by Amir Abdullah — who had been engaged during the Revolt principally in trying to control the growing power of the Wahhabis — was annihilated, Abdullah barely escaping with his life. Ibn Saud would probably have completed the conquest of the Hijaz had not the British government, which was subsidizing both sides, intervened.[53] As Arnold Toynbee put it:

> France and the United Kingdom did not carry their post-war colonial rivalry in the Middle East to the length of engaging in hostilities, but the India Office and the Foreign Office were less self-restrained. In May, 1919, they fought each other by proxy in Arabia, on the border between the Najd and Hijaz, at a place called Turaba. In this battle, the India Office's Arab ('Abdarrahman ibn Sa'id) defeated the Foreign Office's Arab (King Husayn al-Hashimi); but the Foreign Office then appealed to its ally General Allenby; Allenby threatened to send some whippet tanks to the Foreign Office Arab's aid; and the India Office prudently advised its own Arab to retreat.[54]

This disastrous defeat for the forces of King Husayn weakened the bargaining strength of Faisal in his dealings with the French and made the British understandably more hesitant in their support of Faisal, especially so long as he spoke as a representative of his father.

Lawrence stayed only briefly in Cairo in late June and early July of 1919 ("going through the Arab Bureau Archives for materials")[55] before returning to Paris. He was observed at Shepheard's Hotel in Cairo outfitted not as a colonel any longer, but as "a rather ruffled T.E., dressed in uniform but without belt or cap — as a subaltern in something."[56]

We pick up Lawrence's trail in Paris once more on July 15, when he telegraphs Faisal not to come to Paris as "nothing will be done [regarding the settlement of Arab affairs] till about September."[57] Curzon seems to have agreed with this advice since he noted in a wire to Balfour, "It seems possible that if Lawrence were not available, [Faisal] might be induced to renounce his journey."[58] The Foreign Office documents of July and early August reveal a debate within the department on whether Lawrence was an asset or a liability in Paris for the government's efforts to get Faisal to come to an accommodation with the French. The question seems not to have been resolved and Lawrence returned to England in August.[59]

# 23

# Return to England:
# London and All Souls

In New York in March 1919, Lowell Thomas began his film-and-talk shows about the war and his meetings with Allenby and Lawrence during the desert campaigns, thereby making the shy colonel well known in the United States before he became famous in Britain. The wave of popularity in the United States for exotic sun-and-sand commercial films of "Arabia," especially those featuring the Italian-born American actor Rudolph Valentino (*The Sheik*, 1921; *The Son of the Sheik*, 1926), may well have been inspired by Lowell Thomas's reportage of the Palestinian campaigns and of the deeds of Lawrence, whom he had filmed in flowing Arab costume.[1] Thomas told me that he had made a series of film shows, each on a different war theatre, which he booked into the Century Theatre with the backing of the New York *Globe*. The New Yorkers, he said, stayed away when the program was about the Western Front, but whenever he showed the Arab and Palestine campaigns featuring Allenby (sixty percent) and Lawrence (forty percent) "they [the promoters] took busloads of people from the Bronx to see the show," and after several weeks the show was moved to Madison Square Garden.[2] On the last night of the show in New York, Percy Burton, the English impresario who had managed Sarah Bernhardt, came to see it and wished to book it in England. Thomas told him facetiously that he would accept only Covent Garden or Drury Lane, not expecting that Burton would actually arrange it.[3] But Burton went ahead, and about the time Lawrence returned from Paris in August of 1919, Thomas was beginning to popularize the Lawrence legend in nightly film-and-lecture shows at the Royal Opera House in Covent Garden. The show began on August 14 to full houses and seems to have been seen by all the notables of England, including the Royal Family, Lloyd George and his cabinet (Thomas told me Lloyd

George received a minor no-confidence vote for watching the show instead of being at an evening meeting of Parliament), and much of London society. The show was the same as the one in New York, except that an elaborate stage prologue was arranged: a Welsh Guards band played in front of the backdrop of the "Moonlight on the Nile" setting from Sir Thomas Beecham's production of Handel's opera *Joseph and His Brethren.* Thomas estimated that one million people came to see the show in London, which ran for six months instead of the two weeks he had planned. After that he took it on a tour of other English-speaking countries. During the next five years, he published several articles on Lawrence and finally, the first biography of him, which appeared in 1924. Unquestionably, Thomas captured the public imagination and was instrumental in making Lawrence a popular hero.

Lawrence's relationship with Thomas, and his attitude toward the elaborate and fanciful romanticization of his exploits, brought out a central conflict in his character, one which cannot be dismissed with catch phrases of paradox, such as "false modesty" or "backing into the limelight." Thomas has made it clear in his writings — and I questioned him carefully about this — that Lawrence cooperated with him in the creation of his own legend.

Thomas originally left his teaching job at Princeton on a propaganda mission. He was to go to Europe and find material to make Americans more enthusiastic about the war.[4] The carnage of the Western Front offered nothing remotely "optimistic," and Thomas, with his cameraman, Harry Chase, found his way to Allenby in Jerusalem and, with Allenby's help, to Lawrence in Aqaba in the spring of 1918.

According to Lawrence they met twice during the two weeks Thomas was in Arabia.[5] With Allenby and especially with Lawrence, Thomas found material that lent itself to colorful, romantic presentation and storytelling, material that could truly be used to sell the war and make it seem attractive, adventurous and worthwhile. Furthermore, Lawrence was cooperative. He seemed to enjoy posing in his "Sherifian regalia" for Chase's pictures (later he thought they made him look like "a perfect idiot"),[6] introduced Thomas to other British officers and prevailed on them to be photographed, took the Americans into the Arabs' tents, where they observed the Bedouin and their leaders, and showed them around Aqaba. But Lawrence would tell Thomas little about himself or the details of his own exploits (Thomas states specifically in the foreword to his book: "I found it impossible to extract much information from Lawrence regarding his own achievements"), so Thomas was forced to extract information about them and the campaigns at second and third hand from Newcombe, Joyce, Dawnay, Hogarth, Stirling and other "fellow-adventurers."[7] As one might expect, the biographical data in Thomas's book are consequently full of inadvertent inaccuracies.

In the fall and winter of 1919–1920, when Thomas was giving his show, Lawrence came to see it at least five times. When Mrs. Thomas would spy him Lawrence would "blush crimson, laugh in confusion, and hurry away with a stammered word of apology," but he seemed to enjoy the glamour of it all.[8] Characteristically, though, he avoided the spotlight and on one occasion wrote a note to Thomas, "I saw your show last night and thank God the lights were out." Lord Northcliffe, the British newspaper magnate, tried through Percy Burton to get an interview with Lawrence for the press, but Lawrence refused.[9] The following year, when Thomas was working on his book *With Lawrence in Arabia,* Lawrence walked twelve miles to the edge of London and back several times to help Thomas with it. He said he was not planning to write a book of his own but was only "working on his notes." I asked Thomas why he thought Lawrence had been willing to do this in view of his later antagonism to the Thomas book. He replied, "He knew I was doing a job"; and then added, "All topnotch people are willing to talk with a reporter."[10] Lawrence specifically denied that he went over the manuscripts of Thomas's book, in contrast to the thorough editing and rewriting he later did for the biographies that Graves and Liddell Hart wrote.[11] Thomas retains a very positive feeling about Lawrence and wishes that he had done more to help him, especially in view of the enormous service Lawrence did for his career.[12]

The truth seems to be that much as Lawrence was attracted by the glorious image of himself as "the Uncrowned King of Arabia" that was played on the screen and embellished by Lowell Thomas, he was also genuinely repulsed by it. He knew Thomas's picture of him to be false, not because he had not taken part in acts of heroism, but because it was a make-believe, commercial glorification. At a deeper level he felt he deserved a much lower opinion, and the grandiose myth-making he was witnessing only deepened the inner reproaches of his conscience and further provoked his self-contempt. I suspect that the conflicts aroused by the Thomas performances contributed to the despondency and despair that Lawrence suffered from during the fall and winter of 1919–1920.

In January 1920, Lawrence wrote to Archibald Murray, his first commander-in-chief in Arabia, to convey his embarrassment about Thomas's activities, especially passages in articles Thomas was writing that might be critical of the general. He wrote that he had refused to correct the galley proofs because they contained so many misstatements that he "could not possibly pass one tenth of it."[13] The letter, which includes also a request that Murray read the proofs of *Seven Pillars of Wisdom* ("the first draft was stolen and the second is not finished"), concludes: "I could kick his [Lowell Thomas's] card-house down if I got annoyed, and so he has to be polite. As a matter of fact he is a very decent fellow — but an American journalist, scooping."

In March Lawrence wrote to F. N. Doubleday: "You know a Mr. Lowell Thomas made me a kind of matinee idol: so I dropped my name so far as London is concerned and live peacefully in anonymity. Only my people in Oxford know of my address. It isn't that I hate being known — I'd love it — but I can't afford it."[14]

More candidly and with considerable self-awareness he wrote to a man named Greenhill, who had commanded an armored-car company in the Hijaz: "For Lowell Thomas: I don't bear him any grudge. He has invented some silly phantom thing, a sort of matinee idol in fancy dress, that does silly things and is dubbed 'romantic.' Boy scouts and servants love it: and it's so far off the truth that I can go peacefully in its shadow, without being seen. Last Thursday I went to an art gallery where was a ripping portrait of me by [Augustus] John: another man was looking at it: and as I passed he whispered confidentially, 'Bloody looking feller, isn't he?' and I said yes."[15]

In 1927 Lawrence wrote: "Lowell Thomas was 10 days in Arabia. He saw me for two of those, and again one day in Jerusalem: and afterwards I breakfasted with him once or twice in London. His book is silly and inaccurate: sometimes deliberately inaccurate. He meant well."[16] Much of the inaccurate or otherwise offensive material was removed in later editions of Thomas's book.

The actualities that Lawrence faced upon his return to England in August 1919 contrasted starkly with the romantic glow created by Lowell Thomas's performances. At the end of the previous January, Geoffrey Dawson, editor of *The Times* and a dedicated Fellow of All Souls College for twenty years, had written Lawrence offering to propose him for a fellowship at All Souls. The fellowship "would give you rooms in college and certain emoluments," Dawson wrote, "in return, I think, for a general undertaking to reside during stated portions of the year and to pursue some recognized line of duty. I broached this scheme to the warden last Sunday and found him entirely sympathetic."[17] Lawrence found the terms agreeable and replied that he would indeed accept the post if it was offered to him. Dawson promptly wrote the warden formally recommending "my little friend Lawrence of the Hedjaz. . . . He assures me that his one object in life (after the peace Conference is over) is research in his own particular line of study. . . . He is so big a man, so modest, and so eminently fitted to adorn our society, that I do hope that we shall make an effort to elect him."[18] In June Lawrence received a letter from the warden informing him of his election to a research fellowship, which paid a very small stipend, "the conditions of the Fellowship to be that he continues during his tenure thereof to prosecute the researches into the antiquities and ethnology, and the history (ancient and modern) of the Near East."[19]

But in the Near East matters were working against what Lawrence had struggled to protect.[20] The inter-Allied commission, which had finally been established (the so-called King-Crane Commission) visited Syria in June and July, interviewed Faisal, and assessed the feeling of the Syrian populace. Faisal made it clear to the commission that in his opinion a French mandate would mean the death of his country. The Syrians were overwhelmingly opposed to a French mandate and feared French colonial methods.[21] But the commission had become a purely American effort, distrusted by the French and virtually ignored by the British. By the time the final report was delivered to Wilson in late August the American commitment to the Middle East had faded. Even Charles Crane himself, a Chicago millionaire who was a partisan of self-determination, felt that the commission might do harm by arousing hopes "which it would not be possible to fulfill."[22]

In the meantime, over the spring and summer of 1919, Faisal was establishing a Syrian government, and Lloyd George and Lord Balfour, the foreign secretary, were struggling to resist French demands regarding Syria. But because of increasing pressure at home for demobilization, higher priorities given to securing a British mandate for Palestine, and need to make concessions to France in order to protect British access to Mesopotamian oil fields, Lloyd George began to yield to Clemenceau on the question of Syria. The British government cooled toward Faisal and started to look for a way out of their dilemma. Clemenceau, under pressure from conservative colonialist elements in France, was demanding that the British adhere to the terms of the Sykes-Picot Agreement and agree to the French mandate. An eloquent analysis by Lord Balfour in August of the situation "respecting Syria, Palestine and Mesopotamia" questioned "on what historic basis the French claim to Syria really rests," but also made it clear that "a home for the Jews in the valley of the Jordan" and a British zone in Mesopotamia extending "at least as far as Mosul" had become higher priorities than an independent Syria, or Syria under a British or American mandate.[23] Meanwhile, British officers in Syria warned that British withdrawal and French occupation would inevitably lead to violent resistance by the Arab populace, who would not accept a French military presence in the country.[24]

The home Lawrence returned to on Polstead Road in Oxford in August 1919 was much changed from the one he had left in 1914. Two of his brothers had been killed in the war and his father had recently died. His mother's emotional needs became focused upon him, but he could not meet them. Lawrence's cause in the Middle East was going poorly but his continued involvement with its problems (ensured by the terms of the All Souls fellowship) and the writing of his book permitted him no distance from the conflicts aroused by the shattering experiences of the war.

For the first time in many years Lawrence was relatively footloose with no immediate field of action upon which to release his energies or to draw his attention away from himself. He turned inward, and his mother described to David Garnett how during the fall of 1919 and the winter of 1919–1920 Ned would sit for hours in a state of marked despondency without moving or changing his facial expression. Occasionally his usually severe self-control would give way. On one occasion he tripped over a water can and suddenly gave it a kick that sent it flying across the garden.[25]

On September 1, shortly after arriving in Oxford, Lawrence wrote his old friend Richards that he was out of the army that day, would like to avoid thinking about Arab matters, and was interested in setting up with him their printing press on five acres of land at Pole Hill, Chingford, on the edge of Epping Forest, which he had recently paid for.[26] But a week later he was back in the political battle, writing a letter to *The Times* on September 8 (it appeared three days later) in which he referred to himself as "the only informed free-lance European" and listed for the British public (evidently for the first time) the essentials of the McMahon-Husayn correspondence, the Sykes-Picot Agreement, the statement to the Seven Syrians and the Anglo-French Declaration of November 1918, "all produced under stress of military urgency to induce the Arabs to fight on our side."[27]

All these documents contained commitments to areas of Arab independence in the former Ottoman territories. But *The Times*, under Steed's editorship,* hewed closely to the official government line, and Steed suppressed the last part of the letter, in which Lawrence wrote that he expected the British government to live up to its promises to the Arabs and that he wished to inform the Arabs and the British public that he regretted what he had done in the war because the government evidently had no intention of living up to the commitments it had authorized him to make to the Arabs.[28] Steed weakened the impact of Lawrence's letter still further by publishing an accompanying editorial which, in mollifying tones, spoke of the necessity for Anglo-French cooperation in settling "the legacies of the war" and suggested that "the present Conference in Paris" should help to smooth the approaches to these problems.[29]

Nevertheless, Lawrence's letter evidently caused a stir in the Foreign Office, especially as Lloyd George and Clemenceau were about to conclude an agreement in Paris that would in effect turn over the mandate for Syria to France.[30] Lawrence had obviously become something of a thorn in the side of the Foreign Office. A few days earlier a Foreign Office official had penned a note on a letter from Paris to London (the

---

* Lawrence's friend Geoffrey Dawson had resigned in March 1919 after a conflict with Lord Northcliffe, *The Times* proprietor, who, in his failing years, had become a more faithful advocate of British government policy.

letter itself suggested that Lawrence "if properly handled" might be able to get Faisal "into a reasonable frame of mind" to accept the plans that were being devised for him): "The trouble is that it is always Lawrence who does the 'handling.' He has told me quite frankly that he had no belief in an Anglo-French understanding in the East, that he regards France as our natural enemy in those parts and that he has always shaped his action accordingly."[31]

In the agreement between Lloyd George and Clemenceau of September 13, which was supported publicly by the Supreme Council of the Allies in Paris two days later, Britain agreed to evacuate Syria by November 1, 1919, with the understanding that the western (coastal) areas of Syria and Lebanon would be garrisoned by the French, while the cities of Damascus, Homs, Hama and Aleppo would be turned over to Amir Faisal.[32] Lloyd George invited Faisal to London to try to pressure him into accepting the agreement, which Clemenceau regarded as a triumph for the French. But Faisal, fearing any French occupation of his country, wrote two letters to Lloyd George — on September 21 and October 9 — asking that the agreement be abrogated and the coastal areas returned to Arab control. He anticipated a great catastrophe for the Arab world should British troops be withdrawn from Syria.[33]

Meanwhile, seeing that one way or another direct British military control of Syria was going to end, Lawrence wrote to the Foreign Office on September 15 and to Curzon, the foreign secretary, on September 27, in an attempt to make the best of the situation.[34] The Foreign Office remained willing to use Lawrence's influence with Faisal for its purposes as long as "Colonel Lawrence's well-known antipathy to the French" did not interfere with Anglo-French negotiations.[35] He agreed to try to persuade Faisal to accept the French presence in the coastal regions of Syria if Britain would maintain advisors in central Syria and guarantee its commitment to an Arab government in Mesopotamia, where he anticipated a revolt by March (1920) 'if we do not mend our ways." (Actually the revolt did not occur until the summer.) He envisaged Faisal as a kind of centrally placed broker in the region between the French influence on the coast and the British mandated areas to the east and south. To Curzon Lawrence outlined his idea for the eventual leadership of Baghdad over the regions of Western Asia ("the future of Mesopotamia is so immense that if it is cordially ours we can swing the whole Middle East with it").[36] It was in the letter to Curzon that Lawrence made his often-quoted statement: "My own ambition is that the Arabs should be our first brown dominion, and not our last brown colony."[37]

On September 28 Lawrence wrote to Alan Dawnay, by this time a staff officer in Jerusalem, stressing again the importance of keeping Kinahan Cornwallis, the British liaison officer, in Damascus as an advisor, and the capacity of Mesopotamia, because of its agricultural and oil resources, to support a far greater population. He argued for the importance of Arab-Zionist cooperation, and emphasized again the coming of "brown" peoples into the empire, despite the fact that "Australia won't like brown citizens of the Empire — but it's coming anyhow. They are 5,000,000 and the Browns about 300,000,000." The letter concluded with a characteristic disparagement of the French: "The French will hold an uneasy position for a few years on the Syrian coast, like the decadence of the Crusading Kingdom of Jerusalem, or Egypt before the Moroccan bargain — and then: 'No more of me and thee.' "[38] If Lawrence was measuring "a few years" by the clock of human history he was correct. But in less than a year the French had occupied all Syria, driving Faisal out. Independence did not come to the country for a quarter of a century.

William Yale, who had been a member of the King-Crane Commission, was more alarmed by the dangers for peace in the Middle East under the Clemenceau-Lloyd agreement than was Lawrence, who seems to have shifted his focus ahead to Mesopotamia. Yale feared, correctly as it turned out, that the Arabs in Syria would not accept the French anywhere in the country and that the withdrawal of the protective presence of British troops would result in serious local disorders, spreading to other areas of the Middle East. He pleaded for a shift toward a more liberal policy and had a plan of his own. But despite Yale's interviews of countless officials and other leaders of opinion, including Lawrence, his efforts seem to have been of no avail, especially as President Wilson would not invest Yale with any authority.[39] It is not clear whether Lawrence met Faisal during his visit to England in September and October of 1919. In any case, the amir was unchanged in his views. He left after a brief time to negotiate directly with the French and arrived in Paris on October 20.[40]

Rudyard Kipling was more realistic about these sad events and was able to express to Lawrence the disappointment they both felt in a letter he wrote his friend in October:

Dear Lawrence,
Naturally, if you didn't take what was offered you and do what you were wanted to do, you would — from the F.O. point of view — be the worst kind of crook. They don't understand deviations from type. Later on, I expect, you will be accused of having been actuated by "financial motives" in all you did. Wait till you are cussed for being a "venal hireling" — as I was once — in a Legislature.
But we are all sitting in the middle of wrecked hopes and broken dreams. I tried all I knew to put the proper presentation of the American scheme before men over there who, I thought, would help. But one can't expect people whose forebears went West to avoid trouble to stand up to responsibility in a far land for no immediate cash return.
But you will not go out of the game — except for the necessary minute to step aside and vomit. You are young, and the bulk of men now in charge

are "old, cold and of intolerable entrails" and a lot of 'em will be dropping out soon.[41]

Urged by Kipling and others, Lawrence had begun in Paris to "write an account of what happened in Arabia."[42] In the manuscript of *Seven Pillars of Wisdom,* which is in the Bodleian Library, Lawrence stated that he began the first edition of the book on January 10, 1919, in Paris, but in notes penned five years later he wrote that the book was begun in February.[43] Between early 1919 and May 1922 Lawrence wrote three texts of his book. Of these only the third survives.

There are no contemporary notes about Lawrence's early writing activities in Paris. Perhaps the arrival in March of Gertrude Bell, whom Lawrence later credited with his decision to publish a limited edition of the work, played a part in his keeping on with the manuscript. They spent much time together during March discussing the political problems of their Arab friends.[44] Hogarth states that Lawrence did most of the writing in the spring at Faisal's temporary home in the Avenue du Bois de Boulogne.[45] He was aided by a diary he had kept on army telegraph forms (now in the British Museum) which he described to Mrs. Shaw as "nearer a bunch of thorns than a flower."[46]

During his first months back in England in the late summer and early fall of 1919 there is no evidence that Lawrence worked much on his manuscript. Early in November he turned back to Charles Doughty, who had provided so much of his original inspiration and to whom he had first turned for guidance to the East. He wrote cautiously to Doughty's daughter that he had heard her father had been ill (which proved to be untrue) and that "I would very much like to come and see him, and I'm afraid of only being a nuisance."[47] But Doughty himself wrote back immediately: "I rejoice that you have returned safe & sound from the late arduous and anxious years of World-wide warfare, in which you have borne politically and militarily so distinguished a part for your Country with the Friendlies of the South Arabians; & to think of your passing again happy days in the blessed peace & quiet days of Oxford life."[48] Doughty encouraged his young friend to stay with him and his family at his home in Eastbourne.

Later in the month, in another letter to Doughty, Lawrence confessed that he had "lost the MSS of my own adventures in Arabia: it was stolen from me in the train."[49] Lawrence suggested to Liddell Hart that unconscious factors may have been at work in the loss of this first text, which he considered "shorter, snappier and more truthful" than the later versions.[50] Liddell Hart provides these details from his notes of a conversation with Lawrence in 1933: "On a train journey from London to Oxford. Went into refreshment room at Reading, and put bag under the table. Left it. Phoned up from Oxford an hour later, but no sign of the missing bag — it was a bank messenger's bag, the "thing they carry the gold in!' [surely an invitation to theft]." Liddell Hart goes to say, "T.E. wonders did fancy (*involuntarily*) [italics in original] play with it?"[51] Lawrence told Liddell Hart that he had proclaimed joyously to Hogarth, "I've lost the damned thing," and Mrs. Lawrence is said to have found him in the garden cottage laughing in his bed late at night afterwards.[52] But Hogarth was angry, and both he and Doughty urged Lawrence to write it again.[53]

On December 2, 1919, in Oxford, Lawrence began writing the second text of his book (except for the introduction, which "survived"), and "so it was built again with heavy repugnance in London in the winter of 1919–1920 from memory and my surviving notes."[54] He wrote most of the second text during the first two months of 1920, calling it then "the-book-to-build-the-house" because he had not yet given up his vague plans for printing in a medieval hall at Chingford.

Lawrence is somewhat contradictory in his statements about the writing of the second text. The inconsistencies are symptomatic of the ambivalent attitude he retained toward his book and toward the events it described throughout the long history of its various writings and publication. He stated in 1923, for example, that he began *Seven Pillars* in Oxford; to Graves he wrote that none of it was written in Oxford; and in a leaflet he issued with the 1926 edition he wrote that a month or so after he lost the first edition, "I began, in London, to scribble out what I remembered of the first text."[55]

Lawrence seems to have found the atmosphere at home and at All Souls difficult for writing, and chose to draft most of the second text in an attic in Westminster, which his architect friend, Herbert Baker, had provided ("dark and oak-panelled, with a large table and desk as the principal furniture").[56] "I work best utterly by myself," he wrote Richards at the time, "and speak to no one for days."[57] When in London he already was living under a different name (he did not tell what it was). He had assumed the new name, he wrote Newcombe, "to be more quiet and wish I could change my face to be more lovely."[58] To Ezra Pound the reasons were "for peace and cleanliness."[59]

Baker has given this picture of his friend at work over the years in the secluded attic, and the spartan existence he preferred:

"It was the best-and-freest-place I have ever lived in," he wrote when he ceased to live permanently there; and "nobody had found me . . . despite efforts by callers and telephones." He refused all service and comfort, food, fire or hot water; he ate and bathed when he happened to go out; he kept chocolate — it required no cleaning up, he said — for an emergency when through absorption or forgetfulness he failed to do so. He worked time-less and sometimes around the sun; and once he said, for two days without food or sleep, writing at his best, until he became delirious. He wrote most of the

*Seven Pillars of Wisdom* there; he usually slept by day and worked by night; in airman's clothes in winter cold. We who worked in the rooms below never heard a sound; I would look up from my drawing-board in the evening sometimes to see him watching, gnomelike, with a smile; his smile that hid a tragedy.[60]

A decade later Lawrence conveyed to another writer the moral dilemmas and inner psychological obstacles, the struggle "to work out my path again," which accompanied the writing of *Seven Pillars of Wisdom*: "I was a rather clumsy novice at writing, facing what I felt to be a huge subject with hanging over me the political uncertainty of the future of the Arab movement. We had promised them so much; and at the end wanted to give them so little. So for two years there was a dog fight, up and down the dirty passages of Downing St., and then all came out right — only the book was finished. It might have been happier had I foreseen the clean ending. I wrote it in some stress and misery of mind.

"The second complicity was my own moral standing. I had been so much of a free agent, repeatedly deciding what I (and the others) should do: and I wasn't sure if my opportunity (or reality, as I called it) was really justified. Not morally justifiable. I could see it wasn't: but justified by the standard of Lombard St. and Pall Mall. By putting all the troubles and dilemmas on paper, I hoped to work out my path again, and satisfy myself how wrong, or how right, I had been.

"So the book is the self-argument of a man who couldn't then see straight: and who now thinks that perhaps it did not matter: that seeing straight is only an illusion. We do these things in sheer vapidity of mind, not deliberately, not consciously even. To make out that we were reasoned cool minds, ruling our courses and contemporaries, is vanity. Things happen, and we do our best to keep in the saddle."[61]

In drafting the first and second texts, Lawrence apparently wrote at times with great speed and without interruption for many hours. He told his biographer Robert Graves that he did "four to five thousand words a day," and Liddell Hart mentions one marathon of thirty thousand words in twenty-two hours.[62] Book VI — the one that contains the account of his assault at Der'a — Lawrence evidently raced through with particular speed, not wishing perhaps to linger any longer than he had to over these disturbing events. He revised it, however, many times. In *Seven Pillars of Wisdom*, he states that Book VI "was written entire between sunrise and sunrise,"[63] but this is contradicted by his statement in his February 27, 1920, letter to Richards that his book was "on paper in the first draft to the middle of Book VI: and there are seven books in all."[64] In his notes for the 1926 (subscribers') edition, Lawrence refers to ten books in Text II.[65]

These examples of inconsistencies indicate the difficulty of obtaining an accurate history of the writing of *Seven Pillars of Wisdom*, especially during this troubled early period. The book's content is so intimately tied to Lawrence's deepest conflicts that its writing, and the reporting of its writing, were especially prone to neurotic distortion. But he could, on occasion, be quite objective about the book's potential lasting value. He wrote prophetically in January 1920 to his former commander Archibald Murray: "I put on paper my account of what happened to me in Arabia some time ago, but had it stolen from me, and am therefore doing it again, rather differently. It seems to me unfit for publication, but if published it will have some success (for the story is in parts very odd and exciting — there are many strange things) and will probably last a long time, and influence other accounts in the future, for it is not badly written, and is authoritative, in so far as it concerns myself."[66] Lawrence asked Murray if he would agree to read it over, but whatever Murray's reply, the manuscript was evidently never sent to him. Lawrence wrote Liddell Hart that this text was "not circulated," unlike the first one, which had been "read by Meiner [Meinertzhagen], Dawnay, Hogarth."[67]

As indicated to Murray, Lawrence was unclear at this time about his plans to publish the book. His friend Doubleday wrote that "he had the most peculiar notions. . . . First he was going to have one copy printed and put in the B.M. [British Museum], and he made a dozen different plans."[68] Dermot Morrah, with whom Lawrence shared a suite of rooms at All Souls, mentioned that Lawrence considered either having the book published in a cheap edition in America to avoid piracy in England or setting a price so high ($200,000) that no one would buy it. Later, the story went around the college that Lawrence had written the Library of Congress, urging that *Seven Pillars* be included among the obscene books, and threatening to put dirty pictures in the fly leaf so the Library would have no choice.[69]

In the manuscript Lawrence wrote that this second text was completed on May 11, 1920, but "corrected and added to slowly for nearly two years."[70] A contemporary letter to Doubleday of July 21, 1920, states that "the original-and-to-be-kept-secret version was finished on July 12th."[71] But in August he wrote to Richards, "To finish my 'Boy Scout' book by September 30 will mean my spending August and September in All Souls."[72] On October 7, Doubleday wrote Lawrence, "Your M.S. I have put in the hotel safe (Brown's in London)."[73] Through 1920 Lawrence's efforts to have a second edition of Doughty's *Arabia Deserta* published seemed to parallel his struggles over the second writing of his own book and he turned especially to Doubleday for help with both.[74] As it turned out, Lawrence rewrote the book a third time and then destroyed Text II.

As the turmoil-filled year of 1919 drew to a close Lawrence had turned to the waiting opportunity at All Souls to find "the blessed peace and quiet days of Oxford" that Doughty had held out to him. Whether Lawrence found peace and quiet at Oxford in 1920 is, I suppose, a matter of definition. He was there only intermittently, moving back and forth between his isolated attic in Westminster and his rooms at the college. But as a result of his friendships at All Souls, especially with Robert Graves, Lawrence met writers and poets — Siegfried Sassoon, Edmund Blunden, John Buchan and, later, Thomas Hardy. His fame brought him in touch with artists like William Rothenstein and Augustus John, who wished to paint his portrait, and Eric Kennington, whom he sought out. "The painters and sculptors also seemed to Lawrence to have a secret," Graves wrote, and "already at Paris, during the Peace Conference he was getting in touch with them."[75]

In the intellectual atmosphere of Oxford Lawrence copied out the poems that best expressed his tastes and moods. Each of these poems had "had a day with me," he wrote to Mrs. Shaw in 1927, many having come from *The Oxford Book of English Verse,* which Lawrence had kept with him during the desert campaigns. They formed a kind of anthology he called "Minorities."[76] "One necessary qualification" for inclusion, he said, was "that they should be in a minor key."[77]

The "minor key" was also a reflection of Lawrence's mood. Morrah observed (1920) that he was subject to depression and would sit silently for hours in the common room, absorbed in his own thoughts. At times Lawrence's aloofness seemed so intense that some of the All Souls students thought that he was "off his rocker," and depressed even to the point of being suicidal. At other times he would be noticed long after dinnertime flat on his face on the hearth rug, or sitting beside the fire in the common room writing. At these times, according to Morrah, Lawrence would warm up and tell "hair-raising stories" about his experiences in the Middle East. He seemed to take pleasure in exaggerating and would continue to "unbend," talking until the early hours of the morning.[78] Ralph Isham (Boswell's biographer), another friend Lawrence came to know during this period, similarly describes Lawrence's yarning: "He did not lie in the strict sense, but he did indulge in fiction. And he was perfectly aware of it. His tales arrived full-blown."[79] On the other hand, according to Herbert Baker, "He could not be induced to tell of his adventures in the War, except in his kindness to my young son; or as a bait to draw out the adventures of others."[80] Lawrence was apparently selective about whom he would share his war experiences with.

I am of the opinion that this tendency to fictionalize his experiences, to turn his life into a legend, was most prominent when Lawrence was feeling particularly troubled in his self-regard. At these times he would give way to an unconscious need to create a fictional self, drawn on the lines of childish heroism, to replace the troubled self he was experiencing. Most of the time his rational self rejected the fictional one, the "Lawrence of Arabia." In meeting Lawrence for the first time in the summer of 1919, Isham asked him if he knew his "namesake of Arabia." Lawrence "grinned hugely and said, 'I'm afraid I know him much too well.' He enjoyed my discomfiture. I said, 'Well, anyway, you don't look like him.' He replied, 'I know I don't and I don't feel like him.' And we both laughed."[81]

Lawrence tended at All Souls to engage in undergraduate pranks (he was thirty-two at the time). Most of the tales of these escapades — flying the Hijaz flag from the pinnacle of All Souls, ringing the station bell captured at Tell Shahm out his window into the quadrangle, or stealing the Magdalen College deer — have been told by Robert Graves, a well-known fiction-maker himself, but some of them have been confirmed. Arnold Lawrence feels that these pranks were clear indications of his brother's troubled state.[82]

It did look for a time in 1920 as if Lawrence might become the Oxford scholar he had always seemed almost to be. He visited his many friends in Oxford, talked and wrote about books and printing, and called himself a bookworm. He indicated in a letter that he thought of settling down some day to do his history of the Crusades.[83] But his restlessness and discontent proved eventually too profound for such a quiet life. "When I got back I tried Oxford for a bit but gave it up," he wrote at the end of February.[84]

When asked to be the godfather (how often he was a godfather!) to his friend Newcombe's boy he answered: "In the history of the world (cheap edition) I'm a sublimated Aladdin, the thousand and second Knight, a Strand-Magazine strummer. In the eyes of 'those who know' I failed badly in attempting a piece of work which a little more resolution would have pushed through, or left untouched. So either case it is bad for the sprig."[85]

Despite this demurring, he took a godfatherly interest in the "sprig," who was named Stewart Lawrence Newcombe. Wouldn't the child be handicapped by that name? Lawrence asked the father. He soon asked to visit his godson, and was enchanted with him. "Ned loved Jimmy from the time he was born," the mother confided to me, "and bounced him on his knee. He felt Jimmy was something that was his, a familial link."[86]

In March Lawrence wrote to a wartime friend, "I'm out of affairs by request of the Foreign Office which paid me the compliment of calling me the main obstacle to an Arab surrender."[87] On May 14 he wrote to Frederick Stern: "Paris gave me a bad taste in my mouth, and so last May I dropped politics, and have had no touch with British or Arabs or Zionists since. I'm out of them for good, and so my views on Palestine are merely ancient history."[88] But British mismanagement of its Middle Eastern responsibilities had already been drawing Lawrence's attention, and a few days after writing Stern he was once more in the thick of Middle Eastern politics.

While Lawrence was struggling with his memoirs in London and enjoying his friends in Oxford, the situation in Syria and elsewhere in the Middle East was deteriorating. Abandoned by the British to the French in the fall of 1919 (by the end of November all British forces had been withdrawn from Syria), Faisal had turned to the French government to try to negotiate on his own. But in January 1920 his situation became more precarious when Clemenceau was defeated for the presidency and a more conservative, colonialist regime came into power. In March the Syrian congress declared the country's complete independence from France and Faisal was made king. But the assertion was an empty one. On April 25 at the Italian Riviera resort of San Remo the Supreme Council of the Allies met to construct the Turkish treaty and divided Syria into three parts: Lebanon, Palestine and a reduced "Syria." By the terms of this agreement, called the Treaty of Sèvres because it was signed there — near Paris, the mandates for Syria and Lebanon were awarded to France and separate mandates for Palestine and Iraq were assigned to Great Britain. The map of Arab Asia was redrawn, without attention to the wishes of its people. The French interpreted "mandate" as they chose, and soon after the decisions were made public in early May sent an army into Syria, drove Faisal into exile, and occupied Damascus after a bloody battle with Arab resisters.[89]

In late March or early April of 1920, Lawrence received a letter from an archeologist at Carchemish which he must have found distressing. He learned that "everybody, man, woman and child dislikes the French and expressed to me the hope that the English would come back and let the French leave the country."[90] The letter also provided Lawrence with a long account of the progress at the site.

Perhaps this letter, reminding him of his earlier attachments in the Arab East, influenced Lawrence, or perhaps he simply became increasingly distressed over the events in Syria and Mesopotamia. Whatever the reason, he decided to involve himself once more in Arab affairs, at least with his pen. On May 21 he wrote to Philby, inviting him to join a group of "Middle Eastern" colleagues who were petitioning the prime minister (Lloyd George) to take control of Mesopotamia away from the India Office and the Foreign Office, and to place it in the hands of a newly-to-be-created Middle East Department.[91] In the letter to Philby, which has never to my knowledge been published, Lawrence wrote: "It happens to be — politically — the right moment for pressure towards a new Middle East Department, since some re-shuffling of spheres is certain to happen quite soon: and the enclosed [the petition to Lloyd George] is a step taken under advice, to add pressure from outside, to what is going on inside. They have asked me to get your name on the list: other 'experts' invited are Hogarth, Curtis, Toynbee and myself. I have no doubt you will agree, so I won't bother to argue. It is a step necessary before a new policy can be put in force, and when we get it through, then we'll have to open up a battery of advice on the new men. . . . Curzon of course is the enemy: but he's not a very bold enemy, and won't like a rift in his family showing up: I have good hopes of it."[92]

A few days later, Lawrence followed this letter and the petition with the first of three newspaper articles, using the authority of his own name ("Colonel T. E. Lawrence, late British Staff Officer with the Emir Faisal"). Two of the articles appeared in the *Daily Express* and the third in the *Sunday Times*, and all were highly critical of British policy in the Middle East.[93]

In the first, Lawrence attacked the British policy of supporting both Ibn Saud and King Husayn and frankly acknowledged that he had advised his government to support only the latter. He still expected that this latest "outburst of puritanism in the desert" would die away, but was correct in predicting that the European powers would not be able to meet a crisis when it occurred.[94]

In the second, he attacked the paralysis of policy in Middle Eastern affairs that had resulted from a division of responsibility among the Foreign Office, the India Office and the War Office. "The war has had the effect on the offices," he continued, "of making the young men younger, and the old men older. The blood thirstiness of the old men — who did not fight — towards our late enemies is sometimes curiously relieved against the tolerance of those who have fought and wish to avoid making others fight again tomorrow.

"Asia has changed in the war almost as much as Europe, and the men in touch with it today find a great difficulty in speaking a common language with those who have been viceroys or governors long ago.

"The old find it difficult to believe that even before the war the British Empire in Asia was founded, not on troops, but on the passive consent of the greater number of the subjects. They fail to see that Asiatics have fought in the war, not for us, but for their own interests; to give themselves a better standing with us. They do not understand that Russia is also an Asiatic country, and that its revolution is an object-lesson to Asia of a successful rebellion of the half-educated and the poor.

"They have a belief, pathetic if not so dangerous that, 'a few troops' are a medicine for political disease."[95]

The third article, which appeared in the *Sunday Times*, was a bitter attack on the Treaty of Sèvres, which had been made public earlier in the month. Lawrence wrote that after the armistice "everywhere between Russia and the Indian Ocean it was felt that the war cloud had lifted, and that the brown peoples who had chosen to fight beside the Allies would receive their meed of friendship in the work of peace, that new age of freedom of which victory was the dawn." But not only had the framing of a peace treaty with Turkey been delayed, but when it was finally drawn up its terms were "impossible," as its framers admitted. "No account," Lawrence declared, "was taken of the actual conditions of the former Turkish Empire, or of the military and financial strengths of the countries devouring it. Each party making the terms considered only what it could take, or rather what would be most difficult for her neighbors to take or to refuse her, and the document is not the constitution of a new Asia, but a confession, almost an advertisement, of the greeds of the conquerors." He then reviewed the mismanagement of Britain's responsibilities throughout the Middle East, citing especially Lord Curzon, and the loss of "our friendly reputation" in Persia, the Caucasus, Turkey, Mesopotamia, Arabia, Syria and Egypt. In Mesopotamia, Lawrence noted, Britain had 50,000 troops and "nearly 200,000 labourers keeping them alive," at a cost of 30 million pounds a year, "and [they] eat up the country besides."

"Some day," he continued, "by a small increase, we will be able to hold part of Kurdistan and bore there for oil. Meanwhile it is a good training for the troops." He urged in ironic language the consolidation of the management of Britain's Middle Eastern policies under a single department (actually formed later in the year) and predicted (correctly as it turned out) that this would greatly cut the cost of lives and money. The article concluded with a statement of support for Faisal that is one of the most bitingly critical passages he ever wrote:

"He is the moderate in Syria, the constructive stateman who prevents the Arab hot-heads from attacking the French, the Jews, and the British, and his self-control has delayed our settling Syria by a military expedition. However, the Foreign Office have now hit on a new plan, and are tempting him to come to Europe on a business-holiday, for a sum of money running far into six figures. It is not a bribe, but 'arrears of subsidy,' and when he leaves Syria there will be, with luck, another little war, and our expenditure will have justified itself: though I personally, since I know and like Feisal, will regret the part of the money I contribute in taxation towards his downfall. It is not for such policies I fought."[96] Less than two months after Lawrence wrote this letter Faisal was driven from Syria and Lawrence's artist friend Augustus John, who had once painted Faisal for him, must have troubled Lawrence when he asked with seeming innocence, "Why was he beaten by the French — because you were not at his side?"[97]

During the war Arab nationalism had "flickered fitfully in Iraq,"[98] but in Mesopotamia the movement toward independence had received a powerful stimulus from the success of the Arab Revolt (the Arab forces included many Iraqi) and the example of the Bolshevik Revolution to the north. British assurances of independence issued to gain Arab support during the war period — especially the Anglo-French declaration of November 7, 1918, in which the declarers agreed to assist in setting up indigenous governments in Syria and Mesopotamia — provided a further impetus toward self-determination. The autonomous Arab government in Syria during the postwar period had a further influence upon Iraqi nationalist agitation.[99] The announcement in May 1920 of the assignment of the mandate for Iraq to Great Britain further agitated the nationalists and seemed proof that Great Britain had no intention of keeping her earlier promises, although the type of mandate awarded (Class A) promised relatively early independence.

Curzon's statement in the House of Lords in June that "the gift of the mandate . . . rests with the powers who have conquered the territories, which it then falls to them to distribute" reflected British imperialist thinking.[100] The policies of the civil commissioner in Iraq, Arnold Wilson, who advocated large numbers of British personnel to keep the natives in line, was consistent with this thinking. In late June a tribal rebellion broke out on the lower Euphrates and spread through much of the country. Its suppression over the summer of 1920 was a costly tragedy for Great Britain and Iraq in lives and resources, and in the destruction of good will between the Arab and Western worlds.

After the rebellion broke out, Lawrence wrote from All Souls a blistering series of attacks on British Mesopotamian policy, which were published in July and August in *The Times, The Observer* and the *Sunday Times*.[101] During the same period *The Times* published anonymously two additional articles of Lawrence's reviewing in laudatory terms Faisal's contributions to Britain as a leader of the Arabs during the Revolt, and his effective diplomacy of moderation in Syria after the war. These articles are eloquent, stirringly written documents, which reached a British public that was growing intolerant of the cost and bloodshed of mismanagement in Mesopotamia. They played a real part in influencing the government to change its policies and in preparing the ground for Faisal's eventual rulership in Iraq.

"Merit is no qualification for freedom. Bulgars, Afghans and Tahitians have it," Lawrence argued. He urged dominion status for Mesopotamia and the removal of all the thousands of British and Indian soldiers and other personnel then fighting the rebels or running the country, and recommended "tearing up what we have done and beginning again on advisory lines."[102] He knew that his ideas would be called "grotesque," but he advocated making Arabic the government language and raising an army of Arabis — two divisions of volunteers.[103]

As news of the slaughter of Arabs by the British in the rebellion reached him, Lawrence became still more forceful and sarcastic: "We have really no competence in this matter to criticise the French; they have only followed in very humble fashion, in their sphere of Syria, the example we set them in Mesopotamia."[104]

His words rose to a crescendo in the last article (August 22) written while the rebellion was still going on: "We have killed about ten thousand Arabs in this rising this summer. We cannot hope to maintain such an average: it is a poor country, sparsely peopled. . . . Cromer controlled Egypt's six million people with five thousand British troops; Colonel Wilson fails to control Mesopotamia's three million people with ninety thousand troops. . . . We say we are in Mesopotamia to develop it for the benefit of the world. All experts say that the labour supply is the ruling factor in its development. How far will the killing of ten thousand villagers and townspeople this summer hinder the production of wheat, cotton and oil? How long will we permit millions of pounds, thousands of Imperial troops, and tens of thousands of Arabs to be sacrificed on behalf of a form of colonial administration which can benefit nobody but its administrators?"[105]

Lawrence's information about Mesopotamia was sketchy. He had spent little time there and was less familiar with the local conditions and problems of governing the country than he was with those of Syria. He seemed almost to take advantage of incomplete knowledge, turning it into a license for exaggeration in order to strengthen his arguments. His friend Gertrude Bell, who was then serving with the civil administration in Mesopotamia, acknowledged that mistakes had been made. Early in July, before his last barrage of newspaper articles, she had written to Lawrence: "What curious organs [the newspapers] you choose for self expression!" and had criticized his underestimation of Ibn Saud. "However whatever the organs I'm largely in agreement with what you say."[106] She wrote then of her anguish and shared with him her own struggle to shift the direction of British policy in Iraq. She was critical only of his naiveté in failing to recognize that Ibn Saud was far stronger than Husayn and not so easily dealt with.

But by September, Bell was exasperated and frantic over what she felt were misleading statements (not all she objected to are quoted above) and over false impressions she felt Lawrence's articles were making. In her diary entry of September 5 she notes:

> The thing isn't made any easier by the tosh T. E. Lawrence is writing in the papers; to talk of raising an Arab army of two Divisions is *pure nonsense*. . . . I can't think why the India Office lets the rot that's written pass uncontradicted. T.E.L. again: when he says we have forced the English language on the country it's not only a lie but he knows it is. Every jot and tittle of official work is done in Arabic; in schools, law courts, hospitals, no other language is used. It's the first time that has happened since the fall of the Abbasids. . . . we are largely suffering from circumstances over which we couldn't have had any control. The wild drive of discontented nationalism from Syria and of discontented Islam from Turkey might have proved too much for us however far-seeing we had been; but that doesn't excuse us for having been blind.[107]

On September 19 she wrote further in her diary:

> The fact that we are really guilty of an initial mistake makes it difficult to answer letters like those of T. E. Lawrence. I believe them to be wholly mis-

leading, but to know why they're misleading requires such an accurate acquaintance not only with the history of the last two years but also with the country and the people, apart from our dealings with them, that I almost despair of putting public opinion in England right. I can't believe T.E.L. is in ignorance, and I therefore hold him to be guilty of the unpardonable sin of wilfully darkening counsel. We have a difficult enough task before us in this country; he is making it more difficult by leading people to think that it's easy. How can it be easy when you're called upon to reconcile the views and ideals of a tribal population which hasn't changed one shade of thought during the last five thousand years, and of a crude and impatient band of urban politicians who blame you for not setting up universities.[108]

Lawrence received letters of approval for his newspaper campaign from such Arabists as Wilfred Scawen Blunt, the famous Middle East traveler and poet, and from George Lloyd, Doughty and Philby. Blunt wrote, "I was greatly pleased at your letter in the *Times* and, though I have no confidence in the honour of our government, I yet do not quite despair of a victory for Asia or the result of the struggle now going on,"[109] and Lord Lloyd, then governor of Bombay, wrote from India: "No news of you except through the newspapers — Was there ever so fatal and disastrous a muddle over Egypt, Syria, Palestine and Mesopotamia. I am beginning to think that when you and I kept repeating our familiar tags, you 'Alexandretta!' and I 'Gibraltar's not territory' we were not only saying and meaning the same things but right things."[110]

Pleased with the progress of his newspaper campaign, Lawrence wrote in August, before it was over: "It did some good and the Government (very grudgingly and disowning me every step of the road) is doing absolutely the right thing by Mesopotamia now: they are even making the special department in London to look after those districts when they need help!"[111] And to Mrs. Shaw seven years later, he wrote in retrospect: "So I remain unrepentant. I was right to work for Arab self-government through 1919 and 1920: and my methods then, though not beyond criticism were, I think, reasonably justifiable."[112]

During 1920, when he was not writing for the newspapers, Lawrence was busy on other articles. These included his piece on changes in Asia, which he wrote anonymously for Lionel Curtis, the visionary and idealistic editor of the *Round Table,* and an article for Guy Dawnay, editor of *The Army Quarterly,* on his concepts of strategy in guerrilla warfare as applied to the Arab Revolt. In the latter piece, entitled "The Evolution of a Revolt,"[113] Lawrence analyzed the fundamentals of command, breaking them down into scientific or mathematical, biological and psychological aspects (the "kingdoms" that "lay in each man's mind"). The scientific aspect concerned the geography, terrain, populations and forces involved, while the biological concerned the variability of human endurance and capability, "the breaking point, life and death," and the cost and valuation of human life. The psychological aspect he related to that science "of which our propaganda is a stained and ignoble part. Some of it concerns the crowd, the adjustment of spirit to the point where it becomes fit to exploit in action, the prearrangement of a changing opinion to a certain end. *Some of it deals with individuals, and then it becomes a rare art of human kindness* [italics added], transcending, by purposeful emotion, the gradual logical sequence of our minds. It considers the capacity for mood of our men, their complexities and mutability, and the cultivation of what in them profits attention."[114]

Over the summer of 1920 Lawrence's persistent efforts to have a second edition of *Arabia Deserta* published finally met with success, and the Medici Society, which had published booklovers' editions of the classics, agreed to do it, but only if Lawrence would write an introduction, in order presumably, to enhance the chances of commercial success. A decade later H. M. Tomlinson wrote to him, "The simple truth is that your introduction to the 'Arabia Deserta' got that work placed where some of us wanted it to be, but hardly expected to see it."[115] The introduction, really an essay of Lawrence's own on Arabia and the Middle East, was written between August and November 1920, and Lawrence claims it was the "only thing" actually written at All Souls.[116] It provides his most succinct expression of the meaning for him of the desert, the Bedouin way of life and the experience of living among them. He admired in Doughty's pioneering achievement of travel in Arabia not only what he most valued in his own achievements, but also qualities Doughty possessed which he felt he could not emulate. Doughty, like Lawrence, overcame poor health and endured. "None of us triumphed over our bodies as Doughty did," Lawrence wrote.[117] But Doughty was "never morbid, never introspective," as he felt he was himself to a fault, "and the telling is detached, making no parade of good and evil." Doughty, in Lawrence's view, was the kind of Englishman abroad who gave the example of "the complete Englishman, the foreigner intact," in contrast to those like himself who "imitate the native as far as possible," becoming "like the people, not of the people." For Lawrence the attractions and limitations of the Bedouin life and character, the freedom and simplicity, and the "barrenness too harsh for volunteers" combined with narrowness of mind and impulsive subjectivity. Beyond abnegation and self-restraint Lawrence saw in the Bedouin the seeking of pain (which in himself had gone much beyond the renunciation of pleasure), "a self-delight in pain, a cruelty which is more to him than goods." Lawrence wrote almost longingly of some aspects of desert life: the organic connection between social organization and natural circumstances, the candor with which men lived with each other, and the openness of life among the tents ("beside one another . . . the daily hearth of the sheikh's coffee-gathering is their education, a university for every man grown enough to walk and speak").[118]

Gertrude Bell's letter of July 20, 1920, which he received about this time, may have had some impact, for he speaks here admiringly of Ibn Saud. "The Wahabi dynasty of Riath," he wrote near the end of the introduction, "has suddenly revived in this generation, thanks to the courage and energy of Abd el-Aziz [Ibn Saud] the present Emir. He has subdued all Nejd with his arms, has revived the Wahabi sect in new stringency, and bids fair to subject all the inner deserts of the peninsula to his belief." Lawrence concludes the introduction by expressing his indebtedness to Doughty for providing not only a great travel book, but a "military text-book" which "helped to guide us to victory in the East."[119]

By the end of 1920, which he wrote later was an even worse year for him than 1919, matters were looking up for Lawrence. The government had decided upon a change from its inept policies in Iraq, a decision which the press attacks of Lawrence and others had helped to influence. The statesmanlike Percy Cox returned to Baghdad from Persia in October to replace Arnold Wilson, and by the end of the year had instituted a provisional Arab government and other reforms.[120] Plans were being made in London to transfer authority for the region into a newly formed Middle East Department of the Colonial Office under Winston Churchill, thus filling with a single authority what Lawrence had called "the empty space which divides the Foreign Office from the India Office."[121] Lawrence's up-and-down attitude toward his book was on an upturn, and he made plans with the artist Eric Kennington to return with him to the Middle East so that Kennington could illustrate the narrative with drawings of the Arabs and other participants in the campaigns. Kennington was so enthralled with the plans that he spent a month in London studying Lawrence's material on the Revolt and earning money as an artist in order to make the trip at his own expense. Through Lawrence he was captured by a "fantastic Eastern romance" of his own.[122]

Kennington has provided an interesting, romanticized picture of Lawrence at the end of 1920. In their first meeting Kennington observed a nervous giggle, but this subsided eventually in later meetings. Kennington was impressed with Lawrence's

> male dignity, beauty and power. He moved little, using bodily presence just sufficiently to make brain contact. I had never seen so little employment or wastage of physical energy. The wide mouth smiled often, with humor and pleasure, sometimes extending to an unusual upward curve at the corners, a curious menacing curve, warning of danger. The face was almost lineless, and removed from me as a picture of sculpture. . . . The eyes roamed round, above, and might rest on mine or rather travel through mine, but never shared my thoughts, though noting them all. He stayed higher on another

plane of life. It was easy to become his slave. These crystal eyes were almost animal, yet with a complete human understanding. And at moments of thought, when he would ignore the presence of others, retiring into himself, they would diverge slightly. Then, he was alone, and as inscrutable as a lion or a snake. He would return, and graciously attend to one with limitless patience, dealing with our slower brains and limited understanding, our hesitations, and fears, apparently never exasperated by our inefficiency. . . . I realized both his bodily strength and his sensitiveness. Though not broad, he was weighty from shoulders to neck, which jutted, giving a forward placing to the head, and a thrust to the heavy chin. Graves has called his eyes maternal, and I think rightly so, but a near contrast was the power of the frontal bones, and their aggressiveness . . . the fearless eyes were protected by a fighter's bones above and below.[123]

# 24

# Lawrence and Churchill: The Political Settlements in the Middle East

Lawrence's plans to go to Jerusalem ("I'd just got as keen as mustard on going out with Kennington") were cut short by his agreeing to work as a political advisor to Winston Churchill with a "free hand" and a salary of £1,200 a year, which he used for "official purposes" and to pay for Kennington's drawings for his book rather than for his own personal needs.[1] "So I'm a government servant from yesterday," he wrote in a letter to Graves near the start of the new year, "and Palestine goes fut (or phut?)."[2] But Kennington, who had been led by Lawrence — Kennington called it "stumbling after his mind," on an imaginary journey "through Nejd, Yemen, Jerusalem, Damascus, Sunni, Shia, Ash-Kenazim, Saphardim," — was determined to go alone and did so.[3]

Lawrence's work with Winston Churchill in 1921 in a newly created Middle East Department that placed Hashemite rulers at the heads of two new Arab states — he called this later the period "of which I'm proudest" — illustrates most strikingly his political and diplomatic functioning, the strengths and weaknesses of his personal approach to world affairs. As had become characteristic of him, Lawrence worked through another, older, man in a position of power and command, and influenced him toward a solution that carried Lawrence's personal stamp but was spelled out in minute detail ("talk of leaving things to man on spot — we left nothing").[4] Churchill persuaded Lawrence to work with him by "arguments which I could not resist,"[5] and Churchill confounded his astonished colleagues, who included men from the India Office, by returning this "wild ass of the desert" to harness.[6]

A deep mutual admiration and respect grew between Lawrence and Churchill. Churchill admired the patient and calm way Lawrence gave himself to the task, and was able "to sink his personality, to bend his imperious will and pool his knowledge in the common stock . . . he saw the hope of redeeming in large measure the promises he had made to the Arab chiefs and of re-establishing a tolerable measure of peace in those wide regions. In that cause he was capable of becoming — I hazard the word — a humdrum official. The effort was not in vain. His purposes prevailed."[7] Lawrence for his part admired Churchill's courage and his imaginative approach to political problems, his willingness to depart from old ways and to use the best knowledge available to find new solutions. Lawrence also stressed Churchill's kindliness to him and called him "an employer who had been for me so considerate as sometimes to seem more like a senior partner than a master."[8] The only "breeze" (friction) was "when T.E. said Lenin was the greatest man, when W.S.C. was fondling Napoleon's bust."[9]

The solution for Iraq arrived at by Churchill's new Middle East Department had two principal parts: the transfer of responsibility for policing the country from the army to the air force, and the installation of Faisal at the head of an Arab government that would be affiliated with Great Britain and would be given a good deal of opportunity for self-government. The huge army garrison was to be removed (in 1920 alone £38,500,000 was expended to suppress the revolt in Iraq — several times what it cost the British government to finance the entire Arab Revolt), and the policing responsibility taken on by several squadrons of the young RAF at greatly reduced expense.[10]

Churchill appears to have originated the idea of RAF control of Mesopotamia early in 1920, before the revolt of the tribesmen, when he was secretary of state for air and war. The details of how it might be done were developed by Hugh Trenchard, chief of air staff, and Lawrence over the course of the next year.[11] In April 1920, after a dinner meeting with Trenchard, Lawrence wrote to Lord Winterton, "After quite a lot of talk I feel inclined to back his [Trenchard's] scheme."[12]

Even more than the RAF plan, the placement of Faisal upon the throne of Iraq bears the stamp of Lawrence's personal diplomacy. With Faisal in Damascus, Lawrence had proposed to the cabinet at the war's end that Abdullah rule in Baghdad and Lower Mesopotamia and Zayd in Upper Mesopotamia,[13] and continued to support this view at the Peace Conference.[14] But events over the next two years altered his view, and soon after Faisal's expulsion from Damascus, Lawrence began to prepare British opinion for the amir's leadership in Iraq. The suggestion that Faisal rule in Iraq had, ironically, already been made to the government in a telegram sent by Arnold Wilson in July 1920, just after Faisal left Syria.[15]

Lawrence concluded his two anonymous encomiums on Faisal in *The Times* in August 1920 with a statement of his friend's availability: "He now finds himself a free man, with unrivalled experience, great knowledge of war and government, with the reputation of the greatest Arab leader since Saladin, and the prestige of three victorious campaigns behind him. He is 33, vigorous, and not yet at the height of his powers. His ambitions for himself are nothing. He is the most democratic of men, the most charming personality, but he has put all his abilities and strength at the service of the Arab national movement for 10 years, and raised it from an academic question to the principal factor in Western Asia. It will be interesting to see in which direction he turns, to which of all the opportunities at his command he will finally incline."[16]

The direction of Faisal's turning or, more accurately, the direction in which he was turned, was soon determined. In December he came to London, and Kinahan Cornwallis, his former advisor in Damascus, with Curzon's authorization unsuccessfully offered him the throne of Iraq.[17] Thereupon Lawrence and Lord Winterton made another try. Winterton was approached by the prime minister's secretary "unofficially" to obtain the amir's promise of acceptance of the crown of Iraq should it be "officially" offered to him. This Winterton did

> with the invaluable aid of Colonel Lawrence, Lord Harlech, and the late Lord Moyne, at 3 A.M. in my house in the country after five hours continuous discussion. King Feisal was a brave, most talented and charming man, and one of the greatest gentlemen I have ever met, but like most geniuses he was temperamental. For hours, to all our collective persuasion, he made the same answer. He was sick of politics, especially European politics, and indeed of all Europeans except personal friends such as ourselves. He had been abominably treated in Damascus; was there any reason to believe we should treat him any better in Baghdad? At last he assented to our request and said he believed Iraq and Britain could and should work together, which would be his great aim in his new position.[18]

By the time Churchill had gathered the principal figures involved in the affairs of Iraq in Cairo for a conference in March 1921, the main decisions had already been made ("over dinner tables at the Ship Restaurant in Whitehall").[19] It would be proposed to the British cabinet that Faisal rule the country in alliance with Great Britain and the expense of governing it should be reduced by entrusting its defense to the Royal Air Force.[20]

Lawrence wrote early in February of 1921 to Lady Kennet, a sculptor who was making a statuette of him, "I'm tired of the limelight, and [I'm] not ever going to be a public figure again."[21] But by the end of the month he was off to Cairo to play a dramatic role in the conference that was held there in March. "Everybody Middle East is here," he wrote home on March 20, "except Joyce and Hogarth. . . . We're a very happy family: agreed upon everything important: and the trifles are laughed at."[22]

Walter Henry Thompson, a Scotland Yard inspector who had the responsibility of guarding Churchill for nearly twenty years, spent many days and hundreds of hours with Lawrence in Egypt and Palestine in March 1921. He has left a remarkable firsthand record of Lawrence's compelling power among the Arab peoples and the adulation which greeted his return to the lands he had helped to liberate.[23] Thompson had received advance notice that Churchill's life would be in danger in Egypt, but Lawrence, through his knowledge of the Arab countries and people ("in a strange sense it *was* Lawrence's land, by legacy to him from those Arabs") and his sense of the moods of crowds, guided the diplomatic party safely through their journeys.[24]

At Gaza, on the way to Jerusalem, Lawrence settled an unruly-looking mob by having the party detrain and proceed to a hall near the town mosque where, dressed in full Arab regalia, he translated a brief speech for Churchill. Thompson described the "magic" in the atmosphere as the tribal leaders from far-flung parts of the Arab world came to greet Lawrence:

> It is doubtful whether the Arabs, with the unclassifiable admixture here in the mob at Gaza of Lebanese, Iraqi, Alaouites, Djebel Druses, Turks, Syrians, Jews, Armenians, Kurds and Persians — whether more than three or four in the crowd knew which was Churchill. Or much cared. We were just a knot of Europeans with hats on. Lawrence was the man.
>
> No Pope of Rome ever had more command before his own worshippers in the Palazzo. And Colonel Lawrence raised his hand slowly, the first and second fingers lifted above the other two for silence and for blessing. He could have owned their earth. He did own it. Every man froze in respect, in a kind of New Testament adoration of shepherds for a master. It was quite weird and very comforting.
>
> We passed through these murderous-looking men and they parted a way for us without a struggle. Many touched Lawrence as he moved forward among them. Far off, drums were beating, and a horse neighed. A muezzin's cry fell sadly among us from the single minaret in the mosque.[25]

Thompson concluded that at this time in this part of Western Asia, "Lawrence was so greatly loved and so fanatically respected that he could have established his own empire from Alexandretta to the Indus. He knew this, too."[26] And, I might add, it frightened him.

One of the "trifles" Lawrence referred to in his March 20 letter to his mother was how to get Faisal accepted by the Iraqis as their ruler. There were rivals for the throne, such as the *naqib* (head of the provisional government) and Sayyid Talib, but the former was too old and infirm, and too limited in competence or authority, to be acceptable to either the British or the Iraqis, and the latter was feared as an unreliable rabble-rouser with dictatorial ambitions.[27] Faisal's diplomatic and military experience, proved statesmanship, high prestige in the Arab world and friendliness (if dealt with fairly) with the British made him an acceptable candidate to Cox, who had, by the time of the Cairo Conference, already come to "a 'Sharifian' although not definitely a 'Feisalian' conclusion."[28] To Mrs. Shaw in 1927 Lawrence wrote, "In 1921, at the Cairo Conference, [Gertrude Bell] swung all the Mespot. British officials to the Feisal solution, while Winston and I swung the English people."[29]

The implementing of the decisions of the Cairo Conference, especially the installation of Faisal as king of Iraq, was achieved by a combination of British force, diplomacy, manipulation and deception, in which the high commissioner, Sir Percy Cox, and his assistant, Gertrude Bell, played key roles in Iraq, while Churchill managed the difficulties presented by his own government.[30]

Strong national and religious groups in Iraq were either directly opposed to Faisal and favored another candidate, or were at best cool to the prospect of his rule. In April the leading contender, Sayyid Talib, after making a threatening speech was arrested out of fear that he would foment violence among the revolutionary elements of the country. There was considerable delay in making public the British decision to place Faisal on the Iraqi throne, as every effort was made to have his candidacy appear to be the desire of the people themselves. Churchill's speech of June 14 in the British House of Commons, announcing the Cairo decisions, contained the contradictory statements that the British did not intend or desire to force a particular rule on the Iraqi people and that Amir Faisal was "the most suitable candidate in the field." He hoped "that [Faisal] will secure the support of the majority of the people of Iraq."[31]

Faisal arrived in Iraq on June 23 and experienced a cool reception during his trip to Baghdad, but was received there by huge enthusiastic crowds.[32] Under the guidance of the high commissioner a referendum held in August found ninety-six percent of the votes supporting Faisal, but as Sir Percy's biographer noted with masterful understatement, "in the Near and Middle East the results of all such operations are exaggerated and owe much to official prompting or pressure."[33]

Through the force and skill of Faisal's own statesmanship, he was able to reconcile most of the discontented elements of the country to his candidacy, including those that wished complete independence from Britain. He successfully staved off a British effort to shackle his authority and was duly enthroned on August 23 as a military band played "God Save the King" (there was no Arab national anthem), and a twenty-one-gun royal salute was fired.[34] Through this compromised process of democracy-in-action the state of Iraq was created in alliance with Great Britain, and began to move toward full independence.

Faisal owed his throne in Iraq to Lawrence most of all, and it was to Lawrence whom he wrote for advice regarding the details of the treaty between his country and Great Britain, the degree of British control of Iraq's financial and political affairs he should endure, his difficulties effecting changes in his administration, and his frustration with the high commissioner, who, he wrote, had "a perfectly genuine desire, to keep everybody who had served in any office in his position whatever his circumstances are."[35] Faisal's letters to his English friend (Lawrence's letters to the king have not been discovered) are affectionate in tone and convey his deep commitment to his people. He concluded one letter in November 1921:

> And indeed, my dearest Lawrence, I have seen that as the result of the Treaty I shall be able to benefit you and benefit my country and indeed as you know I am not afraid of work or responsibility, and if I saw that I was going to be tied down or gagged and to meet with shame and failure into the bargain I don't wish to be like the Shah of Persia to make a promise and then not stand by my engagements (and I am staking my honour and my love for my people and my love for you on the result) and I should lose everything, nay, I should ask pardon from everybody and become submissive to your directions, whatever they may be. To conclude, Hope you are in good health.
>
> Your friend. Feisul[36]

By 1927 progress toward independence and stable government had been made in Iraq and Lawrence wrote proudly to Mrs. Shaw, who had just met Faisal in London: "I'm awfully glad you liked him. For so long he was only my duckling: and I crow secretly with delight when he gets another inch forward on his road. When you think of the harrassed and distant figure of Wadi Safra in 1916. . . .

"I don't think he wants me really. Not even the nicest man on earth can feel wholly unembarrassed before a fellow to whom he owes too much. Feisal owed me Damascus first of all, and Baghdad second: and between those stages most of his kingcraft and affairs. When with him I am an omnipotent advisor: and while that is very well in the field, it is derogatory to a monarch: especially to a monarch who is not entirely constitutional. . . .

"Also peoples are like people. They teach themselves to walk and to balance by dint of trying and falling down. Irak did a good deal of falling between 1916 and 1921: and since 1921, under Feisal's guidance has done much good trying and no falling. But I don't think it yet walks very well. Nor can any hand save it from making its messes: there is a point where coddling becomes wicked. All my experience of the Arabs was of the ex god-father role: and I think they have outgrown that. If they are to make good as a modern state (how large an 'if') then it must be by virtue of their own desire and excellence. . . .

"What you say about him looking young and happy and peaceful pleases me: of course he has won great credit for himself: and that brings a man to flower. . . .

"You know without my letting [sic] you, how much I liked him. I talk of him always in the past tense, for it will be a long time before we meet again. Indeed I hope sometimes we never will, for it would mean that he was in trouble. I've promised myself to help him, if ever that happens.

"As for Irak . . . well, some day they will be fit for self-government, and then they will not want a king: but whether 7 or 70 or 700 years hence, God knows. Meanwhile Feisal is serving his race as no Arab has served it for many hundred years. He is my very great pride: and it's been my privilege to have helped him to his supremacy, out there, and to have made him a person, for the English-speaking [sic] reading races. Gertrude [Bell] has nobly supported him in his last effort. . . .

"Don't you think he looks the part, perfectly? Was there ever a more graceful walk than his? G.B.S. probably (being an emperor, himself) thinks poorly of kings: but he'd admit that I'd made a good one."[37]

Allowing for the egoism of the letter and some exaggeration of his role as a king- and state-maker, it contains enough uncomfortable reality (from an Arab point of view), and is so revealing of his attitude, as to make understandable the resentment of later Arab nationalists toward Lawrence's political activities in the Middle East.

On March 25 or 26, 1921, Lawrence left Cairo and proceeded via Gaza, Jerusalem and Amman to es-Salt to meet Amir Abdullah, who had gone to Trans-Jordan with "orders from his father to raise the tribes and drive the French out of Syria."[38] Lawrence told Abdullah "that it was impossible for King Faisal to return to Syria,"[39] and brought him through cheering crowds to a meeting in Jerusalem on March 28 with Churchill, Sir Herbert Samuel (the high commissioner of Palestine), and other officials. Abdullah was asked by Churchill to accept the decisions of the Cairo Conference regarding Iraq, but was offered in compensation the amirate of Trans-Jordan as a kind of buffer state, loyal to Great Britain, between Palestine, where a pro-Zionist policy was being implemented, and the anti-Zionist regions of the Arab world.[40] Abdullah proposed the creation of a single Arab state consisting of Palestine and Trans-Jordan, but eventually agreed to the more limited Lawrence-Churchill solution of the amirate of Trans-Jordan after some arm-twisting and the offer of the possible eventual restoration of an Arab administration in Syria.[41] Although Abdullah agreed to try to influence his father to accept the plan, he is said to have held it against Faisal for years afterwards that his brother usurped the crown of Iraq, which Abdullah believed was his by right.[42]

Lawrence seems to have been in good spirits in the early spring of 1921, pleased with his accomplishments at this time and glad to be back again in the desert lands, which were coming into bloom. "The country across Jordan is all in spring," he wrote his family in April, "and the grass and flowers are beautiful. . . . Spent eight days living with Abdullah in his camp. It was rather like the life in wartime, with hundreds of Bedouin coming and going, and a general atmosphere of newness in the air. However the difference was that now everybody is trying to be peaceful."[43]

Kennington captured the excitement with which Lawrence's former desert companions and comrades-in-arms greeted him upon his brief return to Trans-Jordan:

> Their cries . . . become a roar, Aurens — Aurens — Aurens — Aurens! It seemed to me that each had need to touch him. It was half an hour before he was talking to less than a dozen at once. Re-creating the picture, I see him as detached as ever, but with great charm and very gracious. I thought he got warmth and pleasure from their love, but now know his pain also, for they longed for him to lead them again into Damascus, this time to drive out the French. Easily self-controlled, he returned a percentage of the pats, touches and gripping of hands, giving nods, smiles, and sudden wit to chosen friends. He was apart, but they did not know it. They loved him, and gave him all their heart.[44]

Sir Herbert Samuel, the British high commissioner in Palestine, has provided another, more sober, eyewitness recollection of Lawrence's return to Amman: "I was witness of a most affectionate greeting from some of the principal Bedu sheikhs, who had been his associates in the Arab Revolt, when quite unexpectedly they found him among them once more."[45]

Lawrence's good spirits did not last very long. In April and early May he traveled between Egypt, Trans-Jordan and Jerusalem, spending some of the time with Kennington, who was drawing Arabs for the book. He met secretly with Faisal at Port Said to discuss British plans for the amir's enthronement in Iraq and evaluated for the Colonial Office the precarious position and impoverishment of Abdullah's fledgling administration in Amman. He returned to England in May, and wrote Graves, "I'm back in the Colonial Office and hating it."[46] Without an immediate sphere of action Lawrence devoted himself to literary interests, and to help Graves financially by turning over to him the disappointing proceeds of the sale of parts of his narrative of the Arab Revolt to a New York magazine.[47]

Although Lawrence was satisfied with progress in the Middle East from the political standpoint, he recognized that his return there had stirred up troubling memories. "I can't live at home," he wrote his poet friend, "I don't know why: the place makes me utterly intolerable. . . . Our schemes for the betterment of the Middle East race are doing nicely: thanks. . . . I wish I hadn't gone out there: the Arabs are like a page I have turned over: and sequels are rotten things. . . . Meanwhile I'm locked up here: office every day, and much of it, and another trip E. (this time to Jeddah to see the Sherif) looming."[48]

In June Lawrence learned that he was definitely being sent by Churchill as an envoy to try to persuade King Husayn to sign a treaty spelling out the various settlements that had been proposed for the Middle East from the time of the Versailles Treaty. Many of these solutions, such as the British mandate for Palestine, the French presence in Syria, and a general restricting of the king's sovereignty, were obviously intolerable to him, and represented a breach of the agreements and understandings he had been party to with Great Britain since 1914. Lawrence's position was an uncomfortable one and it is somewhat surprising that he accepted the appointment at all. If he were to be completely "successful" from the British point of view, it would have meant selling out his old ally altogether, while encouraging the king would have meant more war with Ibn Saud, who was still receiving subsidization from England.

Lawrence, according to his brother Arnold, chose a middle course and "bitched it up," making sure that his negotiations with Husayn were unsuccessful.[49] Some support for this view is provided by a comment of Lawrence's in a 1927 letter: "It was my action at Jidda in 1921 which made Ibn Saud's advance on Mecca possible. I hope he holds it for some years yet."[50] Later he told a friend in the Tank Corps that this trip to the Hijaz in 1921 was almost too much for him and that the mental strain to which he was subjected during the negotiations with Husayn was worse than anything he had known during the campaign.[51]

Doughty warned Lawrence to "look out for madmen fanatics at Jidda."[52] But early in July Lawrence headed for Jidda anyway and spent two hot, frustrating months there and in Aden. He met several times with the old king. Despite various odd attempts to browbeat Husayn, whose conceit and unrealistic ambitiousness Lawrence now found exasperating, and the contemplation of threats of force or withdrawal of his subsidy, nothing much came of the meetings and no treaty was signed.

The telegraphic correspondence between Lawrence and the Foreign Office from July 23 to September 22 provides a graphic, sometimes amusing, at other times questionable, account of Lawrence's effort to deal with the king.[53] He seems to have been most successful when appealing to the old man's vanity — for example in offering him a yacht for his personal use ("Any news of proposed yacht for Hussein to buy cheap if he behaves himself?"), Italian airplanes (very expensive "rubbish"), or agreeing to a visit from the Prince of Wales. Husayn's sons Zayd and Ali were much more reasonable and seemed to be working with Lawrence toward arriving at some sort of compromise. At one point Lawrence invoked Zayd's authority to recommend suppression of a complaining telegram that Husayn was planning to send to Faisal. It is not clear whether Lawrence had Zayd's authority to do this. When interviewed nearly a half century later, Zayd denied that Lawrence had acted with his knowledge.[54] The contemporary record, however, indicates that Lawrence and Zayd were working in close cooperation. At one point, for example, when Lawrence walked out of a session with the king "with parting remarks," Zayd came to him "with a rough draft of a treaty based on ours for my consideration."[55] When Lawrence left Jidda for Aden on August 12, it appeared that he had made some progress in obtaining the king's acquiescence in the various agreements under discussion.

In late August from Aden, where he had gone to consult the British resident, Lawrence wrote to Kennington, "This is the beastliest trip ever I had: but thank the Lord I took no dress clothes," and sent him an introduction he had written there to a catalogue of the drawings that the artist had made during the past year of the people of the desert for his (Lawrence's) potential book ("something for the future").[56] In this essay Lawrence expressed even more strongly than he had a year before in the introduction in *Arabia Deserta* his preference for the Arabs of the desert, for the Bedouin over the Arabs of the towns or other settled peoples. "He [Kennington] has drawn camel-men," Lawrence wrote, "and princes of the desert, donkey-boys, officers, descendants of the Prophet, a vice-president of the Turkish Chamber, slaves, sheikhs and swordsmen. They represent a fair choice of the real Arab, not the Algerian or Egyptian or Syrian so commonly palmed off on us, not the noisy, luxury-loving, sensual, passionate, greedy person, but a man whose ruling characteristic is hardness of body, mind, heart and head. . . . It is interesting to see that instinctively he drew the men of the desert. Where he was there were ten settled men to every nomad: yet his drawings show nearly ten desert men to every peasant. This has strengthened in me the unflattering suspicion that the nomad is the richer creature. The Arab townsman or villager is like us and our villagers, with our notion of property, our sense of gain and our appetite for material success. He has our premises, as well as our processes. The Bedouin on the other hand, while his sense is as human and his mind as logical as ours, begins with principles quite other than our own, and gets further from us as his character strengthens. He has a creed and practice of not-possessing, which is a tough armour against our modern wiles. It defends him against all sentiment."[57]

On August 29 Lawrence returned to Jidda for more than three additional weeks of fruitless negotiations with King Husayn,[58] who, Lawrence discovered, had gone back on his decision and demanded, among other things, "recognition of his supremacy over all Arab rulers everywhere."[59] Lawrence wired to London: "My reply made him send for a dagger and swear to abdicate and kill himself. I said we would continue negotiations with his successor."[60] Zayd, Ali and the queen ("who is of our party" and "lectures him at night") took "a strong line" and the negotiations became temporarily "friendly" and "rational" once again.

Lawrence seemed to have forgotten or repressed this episode, for when Liddell Hart asked him in 1933 whether there was any truth to the story that the king had called for his sword and threatened to kill himself Lawrence replied: "No truth. Suicide practically unknown amongst ortho-dox Moslems. King Hussein used to threaten to abdicate. I wished he would, but was never funny about it. The old man was a tragic figure, in his way: brave, obstinate, hopelessly out-of-date: exasperating."[61]

In mid-September the Foreign Office was becoming eager for Lawrence to visit Trans-Jordan "as soon as possible" (especially as the British government was under pressure from the French to force Abdullah to arrest the men involved in an assassination attempt on the French commander of Syria) and he sought to wind up his negotiations in Jidda. The king approved each clause of the treaty and announced publicly his plan to sign it. Lawrence wired to London, however, that "when Ali presented him [Husayn] text for ratification he shouted and struck at him, and then sent us eight contradictory sets of prior conditions and stipulations all unacceptable. Ali says the old man is mad, and is preparing with Zeid to obtain his formal abdication. Ali and Zeid have behaved splendidly, and they may change things in the next weeks."[62] On September 22 Lawrence set sail for Egypt and after five days there proceeded by train to Jerusalem.

By the end of the summer of 1921 Lawrence was becoming depressed once again. Abdullah's regime in Trans-Jordan was faltering under the pressures of Syrian and Palestinian politicians, French complaints and the besiegings of his British advisors, to all of whom Abdullah was said to have "smiled sweetly, expressed agreement" and done nothing, earning for himself the nickname of "Sunny Jim."[63] Lawrence was delegated to proceed from his mission with Husayn to view the situation at first hand in Amman and advise Winston Churchill in London regarding the future of the regime.[64] In July he had considered with Herbert Samuel that union with Palestine would be the best future for Trans-Jordan.[65] Lawrence expected that he would recommend ending Abdullah's faltering regime, and wrote to Kennington from Cairo at the beginning of October: "Tomorrow I go to Trans-Jordan, to end that farce. It makes me feel like a baby-killer. . . . I'm bored stiff: and very tired, and a little ill, and sorry to see how mean some people I wanted to respect have grown. The war was good by drawing over our depths that hot surface wish to do or win something. So the cargo of the ship was unseen, and not thought of. This life goes on till February 28 next year."[66] As it turned out, Lawrence proved to be the decisive factor in preserving Abdullah's regime in Trans-Jordan.

At the end of the first week of October, after discussions in Jerusalem with the high commissioner and his staff, Lawrence was still planning to persuade Abdullah to step down.[67] He arrived in Amman on October 12 as the chief British representative to evaluate the situation and obtain the agreement of Abdullah to the treaty his father had been unwilling to sign. He lived with his old friend F. G. Peake, who had served with him in the closing days of the desert campaigns and was now attempting to build up a native army, in a stone-built house at the site of a disintegrating Byzantine church.

During this period, according to Peake, Lawrence was given to shifting moods. Much of the time he amused himself with "Arab cronies" and lived once more the life of the desert and the tribes, but felt "stultified" in his role as a civil servant working with politically minded men who had not the élan or the commitment of his companions in the Revolt.[68] He suffered periods in which he appeared to Peake to be "depressed, incommunicative and obviously weighted down by the cares of fashioning a post-war world in the Middle East."[69]

Lawrence spent little time in the chief representative's office, preferring once more to see for himself the situation in the country. He drove all over the countryside (including a last look at his wartime base and retreat at Azraq) with Peake in his Model T Ford and later with Philby, who arrived at the end of November. After two weeks in Trans-Jordan Lawrence wrote a report to the Colonial Office in which he reviewed critically the administrative, military and political situation in the country. The report is factually detailed, but contains characteristic bits of Laurentian irony. For example: "Peake cannot show his men in public till they are reasonably smart and till they have rifles, for in Trans-Jordania every man of military age carries a rifle as a mark of self-respect, and Peake's, the so-called Military Force, is the only unarmed body of men in the country"; and, a driver, "who is supposed to be qualified, can drive the car forward but is not good at reversing. He is practicing this on the path between the tents."[70] Lawrence found in Trans-Jordan an understandable "distrust of the honesty of our motives," principally out of fear that British Zionist policy would be extended into this region, and he advised that Britain declare herself against such a policy.[71] He also busied himself with mediating various tribal disputes and claims: He destroyed a number of his predecessor's files which he thought would trouble Arab-British relations, including several passports awaiting endorsement (creating much trouble for their owners when they came to collect them); found time to engage a mason to underpin a collapsing Roman arch; and helped to resist from behind the scenes French demands that certain Arab nationalists be turned over to them.[72] To Newcombe, who was on his way to Syria, Lawrence wrote in November:

"There's only one thing to tell the French: that the catching of assassins is no doubt desireable, and one of the functions of government: but that we in Trans-Jordan have first to make the government, and then to make opinion disapprove of political assassination. After this the capture of assassins becomes timely. Meanwhile it would be silly, and I'll have no part in it. We cannot afford to chuck away our hopes of building some-thing to soothe our neighbour's feelings: and the French have made our job here as difficult as possible — if it is possible at all — by their wanton disregard of the common decencies between nations.

"Please remind them that they shot Arab prisoners after Meisalun and plundered the houses and goods of Feisal and his friends. The dirty-dog work has been fairly shared, and I thank what Gods I have that I'm neither an Arab nor a Frenchman — only the poor brute who has to clean up after them. . . .

"If you can, drop over here friendly-fashion some time, and I'll show you the French picture from underneath. Not lovely. à toi."[73]

It was (according to Philby) Lawrence's puckish suggestion that he should be succeeded as chief British representative by Philby, the close advisor of Abdullah's enemy, Ibn Saud,[74] but the choice proved to be a happy one for all concerned, including Amir Abdullah himself.[75] Philby arrived on November 28 and his stay overlapped Lawrence's by ten days. He had nothing but praise for Lawrence's work in Trans-Jordan and while Lawrence remained there left him in charge. On his first day at work Philby wrote in his diary: "I leave all business to Lawrence, who in spite of his repeated assertions that he had handed over the reins of office to me, finds that he cannot divest himself of its functions. He must carry on while he remains here, and I am well content to let him do so. He is excellent, and I am struck with admiration of his intensely practical, yet unbusinesslike, methods."[76]

On December 8, Lawrence's last day in Trans-Jordan, he and Abdullah concluded the Anglo-Hijaz Treaty ("a pompous and portentous docu-ment," Philby called it). But it proved to have little meaning because King Husayn, to whom Lawrence brought the treaty at Jidda the follow-ing day, refused "to accord any kind of recognition to the Jewish National Home Policy in Palestine."[77] Although Lawrence apparently wrote no final report regarding his two months in Amman, he recommended to Churchill that Trans-Jordan be treated as an independent state, freed of control by the high commissioner of Palestine, and that Abdullah be allowed to stay as the head of the new country.[78] Stay he did, as head of the small state of Trans-Jordan, which gradually became free of British authority and achieved independence in 1951, shortly after which Abdul-lah was assassinated. The present able ruler, Husayn, is Abdullah's grandson.

Lawrence left Jidda, spent several days in Jerusalem and Egypt, and returned to England via Paris before Christmas in 1921, and "shook the dust of Arabia from his feet forever."[79] In his diary entry of December 8 Philby wrote: "The departure of Lawrence leaves me in full charge, and at the same time a gap which will not be easy to fill. He knows and is known to everybody in these parts; and many of them have been intimately associated with him for years during the military operations which he conducted up and down the railway. That he has effected a great change in the situation since he came here two months ago admits of no doubt. He has turned a pessimistic outlook into one which is certainly the reverse; the administration which he has encouraged to function is working smoothly."[80]

"In the winter of 1921–1922 Lawrence was in a very nervous condition," Graves wrote, "did not eat or sleep enough, and worked over the *Seven Pillars* again."[81] Arnold Lawrence confirms that in 1922 his brother "came as near as anyone could do to a complete breakdown, after nine years of overworking without a holiday, and several of them under a continuous nervous strain. He cured himself by enlisting."[82]

Lawrence wrote little of the months before his enlistment in August 1922. He told Liddell Hart that he was "nearly dotty" then, and that he spent much time tramping about London.[83] He also made a number of trips to his property (Pole Hill, Chingford) in Epping Forest in Essex, where he and Vyvyan Richards again discussed the possibility of printing *Seven Pillars* on a printing press they would construct there. It was also during this period that Lawrence burned at Pole Hill the second text of *Seven Pillars of Wisdom*. He delighted a group of boys from a nearby school, where Richards was a teacher, with rich stories about the Arabian campaigns, which he so seldom talked about with adults. One of these former boys, whom I had the opportunity recently to meet, recalled more vividly the tales themselves, which appealed enormously to the imagination of a teen-ager, than the man who told them.[84] Lawrence's letters, especially those to Eric Kennington, reflect his increasing frustration with the Colonial Office routine and his desire to get away from it.

There is evidence that in this time Lawrence experienced genuine poverty, created largely by his generosity to his friends and his refusal to use any money from his work in the Colonial Office (as it was concerned with the Arabs and the Middle East) to gratify his own needs. "I ran right out of money in April 1922," he wrote Ralph Isham five years later. "And went along with great difficulty until August, when Trenchard let me into the Royal Air Force. My capital then was 15 pence, and I'd been half-fed for weeks."[85] It was also during these early months of 1922 that he struggled with the dedication to his war book ("To S.A.") and submitted the poem to Robert Graves for poetic revision.

When Graves correctly identified S.A. with Dahoum (whom Lawrence acknowledged in 1922 as having "provided a disproportionate share of the motive for the Arabian adventure"), Lawrence threw him off the track by writing: "You have taken me too literally. S.A. still exists; but out of my reach, because I have changed."[86]

In February 1922, Lawrence became aware that his friend Doughty was once more in difficult straits and went to great lengths to help him. "I feel rather worried about it all," he wrote to Mrs. Doughty.[87] He arranged that Doughty should receive a small government pension and a grant from the Royal Literary Fund, and also put the family in touch with good investment advice on some rubber shares they held. In addition, he obtained £400 with which the British Museum bought from Doughty the manuscript of *Dawn in Britain*, the only manuscript of Doughty's works available, and handled all this so unobtrusively, and with such tact, that Doughty seems never to have felt that he was the recipient of charity, although David Garnett had "reason to think" that Lawrence provided most of the money for the manuscript himself.[88] Several of Doughty's letters reflect without apparent embarrassment his gratitude to his friend, who had spared him being given anything "like to an alms which I could not receive."[89] Lawrence visited Doughty in Eastbourne at the end of March, and according to letters of Doughty's, was to go to Iraq on April 1, but there is no evidence he ever made such a trip.[90]

Dissatisfied with his second version of *Seven Pillars*, Lawrence had begun at the end of 1920 in London the third version, which he had continued to work on in Jidda and later in Amman. Between January and June of 1922, Lawrence had eight copies of *Seven Pillars of Wisdom* (of which five, possibly six, survive) printed privately by the Oxford *Times*. He states that he completed the third text on May 9 and that the following day he burned at Chingford the now-rejected second text.[91] After the book was printed, Lawrence placed the manuscript of the third text in the Bodleian Library, where it may be read. He was still resisting any more general circulation or publication of his work. But in March a fine crop of Kennington's drawings had arrived at the Colonial Office, and Lawrence's friends increased their pressure on him to publish the work. Kennington has offered this version of his peculiar struggle, probably in the spring of 1922, to persuade Lawrence to publish the book, at least for his friends:

"He actually looked not well, and his still seriousness was frightening. 'It is an evil work. . . . I could not refuse you after receiving the Arab portraits from you. It will not disturb you. Next morning you will start your day's work as usual, but you have an odd brain. It is in compartments. I have not let Robert Graves read it. It can never be published. I could not live if it was loosed abroad.' I began to fight. It had to be published. It was a grand, immense masterpiece. He looked more tired. 'How could I go on if it was made public? At Stamford Brook I did not know whether I was trying to throw myself under a train, or trying not to. I intended to throw these volumes off the centre of Hammersmith

Bridge. I have worked myself out and am finished. Every bone in my body had been broken. My lungs are pierced, my heart is weak.' "

Kennington pushed on, but "he began again, gently to prove to me how degraded the book was, and foreseeing defeat in a battle with that brain, I said the book had to be published. He said more gently, 'Give me one good reason — one only.' It seemed, the crisis, and I found one reason, and said it was a book on motive, and necessary at this moment of life; the world had lied till it was blind, and had to be re-educated to see its motives. It sounded futile, but he stopped quiet, and after a pause, said undramatically, 'Not bad' — (giggle) — 'Quite good' — (many giggles) — 'You win.' "[92]

It was not, of course, the end of the struggle, and George Bernard Shaw (whom Lawrence had met in March), Hogarth, Kipling, and other friends also appealed to him to publish the book. "I wrote a book on Arabia," he wrote the young painter Paul Nash in August. "To publish it would involve me in as many libels as there are characters. I move in its pages like St. Anthony among the devils. Also it isn't good enough to publish, but it's good enough for me to make better, till it can be published in the course of years."[93] Years later he brushed aside the influence of all these weighty entreaties, crediting his change of mind and heart to Gertrude Bell's simple request, "Wouldn't you consider publishing it for your friends?"[94]

On July 1, 1922, Churchill agreed to let Lawrence leave the Colonial Office, and three days later Lawrence wrote his formal letter of resignation, declaring himself to be "very glad to leave so prosperous a ship."[95] But it was mid-August before he had worked out with his friend Hugh Trenchard, the air marshal, the details of his enlistment in the RAF. "Winston very agreeable," Lawrence wrote Trenchard. "Hope your lord [Lord Guest, secretary of state for air] was the same."[96] Trenchard replied, "Yes, my Lord was very agreeable."[97] A week later Lawrence presented himself at the RAF Recruiting Depot for enlistment as Aircraftsman J. H. Ross.

With his enlistment, Lawrence left behind for good the politics of the Middle East and his official involvement with Arab affairs. "The life of politics," he wrote Hogarth ten months later, "wearied me out, by worrying me over-much."[98] Once out of the political arena he proceeded, according to his brother Arnold, "to lose interest in the East, not simply with that satiated curiosity with which he turned from his medieval and archaeological interests. For he looked back upon his subjection to the East with horror. His memories were the more painful because of the vividness with which he recollected sights and smells and sounds, creating again in all their poignancy scenes he would have preferred to forget."[99]

In a speech in the House of Commons a few months before the outbreak of World War II, Churchill called Lawrence "the truest champion of Arab rights whom modern times have known,"[100] but not all Arabs would agree with this assessment.

On the one hand, Lawrence was too caught up in Arab causes to be entirely objective, while on the other, his partial withdrawal from public life after the Paris Peace Conference so removed him from what was happening in the Middle East that in 1920 he could become only a propagandist.[101] As a result of the intensely personal quality of all his political activity Lawrence identified too strongly with the purposes of his own government *and at the same time* with the aspirations of the Arab peoples. He was both too visionary and too narrow in his outlook. Modern Arab nationalists have criticized his singleminded backing of the Hashemite family, and Zeine, for example, has pointed out the "blunder on the part of Faisal and Lawrence" in trying to establish after the fall of Damascus a Hashemite government in Beirut and the Lebanon "in the name of the King of the Hedjaz," thus precipitating prematurely a struggle with the French.[102] But Lawrence denied a part in this action and agreed with Zeine's assessment. He wrote in 1929 that the "precipitate occupation of Beyrout and Lebanon wholly threw away the local people's chances" and that Shukri al-Ayyubi was sent to Beirut by Ali Ridah al-Riqabi, the mayor of Damascus.[103] English writers, especially Philby, have stressed how Lawrence backed the wrong horse in continuing to support after 1919 the family of King Husayn while Ibn Saud was consolidating his power in Arabia, and it is possible that personal loyalties stood in the way of a more realistic and objective view ("You can't guard the Hedjaz by backing Husain and dropping I.S. [Ibn Saud]," Gertrude Bell had cautioned him in 1920).[104]

Lawrence's many assessments of his own and Britain's role in the postwar settlements in the Middle East reflect his deep personal involvement in their results, his need for atonement, and perhaps also some rationalization of his abandonment of further involvement with their consequences. "Surely," he wrote to Hugh Trenchard, "my share in helping settle the Middle East atones for my misdeeds in the war. I think so, anyway."[105] Lawrence was aware of the subjectivity of his writings and partisanship, which derived especially from his wartime participation. For example, to one veteran of the campaigns he wrote: "I wish my record of events had been less personal and more a history: but when I tried to be impartial and to weigh the merits of plans and men and action, I found myself disqualified from good writing. I had been so much of a partisan in all the campaign, and been so firmly converted to my private courses, before I embarked on them, that in no case could I have written fairly either of the others or of myself."[106]

In repeated statements Lawrence reiterated his conviction that the settlements worked out with Churchill represented a fulfillment of Britain's wartime pledges and responsibilities to the Arab peoples, that England was "quit of the war-time Eastern adventure with clean hands."[107]

In 1927 he wrote: "I had 18 months of office, and my settlement is knave- (but not fool-) proof. I'd be a poor creature if it wasn't: and a rat, if I'd voluntarily got out before the last of my men. As it was, I could (and did) retire with some self contentment, with the whole job done. I wanted the Arabs to have leave to make their own mess: and not to go on holding their hands to save them from messes. People learn by falling down, like babies."[108] To Mrs. Shaw Lawrence wrote similarly: "The settlement which Winston put through in 1921 and 1922 (mainly because my advocacy supplied him with all the technical advice and arguments necessary) was, I think, the best possible settlement which Great Britain, alone, could achieve at the time. Had we waited for the French to come to their right mind and cooperate in a complete settlement, we would be waiting yet. And after June, 1922, my job was done. I had repaired, so far as it lay in English power to repair it, the damage done to the Arab movement by the signing of the Armistice in November, 1918."[109] In his final statement on the subject in 1935 Lawrence wrote to Graves, "How well the Middle East has done: it, more than any part of the world, has gained from that war."[110]

Lawrence even offered his suffering in Arab services as evidence of the purity of his and Britain's intentions and actions in fulfilling their obligations to the Arab peoples. Late in 1922 he wrote: "I do not wish to publish secret documents, nor to make long explanations: but must put on record my conviction that England is out of the Arab affair with clean hands. Some Arab advocates (the most vociferous joined our ranks after the Armistice) have rejected my judgement on this point. Like a tedious pensioner I showed them my wounds (over sixty I have, each scar evidence of pain incurred in Arab service) as proof I had worked sincerely on their side. They found me out-of-date: and I was happy to withdraw from a political milieu which had never been congenial."[111]

It was in particular Britain's abandonment of Syria to the French and his accommodation with Zionism that make Lawrence's positive summary statements unbalanced and so disturbing to modern Arab nationalists. However, some of those who hold him responsible for this abandonment are misinformed. Lawrence himself appeared later to forget that the postwar settlement in regard to Syria was the result of a deal between Britain and France, and seemed to blame the outcome on the Syrians themselves. In 1927 he wrote: "Between us [with Churchill] we brought a peace in Irak and Transjordan and Palestine which has lasted for five years. That's a good achievement. The Arabs have now a place where they can obtain their full freedom, if they are good enough to use it. As for Damascus — they had Irak's present opportunity in 1920, and threw it away. So the political education of Syria goes on, as it did under the Turks, with bombs and bayonets as text-books" [the Syrians had risen in a bloody rebellion in 1925 against French military rule].[112] And in another letter: "Syria is not our pudding. The Syrians brought the French there, deliberately. Their political education (and France's) is proceeding!"[113]

Yet in the main Lawrence had made "a good achievement" in his effort to start the Arab nations on their road toward psychological and political independence, and it would be hard to argue with his summary: "My part of the Middle East job was done, by 1922, and, on the whole, well done."[114] And the lasting value of his work grew out of the power of his convictions, the extent of his knowledge and the depth of his personal commitment. Its limitations derived from the intense subjectivity of his involvement, his need — in the postwar political settlements, as in the war itself — to resolve in the public domain profound personal issues.

From the personal standpoint the years of Lawrence's Arab service had been devastating, and neither a just political settlement nor the effort at self-cure by writing his book could heal the wounds they had inflicted. Five years after he left the Colonial Office he wrote in a letter, "That Arabian time is now only a bad dream, which, when I get a touch of fever at night, wakes me up sweating and yelling, scaring the other fourteen fellows in our room into very violent curses."[115]

Arnold Lawrence had written that his brother's conscience was satisfied by the creation of autonomous Arab states "with the provision for their ultimate independence in connection with the British Empire." He points out that T.E.'s "friendliness" was not limited to the Arab-speaking peoples of Asia, for "he had helped to secure a peaceful frontier to the Kemalists during their struggle for the new Turkey and afterwards advocated British support for their Turkish Republic."[116] Arnold Lawrence felt that his brother would have adjusted his attitude toward Zionism "to the tremendous spurt in colonization caused by Jewish emigration from Nazi Germany. After he left the Colonial Office he anticipated a long-protracted British administration of Palestine, ending in a comparatively amicable solution of the problem, in favour, I think, of a Jewish majority in the distant future."[117]

These lines were written in 1936.

The Versailles Treaty and the agreements that followed in its wake represented the last major international diplomatic effort in which the Western Great Powers were able to impose settlements upon the peoples of Asia with so little regard for their desires. Since the period in which these agreements were signed, many new countries have merged in Asia and Africa, and self-determination for the formerly colonized regions has become an accepted principle of international relations.

It was not so in 1919. In the period after the Armistice Lawrence's was one of the few voices of conscience — and surely the most effective one — urging Great Britain, France and the other Western powers to uphold certain of their commitments and to respect the right of the Arab peoples to self-determination. He retained a concept of the British Empire but it was an empire of voluntary affiliation for mutual advantage, not one of conquest and control. His prediction that our allies of the future would come from those different from ourselves, even from peoples "most active in agitating against us," is proving generally true, although his hope of collaboration between the Jews of Palestine and their Arab neighbors is far from being fulfilled.

The relations between the formerly colonized peoples and their colonial masters have shifted radically in the half century since Versailles. The residues of nineteenth-century imperialism are vanishing, giving way to new forms of dominance by the major world powers. The "newer men, with a fresher culture," of whom Lincoln Steffens wrote, have in some instances, taken over.

# FIVE

# THE YEARS IN THE RANKS, 1922–1935

# 25

# The Service Years:
# An Overview

There is little that can be said of a period devoted to self-effacement."[1] This statement is the last entry in Lawrence's RAF service record. His biographers seem largely to have agreed with it. The years in which Lawrence served as an enlisted man in the air force and the army have been relatively neglected by them. But I find that although Lawrence's accomplishments were less dramatic than those of the war and postwar political years, this period was equally rich, and formed a vital part of his life and legend. His membership in the ranks became the central focus of his life.

During this time Lawrence published a limited ("subscribers'") edition of *Seven Pillars of Wisdom* and a commercial abridgment of it, *Revolt in the Desert*. He wrote his other original book, *The Mint* (it was not published until after his death), and published a translation of Homer's *Odyssey* (the only work issued under the name of Shaw). He also translated a French book about a California redwood tree, wrote prefaces or introductions to several English works, published anonymously a number of reviews, and wrote great amounts of literary criticism, principally in letters to his friends and literary associates. Lawrence further enriched his personal associations through a number of new friendships, especially with well-known writers.

The most important sources for these years are Lawrence's letters. He wrote several thousand, only a fraction of which have been published, and complained ceaselessly at the task of keeping up his voluminous correspondence. Of particular value are the more than three hundred letters to Charlotte Shaw that are now in the British Museum. The range of his relationships had become enormous by the end of his life. His letters are of particular value in understanding them because of his ability to write in a manner that conveyed the actual quality of his relationship with each of his correspondents. This was deliberate on Lawrence's part. "Each [letter] tries to direct itself as directly as it can towards my picture of the person I am writing to," he wrote Eric Kennington in 1934, "and if it does not seem to me (as I write it) that it makes contact — why then I write no more that night."[2]

Also essential to an appreciation of Lawrence as a human being are the personal accounts of him that I received from the men with whom he served — they were always eager to talk about their friend. In addition, Mrs. Charles Rivington, a friend of mine who had come to know many of these men, had collected their reminiscences and very kindly shared them with me. I regret that her untimely death in 1971 prevented her from writing a full picture, based on her own research, of Lawrence's life in the ranks.[3]

"My ambition to serve in [the air force] dates — concretely — from 1919: and nebulously from early 1917, before there was an Air Force," Lawrence explained to Herbert Baker.[4] His war experience in the Middle East had impressed upon him the potential effectiveness of air power when the military operations had to cover long distances, and his three months with the crew of the Handley-Page squadron in 1919 "put the complete wind up me" about the air and aircraft.[5] Arnold Lawrence confirmed his brother's enthusiasm: "He obviously enjoyed the companionship and appreciated both the mechanics' and pilots' dedication to their jobs and their skill in bringing so many of those worn-out planes to their destination (including the one in which he was)."[6] It is possible that even if T.E. could have been admitted readily into the countries of the Middle East after the peace settlements, he might still have chosen to enlist in the RAF rather than to continue his archeological work.

In earlier conversations with Trenchard after the war Lawrence had spoken of his interest in joining "this air force of yours,"[7] but Trenchard had assumed that Lawrence meant service as an officer. As long as Lawrence was involved in his political strategies in behalf of the Arabs, he put off his plans to enlist. Then on January 5, 1922, he wrote Trenchard that he would "like to join the R.A.F. — in the ranks of course." He wanted to develop his skill as a writer and saw "the sort of subject I need in the beginning of your force . . . and the best place to see a thing from is the ground. It wouldn't 'write' from the officer level."[8] But when he entered the service seven months later, his motives for doing so were far more personal than literary. Even so, he was considered for the post of RAF historian for two years after he enlisted.

Much has been written about Lawrence's motives for joining the RAF. It has been assumed that his reasons were hidden, even from himself. But actually, in his letters and conversations, he revealed — almost casually at times — what the psychological sources of his action were and that he knew, to a considerable extent, what they were. In fact, his insight into the unconscious sources of his motivation was uncommonly deep. As is characteristic, however, of explanations involving psychological processes that relate to unconscious ideas, his revelations seem incomplete. The incompleteness is not just another example of Lawrence's need to tease, to provoke curiosity. Anyone who attempts to convey to himself or anyone else psychological processes that have unconscious origins is bound to come up with only partial explanations. The deeper motives continually act upon each other at a number of levels, both within the personality and in relation to the outside world. They rarely can be viewed satisfactorily by themselves.

By the time Lawrence joined the RAF he was in a deeply troubled state — eating and sleeping poorly, quite agitated, and with no task ahead of him that could fulfill his needs. He had completed recently his third and last version of *Seven Pillars of Wisdom*, and the labor of rewriting, which entailed reliving his war experiences, had "excited" him to the point where he was "nearly dotty."[9] In this shaken state he needed to have basic requirements met — for food, shelter, companionship and security. Furthermore, he regarded himself as guilty, not simply because he felt that his leadership had ended in the betrayal of his Arab followers, or because he had given in to unacceptable sexual and aggressive impulses during the campaigns, but more fundamentally because he continued to be aware in himself of desires, ambitious and erotic, which, to his exacting conscience, were totally repugnant. He entered the ranks to cure himself of wishes, to do penance, and "to kill old Adam," as he phrased it bluntly to another airman.[10]

But Lawrence was not simply a twentieth century anchorite seeking a monastic existence and solitary escape. He remained a creative person, with a need for companionship and a powerful drive to be useful and to be engaged in meaningful work. What he required, therefore, was a situation that could meet his dependency needs, shackle his sinful self in chains, and yet provide opportunities for work he could value, while remaining at a lowly level that offered few conventional worldly rewards. The RAF, supplemented by his personal regimen of penance and self-discipline, fulfilled all these requirements splendidly. He had found after several months in the ranks "that it was a life that suited me exactly and if I could be always healthy I'd wish to keep in it forever."[11]

During his thirteen years as an airman and a private, Lawrence succeeded, in his view, in transforming himself into a person without desire or ambition, yet capable of useful work. He had to a degree escaped his expanding legend, which corresponded so little to his experience of himself. "My 'personality,' like the Arthurian legend, enthralls the mystical-minded. All punk, I'm afraid," he wrote in 1934.[12] But in the service "they regard my legend as a huge joke: If it wasn't *my* legend, I'd do ditto."[13] So thorough, however, was this transformation, and so dependent had he become upon the RAF, that after his discharge Lawrence seemed to have no motive for further activity. Less than three months later he was dead following an accident on his motorcycle.

Lawrence's explanations to his friends of his reasons for joining or remaining in the ranks seemed to vary with his situation and his moods as the years went by; yet if looked at in their totality from the standpoint of his psychology they are internally consistent. In 1922 he sought to find himself "on common ground with other men";[14] in February 1924 it was "the failure" of *Seven Pillars* that "broke my nerve, and sent me into the RAF," and "the assured bread and butter feels better than a gamble outside."[15] Later in 1924 he explained that he had joined because "[I had] looked back on my political record, and found it bad."[16] The following year he wrote Mrs. Shaw that he wished to "tie myself down beyond the hope or power of movement" to "keep my soul in prison, since nowhere else can it exist in safety."[17] In India two years later he gained more objectivity and wrote, "Penance, promise, obstinacy, a vow, self-hypnotisation . . . you catalogue my motives. Isn't it possible I like being in the R.A.F.?"[18] And two months after that he wrote of the RAF: "It has been a real refuge to me, and I am grateful to the Air people for taking me in."[19] After his valuable work began on air-sea rescue boats, which occupied the last six years of his life, he stresses less these inner forces and places more emphasis on his mechanical work in a mechanical age.

Lawrence's fellow airmen and army enlisted men came to accept him naturally as one of their number and seemed to grasp intuitively the needs that his military service fulfilled. But his continuing service in the ranks bewildered his intellectual friends. George Bernard Shaw, for all his witty, often accurate, teasing of his troubled friend, never grasped how essential the RAF was for Lawrence, or the seriousness of his purpose in staying in the ranks. "You suggest that I'm not genuine in the ranks: but I am," Lawrence insisted to Shaw in 1923. "People come into the army often," he explained, "not because it is brutal and licentious, but because they haven't done very well in the fight of daily living, and want to be spared the responsibility of ordering for themselves their homes and food and clothes and work — or even the intensity of their work. Regard it as an asylum for the little-spirited."[20] Five years later he had got no further in making Shaw understand, although he had not given up trying. "Only please don't think it is a game," he wrote from India, "just because I laugh at myself and everybody else. That's Irish, or an attempt to keep sane."[21]

Lawrence had an even more difficult time with Robert Graves, who objected particularly to his assumption of a "plain-man tone" with what Graves considered to be "forced ingenuousness." "Come off it, R.G.!"

Lawrence wrote to him in 1933. "Your letter forgets my present state. It is so long since we met that you are excused knowing that I'm now a fitter, very keen and tolerably skilled on engines, but in no way abstract. I live all of every day with real people, and concern myself only in the concrete. The ancient self-seeking and self-devouring T.E.L. of Oxford (and T.E.S. of the *Seven Pillars* and *The Mint*) is dead. Not regretted either. My last ten years have been the best of my life. I think I shall look back on my 35–45 period as golden."[22]

The meaning for Lawrence of his experience in the ranks naturally evolved and shifted as his situation or station changed and the years passed, but his companionship with the other men was at all times of great importance to him. Each man, including himself, had in some way been "hurt or broken in civvy life, to the point of taking flight from it,"[23] and this fact formed a strong bond with his fellow airmen and tank corpsmen. The barrack rooms and mess halls, where men ate and slept together without differentiation, helped Lawrence achieve his goal of feeling ordinary, of obliterating any sense of being special. He could not have accomplished this as an officer. At Cranwell he wrote Mrs. Shaw: "G.B.S. talks to me as if I were one of his crowd: the policeman (in the guard room) as if I were one of his crowd: and I get frustrated and sorrowful. Hut 105 is balm to this: for there we are all on the same footing. . . . Equality could only exist when it was compulsory."[24]

Lawrence's relationships with the enlisted men and officers he met at the various stations to which he was assigned (more than ten in all) varied greatly, but he seemed never to forget the friendships he had made at previous stations. Once he had formed even an acquaintance with another airman or tank corpsman Lawrence maintained an unending interest in his marriages, love affairs, babies, family life, illnesses and jobs (in and out of the service). If the man was interested in writing, Lawrence's interest extended to it as well, and he used his contact in the publishing world (usually without the man's knowledge) to bring the work to the attention of an appropriate editor or publisher. Lawrence's generosity with money could only be described as saintlike, and he gave away any savings he might accumulate from his wages, royalties or other sources of income so readily that he was in fact constantly quite poor. This extraordinary generosity was not limited to airmen, but was extended to officers and their families (on one occasion to the widow of the chief of air staff), artists with whom he had worked, booksellers and writers — to anyone, in fact, whom he thought in need or who approached him for help.

Most of the enlisted men were younger than he and he seemed to achieve a kind of older brother closeness with several of them. One airman he met at the end of 1922 at Farnborough, R. M. Guy, was a particularly handsome young man ("beautiful, like a Greek God," according to another of his companions),[25] and Lawrence became especially fond of him, as he did of A. E. "Jock" Chambers. On Christmas Day in 1923 Lawrence wrote to Guy, whom he sometimes addressed with pet names such as "Poppet" or "Rabbit," of the closeness they had achieved.

Lawrence's influence upon these men was considerable. Several of his former companions have told me of the difference he made in their lives. Some spoke of being shown aspects of the world they had been ignorant of, while others stressed a kind of moral lift or turn their lives took following the association with Lawrence. Some he introduced to literature, which then became a lifelong interest for them. All experienced an increased confidence and an ability to think things out for themselves as a result of knowing him.

A passage in a letter written in 1924 to Mrs. Shaw, when Lawrence was in the Tank Corps, conveys some of these characteristics of his relationships: "The Air Force fellows are like Oxf. undergrads in their 2nd term . . . buds just opening after the restraint of school and home. Their first questioning. Their first doubt of an established convention or law or practice, opens a floodgate in their minds: for if one thing is doubtful all things are doubtful: the world to them has been a concrete, founded, polished thing: the first crack is portentous. So the Farnborough fellows used to come to me there, after 'lights out,' and sit on the box on my bed, and ask questions about every rule of conduct and experience, about the mind and soul and body: and I, since I was lying on my back could answer succinctly and with illumination. Those who seek me out down here are the keenest ones, and they have been following up the chase of the great why themselves, since I disappeared."[26]

George Bernard Shaw provided a somewhat different view of Lawrence among his enlisted friends: "I must confess that when they invited me to tea he looked very like Colonel Lawrence with several aides-de-camp."[27]

In spite of the depth of these relationships Lawrence never felt that he was altogether "one with my fellows." He was not sure whether this was his "solitary misfortune" or "the common fate of man, and that only myself complains of it more."[28] My own impression is that it was both, and that his critical nature maintained him always at an amused distance from others even when he wished to be closer. He always knew in some part of his mind that he was leading a boy's life in the service and could not give himself over to it completely. "They do not allow, in the services, for grown ups," he wrote E. M. Forster; ". . . the whole treatment and regimen is designed for the immature."[29] But as he wrote Mrs. Shaw in 1932, he had found intimacy in the barracks: "a support of one by the next, great friendliness: and, as G.B.S. so well says, the freedom to do all things that a man's hands were made for. The peace-time soldiering is still the best lay-brotherhood. Look at my life."[30]

Lawrence's influence in the ranks extended beyond his impact on individual men. As in the desert campaigns and the political settlements after the war, his influence was out of proportion to his position, only this time he held no rank higher than the equivalent of corporal. As he had done before, however, Lawrence exerted his influence not by assuming power directly, but by engaging and sometimes capturing the minds of those who held power, and then, through the force of his intellect and personality, persuading these individuals to carry out what he urged. His desire, Lawrence wrote to a member of Parliament who had become his friend, was to make the services "decent for all classes, please, by delivering us of superstitions and callousness."[31]

Although Lawrence did not hesitate to press his arguments for service reforms upon prominent civilian friends like Lady Astor and Ernest Thurtle (Both M.P.'s), Liddell Hart, John Buchan, Churchill and George Bernard Shaw, it was through Hugh Trenchard, chief of air staff from 1919 to 1929 and "Father of the RAF," that Lawrence exerted his most important influence. Trenchard and Lawrence felt an intense mutual respect and liking for one another. "Allenby, Winston and you: That's my gallery of chiefs to date. Now there'll be a come down," he wrote to Trenchard when he learned of Trenchard's plans to retire.[32] "He [Trenchard] is as simply built as Stonehenge," Lawrence wrote to Herbert Baker, in images that must have appealed to his architect friend, "and serves equally as well for a temple, or a public meeting place or monument. Altogether one of my admirations: though I fear he cannot follow the wimbling and wambling of my career. I puzzle Trenchard, and he misunderstands me, often. Not that any such tiny detail could distress him; or blot his greatness, in my eyes."[33] To another friend:

"He sees the R.A.F. from the top, and I see it from the bottom, and each of us no doubt thinks he sees straight enough: but I swear I'm as keen on it as he is: and I do all I can, down here, to make it run smoothly. It's only the little unimportant things in the R.A.F. that make airmen's lives sometimes a misery."[34] And to Thurtle: "Curse the Brass Hats: poor reptiles. They always swear that these things are necessary to discipline. A word in your ear — discipline itself is not necessary. We fight better without it. Yet, being Englishmen we are born with it and can no more lose it than our fingernails."[35]

Lawrence tended to be flattering when writing to Trenchard, especially, it seems, when he was worried the chief was vexed with him. In his letters to Trenchard Lawrence would sometimes enclose lists on separate sheets of "trifles" he thought should be changed as "it is the trifles that irritate and do the most harm,"[36] and he urged Trenchard to communicate more directly with the men in the ranks so he could learn of their needs and hear their complaints.

The dignified Trenchard became on occasion quite annoyed with his

most celebrated aircraftsman. Trenchard had a habit of paying unexpected, unheralded visits to the various RAF stations in order to make,
undetected, his own private inspections. Once he visited a station in a
peculiar horse-drawn carriage, hoping that he would not be identified.
But Lawrence, who was on guard duty, caught a glimpse of the air
marshal inside, presented arms smartly, and yelled, "Guard turn out."
Trenchard's cover was completely blown. Lawrence then proceeded to
arrange a reception for the chief with as many appropriate honors as
could be managed on so short a notice. As Trenchard pulled away in his
carriage he glared fiercely out at Lawrence and boomed indignantly,
"SILLY FOOL!" and slammed down the window.[37]

Many of the service practices that Lawrence urged be corrected were
in fact "trifles," but others were more serious. Some were eliminated as a
result of Lawrence's efforts while he was still serving. Others remained to
be changed after he left the RAF. Among the causes Lawrence championed were the elimination of bayonets from airmen's rifles ("Have a
bayonet put in your IN tray every morning: and say to yourself 'I must
get rid of that today,'" he wrote Trenchard);[38] abolition of the death
penalty for cowardice and desertion in the face of the enemy; the abolition of compulsory church parades; the elimination of swagger sticks for
officers and men; change from monthly to yearly kit inspection; weekend
passes; posting of servicemen to stations nearer their homes; permission
to leave the service voluntarily (this was a provision of his own enlistment, and he felt would encourage officers to treat their men more decently); encouraging the wearing of civvies; less arbitrary deprivation of
leaves; and permission for pillion-riding on motorcycles ("airmen are the
only people in England forbidden it: not soldiers, not sailors. It's rather
an insult to what we fondly hope is the most dangerous service").[39] A
pocket diary found after Lawrence's death and dated 1933 contained jottings of almost a hundred additional service changes and reforms he
thought were needed, some related to those listed above, and some quite
new. Many concerned the construction and fitting of marine craft, especially the air-sea salvage boats on which he was then working.[40]

Perhaps as important as these tangible reforms that Lawrence urged
and sometimes achieved in collaboration with his chiefs and influential
friends, was the subtler influence he seems to have exerted at virtually
each station at which he served. It is hard to convey this quality. His
commanders have characterized it as a morally uplifting influence, a
subtle force that raised the standards of efficiency, improved the quality
of work, and had a beneficial effect upon the tenor of relations on the
base and upon morale generally. In some instances Lawrence's influence
remained, like a legend, bringing about change at a particular station
long after he was gone. The degree to which this almost spiritual force
affected the spirit of the RAF, especially in the ranks, has never, to my

knowledge, been given any attention. Lawrence's achievements in the design, construction, fitting, and overall development of small, maneuverable, fast marine craft for use in the air age — the major achievement of his last six years — also awaits careful and objective study.

Lawrence developed a network of personal relationships outside the RAF and Tank Corps, and somehow was able to maintain his friendships with these "posh" types without evoking resentment among his service friends. It was not simply a matter of isolating or compartmentalizing his various human contacts — although he could be skillful at doing this. Rather, he was able to integrate them smoothly into his own life by bringing together — usually at his cottage, Clouds Hill — men from differing social and economic backgrounds, and thereby he enabled artists, writers, airmen and tank corpsmen to enjoy each other's common humanity. E. M. Forster helped Lawrence look after one tank corpsman who was in difficulty and wrote in this connection, "The lower classes fill me with despair, and if I did not care for them I should lead a calmer life."[41] Yet both Forster and Lawrence grasped an element of falseness in this easy communication across class and economic lines. "How right you are that these chaps, fellows, whatever one calls them, like to be 'posh,'" Forster wrote to his friend, "whereas we are amused by them most when they are dirty, off their guard, and natural. Hence a fundamental insincerity in one's intercourse with them."[42]

During these years Lawrence developed new friendships: with Thomas and Florence Hardy, George Bernard and Charlotte Shaw, David Garnett, E. M. Forster, John Buchan, Noel Coward, Frederic Manning, William Roberts, Edward Elgar, Basil Liddell Hart, and Henry Williamson, and with other writers, artists, actors, booksellers, publishers and political figures. And he kept up, although sometimes intermittently, the friendships he had made earlier in his life.

From the emotional standpoint Lawrence's most important relationship during this period was with Charlotte Shaw. The attachment began in December 1922. She wrote him an ecstatic appreciation of *Seven Pillars of Wisdom* ("I don't believe anything really like it has been written before") while he was still eagerly awaiting G.B.S.'s critique.[43] As a basis for their close association Lawrence and Charlotte Shaw had in common similar Anglo-Irish backgrounds with overwhelming mothers and gentler fathers, inability to come to terms with sexuality and child-rearing and a number of emotional conflicts related in one way or another to consciences that were overly severe. "I have in me (what you have so much more strongly)," Mrs. Shaw wrote to Lawrence in 1927, "a fearful streak of conscience, and sense of duty, complicated by a sensitiveness that is nothing less than a disease."[44]

Because she did not make the same demands as his mother did, and because of the unobtrusiveness of her understanding, Lawrence was able to confide in Mrs. Shaw, although he had to deny any maternal element in the relationship. "Let me acquit you of all suspicion of 'mothering' me," he wrote in the summer of 1928. "With you I have no feeling or suspicion of clash at all. You are (probably) older than me [she was thirty-one years older, actually], you are one of the fixed ones, socially and by right of conquest: yet I talk to you exactly as I feel inclined, without any sense that I'm talking up, or you down. Which is very subtle and successful of you. I think it represents reality too, in your attitude, as well as mine. My mother would be easy with me, too, if she didn't think of mothering."[45]

Lawrence visited the Shaws frequently at their country home at Ayot St. Lawrence in Hertfordshire, but when Lawrence was on distant assignments Charlotte sent him — according to Shaw's secretary, Blanche Patch, who prepared the packages — "chocolates from Gunter's, China tea from Fortnum and Mason's; at Christmas *foie gras* and peach-fed ham to Clouds Hill; to Karachi chocolates, cake and marrons glacés."[46]

It was in long, often highly personal letters, however, that the relationship reached its greatest intensity. Encouraged by Mrs. Shaw's empathy and objectivity, Lawrence shared with her his feelings and conflicts. They exchanged opinions on books, politics, and a wide variety of other subjects, and Lawrence sent her his most treasured writings, including his personal anthology of poems, "Minorities," and the manuscript of *The Mint*. "You are rather like the Semitic God, of whom it is easy to say what isn't, but impossible what is," Lawrence wrote to her in 1929. "I have never tried to describe you in words. Did I tell you that the blend of you and G.B.S. was a symphony of smooth and sharp, like bacon and eggs? Possibly. Conjoined you would be complete humanity. . . . As for feeling 'at home' with you: this is not the word. I do not wish to feel at home. You are more completely restful than anyone I know, and that is surely better? Homes are ties, and with you I am quite free."[47]

Lawrence seems to have written nothing of his own for publication (except his technical treatise for the RAF in 1932 on a type of boat he was developing) after the expansion and reworking of his notes for *The Mint* in 1928, and after completing the translation of the *Odyssey* in 1931, composed no other works of literature. He remained to the end of his life a prolific reader and a lover of books, especially contemporary English and French works (particularly finely printed ones), but seemed often to use reading as a way of substituting an alternative world for the one in which he was living. "I have half an hour in the morning, before breakfast, which I keep for my own reading," he wrote to F. N. Doubleday. "One can't *read* in odd half-hours," he complained, as "reading is to soak oneself hour after hour all day in a single real book, until the book is realler than one's chair or world."[48] Lawrence enjoyed most, however, being a teacher of those not previously exposed to literature and poetry, and a kind of freelance critic and champion of freedom of the press for young writers and poets, who often sent him their works.

Although Lawrence took no official part in political life after his enlistment, he was willing to offer his opinions, especially to his various friends in policy-making positions, when consulted (and sometimes when not) on questions involving the Middle East and other topics. He would also on occasion defend his own part in the war and the postwar settlements if he felt it was being distorted by biased newspaper coverage. His interest in political affairs was, however, quite spotty, which raises some doubt whether he could ever have been willing to take on an important post in public life again had he lived longer. He never once, for example, in his long association with George Bernard Shaw mentioned or expressed curiosity about the Russian Revolution, although Shaw had visited the Soviet Union and Lawrence thought Lenin a very great man. The pattern of these years was not political, but Lawrence continued to be a useful public servant on a smaller, more restricted scale.

Music took on increasing importance for Lawrence, and he loved to sit in rapt concentration letting the sounds wash over him. Although he had felt it necessary to abandon archeology as a profession, he never lost interest in the architecture of the Middle Ages. He enjoyed visiting castles and cathedrals in England, and instructing his companions in their details and history. An interest in fine craftsmanship, dating back to childhood, took on new importance in his later years. His cottage, Clouds Hill, which he repaired and outfitted largely himself, and the RAF boats he worked on after 1929, offered him many opportunities for realizing his desire for perfection in artistic craftsmanship. "If the creative instinct had to have an outlet, it was in the solution of the mechanical difficulties and the gradual refinement of the RAF boats," one of his airmen friends wrote after Lawrence's death.[49]

The first months of Lawrence's indoctrination into the RAF at Uxbridge were torture for him and in many ways traumatic. He maintained his equilibrium by writing notes about his experience each night in the barracks. Later at Karachi in India (1927–1928) he reworked these notes and expanded them with entries from the period at the RAF Cadet College at Cranwell in Lincolnshire (1925–1926) which was, by contrast, more humane. The result was *The Mint*, Lawrence's chronicle of service in the ranks, which was not published in a trade edition until 1955. Lawrence had meant, he wrote Wavell in 1929, "to write a 'big' book (not in size: in matter) about the R.A.F.," but the RAF "threw me out, and so broke the continuity of my experience."[50] He pulled strings and in March 1923 was admitted to the Tanks Corps, where he served until July 1925, when alarms of suicide mobilized his friends to induce the British government to permit him to return to the RAF.

The first months of service in the Tanks Corps, when he had once again to go through basic training, were among the most anguish-filled times of his life. Obtaining Clouds Hill in the summer of 1923 gave Lawrence a place of his own and he was able to find relief there from the grimness of service life. After he was readmitted Lawrence served in the RAF continuously for nearly ten years and retired three months before his death. He was stationed in India for two years, from the beginning of 1927 to the beginning of 1929, a period in which he limited his life to the activities within the camps themselves, began his translation of the *Odyssey*, and attended to the voluminous correspondence he carried on with Mrs. Shaw and other friends. He did not venture from his stations in India, and was observed by the officers and other airmen to have periods of despondency and depression.

Lawrence was brought back to England abruptly early in 1929 as the result of a bout of publicity, linking him incorrectly to a rebellion in Afghanistan. During the remaining six years of RAF service he found a new calling as a sort of marine engineer-mechanic, designing, developing and testing new kinds of boats. He achieved peace and personal equilibrium during these years, but he recognized that its price was a considerable restriction of the range and depth of his activities and sensibilities. "It is the life of the mechanic," he wrote Robert Graves in 1933, "concrete, superficial, every-day: unlike the past excitement into which the war plunged me. I know the excitement in me is dead, and happier so."[51]

During part of this six-year period he was at Mount Batten Station, near Plymouth, where he grew close to Wing Commander Sydney Smith and Mrs. Smith. From Mount Batten Lawrence was posted much of the time after 1930 to Southampton for work at the Scott Paine boatyards, and continued to work there until late in 1934, when he was posted to Bridlington on the Yorkshire coast for the last four months of his service. He had a brief period of retirement at Clouds Hill before the fatal accident occurred. Despite a persistent nihilism during the later years of his life, Lawrence never lost a perceptual sensuousness, an openness to the impression of the world around him. He never lost his ability to enjoy speed, the sting of spray or the taste of ripe blackberries "all cold with rain."[52]

David Garnett, whom Lawrence took on an air-sea rescue operation in one of the motorboats with which he was working, has described the "red-faced, weather-beaten, tough mechanic" that Lawrence had become after a decade in the ranks. "We were happy: eager, unself-conscious," Garnett wrote, "made accomplices by the excitement of the flying spray, the work, the boat herself. . . . I think it was then that I first fully realized how wise he had been to enlist in the ranks of the R.A.F. He had done a great deal for it, but it had done a great deal for him by giving him the ease and intimacy which comes from doing work with other men."[53]

Lawrence had visions of a new age in which mankind would leap forward into its last challenge, the mastery of the air. "For thousands of years nature has held this mastery of the last element in her lap, patiently waiting for our generation, and you and I are of the lucky ones chosen," he wrote to another aircraftsman.[54] In 1933 he wrote a few excited lines about the conquest of the air and of scaling the heavens, "as lords that are expected," seeming to anticipate the event of the entry of man into space.[55] He saw the skilled worker as important in reaching this goal: "The conquest of the last element, the air, seems to me the only major task of our generation; and I have convinced myself that progress today is made not by the single genius, but by the common effort. To me it is the multitude of rough transport drivers, filling all the roads of England every night, who make this the mechanical age. And it is the airmen, the mechanics, who are overcoming the air."[56]

It will, of course, never be known whether Lawrence would have played a part in accomplishing this remaining "major task," whether he would have found a way to make such achievement consistent with his life of renunciation. For only three months after writing these lines T. E. Lawrence was dead.

# 26

# Ross: The First
# RAF Enlistment

Lawrence received proofs of the last eight parts of *Seven Pillars of Wisdom* from the Oxford *Times* printers on July 21, 1922,[1] and eight copies of the book were subsequently printed and bound. The following month he sent a copy for comment to George Bernard Shaw, whom he had recently met for the first time, and another to Edward Garnett of Jonathan Cape, the publishers. With the completion of the book, which Lawrence would continue to perfect for four more years, a phase of his life came to an end. Air Marshal Trenchard made special arrangements for Lawrence's enlistment in the RAF and gave orders to his chief personnel officer, Oliver Swann, to carry them out. "He is taking this step in order to learn what is the life of an airman," Trenchard informed Swann, and "on receipt of any communication from him through any channel, asking for his release orders are to be issued for his discharge forthwith without formality."[2]

Swann informed Lawrence on August 16 of the arrangements and he was inducted secretly two weeks later at the recruiting depot in London under the name of John Hume Ross. (He used this name for his bank account for the rest of his life and for the authorship of his translation of *Le Gigantesque* [*The Forest Giant*] in 1924, although he used it personally for less than five months.) Arnold Lawrence stated that his brother picked the name at home one day when their mother happened to speak about a Mrs. Ross, and "he said that would do — he was looking for a short name."[3]

In *The Mint* Lawrence says that he was so anxious before he went to the enlistment depot that he had a bout of "melting of the bowels," which he revealed had occurred at other times of crisis.[4] According to the account of the chief interviewing officer at the recruitment depot, Lawrence attempted initially to be inducted without using the influence of the Air Ministry that was available to him.[5] But he had no references with him and did not come up to medical standards. His brother has written that Lawrence had reached a state of nervous exhaustion by the time he went to the recruiting depot and had starved himself until he weighed about fifteen pounds less than his usual weight, despite the many lunch and dinner invitations of his friends.[6] Furthermore, he had scars on his back from the floggings at Der'a, which aroused suspicions at the depot ("Hullo, what the hell's those marks? Punishment?' 'No Sir, more like persuasion Sir, I think.' Face, neck, chest getting hot").[7] After the initial rejection Lawrence returned with an Air Ministry messenger bearing orders from higher up and was admitted.[8] Lawrence quickly wrote to Swann to thank him for his help and apologized to him for the trouble he had caused. "If I'd known I was such a wreck I'd have gone off and recovered before joining up," Lawrence wrote; "now the cure and the experiment must proceed together."[9]

Lawrence, like other RAF recruits, was sent to the training depot at Uxbridge, about ten miles west of London, where he underwent two months of grueling basic training, the misery and hardship of which were aggravated by the pain of a bone fragment (a relic of the 1919 Handley-Page crash) that was sticking into the inside of his chest wall.[10] As mentioned previously, Lawrence has described his experience at Uxbridge in *The Mint*, a classic and honest picture of certain aspects of barrack life among enlisted men, a life that, since the literature that grew out of World War II and subsequent wars, has become more familiar to the general public. In *The Mint*, he conveys vividly, with great empathy for his fellow sufferers, the raw brutality, vulgarity and crude four-letter humor that was commonplace in the basic training of enlisted men. Trenchard told Arnold Lawrence that he sacked the commander at Uxbridge after reading *The Mint*.[11]

One must read *The Mint* to appreciate the utter degradation to which Lawrence submitted himself or was subjected at Uxbridge. He seemed at times to degrade himself beyond what was necessary and imposed by the camp authorities. Both figuratively and literally he worked in and became covered with excrement and swill until it "oozed slowly from my soiled things and stagnated in a pool over me."[12] Although he had in a sense put shackles on himself by enlisting in the first place, he had reason to rage at the tyranny of the noncommissioned officers and the abuses of authority that were imposed on the lowly "erks" [airmen]. Lawrence did not rebel ("Rebellious again? Not on your life").[13] He protested bitterly in *The Mint* against the unnecessary humiliations imposed upon him and the other men. Instead he was conscientious and correct, and struggled to master the drill and other routines. He submitted to authority, allowing the RAF to "bray me and re-mould me after its pattern" (the "minting" of the book's title).[14]

In the hut he found a fellowship among the men, sharing with many of them the basic sexual shyness which lay behind their vulgarity and verbal lechery and bravado. "We attain an instant friendliness," he wrote, "and there stuck, three paces short of intimacy."[15] *The Mint* contains familiar psychological themes, recalling the struggles of Lawrence's youth, especially the need to master fear. "The root-trouble is fear," he wrote, "fear of falling, fear of breaking down."[16] And: "Here I have been on my own, and up against it: stretched almost beyond my failing body's bearing to sustain the competition of youth. Depot will have the backward-looking warmth of probably my last trial: survived at least, if not very creditably. Though sometimes I've laughed aloud while I cried hardest into my notebook. And the gain of it is that I shall never be afraid of men, again."[17]

Lawrence worked at Uxbridge to develop photography as a trade, having had considerable earlier experience in it. Gradually he found that the self-imposed limitations of military life were making their mark. "We have grown," he wrote, "to do only what we're told. . . . This learning to be sterile, to bring forth nothing of our own, had been the greater half of our training and the more painful half."[18] As much as possible Lawrence felt that he had shed his past identity and had "attained a flight-entity which is outside our individualities."[19] "The R.A.F.," he wrote, "is now myself," and if someone "offends the others I am indignant. He sins against the air."[20]

But, as among the Arabs, Lawrence's solidarity with the other men was incomplete. "I joined in high hope of sharing their tastes and manners and life: but my nature persists in seeing all things in the mirror of itself, and not with a direct eye. So I shall never be quite happy, with the happiness of these fellows who find their nectar of life, and its elixir, in the deep stirring of some seminal gland. It seems I can get nearest it by proxy, by using my powers (so sharpened by experience and success in war and diplomacy) to help them preserve their native happiness against the Commandants and Pearsons [a sergeant who tormented the airmen] of this world."[21]

"My Uxbridge notes dated from 1922 when it was a different place," Lawrence wrote to an officer there in 1933. "Today's recruits are fairly happy there, and we were NOT!"[22] Perhaps his influence, both directly and through his legend, had helped to achieve some change. "Lawrence was already a fabled ghost at Uxbridge by the time the class of April, 1937, discovered the rigours of that place, and the ghost was a dear one," one former A/C 2, E. B. Metcalfe, wrote in 1955.[23] Change for the better had occurred, but more important than that was the continuing influence of Lawrence's ghost. When a mathematics instructor admonished the 1937 recruits that Lawrence of Arabia had been in their classroom and they should behave in a worthy fashion, "it hardly seemed that the famous erk was on our side. Yet with the days that followed, it quickly became evident that dead as he was, he was the only source we had for any redress of grievance."[24]

Lawrence had developed a reputation for intervention and, according to this ex-erk, his memory gave the men solace for the annoyances of service life. "A large book could be compiled of his acts, apocryphal or not, by which he sought on behalf of some unhappy blighter to get him compassionate leave, excused fatigues, reduction of sentence, or even his ticket. 'That ——— wouldn't have talked to Lawrence like that,' an erk would mutter after having a stripe torn off him for some good or bad reason."[25] Whether or not the stories about Lawrence were true would be "missing the point to ask," Metcalfe continued, "for they bespoke an attitude with which it was pleasant and natural to identify oneself."

There were stories of Lawrence's wrath, successfully expressed against unjust authority, of his showing up at the homes of the great with uncouth RAF types, or of sending the "scruffiest rogue" with a message to represent him with full powers. In 1937 the airmen were convinced that when *The Mint* was published "they" [the officers] would have "had it." "What we believed basically was this: that he [Lawrence] was one of the thousands of skilled groundlings, the one who could hope for and gain recognition; that he had souped up the R.A.F.'s motor-boat section to perfection; and that he was a 'man' who was a man." *Seven Pillars of Wisdom* also had great meaning for the men, "for if such a hero could make himself one of our kind, did it not follow that we could make ourselves one of his kind?"[26]

Lawrence's letters of the Uxbridge period reflect little of the stresses he was undergoing at the camp, and to some of his friends he seems, out of fear of being found out, to have made no mention of his enlistment in the RAF. To others, who did know — Eric Kennington was one — he appeared steadier and more poised in his trim Air Force uniform.[27] His surviving letters of the period are concerned with arrangements for the illustration of *Seven Pillars,* and are a blend of apology for asking his worthier friends to read his inadequate production, and big hopes for the book, even the dream that he had succeeded in producing "an English fourth" on the titanic level of "The Karamazovs, Zarathustra and Moby Dick."[28]

One of the artists, Paul Nash, whom Lawrence asked to do the landscape illustrations from his photographs, wrote enthusiastically of his assignment: "I think its going to be great fun. . . . O what a dream! Lawrence is of the salt of the earth and I know he's doing much of this simply to help painters who find a difficulty in *affording* to paint."[29]

Although he constantly expressed his disappointment with the book and devalued it, Lawrence seemed to understand its value at another level, at least as a personal testimony. He described it to Edward Garnett as "a summary of what I have thought and done and made of myself in these thirty years."[30] And in another letter to Garnett: "It was written in dead earnest and with as much feeling as a 'don possessed' can muster: and I think it's all spiritually true."[31] Garnett was very appreciative and encouraging and wrote to Lawrence, "I feel somehow that your analysis of life may carry us *further:* there's a quality in your brain that suggests a new apprehension of things."[32] Garnett also began work on an abridgment of *Seven Pillars,* which Lawrence planned for a time to publish. At the same time Lawrence made arrangements with the young artist William Roberts to draw portraits of high-ranking British officers who played important roles in the Revolt.[33] "I like the complete book, of course, much better," he wrote to Garnett, "but I realize that artistically it has no shape: and morally I detest its intimacy."[34]

When he did refer to his enlistment in writing to his friends Lawrence stressed the loss of freedom and his plan to adjust to his shackles. "I got sick of things," he wrote to one, "and being penniless hopped off — into a kind of community, which does more work than worship, but is remote and cut off from normal ways. It will perhaps suit me — and if it doesn't I will have to suit it. . . . I haven't told anyone what I'm at, or where, except that I am travelling in China! You see, now I'm not my own master."[35]

On November 8 Lawrence was transferred to the RAF School of Photography at Farnborough. In a contemporary note found in the folds of the manuscript of *The Mint* Lawrence compared Farnborough with Uxbridge: "Odd that Uxbridge has so touched me that when I reached Farnborough its looseness and untidiness were disagreeable. Also, I felt lost (November 8). Small room of 12 beds, long classes and 9 months, saw the intimacy greater. Uxbridge diffident offering politeness. Here an understanding no less kind, but less courteous. Some soreness, resentment at multitudes of soldiers round us. Airmen feel so distinctly that they are not soldiers, and fear that outsiders may not see this so clearly as we do."[36]

Airman A. E. "Jock" Chambers, who became one of Lawrence's closest service friends, had a bunk next to his at Farnborough and found his friend in a very anxious and troubled state on arrival from Uxbridge. Lawrence slept little while at Farnborough, according to Chambers, and was disturbed by nightmares in which he would relive the horrors of his war experience, and Chambers did much to comfort his new friend and settle him down.[37]

Chambers furnished me with this account of his meeting with Lawrence at Farnborough:

> He settled in quite easily; his voice sounded posh and alarmed me at first, as we already had one ex-officer we were trying to educate. I've always liked books and as he emptied his kit bag, I spotted some that looked good, found

they were and borrowed them. Some time later, we were both detailed with two others for guard. I had no misgivings — it was nothing new to me; not so my chum. "Jock," he said, "I'm windy — can't slope arms or do any of the drill."[38] "Shut up," says I patronizingly. "Just watch me, follow my motions; nothing in it"; so we "poshed up" and on to Guard Mounting we went. "New Guard — slope arms": Me, in a whisper, "Sling it up cock." Just then Warren A.C. 2 plonk and very fat crossed the road in full view, dressed in khaki drab and carrying a heavy sack of tins as he staggered along. I couldn't resist saying . . . with *Hassan* in my mind [a book by Flecker, which Lawrence had lent Chambers], "Thou dragger of dead dogs." The next moment I heard Sgt. Major Pierce's voice, trembling with rage. "What the ——— hell are you laughing at, Ross?" He replied, "I wasn't laughing, Sgt. Major, just grinning." The Sgt. Major muttered, "I'll double you round the ——— square after this and we'll ——— see who laughs last!" The tension eased; we took over from the old guard and I became sentry no. 1.[39]

Although Lawrence was relieved to get away from Uxbridge, which his entreaties to Swann may have speeded, and found Farnborough almost "disagreeably loose" by comparison, he was unhappy there nevertheless — "a mean C.O. and a bad show Farnborough was," he wrote several years later.[40] Four days after his arrival there, he wrote Garnett: "Honestly, I hate this dirty living, and yet by the decency of the other fellows, the full dirtiness of it has not met me fairly. Isn't it a sign of feebleness in me, to cry out so against barrack-life? It means that I'm afraid (physically afraid) of other men: their animal spirits seems to me the most terrible companions to haunt a man: and I hate their noise. Noise seems to me horrible. And yet I'm a man, not different from them; certainly not better. What is it that makes me so damnably sensitive and so ready to cry out, and yet so ready to incur more pain? I wouldn't leave the R.A.F. tomorrow, for any job I was offered."[41]

In the meantime Lawrence eagerly pressed George Bernard Shaw for an opinion of his book. Shaw (referring to an episode before the capture of Aqaba) replied, "Patience, patience: do not again shoot your willing camel through the head," and admitted (on December 1, 1922) that he had only a chance to sample the book. His wife, he said, had "seized it first, and ploughed through from Alpha to Omega. It took months and months."[42]

Shaw worried Lawrence by comparing him with Charles "Chinese" Gordon, the fanatical defender of Khartoum. "You are evidently a very dangerous man," Shaw wrote; "most men who are any good are: there is no power for good that is not also a power for evil. You have a conscience which would have prevented you from acting as Gordon did in China; so there will be a deep difference; but I wonder what, after reading the book through, I will decide to do with you if ever I become one of the lords of the east. As I shant, perhaps I shall put you into a play"[43] (as, in fact, he did nine years later in *Too True to Be Good*).

Over the next few weeks Shaw, who still had not read the book through, indicated in subsequent letters that he thought *Seven Pillars* was a great work and should be published in its entirety. But in the meantime Charlotte Shaw had "devoured" the book from cover to cover. In November she wrote Sydney Cockerell, who had introduced Lawrence to the Shaws, that she was carried off her feet by it, and then on the last day of the year wrote Lawrence himself a letter of ecstatic praise, calling the book "one of the most amazingly individual documents that has ever been written."[44] Although Lawrence had continued planning an abridgment on the grounds that he detested "morally" the intimacy of the uncut version, she encouraged him to publish the whole work. Lawrence was naturally very much pleased and encouraged by Mrs. Shaw's letter, but wrote her that to publish the book in its entirety "was as improbable as that I'd walk naked down Piccadilly."[45] He did, however, consider with Edward Garnett a limited edition of two thousand copies of the complete book, but after the publicity about his identity burst in the press, Lawrence canceled plans to publish even an abridgment.[46]

Despite his complaints Lawrence was also finding that the air force contained for him "spots of light, very exciting and full of freshness."[47] He had been anxious about being discovered and while at Uxbridge wrote to William Roberts, "I should have told you before that I'm a photographer-mechanic in the R.A.F. — a tommy — and so cannot dispose of my own movements very certainly." He could not meet Roberts in London because "I'm in blue uniform, and don't want to be known in any of my old feeding-places! Please don't tell anyone that I've enlisted. The press would make a humourous story of it!"[48] This was prophetic, for on December 16 two reporters, who, according to a report of that date by the commanding officer "have certainly got wind of Ross," came to the camp looking for him.

Although his commanding officer and adjutant suspected who he was, "Ross's" identity as "Lawrence of Arabia" was confirmed to them by a staff officer visiting from the Air Ministry. This information was confined, at least at first, to a few officers at Farnborough. One of them, Charles Findlay, the adjutant, has written of what "a heavy responsibility" it was "to have a world-famous character on our hands as an AC2, and many times as I saw his slight, blue-uniformed figure engaged in some menial task I tried with difficulty to reconcile it with the romantic soldier who had inspired the grim, desert peoples to fight so audaciously."[49]

Although the airmen protected Lawrence's identity, it was, according to Chambers, betrayed by a café proprietor who offered Ross sanctuary and then sold the information to a reporter.[50] Lawrence on the other hand declared that it was "one of the beastly officers" who gave him away.[51]

Once his identity was generally known, Findlay wrote, "there is little doubt that his presence in the camp had an unsettling effect upon all ranks. As Adjutant of the School, I was very conscious of this."[52] I have found no evidence to support the assertion of Samuel Hoare, then secretary of state for air (who, Lawrence stated, "first moved to get me out of the RAF"), that Lawrence had given the story to the press himself.[53] The "carelessness" of the Colonial Office in using Lawrence as a consultant in the handling of the 1922 crisis between Turkey and Greece may have played a part in the discovery of his identity in the RAF.[54] Guilfoyle, the commanding officer, in a report to Trenchard in mid-December wondered if "all the conjecture and talk" was worth the damage to discipline.[55]

George Bernard Shaw had been impatient with Lawrence about his RAF enlistment and suggested that if he did not know him better he might conclude that he was simply "a depressed mechanic oiling up fuselages for profanely abusive pilots."[56] He warned Lawrence (the press right then was already, according to Chambers, turning the camp into "a sort of fortress, besieged by a number of press men, and photographers")[57] that "[Lord] Nelson, slightly cracked after his whack on the head in the battle of the Nile, coming home and insisting on being placed at the tiller of a canal barge, and on being treated as nobody in particular, would have embarrassed the Navy far less . . . the thing is ridiculous."[58]

By the end of December the story was out in the press with the predictable uncrowned-king-of-Arabia-war-hero-turns-private headlines.[59] Shaw was not surprised when the story broke and wrote Lawrence realistically though rather unsympathetically:

Like all heroes, and, I must add, all idiots, you greatly exaggerate your power of moulding the universe to your personal convictions. You have just had a crushing demonstration of the utter impossibility of hiding or disguising the monster you have created. It is useless to protest that Lawrence is not your real name. That will not save you. You may be registered as Higg the son of Snell or Brian de Bois Ghilbert or anything else; and if you had only stuck to it or else kept quiet, you might be Higg or Brian still. But you masqueraded as Lawrence and didn't keep quiet; and now Lawrence you will be to the end of your days, and thereafter to the end of what we call modern history. Lawrence may be as great a nuisance to you sometimes as G.B.S. is to me, or as Frankenstein found the man he had manufactured; but you created him, and must now put up with him as best you can.[60]

Trenchard came under increasing pressure to discharge Lawrence from the RAF. He might have been able to resist this had it not been for the junior officers who were concerned that Lawrence was in the RAF as an enlisted man to tell tales about them to their superior officers.[61] Finally Trenchard capitulated and Lawrence was discharged toward the end of January despite his willingness, as he wrote Graves at the time, "to eat dirt, till its taste is normal to me."[62]

# 27

# The Years in the Tanks

Lawrence was deeply distressed by his expulsion and appealed for another chance to the RAF officials. He met with no success, although Trenchard offered him a commission, and Leopold Amery, first lord of the admiralty, proposed giving him a coastguard station or a lighthouse. But either was too isolated even for Lawrence.[1] He concluded his entreaty to the secretary to the chief of air staff by stating, "The last thing I wish to seem is importunate: but I'm so sure that I played up at Farnborough, and did good, rather than harm, to the fellows in the camp there with me, that I venture to put in a last word for myself."[2]

The problem was not, however, with the "fellows" but with the officers. Amery explained, "I had a word with Sam Hoare who assures me that it was nothing but the embarrassment of junior officers and others of knowing what your real identity was that made them decide to drop you out of the Air Force,"[3] and David Hogarth noted to George Bernard Shaw: "Some R.A.F. officers disliked commanding him and thought he laughed at their instructions."[4]

Lawrence returned to London after the ouster and spent six weeks looking for other work, but without success. "No one will offer me a job poor enough for my acceptance," he complained to one of his artist friends.[5] Despite his effort to maintain a cheerful front Lawrence was "in very low water" after his discharge and wrote to William Roberts, another artist, that he felt "rather stranded on the beach, in need of another job very soon, if I'm to go on living. It's rotten not having a trade of any sort."[6] A few days later Lawrence wrote with sardonic humor of his plight to a former friend from Arabian campaign days: "I'm very cheerful, and better off than you, for from my six months in the R.A.F. there survives a Brough [a motorbike], which is the paragon of everything on wheels, and on it I dash frantically about south England. Only the dreadful day creeps nearer when I'll have to eat the poor beast."[7]

Despite his situation (in a sense self-imposed, of course), Lawrence was able to overcome any personal resentment he may have felt and managed to find time to use his influence and prestige to help Trenchard with a problem he was having in relation to Iraq and more generally in regard to the future of the RAF.[8] He spent these weeks "haunting influential acquaintances in the political and literary spheres," primarily in search of another retreat, but he also spoke his mind about the Middle East and the future of the RAF to anyone who asked his opinion and probably to some who did not. The results are described by Andrew Boyle in his biography of Trenchard:

> It would be easy to exaggerate the influence of one man, and an unhappy outsider at that, in improving the climate of opinion within a cautious and still uncommitted Government Committee. . . . Trenchard confirmed Amery's impression that Lawrence contributed something positive to the Iraq Committee's deliberations, almost in spite of himself, because his frankness was accepted as being based partly on experience, partly on disinterested conviction. Trenchard found not a little irony in the fact that Hoare, whose propriety had been outraged by the unmasking of "Air Mechanic Ross," and only slightly placated by his dismissal, presently began to benefit indirectly from Lawrence's freelance advocacy. . . . His expulsion "as a person with altogether too large a publicity factor for the ranks," to use his own phrase, was the only sensational happening that winter which brought the RAF to the public eye.[9]

By the beginning of March 1923, the efforts of Lawrence and his friends proved successful at the War Office and he was admitted into the army as a private in the Tank Corps and posted to Bovington Camp in Dorset. He assumed a new name — "Shaw" — this time. Despite Lawrence's protestation to Graves ("I took the name of Shaw because it was the first one-syllabled one which turned up in the Army List Index") and to others that the new name had no special significance,[10] I am convinced that it was based upon an identification, perhaps unconscious, with the Shaws, to whom Lawrence was becoming strongly attached. Certainly he developed a deepening admiration, approaching adulation, for G.B.S. and a dependence of even greater strength upon Shaw's wife.

Despite his acknowledged aim of self-degradation, Lawrence found life among the ranks in the Tank Corps initially intolerable, especially as he had to endure once again a period of basic training. He seemed to have forgotten his unhappiness at Farnborough and to remember only the positive aspects of his experience there, whereas the army, he felt, was totally hateful. Only his ability to express his feelings through his pen seems to have enabled him to survive these first months. In the first of a remarkable series of letters to Lionel Curtis (which Arnold Lawrence and his wife believe were intended primarily for Mrs. Curtis) Lawrence communicated his personal agonies and philosophical ruminations. "The Army (which I despise with all my mind) is more natural [a word Lawrence frequently used to denote the primitive or bestial aspect of life] than the R.A.F.," Lawrence wrote on March 19 in the first of these letters. "For at Farnborough I grew suddenly on fire with the glory which the air should be, and set to work full steam to make the others vibrate to it like myself. I was winning too, when they chucked me out: indeed I rather suspect I was chucked out for that."[11] Three days later he put the matter more succinctly to Aircraftsman R. M. Guy, his Farnborough friend: "The crowd talk a great deal of twats! and the rest of the time about ballocks."[12] So intense was his distress that he even lost interest in his book.[13]

Lawrence felt no better and wrote to Edward Garnett in April: "The army is unspeakable: more solidly animal than I believed Englishmen could be. I hate them, and the life here." But then he added: "and am sure that it's good medicine for me."[14] He longed for the air force and wrote a poetic, romantic essay based on his memories of the three months spent in 1919 with the Handley-Page squadron in the Mediterranean. Included was this passage: "We in the machine were like souls suspended motionless in unchanging ether, conscious of no movement, of no space, hardly of time — for comparing notes with one another afterwards we could not rightly say if the four hours of our crossing had seemed to us a moment or an age. For that space our minds had ceased to exist."[15]

Early in May Lawrence wrote provocatively to George Bernard Shaw, "I haven't been in a mood for anything lately except high-speed motorbiking on the worst roads." If this distressed G.B.S. he did not let on in his next letter ten days later. Rather, he expressed his impatience at all the time Lawrence was taking collecting pictures for his book and wondered whether he had not yet been identified and thrown out of his new regiment.[16]

By mid-May Lawrence's distress had deepened to despair, and in a letter to Curtis he gave indications of the program of self-discipline and penance upon which he would eventually embark. The lifelong physical self-testing and need to master is again evident, but now it has become clearly linked with Lawrence's sexual conflicts and deep doubts about his self-worth:

"The R.A.F. was foul-mouthed, and the cleanest little mob of fellows. These are foul-mouthed, and behind their mouths is a pervading animality of spirit, whose unmixed bestiality frightens me and hurts me. There is no criticism, indeed it's taken for granted as natural, that you should job a woman's body, or hire out yourself, or abuse yourself in any way. I cried out against it, partly in self-pity because I've condemned myself to grow like them, and partly in premonition of failure, for my masochism remains and will remain, only moral. Physically, I can't do it: indeed I get in denial the gratification they get in indulgence. I react against their example into an abstention even more rigorous than old. Everything bodily is now hateful to me (and in my case hateful is the same as impossible). In the sports lately (they vex us with set exercises) I was put down to jump, and refused because it was an activity of the flesh. Afterwards to myself I wondered if that was the reason, or was I afraid of failing ridiculously: so I went down alone and privily cleared over twenty feet, and was sick of mind at having tried because I was glad to find I still could jump. . . .

"This sort of thing must be madness, and sometimes I wonder how far mad I am, and if a mad-house would not be my next (and merciful) stage. Merciful compared with this place, which hurts me body and soul. It's terrible to hold myself voluntarily here: and yet I want to stay here till it no longer hurts me: till the burnt child no longer feels the fire. . . .

"I sleep less than ever, for the quietness of night imposes thinking on me: I eat breakfast only, and refuse every possible distraction and employment and exercise. When my mood gets too hot and I find myself wandering beyond control I pull out my motor-bike and hurl it top-speed through these unfit roads for hour after hour. My nerves are jaded and gone near dead, so that nothing less than hours of voluntary danger will prick them into life: and the 'life' they reach then is a melancholy joy at risking something worth exactly 2/9 a day.

"It's odd, again, that craving for real risk: because in the gymnasium I funk jumping the horse, more than poison. That is physical, which is why it is: I'm ashamed of doing it and of not doing it, unwilling to do it: and most of all ashamed (afraid) of doing it well.

"A nice neurotic letter! What you've done to deserve its receipt God knows. . . . perhaps you have listened to me too friendly-like at earlier times. Sorry, and all that. You are a kind of safety-valve perhaps. I wish you were an alienist, and could tell me where or how this ferment will end."[17]

Two weeks later he wrote again to Curtis that he intended to continue to try to find some relief from the torments of his sickly conscience through the shackles of military authority, but expected that this subjugation would also fail to bring peace:

"You know with neurosis the causeless ones are worst. If my success had not been so great, and so easy, I would despise it less: and when to my success in action there was added (according to those whose judgement I asked) success in book-writing, also at first venture — why then I broke down, and ran here to hide myself. . . .

"Conscience in healthy men is a balanced sadism, the bitter sauce which makes more tasteful the ordinary sweets of life: and in sick stomachs the desire of condiment becomes a craving, till what is hateful feels therefore pure and righteous and to be pursued. So because my senses hate it, my will forces me to it and a comfortable life would seem now to me sinful. . . .

"I have to answer here only for my cleanness of skin, cleanness of clothes, and a certain mechanical neatness of physical evolution upon the barrack-square. There has not been presented to me, since I have been here, a single choice: everything is ordained — except that harrowing choice of going away from here the moment my will to stay breaks down. With this exception it would be determinism complete — and perhaps in determinism complete there lies the perfect peace I have so longed for. Free-will I've tried, and rejected: authority I've rejected (not obedience, for that is my present effort, to find equality only in subordination. It is dominion whose taste I have been cloyed with): action I've rejected: and the intellectual life: and the receptive senses: and the battle of wits. They were all failures, and my reason tells me therefore that obedience, nescience, will also fail, since the roots of common failure must lie in myself — and yet in spite of reason I am trying it."[18]

The day after this letter was written George Bernard Shaw wrote a memorandum to Stanley Baldwin, then the prime minister, expressing concern about Lawrence's poverty: "It strikes all who know about it as a scandal that should be put an end to by some means." Shaw went on to insist that "the private soldier business is a shocking tomfoolery," and urged that Lawrence be given "a position of a pensioned commanding officer in dignified private circumstances."[19] Shaw had discussed the matter with Lawrence, who apparently had indicated his willingness to accept a modest pension, if offered, while remaining in the ranks.[20]

One benefit of being stationed at Bovington in Dorsetshire was that Lawrence was able to develop a friendship with Thomas Hardy and his wife, who lived nearby; the three quickly became fond of one another. "Lawrence came to see us a fortnight ago, and is coming — I think — this Sunday," Mrs. Hardy wrote about a year after their first meeting. "He is one of the few entirely satisfactory people in the world. He can be so very kind. He has had influenza but looks well, and has a most powerful motorcycle."[21]

Lawrence was introduced to Hardy in the spring of 1923 through Robert Graves and wrote several months later: "Hardy is so pale, so quiet, so refined in essence: and camp is such a hurly-burly. When I come back I feel as if I'd woken up from a sleep: not an exciting sleep, but a restful one. There is an unbelievable dignity and ripeness about Hardy: he is waiting so tranquilly for death, without a desire or ambition left in his spirit as far as I can feel it. . . . It is strange to pass from the noise and thoughtlessness of sergeants company into a peace so secure that in it not even Mrs. Hardy's tea-cups rattle on the tray: and from a barrack of hollow senseless bustle to the cheerful calm of T.H. thinking aloud about life to two or three of us."[22]

By the end of June Lawrence seemed more reconciled to the Tank Corps and was able to write to Hogarth, who had been trying to help him get back into the RAF: "It is probably not worse than the reality of any other unit. It's only that the R.A.F. is much better."[23] To Curtis he wrote: "It isn't all misery here either. There is the famous motor-bike as a temporary escape. Last Sunday was fine, and another day-slave and myself went off with it after church-parade. Wells we got to [over two hundred miles] and very beautiful it was: — a grey and sober town, stiffly built of prim houses, but with nothing of the artificial in it."[24] He watched a white-frocked child playing with a ball in front of the cathedral and observed: "The child was quite unconscious of the cathedral (feeling only the pleasure of smooth grass) but from my distance she was so small that she looked no more than a tumbling daisy at the tower-foot: I knew of course that she was animal: and I began in my hatred of animals to balance her against the cathedral: and knew then that I'd destroy the building to save her. That's as irrational as what happened on our coming here, when I swerved at 60 M.P.H. on to the grass by the roadside, trying vainly to save a bird which dashed out its life against my side car. And yet had the world been mine I'd have left out animal life upon it."[25]

Lawrence revealed little evidence of his distress to his Tank Corps companions. They remembered, rather, his quiet and reserve coupled with a sense of fun, and, inevitably, his kindness and generosity.[26] Only to Eric Kennington and his wife does Lawrence seem to have shown in face-to-face contact the distress he was undergoing. Ordinarily Lawrence would joke about his "Tank Town troubles," but on occasion with the Kenningtons he "dropped all defenses" and revealed "a wall of pain between him and us." Lawrence then gave forth with a barrage of nihilistic thoughts, which had been unfamiliar to Kennington before. "Everything was attacked," Kennington wrote. "Life itself. Marriage, parenthood, work, morality, and especially Hope. Of course, we suffered and were unable to cope with the situation."[27]

Alec Dixon, who was a corporal in the Tank Corps when Lawrence arrived at Bovington, got to know him as well as anyone in the camp, and spent most weekends and two or three evenings a week with Lawrence at Clouds Hill. "Solemnity and an air of melancholy distinguished his behavior during his early months at Bovington camp," Dixon wrote me.[28] But despite the great suffering Lawrence revealed in his letters to Curtis, he never complained to anyone in the camp. He carried out his duties "efficiently and quietly, in a manner that contrasted oddly with the clamorous and slapdash methods of his younger companions."[29] Very few of the men at Bovington, including Dixon, knew, at least at first, of Lawrence's past history, although his skill and speed with a motorcycle earned him a different sort of fame — "seventy miles an hour was nothing to Shaw and couldn't that little bloke ride a motorbike!"[30] Later, after they knew, they would protect him from prying reporters by warning him of their arrival while pretending to look for him.[31] Shaw took Dixon and the other soldiers for rides on his built-to-order motorcycle and he soon became known as "Broughie" Shaw.

Dixon became curious about Private Shaw when he saw the remarkable influence he had on the other recruits. He noted especially that they "eschewed swearing and smutty backchat whenever Shaw paid them a visit."[32] One day Shaw took Dixon for a ride to nearby Salisbury. They roared out of camp at a terrific speed. It was raining and when the speedometer reached eighty-three, Dixon felt the stinging drops tear into his face "as though they had been hailstones. Shaw leaned over to hand me his goggles, puckering his eyes against the driving rain. Through the rain-blurred glass I saw that the speedometer was still at seventy-five."[33] They stopped for tea at a pleasant shop in Salisbury and talked of architecture, the Crusades and many other subjects, and finally of airmen and the air.* "Talk of airmen," Dixon wrote, "reminded me of 'that fellow Lawrence' who had enlisted in the Royal Air Force as a mechanic. That was an extraordinary affair, wasn't it? What on earth, I wondered, could have induced a man of his calibre to demote himself in that absurd fashion. 'Do you suppose it was a stunt on his part?' I asked casually. Shaw giggled at the suggestion. 'Stunt?' he repeated slowly, as if weighing the word. 'No, I shouldn't call it a stunt.' He munched bread and butter for a moment or two, eyeing me thoughtfully. 'That was a difficult question,' he said. 'You see ... I *am* Lawrence.'"[34]

Dixon described Lawrence as being "as good a soldier as any man in the Depot," but looking small and humble beside his burly fellow recruits. He was very popular with the other men, in part because of the keenness of his sympathy for the underdog.[35] According to Dixon,

> he never leaned or lounged, and I never saw him to relax. He was surely a man with "ants in his pants," if ever there was one. When walking about the Camp his normal bearing was very noticeable for, except when on a drill parade, he did not swing his arms as he walked in the approved manner — an oddity which singled him out from all of us. He walked "all of a piece" as it were, with an air of tidiness; his arms were close to his body and his toes well turned out, though not exaggeratedly so. As he walked he appeared to see no one about him; his head was slightly tilted and the blue-grey eyes steady, looking neither to the right nor to the left.[36]

Toward the end of his Tank Corps recruit training Lawrence was assigned to the quartermaster's stores ("a sort of half clerk, half storeman," he wrote his family),[37] where he worked for about two years and was "the driving force" behind its function and reorganization.[38]

---

* Dixon later wrote me that he considered Lawrence's view of the differences between the Tank Corps and the RAF greatly exaggerated, "a ripe piece of T.E. humbug" (June 25, 1967).

In the summer of 1923 he was able once more to consider the publication of *Seven Pillars of Wisdom*. "It is meant to be the true history of a political movement whose essence was a fraud," he wrote Mrs. Hardy, "in the sense that its leaders did not believe the arguments with which they moved its rank and file: and also the true history of a campaign, to show how unlovely the back of a commander's mind must be."[39] And he sought further advice from the Hardys, Hogarth and others about publishing. By mid-September he had decided upon publishing a private limited edition of one hundred to three hundred copies for friends and others willing to subscribe to an expensive book, although he still felt *Seven Pillars* to be "a pessimistic unworthy book, full of the neurosis of war," and hated the idea of selling it.[40] But Lawrence feared, among other things, the book that Lowell Thomas would publish and thought "it might be better to get my blow in first."[41]*

In September 1923, Lawrence rented for two shillings sixpence a week from a distant cousin on the Chapman side of the family a thatched brick cottage near the camp. The land on which the cottage stood had been in the possession of the family since the fourteenth century,[42] and the cottage itself, called Clouds Hill, was built in 1808. Lawrence remarked on this family connection in a letter home: "Quaint how these people are settled all about here. The daughter of the rector of the South Hill parish it was who knew all about us."[43]†

The cottage was nestled against a small hillside in lovely heath country, and was almost buried by an unruly thicket of rhododendron. (The rhododendron is today as thick as it ever was, but the nearby countryside is scarified and denuded by tank tracks.) The cottage was in a ruined state when Lawrence took it, and he soon began to fit it up "with the hope of having a warm solitary place to hide in sometimes on winter evenings."[44] He used the money from selling a gold dagger he had obtained in Mecca in 1918 to Lionel Curtis to repair the floor and roof and make the cottage habitable.[45]

Lawrence was extraordinarily generous in permitting his friends — those from the service as well as those of the English literary world — to use Clouds Hill whether he was in residence or not, and these disparate types mingled comfortably there. "I wish there was a Clouds Hill in every camp, assigned for the use of aircraft hands," he wrote to one such service friend in 1929.[46] The cottage seems to have been a second home, or even the only home for many of Lawrence's airmen and army friends, and he often encouraged them to stay in the cottage when he was away and could not use it. Jock Chambers and others have described to me in loving

* Actually, the subscribers' edition took so long to publish that Lowell Thomas's book was out for at least two years before the two hundred or so copies of *Seven Pillars* saw the light of day in 1926.

† It will be recalled that South Hill was the name of the manor house in County Westmeath, Ireland, which Lawrence's father left behind. This is the only mention of South Hill by Lawrence of which I am aware.

detail the aspects of the cottage rooms and the relaxed pleasure they experienced sitting around the fire, talking or listening to the expanding collection of gramophone records.

E. M. Forster, who first came to the cottage in 1924, has written about the silence, peace and "happy casualness" of the place, as he and other friends ate (from cans), slept, bathed and talked there. "T.E.'s kindness and consideration over trifles were endless," Forster recalls, "and after he had returned to camp one would find a hot bottle in the bed, which he put there in case his precious visitor's feet should be cold. That was like him. The harder he lived himself, the more anxious he was that others should fall soft. He would take any amount of trouble to save them."[47] Dixon has written similarly:

> Two or three other men — sometimes more — of widely differing types were among the regular visitors to Clouds Hill in those days. T.E. was an expert at "mixed grills" where men were concerned. He presided over the company, settling arguments, patiently answering all manner of questions, feeding the gramophone, making tea, stoking the fire and, by some magic of his own, managing without effort to keep everyone in good humour. There were many picnic meals (stuffed olives, salted almonds and Heinz baked beans were regular features) washed down with T.E.'s own blend of China tea. Some of us used chairs, others the floor while T.E. always ate standing by the end of the wide oak mantelshelf which had been fitted at a height convenient to him.[48]

To Chambers, in inviting him to the cottage, Lawrence wrote: "I don't sleep here, but come out 4:30 P.M. till 9 P.M. nearly every evening, and dream, or write or read by the fire, or play Beethoven and Mozart to myself on the box. Sometimes one or two Tank-Corps-slaves arrive and listen with me . . . but few of them care for abstract things."[49] Over the door he carved the Greek words OY ΦPONTIΣ, meaning "does not care," and explained to Forster and other friends that he had taken this motto out of the story of Hippocleides in Herodotus.[50] "The jape on the architrave," Lawrence wrote in 1932, "means that nothing in Clouds Hill is to be a care upon its habitant. While I have it there shall be nothing exquisite or unique in it. Nothing to anchor me."[51]

Lawrence's friends were becoming impatient with his vacillations about *Seven Pillars*. The poet Siegfried Sassoon wrote him in November 1923: "Damn you, how long do you expect me to go on reassuring you about your bloody masterpiece: It is a GREAT BOOK, blast you. Are you satisfied?, you tank-vestigating eremite."[52]

Toward the end of the year Lawrence made David Hogarth his literary executor and plans for the subscribers' edition were completed.[53] "The business will be done as crazily as you feared," Lawrence warned Shaw, and added, "your subscription will not be accepted, since I'm gunning only at the ungodly rich."[54] On December 19 Lawrence sent out a notice to prospective "discreet subscribers" that one hundred copies of the book would, he expected, be ready in a year or a year and a half (actually it was three years). The book would be elaborately printed and illustrated, and would cost thirty guineas.[55] He estimated that the production would cost him about £3,000 and be covered therefore by the subscribers. Actually, it cost £13,000, part of which resulted from the fact that he gave away over one hundred copies to friends who could not afford the thirty guineas or who might benefit from selling their copies at the enormously inflated price which this rare and notorious collector's item was soon to bring.

Meanwhile, Lawrence continued his campaign to get back into the RAF and never ceased to resent his expulsion bitterly. "If Hoare dies horribly some day you will know it's my bad wishes dogging him," Lawrence wrote to Lord Winterton.[56] He spent Christmas in his cottage ("I refused Max Gate [Hardy's home]," he wrote Sydney Cockerell. "It's not good to be too happy often.")[57] He did "rations and coalyard" to set the other men "free for their orgy. . . . Xmas means something to them. My pernickety mind discovers an incompatibility between their joint professions of Soldier and Christian."[58]

Lawrence assessed his situation in a letter to R. M. Guy: "Xmas — spent alone in my new-old cottage — has been a quiet time of simply thinking. It seems to me that I've climbed down very far from two years ago: and a little from a year ago. I was in the guard room of Farnborough that night, and the next day the newspapers blew up and destroyed my peace. So it's a bad anniversary for me.

"Yes Trenchard writes to me sometimes, but it won't be to have me back.[59] Baldwin [the Prime Minister] tried to persuade him and failed."[60]

George Bernard Shaw continued his efforts to persuade Baldwin to secure a pension for Lawrence. At the same time he never ceased ragging Lawrence about serving in the ranks — "your success in making the army ridiculous" he called it.[61] Lawrence finally had enough of this, and became bothered by Shaw's refusal to take his purposes seriously. "It's awfully good of you . . . but awfully bad for me," he wrote in January 1924. "Please let up on it all. The army is more or less what I ought to have, and in time I'll get to feel at home in it."[62] He also wrote to Hogarth of Shaw: "Such sureness of success has closed his pores."[63]

In February Lawrence received a detailed and very valuable critique of *Seven Pillars of Wisdom* in a long letter from E. M. Forster. He found Forster's appreciation of the book so gratifying that "a miracle happened" when he read the letter. He had been suffering from a bout of malaria and "the fever left me and I sat up and read it all."[64] Forster offered in a meeting to try to help Lawrence "to get rid of" the book. He recognized the anguish it was causing his friend and wrote: "I can't cheer you up over the book. No one could. You have got depressed and muddled over it and are quite incapable of seeing how good it is."[65] Eight years later Lawrence wrote to a young author: "I found Forster a very subtle and helpful critic, over my *Seven Pillars*. Hardly anybody else (of the dozens of critics who dealt with that or *Revolt in the Desert*) said anything that wasn't just useless pap. . . . After all, he writes, and so knows what authors are up against."[66]

An American firm had pirated Lawrence's introduction to Doughty's *Arabia Deserta*, and he became anxious lest the same thing might happen to *Seven Pillars of Wisdom* after the extraordinary expense and effort he had expended in the printing, illustrating, binding and producing of the elaborate subscribers' edition. In April he wrote to F. N. Doubleday: "It's the U.S.A. Copyright law which concerns me. In England the thing is copyright, for subscription printing isn't publication: and the public libraries can't demand copies. But the U.S.A. Land of pirates!

"I'm set on never making a brass farthing for myself out of that scabious Arabian Adventure; . . . but, also, I'd grudge anyone else making any. How can I circumvent the American Pirate? . . .

"The idea that came to me was this. To print every other page (or every other paragraph) of the English edition, at yours or another less reputable works: print them carelessly, so that they should be not merely unreadable, but obviously unreadable. Print perhaps six copies. Price them at 700 dollars (or 7000 dollars, or 7000000 dollars . . . anything so long as it was impossible) and tell the Copyright Department, when it asked, that the edition was still on sale (in fact, not selling well). It wouldn't be worth any pirate's while (so I think) to print the unreadable other half of the English Edition: nor would he be allowed to put the pieces together and print a connected text, since the disjointed first parts would be your right."[67]

Doubleday modified this plan into an appropriate arrangement that would secure the American copyright, and then was surprised to discover that Lawrence had turned the project over to his literary agent, Raymond Savage.[68] Doubleday was even more astonished when he learned that George Doran in New York had secured the publication rights of the book and had signed a contract with Lawrence in September 1925 for the printing of twenty-two copies.[69] Doran was to keep four copies, Lawrence six, two were to be deposited in the Library of Congress (where they remain in the Rare Book Division),[70] and ten were put up for sale at $20,000 per copy, at which price they would naturally not be sold. It appears that Doran was willing to make such an outlandish agreement because he knew that an abridgment of *Seven Pillars* that would be sold to the general public was in the offing. When in fact the abridgment, entitled *Revolt in the Desert*, was published — in 1927 by Doran in the United

States — it sold handsomely at $3.00 a copy, the earlier publicity attending the publication of the "$20,000 edition" having done an excellent job of advance promotion.[71] Doran regarded this as a calculated move on Lawrence's part, although this seems unlikely. "Lawrence had a capacity for superbly arrogant modesty," Doran observed.[72]

Doughty had repeatedly asked to see Lawrence's book on his war experiences ("I have remained in utter painful darkness as to your great Campaign in Arabia," he wrote upon learning he would receive it to read), and in late April Lawrence finally agreed to have a copy of the Oxford proofs sent to him. "My experiences in Arabia were horrible," Lawrence wrote the aging poet, "and I put them down as they happened to me. Consequently the book is not fit for general reading. I've never asked anyone to read it . . . and don't expect you to do so. At the same time you are one of the people whose wishes I cannot refuse."[73]

The desert campaigns proved not to have been what Doughty had expected, and he wrote his friend in biblical cadences, "I am able to view your vast war-work near at hand, with its almost daily multifarious terrible and difficult haps, experiences, physical and mental strains, and sufferings and dark chances that must needs be taken, in meeting and circumventing enemies, in the anxious Leadership of an Armada of discordant elements, as often naturally hostile among themselves of Arab Tribes; until, after two years, you won through to the triumph of Damascus, after enduring all that human life can endure to the end."[74] Then Doughty added, "I trust, that the long endurance of so many mischiefs may have left no permanent injury to your health."

Doughty, according to his biographer, Hogarth, could not approve *Seven Pillars of Wisdom*, "deeply attached to his strange follower though he was." Doughty told Sydney Cockerell that he thought in Lawrence's own interests a good many passages should be omitted.[75]

On this somewhat discordant note the relationship between the two famous Eastern travelers ended. Doughty died in February 1926. Lawrence attended the funeral and afterwards wrote to Mrs. Shaw: "Doughty's funeral made me miserable: not at the fuss of disposing of the body (something has to be done to get *rid* of the huge chunk) but at the sight of Mrs. D. so crushed. She had been very proud and careful of her great man, and now he has fallen. The ride back was miserable, accordingly."[76]

Lawrence was in bed much of May with malaria, and also dislocated his knee. His mood took a downward turn and he described a listlessness and apathy in letters to Graves and Hogarth. He felt, he said, "purged quite suddenly of all desire."[77] He also learned that Hogarth was ill as a result of diabetes, which further troubled him. He was discouraged initially by the extraordinary difficulties of producing his book virtually by himself (he chose the type and the typesetter, and dummied the entire text), especially when subscribers were slow at first in coming and he saw, that even fully subscribed, the book, produced in this way, would not pay for itself.[78] He was helped in financing the book by Robin Buxton, his banker and former wartime comrade-in-arms, and the two carried on a voluminous correspondence regarding the details of the book's production.[79] The next year Lawrence put his property at Chingford up for sale and began planning an abridgment (for which Cape paid an advance of £3,000) in order to pay for the subscribers' edition.

But by the end of the summer of 1924, thirty-guinea subscriptions were "rolling in merrily . . . at a rate of ten or twelve a month," and Lawrence saw that he could have sold two hundred copies if he had wished.[80] Often he discouraged people from subscribing. To one potential customer he wrote, for example: "If you subscribe for the book you are risking thirty guineas on what may be a very disappointing production, when you see it. I strongly advise no one to get it unless he is particularly rich, and a curio-hunter. Incidentally there are no political indiscretions in it: no special lewdness: some horror, and much dullness and hysteria. It's a war book, in other words."[81]

In October 1924, Lawrence received finally from Bernard Shaw the detailed criticism and page-by-page correction of the Oxford proofs of *Seven Pillars* for which he had been waiting more than a year. "Confound you and your book: you are no more to be trusted with a pen than a child with a torpedo," Shaw scolded, and proceeded to lecture Lawrence humorously on the fundamentals of punctuation, especially the use of colons and semicolons.[82] Shaw also warned Lawrence about libelous passages that had to be removed, and urged that he "swallow" these suggestions "literally with what wry faces you cannot control." On the flyleaves of Charlotte Shaw's copy of the subscribers' edition of *Seven Pillars of Wisdom*, Shaw noted: "I rewrote these passages for him in terms that were not actionable. He adapted my versions, but, much amused by them, shewed them with his own text to the victims, as first rate jokes."[83] Shaw also told Lawrence to cut out his moving first chapter, not to "suppress" it but because in Shaw's view it did not properly introduce "the who and when and where and how and what which readers must know if they are to understand what they are reading."[84]

At this time Lawrence wrote to W. F. Stirling — he had sent Stirling the book for corrections and had just received it back: "I hate and despise myself more and more for the part I played in it [the Revolt]. Today my wish is to strip off from the yarn all the little decorations and tricks and ornaments with which I have made it ever-so-little exciting: so that the core of it should stand out as a disenchanting, rather squalid, experience. That's today: and the book is being printed today for the final time. If I waited till tomorrow probably I'd give effect to this wish, and gut the whole yarn of its adventitiousness: and then all would cry out that I'd spoiled it. So the way of least resistance is to let it, generally, alone."[85]

Early in 1925 Lawrence resumed his efforts to get back into the RAF. He wrote to Trenchard: "I've lived carefully, and am in clean trim, mind and body. No worse value, as an Aircraft hand, than I was.... The war-worry and middle-east are finished." Lawrence pointed to this two years without difficulty in the army, and entreated: "I'm not the only misfit one meets (and is usually sorry for). There is nothing portentous about my small self.... Being 'bottom dog' isn't a whim or a phase with me. It's for my duration, I think." Lawrence concluded the letter with an apologetic threat to use influence to get his way: "Please don't turn me down just because you did so last year and the year before. Time has changed us both, and the R.A.F., since then. I could easily get other people to help me appeal to you: only it doesn't seem fair, and I don't really believe that you will go on refusing me for ever. People who want a thing as long and as badly as I want the R.A.F. must get it some time. I only fear that my turn won't come till I'm too old to enjoy it. That's why I keep on writing."[86]

In June Lawrence learned that his latest effort to return to the RAF had been turned down once more, despite appeals to Churchill and Hoare, whom he again held responsible for his failure (this hope was his only reason for staying in the army he wrote Buxton, and made plans to leave the Tank Corps).[87] He became increasingly distraught and focused his despair upon the "muck, irredeemable, irremediable" of the *Seven Pillars*.[88] On June 1 he had written to his waiting subscribers that the time estimated to produce the *Seven Pillars* had proved wrong and offered them the chance to get their money back if they did not wish to wait. "I am still unable to promise anything," he told them, "and any subscriber who for any reason does not wish to wait the ending of the performance can have his money back on applying to me ... but naturally I shall regret the loss of those who were willing to risk their money on what the Arabs would term 'fish yet in the sea.' "[89]

As the days went by without any sign that he was to be readmitted to the RAF, Lawrence's despair deepened and on June 13 in a letter to Edward Garnett he threatened suicide: "Trenchard withdrew his objection to my rejoining the Air Force. I got Seventh-heaven for two weeks: but then Sam Hoare came back from Mespot and refused to entertain the idea. That, and the close acquaintance with *The Seven Pillars* (which I now know better than anyone ever will) have together convinced me that I'm no bloody good on earth. So I'm going to quit: but in my usual comic fashion I'm going to finish the reprint and square up with Cape before I hop it! There is nothing like deliberation, order and regularity in these things.

"I shall bequeath you my notes on life in the recruits camp of the R.A.F. They will disappoint you."[90]

In May Lawrence had met John Buchan by chance in the street and had followed this up with a passionate letter pleading that Buchan use his influence to help him return to the RAF. Buchan wrote to Baldwin, who answered, "Come and see me about that exceedingly difficult friend of yours."[91] Buchan's personal intervention and a card from George Bernard Shaw to the prime minister, which threatened "the possibility of an appalling scandal" if Lawrence did commit suicide, turned the tide.[92]

Lawrence wrote a friend in November that while at Bovington that spring he had made up his mind "to come to a natural end about Xmas when the reprint of my book would have been finished."[93] I believe that this was no idle threat and that his despair, increased once again by working over and over the material of his book, especially the Der'a chapter, which he was revising for the ninth time in July, might well have led him to carry it out. But permission for transfer was urged by Trenchard and granted in July despite strenuous objections from Hoare, and Lawrence reentered the RAF on August 19, posted to the Cadet's College at Cranwell in Lincolnshire.[94] The news of the permission felt, Lawrence wrote Buchan in a letter expressing his deep gratitude, "like a sudden port, after a voyage all out of reckoning."[95] Lawrence stayed as an airman in the ranks of the RAF for the remaining ten years of his life. He never again experienced the degree of despair that he had suffered during his years in the Tanks Corps.

# 28

# Cranwell

Lawrence's early letters from Cranwell ("a very comfortable, peaceful, cleanly camp [which] will be glorious when I have settled into it")[1] reflect his exhilaration and relief at being back in the RAF, even as a flight clerk, and he related to friends with relish, humor and a sense of triumph the reinduction process. "A miracle (called Baldwin, I believe, in the directory, but surely a thing with wings and white robe and golden harp)," Lawrence wrote to Edward Marsh in November, "put me back suddenly in the R.A.F., when I had completely lost hope. And now I'm a ludicrously contented airman: It's like old ship Argo, on the beach after all her wanderings, happily dropping to pieces."[2] Two years after he left Cranwell he referred to his fifteen months there as one of the two golden periods of his life (the other was Carchemish).[3]

"Well, you're in luck here: this place is cushy. Any bed you like," was the pleasant greeting Lawrence received at Cranwell.[4] Lawrence seemed at the Cadet College to be, at least outwardly, cheerful and happy. Sensing the suspiciousness with which the men there regarded his unusual past, Lawrence broke the ice socially by playing the most awful-sounding records he could find on his gramophone, and listening without any facial expression while the men suffered. When they realized it was a leg-pull the tension was relaxed and he was accepted into the flight.[5] "Everywhere a relationship: no loneliness anymore," he wrote contentedly.[6]

The mission of the station — to maintain the aircraft which the cadets were learning to fly — was meaningful to Lawrence, and he made a point of flying with the officers in the flight whenever he had an opportunity. Although he was assigned to an office, he would "leave the office at times, shove overalls on," and scrub and wash machines in the hangar despite the fact that "there was never any need to do so."[7]

Sergeant Pugh of "B" Flight at Cranwell reported that in his clerk's job Lawrence mastered and took care of "every conceivable kind of job." Less than a year after Lawrence left Cranwell for India, Pugh wrote Graves: "His sheer force of personality got him undreamed of odds and ends necessary for us in our work, which seemed unattainable to any Sergeant to say the most, and never an aircraft hand."[8] Lawrence would not, however, hear of promotion.

As at other bases, despite his often exaggeratedly literal obedience to authority, Lawrence was the champion of the men against unreasonable authority or regulations. Although he liked, for example, the church at Cranwell, he had no use for the sermons and amused the enlisted men with his employment of the device of "apparent stupidity" in his resistance to mandatory churchgoing.[9] He also astounded the other men by his successful protest to the superintendent of police at Cranwell over being unjustly held up on his motorcycle by the "copper" in the town.[10] Such arguments with civilian authority were unheard of for enlisted men in uniform at that time and provided them with an exhilarating example with which to identify.

Sometimes, according to Sergeant Pugh, Lawrence would head off into the night on his Brough, summer or winter. He would return "loaded up with good things for his roommates," but then make his own supper of "Smith's crisps" (potato chips) at the camp canteen. At other times he would "smoke" down to London on the Brough to look after the printing of his book and would sleep at the Union Jack Club. On at least one occasion, when the club was full, he was packed among other enlisted men in varying states of drunkenness.[11]

Sergeant Pugh offered this summary of Lawrence at Cranwell:

> It seemed his sole purpose was to be an airman of the lowest grade and rank and to be left alone with his Brough at "B" Flight, Cranwell. He was hero-worshipped by all the flight for his never failing cheery disposition, ability to get all he could for their benefit, never complaining, and his generosity to all concerned till at times it appeared that he was doing too much for everyone and all were out to do their best for him. Quarrels ceased and the flight had to pull together for the sheer joy of remaining in his company and being with him for his companionship, help, habits, fun and teaching one and all to play straight. He fathered us and left us a sorrowful crowd awaiting letters or his return.[12]

But beneath the outwardly happy state of mind that Lawrence conveyed at Cranwell his inner sense of failure and deep personal distress remained. "Behind us, in our trial of civvy life, is the shadow of failure," he wrote of Cranwell. "Bitterly we know, of experience, that we are not as good as the men outside."[13] To Mrs. Shaw he wrote just a month after arriving at Cranwell: "Do you know what it is when you see, suddenly, that your life is all a ruin? Tonight it is cold, and the hut is dark and empty, with all the fellows out somewhere. Everyday I haunt their company, because the noise stops me thinking. Thinking drives me mad, because of the invisible ties about me which limit my moving, my wishing, my imagining. All these bonds I have tied myself, deliberately, wishing to tie myself down beyond the hope or power of movement. And the deliberation, this intention, rests. It is stronger than anything else in me, than everything else put together. So long as there is breath in my body my strength will be exerted to keep my soul in prison, since nowhere else can it exist in safety. The terror of being run away with, in the liberty of power, lies at the back of these many renunciations of my later life. I am afraid, of myself. Is this madness? [The latter phrase was written in small, wobbly letters.] The trouble tonite [sic] is the reaction against yesterday when I went mad."[14]

Lawrence went on to tell how he had gone to London, seen Faisal, who was visiting there, and Winterton, and spent a solitary night in a rooming house, but realized only how much that life was behind him, although Winterton had attempted to recall old times. "From henceforward," the letter continues, "my way will lie with these fellows here, degrading myself (for in their eyes and your eyes and Winterton's eyes I see that it is a degradation) in the hope that some day I will feel really degraded, be degraded, to their level. I long for people to look down upon me and despise me, and I'm too shy to take the filthy steps which would publicly shame me, and put me in their contempt. I want to dirty myself outwardly, so that my person may properly reflect the dirtiness which it conceals . . . and I shrink from dirtying the outside, while I've eaten, avidly eaten, every filthy morsel which chance threw in my way."[15]

Early in December Lawrence had a crash while riding his motorcycle, which, in retrospect, seems to anticipate the accident that led to his death ten years later: "Knee: ankle: elbow: being repaired. Tunic and breeches being repaired. Front mudguard, name-plate, handlebars, footrest, renewed. Ski on ice at 55 m.p.h. Dark: wet: most miserable. Hobble like a cripple now."[16]

At Christmastime Lawrence was still wrestling with the Der'a passages during the final corrections of the subscribers' edition of *Seven Pillars*. "That's the 'bad' book" [Book VI], he wrote Mrs. Shaw, "with the Deraa Chapter. Working on it always makes me sick. The two impulses fight so upon it. Self-respect would close it: self-expression seeks to open it. It's a case in which you can't let yourself write as well as you could."[17] And to his agent he wrote several days later: "The book. It crawls. The distractions are too many, and I hate the beastly thing."[18]

His mother looked to him at this time for more expressions of closeness, but Lawrence could not, would not, give them and held her away firmly and abruptly: "You talk of 'sharing my life' in letters," Lawrence wrote, "but that I won't allow. It is only my own business. Nor can anybody turn on or off the tap of 'love' so called. I haven't any in me, for anything. Once I used to like *things* (not people) and *ideas*. Now I don't care for anything at all."[19]

Cranwell brought Lawrence a period of calm he had not experienced for many years, especially during the "interim misfortunes" of the Tank Corps period. In January he wrote Mrs. Shaw like an exultant schoolboy bringing home a good report card: "My R.A.F. character has been assessed (for last year) as 'exceptional.' This is the highest grade. It shows you how I can behave for four months. Down with the Sam Hoares!"[20] Cranwell lacked only privacy — "why there isn't a lock in my power at Cranwell, not even on the shit-house door!" he complained to a friend.[21] But this was made up for by the kind loan, if temporary, of a London apartment: "The place so quiet, so absolutely mine, and the door locked downstairs, so that it was really mine."[22]

Lawrence was able at Cranwell to permit himself once more the sensuous yet objective appreciation of the qualities of the world around him as he had not for years. "I went to a Lyons shop, and ordered tea," he wrote to Mrs. Shaw in February, "the other people were amusing. They hadn't come from my planet, I think. The only friendly person was a black cat, who sat beside me, and was exceedingly insistent upon the point of food. I bought an eclair, and split it open down its length, like two little dugout canoes. The cat flung itself upon them, and hollowed out all the pith with its grating tongue. When it got down to the brown shell it sat back on its hind legs and licked its face lovingly. A man on the opposite seat, also had cream on his cheek and tried horribly hard to lick it. Only his tongue was too short. Not really short, you know: only for that ... the cat was a very excellent animal. The human beings were gross, noisy, vulgar: they did the same things as the cat, but in a clumsy blatant way.... Heaven knows why I've bothered to write you this nonsense. The moral spoils it."[23]

Early in March 1926, Lawrence completed the correction of the text of *Seven Pillars* and soon began work on the popular abridgment for Cape, *Revolt in the Desert*, that was to pay the bills of the lavishly produced subscribers' edition. Actually the latter edition was itself an abridgment of the Oxford text from which Lawrence, incorporating many of George Bernard Shaw's suggestions, had cut out about fifteen percent or fifty thousand words.[24] To a new friend and reader of the book, the Cambridge poet F. L. Lucas, Lawrence wrote: "I always had the ambition to write something good, and when the Revolt gave me a subject I tried to make up for what I felt to be my lack of instinct by taking immense pains: by studying how other people got their effects, and using their experience. So I built an enormous mass of second-hand ornaments into my skeleton . . . and completely hid the skeleton under them. . . . It sounds very conceited, that I should go on believing the book rotten, when you have written in the contrary sense. S.S. [Siegfried Sassoon] also called it epical (though an epic hasn't yet been built on the feelings, as aside from the actions of men)."[25]

A day or two after this was written (in mid-March) Lawrence broke his right wrist trying to help out in an auto accident. He was forced, therefore, to write much of the abridgment, what he called his book "for boy scouts," with his left hand "in a pencilled scrawl"[26] (Lawrence called it "a drunken script") while his right hand hurt horribly.[27] In making his abridgment (which he claimed to have done in seven hours with the help of two airmen),[28] Lawrence ignored Edward Garnett's earlier abridgment and reduced the text to less than half by taking a set of sheets from the subscribers' edition and, "with a brush and Indian ink" obliterating "whole slabs of the text."[29] Omitted were the emotionally laden, introspective or personal parts, or any sections which might reveal himself or otherwise provoke, shock or disturb his readers. "I cut out all the high emotion," Lawrence wrote Edward Garnett, and "whittled it into nonentity."[30] Since most of his self-criticism derived from precisely these personal elements of the narrative, and from the disturbing occurrences they described, it is not surprising that Lawrence declared the abridgment on occasion to be better than the complete text. "Half a calamity is better than a whole one," he wrote David Garnett. "By excising heights and depths I have made a balanced thing: yet I share your difficulty of seeing the shorter version's real shape across the gaps."[31] Remarkably, according to Howard, "his cuts required scarcely any interpolations to form linkages and very few words were written in."[32]

In order to avoid the publicity that would attend the publication of *Revolt in the Desert*, scheduled to appear the following March (1927) after serialization in the *Daily Telegraph* in December 1926 and January 1927, Lawrence made plans with his superiors to be transferred to India at the end of 1926. There are few letters from this period, in part because after three months his right wrist still throbbed painfully. In June he wrote to Mrs. Shaw: "I can only keep happy in the R.A.F. by holding myself a little below par: if it's much below I mizzle: grow sorry for myself. This happens if I get ill or hurt, or am chased over much by some N.C.O. with a grievance to hand on."[33] Early in July he told his mother of the plans for India, explaining that "the Air Force authorities drag too slowly" and that he wished to be definite before letting her know the news. "It is always difficult to get away," he wrote, "and I've been long drawing in my horns inch by inch, like a snail. India will let me finish the business."[34]

In August, in preparation for leaving the country, Lawrence had his solicitors draw up a Last Will and Testament ("of me THOMAS EDWARD SHAW otherwise called THOMAS EDWARD LAWRENCE or JOHN HUME ROSS of Clouds Hill, Moreton"). He appointed his younger brother and his solicitor as executors and willed each of them £100 and a copy of Shelley's poems in the Kelmscott Edition by William Morris. He left the land and buildings at Pole Hill, Chingford, in Essex to Vyvyan Richards and the residue of his property to his younger brother Arnold and Arnold's children.[35]

On November 3 Lawrence left Cranwell, which had become his "home for lost dogs,"[36] and took a month's leave to prepare his departure for India. The December date of his departure coincided with the completion of the production of the subscribers' edition of Seven Pillars: "I had an awful month," he wrote one friend, "real hard labor upon my old man of the sea: final printings, plates, collection, collation, issue to binders, correction of subscribers' lists, allotment of copies. Yet though I sweated it at every possible hour of the day and night, seeing no one and doing nothing else, even now it is not finished. About 20 copies have gone out, and most of the rest will go out about Christmas time ["my Christmas pudding" he called it in another letter][37] but the very special copies will hang on till the New Year. I think my experience is almost a conclusive demonstration that publishing is not a suitable hobby for an airman."[38] "It is a strangely empty feeling to have finished with it, after all these years," he wrote to Dick Knowles, his Clouds Hill neighbor, just before his departure.[39]

Lawrence's mother, who was with Robert Lawrence in China on medical missionary work, had urged Lawrence to leave the RAF when she heard he was going to India. But he replied that "the bustle and enforced duty of the R.A.F. is good for me. I wish it was not India — an experiment which has lasted too long and where we are failing." He then lectured them both — the first of a series of dressings down he gave them — about the evils of missionary work and medicine in general and interfering with the destiny of other peoples, all of which his medical missionary brother not unexpectedly cut from the printed edition of these letters. Lawrence gave many of his books to Vyvyan Richards and a gift copy of Seven Pillars in heavy morocco binding to Robert Graves, and also sent copies to Trenchard, King George ("he wanted one") and, via John Buchan, to the prime minister. On board ship he wrote to Sergeant Pugh (of his flight at Cranwell) of Trenchard's last-minute offer of a choice about whether or not to go to India, but "I had to choose to go, of course, damn it. I'm always hurting myself or my interests."[40]

The trip to India aboard the crowded troopship Derbyshire was a foul and fetid one, with "wave upon wave of the smell of stabled humanity" from which Lawrence sought to isolate himself by writing further autobiographical notes.[41] What seemed to represent for him the quintessence of its horror was the problem of unplugging a latrine in close quarters stopped up by a sanitary napkin ("the horror of almost final squalidity").[42] The only relief was a brief affectionate meeting in Port Said with the Newcombes, who took him away for several hours into the harbor where he could escape the smell of the ship.[43]

# 29

# India

Lawrence was posted to an RAF depot at Drigh Road near Karachi in the western desert portion of what is now Pakistan. He arrived early in January 1927 and remained there for sixteen months, during which time he left the base rarely, in part because the region reminded him unpleasantly of his earlier experiences in the East. He found the area even more objectionable because of the squalor resulting from its greater density of population and the culturally destructive contact with European civilization. "It is a desert, very like Arabia," he wrote Mrs. Shaw, "and all sorts of haunting likenesses (pack-donkeys, the colour and cut of men's clothes, an oleander bush in flower in the valley, camel-saddles, tamarisk) try to remind me of what I've been for eight years desperately fighting out of my mind."[1]

Although he himself had sought this additional isolation for a specific purpose, and further restriction on the range of his opportunities, Lawrence often longed for England and was sometimes observed to be "oppressed and utterly cast down" or suffering from "fits of depression" during the period at Karachi.[2] His principal job assignment was to the Engine Repair Section, where his intellectual talents were soon put to use helping the officer in charge write reports and memoranda. "Coldly routine subjects developed into reasoned expositions of the pros and cons of every side issue" in Lawrence's reports, and, the adjutant tells us, "many a trivial subject, in itself unworthy of argument beyond the merest yea or nay, was kept alive on paper for the sake of the mysterious stamp of erudition which marked the reports now coming from the E.R.S. officer." From Karachi Lawrence asked Trenchard, "Wouldn't you like the future anthologies of English prose to include passages from technical orders?"[3]

Lawrence's arrival in India was naturally preceded by the expectation that he would be at least "a queer fish." But several of his RAF companions there have described his quiet and unobtrusive ways, and the friendly, natural and unposed manner in which he conversed openly on a variety of subjects once he knew he was being accepted for himself and not regarded as a curiosity or being pumped for information. "He was, like most great readers, extraordinarily well informed over a tremendous range," one officer wrote, "and as he had the sort of mind which forms some useful thought on small as well as large matters and enjoyed an argument even on trivialities, he was most enjoyable to listen to."[4] Private Shaw's need for privacy was accepted by both officers and enlisted men, and one officer noted his "pitiful vulnerability, the barrier which was there ready to be shut down at once as the only shield against probes into his privacy." Although "monastic traits" were noted in Lawrence in India as before, his need for "open spaces" in "community with his fellow-men" has always made the analogy less than completely accurate.[5]

Lawrence worked hard at Karachi, as he always seems to have done in the RAF, and as one officer observed, since he "packed into his working hours an amount of labour out of all proportion to his rank and trade" he was a "magnificent investment at about two shillings a day!"[6] At Karachi even more than at the stations in England Lawrence demonstrated his inventiveness in rigging up extra lighting or special baths, finding methods of insect extermination or discovering ingenious ways to circumvent, while not actually flouting, orders and regulations. Despite his cultured voice and manner, there was not, as one airman stated, "the slightest vestige of superiority in his make-up,"[7] and he adapted with ease to all of the varied types with which he came in contact. This was a principal reason why at Karachi, as at all his stations, Lawrence was so well liked and respected by military personnel at different levels.

The station was in Lawrence's words a "dry hole, on the edge of the Sind desert, which desert is a waste of sand and sandstone, with a plentiful stubble of cactus on its flat parts, and of tamarisk in its valleys. Over it blow hot and cold winds, very heavily laden with dust. We eat dust and breathe dust and think dust and hate dust on the days when dust-storms blow."[8] He wrote to Fareedah el Akle (to whom he regretted not having been able to devote more personal attention during her recent trip to Europe as the representative of Syria to the first Council of Women in Paris): "India is squalid, with much of the dirty industrialism of Europe, with all its native things decaying, or being forcibly adjusted to Western conditions."[9]

Lawrence especially deplored the traditional, shortsighted attitudes of the British colonialists toward the Indians and expressed concisely to Mrs. Shaw his own anticolonialist philosophy of enabling: "On a priori grounds I would reply, that no native troops are loyal to their foreign masters: or rather, only those who had no self-respect would be loyal, and men without self-respect aren't capable of loyalty. The better the Indian, the less happy he could be as an agent of repression. Not one British officer in a thousand ever sees the contradiction of his profession with possibility. We are here for the good of India. The only good of mankind is responsibility: therefore the good we will eventually do India is to *enable* it to do without us" (Lawrence's emphasis).[10]

"I am a sort of messenger, runner they call me," he wrote to Jimmy Newcombe, six and a half years old, with apparent cheerfulness, "but I do not run: just waddle like a blue duck."[11] But on the same day he wrote about himself in the third person to a former RAF companion: "It is misery and shame being here again in the East where he did so blacken his character in 1917 and 1918, and he skulks among the airmen out of sight, very remorseful. There are no good roads: and no cream doughnuts. No good records [soon remedied]. No dogs (hot). No nothing."[12]

During this first winter in a colonialized country Lawrence delivered long sermons to his mother and brother in China against all "endeavours to influence the national life of another people by one's own," and observed, accurately as it turned out, that ultimately the rise of the Chinese Nationalists would bring the end of the "foreign" period in China. "The English," he noted dryly, "with their usual genius for beginning on the wrong side, are fighting the Nationalists, the party which must in the end (this year, next year, fifty years hence) prevail."[13] He was equally cynical about the medical work itself and he urged them both to leave the country before they were forced to leave. "There cannot be any conception of duty to compel him [Bob] to stay. In olden days doctors and medicine were respectable mysteries; but science is rather out of fashion now: and it seems to me that the fate of everyone upon earth is only their own concern. It is no merit to prolong life, or alleviate suffering: — any more than it is a merit to shorten life or inflict suffering. These details are supremely unimportant."[14]

The expression of these nihilistic thoughts to his family fitted well the personal renunciation of feeling and desire he believed he was finally realizing in the "clean emptiness" of Karachi. "I've learned a lot about living in the last five years," he wrote Robin Buxton early in March, "and have a curious confidence that I need not worry at all. Desires and ambitions and hopes and envy . . . do you know I haven't any more of these things now in me, for as deep down as I can reach? I am happy when I'm sitting still, in complete emptiness of mind. This may sound to you very selfish . . . but the other fellows find me human, and manage to live with me all right. I like so much the being left alone that I tend to leave other people alone, too."[15]

Early in March, *Revolt in the Desert* was published at about the same time that distribution of the full book to its subscribers was completed.

George Bernard Shaw in an early review of *Revolt* wrote: "The book does not, like the original, leave you with a sense of having spent many toilsome and fateful years in the desert struggling with Nature in her most unearthly moods, tormented by insomnia of the conscience: indeed, it is positively breezy; but that will not be a drawback to people who, having no turn for 'salutary self-torture,' prefer a book that can be read in a week to one that makes a considerable inroad on a lifetime."[16]

Lawrence regarded the reviews of *Revolt in the Desert* as "mostly slobber" and delighted in quoting excerpts from them in his letters for the purpose of making the reviewer look confused and silly. "The reviewers have none of them given me credit for being a bag of tricks — too rich and full a bag for them to control," he wrote Mrs. Shaw.[17] Lawrence did however, object seriously to being accused of imitating Doughty. Doughty, he wrote, "was keen only on death and life, and I was keen on psychology and politics. So we quarter different fields."[18] By the end of June, *Revolt*, which was bought up like "ripe apples," had sold 30,000 copies in England and 120,000 in America and had more than paid off the debts Lawrence had accrued during the production of the subscribers' edition.[19]

Except for a few essays by insiders, the rare subscribers' edition of *Seven Pillars* received few reviews, and Lawrence had to depend on the personal comments and letters of his friends for criticism of the work. "Do you know I'm absolutely hungry to know what people think of it," he had written to Lionel Curtis in 1923 — "not when they are telling me, but what they tell to one another."[20] George Bernard Shaw, sensing how seriously Lawrence took the book, liked to tease him about it. "I used to tell Lawrence that what happened was that an Italian Opera Company had been lost in the desert and bred a posterity of Beduwy," he wrote Sydney Cockerell many years later. "Auda, for instance, was clearly a Verdi baritone."[21]

Lawrence recognized that there was to be a sizable profit from the sales of *Revolt*, which he refused to take for himself, and £4,000 to £5,000 more than was needed to cover his debts had been received by mid-August 1927.[22] "The line of least resistance is the R.A.F. Memorial," he wrote Hogarth, and made substantial contributions to this fund, "but let's have some fun with it," he suggested.[23] By "fun" he meant nothing less than giving away money freely to airmen and other friends who were in financial need. He considered threatening to terminate sales on *Revolt* in June as a kind of blackmail scheme aimed at Cape in order to get his firm to help Pike, the printer of *Seven Pillars*, who was now in financial difficulty. At Lawrence's request sales were stopped after the book had served its purpose. Although Cape had more than fifty thousand additional copies on hand, the book had to be declared out of print. Nevertheless, the profits of the company rose from £2,000 to £28,000 for the year and the company's success may be traced directly to *Revolt in the Desert*.[24]

The limited number of available copies of the larger book (soon selling "thanks to the speculative book sellers" for three or four hundred pounds), and the confused legal status of its copyright, seem to have given Lawrence a perverse delight. "I've had two or three peevish letters from people who failed to subscribe, or whom I refused," he wrote to Buxton. "What matter? My book: I gave it to anybody I pleased: Tell your millionaires, if they pester you, that copies are on sale with Doran of New York! It's not as though the book was out of print. Anybody (with twenty thousand dollars) can get a copy. Ha. Ha.!"[25] Of the subscribers themselves, Lawrence was particularly pleased to receive a "jolly letter," from Allenby, "not peevish at all, so far as I could guess," seeming to accept the account of the campaigns in the book.[26]

With *Revolt in the Desert* published and *Seven Pillars of Wisdom* distributed, Lawrence's mood in the isolation of the Indian desert took a downward turn. "You cannot conceive how empty, uprooted, withering, I feel out here," he wrote Charlotte Shaw; "it is really a case of having come to a stand."[27] It was in April of 1927 that Lawrence wrote her perhaps the most self-exploring and revealing letter he ever wrote about his family relationships and their meaning to him.* He also wrote her that he was concerned that other airmen might discover and read her letters to him. "I feel that they belong utterly to me . . . I don't want the others to share in what I feel about them," he wrote to her.[28]

At the end of April, Mrs. Lawrence and Bob started home from China. "Good news from China," he wrote Fareedah el Akle. "My mother and brother have left it, and are on their way home. I sincerely hope that they will not return. The Chinese are waking up, at last — and the fewer foreigners that they have there the better — well intentioned foreigners, that is. Foreign enemies do no harm to a race just beginning to feel national. By their opposition they inflame the race-consciousness of the local people: but foreign friends! Oh, they are a disaster."[29]

After his mother and brother had returned, Lawrence wrote to them in concern that an airman might have read one of their letters to him which had gone astray. He hoped "there was nothing in the letters which the man who got them shouldn't read. Airmen, you know, dislike the mention of Love and God because they care about these things, and people should never talk or write about what is important."[30] Also omitted by Robert Lawrence from the printed letter was this passage: "The civil wars will last for a while yet, and after that a violently national Government will want to restore Manchuria and Korea. So for a long time China will look after herself: indeed I think probably there will not be much more missionary work done anywhere in future. The time has passed. We used to think foreigners were black beetles, and coloured races were heathen: whereas now we respect and admire and study their

* Most of this letter has already been quoted on pages 12, 27–28, 31.

beliefs and manners. It's the revenge of the world upon the civilization of Europe."[31]

Knowing Lawrence would soon withdraw *Revolt in the Desert*, and in order to forestall other attempts to capitalize on the story, Cape and Doran commissioned Robert Graves in June to write a popular version of the Revolt, based on Lawrence's own account of it.[32] "Robert Graves, a decent poet," was writing the new book about him, "as the result of a conspiracy of my friends, to keep the job out of bad hands," Lawrence wrote to his Clouds Hill neighbor at the end of June.[33] By the terms of his contract Graves had only six weeks to collect his material and Lawrence, understanding this, supplied him with great amounts of biographical information concerning the Revolt and other aspects of his life in long letters in June and July.[34] Furthermore, in order that the book, which was published as *Lawrence and the Arabs* about Christmastime, contain as few distortions as possible, Lawrence went over the drafts of the text in detail, making numerous changes and additions. While this was going on, Lawrence wrote to Lionel Curtis that Graves perhaps "will think out some psychologically plausible explanation of my spiritual divagations."[35]

Although after five or six months at Karachi (Lawrence had noted that it usually took him about six months to adjust to a new camp) he was reasonably content, he longed increasingly for England. "It will amuse you to know that my satisfaction with R.A.F. life keeps me contented in this dismal station and country," he wrote to John Buchan. "We spend much of our time playing infantry-games! However, it is only for a term of years: and my appetite for England will grow and grow and grow, till, upon my return, I'll lie down in the Strand and start eating the pavement in happy delight."[36] At the end of June he summed up his situation to Trenchard: "I'm sure I was wise to come overseas. There is no local press, and I arouse no interest in camp. Karachi I haven't visited. So nobody outside the depot has seen me. Service character still good, and I've not yet been in real trouble: nor sick."[37]

In July Lawrence indicated what he had in mind for himself for future employment after completion of his service period. "Didn't I tell you what I hope for, when I come out of the R.A.F.?" he asked Edward Garnett. "Robin Buxton, my banker, now Trustee, is going to try and get me a night job in the city, either as watchman in a Bank, or caretaker in a group of offices. They pay fairly: it is a quiet employment, whose only necessary qualification is honesty: and the work is not hard. I expect, you know, to fall into age quite suddenly, as I did into middle age on landing here. My eyes are troubling me so that I can't read much, or see clearly what I write. I'm going a bit deaf: and they say (I can't see my own head) that my hair is now thick with white hairs. I take it quite likely by 1935 I'll require an occupation which is slow, and full of sitting down. On the other hand, return to England might cheer me up to a few more years of motor-madness. Who knows?"[38]

His close participation in the creation of Robert Graves's book about him revived once again for Lawrence the painful memories and feelings associated with the war experiences. "Reading it," he wrote to Mrs. Shaw, "is like the memory of last night's sardine which sometimes comes to a man, unasked, just before breakfast, when the day is clean."[39] The book was "too laudatory" for the strict economy of his fiercely critical self-judgment. "So soon as I insulate myself," he wrote Mrs. Shaw in August 1927 the day after he received the proofs of *Lawrence and the Arabs,* "the needle swings back to self-condemnation."[40] In the same letter he told her that he had completed papers to change his name officially to Shaw. "Oh, I am so tired," he wrote, "I'd like to go off and turn into a lizard, and champ myself a long and cool and dark twisty hole under one of those immemorial cactus clumps, and sleep there in the bottom of it until the world was empty of all my kind. . . . By the way I executed a fearsome insect the other day, a legal insect of ———'s [his solicitor's] inventing, called a deed poll, by virtue of which my name is now Shaw only."[41]

In October Lawrence allowed himself after five years of service to be promoted from AC/2 to AC/1, equivalent to corporal and the highest rank he permitted himself, but his letters reveal an increasing nihilism and self-disparagement during the Karachi period, which the news of Hogarth's death in November only served to deepen.

David Hogarth died on November 6, 1927, and Lawrence learned about it three days later. Although the news was not unexpected, as Hogarth had been quite ill for many months, Lawrence's initial reaction was one of shock. "Yesterday Buxton wired me that Hogarth is dead," he wrote Mrs. Shaw, "and that means that the background of my life before I enlisted has gone." He recounted all the jobs he owed to Hogarth or had worked on with him. Since the war, he wrote, "whenever I was in a dangerous position I used to make up my mind after coming away from his advice."[42] Hogarth's wife, Laura, wrote to him in December: "I know you will miss him, more than perhaps anyone else, except Billie and me."[43]

A week after learning of Hogarth's death Lawrence sent the manuscript of his private anthology of poetry, "Minorities," to Mrs. Shaw in return for her private anthology of meditations. He apologized that "the weakness of spirit in this collection will only anger you: and then my notebook will not be a fair return for your notebook. In my eyes it is: for I'm not so intellectual as to put brain-work above feeling: indeed as you know, I don't like these subdivisions of that essential unity, man."[44]

Lawrence's letters during this period are filled with open expressions of his grief. "But I cannot write today," he wrote to H. S. Ede, an art critic at the Tate Gallery who had written to him after reading his contribution to the catalogue introducing Kennington's exhibition of paintings at the Leicester Galleries in London. "There was a man called Hogarth, who did everything for me for about 12 years, while I was growing up: and he died lately leaving me with a queer feeling that I had lost it all again. It's like being once more on one's own: and it will take me a few weeks to get square again."[45]

But three weeks later his grief had not lessened. "My bed-fellows tell me that I cry in bed at nights," he wrote Mrs. Shaw, "in the early hours of the night before they go to sleep and before I wake up. They begin to suspect me of secret griefs."[46] Hogarth represented for Lawrence what he valued most about Oxford, a civilized don who was worldly, scholarly but not bookish. "It was because he lived there that I liked Oxford," he wrote Trenchard, "and now I shall be afraid to go back to it."[47]

Perhaps the most moving expression of his feelings about Hogarth's loss came in a letter to Edward Garnett written just before Christmas: "Hogarth's death did, as you expected, bring me to a standstill. He meant very much to me; indeed he was the only man I had never to let into my confidence. He would get there naturally. Also I like him, almost un-healthily well; and owed him all I ever had, before 1922. After I had enlisted, my need of help and of friends much declined; so I saw little of him in the last five years; but the knowledge of that tower of understanding fellowship was reserve to me, and I feel orphaned in his going. There are expressing artists whose deaths one cannot bitterly deplore: — Conrads, or Hudsons, or Hardys; behind them is more harvest of ideas and emotion than most of us have leisure to gather in. But Hogarth carried his rareness in his mouth and eyes; — and he is wholly lost."[48]

In the meantime in the barracks Sophie Tucker was providing a respite for the airmen from Lawrence's more classical tastes in music. "She was worn to the bone, after about 200 playings," Lawrence wrote Graves, "and I find her just as intellectually suggestive when she comes down the wind to us from the next barrack-block ninety yards away. A splendid woman, doubtless, but she inclines me against matrimony. Imagine her greeting you at breakfast, day after day."[49]

As his first year in India drew to a close Lawrence still found much of the service routine difficult and he continued to resist it. Guard duty in particular remained a "beastly ordeal," which drove him into "a shaking funk," even though he knew the movements well — "something always comes to flurry me, when it is a performance with witnesses,"[50] and E. M. Forster suggested that perhaps "you and I may be wrong in hankering at all after this notion of escaping."[51] By the end of the year also, Lawrence formed a notion (never realized) of doing a biographical study of the revolutionary Roger Casement, with whom he seems, in curious ways, to have identified himself. "He could be made the epitome of all the patriotisms and greeds and lusts of man-imperial," he wrote Mrs. Shaw. "I suppose if I got all the materials and wrote it, white hot, that it would never find a publisher."[52] It is not clear whether Lawrence knew of the irregular sexual practices of which Casement wrote in his suppressed "Black Diaries."

During the first year at Karachi, Lawrence also took up his Uxbridge notes once again to make them into a book, *The Mint*. In August 1927, he had written to Edward Garnett that he was copying the notes into a notebook "as a Christmas (which Christmas?) gift for you."[53] A year later, after Ede and several other friends and acquaintances had read the notes and written long commentaries to the author in India, Lawrence wrote to Ede: "It is my only book, the only time I've said, to myself 'I'll write something about this.' Every evening at Uxbridge after I'd get into bed (the shedding those harsh trousers and tight tunics, and the stretching my legs into the looseness of bed were heavenly freedoms), I'd prop a pad on my drawn-up knees and scribble what had impressed me, in the day: or if nothing had impressed me, I'd jot down a conversation going on a bed or two away. So the Mint is really journalism, and I enjoyed it, as a new adventure."[54] At Karachi Lawrence added extracts, mainly from private letters, describing his experiences at Cranwell, in order to show, in contrast to the savagery of Uxbridge, "how humane life in a cadet college was."[55]

With Hogarth's death Lawrence suspended work on the notes. But on January 2 of the new year (1928) he sent to Mrs. Shaw a draft he had typed in October for her and G.B.S. to read and comment upon. Lawrence would not permit these notes to be published during his lifetime, principally because of the betrayal of trust in regard to his fellow airmen he felt making them public would represent. He wrote of these feelings to Mrs. Shaw in the letter which accompanied the manuscript: "Please regard yourself (in reading it) as being in an equivocal position, eavesdropping in a men's barrack. Those of us who live together have to depend on each other's decency to respect our inevitable confidence. We are all in the mire, together. The rest relied on me, to keep their custom, and I break it. What is given away is not myself, as in the *Seven Pillars*, but my fellows. I take you into their confidence, showing only just so much of myself as seems to illuminate their dark plans. I fear you will not like them. Yet I have censored out their secretest things, their best or worst intimacies. So many of them come to confide in my greater age and experience. What I have left is too much: to my informed mind there are things, poignantly unbearable, suggested behind these notes: and a great and lovely cleanness of spirit. So gay.

"I wrote them for myself, and copied them for Garnett: and was going to ask him not to lend them except to two specific people. Now there will be you and G.B.S. (if you wish) added. I do not want others even to know that the notes exist: least of all that they exist in book-form. You see, all the men are living airmen: only their names have been changed twice or thrice, after the S.P. [*Seven Pillars*] fashion. But we lived together, really, in the huts I mention and we said and did and suffered these things. There is nothing added — and only the intimacies subtracted. They talked like this to me, because I was one of them. Before you they would have been different: and they would be angry to think that a woman had shared their life. They cannot have the privilege of knowing you: nor would all of them have the largeness to understand you, if they did. It has been bred into them that a woman is different: holy almost, despite the soilings they receive when men handle them."[56]

In responding to a first reading of the notes, Mrs. Shaw remarked upon Lawrence's unusual sensitiveness. He replied: "Every one of us thinks he's very sensitive. I fancy we all feel very much the same. I was the only one to put in (unspoken) words, and write it down: that perhaps relieved my feelings: acted as a safety valve. If a fellow cries when he's hurt, it notably eases the pain: though it is not thought brave of him. So perhaps I suffered less than the rest of the squad. . . . I pretended to be one of them: that I might write down what they said and felt. Oh, that was the difficult part. If I'd forgotten my reproducing business, and gone properly with them, I'd have been dumb, too."[57]

On March 15 Lawrence wrote to Edward Garnett that the "R.A.F. notes" were on their way to him, carefully written out by hand and bound in blue morocco — "the blue we wear, and you can imagine the tooling is our brass buttons."[58] Two days later he wrote Trenchard what he had done and tried to reassure him that these candid revelations of barracks life would not embarrass him as he had "made a lovely bonfire of the originals" and "Garnett will not hawk the thing about." He had no intention of publishing them during his lifetime, he reassured the chief, and gave repeated instructions to Arnold Lawrence not to publish the notes before 1950.[59] But Trenchard was not reassured. He felt saddened after receiving Lawrence's letter, and worried about what would happen to the work he had done in building up the young air force should the press get hold of this revealing material, which he had not, as yet, read himself. He claimed not to be annoyed at Lawrence and consulted him for advice about raids that were going on between the tribes under Faisal and Ibn Saud.[60]

Shortly after this, however, Lawrence received encouragement from George Bernard Shaw and an ecstatic critique of *The Mint* from Edward Garnett. Shaw wrote, "There is not the slightest reason why it should not be shewn to anyone interested in the manners and customs of soldiers, or the psychology of military professionalism, or the history of initiation rituals, or the taming of animals, or half a dozen other departments of history and science. The slightest reticence or self-consciousness about it would be misplaced and unpardonable."[61] Shaw also suggested various ways to secure the manuscript from destruction and for the publication of a limited edition. Garnett wrote, "the book has perfect spiritual balance."[62] In a follow-up letter, Garnett described to Lawrence a meeting he had with Trenchard and Edward Marsh that Trenchard had requested because of his anxiety about *The Mint.* Concerned as he was that enemies of the air force might use the book to damage the service, Trenchard was, understandably, strongly opposed to publication. "He might sit for a picture of Mars," Garnett noted caustically.[63]

Meanwhile, in another letter Lawrence tried further to allay Trenchard's anxieties by assuring him of his loyalty and insisting on the private nature of the gift of the manuscript to Garnett. The book would not be published before 1950, or 1970 if Trenchard preferred, and anyway the RAF had become so strong and good, thanks to "your single work," that Trenchard need not worry about its failure or damage to its reputation.[64] There followed a long passage of advice concerning the handling of a new desert crisis.[65]

Lawrence was pleased to receive Shaw's praise of *The Mint*, but not happy with his suggestions about saving it from destruction or placing it on record, especially an idea Shaw had of putting it in a library. "Libraries like the W.O. [War Office] (to which you suggest a copy might go)," he wrote Shaw, "are open only to the officer-class, whose supremacy is based on their not knowing or caring what the men think and feel."[66]

It is not clear how many readers Edward Garnett and his son, David, loaned the manuscript to while Lawrence was in India, or how many friends Lawrence himself allowed to read it after he returned. "Show it to whom you think fit," he urged Edward Garnett, "under promise that they will not gossip about it."[67] Lawrence enjoyed in particular a correspondence with E. M. Forster regarding the book, and David Garnett had his wife type a copy ("slowly so T [Trenchard] won't get it for awhile") from the handwritten manuscript.[68]

Toward the end of his life Lawrence took the book up once again and made further revisions, and a few copies were privately printed soon after his death to prevent piracy in the United States.[69] By 1937 its existence was well known at Uxbridge, where it took on a legendary value as an exposé of abuses by the officers against the men. No edition reached the general public until 1955, one in which the names of characters were changed, and an unexpurgated text was issued only in a limited edition. Not until 1973 was a corrected, unexpurgated edition published without limitation.

The book is a starkly vivid, and unprecedentedly honest, revelation of barracks life. In 1928 E. M. Forster called *The Mint* "what is needed to express the guts of men, and they have never been expressed before,"[70] and in 1935, two months before Lawrence's death, John Buchan wrote him: "I have read your Air Force notes with acute interest and great admiration. It is the kind of document which has never been produced before about any service."[71]

*The Mint* is also an expression of Lawrence's personal ordeal, and his need for it — for what R. P. Blackmur called his "cultivation of the intolerable" — and "an essay in moral immolation and intellectual asceticism," Lawrence's personal, "minting the soul."[72]

In January 1928, Lawrence learned of the death of Thomas Hardy, and wrote a kindly letter to Mrs. Hardy. He understood her devotion to her treasured man: "You have given up so much of your own life and richness to a service of self-sacrifice. . . . Oh, you will be miserably troubled now, with jackal things that don't matter: You who have helped so many people, and whom therefore no one can help. I am so sorry."[73] Mrs. Hardy replied: "He was devoted to you. Somehow I think he might have lived had you been here. . . . You seem nearer to him, somehow, than anyone else, certainly more akin."[74]

In December 1927, Ralph Isham, on behalf of the American typographer Bruce Rogers, inquired of Lawrence whether he would undertake for £800 a new translation of the *Odyssey*. Rogers had read *Seven Pillars of Wisdom* and decided: "Here, at last was a man who could make Homer live again — a man of action who was also a scholar and who could write swift and graphic English."[75] Lawrence's reply to Isham was a classic example of his self-effacement. He listed the difficulties involved for him, that he "could not," for example, "sign it with any one of my hitherto names. It must go out blank, or with a virgin name on it." Furthermore, he wrote Isham, "I am nothing like good enough for so great a work of art as the Odyssey. Nor, incidentally, to be printed by B.R. [Bruce Rogers]." The letter concluded: "Your kindness remains overwhelming. Do realize I have no confidence in myself."[76]

He left the door open, and Rogers wrote in March a long letter setting forth the terms of the proposal. Lawrence replied in April, "I want to do it, and am afraid," and insisted upon the identity of the translator remaining anonymous.[77] An agreement was reached and Lawrence began work slowly on the translation late in the spring of 1928. As work progressed he came to think less of Homer and more of his own work, despite the usual self-disparagement.

In April Lawrence asked Sir Geoffrey Salmond, the air chief in India whom he had known "from Palestine days," that he be transferred from Karachi to another station. "Salmond has so large a stock of stations to which he can post me, that I can't even guess which it will be," he wrote his family.[78] He requested the transfer not just because of the heat and dust of Drigh Road, but also because "my personal relations in that camp were not improved by the summer postings."[79] He never explained this cryptic statement.

Miranshah, the new post, was in a remote corner of northwest India ten miles from the Afghanistan border, the smallest RAF station in the country, with only twenty-five RAF personnel (including three officers), and seven hundred Indian irregulars. Lawrence enjoyed the enforced isolation of the station in its mountain fastness and wrote that it was "easier for me behind walls than in an open camp."[80] To his former chief in the Hijaz, Pierce Joyce, who would understand the comparison, he likened the Afghan hills to the Wadi Itm near Aqaba, the place possessing a "quietness so intense that I rub my ears wondering if I am going deaf."[81] To Trenchard, who seems not to have been personally involved in this move, Lawrence wrote after four months: "We are behind barbed wire, and walls with towers, and sentried and searchlit every night. It is like having fallen over the edge of the world. A peace and hush which can be felt. Lovely. I hope to stay here for the rest of my overseas spell."[82] He was allowed, however, to remain in this retreat for fewer than eight months.

As the only airman there who could type, Lawrence was assigned office work, to "act postman, and pay clerk, and bottle-washer."[83] He found the commanding officer at Miranshah, I. E. Brodie, to be "the best and kindest C.O. of my experience."[84] Brodie returned the feeling. He liked and admired his "excellent orderly room clerk — excellent because he never produced a letter or a signal without the appropriate answer already typed and ready for signature." Brodie also noted with apparent sympathy that Lawrence had no respect for "barrack-square-type" authority and gave examples of his gentle mocking of silly instructions, usually by an exaggerated compliance which only pointed up their foolishness. Brodie also observed that Lawrence had "a steadying influence — magnetic — unseen and unheard. On the station he was not a hero — he was just 'a jolly good scout.' "[85] Lawrence was the first serviceman to show that there was no medical necessity for helmets and spine pads to fend off sunstroke. He went about bare-headed.[86]

Lawrence's struggles over *The Mint* continued at Miranshah. By July Trenchard had read the book and was still not reassured. "It was what I expected to read," he observed, and with deep sincerity wrote again to Lawrence of his concern that the book could be misunderstood and used to damage the RAF if its contents were made public. He described the reforms in the service he still wished to effect, and wrote of his wish to have air power lead to the prevention of massive killing and unnecessary casualties in war.[87]

Although Lawrence continued to luxuriate in the praise of the book he received from his literary friends, and was under pressure from Cape to permit some form of publication, he held fast to his promise to Trenchard not to publish it, and gave out that he himself was responsible for keeping his book in manuscript. "Trenchard isn't the difficulty," he wrote Jonathan Cape, "at least only a minor one. I am the prime stumbling block. All the fellows in the hut are in the book: and they would regard the record of themselves as a betrayal of confidence. When that sort of man goes to be photographed he puts on what he calls 'best': — a special suit of clothes: — and they wouldn't relish the birthday suits in which I draw them."[88]

Of greater significance for Lawrence was the debate he was undergoing with himself, shared as was his way in letters, about whether he was "a writer." Edward and David Garnett could call him one; E. M. Forster and George Bernard Shaw could speak of his works as masterpieces, even specifying in detail the elements of style and the passages they liked best; and H. M. Tomlinson could remind him of his responsibility to a whole postwar generation to tell the realities of service life.[89] It did not matter. Since praise or even encouragement only intensified his self-criticism, Lawrence could still dismiss *The Mint*, after all these comments, as "a vulgar little book, full of bad words."[90]

The problem, of course, had little — except in his own eyes — to do with the objective value of his works. It lay rather in the fact that Lawrence could no longer consider that he had anything of value or, for that matter, much of anything at all remaining within himself. "I'm all smash inside," he wrote, and "there never was an orange squeezed dryer than myself. Not a kick in the entire body. I'll write nothing else I'm sure." Or: "The great geyser in Iceland used to erupt when visitors threw soap into its mouth. This morning I got a mouthful of Pears [an old English soap] and only sputtered. I think that's a significant picture."[91]

On his fortieth birthday Lawrence summed up his view of himself to Mrs. Shaw: "Growing old too late . . . tragic, isn't it? However, it comforts me to be well over half-way. This forty years has gone quickly. I hope the residue will be less, and will go as quickly. It is not nice to feel decay getting hold of your faculties, though. I grudge my eyes their failing. As far as my arms and legs go, I'm all fit, as yet. Nor am I less elastic-stomached, and I have not got a tropic liver. Nor do I notice any change in my head yet. If only I was not always tired. I have been so, ever since the end of *The Mint*. Does GB go weary after his books? Of course he's so fertile, and I so thin in harvest, that it is not a fair comparison. A light soil soon exhausts itself if one heavy crop is taken out of it, and my *Seven Pillars* was a bit heavy."[92]

At the end of August Lawrence gave what may be taken as his final verdict on himself as a writer to Edward Garnett, his most steadfast supporter: "I am in the R.A.F. for so long as it will keep me. There is no question of my being a writer. 'Writes too' as Whistler or someone said. No more than that.

1.) E. M. Forster wants me to write about women.

2.) D. Garnett wants me to write a fairy tale.

3.) E.G. wants me to write a history of the Versailles Conference.

4.) Actually, I have begun to translate the Odyssey."[93]

This translation was to be his last published work.

Lawrence's RAF service was scheduled to terminate in 1930, and his friend Herbert Baker had even arranged for a permanent job for him as a nightwatchman in the Bank of England. But in September of 1928, Lawrence applied to Trenchard for and was granted a five-year extension of his RAF service to 1935. "The R.A.F. is like a life-line to which I cling," he wrote to Alan Dawnay. "Odd isn't it? If I hadn't tried it, I'd never have guessed that the ranks were my natural home."[94] At times Lawrence seemed to attribute his continuing commitment to the RAF to impersonal forces, beyond his control. "I am distressed for myself, and yet feel that the course is inevitable," he wrote Mrs. Shaw in November, "if only there could be an end in sight. I would so like to be comfortable, and respected. The world would pardon me enlisting for a 'stunt': but not for a vocation. Yet there it is. I'm going to let the force which governs me have its will. There is a governing force: that I'm sure. Of my own choice I would never stay in the wilderness."[95]

In the fall of 1928 Lawrence's work on the *Odyssey* ("mock-heroic" he called its style) picked up in pace, and by Christmas he had spent five hundred hours in translating the first three books. "I think my version is richer, on the whole, than the original," he wrote to the printer and pondered the sex of the author. "He or she? Honestly I don't care. No great sexualist, either way: no great lover of mankind. Could have been written by a snipped great ape. A marvelous crafty tale, mixed just to the right point with all the ingredients which would mix in. The translators aren't catholic like their master. Each of us leans toward his private fancy."[96]

Lawrence was much affected by learning of Trenchard's plan to retire, scheduled for the end of 1929, and wrote him about it as if it were a fait accompli over a year before the projected date. In an expressive letter he drew upon the image of birds and their chicks he often used when writing about the process of growth and to describe his mother's relationship with her children:

"I am very sorry you are going: it ends an epoch: and I had a personal pride in seeing you make the service, and helping you make it, from the bottom, and in being made by it, too. But I'm a believer in the parent birds getting out, when the chick's done his first solo. You may remember my getting right out of the Arab business, so soon as it seemed a going concern. Arab Nationality was as much my creation as the R.A.F. is yours. [One wonders how the Arabs feel about that statement.]

"A careless parent does no harm to the grown-up child: but the more one has cared, the more one tends to keep excessive hold of the leading strings: and the only way a kid can learn to walk is by falling down and struggling up again. Your chicken is so fit, that a bit of tumbling will do it good."[97]

# 30

# Mount Batten

On January 8, 1929, Lawrence's tour of duty in India was abruptly cut short when he was whisked by air from Miranshah to Lahore. On the twelfth he was on board the S.S. *Rajputana* on his way back to England. What had occasioned this abrupt decision by the Air Ministry were rumors in the worldwide press that Lawrence was involved in a government-instigated rebellion against Amanullah, the emir of Afghanistan, a rebellion inspired perhaps by the fact that the ruler had become too friendly with the Soviet Union.[1] Lawrence, the man of mystery, the arch-spy, was being used once again, some claimed, as an instrument of imperial policy to foment rebellion, this time in the remote mountains of Asia. "Somewhere in the wild hills of Afghanistan up the rocky slopes by the cave dwellers," claimed one article, "perched high by the banks of mountain streams, a gaunt holyman wearing the symbols of the pilgrim and a man of prayer proceeds along his lonely pilgrimage. He is Col. Lawrence, the most mysterious man in the Empire. He is really the ultimate pro-consul of Britain in the East."[2]

The uproar grew in intensity, and Lawrence was even burned in effigy by Socialists on Tower Hill in London. Although neither the cabinet nor the British government in India suspected Lawrence of any complicity in the Afghan rebellion (he never, as far as one can tell, left the camp enclosure at Miranshah) he was brought home, nevertheless, to quiet the furor. Lawrence was not to be free of newspaper publicity and other notoriety related to his legend — some of it highly noxious to him personally — for the remaining six years of his life.

Secret arrangements were made to have Lawrence (who spent most of his time on board ship in his cabin working on his translation or reading) brought back quietly and taken ashore at Plymouth without publicity.

But there was a commotion when the ship put in at Port Said, and confusion in Plymouth Harbor when Wing Commander Sydney Smith of nearby Cattewater Air Station, the man delegated to bring Lawrence ashore in a motor launch, sought to avoid the hotly pursuing press boats.[3] All this secrecy stimulated rather than quieted publicity, and a chase to elude reporters ensued, which was led by Wing Commander Smith. Much to Lawrence's amusement, it ended in London when he crashed across the threshold of Smith's sister-in-law's apartment and into his wife, almost knocking her off her feet. From there Lawrence was smuggled out the back way and finally to the safety of Herbert Baker's flat on Barton Street. Thus began a friendship between Lawrence and the Sydney Smiths, about which Mrs. Smith has written lovingly in her book, *The Golden Reign.*

Meanwhile, questions were being asked in Parliament about Lawrence's enlistment under a false name and his service activities. Not only was he afraid that he would be sacked from the RAF, but also that the facts regarding his illegitimacy and family background might be brought out. Soon after coming to London he made a midnight telephone call to Ernest Thurtle, the most aggressive questioner regarding his identity, and arranged a meeting with him for the following day at the House of Commons. He explained his situation to Thurtle and several associates, convincingly as it turned out, so that the publicity and questioning slacked off, and loaned Thurtle copies of *Seven Pillars of Wisdom* and *The Mint* in typescript.

After the meeting with Thurtle, Lawrence wrote to Trenchard, "I want to tell you, too, that I have explained to Mr. Thurtle, privately, the marriage tangles of my father (*you* probably know of them: *he* didn't, and is asking the questions which might have dragged the whole story into the light) and I hope he will respect my confidence, and stop asking questions in the House."[4] The visit to Parliament, for which Lawrence received a reprimand from the Air Ministry, resulted in a close friendship with Thurtle, and Lawrence found him a valuable figure in the government through whom he could channel his ideas about service reform. He was soon writing Thurtle long letters espousing various changes. Trenchard, after discussion with Lawrence and the Smiths, agreed that the best arrangement would be for him to be assigned to Smith's station near Plymouth.

Lawrence arrived at his new station early in March 1929, on a Brough motorcycle given to him by George Bernard and Charlotte Shaw. The camp was located on a peninsula near Plymouth: "a spine of rock and grass, like a lizard suddenly fossilized as he tried to swim across Plymouth Sound. The liners come into the harbor and tie up just below our huts, and moo through the morning mist like sea-lions in labour."[5]

Despite the intense cold, which disturbed him, and the fact that "the sea is all over the camp if a gale blows from the South,"[6] Lawrence was more contented at Cattewater (he and Wing Commander Smith soon arranged that the name be changed to Mount Batten) than he had been since Cranwell. This was due in part to the tender relationships and many shared interests he developed with the Smiths. The commanding officer was "a treat" and "a trump," and the two men formed an effective working partnership. Lawrence also was able to find pleasure in being near the sea, related perhaps to the years of his childhood spent near the water, and found a deep gratification in valuable work with boats and marine engines.

In *The Golden Reign,* which contains an introduction by Lawrence's mother, Clare Sydney Smith describes the many hours spent with Lawrence listening to music, following the waterways along the south coast, and exploring the countryside of Devon and Cornwall. The "golden reign," according to Lawrence's mother, was what he called this period, and the Smiths' house, which he christened "The Fisherman's Arms," became for almost three years another home.

Lawrence managed through his natural manner to gain the affection and respect of the men at Mount Batten, who seemed to accept without resentment his special relationship with the Smiths, perhaps in part because he never traded on it to receive special favors. His generosity also endeared him to the men at Plymouth. Sergeant W. Bradbury, who worked closely with Lawrence at Plymouth and Southhampton, wrote after his death: "The troops at Plymouth had many a snack from Shaw's parcels and he enjoyed watching them eat it. His books were returned to him but he lost a good number. His gramophone records were his pets, yet he would lend them to anyone who cared to borrow them; he only stipulated that they use special needles and he even provided them with these. He often did a night duty for fellows who wanted to go out but could not do so owing to the fact that it was their duty night."[7] Later, Lawrence was to work successfully without Bradbury's knowledge to have this younger airman succeed him in his work at the boatyards at Southampton, a position he knew Bradbury wanted.

Tommy Jordan, the former coxswain of one of the boats at Mount Batten, offered, more than thirty years later, these vivid recollections of Lawrence: "He was a bloke on the job and a good bloke on the job. He was a natural conversationalist. He'd get on the men's level, yet he kept that little bit of reserve. A natural man's man. Lawrence of Arabia? No, he was just a man we were working with."[8] According to this former enlisted man Lawrence and Smith worked successfully to achieve an atmosphere of mutual respect between officers and men at Mount Batten. The feeling between the two groups was comfortable and easy, with little consciousness of rank. This climate, Jordan stated, persisted at Mount Batten for many years after Lawrence's death.

During the spring of 1929 Lawrence taught himself to be an expert mechanic by overhauling a Biscayne Baby speedboat, The *Biscuit,* which an English millionaire had given him to use. He kept the boat finely tuned and it was in this craft that he would take Mrs. Smith and other friends on memorable trips in the vicinity of Plymouth. Work also continued on the *Odyssey*, although he found Zeus and Athena too "social" to suit his tastes, and he would have liked "the style to quicken a little, and be business-like: only Homer, alas, was not of my view. It's all the same all through."⁹ When the weather grew warmer Lawrence mastered a fear of swimming that had prevented his going in the water since Aqaba, and he swam every evening off the side of a motor yacht until he conquered the problem.

It was also in the spring of 1929 that Lawrence came to know the military historian Captain Basil Liddell Hart. (They had corresponded previously about an article on guerrilla warfare for the *Encyclopaedia Britannica*, written by Liddell Hart and based on Lawrence's 1921 piece for the *Army Quarterly*. But they had not met.) Liddell Hart sought Lawrence out to discuss aspects of military history and strategy, but their discussions reached over such a wide range of subjects that Liddell Hart eventually became interested in writing a full-length biography of Lawrence. Liddell Hart became another valuable person to whom Lawrence could press his ideas about service reform. He also got to know Lady Nancy Astor, M.P. for Plymouth, whom he took for rides on his motorcycle. Lawrence developed a lighthearted friendship with her that continued until his death.

Lawrence was not prevented by his relative isolation at Mount Batten from maintaining a continuing interest in public life, and he did not hesitate to try to influence the course of events, particularly through Thurtle and Lady Astor, if he saw an opportunity. "I am hoping especially that you will let Trotsky into England," he wrote Thurtle in June, "that you will abolish the death penalty for cowardice in war. I have run too far and too fast (but never fast enough to please me at the time) under fire, to throw a stone at the fearfullest creature. You see, if I did, I might hit myself in the eye!"¹⁰ Characteristically, Lawrence related his views on social and political issues to his own personal experience.

During the summer of 1929 Lawrence was kept furiously busy assisting Wing Commander Smith with preparations for the Schneider Cup Trophy Race, a competition among marine aircraft of the United States, Great Britain, France and Italy. The race went smoothly and was won by the English seaplane. Lawrence, however, got into difficulty and was almost thrown out of the RAF once again. The new air minister, Lord Thomson, was not pleased to have Lawrence in the RAF and used the pretext of his being seen publicly talking to the Italian air marshal, General Balbo, to crack down on him. The RAF crews had left some slippery green scum on the Italians' slipway and the Italians asked him to have a crew clean it up before the race, which he did.¹¹ It required fairly extensive negotiations in London before Lawrence was permitted to remain in the RAF and he was allowed to stay only if he stopped hobnobbing with important people, a requirement that could hardly be practically enforced since, as Graves dryly commented, these "included most of Lord Thomson's political opponents."[12] He was also forbidden to fly in government aircraft.

The fall of 1929 was a peaceful, uneventful time for Lawrence, during which he seemed, according to Mrs. Smith, to become more relaxed and "better integrated." Sometimes he took her daughter, nicknamed Squeak, in the boat. "He seemed to inspire confidence, not only in himself, but one's own self as well," Mrs. Smith wrote. "Squeak says just the same. He sometimes took her out in the *Biscuit* and let her take the wheel, even though she was a child, and she never felt in the least nervous when she was with him."[13]

Lawrence's mother moved into rooms in London in September "so that we can be near together!" ("There I am, beset," he objected to Mrs. Shaw.)[14] Also during this period he worked furiously on the *Odyssey* — as much as forty hours a week, he wrote Rogers — and complained to Mrs. Shaw, "I am so bored with the resourceful Odysseus," and, in another letter, "what a set of worms the ancient Greeks paint themselves to be."[15] Lawrence's usual capacity to upgrade the intellectual diet of the airmen was having its effect on Mount Batten as at previous camps. "The airmen are reading more," he wrote to Mrs. Shaw, "they come in to my bed, and say 'can you lend us a book?' and if there's anything just returned, I thrust it towards them."[16] As the year drew to a close Lawrence agreed to be godfather to still another child, this time the baby son of W. H. Brook, his Stokes gunner in Arabia. "Infant camels," he reminded Brook, "can walk three hours after birth. One up on them."[17]

The next year, 1930, would turn out to be quieter and happier, "the first for ten years," he wrote to Mrs. Shaw, "to leave me quite at peace."[18] As the year began he summed up his situation to an aircraftsman at Miranshah: "Life here goes smoothly. In November I had a tiff with Lord T. our present boss. He tried to sling me out: I double crossed him. So am airmanning on. Our C.O. here is a treat. Grub is better than Miranshah grub. Plymouth is a rotten hole; the sea is lovely in summer and hell in winter: and its work, work, work. I wish Greek had never been invented."[19]

Work on the "Greek" continued throughout the year, and Lawrence struggled to maintain the effort at the level of his exacting expectations, often making many drafts before sending Rogers a final version. "I've struggled with it till I'm sick," he wrote Mrs. Shaw in January. "The original is not great stuff: or that is the sad feeling I have: yet I'd like mine to be first rate."[20] To Rogers he wrote: "I don't use any obsolete words, I think, or even archaic words — or hope I don't! The thing tries to be straightforward."[21]

In two other letters to Rogers, Lawrence suggests a psychological link between his doubts about the value of his work on the *Odyssey* and his personal effort (never fully successful) to surmount self-doubts deriving from his illegitimacy. "Alas and Alack! I am going to be really proud of my *Odyssey*. It shall remain illegitimate," he wrote.[22] Several months later he again insisted that his name not appear on the work and asserted, "It's everybody's secret that I have done it, and I don't care; but between that and legitimatising the child is a great gulf!"[23] He suggested facetiously to David Garnett that he might call the translation *Chapman's Homer*.[24] Although he was "tired of all Homer's namby-pamby men and women,"[25] by the end of 1930 he felt better about his own work. "It's going to be a peach of a book," he wrote Rogers, and then added, "I had so much spare time. But in England an airman has no right to undertake a version of the *Odyssey*. I am sorry to have been so long."[26] By the end of November the work on the *Odyssey* was "¾ done."[27]

Lawrence's kindliness proved helpful to his friend, H. S. Ede, at the Tate Gallery. The two had corresponded since 1927, but did not meet until Lawrence returned from India. Ede suffered an emotional disturbance in the latter part of 1929 and wrote that Lawrence "by his kindly sanity on his various visits helped me considerably at this period."[28] In his effort to help Ede obtain a balanced perspective (Ede tended to blame the war for his difficulties), Lawrence wrote him letters which suggest that he had gained some insight and distance with regard to the conflicts and emotional injuries left by his own war experiences: "I cannot put *all* our troubles down to war. As the war gets more distant, it gets more horrible truly: at the time we did not feel it as hardly as we do now. Yet I feel that change is in ourselves, not in the war. Blame your illness rather on doing too many things. Book-writing is the world's most exhausting toil, and you tried to double it with the Tate. After G-B [Gaudier-Brzeska] is behind you, your health will come to you as before."[29]

But privately to Mrs. Shaw Lawrence indicated that his own emotional conflicts related to the war remained a source of anguish, at least during the night, despite his contented life at Mount Batten: "The war is so long over, that we should be all recovered from it now, only we aren't. It wakes me up in the early hours, sometimes, in a terror."[30] He shared with Ede his view of his own work, that had been such a great emotional strain for him to produce: "Surely you over-estimate *Seven Pillars* — a story of adventure, modern man facing troubles moral, mental and physical. It interests you because we are aware of one generation: but the future will not comprehend what you saw in it, or what I put in it, as they will have travelled past all these things."[31]

Lawrence continued, quietly, to help other people. In February 1930, he recommended his brother Arnold to David Garnett, who was looking for someone to edit an edition of Herodotus for the Nonesuch Press, and wrote to his childhood neighbor, A. S. Kerry, now a mathematician at Eton in behalf of the Newcombes, who were seeking admission for their son, Jimmy. Both of these efforts turned out to be successful.

Mrs. Smith offers this picture of Lawrence in the early spring of 1930, after a year at Mount Batten: "In this year he lost his self-consciousness and much of his nervousness and became a more integrated personality, able to enjoy simple things of life and less tortured by doubt and by thought. He loved, when I knew him, the composition of a view and the atmosphere that a particular day's combination of cloud and sunlight created. He could sit and lose himself in music for hours at a time; he was fulfilled and happy in his work, and he met people naturally — drawing them out if they were simple and inarticulate, teasing them if they took themselves over-solemnly, pricking the bubble of their self-importance with some acute words spoken in an innocent voice with his chin in the air and an amused smile lurking at the corners of his mouth, contracting and hiding in a shell of silence and withdrawal if they jarred or grated on his sensibilities, talking with animation and conviction if they were people of his own calibre of brain and achievement — and holding such an audience in a web of interest at his talk and personality, the Irishman in him thoroughly revelling in holding his audience and winning its approval."[32]

It was in 1930 that Lawrence developed an important friendship with the Australian writer Frederic Manning. "Manning is a very exquisite person: so queer," he wrote to Mrs. Shaw in February.[33] Somehow Lawrence penetrated the anonymity of Manning's war novel, *Her Privates We*. Peter Davies, its publisher, used extracts from a telephone conversation and a letter from Lawrence praising the book to help its sales, and introduced Lawrence to Manning.[34]

It is not clear how often Lawrence and Manning actually met, but they shared many personal thoughts in their correspondence on contemporary literary, social and political questions. Lawrence wrote Manning that the hero of *Her Privates We* said and thought a lot of the things he wanted to say but did not or could not.

In May Lawrence shared with Manning, in connection with a consideration of *Seven Pillars*, the impact upon him of his war experiences, and his lingering moral and political conflicts in relation to these years. He was as usual self-disparaging, but acknowledged his love of Arabia: "I wake up now, often, in Arabia: the place has stayed with me much more than the men and the deeds. Whenever a landscape or colour in England gets into me deeply, more often than not it is because something of it recalls Arabia. It was a tremendous country and I cared for it more than I admired my role as man of action. More acting than action, I fancy, there."[35]

In July he confided to Manning that he was considering having Peter Davies print a copy of *The Mint* but decided against publishing the notes as they were too "scrappy and arty and incompetent," and he could not afford the £120 the project would cost.[36] He also confided to Manning such private opinions as that he found the tone of Graves's latest book (*I Claudius*) "sickening" and that G.B.S. "finds it so easy to be brilliant-surfaced that he never bothers to go underskin. His characters are characters, all right, but have only the one mind among them."[37] Lawrence considered Manning "as satisfying a writer, as anyone who has ever written,"[38] and wrote Graves in 1933, "I think Frederic Manning, and an Armenian, called Altounyan, and E. M. Forster are the three I most care for, since Hogarth died."[39]

At the beginning of March 1930, St. Andrews University offered Lawrence the honorary degree of Doctor of Laws on the occasion of the installation of Stanley Baldwin as chancellor. Acceptance would have involved traveling to St. Andrews in May for the award.[40] He did not — or chose not — to believe the offer was serious, and quickly refused. He told a friend four years later that the invitation was "oddly worded and came in a very crumpled envelope . . . containing a very crumpled single sheet of typewriter size letter paper."[41] A second letter, correctly worded and neater, convinced him the invitation had been in earnest. When he learned that his quick refusal caused embarrassment at the University and for John Buchan and his other friends who were behind the offer, Lawrence promptly wrote Buchan, "I naturally concluded it was a student leg-pull, and sent it cheerfully back to the address given, saying that it was no go. How could I be expected to imagine it was serious?"[42]

Fearing the damage that the publicity attaching to the degree would cause to his air force status, still precarious at this point, Lawrence clung to his refusal, although he appreciated "the mere being taken into consideration for an honorary degree."[43] Lawrence joked later with his friend Reginald Sims about how inappropriate it would be for an airman to become a Doctor of Laws:

"Should I be A/C 1 Doctor Shaw???
     Doctor A/C 1 Shaw???
     A/C Doc Shaw???
and if ever I were made Leading Aircraftman, how would
LAC DOC SHAW or DOC LAC SHAW sound?"[44]

He was "staggered" some time afterwards to receive a similar offer of a degree from Glasglow University, but refused again on the same grounds, adding that as his own university had not seen its way to recognizing any literary merit of his, it would be "impolitic" to accept such an honor from "a rival university."[45]

Lawrence had discussed and exchanged correspondence with Trenchard regarding the use of air power as a means of reducing casualties in battles. In his desire to see air power in a humane light he seems not to have anticipated the monstrous use to which bombing would be put for the destruction of mankind. In June 1930 he wrote to Liddell Hart in response to a question about the *Arab* reaction to bombing: "There is something cold, chilling, impersonally fateful, about air bombing. It is not punishment, but a misfortune from heaven striking the community. The R.A.F. recognizes this, and bombs only after 24 hours notice is given. So the damage falls only on immovables.

"It is of course infinitely more merciful than police or military action, as hardly anyone is ever killed — and the killed are as likely to be negligible women and children, as the really important men. Only this is too oriental a mood for us to feel very clearly. An Arab would rather offer up his wife than himself, to expiate a civil offense."[46]

Lawrence had continued to visit the Doubledays when they were in England, although F. N. Doubleday was not well. During the summer of 1930 Doubleday underwent a serious operation and Lawrence wrote him several much-appreciated letters, filled with news of his activities, which included the fact that he had broken two chest ribs ("worse than stomach ribs").

In October Lawrence learned that Lord Thomson had been killed in the crash of an *R101*, a lighter-than-air gasbag. With Lord Thomson's death the restrictions he had imposed upon Lawrence against flying in government aircraft and visiting his prominent friends were, in effect, removed and he was soon flying and socializing on leave with Nancy Astor and others. "I continue in Plymouth, moderately quiet and immoderately happy," he wrote to Thurtle at the end of October.[47]

In November Lawrence took part in the first of a series of seaplane rescue operations, which contributed to his growing interest in developing fast, maneuverable boats, smaller than the ones the services were using, in order to effect more rapid rescues of pilots and crews. On this occasion there was no loss of life. Despite the bitter cold of the November sea Lawrence dived into the water and got a hawser around the hull of the plane, which lay in quite deep water, so that it could then be hauled out.[48]

At the end of November Lawrence was saddened to learn that in the Soviet Union the Russians had arrested several men and elicited confessions from them that they had had conversations with him in England during the time that he was actually in India.[49] He tried to counteract this unfortunate by-product of his notoriety through letters to Thurtle, but there was very little he or Thurtle could do about the situation. "They may hang these poor creatures for all I know," he wrote Thurtle. It is not known how the trial came out.

Before Christmas Mrs. Smith and her sister were in Paris. "I've forgotten to hope that Paris will be a success," Lawrence wrote them a little sardonically. "I never liked it greatly, but then, there were political reasons for that!"[50]

The new year — 1931 — began pleasantly. Mrs. Smith has described a delightful time of fishing for myriads of mackerel with Lawrence off a breakwater at Mount Batten. She fished and he unhooked the fish and baited the line. But this peace was shattered one day in February when an Iris III seaplane from the air station nose-dived into Plymouth Sound before their eyes. Mrs. Smith has described Lawrence's quick assumption of command of the situation, and his mastery of the rescue operation in which he dived with the other rescuers. Wing Commander Smith's orders for each step of the operation followed Lawrence's suggestions. Six of the twelve men aboard the plane were rescued but the rest drowned.[51] The incident, including Lawrence's part in the rescue operation, brought him new unwelcome publicity.

It may have been this incident that prompted George Bernard Shaw the following month to begin his play *Too True To Be Good*. The central character, Private Meek, who was modeled upon Lawrence, demonstrated that a private could control a regiment more effectively than a colonel. Shortly after the crash, when he learned that Lawrence would have to testify at an inquest, Shaw wrote to him: "As to the crash, you seem to be in the position of the sentinel in Macbeth who, having seen Birnam Wood start to walk, could say only, 'I should report that which I say I saw, but know not how to do it.' You are a simple aircraftsman: nothing but an eyewitness's police report can be extorted from you. However, as you will probably insist on conducting the enquiry, and as you will want to save your ambitious commander from being sacrificed, the future, to my vision, is on the knees of the gods. Pray heaven they sack you!"[52]

In addition to his matter-of-fact descriptions of the crash at the inquest, Lawrence did make behind-the-scenes efforts, through Lady Astor and other influential friends, to protect his commander, and turned the tragic incident into an opportunity to achieve needed reforms, especially in the methods of air-sea rescue.[53] At about the same time he was also drawn into a debate with an Homeric expert, employed by the publishers of his translation, over archeological and other technical questions presented in the *Odyssey*. He refused to accept the authority of any other translator and argued to Rogers that his life's experiences had placed him in as strong a position "vis-à-vis Homer" as other translators: "For years we were digging up a city roughly of the Odysseus period. I have handled the weapons, armour, utensils of those times, explored their houses, planned their cities. I have hunted wild boars and watched wild lions, sailed the Aegean (and sailed ships), bent bows, lived with pastoral peoples, woven textiles, built boats and killed many men. So I have odd knowledges that qualify me to understand the *Odyssey*, and odd experiences that interpret it to me. Therefore a certain headiness in rejecting help."[54]

In March the Shaws took a long trip overseas, which included visits to

Syria and the Holy Land. This trip highlighted for Lawrence the contrast between his present activities and his former life in the Middle East. "Yesterday I had your card from Damascus," he wrote Mrs. Shaw. "How queer it feels that you should have got there. I have to shake myself awake to realize I used to be there once. That was another life, and it was so long ago. Often I fancy that Colonel Lawrence still goes on, and it is only me who has stepped out of the way . . . picture me just as a sailor nowadays."[55]

# 31

# "Boats, Boats, Boats"

Through Flight Lieutenant W. E. G. Beauforte-Greenwood, head of the Marine Equipment Branch of the Air Ministry, Lawrence had begun work in the fall of 1930 testing and tuning speedier experimental boats, which were being produced for the armed services by private contractors. Lawrence had been attempting for some months to influence the Air Ministry to let these contracts, and their development was a victory for his cause.[1] There was a constancy, even monotony, about this work, which was to occupy Lawrence until his retirement. "My life is as before: boats, boats, boats," he wrote to Bruce Rogers eight months before he left the RAF. "They grow more and better daily."[2] In April 1931, Lawrence was given an assignment by Wing Commander Smith to the Scott Paine yard at Hythe, Southampton, where he was to spend about half the remaining months of his life. On this occasion he spent two months in Southampton tuning and testing the new types of boat engines. In May he wrote to Curtis: "We work all day all week, and have no means of amusement and no leisure for it. I am glad to do the job, as the boats are of the sorts I have been pressing upon the service for many months, personally and by reports: and they are proving what I had hoped."[3] The same month he wrote the Smiths: "To confess the truth I have had almost all the speed-boating the most confirmed water rat could want. Something quiet would be my choice now; a country walk perhaps, and some flowers to pick. I am sick of salt water, and the burn of spray."[4]

Sergeant W. Bradbury, who worked with Lawrence at Southampton at this and other times recalls: "He never referred to anything as regards boats in their correct nautical terms, the bow and stern were always the thin and thick end, port and starboard were left and right, and he would never refer to bow and stern lines as such, it was always a piece of string.

If he wanted to know about an engine he would strip it down to the last nut and bolt and go into the smallest part, work on it until he had it correct and then was satisfied."[5] Lawrence's objections to the ways of the "regulars" seem to have persisted throughout his life. But this inattention to technical language did not carry over to Lawrence's *writings* about boats and boat engines. In the spring of 1931 he began a masterful technical report for Beauforte-Greenwood in which he dealt exhaustively with all aspects of the RAF 200 boat he was developing.[6]

Perhaps the too-earnest tone of the treatise struck him as ludicrous and inspired him to write at Southampton a brief satirical essay on an autogyro of the future for the burlesque novel *No Decency Left*, which Robert Graves was writing with Laura Riding. The machine would be designed by a Spanish dressmaker "to provide the ultimate degree of private comfort consistent with safety and speed," and its usual technical features would include beam-antennae (anticipating radar) which would indicate by sound signal the presence of anybody of more than atmospheric density within three hundred meters.[7]

In June 1931, Lawrence returned to Plymouth, and the matter-of-fact tone of a letter to a former companion in the desert indicates how far he had come in molding himself into the role of the uncomplicated aircraftsman: "What's happened to you? I enlisted in 1922 and have been quite happy since, except when badgered by press enquiries into my present or past. It's not comfortable nor well paid: but I like mucking about and the other fellows are decent. Peace time airforcing isn't like the army in war you know. . . . By the way, if you answer this forget the 'Col' and the rest of it. I'm a very plain sort of creature now."[8]

Over the summer Lawrence wrestled with the problem presented to him by the author James Hanley in regard to a novel, *Boy*, which dealt candidly with sexual, including homosexual, feelings and activities. Although he thought Hanley went rather too far in places ("Now, honestly, you overdo the lechery of bus-conductors. A decent, wearied, cynical, and rather hasty-tempered class of men"),[9] Lawrence admired his writing. His letters to Hanley contain this interesting passage: "Your sanity and general wholesomeness stick up out of your books a mile high: people with dirty patches in them skirt round and round them, alluding but never speaking right out."[10] Lawrence sought (unsuccessfully, despite the fact that he did some revamping of the book himself) to keep Hanley out of the courts by having his publisher "even out" the actionable passages ("I far prefer censorship by the publisher to censorship by the police," he wrote one of the publishing partners).[11]

Work on the *Odyssey* was halted by Lawrence's assignment to Southampton. He took it up again when he returned in June to Plymouth and by mid-August had brought the translation near to completion. At the beginning of August he took a leave and buried himself with the *Odyssey* at Barton Street until he was "sicker than ever of that great work."[12] On August 12 he wrote the Smiths, "*Odyssey* creeps slowly over the ground, like a snake with glanders,"[13] but on August 15 he inscribed the last page for the publisher and printer (although he would continue to work on the text until late in October).[14]*

Lawrence felt a "half-regretful sense of loss" as he was unburdened of the work. The requirement of anonymous authorship had been dropped along the way, and the *Odyssey* translation would be the only published work to bear the name of T. E. Shaw. Lawrence had looked to the *Odyssey* for epic greatness when he was younger and now found Homer and his heroes of insufficient stature for his ideals. This disappointment colored his view of the work and therefore to some degree his own achievement as a translator. He comments at the beginning of the volume that "the twenty-eighth English rendering of the *Odyssey* can hardly be a literary event, especially when it aims to be essentially a straightforward translation." His translator's note continues: "Crafty, exquisite, homogeneous — whatever great art may be, these are not its attributes. In this tale every big situation is burked and the writing is soft."[15]

Lawrence, like an early psycho-biographer, sought to deduce Homer from his work, and found him "a book-worm, no longer young, living from home, a mainlander, city-bred and domestic. Married but not exclusively, a dog-lover, often hungry and thirsty, dark harried." And went on to suggest that Homer, "like William Morris, was driven by his age to legend, where he found men living untrammeled under the God-possessed skies."[16] The translator's note concludes with Lawrence's unrelenting expression of disappointment in the examples of the *Odyssey*'s principal characters — "the sly, cattish wife, that cold-blooded egotist Odysseus, and the priggish son who yet met his master-prig in Menelaus. It is sorrowful to believe that these were really Homer's heroes and exemplars."[17]

In July Lawrence learned that the "Golden Reign" was soon to come to an end, and that Wing Commander Sydney Smith and his family were to be assigned to another post. Clare Sydney Smith felt poignantly her own loss at the end of the close association. Lawrence has left no record of his own feelings. She tried to persuade him to transfer with them, but Lawrence wished to continue his work in designing speedboats and also did not want to leave his other friends at Mount Batten.[18] The Smiths were transferred to Manston, another base in England, in October, and as a parting present Lawrence gave them a copy of *Seven Pillars of Wisdom* (a very valuable gift by this time) inscribed on the flyleaf: "From T.E.S. to S.W.S. on dissolution of partnership."[19] At the end of the month he wrote them, after spending two weeks helping Mrs. Smith move into

---

* See the illustrations between pages 420 and 421 for a reproduction of the final page of Lawrence's translation of the *Odyssey*.

her new home (under "temporary orders"):[20] "Since life is all growing
roots and tearing them up every time I reach a new station, I vow that I
will not put down roots, to save pain — but the things grow in the dark,
all unknowing."[21] Also, in the fall of 1931 Mrs. Shaw visited Lawrence
twice at Clouds Hill, and his mother and Robert, against Lawrence's
wishes, made plans to return to China.

At the end of November Lawrence wrote a foreword to Bertram
Thomas's *Arabia Felix*, the author's account of his crossing — the first
ever — of the Rub' al Khali, the great Empty Quarter of the Arabian
Desert. Two years earlier Lawrence had urged Trenchard to have this
desert, one of the last remaining uncharted lands on earth, crossed by an
RAF dirigible: "Let us get the credit: and for the Lord's sake do it
quietly."[22] But nothing had come of his suggestion. When Thomas, then
the British agent in Muscat, accomplished his feat, not by air but by
camel, Lawrence was enthusiastic and urged through Edward Marsh,
Churchill's secretary, that the British government honor him appropriately: "Do not let the swag be all carried off by the Rositas [Rosita
Forbes, another Arabian traveler] and Lawrences of the vulgar Press.
Here is one of your own men doing a marvel."[23] In his foreword Lawrence
cited the great Arabian travelers of the past and apologized that only
because they had all died must Thomas come down to him for the writing
of a foreword. He offered the thought, but did not elaborate on it, that
"the mere wishing to be an Arabian betrays the roots of a quirk."[24]

In November Lawrence was reassigned to Hythe, Southampton, to
work on a new dinghy engine and remained there until after Easter of
1932. "I am becoming an exile from people," he wrote to Mrs. Shaw soon
after returning to Southampton, "or am beginning to feel remote, which
is worse, perhaps. The more I like engines . . ." — the rest of the thought
was left for her to complete.[25] At the end of the year he expressed concern about his RAF discharge, although he knew it to be more than three
years away. "Service life is all making and losing friends, a wandering."
he wrote to the Sydney Smiths. "I shall not dispose of myself and grow
fixed until 1935. Only this is 1932, almost. It grows fearfully near."[26]

In a letter of January 9, 1932, to Mrs. Shaw, Lawrence wrote a detailed
critique of G.B.S.'s new play, *Too True to Be Good*, with an attached
sheet of textual corrections based on his knowledge of the services.[27] This
was, as Stanley Weintraub has discussed in his book *Private Shaw and
Public Shaw*, the first play Lawrence had "worried over" with Shaw, and
as early as June of the previous year had offered him criticisms about
military dialogue and various aspects of service protocol depicted in the
play.[28] Lawrence was enthusiastic about the play, which provides a
satirical view of the functioning of a military establishment, but objected

to Shaw's view of the services in the postwar period. In his criticism he provides a clear analysis of what service life meant to him: "Only at one point did my nature want to say 'no' to G.B.S.: Where he said that the war had spoiled the services. It did alter them profoundly, for the time. After troops had left England for one of the fronts there was no brotherhood remaining. It was the fighting spoilt it. But after peace came, the pre-war mood returned. Relative to civil life the service today is more serene than it was of old. I cannot clearly tell you why this is. People dare not analyze their contentment. Partly because we feel eternal. The army's always aged about 20: no illness: no death: no old or young. All of a sort, all dressed, paid, fed, worked alike. The security of years of sameness before us. The common subjection to arbitrary power, and its assumption of all responsibility. . . . The male society, men's minds being slow and inflexible. Women, when we want them, we can encounter: but of our own will, only. They cannot come to us. Also there is an intimacy in barracks, a support of one by the next, great friendliness: and, as G.B.S. so well says, the freedom to do all things that a man's hands were made for. The peacetime soldiering is still the best lay-brotherhood. Look at my life."[29]

Although the character of Private Meek was based on Lawrence, Weintraub has pointed out that the figure of Aubrey Bagot, the ex-RAF combat officer who has been warped by military experience to the point where he cannot adjust to civilian life, is also shaped from aspects of Lawrence's character.[30] Shaw incorporated all Lawrence's suggestions, which continued in another letter at the end of January, into a revised text of the play. Lawrence read the play over and over again. "It gave me inexpressible pleasure," he wrote Mrs. Shaw. "I went about for days with a feeling that some great unknown benefit to me had happened. And that does not mean Pvt. Meek!"[31]

At the same time that Lawrence was offering Shaw technical criticisms of his play, he was completing his own detailed technical treatise for the RAF on the 37½-foot cruiser he had been developing. By the beginning of March it was completed, and, as usual, subject to his devaluation. "Ever so dull, the notes, and entirely impersonal," he wrote the Smiths. "Nobody could guess that anybody had written them. They seem just to have collected themselves."[32]

After completing his report Lawrence took up once again his struggle to get his ideas about marine craft accepted in the services, especially by the navy.[33] Lawrence suggested that Dawson send his "marine man" down to Southampton to see the boats for the purpose of writing them up in the paper, and offered to have the reporters picked up and "given a show. My name, of course, not to be mentioned." Dawson followed through as Lawrence wished, and in April (1932) a reporter visited the boatyards and wrote two articles in *The Times* about what he had discovered. Although the articles did not mention Lawrence by name, he could not, as it turned out, remain dissociated from these revolutionary developments in marine engineering.

Over the next few months Lawrence was rewarded for his efforts by a hectic period (which he seems to have enjoyed despite complaints that "my head is like a pudding") of running the new boats hundreds of miles to various coastal stations in England and Scotland, where he instructed new crews in their operation and ran trials of target boats. There are few letters from this period. So busy was he that when he heard in June from a friend that St. John Philby had crossed the Empty Quarter of Arabia by a route more difficult than Bertram Thomas's, Lawrence replied: "Only vaguely I heard he was dead. Good he isn't for Philby is a decent creature."[34]

In August Lawrence returned to Southampton and described himself to Ede as "part mechanic, part water-chauffeur, but very busy, and not useless, though an ephemeris."[35] *Too True to Be Good* played for the first time in August in Malvern, then moved to Birmingham, where Lawrence saw it, before opening in London in September. Lawrence saw the play again in London and this time went backstage to thank Walter Hudd, the actor who played Private Meek, "for making the part neither impudent or servile (its dangers) and tried to hide my regret that the counterfeit was so much nicer than my original."[36] Hudd wrote to Stanley Weintraub of his meeting with Lawrence. "His most striking characteristic appeared to be his *repose*. This aspect of him I had already used, however. He spoke briefly and quietly, examined me curiously, and then shyly withdrew."[37]

In September Lawrence was asked by W. B. Yeats if he would consent to being nominated for membership in the Irish Academy of Letters, to which he was eligible by virtue of being the son of an Irishman. This was one honor which Lawrence did not decline ("I am Irish and it has been a chance to admit it publicly," he wrote Yeats), and his acceptance was communicated to Yeats through Mrs. Shaw. Yeats then wrote to Lawrence: "Your acceptance of our nomination has given me great pleasure, for you are among my chief of men, being one of the few charming and gallant figures of our time, and as considerable in intellect as in gallantry and charm. I thank you."[38]

But complete happiness, as Lawrence wrote to Ede at the time, "is like a boom: it involves a slump before and after."[39] In October he was sent by the Air Ministry from Southampton back to his base at Plymouth, "chased" out of his job and lodgings at Hythe by newspaper headlines concerning his exciting work with speedboats "that said more than the truth."[40] As David Garnett pointed out, it seems never to have occurred to the British government that they had in their famous Lawrence of Arabia, working diligently in the ranks, not only a threat but an extraordinary moral example and a priceless asset for recruitment of men of high caliber into the armed services.

At first Lawrence seems to have enjoyed his relative leisure at Plymouth, where he was engaged in routine activities not concerned with boat-building. For the first time in many months he had time to listen to records, catch up on his correspondence and reading, and take his friends on boatrides for pleasure. "My life is full of books," he wrote Aircraftsman-poet G. W. M. Dunn in November 1932, "and I get heaps of them, every week. There must be 2000 in the cottage, all going to waste in the hope that I will live there after 1935 when I leave the R.A.F."[41]

Also in November his translation of the *Odyssey* was published in the United States by the Oxford University Press. Although the work was reviewed favorably on the whole (except by the most decorous of classical scholars) and praised in particular for its freshness, readability and vital-ity, Lawrence as usual derogated his production.[42] He gave copies to several of his friends with demureness and insisted that he had done this laborious work only for the purpose of getting enough money to pay for improvements at Clouds Hill. "The *Odyssey* to me represents — a bath, a hot-water plant and book-shelves in my cottage," he wrote to one friend in December 1932,[43] and to Rogers he wrote in February, "Please do let the bathroom be furnished by Odysseus himself."[44] Lawrence's perfec-tionist conclusion was: "The translation just isn't good enough, though it is the best I can do."[45] By February 1933, the translation had sold eleven thousand copies and soon after this a new edition for use in secondary schools was under way.

During his two-week stay in Scotland in April 1932, Lawrence had become friendly with a retired group captain at the coastal station he had visited at Donibristle. This gentleman had taken a hand at farming, un-successfully as it soon turned out, and had also written a book about it. Not only did Lawrence write him detailed letters offering criticism of the book, but also sent him £200 in advance of receiving royalty payments from sales of the *Odyssey* ("to stave off bankruptcy from him").[46] "Re-ceipts, arrangements . . . no good," Lawrence wrote the officer. "Treat it as your own, and shove it back on me as and when you can with con-venience . . . this *Odyssey* translation is likely to bring me in this much in 1933."[47]

Early in 1933 the lack of any useful application of his talents began to wear on Lawrence and he considered leaving the RAF. As the cold winter wore on he became increasingly frustrated, restless and troubled. Another Iris crash, with the loss of a life, involved him once again in a round of salvage operations, a court of inquiry and an inquest. As Mrs. Smith wrote, no one at Mount Batten seemed to know how to make use of him.[48]

Early in March he applied for discharge. He was trying to force the issue, but was prepared to leave if no useful work could be found for him to do. "Actually I have been in the R.A.F. for eleven years now," he wrote Ede, "and the last year or two are only slow dying: So I should not fight for them. I must leave early in 1935, anyhow: and might almost as well leave in 1933. But there are two more types of boats I would be glad to make for them, and other trifles in my power and competence."[49] In March and April Lawrence wrote to air force officials and met with the chief of air staff, Geoffrey Salmond, and then with Salmond's brother John, who became chief when the former retired because of illness. He refused, he told Geoffrey Salmond at the end of March, to continue to do routine assignments at Mount Batten and wished to work further on boatbuilding or to do a long "flying boat" voyage and write a log of it.[50] Lawrence permitted the planned date of discharge — April 6 — to come and go without any action either on his part or the RAF's. But on April 21 he talked with John Salmond, who agreed that he would be posted first to the marine craft contractor's yard at Felixtowe in Suffolk, and then to another experimental station at East Cowes on the Isle of Wight in May. Once again Lawrence was building motorboats. "They are life-saving in object, not war weapons," he wrote Thurtle, and added with rather bitter irony, "Every true pacifist supports the R.A.F. In case of war we will destroy

(1) fleets
(2) civilians
(3) soldiers

in that order!"[51]

In the spring of 1933 Liddell Hart began writing his biography of Lawrence. As in the case of Graves's book Lawrence collaborated in providing information to Liddell Hart and corrected his proofs, but he maintained an ambivalent attitude toward this work as he did toward any work which called public attention to himself. He had enjoyed talking with Liddell Hart in their several meetings about various aspects of military history and strategy, and seems to have permitted the book on the grounds that it would emphasize this aspect of his life, but he resented the personal aspects of the writing. "I like Liddell Hart, yet I fear him," Lawrence wrote Mrs. Shaw in June. "He is too serious. His book on me is very interesting, where it is military, and *awful* (to my hidden self regard) where it deals with me as a human being."[52] After the writing was completed he wrote the publisher: "My reading Liddell Hart's effort does not imply either approval or collaboration. I regret it and apprehend it keenly."[53]

At the end of July 1933, Lawrence returned to Southampton, where he took lodgings in a rooming house. They remained his headquarters for the next sixteen months, although his new assignments in the development of

marine craft would take him to other boatyards and testing stations in
various parts of the British Isles to supervise RAF boatbuilding contracts.
"I work at boats always," he wrote his mother in November, "and am now
getting my ideas generally accepted. Even our stick-in-the-mud Admiralty
wants to borrow one! When I have evening time I try to revise the
*Odyssey* for publication in U.S.A. as a school-book: but I have been all
the summer on this, without getting half-way. There are no free evenings."[54] When he was at Southampton, Lawrence (and therefore his
friends) were kept well supplied with cakes, candy and pudding by Mrs.
Shaw and other friends.

The increased stability of his existence permitted Lawrence to devote
himself to "domestic" concerns, especially the installation in his cottage
of such improvements as a new bathtub, a pool and an ingenious small
ram (a pump to drive water uphill) connected with a spring. "Cottage all
a ruin now, with the new water works in progress," he wrote Buxton in
August. "Soon I shall have my very own bath! The first I have ever owned
in exclusiveness. A milestone in my life."[55] There were a drought and
heath fires near the cottage, but not nearly as severe as the following
year, and generally it was a "marvelous summer" for weather.[56] More
than ever before, Lawrence looked after friends and acquaintances who
were in financial need, and even offered help with the education of the
son of the dying chief of air staff, Geoffrey Salmond.[57] At times the various names he had used in his life became a nuisance in the handling of
his complicated finances. "All these Rosses and Lawrences and Shaws
make my head swim, and its a perpetual miracle how anything ever gets
in the right place — if it does!" he wrote Buxton.[58]

In November a magazine called *British Legion Journal* printed the last
three chapters (not a précis of these as Lawrence stated in a published
letter)[59] of *The Mint* as an article by "Lawrence of Arabia" entitled
"Service Life."[60] Although the content of the passages was innocuous,
being concerned mainly with Lawrence's pleasure in rushing around the
countryside on his Brough and his contentment with his comradeship
among the men at Cranwell, unauthorized publication of the material got
him into various sorts of difficulty. "I've got into awful trouble," Lawrence
wrote in an unpublished letter, "with the Air Ministry, for publishing
opinions about service matters without permission — with Lord Trenchard, for publishing part of *The Mint* against my most solemn promise to
keep it private till 1950 at least — with Jonathan Cape, of piece-meal
disclosure of matter upon which they hold an option. In fact my name is
mud, everywhere, and I may be civvy next week because of it."[61]

The problem was in part of his own making: he had lent the manuscript to so many people to read. Before he found out who gave it to the
*Journal* after "sub-loan upon sub-loan," he suspected David Garnett of
leaking the material, but Garnett told him that he was not responsible for
it. "As I was explaining this," Garnett wrote, "T.E. looked hard into my

eyes. For a moment his blazed with blue fire, full of compelling force, unlike anything I have ever seen before or since in other men. I felt no fear or embarrassment and gazed back at him with astonishment and at that moment there was suddenly no barrier between us. The power, possibly hypnotic, possibly just rage, went out of him. T.E. was satisfied I was speaking the truth."[62] Lawrence did not end up in civvies over this incident: the damage appears to have been fairly readily undone by the *Legion Journal's* agreement to assume responsibility for publishing the piece.

In December Lawrence seems to have become inspired briefly to write a major autobiographical book about his years in the RAF and the significance of man's entry into the "element of the air." A few paragraphs of the beginning of a work with this title have been preserved,[63] but there is no evidence that Lawrence did much more with the idea during the remaining year and a half of his life. Two months later the project had been downgraded to "sometimes I think of writing a little picture of the R.A.F."[64] The entry into the air and beyond the atmosphere into space has, of course, been the purpose more of this age than of his.

As 1933 drew to a close, Lawrence spoke of himself as a man troubled about growing old and looking forward to death. "I grow fat and stiff and white-haired," he wrote a former companion of the desert campaigns. "Hard luck, again. Time all of us relics of the great war were broken up."[65] On the last day of the year he wrote to Ede that his work with boats "will be the last tangible things I do."[66]

On this same day Lawrence also wrote to his two closest women friends, Lady Astor and Mrs. Shaw, both older than himself, about his problems with love. "This Christmas there has been an epidemic of love amongst my friends, male and female," he wrote Mrs. Shaw. "It makes me feel all shuddery, to be so cold and hostile to it. What can one do? If I turn hard they mope like the owls to the moon! and if I talk gently they beg for more."[67] To Lady Astor, he was more specific about a lady to whom he was rumored to have lost his heart. "Probably it would be wholesome for me to lose my heart," he wrote, ". . . if that monstrous piece of machinery is capable of losing itself: for till now it has never cared for anyone, though much for places and things. Indeed I doubt these words of 'hearts.' People seem to my judgment to lose their heads rather than their hearts. Over the Christmas season two men and four women have sent me fervent messages of love. Love carnal, not love rarefied, you know: and I am uncomfortable towards six more of the people I meet, therefore. It's a form of lunacy, I believe, to fancy that all comers are one's lovers: but what am I to make of it when they write it in black on white? If only one might never come nearer to people than in the street. Miss Garbo sounds a really sympathetic woman! The poor soul. I feel for her."[68]

Early in 1934 Lawrence was sent for nearly three weeks to work at a boat-engine yard at Wolverhampton in the industrial Midlands. Although his retirement was still a year away he wrote his mother: "I have a queer sense that it is all over — all the active part of my life, I mean; and that retirement from the R.A.F. is also retirement from the stream. I shall be 46; which is neither young nor old; too young to be happy doing nothing, but too old for a fresh start."[69] On the same day he wrote to Mrs. Shaw: "In the light of knowledge I see so clearly that what I once took for contentment is resignation: and what I thought was happiness is sense of failure."[70]

These brooding thoughts did not prevent Lawrence from continuing to work productively in the development of motorboat engines and target boats. Although still an A/C 1, Lawrence's influence and authority in boatbuilding had increased to the point where he was given quite a free hand by the Air Ministry ("they get the boats and engines that I want, and not always what they want").[71] Sometimes he would be called to London for high-level conferences at the Air Ministry concerning planning in his field of expertise. At these times he would stay at the Union Jack Club (a hostelry for servicemen) and book as 353172 A/2 Smith, RAF, because "aircraftman Shaw is becoming too popular a chap!"[72] He also managed to find time to "throw pots" in nearby Poole in order to make his own "decent" tea service for Clouds Hill.[73]

Early in 1934 Nazi Germany was becoming a sinister threat on the international horizon and efforts were made by former friends of Lawrence's from the All Souls days, among them Lionel Curtis and Philip Kerr, to draw Lawrence into assuming an active political role. He declined such invitations, but did write an extraordinary letter to Curtis in mid-March offering sound criticisms of Britain's defense preparations and recommending the direction of necessary RAF and naval development and expansion to meet the threat of possible future attack from Germany. He urged that Britain develop (sooner than she actually did) the air capacity to thwart a German attack. He had already had an important personal hand in developing a type of high-speed maneuverable naval craft, the forerunner of the P.T. boat of World War II, that would be less vulnerable to air attack than capital ships.[74]

More than ever during these last months of his life Lawrence was involved in acts of kindness and altruism in behalf of friends and acquaintances. His letters of this period, largely unpublished, are filled with efforts to help others: advice to a friend, for example, too dizzy with "the diet of cocktails" of a doomed love affair to think realistically; offers of the use of his cottage; explanations of enclosed checks meant to help someone in need; or critiques of the work of the many poets and writers who consulted him as his fame grew and his willingness to help became known. Always Lawrence's words seem to have been carefully chosen with attention to the feelings of the person to whom he was writing. He sought to be useful without wounding the self-regard of others.

The publication of Liddell Hart's book early in 1934 brought a new wave of idolization and lionization to further complicate Lawrence's life. The book disappointed him, he wrote, "because it fails to criticize anything. One could swallow praise, if it was moved with a reasonable amount of blame; but as one knows that not everything was well done, one cannot trust his judgement."[75]

One idolator of the period was the young dancer and writer Lincoln Kirstein, a pioneer of modern ballet production, and one of the reviewers of Liddell Hart's book. He had written to Lawrence in December that he regarded him as the only man he knew of who had accomplished in life what he had set out to do, and one of four men with whom he had been obsessed.[76] In April Lawrence, surfeited with the praise of Liddell Hart's book, replied in detail to Kirstein, disavowing the value in himself or his writings that Kirstein had ascribed. "You scare me, with your over-impression," Lawrence wrote. "Please come and see me, if you get to England again; and then you will see I am your own size — and everybody else's. . . . 'Man of action' you call me . . . do for heaven's sake, travel down to where I am and put these ideas straight. We are all poor silly things trying to keep our feet in the swirl."[77] Kirstein, undaunted, wrote that he was concerned with "how men act: a subject so few care to consider — and as I understand it — one of your prime interests."[78] Lawrence replied with more self-criticism: "The worst of being oneself is that one knows all one's vices too! . . . There ain't any such super-creatures as you would fain see."[79] They never met, but Kirstein recalled thirty-five years later, "He was a terrific hero to me in my youth."[80]

In addition to the worshippers male and female (a variant of the latter were a number of women who wrote letters to Lawrence accusing him of having "taken some advantage" of them),[81] Lawrence and his solicitors were made aware by Liddell Hart himself of a man who was going about impersonating Lawrence. They tracked the man down (it turned out he was a discharged mental-hospital patient receiving psychiatric treatment under the name of Lawrence) and persuaded him to give up the imposture. "I am not flattered at the thought that he got away with it successfully. An obviously feeble creature, with the wrinkling face of a chimpanzee," Lawrence wrote hastily after the episode was ended.[82]

Over the remaining months of the spring and summer of 1934 Lawrence turned his thoughts increasingly toward his air force retirement, now only a few months away. Although he was unable to spend as much time at Clouds Hill as he would have wished, he fussed over details of its furnishing, equipment and bedding for William Roberts and several others to whom he lent it freely whether he was there or not. He felt acutely the loss of friends who had died or who, like the Smiths and Robert Graves, were overseas. At the end of May he wrote the Smiths in Singapore: "There comes over me that sense of hopeless space and lack of contact. One changes in a week, you know, and unless in daily touch, how can either of us visualize the sort of mind which receives the letter, after weeks and weeks of posting?"[83]

A conversation with Liddell Hart early in June seemed to anticipate the manner of Lawrence's death a year later. He talked of the way he would try to avoid running over a hen on his motorcycle, although to swerve was a risk — "only on a motorcycle was the driver compelled to take a fair proportion of risk."[84] During another conversation later in the month he told Liddell Hart that the British "Fascists had been after him." He would not help them to power, he said, but if they did come to power he "would agree to become 'dictator of the press' — for a fortnight." That would suffice, he wrote, to settle the quarrel between the press and him.[85]

In a letter to Eric Kennington in August Lawrence showed that the absolutism of the standards by which he continued to measure himself had not softened or been modified in the slightest during his twelve years in the ranks; his inner dissatisfaction remained, therefore, unchanged. "One of the sorest things in life is to come to realise that one is just not good enough," he wrote; "better perhaps than some, than many, almost — but I do not care for relatives, for matching myself against my kind. There is an ideal standard somewhere and only that matters: and I cannot find it. Hence this aimlessness."[86]

During his last months based at Southampton Lawrence moved around a great deal, traveling to Wolverhampton, Kent, Nottingham, London and Plymouth to complete his work on small boats and to test "a rather exciting new" diesel engine.[87] He continued to struggle with the "mulish" navy and "pulled string after string" to get them to accept the faster Scott Paine motorboats as "set against their primitive junks."[88] He grew tired and despondent and longed for the peace of Clouds Hill — "the best part of the picture" — yet managed to find the energy and interest to write for his old friend of the Cairo days, George Lord Lloyd, former high commissioner of Egypt, a long critique of Lloyd's recent book, *Egypt Since Cromer*.[89] "How bored I'm going to be!" (in retirement), he wrote Liddell Hart. "Think of it: a really new experience, for hitherto I've never been bored."[90]

In November 1934, Lawrence was transferred to Bridlington, a summer resort on the North Sea, to supervise the overhauling in a huge garage of ten RAF boats that were working a bomber range. He was stationed at Bridlington for the less than four months that remained of his RAF service. Lawrence felt that it was time he retired: he found himself becoming "censorious" and could "see nothing which could not be better done, whether it is my own old work, or another's."[91] Yet, as he wrote to Mrs. Shaw, he wished he could avoid the inevitable and that "the world did not change. This blue protective coating has meant so much to me. I go back to the self of 1920 and 1921, a crazy pelican feeding not its young but its spirit creations upon its bodily strength. I had hoped all these years that I was not going to be alone again."[92]

The short period of Lawrence's stay at Bridlington is well described by the recollections of men with whom he worked, especially in the notes made after his death by Flight Lieutenant Reginald Sims, an equipment officer stationed there whose family Lawrence visited about once a week. The pattern of earlier recollections of Lawrence in the ranks is not broken by these accounts — the soft, silent manner; the precise, craftsmanlike use of language; the irreverent stories telling of the deflation of lofty personages ("big noises"); the elevating influence on the standards of conduct of officers and men; the abstemious habits; and the unvarying patience and sense of humor. Although his face had become red and roughened, "sandblasted," as Lawrence put it, the blazing blue eyes and impression of eternal youthfulness were unchanged. Lawrence had accumulated by this time an enormous knowledge on a vast variety of technical and other subjects which, combined with considerable practical experience, made him invaluable to the detachment. He loved tools and acquired a perfect fitter's tool kit, selecting its items as much for the beauty of their materials as for the fineness of their craftsmanship.

He had become by this period a still more seasoned storyteller and was apparently less reticent in talking about his past, as the many stories recorded by Sims well document. "He ranged the world for us," Sims wrote, and gave his entranced audiences "in brilliant cameo, sketches of kings, beggars, celebrities, underdogs, artists, murderers, and friends." He did not speak of enemies. "With a slight movement or expression, he would conjure up persons, so that we could almost see them before us, while the faint grin, and elfish look that accompanied some of his descriptions, were part of that birth right with which the Fairies had dowered him."[93]

Although Lawrence did not at Bridlington appear despondent or depressed as he had at earlier posts he still seemed, to Sims, to be "working out some difficult problem of his own at the same moment, that was not even remotely connected with the story he was telling or the life he was leading."[94] His past, Lawrence had once remarked, was like a tin can tied to the tail of a dog that rattled whatever he did.[95] Perhaps the rattle seemed less harsh to him now.

One story Lawrence told Sims — one of the rare ones that concerned his childhood — provides insight into his intense interest in fast boats and his long struggle with the admiralty to have his ideas accepted. When he was eight (the family was by then living in Oxford) his parents took him to see a review of the fleet at Spithead near Southampton on the occasion of the Diamond Jubilee of Queen Victoria. There was a vast array of the latest naval ships in perfect alignment to be reviewed. About half an hour before the Queen was to make her inspection "a small, evil-looking, squat, ugly little steamer, clearly non-service, and simply belching out clouds of dense smoke" made a straight line for the fleet from the shadow of a nearby headland. Greatly alarmed, the senior naval officer in charge dispatched one fast naval vessel after another to head off or even destroy the little steamer that was threatening to ruin the formation. But the little steamer led her pursuing armada out to sea and disappeared over the horizon as she maintained and even increased her lead. This proved to be a dramatic demonstration by a Mr. Parsons, who had invented the turbine engine, but who had been unable until that time to get the admiralty interested in it. After the drama was over — he had spent every farthing he could scrape together on it — the admiralty fined him £200 for the disturbance but gave him a million-pound order for turbine engines. Lawrence had wished to repeat history at the next fleet review at Spithead on the occasion of King George V's Jubilee by demonstrating a speedy motorboat he had developed, but knew he would no longer be in the RAF at that time. He had to be content with a more gradual persuasion of the admiralty to his point of view.[96]

As Lawrence's discharge date approached, a number of his friends became concerned about what he was going to do after retirement and were eager to prevent his vegetating and going to seed. One of these, Lord Rennell of Rodd, a banker, was in close touch with Montague Norman, governor of the Bank of England. Norman in the summer of 1934 was concerned with filling the post of secretary of the bank. The person chosen need not have a technical, financial or economic background but had to be able to provide leadership: "He had to be a man."[97] One day, on the urging of Herbert Baker, who also was concerned about Lawrence's future, Norman called Rodd and asked him to inquire of Lawrence privately whether he would consider "the offer of an appointment to the Bank of England with a view to becoming Secretary of the Governor and Company of the Bank" after his RAF service was over.[98]

Rodd observed that Lawrence had no business experience, but Norman held firm on the "Elizabethan" ground that a man who was good at one thing would be good at another. Rodd wrote to T.E. in the early fall, but owing to the latter's moving about received no reply until a letter from Lawrence dated November 23 came from Bridlington. Lawrence was clearly moved by the offer but, despite his anticipation that he would feel "unutterably lost" out of uniform, refused it. "Will you please say No, for me, but not a plain No," he wrote Rodd. "Make it a coloured No, for the Elizabethan of Baker's naming has given me a moment of very rare pleasure which I shall not tell to anyone, nor forget."[99]

Cheered by the anticipation of a few days at Clouds Hill at Christmastime Lawrence wrote a delightful letter to Jimmy Newcombe, now fourteen and a full-fledged Etonian, which is filled with gentle parodies of Christmas conventions. He urged young Newcombe to watch over his parents and prevent their gluttony at the dinner table: "If they bring in plum puddings and things, remark in a blasé accent . . . the normal speech, I mean, of Eton . . . 'Isn't it jolly, papa, to keep up these old customs? It's like Dickens, isn't it, I mean, what?' That will throw a chill over the whole meal-time — I mean orgy. You owe a duty to your family at Christmas." The letter concluded: "Don't wish them any sort of celebration of the birth of Christ. I only do one Xmas letter per year, and that's not really a letter. I send Lady Astor a reply-paid wire of 'Merry Xmas' and she wires back 'Same to you.' "[100] During the Christmas holidays Lawrence talked with his neighbor, Pat Knowles, about plans for building a printing press, and Knowles even began to gather materials for a shed to house it.[101]

As the year drew to a close the future did not look cheerful to Lawrence. "The R.A.F. leaves me out of its rolls in February next, and I'm facing rather a blank future in something like unhappiness," he wrote the poet Maurice Baring. "I've been serving for 12 years, and the assurance has stayed me, like his shell a hermit crab. Now life's to begin again, with all the 24 hours of the day given to me — and I particularly don't want so much."[102] He still thought sometimes of doing a short book about Roger Casement. "As I see it, his was a heroic nature. I should like to write upon him subtly, so his enemies would think I was with them til they finished my book and rose from reading to call him a hero. He had the appeal of a broken archangel."[103]

On January 3 of the new year (1935) Lawrence wrote to Ede: "Early in March I 'get my ticket.' It's like a blank wall beyond which I cannot even imagine. Exactly what leisure is like, whether it will madden me or suit me. What it means to wake up every day and know there is no compulsion to get out of bed . . . it's no good. When it comes, I shall try to deal with it; but now, beforehand, I can only say that I wish it had not to be."[104]

Other letters in the early weeks of 1935 also express Lawrence's anxiety about leaving the RAF and a sense that time was running out on him and that his life "in the real sense" was over. "The sands run out, continually," he wrote to the Smiths in Singapore. "Another six weeks and the R.A.F. loses its smallest ornament. Meanwhile I work away at the boats, and find myself everlastingly putting up suggestions for new devices or improvements. I forget I'm going out, whenever there is anything to do."[105] Elsewhere he noted that he was constantly tripping himself up "in some research or advice concerning boats, something that might take weeks to fruition."[106]

Lawrence remained "fully engaged" in his work on motorboats until he left the camp, but was also busy with several other matters. He successfully staved off an effort by the film producer Alexander Korda to make a movie of his life. He met Korda, "the film king," and persuaded him of his desire to be left alone. "He was quite unexpectedly sensitive, for a king," Lawrence wrote Mrs. Shaw.[107] Lawrence told the Simses that the only film he could have borne to have done about his Arabian campaign would be one by Walt Disney in the style of *Three Little Pigs* and *The Grasshopper and the Ant* — "Me and my army jogging across a skyline on camels could have been very amusing."[108]

At the end of January he learned that the publishers of Hanley's novel *Boy* were successfully prosecuted for indecency by local police. Lawrence was clearly troubled about this on principle and alarmed at the precedent of putting writers and publishers "at the mercy of the discretion of any Police Chief at any time."[109] He sought to mobilize a protest of publishers against the police action and was still engaged in this effort when he was fatally injured.

Also he had what he called "a dust-up" with the chief constable in one city over the matter of an eccentric widow of fifty-three who kept writing him letters, calling him "Jim," and begging him to return and that all would be forgiven. She would not take no for an answer and kept writing twice a week, so Lawrence asked the chief constable to help him out. The chief seems to have believed the lady's story that Lawrence had lived with her during the 1914–1918 war and had left her with two sons, and he wrote to Lawrence's "C.O." at Bridlington. There being no such officer, the letter came to Lawrence, who wrote the "Chief Copper" a blistering letter telling him that his action could have caused him much gossip and embarrassment. He never heard further from the widow or the constable.[110]

Early in February Lawrence wrote to Robert Graves, who had always been critical of his decision to remain in the ranks, a justification of his air force years, especially his success, achieved with others, of having new concepts of boat design accepted by the admiralty and by the navies of other governments. From the personal standpoint he offered this summary of his years in the ranks:

"I went into the R.A.F. to serve a mechanical purpose, not as a leader but as a cog of the machine. The key-word, I think, is machine. I have been mechanical since, and a good mechanic, for my self-training to become an artist has greatly widened my field of view. I leave it to others to say whether I chose well or not: one of the benefits of being part of the machine is that one learns that one doesn't matter!

"One thing more. You remember me writing to you when I first went into the R.A.F. that it was the nearest modern equivalent of going into a monastery in the Middle Ages. That was right in more than one sense. Being a mechanic cuts one off from all real communication with women. There are no women in the machines, in any machine. No woman, I believe, can understand a mechanic's happiness in serving his bits and pieces."[111]

Lawrence, as is well known, rarely drank, but he was invited by the officers and his fellow airmen to a party shortly before he left Bridlington. The group went to a local theatre and then visited a nearby club for "ginning-up." Lawrence did not have a drink, but ate a cherry on a stick from one of his friend's glasses. A waitress then brought him an entire dish of cherries, "and he ate every one with the zest of a schoolboy raiding a tuck shop."[112]

In February Lawrence had a card printed, which read, "To tell you that in future I shall write very few letters," and planned to put one in each letter that he wrote over the next six months.[113] In order to avoid publicity, plans were made to have Lawrence leave Bridlington at the end of February rather than on his scheduled date of March 11. He had been corresponding, however, with a former serviceman from the days of the Arabian campaigns who had offered to be his valet. Lawrence declined the offer ("No, Clouds Hill wouldn't look right with a valet!"), but let his friend know of his plans to leave Bridlington in a month. Somehow the press found out, for on February 25, the day before Lawrence was to leave, reporters were "scurrying about" Bridlington and also at Clouds Hill.[114]

There is irony in a conversation that occurred not long before Lawrence left Bridlington, recalled afterwards by a ship contractor, Ian Deheer, with whom he had worked there. "'I have brought my bike up, would you like to see it?'" Lawrence asked. "'Most certainly,'" Deheer replied. "He took me up to the cycle, which with him standing alongside, looked enormous. I was taken aback at the size of it and remarked, 'You will be breaking your blinking neck on it,' and his reply was, 'Well, better than dying in bed.'"[115]

# 32

# Retirement and Death

From the standpoint of the service at least, Lawrence's years had been successful, for his discharge forms contained this summary: "He is an exceptional airman in every respect and his character and general conduct have at all times been 'very good.'" A document from the Ministry of Labor among his discharge papers was more specific and conveys a sense that his transformation was quite complete: "This airman has a habit of pushing any job too far. He can do rather too many things. He prefers a small job to a big one. Job preferred: motor yacht hand. Seasonally only and in a small craft. . . . References: None — best reference probably manager British Power Boat Company or Wing Commander."[1]

On February 26 Lawrence left Bridlington on his bicycle, having decided that his income from investments of twenty-five shillings a week would make it difficult to maintain his motorcycle. "I'm riding out of Bridlington at this moment, aiming South but with no destination in view," he wrote to an RAF sergeant.[2] He dropped in (as was his way) on the Arnold Lawrences in Cambridge the next day (it was the last time the brothers were to see each other). He seemed steady, at ease and content, and spoke of passing the time exploring the countryside or printing.[3] He intended to go to Clouds Hill for a time, but otherwise his plans were curiously indefinite. To one person or another he had told of his desire to visit Iceland, take up his dream of printing, tour the Midlands,[4] travel in England with Eric Kennington, or just "wander for most of this year about England."[5]

He had planned to visit Frederic Manning on his way south but discovered that Manning had recently died. He quickly sent off a letter to Manning's friend and publisher, Peter Davies, expressing his sadness and regret that Manning had died unknown and unappreciated. Lawrence's grief over Manning's death blended with his sense of loss with regard to the air force and he wrote to Davies of his longing for death: "I find myself wishing all the time that my own curtain would fall."[6]

As Lawrence disliked wearing a crash helmet when he rode his Brough, Jock Chambers was relieved to hear that Lawrence traveled by bicycle on this trip.[7] Staying in youth hostels along the way, Lawrence arrived in London in the first days of March, having been shocked to discover en route that Clouds Hill was besieged with reporters and photographers, who damaged the roof of the cottage and trampled the land. He took an apartment in London under the name of E. Smith (he had used this before), went about London feeling quite lost,[8] and spent much of the month "wandering about the South Country."[9] The reporters left and he returned to the cottage in mid-March, but so did they.[10] They refused to leave and insisted on interviewing and photographing him. He punched "the most exigent" one of them in the eye so hard that the man had to see a doctor, and rode off on his bicycle back to London with a sore hand.

On March 22 Lawrence suggested to Liddell Hart that he write a book to be called "Fifteen Decisive British Defeats,"[11] and on the same day had a long conversation with Ralph Isham in which they talked about the threat of European war and the more imminent concern about war between Italy and Ethiopia. Lawrence predicted that if war came in Ethiopia conflict between dark and white races would spread over the world.[12] Lawrence himself was approached by the government on whether he might be interested in taking part in the reorganization of Home Defense by serving as the deputy and eventual successor on the defense side to Lord Hankey.[13] He toyed with the idea for a while, and expressed in a conversation with Herbert Baker "a desire to serve in the guiding of it."[14] But, in his brother's words, "after oppressed hesitation he saw means to avoid an active participation in the replanning of national defence — which began immediately with a great expansion of the Air Force."[15]

At the end of March Lawrence visited Ede, who gave him a check for twenty or thirty pounds so that he could afford his motorbike. Although Lawrence thanked him and accepted the check initially, it was found in his cottage uncashed after his death. Ede wrote that he "felt very strongly" after their conversation that Lawrence "really had at last come through the war, or almost so, and I kept thinking that two years, or three of country life would see him embarked on some new activity which would swamp out his previous record."[16]

Lawrence's view of himself at this time was different: "I'm gray-haired and toothless, half blind and shaking at the knees," he wrote to one serviceman, and to another: "The active part of life is over."[17]

Finally, through a combination of writing and personal visits he was able to achieve an "unholy compact" with the Newspaper Proprietor's Association and a precarious peace with the reporters that enabled him to return to Clouds Hill at the end of March. In the weeks of April and May that remained, Lawrence sought the peaceful existence that had always eluded him. He does not in fact seem to have done very much during these last weeks. He spent his time "inventing odd jobs," such as cutting and gathering wood, laying pipe, and building. He fitted the cottage with a large porthole, and tried unsuccessfully to drive off a persistent small bird which fluttered for hours a day against a windowpane. ("First I thought he was a bird-pressman, trying to get a story: then a narcissist, admiring his figure in the glass. Now I think he is just mad.")[18]

Although Lawrence continued to feel "like a lost dog" he was pleased that the navy was ordering "by the dozen for all ships" the fast small dinghies he had developed. He thought the hulls of ships like destroyers should be redesigned so that they could plane (like hovercraft) and thus achieve speeds of 70 knots.[19] At the end of April he traveled to Hythe for a last meeting with Beauforte-Greenwood and Flight Lieutenant Norrington to accept a gift of stainless steel candlesticks in commemoration of their association in the building of the dinghies.[20]

As he began his second month of leisure the pain Lawrence experienced over the loss of the RAF had grown "worse instead of healing over,"[21] and this made him feel "queer and baffled."[22] To Bruce Rogers he wrote on May 6: "I'm 'out' now of the R.A.F. and sitting in my cottage rather puzzled to find out what has happened to me, is happening and will happen. At present the feeling is mere bewilderment. I imagine leaves must feel like this after they have fallen from the tree and until they die. Let's hope that will not be my continuing state."[23] He used the same image in a letter to Eric Kennington: "What I have done, what I am doing, what I am going to do, puzzle me and bewilder me. Have you ever been a leaf and fallen from your tree in autumn and been really puzzled about it? That's the feeling."[24]

Lady Astor made a last effort to draw Lawrence to Cliveden to discuss his role in the reorganization of the defense forces. But he was not interested. "No," he replied to her letter on May 8, "wild mares would not at present take me away from Clouds Hill. . . . Also there is something broken in the works, as I told you: my will, I think. In this mood I would not take on any job at all."[25]

Lawrence made plans to have various visitors at his cottage — E. M. Forster and Aircraftsman Dunn among others — but does not seem to have had any guests during these days. On May 12, the day before his fatal accident he wrote, "At present I'm sitting in my cottage and getting used to an empty life."[26]

One of his visitors was to be Henry Williamson, who wished to come to Clouds Hill to discuss his ideas about Anglo-German relations. Williamson wrote to Lawrence that he would arrive as planned unless the day was rainy. I discussed with Williamson in 1965 his recollections of what he had in mind in requesting such a meeting. Williamson was a friend of the English fascist Oswald Mosley, and he and Mosley had talked about Hitler, whom Williamson regarded as unbalanced or unstable mentally, but who had a capacity to accomplish something positive for Europe if "someone could send him along the proper track." Somehow Williamson got into his head the notion that only Lawrence could send Hitler along this "proper track," although Lawrence — Williamson stated this explicitly — had no sympathy with the dictator or with the German government. Williamson did not recall what he put into his letter, whether in fact it contained any references to these political fantasies. The letter was not discovered among Lawrence's possessions after his death. Its disappearance gave rise to speculation that it was taken by a newspaperman or suppressed. It has never been found.[27]

On the morning of May 13, Lawrence rode on the Brough (he had recently begun to use it again) to Bovington Camp about a mile from Clouds Hill to wire Williamson to come ahead for lunch the next day, whether it was wet or fine. There is no evidence that Lawrence's interest in such a meeting had anything to do with a wish to discuss Williamson's political schemes. They were friends, Lawrence was lonely and lacking in companionship at this time, and, as Knightley and Simpson have pointed out, the two had common literary interests.[28]

On the return trip from Bovington Lawrence was traveling at 50 to 60 miles an hour[29] — an unsafe speed, but one he could ordinarily have managed — when he came suddenly upon two boys at a rise in the road just before the cottage. They were on bicycles, going one behind the other, in the same direction he was. A black car or delivery van had just passed, going in the opposite direction, and may have been distracting. Lawrence swerved suddenly to avoid the boys, flew over the handlebars, and fell in the road, suffering fatal head injuries.[30] He lingered for nearly six days in a coma at the Bovington Camp hospital and died on the morning of May 19, 1935. To avoid publicity visitors were limited. A few friends, among them Colonel Newcombe and Lord Carlow, stayed at the bedside to the end. The King telephoned the hospital to inquire about the fallen hero, and when Lawrence's death was known wrote to Arnold Lawrence, "His name will live in history."

The funeral was held at the Moreton village church on the afternoon of May 21 near Clouds Hill and was attended by mourners who had known Lawrence in various phases of his career: former comrades-in-arms, government dignitaries, artists, writers, military officers and enlisted men. The service was simple and brief, and the parson faltered as if overcome with emotion. The coffin was buried in a leaf-lined churchyard grave.[31]

Clare Sydney Smith's letter to Mrs. Shaw the day after Lawrence's death is characteristic of the reactions of his friends: "For myself I am heartbroken," she wrote. "For him I cannot feel sad. He wasn't a happy man, and he was lonely — But what a loss, and I know you and your husband will feel it sadly."[32] On the same day as this letter was written the New York *Times* reported a statement of 'Ata Amin, chargé d'affaires at the Iraqi Embassy in New York: "The Arab nation has lost a great friend. . . . Lawrence did his utmost in striving for the independence of our nation, he was the champion of the Arab's cause not only during the war but afterward at the Peace Conference."[33] Trenchard also wrote to Arnold Lawrence the day after T.E.'s death, "His influence for the Air Force was all for good," but Lawrence's service file contains a note, written the day after the funeral, stating that nothing would be published "dealing with Lawrence's service in the R.A.F. since there is little that can be said of a period devoted to self-effacement."[34] Seven months later a memorial service was held for Lawrence in St. Paul's Cathedral, London, at which a bust of him was unveiled in the crypt. Mrs. Lawrence offered to pay the railway fare of any of her son's service friends who wished to attend but could not afford to.[35]

Soon dramatic stories, some with sinister political implications, were spread about the circumstances of his death, but I could find no information to substantiate them.[36]

The question of a possible self-destructive or suicidal element in Lawrence's death is more complex. Arnold Lawrence has written of the "despondency" that overshadowed his brother after retirement and that had not lifted by the time of the accident. He suggests that Lawrence rode at a somewhat excessive speed to "forget himself for a few seconds" and that he thus rode "into a catastrophe which the normal quickness of his brain might possibly have averted; as it was, he saved others from injury."[37] The pattern of letters in the last months of Lawrence's life, especially those written after his RAF retirement, suggest a continuing and progressive despair and emptiness. There is no relieving plan, nothing to suggest a revival of new interest in living. It is hard for me to agree with Churchill's opinion that had he lived "some overpowering need would draw him from the modest path he chose to tread and set him once again in full action at the centre of memorable events."[38] It is a useless argument.

There is no evidence of a direct suicidal intent in the accident. But it is known that men who are living without hope or interest in their lives, or have suffered a recent severe loss, like Lawrence's loss of his work in the RAF, are more prone to accidents. The self becomes less attentive to its own preservation. The immediate period of retirement is a well-known time of depression, despair and even suicide for men leaving the security of the armed forces. The RAF had furnished Lawrence with certainty, security and companionship, and a life containing worthwhile work and activities; at the same time it provided relief from larger responsibilities. He had found nothing to take its place, and in his despondency and increasing nihilism was prone to "forget himself," as his brother has described.

Lawrence did not, in my opinion, commit suicide. He was, however, less vigorous in preserving his own life than he might once have been. When he suddenly became aware of the boys on bicycles in front of him his natural response was to protect them from injury, even at the risk of his own safety. Mrs. Smith wrote at the end of *The Golden Reign*, "His strongest impulse was to save life, and he lost his own in doing so."[39]

# SIX

# FURTHER  DIMENSIONS

# 33

# Intimacy, Sexuality and Penance

Every biographer confronts aspects of his subject's life that do not lend themselves to treatment within the chronological sequence of events. This is especially true of themes that relate to the subject's character, or to his intimate or private life. Although these more personal, more psychological, dimensions may be only intermittently apparent or may be visible for the first time relatively late in the subject's life, they usually are organically related to other, earlier times and experiences, even childhood ones. They grow out of the very fabric of the personality.

As I have tried to show in various parts of this book, there are demonstrable connections between elements of Lawrence's personal history and psychology and his actions that have historical importance. I suspect that all public figures are like Lawrence in this respect, although these connections are perhaps more readily discernible in Lawrence's life because of the conflicts with which he struggled and his gifts as an introspective psychologist.

In this section I will deal with some of these personal, more private dimensions, which do not readily find a place in any single part of this narrative. Although they may at times make for painful reading, I feel that their inclusion in this work is necessary if Lawrence is to be fully understood and appreciated.

Arnold Lawrence once concluded a letter to me at a time when we were trying to place his brother's beating problem in a broader psychological perspective, "I don't see why a man's choice of sexual outlet should matter much biographically; everyone has one, or should, and his was predetermined by accidental circumstances."[1] This statement, linking the flagellation disorder with the Der'a incident, raises an important question. Despite the current public openness about sex, a person's sexuality, like the rest of his personal or intimate life, remains his private business, and the biographer may be required to have some justification beyond the potential interest of his readers for making its details public.

Nor is a purely clinical interest adequate, for in professional journals the publication of intimate personal or physical details for the purposes of advancing scientific knowledge is done with accepted safeguards of anonymity and privacy. Obviously, for a public figure like Lawrence no disguise of identity is possible, and the effect of such disclosures on the sensibilities and feelings of relatives and friends, and upon the continuing rights of the dead to remain interred with some privacy respected, merits careful consideration.

The biographer's justification for exploring the sexual (or any other intimate aspect of the life of the person being studied) is his belief that it is vitally related to his public life, that understanding it is essential to understanding the subject's character in general, or that in itself its details are potentially of such unique scientific or humanitarian interest that publication will be of value. In my opinion all of these conditions pertain to some degree in Lawrence's case. Up to the time of the war, it is difficult to establish precise connections between Lawrence's sexuality and its related conflicts and the directions of his life, although I believe such connections exist. After the war, however, they are unmistakable. Furthermore, the intricacies of Lawrence's sexual life are so fundamentally bound up with other aspects of his character that it is not possible to understand the latter fully without some exploration of the sexual aspect. The converse is also, of course, true — that his sexuality is not explicable without a full understanding of his development as a person. In its details and in the elaboration of related rituals, Lawrence's sexuality, though by no means unique, seems to me sufficiently unusual and revealing of the relationship between private psychology and public action as to warrant examination in its own right. Finally, I believe that much of his suffering, which he felt obliged to hide, was the outcome of his early development. Insofar as his early development was affected by prevailing social attitudes, it is of value to show candidly what misery they caused him, if only to contribute to their modification in the future.

Freud, wishing perhaps to be faithful to his medical background and profession, clung for several decades to a rather narrow biological view of sexuality, although he recognized its obvious links to love and to many human relationships. In recent decades psychoanalysts, dynamic psychologists and other students of psycho-sexuality have given increasing attention to aspects of early sexual development and family life, to the part played by sexuality in a wide range of human relationships, and to the links between sexuality and other human drives and emotions, for example, love, fear, ambition, power and aggression. Perhaps the problem is not only one of definition. Sexuality in its biological sense may be narrowly defined, yet also be approached broadly in terms of its importance to the image an individual has of himself and to his personal, professional, social and political relationships.

My own approach to the study of sexuality in general and Lawrence's in particular combines humanistic, psychoanalytic and medical perspectives, and is both narrow and comprehensive. It is narrow in limiting "sexuality" to specifically sexual attitudes and practices; it is broad in seeing these attitudes and practices in a variety of perspectives and contexts. These include most prominently a developmental approach (that is, the view of adult sexuality as emerging from family influences and from relationships in childhood or other earlier developmental stages); a respect for the role of what in his brother's case Arnold Lawrence called "accidental circumstances" in shaping the direction of a person's sexuality; the recognition of inborn genetic or biological factors; a stress on the links between sexuality and love (and other emotions) in human relationships; and, finally, the influence of society, culture and even politics upon sexual attitudes, choices and decisions.

Lawrence was a child of his age. His childhood in Oxford was spent during the decades of late Victorian England, which saw Oscar Wilde's career destroyed when his homosexual practices were revealed. It was an age burdened by a religiosity, an extreme form of which Edmund Gosse, one of the period's most devastating critics, describes as a social force which invented virtues, both "sterile and cruel," sins "which are no sins at all," and darkened "the heaven of innocent joy with futile clouds of remorse."[2] For Lawrence, the strict social and religious codes which prevailed in England around the turn of the century were augmented by the profound personal sense of sin with which his parents were afflicted as a result of their liaison, what he called "the uprooting of their lives and principles."

One of the central developmental tasks of childhood, especially for boys, is to establish sufficient emotional distance from the mother to allow the pursuit of an independent life. Ideally this life would include the choice of a partner sufficiently distinguished from the mother not to fall under the prohibitions of the incest taboos or be made otherwise intolerable by associations with her. The schoolboy years before adolescence are those in which the boy is turning away from the intimacies of early childhood and pursuing instead a variety of nonsexual relationships and interests in school or in other situations outside the home. The onset of puberty is followed generally by the search for sexual contact, again outside the home. The persistence of attachment to the mother may be discerned principally through idealized comparisons of the partner with her, in the choice of a partner who is valued as the mother (or sister) was, or who may even share her valued attributes. The conveying of standards and values by parents, and the various rebuffs and scoldings which so irritate their sons, serve among other things to aid this process of establishing distance.

Now let us examine what happened to Lawrence. As far as we can tell, intimacy with the mother was present in his early childhood, although he received physical affection more continuously from nurses. Religious and intellectual values and devotion of the members of the family to each other were exaggerated as a result of parental guilt and self-imposed social isolation. The boys were strictly brought up in an atmosphere that stressed a high degree of propriety, if not chastity, and they were encouraged to develop a great range of interests and skills outside of the home, in which the father constructively shared. It was in this context that Lawrence gradually discovered the discrepancy between the fundamentalist values the parents taught him, and purported to follow themselves, and the reality of their actual situation. The same mother for whom Oscar Wilde was a dirty word and who disapproved of theatres and dancing was herself living in an adulterous relationship, to which the father had also subscribed. During a period in which he was attempting to achieve distance from his mother and to put his emotional attachment to her behind him, Lawrence was reminded of the illicit nature of her relationship with his father and of the contradictions inherent in it. In addition, to fulfill her own needs, Mrs. Lawrence seems to have been unusually demanding of her sons for intimacy and expressions of love, a trait which was most clearly evident after she had lost two of them in the war.

Lawrence leaves little doubt that the discovery of his illegitimacy and his relationship with his mother had a profound effect upon his subsequent development. When he was nearly forty years old, he could still write Mrs. Shaw that he found his mother "very exciting" and that "probably she is exactly like me; otherwise we wouldn't so hanker after one another, whenever we are wise enough to keep apart." His inability to find a mate who would bear his children Lawrence attributed directly to his relationship with his mother. "Knowledge of her," he wrote Mrs. Shaw, "will prevent my ever making any woman a mother, and the cause of children." Thomas Lawrence could not have helped his son in this struggle, even if he had understood it, for he was viewed by Lawrence as "her trophy of power."

We have seen how during adolescence Lawrence did not seek out what opportunities for contact with the opposite sex were available to him (certainly fewer in the Oxford of his youth than they would be in the present day), and devoted his energies to nonsexual pursuits, to testing and inuring himself, and to mastering a great variety of skills, as if in preparation for some great task. Lawrence's one attempt to form a heterosexual bond during his youth was with an early childhood friend, Janet

Laurie, and ended in failure. Hurt by the rejection, Lawrence feigned, like Hippocleides, not to care. He went to live and work in the Middle East, where he immersed himself in a culture in which women, if not openly devalued, were at least made largely inconspicuous. Association with men was more congenial to him in any event: he had been brought up in a family of five boys and had attended an all-male school and college. Thereafter, he lived largely in societies of men. The circumstances of life at Carchemish necessitated that daily contact be primarily with men, although Lawrence established valuable friendships with women at the mission school at Jebail, and he showed great consideration and kindness toward Mrs. Fontana and other female visitors to the site. At Cairo and during the campaigns his contacts were also principally with men, war being almost exclusively a male exercise. In the peacetime armed forces Lawrence chose an all-male society, quite removed from the company of women.

In *Seven Pillars of Wisdom* Lawrence acknowledged his "craving to be liked — so strong and nervous that never could I open myself friendly to another," yet made it clear that he had shrunk from physical intimacy in any form: "The lower creation I avoided as a reflection upon our failure to attain real intellectuality. If they forced themselves on me I hated them.[3] To put my hand on a living thing was defilement; and it made me tremble if they touched me or took too quick an interest in me. This was an atomic repulsion, like the intact course of a snowflake. The opposite would have been my choice if my head had not been tyrannous. I had a longing for the absolutism of women and animals, and lamented myself most when I saw a soldier with a girl, or a man fondling a dog, because my wish was to be as superficial, as perfected; and my jailer held me back. Always feeling and illusion were at war within me, reasons strong enough to win. . . . I liked the things underneath me and took my pleasures downward. There seemed a certainty in degradation, a final safety. Man could rise to any height, but there was an animal level beneath which he could not fall."[4]

The assault by the Turks at Der'a was, as we know, a shattering experience for Lawrence. The memory of it haunted him, and he described its impact to Mrs. Shaw in terms reminiscent of his brother's account of the mother's childhood beatings, done to break Lawrence's will. More than six years after the incident Lawrence wrote of it to Mrs. Shaw in connection with the trial scene of Shaw's *Saint Joan*. Lawrence seems to have identified himself with Joan: "Poor Joan. I was thinking of her as a person, not as a moral lesson. The pain meant more to her than the example. You instance my night at Deraa. Well, I'm always afraid of being hurt: and to me, while I live, the force of that night will lie in the agony which broke me, and made me surrender. It's the individual view. You can't share it.

"About that night. I shouldn't tell you, because decent men don't talk about such things. I wanted to put it plain in the book, wrestled for days with my self respect . . . which wouldn't, hasn't let me. For fear of being hurt, or rather to earn five minutes respite from a pain which drove me mad, I gave away the only possession we are born into the world with — our bodily integrity. It's an unforgiveable matter, an irrecoverable position: and it's that which has made me foreswear decent living, and the exercise of my not-contemptible wits and talents.

"You may call this morbid: but think of the offence, and the intensity of my brooding over it for these years. It will hang about me while I live, and afterwards if our personality survives. Consider wandering among the decent ghosts hereafter, crying 'Unclean, Unclean!' "[5]

I do not find any inconsistency between this account and the more lurid and dramatic one in *Seven Pillars;* nor do I find substantiation in this passage of Aldington's assertion that Lawrence "yielded to the Bey's pederasty" rather than to the soldiers as described in the earlier version. More significant, the emphasis in the letter to Mrs. Shaw upon the overwhelming of his "bodily integrity," or in *Seven Pillars,* upon the loss of "the citadel of my integrity," is very similar to the way in which Lawrence viewed the threat of intimacy with his mother.

"I think I'm afraid of letting her get, ever so little inside the circle of my integrity," he wrote in 1928, "and she is always hammering and sapping to get in"; and, three months later, "I always felt that she was laying siege to me, and would conquer, if I left a chink unguarded."[6] These passages about his mother were written, of course, long after the Der'a episode, but they suggest that at the very least the incident aroused or revived earlier conflicts in Lawrence's relationship with his mother, a need to avoid surrendering to her desires and demands which, in view of the childhood beatings at her hands, may also have had the meaning of self-surrender. In any event, the flagellation disorder with which Lawrence was afflicted during his years in the ranks, and which will be discussed later in this chapter, appears to have been directly connected to the Der'a episode. In the absence of direct evidence, the linking of this disorder with Lawrence's relationship to his mother and to the childhood beatings becomes a matter of likelihood or of interpretation, for which no further evidence will probably be forthcoming.[7]

I have found no evidence that Lawrence ever as an adult entered voluntarily into a sexual relationship for the purpose of achieving intimacy or pleasure. This applies equally to heterosexual and homosexual relationships. There are a few passages in his letters and notes which indicate a longing for sexual experience, but no evidence that he could act on these longings, and much evidence that he could not. The evidence certainly does not support the view that Lawrence was "asexual," but rather that

British forces entering
Damascus, October 1918.
Below: The Damascus Town
Hall soon after the surrender
of the city. From the Bodleian
Library, Oxford

McBey portrait of Lawrence at the time of the capture of Damascus.
The picture hangs in the Old Bursary at Jesus College, Oxford.
Courtesy of the Principal and Fellows of Jesus College, Oxford

Statuette of Lawrence by Lady Kennet, 1921, which was formerly
in the City of Oxford High School. Photograph by the author

Lawrence (second from left), Sir Herbert Samuel (third from left), Abdullah (next to Samuel) and others at Amman, April 1921. From the Imperial War Museum, London

Queen Mary, Trenchard and other officers walk past aircraft at St. Omer, July 1917. From the Imperial War Museum, London

The story which follows was first written out in Paris during the Peace Conference, from notes (mainly of impressions) jotted daily on the march, strengthened by some reports sent to my chiefs in Cairo. Afterwards, in the autumn of 1919, this first draft and some of the notes were lost. It seemed to me needful to reproduce the tale for historical purposes, as perhaps no one but myself in Feisal's army had thought of writing down at the time what we felt, what we hoped, what we tried. So it was all built up again in London in the winter of 1919-20, from memory and my surviving notes. The record of events was not dull in me, and perhaps few actual mistakes crept in—except in details of dates or numbers—but the outlines and significance of things had lost edge in the haze of new interests, and consequently the story lacked force. However, this was inevitable, and, as hardly anyone but myself saw the original edition, it would be silly to grow sorry for its loss.

*First page of the 1922 (Oxford) edition of Seven Pillars of Wisdom. This was the copy from which Edward Garnett made his unpublished abridgment in 1922. The deletions are Garnett's. Courtesy of the Harvard College Library*

Lawrence's draft preface for Edward Garnett's 1922 abridgment of *Seven Pillars of Wisdom*. Courtesy of the Harvard College Library

Clouds Hill, Lawrence's cottage. The Greek words over the front door,
which were carved by Lawrence himself, mean "Does Not Care."
From the Bodleian Library, Oxford

Miranshah, the remote Indian fort in the foothills of the Himalayas, where Lawrence was posted in 1928. From the Bodleian Library, Oxford

Lawrence at Miranshah.
From the National Portrait Gallery

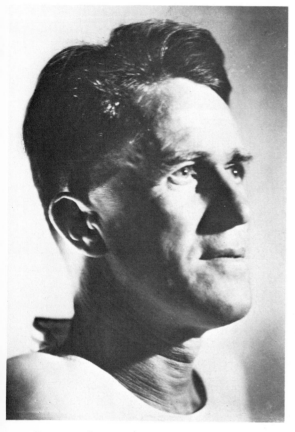

Portrait of Lawrence by Howard Costa,
done around 1930. Courtesy of the
Harvard College Library

With friends in Devonshire. From *The Golden Reign*
by Clare Sydney Smith

T. E. S.

Lawrence at Plymouth in 1930. From *The Golden
Reign* by Clare Sydney Smith

Squeak, 🦢
Squeak, 🦢
Squeak 🦢.

from

T.

E.

S.

Inscription by Lawrence on the
front page of *Child of the Deep*
by Joan Lowell. The book
belonged to Sydney Smith's
daughter, nicknamed "Squeak."
From *The Golden Reign* by
Clare Sydney Smith

RAF 200 leaving from Plymouth. On board are
Fl/Lt. Beaufort-Greenwood, Wing Commander De Courcey,
A/Lt. Norrington, Corporal Bradbury and Aircraftsman Shaw.
This boat put up a new record between Southampton and
Plymouth. From the Bodleian Library, Oxford

For

Sir Emery Walker:                    Wilfred Merton
        Knight            |              Treasurer

Bruce Rogers          —          Miss Saunders
      Printer                              Scribe

This last page of my version of the
O D Y S S E Y
upon which I have spent almost as long as
O D Y S S E U S
and travelled further......

x  x  x  x  x  x  x

Which has furnished me with luxuries for five years
And so wholly occupied my hours off duty that I have had no leisure
to enjoy them....

is
affectionately, kindly,
gratefully,
gladly
and
with enormous relief & glee
P R E S E N T E D .....

                                    T. E. Shaw
Note by Sir Emery              15 · VIII · 31.

Some three years late on the contract! Otherwise well!

The final page of Lawrence's translation of the
*Odyssey*. Courtesy of the Bodleian Library, Oxford

Lawrence (left) and Captain
Basil Liddell Hart in 1933.
Courtesy of Arnold Lawrence

Lawrence at Bridlington,
December 1934. Photograph by
Reginald Sims. courtesy of
Mrs. Hilda Sims

Bust of Lawrence by Eric Kennington (copy) in the chapel of
Jesus College. The original is in the crypt of St. Paul's Cathedral in
London. Photograph by the author

his early development brought about a deep need to reject and devalue all intimacy between the sexes, and gave rise to intense fears and inhibitions that prevented action.

The clearest statement of Lawrence's sexual puritanism, inhibition and conflict occurs in a letter to Mrs. Shaw in 1925: "I'm *too shy* to go looking for dirt. I'm afraid of seeming a novice in it, when I found it. That's why I can't go off stewing in the Lincoln or Navenly brothels with the fellows. They think it's because I'm superior, proud, or peculiar or 'posh,' as they say: and it's because I wouldn't know what to do, how to carry myself, where to stop. Fear again: fear everywhere. Garnett once said that I was two people, in my book: one wanting to go on, the other wanting to go back. That is not right. Naturally the very strong one, Say 'No,' the Puritan, is in firm charge, and the other poor little vicious fellow, can't get a word in, for fear of him. My reason tells me all the while, dins into me day and night, a sense of how I've crashed my life and self and gone hopelessly wrong: and hopelessly it is, for I'm never coming back, and I want to: Oh dear Oh dear, what a coil. Here come the rest [the other airmen in the barracks]: so here endeth the wail. No more thinking for awhile. I'm pitching it straight away to you as written, because in an hour I'll burn it, if I can get my hands on it."[8]

Lawrence strove to isolate psychologically the physical aspect of sex from its emotional and intimate dimensions, thus vulgarizing and demeaning the act and reducing it to a mechanical and trivial performance. He retained a scatalogical view of sexuality that reflected the persistence of a schoolboy attitude. Although this attitude was naturally defensive — that is, protected him from having to deal with the emotional meaning of love linked with mature sexuality — it was a view so tenaciously held, and so frequently elaborated, as to become a matter of conviction and personal philosophy. Even in *Seven Pillars of Wisdom* Lawrence wrote that he chided the venerable 'Awdah abu-Tayyi: "To gain ground with him, I began to jeer at the old man for being so old and yet so foolish like the rest of his race, who regarded our comic reproductive processes not as an unhygienic pleasure, but as a main business of life."[9]

In *The Mint* Lawrence wrote candidly of his ignorance of the realities of the sexual act, which he claims to have shared with many other enlisted men: "Sound momentary: sight momentary: smell? Why, a minute after our personality returns home from an absence, we do not even smell ourselves. Touch? I do not know. I fear and shun touch most, of my senses. At Oxford the select preacher, one evening service, speaking of venery, said, 'And let me implore you, my young friends, not to imperil your immortal souls upon a pleasure which, *so I am credibly informed*, lasts less than one and three-quarter minutes.' Of direct experience I cannot speak, never having been tempted so to peril my mortal soul: and six out of ten enlisted fellows share my ignorance, despite their flaming talk.

Shyness and a wish to be clean have imposed chastity on so many of the younger airmen, whose life spends itself and is spent in the enforced celibacy of their blankets' harsh embrace. But if the perfect partnership, indulgence with a living body, is as brief as the solitary act, then the climax is indeed no more than a convulsion, a razor-edge of time, which palls so on return that the temptation flickers out into the indifference of tired disgust once a blue moon, when nature compels it."[10]

Lawrence's friend F. L. Lucas, a Cambridge don and poet, read *The Mint* in 1929 and questioned these inaccurate speculations in a letter. "Is that genuine ignorance?" he inquired. "I mean the reader cries 'Oh he *must* learn better, if only by hearsay.' Anything up to several hours, they say, in India."[11] Lawrence, sticking to his guns, replied: "The period of enjoyment, in sex, seems to be a very doubtful one. I've asked the fellows in this hut (three or four go with women regularly). They are not sure: but they say it's all over in ten minutes: and the preliminaries — which I discounted — take up most of the ten minutes. For myself, I haven't tried it, and hope not to. I doubt if any man could time his excitement without a stop watch: and that's a cold-blooded sort of notion."[12]

To Robert Graves, who had also read *The Mint* and also challenged Lawrence's assertions about the sex act, Lawrence was even more explicit in defending his views: "Your last page, about fucking, defeats me wholly. As I wrote (with some courage, I think: few people admit the damaging ignorance) I haven't ever and don't much want to. 1-¾ minutes was the Bishop's remark: judging from the way people talk it's transient, if 2-¾ or 3-¾ or 3 hours + ¾s. So I don't feel I miss much; and it must have a dirty feeling, too. However, your positive, comparative, superlative (we make it fucking good

        bastard good

        f. bastard good)

    defeats me wholly."[13]

Although he had many women acquaintances with whom he got along well, especially among the wives of his friends, Lawrence's attitudes toward marriage and toward women in their sexual and reproductive functions grew out of his personal history and conflicts. At the same time these conflicts allowed him to question and challenge the sanctity of marriage. "Marriage-contracts should have a clause terminating the engagement upon nine months notice by either party," he wrote Edward Garnett in 1923.[14] And in *The Mint*: "An idea (as of the normality of marriage, which gives the man a natural, cheap, sure and ready bed-partner), if they [the enlisted men] have grown up with it, has become already, at their age of twenty, enthroned and unchallengeable, by mere use."[15]

Despite his appreciation of many women as human beings (clearly he appraised women as individuals on their own merit and "had more respect for women as *people* than many men"),[16] Lawrence seemed often to devalue the entire sex, if no more than by the implications of his cynicism. "I'm frigid toward woman so that I can withstand her: so that I want to withstand her," he wrote to Sydney Cockerell in 1924.[17] Five years later, in irritation at the implications of newspaper stories about his RAF service he wrote: "Because I don't drink or smoke or dance, all things can be invented. Please believe that I don't either love or hate the entire sex of women. There are good ones and bad ones, I find: much the same as men and dogs and motor bicycles."[18]

Although he was deeply understanding of the struggles and sufferings of women in their reproductive roles — especially when they had failed — Lawrence found the functions related to childbirth, like all other aspects of the sexual and reproductive processes, somehow demeaning. Yet he recognized that his attitudes grew out of the painful history of his own life. In 1924 he wrote to Mrs. Shaw his views on these matters: "Birth . . . seems to me so sorry and squalid an accident . . . if fathers and mothers took thought before bringing children into this misery of a world, only the monsters among them would dare to go through with it. The motive which brings the sexes together is 99% sexual pleasure, and only 1% the desire of children, in men, so far as I can learn. As I told you, I haven't been carried away in that sense, so that I'm a bad subject to treat of it. Perhaps the possibility of a child relieves sometimes what otherwise must seem an unbearable humiliation to the woman: — for I presume it's unbearable. However, here I'm trenching on dangerous ground, with my own ache coming to life again. I hate and detest this animal side — and I can't find comfort in your compartmenting up our personalities. Mind, spirit, soul, body, sense and consciousness — angles of one identity, seen from different points of the compass."[19]

Lawrence was contemptuous of women as writers: "All the women who ever wrote original stuff could have been strangled at birth, and the history of English literature (and my bookshelves) would be unchanged,"[20] an exaggerated attitude which may have been influenced by other feelings about women. In a letter to Harley Granville-Barker Lawrence linked (as many do unconsciously) literary productivity to biological reproduction: "I can't write, and wouldn't if I could, since creation, without conviction, is only a nasty vice. You have to be very eager-spirited to overcome the disgust of reproduction."[21] This comment may contribute to the understanding of Lawrence's intense conflicts and inhibitions concerning literary production: as he was repelled by the biological process, so too he often looked with disgust upon his own efforts to produce literary works.

One of the appeals the society of enlisted men had for Lawrence was probably the fact that, although active sexually where he was not, the other enlisted men shared in many respects his immature and limited views of sexual functioning, and his need to separate the physical aspect of sex from its emotional significance. To the writer James Hanley, Lawrence wrote in 1931: "I've lived in barracks now, for nine years: preferring the plain man to the elaborated man. I find them forthcoming, honest, friendly, and so comfortable. They do not pretend at all, and with them I have not to pretend. Sex, with them, is something you put on (and take off) with your walking-out dress: on Friday night, certainly: and if you are lucky on Saturday afternoon, and most of Sunday. Work begins on Monday again, and is really important."[22]

This trivialization of sexuality occurs over and over again in Lawrence's letters. He even went to the lengths of denying differences between women and men. To Ernest Thurtle, his friend in the House of Commons, he wrote, "Women? I like some women. I don't like their sex: any more than I like the monstrous regiment of men. There is no difference that I can feel between a woman and a man. They look different, granted: but if you work with them there doesn't seem any difference at all. I can't understand all the fuss about sex. It's as obvious as red hair: and as little fundamental, I fancy."[23] Or, still more stridently, two weeks later, to Edward Marsh (Churchill's secretary) upon rereading *Lady Chatterley's Lover*: "I'm deeply puzzled and hurt by this Lady Chatterley of his. Surely the sex business isn't worth all this damned fuss? I've met only a handful of people who really cared a biscuit for it."[24]

Although he was as inhibited in relation to direct physical intimacy with men as with women, I believe it is accurate to say that Lawrence was less uncomfortable with homosexual than with heterosexual concepts and behavior. "Homosexuality disgusted him far less than the abuse of normal sex and the attitude of some of the men in the huts in the R.A.F. or Tank Corps," his brother has written.[25] And Lawrence himself wrote to Charlotte Shaw: "I've seen lots of man-and-man loves: very lovely and fortunate some of them were. I take it women can be the same. And if our minds so go, why not our bodies? There's only a wall between farm and farmyard."[26]

Lawrence's closest attachments were with men, whom he was far more likely to take seriously or idealize. It was, however, nonsexual friendship or intimacy, even playfulness, surely companionship, and sometimes intellectual stimulation, that Lawrence sought in these attachments, rather than erotic contact. His airman friend A. E. "Jock" Chambers has described to me Lawrence's discomfort with physical openness or intimacy, even of a playful kind. Lawrence seemed embarrassed to be seen naked, even by Chambers, who shared in many respects his older friend's repudiation of physical sexuality. Once Chambers gave Lawrence a bear hug from behind in playful roughhousing, pinning his arms briefly behind his back. He could sense immediately that Lawrence did not like it and so quickly stopped.[27]

Lawrence indicated the greater conscious physical appeal of men to him in notes that have been preserved in his private papers, jotted down perhaps in the course of making notes for an autobiography to be called "Confessions of Faith": "Occasionally my eyes seem suddenly switched on to my brain, and I see a thing all the more clear in contrast with the former mustiness, in these things nearly always shapes — rocks or trees or figures of living things — not small things like flowers . . . : and in the figures always men. I take no pleasure in women. I have never thought twice or even once of the shape of a woman: but men's bodies, in repose or in movement — especially the former, appeal to me directly and very generally."[28]

Lawrence's sexual constriction and inhibition contrast sharply with his tolerance and acceptance of the sexuality of others, and his willingness to deal with the subject directly and openly in his writings ("a sexual frankness which would cause most authors to be run in by the police," E. M. Forster wrote in his review of *Seven Pillars of Wisdom*).[29] The tolerance of the sexual practices of others, which he knew often caused much anguish as well as pleasure, was part of Lawrence's deep compassion for human beings, and his understanding of the drives and passions of which they were as often the victims as the masters. His literary candor concerning sexual activities and other body functions also reflects a fundamental intellectual honesty and integrity which must not be confused, as it has often been, with what Lawrence would or could tolerate in himself. His candid descriptions of the homosexual practices of Bedouin youth in the desert in *Seven Pillars of Wisdom* have, in my opinion, been mistakenly offered as evidence of his own participation in these activities. The evidence is strongly to the contrary, however sympathetic Lawrence may have been to the intimacy of these youths, which he saw growing out of their privation, the absence of suitable women, and the "welding" of "souls and spirits in one flaming effort" in the enterprise of the Arab Revolt.

Lawrence's clearest statement of his humanitarian view of sexuality, and his appreciation of the destructive effect of intolerant social and moral attitudes toward this vital aspect of life, is contained in a letter to Henry Williamson about the novel *Lady Chatterley's Lover*: "What D. H. Lawrence means by *Lady Chatterley's Lover* is that the idea of sex, and the whole strong vital instinct, being considered indecent causes men to lose what might be their vital strength and pride of life — their integrity. Conversely, the idea of 'genitals being beauty' in the Blakian sense would free humanity from its lowering and disintegrating immorality of deed and thought. Lawrence wilted and was made writhen by the 'miners-chapel-dirty little boy, you' environment: he was ruined by it: and in most of his work he is striving to straighten himself, and to become beautiful. Ironically, or paradoxically, in a humanity where 'genitals are beauty' there would be a minimum of 'sex' and a maximum of beauty, or Art. This is what Lawrence means, surely."[30] Freud himself never stated in clearer terms the essence of his view of the human cost of neurotic conflict.

Despite his personal revulsion, Lawrence exhibited similar tolerance of the sexuality of the men with whom he lived in the barracks in the Tank Corps and the RAF, recognizing that his own attitudes were odd or exceptional. During a period when he was particularly troubled, having recently had to leave the RAF to join the Tank Corps, he wrote to his friend Lionel Curtis at All Souls: "A filthy business all of it, and yet Hut 12 shows me the truth behind Freud. Sex is an integer in all of us, and the nearer nature we are, the more constantly, the more completely the product of that integer. These fellows are the reality, and you and I, the selves who used to meet in London and talk of fleshless things, are only the outward wrapping of a core like these fellows. They let light and air play always upon their selves, and consequently have grown very lustily, but have at the same time achieved health and strength in their growing. Whereas our wrappings and bandages have stunted and deformed ourselves, and hardened them to an apparent insensitiveness . . . but it's a callousness, crippling, only to be yea-said by aesthetes who prefer clothes to bodies, surfaces to intentions."[31]

Arnold Lawrence wrote after his brother's death that for T.E. there was "no fate he would have more gladly accepted for himself" than a happy marriage,[32] and he once told me on another occasion that his mother had thought that the widow of Robert Scott, the explorer, would have made a good wife for T.E. and would have had the right sort of steadying influence. She was disappointed when Mrs. Scott remarried.[33] There is no information about what T.E. thought of this suggestion, if it was ever made to him. Arnold Lawrence's wife, Barbara, believes that a heterosexual relation might have been possible, though difficult, with the right woman.[34] But the evidence seems to me convincing that no matter how suitable the woman, Lawrence's sexual conflicts were such that he could never have dealt with a marital relationship if it required heterosexual intimacy.

Lawrence's friend David Garnett has perhaps captured best the sad limitations that Lawrence's sexual conflict imposed upon him: "Lawrence did not strive to satisfy the sexual appetite. As a result he did not know love and desire,* and all the range of tenderness between them; he did not know the ecstasies and contentments of physical intimacy or the sharp joys or alarms of parenthood. These were severe limitations and sometimes, like some of the repulsive saints, he seemed to be an enemy of life. The reproductive urge manifesting itself in the whole of nature either disgusted him, or meant little. Yet his imagination and capacity for sympathy

---

* Here I would disagree with Garnett.

enabled him to overcome this disability."[35] T.E.'s exceptionally strong feeling for children, Arnold Lawrence has pointed out, came near to vicarious parenthood.

The passage from *Seven Pillars of Wisdom* that describes the traumatic assault at Der'a (quoted on pages 230–231) points in vivid language to the precipitation in Lawrence of a flagellation disorder.[36] His powerful identification with his guilt-ridden mother; the childhood experience of being beaten repeatedly by her in a manner to break his will; the lifetime fascination with, dread of, and need to master pain; the absence of any offsetting heterosexual adaptation; the guilt and shame which resulted from the war experience; and conceivably, a biologically rooted masochistic predisposition — all of these combined to make Lawrence vulnerable to this disorder, the form of which reflects his youthful familiarity with medieval flagellation practices. There is no evidence that Lawrence suffered from this "morbid desire" prior to the Der'a experience, nor is there evidence that he acted upon it before he enlisted in the Tank Corps in 1923. He may have done so, but the information is not available to me or to anyone I have consulted.[37] Perhaps the political struggles of the postwar period and the feverish efforts to write down his experience of the campaigns in his book helped to prevent earlier manifestations of the problem.

Flagellation or whipping was used in ancient times to revive or resuscitate persons who were medically stricken or unconscious.[38] In the early Christian era and into medieval times in Europe, it was used for mortification of the flesh. "Self-punishment of various kinds were favorite methods adopted by the early saints to subdue sexual thoughts and cravings," one authority on the subject has written.[39] The medieval flagellants sought purification through the practice. Even into the twentieth century the English seem to have found whipping particularly appealing for disciplining children and punishing criminals. The stimulation of latent erotic tendencies by such beatings created a white-slave traffic in flagellation in Victorian England, which provided a field day for such social critics as Bernard Shaw, who noted with pointed irony in one of his several articles deploring the practice that the act which allowed flogging "is a final triumph of the vice it pretends to repress."[40] The punisher collaborates in effect with the unconscious masochistic impulses of the offender while acting out sadistic impulses of his own.

The practice of flagellation by individuals for erotic pleasure is commonplace, being perhaps more frequent in societies that have a medieval tradition of such behavior and use it in rearing children and punishing criminals. Furthermore, erotic flagellation, with rare exceptions, is not severe.[41] Rarer still is the self-determined use of flagellation for personal penance — Lawrence's disorder. Lawrence, as far as I can tell, was not whipped in his school, birching in English schools having been curtailed somewhat after the mid-nineteenth century because of Victorian prudery about the exposure of bare bottoms. He was, though, as has been mentioned, whipped severely as a child by his mother, and he was a student of the Middle Ages. As Arnold Lawrence wrote in 1937 (cryptically at the time because Lawrence's flagellation problem was not publicly known): "His subjection of the body was achieved by methods advocated by the saints whose lives he had read."[42]

In May 1935, about the time of his brother's death at the Bovington Camp hospital, Arnold Lawrence received a letter from John Bruce, a young Scotsman who had joined the Tank Corps near to the time that Lawrence did in 1923. In the letter, which was superscribed with an Aberdeen, Scotland, address, Bruce expressed disappointment that he could not get from the hospital a daily report on Lawrence's condition. The letter, written on May 17, two days before Lawrence's death, referred to an "uncle" of "Ted's" (a nickname given Lawrence by some of his service friends), whom Bruce wished help in contacting, as his correspondence with the uncle had gone through "Ted." In a second letter, written on May 19 after hearing of Lawrence's death, Bruce referred to Lawrence as his greatest friend, regretted not being able to attend the funeral, and wrote that for financial reasons he wished to remain in touch as he might have a statement to make later.

Arnold Lawrence found these letters highly puzzling. In spite of his closeness to his brother, Arnold had not known of Bruce, and by 1920 he and his brothers had no recognized living male relatives, other than a third or fourth cousin, younger than T.E. and whom T.E. had never met.[43] He requested that Bruce direct all future communications through the Lawrence solicitors. "In the meantime," Arnold Lawrence wrote, "I had noticed the passage in the Oxford text of 1922 of *Seven Pillars* which declares the beating he received at Deraa resulted in a longing for a repetition of the experience."[44] After comparing Bruce's letters with earlier ones of his to Lawrence, and with other documents found at Clouds Hill, Arnold Lawrence "realized that my brother had invented a living uncle and that the 'nephew,' who was to be punished by beating and other trials, was T.E. himself."[45]

Meanwhile, Bruce continued writing letters to the family solicitor, in which he expressed his wish to be put in touch with T.E.'s uncle (who apparently had paid Bruce for services performed on behalf of his nephew) regarding his interest in writing a book about Lawrence's private life. He planned to base the work on his personal experiences with Lawrence and on more than two hundred letters and a diary. A meeting was arranged between Bruce, Arnold Lawrence and the solicitor, which was to be held at the firm in July 1935. Bruce "did not come to the office as arranged but telephoned to ask me to meet him alone at a railway station, where we spent, I suppose, an hour together. I did not wish to reveal that the uncle was imaginary, and so could not put direct questions freely (in case they should, by chance, show undue ignorance of matters I might be expected to know about), but the main lines of the story became clear. The 'nephew' had committed some serious offence in law — a financial fraud, it seemed — against his uncle or uncle's wife; they decided not to prosecute, since that would involve public disgrace. Instead, they insisted on his under-going a course of expiation which they themselves devised. I think Bruce said (but I am not sure I have not interpolated this item from data that came to me recently) that they ordered him to enlist. Once enlisted, they — this Bruce certainly told me — arranged for periodic beatings by Bruce, after which T.E. had to show the marks to a doctor who would then report to the uncle and aunt that the punishment had been severe enough. I had no doubt that Bruce believed all this."[46] Arnold Lawrence never met Bruce again.

Bruce did not turn over to Arnold Lawrence any documents at the rail-way station, though in a letter to the solicitor written two days later, he announced his decision to burn the letters he had in his possession. In De-cember 1935, Arnold Lawrence's solicitor wrote Bruce, expressing con-cern that Bruce had not, as planned, destroyed the letters.

Bruce responded in indignant and hurt tones: as Lawrence had been his friend in life so he would be his in death; his story never was or would be for sale; and anyway, he had burned it along with the letters he had been tricked into destroying; and so forth. (As we shall see, Bruce sold a docu-ment describing in detail his alleged relationship with Lawrence for a considerable amount to the *Sunday Times* in 1968, and the following year wrote to me that he planned to publish someday Lawrence's letters to him.)[47] After 1936 Bruce was not heard from by the Lawrence family for twenty-six years. In 1937, for reasons that are not clear, he wrote a letter to Ronald Storrs, claiming to have been Lawrence's closest friend during the last twelve years of Lawrence's life. In August 1938, Bruce had an article, probably written for him by a journalist, published in a magazine, *The Scottish Field*. In it there are obviously fictitious anecdotes, and the claim, inconsistent with the 1935 letters, that he visited Lawrence at Bovington Camp hospital the day before Lawrence died.[48]

In December 1962, about the time that the film *Lawrence of Arabia* was evoking renewed interest in T.E., Bruce wrote again to Arnold Lawrence. Lawrence did not reply, and two months later Bruce wrote again, enclosing a gossip column clipping from a local newspaper of the town of Helensburgh, Scotland. The article states that Bruce had known Lawrence intimately "as his personal bodyguard," and was about to have a book about him published to be titled "Lawrence after Arabia," which had been ghostwritten by an eminent Scottish author.[49]

Nothing further was heard of or from Bruce until February 1967, when without accompanying explanation or covering letter, a copy of an eighty-three-page typescript, written in the first person and giving Bruce's version of his relationship with Lawrence, arrived at the offices of Arnold Lawrence's solicitors. In a subsequent letter to me, Bruce stated that this was an accident and said that it resulted from mixed-up addresses and other errors whereby the document was mistakenly sent to the firm.

On January 1, 1968, Bruce wrote to the Lawrence solicitors asking if there would be any objection to his writing of his friendship with T.E. and that circumstances beyond his control, specifically illness and poverty, made it necessary for him to break his long silence. He wished for the blessings of the "title holder" of *Seven Pillars of Wisdom.* In their reply the solicitors stated their objections to publication and made reference to the typescript they had received. Bruce wrote letters again on January 8 and 25, offering a puzzling explanation of how the typescript had come to the firm, and closed the second letter with the statement that he had hoped on his death to have handed over the story to the Lawrence family. In reply the solicitor observed that he did not see what prevented Bruce from turning over his story to the family now.

At about this time Bruce sold his story to the *Sunday Times* in the form of a typescript similar to the one that Arnold Lawrence's solicitors had received. The *Sunday Times* incorporated this material in four articles, which were published in June under the general title "The Secret Life of Lawrence of Arabia."[50]

Early in March 1968, Arnold Lawrence learned that the *Sunday Times* had bought Bruce's story and was planning to put together quickly a series of articles based on it, but one that would also include such other subjects as Lawrence's family background, alleged espionage activities, and relationship with Mrs. Shaw.[51] Arnold Lawrence "felt desperate at the prospect of there being no background depicted, so that the story would seem just dirt"[52] and was eager for the *Sunday Times* to have me write a companion article that would place the story of the beatings in an appropriate psychological and historical perspective. We both worked toward this end but unsuccessfully: the story was first made public in a very sensational form on June 23 under the title "How Lawrence of Arabia Cracked Up."[53] It contained a number of the inaccuracies that were in Bruce's original typescript.

It would be a mistake to emphasize Bruce's personal role too strongly. Bruce, whose family had owned a dairy near Aberdeen, was only nineteen when he met Lawrence. It is clear that he valued the relationship at the time, not only because of the money he received for performing his services, but also, as he told me himself, because T. E. Lawrence was the first person of the upper classes who did not look down upon him or impress upon him his higher status.[54]

What Bruce believed was a close personal relationship seems to have been primarily a business arrangement. He was hired to administer the beatings and to help Lawrence carry out certain other penances that he had invented for himself. Bruce was particularly qualified to perform these services because he needed money and he was gullible — he believed at the time, and as recently as his last letter to me (written in February of 1969), that he was serving an "Old Man" or "uncle" of Lawrence's who demanded this barbaric treatment.

Bruce's army records show that he enlisted in the Tank Corps in Aberdeen on March 9, 1923, and was posted to Bovington Camp in Dorset, where all recruits went for their initial training. Since Lawrence enlisted in the Tank Corps three days after Bruce did, and was also posted to Bovington, it is likely that the two met at this time.[55]

Fifteen letters from Bruce and one from Mrs. Bruce were found among Lawrence's possessions at Clouds Hill after his death. Two of the letters were written from Scotland to Lawrence in India in April and May of 1927. They indicate a long period since the last meeting or communication, presumably since Bruce's discharge from the Tank Corps in March 1925. The others date from 1933 and 1934. In the letters Bruce tells Lawrence of his recent marriage, expresses gratitude to him, assures him that his secret is safe, and states that he does not want to lose touch with Lawrence. Nine of the letters are from Bruce to Lawrence directly, and concern various business arrangements regarding the performance of his duties on the "Old Man's" behalf. Instructions from the "Old Man" were, according to these letters, to be sent through T.E. and presumably unopened by him. They were to be *returned* by Bruce through T.E. to the Old Man, also unopened. Therefore Bruce would not possess letters from the "Old Man."

Four letters to the "Old Man," to be transmitted by Lawrence, reveal Bruce as trying to please the Old Man by his faithfulness to his instructions in carrying out the beatings and in arranging for swimming, boxing, and physical therapy instruction for his sinful nephew. In one letter he apologizes for exceeding his instructions and overdoing the beatings (October 10, 1933). Similar communications may have occurred in 1931 and 1932 but would not have been found at Clouds Hill, as Lawrence's mother and older brother occupied the cottage from April 1931 to the end of 1932.[56]

There is no conclusive information on how many times Lawrence underwent floggings at the hands of Bruce or anyone else.[57] Bruce has recalled seven to nine occasions between 1923 and 1935 when beatings occurred. Diary jottings of Lawrence's found after his death at Clouds Hill suggest five incidents of flogging between June and October 1933. Lawrence had noted, for example, "Saturday 23rd June, 30 from Jock" (Bruce's nickname). All of the other floggings were also by "Jock" (with numbers from thirty to seventy-five indicating presumably the number of lashes) except four by "G."[58]

It is understandable that the beatings Bruce administered should have

begun in 1923 after Lawrence entered the Tank Corps. Expulsion from
the RAF had recently taken from him not only valued work, but a way
of life that had provided him with needed stability.[59] Lawrence's letters
of this period, especially those to Lionel Curtis, reflect his despair. A week
after he entered the Tank Corps he had written that in the RAF he had
"grown suddenly on fire with the glory which the air should be." The
army, by contrast "seems safe against enthusiasm. It's a horrible life, and
the other fellows fit it. I said to one, 'They're the sort who instinctively
fling stones at cats' . . . and he said, 'Why what do you throw?' "[60] He
wrote Curtis of his joining the Tanks Corps for "mind suicide" and that
"self-degradation is my aim." A week later he continued in this vein: "We
are social bed-rock, those un-fit for life-by-competition: and each of us
values the rest as cheap as he knows himself to be."[61] And two months
later: "Do you think there have been lay monks of my persuasion? One
used to think that such frames of mind would have perished with the age
of religion: and yet here they rise up purely secular. It's a lurid flash into
the Nitrian desert: seems almost to strip the sainthood from Anthony.
How about Teresa?"[62]

And surely, like Saint Teresa of Avila, Lawrence turned to flagellation
for the suppression of sexual needs and the purification of his soul through
mortification of the body. Bruce allegedly told the *Sunday Times* in 1968
that Lawrence was revising the Der'a chapter in 1923 and had nightmares
five nights running, which angered the other occupants of the hut. Lawrence then induced Bruce to repeat the Der'a punishment.[63] This was
the occasion of the first beating. The beatings seem again to have been
more frequent in 1933 and Arnold Lawrence, understanding the economi-
cal balance of pleasure and pain required by Lawrence's conscience, has
suggested that "the boats involved an enormous amount of physical exer-
tion in fresh air, and perhaps the healthiness so induced aroused more
need for Bruce's treatment."[64] The imminent publication of Liddell Hart's
book, extolling his virtues, may have been another reason for Lawrence's
greater need for the punishments at that time.

Bruce seemed husky and fit at sixty-four, the only time I met with him
(a two-hour talk in the summer of 1968 at Bruce's home and in a coffee
shop in Wrexham in Wales where he was then living), although he said
he had been unable to work for nine years because of emphysema and
bronchitis. He was proud of his association with Lawrence, expressed
fondness for him, and said that Lawrence had often bawled him out and
"was like a father to me." Although Bruce claimed to be the only person
"who really knew Lawrence's life after 1922," he actually seemed to know
very little about Lawrence and the Lawrence family. He stated once
again that he had performed the beatings entirely to serve "Ted," and to
protect him from this cruel "Old Man" who threatened to cause a family
scandal by revealing Lawrence's illegitimacy. He claimed to know who

the "Old Man" was and to have met him in T.E.'s company, but would not tell me whom he suspected. He also believed the Old Man responsible for Lawrence's death and connected the black car described at the inquest with the Old Man, who, he said, had to do with chauffeuring it.

Bruce said he believed he had been selected to administer the beatings because he was strong and trustworthy, and because Lawrence was afraid of someone the Old Man might select. Although he stuck to the story that he had protected Lawrence as early as 1922, he said spontaneously that he had known him during the last twelve years of his life, not noting the contradiction. The beatings in any event did not begin until 1923, at a time when T.E. was under much strain. And Bruce had said elsewhere that there were very few beatings before Lawrence left for India at the end of 1926.[65] He said that Lawrence seemed to get no pleasure from the beatings and that he was not "homosexual." Bruce was unaware that anyone else had performed the beatings, except possibly someone the Old Man might have employed because of the distance to Bruce in Scotland.

I will now turn from what Bruce has supplied to the independent observations of a service companion and to material left at Clouds Hill by Lawrence himself.

Lawrence approached this companion in 1931 in great distress, explaining that he had stolen £150 from an "uncle," or "old man," who came to be known to the companion as "R." The Old Man had allegedly threatened to reveal to the world that Lawrence was illegitimate unless he either returned the money, which he was not in a position to do, or submitted to severe floggings. The companion's role was to witness the beatings, and report to "R" in order to assure that "R"'s instructions were being properly carried out. The presence of a witness seems also to have served the purpose of providing a restraint to any excesses of Bruce's in carrying out the floggings.

The companion observed three beatings with a metal whip between 1931 and 1934. They were brutal, delivered on the bare buttocks, and a precise number of lashes was required. Lawrence submitted to them "like a schoolboy," registered obvious fear and agony, but did not scream or cry out. He required that the beatings be severe enough to produce a seminal emission.

Three letters, purporting to be from "R" to the companion, and returned by him to Lawrence, have survived. In addition to the other instructions to the companion they contain — instructions meticulously composed to sustain the fiction of the "Old Man" — the letters seem also to be attempts to deal, through the companion, with the possibility that the beatings might become too severe. Written of course by Lawrence himself, these letters are remarkable psychological documents, revealing the sadness and pathos of this terrible problem, from which Lawrence, even up to the months before his death, seemed unable to free himself. They reveal his bitter hostility toward himself, his profound self-contempt, his wish to know his own reactions, and, finally, a pathetic desire for some vindicating judgment that would free him of the conflict. The last letter suggests that he was having some success in breaking away from his ordeal.

26 Oct 1934

Dear Sir,

I am very much obliged to you for the long and careful report you have sent me on your visit to Scotland with Ted; and for your kindness in agreeing to go there with the lad and look after him while he got his deserts. I am enclosing a fee of three pounds which I hope you will accept as some compensation for your trouble and inconvenience.

From what you tell me, and from the reports of those who have examined Ted since, it is clear that he had a sound thrashing, which was after all what he wanted. I hope he will take the lesson to heart, and not make it necessary for us to repeat it. Please take any chance his friendship for you gives, to impress upon him how wrong it is for him, at his age and standing, to force us to use these schoolboy measures against him. He should be ashamed to hold his head up amongst his fellows, knowing that he had suffered so humiliating and undignified a punishment. Try and drive some sense into his head. [Details of the whippings follow.]

. . . . .

After being loosed, did Ted stand quite steadily, or did he show any signs of trembling on his way from the club-room to the cafe or the train. Also you say that when they met you at the station, Ted was not looking too happy. Did his face remain pale to the end of his punishment, and after it? Did he say anything about his being glad the business was over?

Hills [Bruce] reports that after the birching Ted cried out quite loudly, and begged for mercy. Can you confirm this, and do you recollect in what terms his plea was made? . . .

. . . Does he take his whipping as something he has earned? Is he sorry after it? Does he feel justly treated? Has this year of harsh treatment made an improvement in his bearing?

I am sorry to bother you with all these difficult questions, but you have seen so much of Ted's private history this last twelve month, that your opinion is worth a great deal. One last question, too, if you say Yes to the main principle — are we at the end of our troubles with the lad? If not, must we give Hills his free hand, or will limited measures suffice? Can Hills be trusted again, or must I look elsewhere? And in that case, do you think your friend would be available or suitable?

With further thanks for your kindness.
Believe me
Yours very sincerely,
R

16 November 1934

Dear Sir,

I must apologize for having taken so long to answer the additional report you were good enough to send me. Your information was exactly what I needed and I am most grateful.

You have aroused my curiosity by your remark that from your service with Ted you know something that might replace corporal punishment in making him behave himself. You must understand that this is a matter of the first importance to me and to Ted. By his wishes which I must respect, according to my promise, we are prevented from meeting; but if you can get your information on paper, you would put me further into your debt.

I note what you say about Hills, and it only confirms my own impression. You will recollect how he came to go to him this time. Ted's punishment at X had proved not enough, due to the inadequacy of a belt for use upon a grown lad, and not through any fault of yours or your friend's. Unfortunately you could not arrange another dose at the time, and while we were thinking about it Ted allowed himself to give offense upon quite another subject. It was with this second offence that Hills dealt with last month. Ted still owes us (as he very well knows) proper payment for his very mean action in trying to steal money in transit from me to you.

I do not know, of course, what your hinted remedy is worth, as a corrective. If it proved effective I might save you and me from a repetition of his punishment. I gather that your friend is not yet available, and it is not fair to the lad himself to keep such a punishment hanging over him for month after month. Yet it is equally impossible for me, having solemnly promised it to him. I always do what I promise, and I have brought Ted to know it.

So will you please try to take me into your confidence on this alternative; and please also enquire into the arrangements of the friend who helped you last time, so that we may fall back on him, if necessary.

Yours sincerely,

R

11 January 1935

Dear Sir,

Your letter showed me that I was perhaps being rather hard on Ted, by repeating that punishment at short interval. So upon reconsideration I informed him that it will be indefinitely postponed. I asked him to give you prompt notice that your help would not be immediately required. We will hold our hands and watch to see if the lad justifies this kindness.

I need not say that I am very much obliged to you for being ready to take the further responsibility. I shall call upon you with confidence if Ted again makes it necessary. Please let me correct one misapprehension in your letter, however. Unless he strips, the birch is quite ineffective.

The twigs are so light that even the thinnest clothing prevents their hurting. I fully understand your reluctance to strip him; so I was making up my mind to ask you to use either your friend's jute whip (which you mentioned to me in a former letter) or a useful little dogwhip which I could send you by post.

If the emergency arises, I shall agree to Ted's coming to you in flannels.

Yours sincerely,

R

These letters demonstrate the dimensions of Lawrence's continuing struggle. Although meant to guide the companion and, through him, Bruce, they also show a kind of internal debate, as Lawrence wrestles with the various sides of his dilemma. The deleted portion of the first letter reveals clearly his genuine distress at and fear of the severity of the beatings. Yet at the same time he continued to use Bruce's services precisely because Bruce was willing to administer severe beatings. Even in the last letter, in which Lawrence does seem to be struggling to escape from his need for "corporal punishment," he reminds the companion that "unless he strips, the birch is quite ineffective" and "even the thinnest clothing prevents [its] hurting."

That Lawrence asks in the letters for details of "Ted's" responses to the beatings suggests that his consciousness or self-awareness was disturbed during them to the extent that he could not monitor his own reactions. In addition, however, a number of his questions — "did he show any signs of trembling" or "did he say anything about being glad the business was over" — reveal Lawrence's continuing struggle to achieve mastery over pain. The need for pain, and at the same time to surmount it, are shown side by side with the fear of fatal injury and the need for protection by the companion.

Lawrence makes it clear that the humiliation of self is as important an aspect of the penance as the physical pain. His contempt for "the lad's dignity" may usefully be compared with the several instances in which Lawrence wrote of his "integrity" and its destruction, and the link with "schoolboy measures" is evident. Here he seems to relish humiliation and writes that "the more we can hurt his feelings the better." Yet along with this need for renewed humiliation and shame, Lawrence seems also to be striving to overcome his conflict ("Please take any chance his friendship with you gives to impress upon him how wrong it is for him, at his age and standing, to force us to use these schoolboy measures against him.") But the debate over the justice of these inordinately severe sentences seems to have gone on eternally within Lawrence's tormented spirit. Only six months before his death he still needed to turn to the authority of a humble service companion for a relieving, more objective judgment, a judgment, one should add, that could probably never have had a lasting impact. "Does he take his whipping as something he has earned?" Lawrence asked. "Is he sorry after it? Does he feel justly treated? Has this year of harsh treatment made an improvement in his bearing?"

Although the floggings were the most dramatic and unusual form of penance that Lawrence imposed upon himself, they were not the only one. In addition, he left documentation at Clouds Hill of other "training" rituals which, taken altogether, comprised an elaborate rehabilitation program. Lawrence wrote to various institutions and individuals, including a riding and hunting establishment, a swimming instructor, physiotherapists, a diet expert, and a "remedial gymnasium" specializing in Swedish massage and "medical electricity." As he did in arranging the floggings, Lawrence would write as the uncle ("Mr. E. Shaw") of a recalcitrant nephew for whom severe discipline was necessary, and would ask for a report from the instructor or manager as to "Ted's" progress. For example, to a riding establishment:

Dear Sir:
Some while ago when I asked about Riding Schools in Southampton, I was advised to write to you. I want my nephew taught to ride, for it will be useful to him in an appointment ahead that I have in mind for him.
I think he has been only once or twice upon a horse, so there will be everything to learn. Probably he could come to you early — to finish 10:30 at latest — or in the evening for an hour or two, several days a week for a while. I would like private lessons, best of all in a riding school, if possible, or in some quiet field: not a road or public park. I must warn you that he will not be an easy pupil, but I can help you a good deal with my authority. However, we can discuss that later, if you are able to undertake the work. Terms we can consider after we settle exactly what is needed. Perhaps you will let me know.[66]

The need for secrecy is evident. Replies from the instructors and establishments were also sent to Mr. E. Shaw, in which the nephew's various treatments, exercises and diets were described and the uncle assured of Ted's improvement. Besides all of these activities Lawrence also subjected himself to swimming in the frigid waters of the North Sea in the fall, under Bruce's supervision.

I fear that I shall disappoint those who have borne with me patiently to this point in the expectation that I will find in the documentation of this aspect of Lawrence's life definitive explanations of his character or of other actions which have puzzled his biographers. Perhaps some readers will choose to go further than I will in their own formulations, but I am bound by the data and by my concern lest this most tortured aspect of Lawrence's life be given too great an emphasis.

We may start by asking with justification, what is this all about? For what crime did Lawrence need to be punished and to carry out upon himself such an elaborate program of penance and expiation? Furthermore, how are we to understand the beatings and their function? Are they "sexual," and if so, in what sense? What is the need for and the meaning of the elaborate story of the "Old Man," and what does it tell us about Lawrence's psychology? Finally, what larger significance does this aspect of Lawrence's psychology hold for his life as a whole and what effect did it have upon his historical contribution?

As for the question of the "crime," the most direct statement we have from Lawrence is contained in the letter to Mrs. Shaw of March 26, 1924, written within a year of the beginning of the severe beatings, if our reckoning is correct. In that letter Lawrence makes it clear that the "unforgiveable matter" was the sexual surrender at Der'a out of fear of pain. In this overwhelming traumatic experience Lawrence felt that he surrendered not only sexually, but gave away the fundamental integrity of self, a self which he had striven so hard to perfect and protect. What made "the offense" even worse was that he had found the experience, the mingling of sexual assault and pain, to be pleasurable, "a delicious warmth . . . swelling through me."[67] The traumatic intensity of the experience, with its overwhelming of psychic defenses, led to the permanent welding for Lawrence of sexual pleasure and pain, so that he was plagued not only by the memory of the incident, but by the continuous desire for its repetition.

The reader who has followed Lawrence's history will not have difficulty appreciating that the linking of pain, which he had always feared and tried to master, with sexual pleasure would occasion much guilt in someone with his puritanical background and scrupulous conscience. The problem, however, became for him intrinsically insoluble. The desire for repetition of the experience proved to be overwhelming, especially at times of despair. But this very desire only aggravated the deep guilt that was already active within him. Yet the only punishment that was sufficiently severe to allay the guilt included the repetition of the experience itself — that is, the pain of the beatings. But this in turn brought about, indeed required, a repetition of the sexual aspect of the experience, thereby deepening the guilt and leading ultimately to a need to repeat the beatings. I believe that in insisting that the beatings be so severe and painful Lawrence was trying (short of emasculating or killing himself) to destroy his sexuality. I have no evidence that in any conscious sense Lawrence's insistence that the beatings be of such intensity was for any purpose other than for penance and to get rid of or eliminate his sexuality, that he did not at a conscious level seek or even experience pleasure in these episodes. Sexuality, however, like most bodily functions, replenishes itself, and more importantly, the association of sexuality with terribly painful beatings, only served to gratify, at an unconscious level, the very desire for which Lawrence needed to be punished. The swims in the freezing North Sea, and other elements of Lawrence's rehabilitation program, had the advantage of being measures that were severely disciplinary without containing a sexual component.

I do not wish to imply that Lawrence's guilt, or his desire for punishment, derived entirely from these sexual sources. We have seen in other chapters his lifelong struggle with problems of self-regard, and with the sense that whatever he was or did was never good enough to live up to the inflexible ideal standards that he had begun to set for himself in childhood. Lawrence's whole involvement in the Arab campaigns, with its deception and horror, came to fill him with a profound sense of guilt and a desire for retreat. The loss of control at Tafas, which was linked, I believe, with the Der'a experience, was also a source of profound guilt. But we are concerned here with the specific forms of the punishments, and with their sexual character as suited to a sexual crime.

Just as the beating ritual itself seems to derive from multiple psychological determinants, the myth of the "Old Man" or uncle is similarly complex and revealing. The elements of the invention, whose enactment involved several other people and elaborate planning and staging, demonstrate a weaving together of conscious and unconscious elements and of childhood and adult features. Lawrence is once more a schoolboy to be punished, a wayward youth to be whipped and otherwise disciplined, not for a deeply disturbing adult sexual conflict, but for a petty, childlike misdemeanor, the "filching" of varying amounts of money from a relative. He also talked with the persons he involved in his plan about an inheritance and about who was the rightful heir, which had a garbled foundation in Lawrence's own life.[68] Not surprisingly, it is once again the shame of the illegitimacy, with its link to childhood, that the "Old Man" threatens to reveal. In the "Old Man's" letters to the companion, Lawrence refers to "schoolboy measures," and the whole tone of the letters is that of a disappointed parent with a chronically and incorrigibly recalcitrant child. These letters in particular reveal vividly the split in Lawrence's mentality between the adult and childhood aspects of himself, which, in actuality, he never fully integrated.

The concoction of the Old Man story, an elaborate fiction but bearing a certain relation to reality, solved practical problems for Lawrence. It protected Bruce and the others Lawrence involved from any direct personal responsibility for the parts they were asked to play. They were not administering or taking part in cruelties to their friend or fellow serviceman: their actions were demanded by the Old Man, and they were simply helping to protect Lawrence from worse threats and punishments. The elaborate story was also conceived in such a way as to minimize any suspicion of Lawrence's real purposes: the Old Man made it explicit that he and the others were never to meet. Even though the men drawn into these rituals were uneducated, it is nevertheless a testimony to Lawrence's persuasiveness that none of them seems to have ever doubted the story. Perhaps an even more remarkable tribute to Lawrence's personality is the fact that they maintained respect for a man they believed to be a thief and had seen repeatedly humiliated.[69]

Over and above these practical considerations, the Old Man fantasy is characteristic of Lawrence's inventiveness and creativity. His elaborate imagination and rich fantasy life is welded as usual with action, and his extraordinary capacity to adapt his personal psychological purposes to the realities and needs of other people's lives is again in evidence. As in the desert campaigns, complex systems of transmitting messages and other communications were worked out by Lawrence in extraordinary detail, forming a tight "system" that has been difficult to unravel. Childhood and adult elements, the medieval flagellation rituals with which he became familiar in his youth, and his own complex psychological conflicts and inventiveness were all drawn together by Lawrence in his creative psychopathology.

It is tempting to speculate about whom the Old Man and his associates represent. "The Old Man" often designates the father in some American and British circles, but I know of no such reference by Lawrence to his own father. In actuality it was his mother who was the more severe disciplinarian and administered physical punishment, while the father is remembered by Arnold Lawrence as stopping a carter from beating a horse. Accordingly, it is most likely not Mr. Lawrence (as Lawrence knew him) who furnishes the character of the Old Man, but a sterner figure: the product of T.E.'s imagination and of his own severe conscience, with which he strove to exist more comfortably. The link to his mother's childhood beatings is obvious, but the adult beaters are also associated with the Turkish soldiers who imposed the traumatic assault.

I believe Lawrence could not have allowed himself to be beaten by a woman (the masochism of many men does take this form), for the beatings, perverse, brutal and pathetic as they seem, are nevertheless a form of closeness, selected for the fusion of intimacy and simultaneous desecration they represent. The taboo against intimacy with women was, as we have seen earlier in this chapter, always intense for Lawrence. Lawrence was generally more comfortable with closeness among men, and could tolerate perhaps a perverse form of intimacy with certain men in a way that he could never have tolerated with a woman. Only in the link between the flagellation ritual and the childhood beatings at the hands of the mother does the never-resolved conflict over the attachment to her remain in evidence.

Penitent rituals such as Lawrence's are not unusual and may be associated with a wide range of talents and personalities. Typically they recreate childhood scenes, relationships and conflicts that have been revived by the events and traumata of adult life. The sufferer inevitably draws into his private drama other individuals who form a kind of cast of characters that fulfill specific roles under his personal direction. Lawrence's ritual carried his particular stamp. It was thoroughly compartmentalized and highly creative. He took great pains to protect the others whom he involved from injury or embarrassment.

We are, I believe, justified in presuming that Lawrence was fully aware of the limitations he had imposed upon his public career by involving Bruce in an intimate part of his private life. Once he permitted himself to be involved with Bruce he could no longer return to public life, even if he had so chosen.

There were other consequences of these conflicts for Lawrence. Perhaps most importantly, he was forced in dealing with them to squander a certain amount of psychic energy, however rarely the actual beatings may have occurred. Even though Lawrence touched many people's lives during his years in the ranks, contributed to many reforms in the RAF, and developed new rescue boats, which may ultimately have saved hundreds of lives, his horizons were specifically limited by his personal conflicts.

After Lawrence's death Arnold Lawrence discussed his brother's struggle to maintain a balance between spirit, intellect and body. "The details of his life," he wrote, "were consistent to his plan, but in my opinion he neglected the body's claims unfairly. He maintained this 'balance' at a cost so terrible in waste and suffering, that its author would himself, I believe, have agreed that it was a failure."[70] He was, indeed, as Ralph Isham once remarked, "a battlefield between purity and passion."[71]

# 34

# Lawrence Assayed

When I was first becoming interested in T. E. Lawrence, I watched Arnold Lawrence being interviewed on television. He said of his brother: "He was one of the nicest, kindest, and most exhilarating people I've known. He often appeared cheerful when he was unhappy."[1] I was much affected by this simple observation, but did not know at the time how to place it in relation to the qualities that seemed most immediately related to Lawrence's accomplishments and fame — his courage, his capacity to lead through influencing others, his tendency to dramatize, and the like. Later, A. E. Chambers said to me: "He was my only real friend, the only one I've ever had. He was one of the finest men who've ever trod the globe, better than Christ or any of them. He hated injustice."[2]

In a curious way I felt that personal statements like these were fundamental to an appreciation of Lawrence as a historical figure, that the private Lawrence and the public Lawrence were related. In *Seven Pillars of Wisdom* Lawrence had written of the Arabs that "no man could be their leader except he ate the ranks' food, wore their clothes, lived level with them, and yet appeared better in himself."[3] This passage seemed to provide a clue to the link between the valued personal traits that Arnold Lawrence and Chambers had described and an essential dimension of Lawrence's greatness and historical importance.

There has been a shift in the field of psychoanalysis with the last decade: from discussing human beings and their difficulties through the use of such terms as ego, superego and narcissism, to speaking of them in language closer to sentience and actuality. Traditional psychoanalytic terms have a mechanistic or static quality, and seem to derive in part from an effort to treat human functioning in the concrete terms of the physical sciences. Although such concepts as "self," "identity" or even "ideal self" may be less than perfect alternatives, they are at least dynamic and imply the relationship between a person — or the image or idea of a person — and other beings or selves. The appreciation of these relationships lies at the core of understanding the qualities of public figures with a significant capacity for leadership, whether or not the additional elements of heroism and legend form around them.

We have seen how from an early age Lawrence took the development of himself, the perfection of self, as the principal task of his life. In conventional terms there is a certain egotism or "narcissism" in Lawrence's focus upon the ideal evolution of self. In his unwillingness to compromise the idealistic expectations of being and accomplishment that he developed in his youth he displays considerable immaturity in the classical sense. But there is beyond these hygienic banalities a deeper, more urgent set of realities to consider when a self, in action, becomes public property or is devoted to public service. Lawrence throughout his life offered his extraordinary abilities, his essential self, and even his conflicts to others for them to use according to their own need — to emulate, to learn and to grow. This was true from the time of his earliest boyhood, through the Carchemish period, the war and his years in the ranks. It lies at the heart of his greatness. He wrote, simply, to Dick Knowles, his Clouds Hill neighbor in 1927, "It's my experience that the actual work or position or reward one has, doesn't have much effect on the inner being which is the important thing for us to cultivate."[4]

A person who, like Lawrence, is provided through his extraordinary capacities the opportunity to offer (not sacrifice, which is, as Lawrence well understood, a destructive degradation of the process being considered here) himself to other individuals or whole peoples — and hopes thereby to fulfill ideal expectations for himself through enabling others to achieve the fulfillment of their selves — puts himself in a particularly vulnerable position. As he stretches the limit of possibility in the process of self-testing he may overstep his firm ground and expose himself to people with whom he shares no bond of mutual trust, expectation or fulfillment. He may then be exploited by those who are indifferent or even inimical to him, as happened to Lawrence at Der'a. There is the additional danger that he may not only arouse dormant hopes and dreams but also violent impulses, which may get out of hand, as they did at Tafas and at other times in the campaigns.

This exploitation — rape being its paradigm — and loss of control can be, as we have seen, painful and shattering to an idealist. But they need not, as indicated by Lawrence's letter to Knowles and, in fact, by the entire pattern of his life after the war, result in his abandoning the effort to cultivate the "inner being." Rather they may result in a retreat from any grand design for fulfillment and to renunciation of the desires and ambitions that seem to be the cause of the pain. We have seen how Lawrence's retreat into the ranks enabled him to continue to offer himself to others in fulfilling goals, which they all shared, of useful work and self-development without the risk or temptation of ambition and exploitation.

The question of identity has run through the pages of this book. It is a concept useful to the historian and the psychologist, for in its reference to the central characteristics of the self it may draw into the scope of its meaning the continuity of the individual with the past and the future. The concept of identity is also useful in considering the relation between one person and another, or between one individual and a group or a people, and lends itself to the study of how one man may play a part in the shifting development of other selves or other identities.

The sense of self, of "I" and of "who I am," begins to form in the second, even in the first year of life. Its central shape or character, the identity of the self, is established in childhood and adolescence to a large degree, although this identity can develop and shift throughout adult life. A sense of personal identity develops in childhood as the child tries out his native endowment in an environment of family members (and later of other adults and children), who may love and encourage or, conversely, attack or hinder his unfolding. The elements of this identity take further definition as the child finds in the parents examples of what to be like or to reject. His identification is based not simply upon what his parents are in actuality, or how they behave, but also upon the values they represent to him and the rich dimension that family members contribute through recalling the memories of specific ancestors. For Lawrence, the past, the family history on both sides, was obscured and distorted by the parents' guilt.

Except for the many moves during the years before the family settled in Oxford and the departure of a nurse of whom he was the favorite, Lawrence's early childhood was quite secure. The available evidence suggests that he emerged from it with a sure sense of himself and a strong will, although even then a friend noted that he had "a secret something of unhappiness about him." The cloudiness of the family background; the uncertainty about his mother's origins; the discovery of his own illegitimacy and the related discrepancy between his parents' values and ideals and their violation of social codes; the deception of their silence on these matters; the perceived dominance of his father by his mother; his mother's deep need to find redemption for her sins through Lawrence and his brothers; perhaps the rejection experience in his only attempt as a young man to find a mate — all these adverse influences distorted, damaged, and interfered with Lawrence's development of his own self and left him vulnerable to the later problems which the traumata of the war years brought about.

His name, and the uncertainties which attached to it and to which he contributed, became the focus of some of the more fundamental questions about his identity. "The Lawrence thing hasn't any better foundation than my father's whim," he wrote to Mrs. Shaw in 1925,[5] and two years later he noted that he was not "legally entitled" to use the name "and never again will."[6] In 1926 he wrote jokingly to the Newcombes' six-year-old son: "It's time for you [sic] to change your name once more. In 1920 Lawrence was current. In 1921 our names became Ross. In 1923 we changed to Shaw. What shall we become next year?"[7]

He ended up treating the question of his identity as one of little consequence and summarized the matter succinctly to Harley Granville-Barker in 1924: "My genuine, birth-day, initials are T.E.C. The C. became L. when I was quite young:[8] and as L. I went to Oxford and through the war. After the war it became a legend: and to dodge its load of legendary inaccuracy I changed it to R. In due course R. became too hot to hold. So now I'm Shaw: but to me there seems no virtue in one name more than another. Anyone can be used by anyone, and I'll answer to it."[9]

And yet it would be an error, or a missed opportunity, if these disturbances of identity, from which Lawrence undoubtedly suffered, were looked at simply from the standpoint of his personal psychopathology. The multifaceted nature of his sense of self, the varied aspects of his identity, the absence of clearly established social roles or regular directions of his professional life — all related to Lawrence's creativity, to his capacity to give others "new values," as one friend put it, and to find new solutions.[10] I have little doubt that his extraordinary capacity to move flexibly among peoples of other classes and races, to understand or intuit their needs and hopes, their feelings and dreams, derived to a large degree from the complex and unsettled elements of his own identity. This capacity seemed to know no bounds. He could be what people needed him to be, for he knew what they felt, what they were. This flexibility was not limited to his work among the Arabs. It is easily observed in his relationships among Easterners and Westerners alike after the war and in his associations during the years in the ranks.

Lawrence's extraordinary capacity for empathy with the feelings of other people —for genuine compassion — little stressed in recent biographies, was attested to time and again to me by family members, and by his friends in their writings and in interviews. The old, the very young, the poor and the weak, mothers and sons — none were exempt from his understanding. "After 70 an unearthly richness attacks most of our elders," he wrote Mrs. Shaw, "and they become wells of satisfaction to me. Only then one gets to like them too much and away they go and die."[11]

He had a strong feminine side, which enabled him to understand the feelings and conflicts of women as well as of men, and to take care of people. Mrs. Kennington has written of how, when she had a bad miscarriage, was terribly ill and did not want to go on living, Lawrence came to her bedside and helped her with his understanding through her loss.[12]

In the later years of his life Lawrence felt more firmly his identity as an Irishman, and as we have seen, was pleased to be invited to join the Irish Academy of Letters. Of his biographers Robert Graves in particular thought that Lawrence in his character "had all the marks of the Irishman."[13] Lawrence thought that his tendency to laugh at himself was typically Irish.[14] He had toyed with the idea of helping the Irish Free State, and wrote to Mrs. Shaw in 1927, "I like England so much as I do because I am not English: whenever the point crops up succinctly I know that I'm Irish."[15] Similarly, Lady Pansy Lamb, one of my correspondents, told this story of meeting Lawrence toward the end of his life:

> Finally I met Lawrence — I can't remember exactly when, but not long before his death. It was a Christmas dinner at the Johns. There was a crowd of people, amongst them a little bright-eyed man in a white sweater, who I thought was perhaps the local garage-man whom the Johns were befriending — No introductions, but we all had our places marked with our names and my younger sister found herself next to the stranger. This was her account of his conversation — He picked up his name ticket and said, "Ah — Shaw — I wondered what name they would put." My sister, in the dark, thought he was joking, and asked, "Have you many aliases?" He replied, "Quite a few." "And many nationalities?" "Always Irish," he answered firmly.[16]

In 1929 he wrote to Pierce Joyce, an Irishman himself, of his longing to visit Ireland on leave, but he never did. "How is Ireland?" he asked Joyce. "I dream of spending my next month's leave (autumn perhaps) partly there. Are there roads in Ireland, fit for motorbikes?"[17] In thanking Yeats for the invitation to join the Irish Academy of Letters he apologized: "It's not my fault, wholly, if I am not more Irish: family, political, even money obstacles will hold me in England always. I wish it were not so."[18] And he wrote Edward Garnett in 1933: "Irishmen are disappointing men. They go so far, magnificently, and cease to grow."[19] But he then amended this harsh judgment six months later to Lady Astor in a critique of a play by Sean O'Casey: "When a rare Irishman does go on growing, you see, he surpasses most men. Alas that they are so rare."[20]

There is a temptation in this age of science and psychology to try to explain everything about human beings, or to show how each of the parts of a person's personality relates to the others. There is a false scientism in this, for we are not integrated in our personalities to nearly the same extent as we are in our bodies. Some qualities in all of us — in Lawrence certainly — must stand by themselves without explanation. The insistence on seeing Lawrence as "mysterious" derives from this need for explanation, contributed to by Lawrence himself. His life and complex personality seemed, more than those of most people, to have discernible form, and he tended often to hint in his teasing way that there were explanations for everything about him if only the hunter would look long and hard enough.

The moral dilemmas that grew for Lawrence out of his personal experiences during the war and in the years immediately afterwards led to an accentuation of his code of renunciation. "There is absolutely nothing I want for myself," he wrote Graves in 1928.[21] Although the severity of his self-denial, the degree of self-punitiveness, and the ritual of flagellation to which he subjected himself may, like his identity problems, be looked at from the standpoint of psychopathology, to do so without considering at the same time the great value for other people contained in certain elements of Lawrence's character that related to these struggles would be an equally unfortunate distortion. Lawrence rejected the Christianity of his parents and of his culture in the formal sense. But he preserved through his conscious choice of values, and through the personal example of his life, the elements in the Judeo-Christian tradition that are morally lasting.

He did not exaggerate much when he wrote Edward Garnett that he had "brick by brick . . . sold or given away or lost everything I possessed."[22] Lionel Curtis wrote that "Lawrence was always giving, himself, his friendship, his time, his brains, his possessions, and especially money when he had it."[23] And Lawrence told Liddell Hart, simply, "I like giving."[24] His RAF and Tank Corps companions have repeatedly attested to his sympathy for the underdog and his ready willingness to use his wiles to right injustices of all sorts in the ranks.[25]

I am convinced that much of what Lawrence accomplished, perhaps the central importance of his life, derived from the force of his moral example, what was known in an earlier time as "character." Mrs. Hardy expressed this best perhaps in a letter to Robert Graves in 1927 about Lawrence: "I consider him the most marvelous human being I have ever met. It is not his exploits in Arabia that attract me, nor the fact that he is a celebrity: it is his character that is so splendid."[26]

Lawrence's sensitivity to the feelings of other people continued during his service years to be accompanied by considerable self-consciousness and shyness about himself. He wrote typically to E. M. Forster in 1927, "If you knew all about me (perhaps you do: your subtlety is very great: shall I put it 'if I knew that you knew . . .'?) you'd think very little of me."[27] He had written similar passages in *Seven Pillars of Wisdom* eight years earlier. This basic doubt about his worth, the feeling of being somehow second-rate, was accompanied by a craving for praise and continued in Lawrence until the end. He rarely referred to his body in his writings. When he did so — invariably in humor — he tended to refer to the limitations of his height or what he considered oddities of his stature. On the occasion of parades, he wrote to Sergeant Pugh of Cranwell: "A group of six-foot people take station behind my back, and use me as a convenient low shelf for leaning on to view the procession."[28] When a young female artist with whom he was not acquainted sought his cooperation in being her model, Lawrence replied that it would be all right if she "can't afford a proper model" for "apparently I'm shaped rather like a tadpole."[29]

Lawrence could, of course, "feel things passionately," as he wrote to Bernard Shaw, but guarded intensely against sentimentality or subjectivity, what he called "the stink of personality" in literature or human relations.[30] He found such extravagant expressions of emotion as Laura Riding's suicide leap from love of Phibbs-Barnett rather appalling and called them "mad-house minds: no, not so much minds as appetites."[31] Yet he could feel compassion for the sufferers. He seems to have given more love, or even to have felt it more, than most people. But he could not abandon himself to giving in love, especially in an erotic sense. When one of his friends became troubled over his passion for a woman who was not his wife, Lawrence wrote to him: "The *matter* puzzles me: you must be patient there with my inadequacy. I do not love anybody and have not, I think ever — or hardly ever. It is difficult to share with people what one gives wholeheartedly to places or people or things. Nor have ever, I think, except momentarily-and-with-the-eye lusted. Altogether I'm a bad subject for feeling."[32]

Children were the group with whom Lawrence found it easiest to be open. He grasped readily what would interest a child, and his many letters to children of his friends and colleagues are directed in their style and content to the level of the child's thoughts and imagination. Lawrence's gift of vivid sensory perception and his unusual ability to impose a creative imagination upon the natural world and upon things and beings *in action* made communication with children easy. Animals, battles, scenes in nature all come alive in amusing directness in Lawrence's letters to young friends.

Lawrence lamented at the same time his inability to create works of the imagination in sculpture, painting or poetry.[33] But his creativity seemed to depend on the application of a vivid sensuous imagination to real things, events and creatures in the world of actuality. Even when he was writing of human feelings he was more invested, as he himself recognized, in what "various people did — in the expressions of their moods in action, than in the moods themselves."[34]

Lawrence was an artist of the world in action. His continuing interest as an adult in polarities of value — the ideal and its failure to be attained, or heroism and its betrayal — also facilitated his meeting of the mind with children. For young children in their moral development are much concerned with extremes of value and achievement, and with polarities of good and evil. They have not yet learned to tolerate within themselves —

nor did Lawrence ever learn — personal compromises on matters of value and morality. Reginald Sims recalled his small son and Lawrence happily discussing "the comparative merits of certain persons included in a book entitled *Heroes of Modern Adventure*."[35] It would have been an amusing conversation to have overheard.

Many have recalled the pleasure T.E. gave them when he shared their childhood interests, taught them to paddle a canoe or to shoot,[36] or took them on speedboat rides or other exciting adventures. The childlike side of his own nature and his sense of fun always remained alive just below the surface, and he could easily share a child's pleasure in simple activities, to which he brought his ingenuity and vast technical knowledge. "He could talk to me in child's language and always interest me," Flight Lieutenant Norrington's daughter wrote.[37] Lawrence would readily go out of his way to do something for a child. Much as he was troubled, for example, about the hero-worshipping of Colonel Lawrence or "Lawrence of Arabia," he readily wrote and signed a charming inscription of a copy of Liddell Hart's book for a crippled boy when the boy's sister indicated that an autographed copy would help the child's spirits.[38]

I talked with Colonel Newcombe's son, Stewart, Jr. (Jimmy) about his recollections of T.E. (Lawrence took a special interest in this particular godson and wrote him many letters, from the time Jimmy was six until he was fourteen). Newcombe recalled his enjoyment of Lawrence's company, especially the speedboat and motorcycle rides. Lawrence seemed to like their excursions and to take pleasure in the uncomplicated nature of the relationship. He seemed to have "a yen" for educating a child and sometimes liked to shock. Newcombe found Lawrence an easy adult to be with compared to most others, not the sort who made you feel frightened or awkward, not knowing what to say next. The conversation would proceed naturally, growing out of subjects they were both interested in, such as battleships or early ideas about boats that skimmed over the surface of the water with little resistance (hovercraft). They also enjoyed poking fun together at the pomposity of most adults.[39]

Hot baths and motorcycle riding were pleasures in which Lawrence permitted himself to indulge fully when baths were available and he could afford to maintain his machine. He would go to great lengths to arrange a bath where a camp had none readily available and was much bothered by cold. "Hot water is very near heaven," he wrote Buxton after rigging up his ingenious electrical hot water heater at Karachi.[40] "I'm very susceptible to cold," he wrote Thurtle later. "In England I'm always getting into hot baths, whenever they are available: because then only I am warm enough. Yet I never get what they call 'a chill.' Odd: because usually I get all the infections going."[41] As Sergeant Pugh put it: "Baths are his God." Lawrence would even bribe the "stoker" at Cranwell to tend to the fires for his bath before those of the others.[42]

Lawrence's love of motorcycle riding was more complex and served many functions. He had George Brough build for him eight very fine Brough Superior motorcycles during his years in the ranks, although his death came before he had a chance to ride the last one.[43] He was fussy about the care of his bikes, and according to a tank corpsman who garaged the Broughs for him near Bovington, gave away his wages in return for help in looking after them.[44] He would, nevertheless, sometimes lend his bikes to other enlisted men who took less good care of them than he did. Lawrence was an extremely fine motorcycle rider, with a great technical knowledge of the subject, and wrote several articles on cycling that were never published. The fine machinery itself gave him great pleasure, and he took pains to master the mechanical details. He also delighted in covering great distances in record times.

Speed itself, achieved on his bikes, gave Lawrence obvious sensual pleasure, which he described to Graves: "When I open out a little more, as for instance across Salisbury Plain at 80 or so, I feel the earth moulding herself under me. It is me piling up this hill, hollowing this valley, stretching out this level place. Almost the earth comes alive, heaving and tossing on each side like a sea. That is a thing that the slow coach will never feel. It is the reward of speed. I could write you pages on the lustfulness of moving swiftly."[45] To Liddell Hart he wrote a brief treatise on the lure of speed and man's historical love of finding any means to go faster. "Speed is the second oldest [next to sex presumably] craving in our nature. Every natural man cultivates the speed that appeals to him. I have a motor-bike income."[46]

His motorcycles afforded Lawrence an opportunity to escape from the dullness and oppression of the camp routine ("a hundred fast miles seem to make camp feel less confined afterwards").[47] On his bike he felt free and released. *The Mint* contains what is virtually a five-page eulogy to his fine machine, and includes an exhilarating race with an airplane overhead.[48]

Sometimes he enjoyed taking others with him for companionship, pillion-style, on his bike. But above all the bike represented for Lawrence an extension or prolongation of himself, an element with which (or with whom) he could maintain a comfortably intimate relationship. His various bikes were given pet names — Boanerges, Boa, or George I, II, III, IV, V, VI, or VII — and he spoke of or to them as if they were living things. Before traveling to India, for example, Lawrence was proud of "Boa" for winning a race against fast automobiles, during which he reached a speed of 120 miles an hour. "Never has Boa gone better," he wrote Mrs. Shaw. "I kept on patting him, and opening his throttle, knowing all the while in a month or two he will be someone's else's, and myself in a land without roads or speed. If I were rich he should have a warm dog garage, and no work until his old age. An almost human machine . . . a real prolongation of my own faculties: and so handsome and efficient. Never have I had anything like him."[49] Lawrence succeeded in damaging this particular bike by crashing it on a slippery street, thereby making parting with it for £100 just before he left for India somewhat less troubling.[50] In *The Mint* Lawrence wrote even more warmly of his pet: "Because Boa loves me, he gives me five more miles of speed than a stranger would get from him."[51]

Although Brough himself stated that he never saw Lawrence "take a single risk nor put any other rider or driver to the slightest inconvenience," Lawrence would clearly expose himself to danger on his motorcycles, especially when he was troubled. He acknowledged to Curtis during the difficult months in the Tank Corps: "When my mood gets too hot and I find myself wandering beyond control I pull out my motor-bike and hurl it top-speed through these unfit roads for hour after hour. My nerves are jaded and gone near dead, so that nothing less than hours of voluntary danger will prick them into life."[52] It was only his skill, and perhaps an element of luck, that kept Lawrence from more serious injury over the years, for he had several accidents and disliked wearing a crash helmet.[53]

Lawrence cultivated a philosophical side of his nature as he grew older. Many of his opinions on the great questions of man and nature have the freshness and immediacy characteristic of his original mind. But as in his personal loves and hates, subjectivity and feeling tended to dominate his views, and feeling was not far behind action. Although he set great store upon feeling being accompanied — preferably preceded — by reason and logic, he acknowledged his "bad habit, if I feel a thing, of acting it straightway, very unacademic, I assure you."[54] Although he was a great reader and a fine judge of literature, here too Lawrence tended to be an impressionistic rather than a formal critic, "one who reacts with his feelings to the quality of a writer's world rather than with his mind to meaning and form in any detached or orderly way."[55] He had a great interest in the craft of writing, in the strategies of literary technique, and as in his personal conduct and being, he sought absolute standards of excellence. As Edward Garnett remarked, "Lawrence to the end was a critic in action."[56]

Lawrence's view of human affairs, based as it was upon his life experience and internal state, became fundamentally a pessimistic one. He understood deeply the difference between ideal conceptions, especially in politics, and effective change. "The ideals of a policy are entrancing, heady things," he wrote toward the end of his life, but "translating them into terms of compromise with the social structure as it has evolved is pretty second-rate work. I have never met people more honest and devoted than our politicians — but I'd rather be a dustman. A decent nihilism is what I hope for, generally. I think an established land, like ours, can do with 1% monists or nihilists. That leaves room for me."[57]

Explanatory formulations of the causes of historical change tend to diminish in power as the student enriches his knowledge and gains a fuller picture of events. New elements emerge; further information must be considered; the plot thickens. The same limitation occurs, I believe, in the study of historical figures: in attempting to understand the subject, we must add to the data of biography and psychology, the influence of events, of politics and of historical circumstances — of reality in the broadest sense.

Still more difficult is it, then, to identify with confidence the links between the psychology of the individual historical figure and the events in which he played a crucial part. Yet such connections do exist. Few would deny that highly motivated persons critically placed by circumstance can affect the course of history as they live out their private dreams and needs on the stage of public life. The students of these relationships are in the position of detectives who know how the story came out and seek in the reconstruction to find patterns of meaning and influence.

Early in the development of this study I sought to demonstrate the contributions that a thorough study of the psychology of an individual historical figure might make to the understanding of historical events and change. I still believe that dynamic psychology can contribute a great deal to biography and to the understanding of history. I have ended believing as much, however, in what the methods of historical biography may contribute to my own field of psychiatry or psychoanalysis.

The basic instrument of psychological understanding is, broadly speaking, the analysis of the individual patient or subject through the data which he brings — his "material." But this material, though it may convey the patient's psychological state and his perceptions of reality, provides a distorted conception of the outside world as objective data: it is, in short, essentially self-serving. The patient communicates it in order to establish empathic sharing of pain with a doctor or therapist, for self-justification, or to defend himself through a variety of mechanisms against uncongenial self-awareness. The therapist's role is, thus, to understand these necessary distortions and to help the patient to accept a view of reality that allows him more latitude in mastering it and ultimately more personal gratification.

But even in his therapeutic role, the analyst is handicapped by the fact that he is furnished data chiefly by the patient and thus knows only the view of reality, past and present, which the patient presents to him, unless he can apply corrective judgments of his own. The exception to this limitation would be those instances in which the patient's misrepresentations apply to the therapist himself and he is helped to correct the distortion within the treatment relationship.

As for the therapeutic process — and I am talking principally about the understanding of individuals rather than groups — it is argued that the misunderstanding of reality and of events *as such* does not matter a great deal, since what is of chief importance is the patient's mental state, his view of reality, and its meaning for him. I would maintain, however, that it is often extremely difficult to understand the patient's mental state, the distortion of reality he is communicating, and the psychological mechanisms he is using to do so if the therapist is kept in the dark about the patient's actuality, present and past. Often — and I have experienced this frequently myself — the therapist finds himself subtly caught up in an unconscious participation in the patient's distorting mental mechanisms, complying with a misrepresentation of the outside world which might not be so unfortunate if it were therapeutic. But more often than not this compact is not only untherapeutic: it confirms the patient in maladaptive approaches to the world around him.

Historical biography, in contrast to the therapeutic priority required in work with individual patients, demands an objective depiction of reality. Here, too, psychological mechanisms are analyzed — although the voluntary yield of data that a motivated patient provides is not, of course, available. But these psychological phenomena are understood in conjunction with information about the reality of the subject's life. Information about family members, childhood influences, cultural, political and economic forces affecting the individual throughout his life is obtained in order more thoroughly to understand the subject and his impact upon the outside world. His actions and writings and even his deepest thoughts and feelings are all perceived in a context of reality, which helps to make them more intelligible. We learn more, I contend, about such a subject in this way than through the products of his own mind alone, for we see it in relation to the actual elements which helped to create it.

Present-day psychiatrists and other mental health professionals sometimes obtain information from family members, teachers, neighbors, and even employers, especially of hospitalized patients, or of patients treated at centers that use the approaches of community psychiatry. But I would remind the reader that virtually the entire psychoanalytic view of man, with the exception of some early work with children and their families, was built up through information obtained by the analysis of a selected sample of individual patients without obtaining information about them from other sources. It can be argued that generalizations arrived at in this way might well be invalidated by data regarding patients and subjects obtained from other sources. It can also be argued that the methods and approaches of psychologically oriented biography might have applicability not only to the understanding of historical figures but to the study of a variety of other individuals and character types as well.

Not infrequently, in the course of history, an extraordinary person has been able for a time to impose his will upon events, to seem even to shape these events in the direction of his private purpose. It is rare for such persons to reveal the working of their minds and thus permit us to gain insight into the inner forces that propelled them. T. E. Lawrence was — I often think — unique in combining these attributes.

I have tried to show in this book how Lawrence was able to adapt his talents, conflicts and private needs to the requirements of a series of historical situations, above all in the 1914–1918 war in the Middle East and in the diplomatic maneuverings that followed. The outcome of the Arab Revolt and the shape of the post–World War I settlements were influenced by his efforts. He required an arena of great happenings for the maximum use of his talents, "the current of cataclysmic events to chafe into me any sparkle of light," as he once wrote to Charlotte Shaw.[58]

Lawrence is most immediately associated with his achievements as a modern guerrilla leader and one of the first political strategists of the emerging nations. Yet if it is possible to divide historical figures into men who are known for what they did and those whose importance lies in what they represented, surely Lawrence may, with equal justification be placed in the second category. For his central, his unique, achievement derives from an effort to perfect the self, a shaping of his personality into an instrument of accomplishment, example and change. He sought *new possibilities* for the self.

By the onset of World War I Lawrence had equipped himself for any task that would test his powers. In the Arab Revolt he found a challenge matched to his capabilities and was able to combine the heroic fantasies of his youth with the historical exigencies and opportunities of the British war effort. He did indeed lead the Arabs "madly" to the final victory in Syria however much they may now criticize his approach to their political destinies after the war was over.

Connections can be found, as we have seen, between the elements in Lawrence's ancestral and family background and childhood development and many of the directions and conflicts of his adult life — links that were as vitalizing as they were impeding. Yet it is also clear that if Lawrence derived strength and purpose from his background and childhood, he was left with certain vulnerabilities — what the British writer John Buchan called "a crack in the firing." Unknowingly, he became burdened with the sin of his parents, especially his mother's, and was driven to redeem their fallen souls along with his own. He became aware at an early age that his parents were not married, despite the strictness of their personal codes. This discovery became a source of irreconcilable conflict in Lawrence, perhaps even as it contributed to his unusual tolerance of contradiction, ambiguity, and oddness in others. Having had such a deception imposed upon himself, Lawrence became deeply troubled about his own later role in the deception of the Arabs, whom he had encouraged in the Revolt while possessing the knowledge that secret agreements might ultimately vitiate their accomplishments.

The powerful and devouring personality of his mother was a source of strength for him, but confronted Lawrence with a formidable developmental challenge. She dominated his childhood and whipped him many times in a fashion to break his will. He maintained his integrity and avoided being totally absorbed by her (unlike his older brother) by identifying with many aspects of her personality, while keeping his distance from her as much as possible. This identification enabled Lawrence to develop richly empathic and nurturing qualities — aspects of personality ordinarily thought to be "motherly," or associated with women — that were fundamental to his achievements. It also left him confused in his sexual identity and vulnerable to the precipitation of a masochistic disorder that grew out of his identification with the passive feminine elements of the mother.

Lawrence was eternally engaged in struggles over value and self-worth. As a child he incorporated into his self-regard the guilt, the burden of sin and the shared family shame of illegitimacy, while absorbing at the same time the merciless expectation of exemplary ethical conduct, which was contained in the severe familial moral and religious tenets. He sought always to eliminate through the conduct of his life the gulf between his actual view of himself and his merciless ideal expectations. This gulf, this internal tension, provided an impetus for some of Lawrence's extraordinary strivings, especially his drive to achieve heroic deeds of a scale and form consistent with the chivalric and epic codes of his youthful readings.

To a certain extent, Lawrence was successful, at least from an objective standpoint. He possessed extraordinary courage and stamina (he once wrote Mrs. Shaw that he had sustained more, and fiercer, physical ordeals than any man he had known),[59] and the resourcefulness of Odysseus. He combined these qualities with an array of talents for leadership and a willingness to assume during the desert campaigns and thereafter responsibility to an extraordinary degree.

But there is always danger in trying to impose internal, private purposes upon the outside world, especially on a national or international scale. Events and peoples rarely conform for long to such purposes, and reality soon moves beyond the control of the individual. For Lawrence, the international politics of the struggles of the Middle East had already assured that he would be disappointed even before he had embarked upon his course of leadership in the Hijaz. He knew before he had been actively engaged in the desert campaigns for a year that he was an instrument of deception, encouraging the Arabs in the belief that their accomplishments on the battlefield would be honored at the conference table after the war. Furthermore, the Arabs, though ready to use Lawrence's guidance in achieving their own liberation, often did not conform to the epic ideal in their actual behavior during the war, despite his characterization of certain of their leaders as epic heroes in *Seven Pillars of Wisdom*.

The war left Lawrence troubled by guilt and shame. Not only had he been a party to deceiving, to exploiting, the Arabs — a desecration of his high mission — but he had violated his conscience in other ways: settling blood disputes with his own hand, putting to death his suffering companion, giving the "no prisoners" order at Tafas. The traumatic sexual attack by the Turks at Der'a confronted him with disturbing elements in his nature and reactivated the very doubts about his self-worth that he had sought to remove. It also left him with a disorder that required a repetition of the experience through complex, medieval and ritualistic forms of penance.

The campaigns in Arabia not only failed to resolve Lawrence's conflicts about his self-worth, they left him with far deeper doubts and self-questioning than he had ever had before — "behind the laughing eyes a dreadful haunting."[60] But from this self-questioning has come what I believe to be Lawrence's central importance for our time.

The disillusionment and traumatic experiences of the campaigns led Lawrence to profound introspection, which found its fullest expression in *Seven Pillars of Wisdom*. In this work and in some of his letters, Lawrence examines mercilessly the deeper psychological sources of his efforts on behalf of the Allies and the Arabs during the campaigns. He has told us something important, I believe, about the egoistic roots of leadership, "how unlovely the back of a commander's mind must be," and has laid bare the selfishness of self-sacrifice, in which the minds of the followers are coopted in order to fulfill the private purposes of the leader. By assuming an exaggerated responsibility for murder he did not commit, in a war that was not to begin with his responsibility, Lawrence helped to undermine potentially the rationale — essential in the use of war for political purposes — that killing may be justifiable if the cause is worthy or the killer is merely following orders.

Through his self-questioning Lawrence helped to make out of date the romantic heroism of the nineteenth century, which adhered to an archaic blind patriotism and glorification of war, little adapted to the modern world viewed as a community of nations. Lawrence's exaggerated concern with the leader's responsibility for life may be of use to our age and to those of the future in defining what we expect of our heroes and perhaps how we come to regard heroism in a world that cannot tolerate — or even survive — the glorification and the achievements of war. His exaggerated sense of responsibility may serve as a moral example for the ideals of future leadership.

Lawrence always offered a great deal of himself as public property, his conflicts and his sufferings, as well as his hopes and achievements. Even after he had chosen to retreat from public life and from the full exercise of his personal powers, Lawrence offered his values and his solutions to others. Over and over again in talks with those who knew Lawrence or whose lives he had touched, I heard how he had changed their views of themselves, had helped them to find new approaches to their personal dilemmas and moral struggles.

Recognizing the essentially private nature of man's quest for a sense of personal worth, Lawrence seems to have been able to offer his tastes, his abilities and his moral values — especially his deeply felt code of renunciation — for others to use without imposing his values upon them. He could, like the saints with whose lives he was so familiar, give away everything he possessed — talents, advice, money — without leaving the recipient feeling in his debt.

Part of Lawrence's success in helping others grew out of his ability to keep his personal suffering apart from the daily congress of his life. He seems to have wrestled with his personal torments on his own time, and to have communicated them selectively in his writings, or in personal letters to friends. To other people he conveyed most often a sense of harmony, and seems to have spared them the knowledge of his compelling need for self-degradation and his nihilism. How was the "miracle of harmony" achieved in a man who was "at once prophet, poet, jester, crusader?" one friend wondered but was at a loss to explain.[61]

Lawrence's personality was replete with paradoxes and contradictions. These relate to the complexities and ambiguities of his origins, family relationships, and childhood development, but are not explained by them. They have made him fascinating to biographers and may account in part for the attraction of his example. He retained on the one hand a childlike immaturity — like a gifted schoolboy — and a responsiveness to the child's world, while at the same time he assumed throughout his life extraordinary adult responsibilities. He possessed an unusual capacity for relationships with many different sorts of human beings, while retaining an essential isolation and aloofness. He was highly open to sensuous experience yet remained always an ascetic who rejected many of the pleasures of the flesh, especially sexual ones. Self-absorbed and egocentric, he was nevertheless unselfish in giving of himself. He suffered troubling forms of psychopathology and was "neurotic" in many ways. Yet out of his sufferings he found new solutions and values, and was often able to convert his personal pathology to creative public endeavors. His own moral conflicts became irreconcilable and he never fully recovered a full sense of his own worth. Yet he continuously helped others feel more worthwhile in themselves.

Lawrence was a great creator of myths in the sense that his exploits and his own rich account of them — so vivid at times as to give the impression of fiction — served as the basis for the creation by others of the distorted legend that grew around him. Yet he represented such fundamental truthfulness in his being that David Garnett once told me Lawrence was the only man he had known in whose presence he could never lie. He was to a degree a hero fashioned along the lines of the Victorian revival of medieval romanticism. Yet he may contribute ultimately to the destruction of this form of heroism and help to replace it with a model of a hero more self-aware, responsible and realistic. He was the representative of British colonialism in the Middle East, but became a spokesman for the end of traditional imperialism. A war hero and modern military leader — perhaps, next to Churchill, Britain's best known — Lawrence could become a figure who represents the renunciation of war.

Lawrence was always influencing people. This power to influence lies close to the heart of his effectiveness as a leader and of his historical importance. Besides his influence upon Arabs and British alike during the war in the Middle East and after it, he influenced the development of the RAF and was able to convince the admiralty to use for air-sea rescue the smaller, faster boats he helped to design. Individual airmen and tank corpsmen and other friends have related to me how their acquaintance with Lawrence profoundly altered their lives, helped them to find new purpose and meaning. One airman told me that he had led a derelict life and was in constant difficulty with the authorities until he got to know Lawrence. But through the gentle influence and example of his friend he had steadied himself and had developed a rich and lasting interest in literature. Others ask themselves at difficult moments, "What would Lawrence have done?" and feel guided by the memory of his example.

In 1927 Lawrence asked a friend, "How long do you think, before they forget?"[62] But his influence continues, especially through the written legacy of his experience. Arnold Lawrence still receives letters from people who were enabled to do something useful with their lives, or found a new, deeper meaning through Lawrence's writings and personal example. He had a way of giving people the sense that he had experienced or suffered what they had endured. As he wrote Mrs. Shaw in 1931, "Colonel Lawrence still goes on, and it is only me who has stepped out of the way."[63]

It is difficult, if not impossible, to estimate Lawrence's influence in a larger sense. As one of his biographers I am a part of the process by which he becomes known to his historical audience. The selection of Lawrence for such intensive study bespeaks in itself my belief in his value and importance, and I would wish naturally to have documented the basis for this conviction and to have communicated it effectively. I have in mind not only Lawrence's accomplishments as a military and political leader and writer, or even his achievements in the RAF period, but just as important, I have chosen to stress those aspects of Lawrence's place in history that have been more meaningful to me — the intangible qualities of personality, the example of self through which Lawrence drew others to him and enabled them to change. As Erik Erikson has taught us, the evaluation of the meaning of a man's life viewed in these terms will shift according to the requirements of each age and culture, and every biographer embodies to some extent the values and points of view of his own society in his interpretations of a subject.

Lawrence has been hurt by both his idolators and his denigrators. The latter, especially Richard Aldington and Malcolm Muggeridge, have found Lawrence to be a charlatan and a liar.[64] My own examination of the evidence has led me to different conclusions. Lawrence had a compelling need to tell stories, which grew in part out of his deep doubts about his self-worth. Profoundly uncertain about his value, he laid the foundation for the creation alongside of the actual Lawrence of a legendary personality built on the dramatizations and elaborations of his tales. So extraordinary are some of these stories that they have seemed at times to have been made up. Yet my research led me repeatedly to the conclusion that Lawrence's accounts of his accomplishments were largely accurate and, if anything, he would customarily leave out information that was to his credit, or allow to stand distorted depictions of events that have invited the attacks of his detractors. I have not found Lawrence to be a liar.

Lawrence's struggles form one of the most moving personal sagas I have ever encountered. He could not ultimately resolve his inner personal disorder. Had he been able to, he might have lived to make a contribution in Britain's hour of need in World War II. But though he could not quiet his own inner demons, he was, in Irving Howe's words, a "prince of our disorder" and one of its civilizing forces.

A poet friend wrote to Lawrence once: "You are a kind of double personality for me (a) a charming friendly character given to sudden appearances on inordinate motor-bicycles; (b) a sort of mythological figure or a force of nature — so that I feel as if I were being addressed by an earthquake, in however still and small a voice."[65] Lawrence was tragic and introspective, a master craftsman and technician on the one hand, and a saint with humor on the other. Churchill deemed him one of the greatest beings alive in his time, while David Garnett told me simply, "He was of a higher value."[66]

Others found different riches in Lawrence's nature, other dimensions of themselves. Unable to establish firmly the core of his own identity, he was able to draw men and women to him to offer for their pleasure and development the many currents of his personality. John Buchan captured best this central characteristic of Lawrence's: "I am not a very tractable person or much of a hero-worshipper, but I could have followed Lawrence over the edge of the world. I loved him for himself, and also because there seemed to be reborn in him all the lost friends of my youth."[67]

# APPENDIX

# Appendix

## Twenty-seven Articles*

The following notes have been expressed in commandment form for greater clarity and to save words. They are however only my personal conclusions, arrived at gradually while I worked in the Hedjaz and now put on paper as stalking horses for beginners in the Arab armies. They are meant to apply only to Bedu: townspeople or Syrians require totally different treatment. They are of course not suitable to any other person's need, or applicable unchanged in any particular situation. Handling Hedjaz Arabs is an art, not a science, with exceptions and no obvious rules. At the same time we have a great chance there: the Sherif trusts us, and has given us the position (towards his Government) which the Germans wanted to win in Turkey. If we are tactful we can at once retain his good will, and carry out our job — but to succeed we have got to put into it all the interest and energy and skill *we possess.*

1. Go easy just for the first few weeks. A bad start is difficult to atone for, and the Arabs form their judgments on externals that we ignore. When you have reached the inner circle in a tribe you can do as you please with yourself and them.

2. Learn all you can about your Ashraf and Bedu. Get to know their families, clans and tribes, friends and enemies, wells, hills and roads. Do all this by listening and by indirect inquiry. Do not ask questions. Get to speak their dialect of Arabic, not yours. Until you can understand their allusions avoid getting deep into conversation, or you will drop bricks. Be a little stiff at first.

3. In matters of business deal only with the commander of the Army, column, or party in which you serve. Never give orders to anyone at all, and reserve your directions or advice for the C.O., however great the temptation (for efficiency's sake) of dealing direct with his underlings. Your place is advisory, and

* First published in the *Arab Bulletin* #60, August 20, 1917; reprinted in Lawrence's *Secret Dispatches from Arabia* (1937), pp. 126–133; reprinted in part in Basil Liddell Hart's 'T. E. Lawrence,' pp. 142–147. The original manuscript is in the PRO/FO 882/7.

your advice is due to the commander alone. Let him see that this is your conception of your duty, and that his is to be the sole executive of your joint plans.

4. Win and keep the confidence of your leader. Strengthen his prestige at your expense before others when you can. Never refuse or quash schemes he may put forward: but ensure that they are put forward in the first instance privately to you. Always approve them, and after praise modify them insensibly, causing the suggestions to come from him, until they are in accord with your own opinion. When you attain this point, hold him to it, keep a tight grip of [sic] his ideas, and push him forward as firmly as possible, but secretly so that no one but himself (and he not too clearly) is aware of your pressure.

5. Remain in touch with your leader as constantly and unobtrusively as you can. Live with him, that at meal times and at audiences you may be naturally with him in his tent. Formal visits to give advice are not so good as the constant dropping of ideas in casual talk. When stronger sheikhs come in for the first time to swear allegiance and offer services, clear out of the tent. If their first impression is of foreigners in the confidence of the Sherif, it will do the Arab cause much harm.

6. Be shy of too close relations with the subordinates of the expedition. Continued intercourse with them will make it impossible for you to avoid going behind or beyond the instruction that the Arab C.O. has given them on your advice: and in so disclosing the weakness of his position you altogether destroy your own.

7. Treat the sub-chiefs of your force quite easily and lightly. In this way you hold yourself above their level. Treat the leader, if a Sherif, with respect. He will return your manner, and you and he will then be alike, and above the rest. Precedence is a serious matter among the Arabs, and you must attain it.

8. Your ideal position is when you are present and not noticed. Do not be too intimate, too prominent, or too earnest. Avoid being identified too long or too often with any tribal sheikh, even if C.O. of the expedition. To do your work you must be above jealousies, and you lose prestige if you are associated with a tribe or clan, and its inevitable feuds. Sherifs are above all blood-feuds and local rivalries, and form the only principle of unity among the Arabs. Let your name, therefore, be coupled always with a Sherif's, and share his attitude towards the tribe. When the moment comes for action put yourself publicly under his orders. The Bedu will then follow suit.

9. Magnify and develop the growing conception of the Sherifs as the natural aristocracy of the Arabs. Inter-tribal jealousies make it impossible for any sheikh to attain a commanding position, and the only hope of union in nomad Arabia is that the Ashraf be universally acknowledged as the ruling class. Sherifs are half townsmen, half-nomad, in manner and life, and have the instinct of command. Mere merit and money would be insufficient to obtain such recognition: but the Arab reverence for pedigree and the prophet gives hope for the ultimate success of the Ashraf.

10. Call your Sherif "Sidi" in public and in private. Call other people by their ordinary names, without title. In intimate conversation call a Sheikh "Abu Annad," "Akhu Alia" or some similar by-name.

11. The foreigner and Christian is not a popular person in Arabia. However friendly and informal the treatment of yourself may be, remember always that

your foundations are very sandy ones. Wave a Sherif in front of you like a banner, and hide your own mind and person. If you succeed you will have hundreds of miles of country and thousands of men under your orders, and for this it is worth bartering the outward show.

12. Cling tight to your sense of humor. You will need it every day. A dry irony is the most useful type, and repartee of a personal and not too broad character will double your influence with the Chiefs. Reproof if wrapped up in some smiling form will carry further and last longer than the most violent speech. The power of mimicry or parody is valuable but use it sparingly for it is more dignified than humor. Do not cause a laugh at a Sherif except amongst Sherifs.

13. Never lay hands on an Arab — you degrade yourself. You may think the resultant obvious increase of outward respect a gain to you: but what you have really done is to build a wall between you and their inner selves. It is difficult to keep quiet when everything is being done wrong, but the less you lose your temper the greater your advantage. Also then you will not go mad yourself.

14. While very difficult to drive, the Bedu are easy to lead, if you have the patience to bear with them. The less apparent your interferences the more you influence. They are willing to follow your advice and do what you wish, but they do not mean you or anyone else to be aware of that. It is only after the end of all annoyances that you find at bottom their real fund of good will.

15. Do not try to do too much with your own hands. Better the Arabs do it tolerably than that you do it perfectly. It is their war, and you are to help them, not to win it for them. Actually also under the very odd conditions of Arabia, your practical work will not be as good as perhaps, you think it is.

16. If you can, without being too lavish, forestall presents to yourself. A well placed gift is often most effective in winning over a suspicious Sheikh. Never receive a present without giving a liberal return, but you may delay this return (while letting its ultimate certainty be known) if you require a particular service from the giver. Do not let them ask you for things, since their greed will then make them look upon you only as a cow to milk.

17. Wear an Arab headcloth when with a tribe. Bedu have a malignant prejudice against the hat, and believe that our persistence in wearing it (due probably to British obstinacy of dictation) is founded on some immoral or irreligious principle. A thick headcloth forms a good protection against the sun, and if you wear a hat your best Arab friends will be ashamed of you in public.

18. Disguise is not advisable. Except in special areas let it be clearly known that you are a British officer and a Christian. At the same time if you can wear Arab kit when with the tribes you will acquire their trust and intimacy to a degree impossible in uniform. It is however dangerous and difficult. They make no special allowances for you when you dress like them. Breaches of etiquette not charged against a foreigner are not condoned to you in Arab clothes. You will be like an actor in a foreign theatre, playing a part day and night for months, without rest, and for an anxious stake. Complete success, which is when the Arabs forget your strangeness and speak naturally before you, counting you one of themselves, is perhaps only attainable in character: while half success (all that most of us will strive for — the other costs too much) is easier to win in British things, and you yourself will last longer, physically and mentally, in

the comfort that they mean. Also then the Turks will not hang you, when you're caught.

19. If you wear Arab things wear the best. Clothes are significant among the tribes, and you must wear the appropriate, and appear at ease in them. Dress like a Sherif — if they agree to it.

20. If you wear Arab things at all, go the whole way. Leave your English friends and customs on the coast, and fall back on Arab habits entirely. It is possible, starting thus to level with them, for the Europeans to beat the Arabs at their own game, for we had stronger motives for our action, and put more heart into it than they. If you can surpass them, you have taken an immense stride toward complete success, but the strain of living and thinking in a foreign and half-understood language, the savage food, strange clothes, and still stranger ways, with the complete loss of privacy and quiet, and the impossibility of ever realizing your watchful imitation of the others for months on end, provide such an added stress to the ordinary difficulties of dealing with the Bedu, the climate, and the Turks, that this road should not be chosen without serious thought.

21. Religious discussions will be fairly frequent. Say what you like about your own side, and avoid criticism of theirs, unless you know that the point is external, when you may score heavily by proving it so. With the Bedu Islam is so all-pervading an element that there is with religiosity, little fervour, and no regard for externals. Do not think, from their conduct that they are careless. Their conviction of the truth of their faith, and its share in every act and thought and principle of their daily life is so intimate and intense as to be unconscious, unless roused by opposition. Their religion is as much a part of nature to them as is sleep, or food.

22. Do not try to trade on what you know of fighting. The Hedjaz confounds ordinary tactics. Learn the Bedu principles of war as thoroughly and as quickly as you can, for till you know them your advice will be no good to the Sherif. Unnumbered generations of tribal raids have taught them more about some parts of the business than we will ever know. In familiar conditions they fight well, but strange events cause panic. Keep your unit small. Their raiding parties are usually from one hundred to two hundred men, and if you take a crowd they only get confused. Also their sheikhs, while admirable company commandoes, are too set to learn to handle the equivalents of battalions or regiments. Don't attempt unusual things, unless they appeal to the sporting instinct Bedu have so strongly, or unless success is obvious. If the objective is a good one (booty) they will attack like fiends: they are splendid scouts, their mobility gives you the advantage that will win your local war, they make proper use of their knowledge of the country (don't take tribesmen to places they do not know), and the gazelle-hunters, who form a proportion of the better men, are great shots at visible targets. A Sheikh from one tribe cannot give orders to men from another: a Sherif is necessary to command a mixed tribal force. If there is plunder in prospect, and the odds are at all equal, you will win. Do not waste Bedu attacking trenches (they will not stand casualties) or in trying to defend a position, for they cannot sit still without slacking. The more unorthodox and Arab your proceedings the more likely you are to have the Turks cold, for they lack initiative and expect you to. Don't play for safety.

23. The open reason that Bedu give you for action or inaction may be true, but always there will be better reasons left for you to divine. You must find these inner reasons (they will be denied, but are none the less in operation) before shaping your arguments for one course or others. Allusion is more effective than logical exposition: they dislike concise expression. Their minds work just as ours do, but on different premises. There is nothing unreasonable, incomprehensible, or inscrutable, in the Arab. Experience of them, and knowledge of their prejudices will enable you to foresee their attitude and possible course of action in nearly every case.

24. Do not mix Bedu and Syrians, or trained men and tribesmen. You will get work out of neither, for they hate each other. I have never seen a successful combined operation, but many failures. In particular, ex-officers of the Turkish army however Arab in feeling and blood and language, are hopeless with Bedu. They are narrow-minded in tactics, unable to adjust themselves to irregular warfare, clumsy in Arab etiquette, swollen-headed to the extent of being incapable of politeness to a tribesman for more than a few minutes, impatient, and usually helpless on the road, in action. Your orders (if you were unwise enough to give any) would be more readily obeyed by Bedouins than those of any Mohammedan Syrian officer. Arab townsmen and Arab tribesmen regard each other mutually as poor relations — and poor relations are much more objectionable than poor strangers.

25. In spite of ordinary Arab example avoid too free talk about women. It is as difficult a subject as religion, and their standards are so unlike our own, that a remark harmless in English may appear as unrestrained to them, as some of their statements would look to us, if translated literally.

26. Be as careful of your servants as of yourself. If you want a sophisticated one you will probably have to take an Egyptian, or a Sudani, and unless you are very lucky he will undo on trek much of the good you so laboriously effect. Arabs will cook rice and make coffee for you, and leave you if required to do unmanly work like cleaning boots or washing. They are only really possible if you are in Arab kit. A slave brought up in the Hedjaz is the best servant, but there are rules against British subjects owning them, so they have to be lent to you. In any case take with you an Ageyli or two when you go up country. They are the most efficient couriers in Arabia, and understand camels.

27. The beginning and ending of the secret of handling Arabs is unremitting study of them. Keep always on your guard; never say an inconsidered thing, or do an unnecessary thing: watch yourself and your companions all the time: hear all that passes, search out what is going on beneath the surface, read their characters, discover their tastes and their weaknesses, and keep everything you find out to yourself. Bury yourself in Arab circles, have no interests and no ideas except the work in hand, so that your brain shall be saturated with one thing only, and you realize your part deeply enough to avoid the little slips that would undo the work of weeks. Your success will be just proportioned to the amount of mental effort you devote to it.

# CHAPTER NOTES

# Chapter Notes

The following abbreviations are used in the notes:

| | |
|---|---|
| BM Add MSS | British Museum Additional Manuscripts |
| Bod Res MSS | The large collection of Lawrence's papers on reserve in the Bodleian Library, Oxford |
| CAB | Cabinet Papers |
| *Friends* | Arnold W. Lawrence, ed., *T. E. Lawrence by His Friends* |
| FO | Foreign Office Papers |
| *Home Letters* | M. Robert Lawrence, ed., *The Home Letters of T. E. Lawrence and His Brothers* |
| *Letters* | *The Letters of T. E. Lawrence,* edited by David Garnett |
| *Letters to TEL* | Arnold W. Lawrence, ed., *Letters to T. E. Lawrence* |
| LHB | Basil Liddell Hart, *T. E. Lawrence to his Biographer, Liddell Hart* |
| *Mint* | Lawrence's *The Mint* |
| PRO | Public Record Office |
| RGB | Robert Graves, *T. E. Lawrence to His Biographer, Robert Graves* |
| *Secret Dispatches* | Lawrence's *Secret Dispatches from Arabia* |
| *Secret Lives* | Phillip Knightley and Colin Simpson, *The Secret Lives of Lawrence of Arabia* |
| *Seven Pillars* | Lawrence's *Seven Pillars of Wisdom* |

INTRODUCTION

1. In an essay, "Psychopathic Characters on the Stage," published posthumously, Freud discusses the relationship between dramatic heroes on the stage and the theatre audience, which identifies with the personal conflicts of the protagonist. The spectator, Freud notes, usually feels that there is little of importance in his life and "longs to feel and to act and to arrange things according to his desires — in short to be a hero." The hero on the stage furnishes the opportunity to surmount these limitations through identification with his struggles. Freud does not extend his discussion to the relationship between the "spectator" in society and the public figures with whom he identifies. (*Standard Edition of the Complete Psychological Works of Sigmund Freud*, VII [1942, but written in 1905 or 1906]: 305–310.)

2. *Letters*, p. 651.

3. Isaiah Berlin, *Historical Inevitability*, p. 53.

4. *Letters*, p. 825.

5. Ibid., p. 427.

6. *Seven Pillars*, p. 6.

7. *Letters*, p. 559.

8. A fuller discussion of the history of psychoanalytic approaches to biographical study is provided in an essay by the author, "Psychoanalysis and Historical Biography," *Journal of the American Psychoanalytic Association* 19 (January 1971): 143–179.

1. CHAPMANS AND LAWRENCES

1. LHB, p. 78.

2. RGB, p. 60.

3. RGB, p. 50.

4. LHB, p. 55.

5. Lawrence to John Buchan, June 20, 1927, Bod Res MSS, b55. In 1926 Lawrence also supplied basic biographical data in a humorous letter to David G. Hogarth, who was then preparing an entry on him for the *Dictionary of National Biography* (*Letters*, p. 491–492).

6. Early in my investigations I was led by David Garnett, editor of the Lawrence letters, on to the trail of several members of the Anglo-Irish nobility who had been neighbors of the Chapmans in County Westmeath. They kindly shared with me their recollections of Lady Chapman and her daughters and of the stilted, old-fashioned existence they carried on at South Hill long after Thomas Chapman had eloped with Sarah. "My family and the Chapmans lived about 12 miles apart and probably only met occasionally," one lady wrote me. "I had always understood [Thomas Chapman] had . . . run off with the future Mrs. Lawrence, who was variously described as the 'Italian maid' and 'the Scotch governess'. . . . Meanwhile Lady Chapman and her four daughters had passed a twilight sort of existence and it is not surprising if they grew a little eccentric as they got older. . . . My own first contact with the Chapmans was in 1924 [at a dance]. . . . They [the daughters] certainly looked a bit dishevelled and old-fashioned in dress, but were full of spirit and put up a good show for middle-aged spinsters who had spent their life mewed up in a decayed country house with a decaying mother." A year later the letter writer found "old Lady Chapman, sitting rigidly in an upright chair and looking as if she and her surroundings had not altered since Sir Thomas Chapman eloped. She made polite small talk . . . evidently under the impression that Queen Victoria was still alive" (Lady Pansy Lamb to the author, December 19, 1964). The daughters remembered their mother as cruelly restrictive and punitive. She would make them look away if a man passed in the street, and she once forced the youngest daughter to hang a chamber pot around her neck as punishment when she did something wrong (interview in Dublin with Mrs. Seaton Pringle, a former companion of one of the Chapman daughters, March 19, 1965). She actually drove two of her daughters out of the home for a two-year period. Despite the intolerance of the Victorian era in which she lived, her extreme behavior has led to speculation that Edith Chapman might have been mentally ill. Phillip Knightley and Colin Simpson in *The Secret Lives of Lawrence of Arabia* provide from their researches other accounts of her behavior.

7. *Burke's Peerage*, 1887.

8. Interview with Miss Fitzsimon, Delvin, County Westmeath, March 19, 1965.

9. Lawrence to Charlotte Shaw, March 18, 1927, BM Add MCC, 45903.

10. Lawrence to Edward Garnett, August 27, 1924, Bod Res MSS, d54.

11. Lawrence to Charlotte Shaw, August 24, 1926, BM Add MSS, 45903.

12. Interview on March 20, 1965, with Lily Montgomery, family companion of the Chapman daughters, 1937–1953.

13. Interview with Christine Longford, former neighbor of the Chapmans, March 18, 1965.

14. Interview with Lily Montgomery, March 20, 1965, and letter from her to the author, September 17, 1965.

15. Ibid.

16. Letter to Arabella Rivington from a cousin of Lady Chapman's and the transcription of Mrs. Rivington's interview with the cousin, in the *Sunday Times* research materials, Imperial War Museum, London.

17. Lawrence to Robin Buxton, November 25, 1924, Jesus College Library, Oxford University.

18. Birth record of William Lawrence, Kirkudbright, Scotland.

19. Mrs. Stewart (Elsie) Newcombe to the author, January 5, 1965.

20. LHB, p. 67.

21. Lawrence to Charlotte Shaw, April 14, 1927, BM Add MSS, 45903.

22. Lawrence to Hugh Trenchard, May 1, 1928, Bod Res MSS, d46.

23. Lawrence to Charlotte Shaw, August 28, 1928, BM Add MSS, 45904.

24. Interview with Janet Laurie Hallsmith, March 25, 1965.

25. Interview with Robert Lawrence, March 24, 1965.

26. Interview with Andrew Laurie, March 26, 1965.

27. Interview with Robert Lawrence, March 24, 1965.

28. Ibid.

29. Interview with Theo and Hilda Chaundy, August 24, 1964.

30. An interesting observation in view of the fact that T. E. later took the name Shaw as his own.

31. Comments of A. H. Kerry on a BBC television broadcast, November 27, 1962; interview with Kerry, March 25, 1965.

32. Interview with Janet Laurie Hallsmith and Mollie Laurie, December 17, 1965; interview with C. F. C. Beeson, March 22, 1965.

33. Robert Graves, *Lawrence and the Arabs*, p. 17.

34. Interview with Arnold Lawrence, August 25, 1964.

35. Sarah Lawrence did not live in Oxford after 1923, when the house on Polstead Road was sold. She and Bob soon traveled to China and lived there until they were expelled in 1927. They returned in 1933 and were there when news came of T.E.'s death in 1935. During the interim period and after 1935 Sarah and Bob had a peripatetic existence — in Oxfordshire, Wiltshire, Dorset, London and Malta (where Bob took a post in the Naval Hospital). It was in Malta that Mrs. Lawrence became close to Stewart and Elsie Newcombe. Mrs. Newcombe, because of her close friendship with Sarah, was able to provide valuable information and insights.

36. Interview with Sir Basil Blackwell, Oxford, March 21, 1965.

37. Interview with Basil Liddell Hart, March 27, 1965.

38. Birth record, Sunderland District, England. Mrs. Lawrence concealed her own origins as much as she did the details of her family situation with Lawrence's father. When the *Dictionary of National Biography* required in its entry on Lawrence some mention of the parents' names, Ronald Storrs, the author of the piece, inquired of Arnold Lawrence for information about his mother's maiden name. Arnold knew few details, but discouraged Storrs from asking his mother. "It certainly is no use telling her I approve," he wrote Storrs, "she'd say I ought not to" (letter of April 1946). When she learned from Arnold about the planned article Mrs. Lawrence wrote Storrs to request that if he would say nothing about Lawrence's antecedents other than that his father was Irish and his mother Scottish he would "make an old woman of 85 most grateful" (letter of August 29, 1946). Both letters are among the *Sunday Times* research materials, Imperial War Museum, London.

39. Personal communication from Arnold Lawrence, July 15, 1968.

40. Interview with Arnold Lawrence, August 26, 1972.

41. Interview with Elsie Newcombe, August 27, 1964; Elsie Newcombe to the author, October 3, 1964.

42 Interview with Mollie Laurie, March 25, 1965.

43. Interview with Janet Laurie Hallsmith, March 25, 1965.

44. Florence Hardy to T. E. Lawrence, March 5, 1928, Bod Res MSS, d60.

45. Interview with Elsie Newcombe, August 20, 1972.

46. Ibid.

47. Interview with Dr. and Mrs. Theo Chaundy, August 26, 1964.

48. Interview with David Garnett, October 30, 1964.

49. Interview with Elsie Newcombe, August 20, 1972.

50. When Arnold Lawrence was in Athens six weeks after having written his mother of his marriage, he awoke one morning to discover that he did not know where he was. He went out into the garden in order "to try to get back some feeling." This was about the day that his mother, whose fierce disapproval of his marriage plans he had not anticipated, would have received his letter. Arnold's theory was that her influence upon him was so powerful that she had succeeded in absorbing him. In contrast, other people, especially women, have testified repeatedly to a sweet, kind and loving quality in Mrs. Lawrence, which, despite her disciplined and forceful ways, commanded affection from both adults and children.

51. Robert Lawrence once asked one of his friends, who was familiar with the family background, quite unexpectedly, "Did you know my father's name?" "Thomas Chapman," the friend told him (interview with Elsie Newcombe, August 20, 1972).

52. Interview with Theo and Hilda Chaundy, August 26, 1964.

53. Celandine Kennington to Lady Hardinge, July 30, 1954, in the *Sunday Times* research materials, Imperial War Museum, London.

54. Interview with Elsie Newcombe, August 20, 1972.

55. Interview with Arnold Lawrence, December 8, 1965.

56. Interviews with Elsie Newcombe, August 27, 1964, and August 20, 1972.

57. Lawrence's statement does not agree with the facts as given to me by Arnold and Robert Lawrence, and by Elsie Newcombe, in whom Mrs. Lawrence confided. They all agree that she was brought up in Scotland by an aunt who was married to the rector of an Evangelical ("low church") parish.

58. Lawrence to Charlotte Shaw, May 17, 1928, BM Add MSS, 45904.

59. Lawrence to Charlotte Shaw, April 14, 1927, BM Add MSS, 45903.

60. Lawrence to Charlotte Shaw, August 28, 1928, BM Add MSS, 45904.

61. Arnold Lawrence, "Knowledge of Illegitimacy" (February 1963), Bod Res MSS, b56.

62. LHB, p. 78.

63. Interview with Robert Lawrence, August 24, 1964; *Friends*, p. 31.

64. Interview with Sir Basil Blackwell, March 21, 1965.

65. Interview with Arnold and Barbara Lawrence, March 16, 1965.

66. Personal communication from Arnold Lawrence, July 21, 1968.

67. Interview with C. F. C. Beeson, March 22, 1965.

68. Interviews with Janet Laurie Hallsmith, March 25, 1965, and E. F. Hall, December 16, 1965.

69. Interview with Arnold Lawrence, March 16, 1965.

70. Arnold Lawrence wrote of the difference in his parents' religiosity as follows: "My mother . . . held religious convictions profoundly. She totally accepted the tenets of her brand of Christianity and had no doubt they constituted a complete code of binding rules for conduct; but she could only in small part share in my father's emotional, almost mystical, religious feeling" (letter to the author, November 1, 1968).

71. J. S. Reynolds, *Canon Christopher of St. Aldates, Oxford*, p. 451.

72. Interview with Robert Lawrence, March 24, 1965.

73. *Friends*, p. 28.

74. LHB, pp. 78–79.

75. This information comes from an interview with Stewart L. Newcombe, March 20, 1965, and from a reminiscence by F. C. Lay in the *Jesus College Record*, 1971 (the year of Robert Lawrence's death).

76. Lawrence to Charlotte Shaw, undated, but clearly June or July 1928, BM Add MSS, 45904.

77. Arnold Lawrence wrote the author (July 23, 1973) that he and T.E. once observed together how amusing it might have been had Bob become the eighth Chapman baronet.

78. This passage appears in the manuscript of Graves's biography of Lawrence (Bod Res MSS, c20), but was omitted from the published version.

79. T.E. to Will Lawrence, August 6, 1906, *Home Letters*, p. 21.

80. Interview with E. F. Hall, December 16, 1965.

81. Accounts by F. C. Lay in the *Jesus*

College Record, 1971, and by Sir Ernest Barker in *Home Letters*, pp. 395–397.

82. Interview with E. F. Hall, December 16, 1965.

83. Ibid.

84. F. C. Lay in the *Jesus College Record*, 1971, p. 25.

85. Interview with Arnold Lawrence, July 21, 1968.

86. He has a wry sense of humor. Once, when we were driving together along an English motorway, he noticed a high-tension power station with its usual concentration of metal towers and structural lattice work. "Those would make wonderful ruins," he remarked.

87. Lawrence to Charlotte Shaw, May 12, 1927, BM Add MSS, 45903.

### 2. CHILDHOOD AND ADOLESCENCE

1. *Friends*, p. 25.

2. Ibid., pp. 25–30, 31–35.

3. For example, LHB, pp. 77–79, and *Letters*, p. 148.

4. *Friends*, p. 31.

5. Bod Res MSS, c54. The photograph opposite p. 54 in *Secret Lives*, which shows a little boy in a sailor's shirt and cap and bears the caption "Lawrence the boy," is not of Lawrence. It was supplied by a woman in North Wales who believed it to be of Lawrence. The photograph does not resemble him at all.

6. Interview with Robert Lawrence, March 24, 1965.

7. *Friends*, p. 25.

8. Interview with Robert Lawrence, August 24, 1964; also, *Friends*, p. 31.

9. Ibid.

10. Ibid.

11. *Letters*, pp. 112–113, 153, 161–162.

12. Richard Aldington, *Lawrence of Arabia*, pp. 26–31.

13. *Friends*, pp. 25, 32; Mrs. Lawrence's preface to T.E.'s *Crusader Castles*, II, 5.

14. *Letters*, p. 148.

15. LHB, p. 51.

16. Ibid.

17. *Letters*, p. 148. In his effort to discredit Lawrence, Aldington deliberately omits the not-infrequent disclaimers that Lawrence includes in his statements about his unusual abilities. For example, the full statement of his experience in learning Latin, which is contained in a 1911 letter to Mrs. Rieder, herself a language teacher at the American mission school at Jebail in Syria, was as follows: "I was reading (chiefly police news) at four, and learning Latin at five, and at seventeen I was no more forward than the rest of the school, beginning Latin at eight and one half" (*Letters*, p. 25). His mother confirms that a schoolmaster gave the boys Latin lessons in Langley, to which the family moved before T.E. was six, "to prepare them for going to school." Sometimes it is Lawrence's biographers who are responsible for the distortion, exaggeration or errors that appear in their work. Robert Graves, for example, wrote in his biography of Lawrence: "In six years he read every book in the library of the Oxford Union — the best part of 50,000 volumes, probably" (*Lawrence and the Arabs*, p. 24). Lawrence's actual statement to Graves, upon which this passage was based, was "I read every book *which interested me* [italics mine] in the library of the Oxford Union (best part of 50,000 volumes I expect) in six years" (RGB, p. 64). The exaggeration by Lawrence is still evident but the meaning is different. Aldington chooses to cite this as entirely Lawrence's exaggeration, referring to the fact that Graves said Lawrence passed on every word in the manuscript, despite Liddell Hart's published assertion that this was a proofreading error on Graves's part (LHB, p. 210). The most it seems that Lawrence could be accused of, if indeed he saw the passage in the manuscript, was of failing to correct it himself. In their more recent book, Knightley and Simpson simply reject out of hand the notion of Lawrence's precocity with the statement, "Despite what numerous biographers have written, he was neither a prodigy nor a prig" (*Secret Lives*, p. 9). They do not provide the evidence upon which this assertion is based.

I have gone into considerable detail on this matter because it is part of a larger problem one encounters in trying to understand Lawrence. As a result of central problems of self-esteem in his psychology, statements about his ability, worth, skill and adventurous exploits loom large in his remarks about himself. The difficulties of assessing matters of fact are made still more difficult if his biographers add emotionally toned denigrations or distortions to Lawrence's own inevitable embellishments or dramatic exaggerations.

18. *Friends*, p. 32.

19. Interview with Robert Lawrence, August 24, 1964.

20. Interview with Janet Laurie Hallsmith, March 25, 1965.

21. Ibid.

22. *Friends*, p. 33.

23. Handwritten essay in the front of Charlotte Shaw's copy of *Seven Pillars*, Arents Collection, New York Public Library. Definitions of adolescence as a stage of development rather than simply as a chronological period are affected by cultural determinants. Insofar as adolescence is a time of transition from childhood to adulthood, its characteristics depend on what is expected of children and adults in a given culture, the rapidity with which the transition from childhood to adulthood is made, and the extent to which aspects of this development are left to later realization. Adolescence in America in the 1970's is different from adolescence in England in the first decade of the twentieth century. There are, however, certain changes that are common to adolescents regardless of culture. In addition to the changes of puberty (the time and nature of their occurrence being affected by such factors as climate, general health and, possibly, sexual stimulation), adolescence is generally a time when the establishment of a firm personal identity occurs, when questions of adult sexuality are being faced, when a comfortable emotional distance from one's parents is being established, childhood ideals are brought into harmony with adult realities, and most childhood fantasies are given up. In none of these respects did Lawrence seem to undergo a clearcut adolescence, either physiologically or emotionally.

24. Interview with C. F. C. Beeson, March 22, 1965.

25. *Friends*, p. 52.

26. In the issue dated March 1904.

27. George Bernard Shaw's handwritten essay in the front of Charlotte Shaw's copy of *Seven Pillars*, Arents Collection, New York Public Library.

28. Interviews with C. F. C. Beeson, March 22, 1965; Theo Chaundy, August 26, 1964; and Janet Laurie Hallsmith, March 25, 1965.

29. Interview with Mr. R. W. Bodey, headmaster, City of Oxford High School, August 27, 1964.

30. In the 1930's the Lawrence family endowed a scholarship to enable City of Oxford High School students of little means to go to Oxford.

31. Interview with C. F. C. Beeson, March 22, 1965; *Friends*, p. 46.

32. *Friends*, p. 46.

33. Lawrence to Charlotte Shaw, August 24, 1926, BM Add MSS, 45903.

34. Telephone conversation in 1973 with Fred George, a former City of Oxford High School student during Lawrence's years there; Mrs. Lawrence's preface to T.E.'s *Crusader Castles* II, 5; *Letters*, p. 38.

35. "Playground Cricket," *City of Oxford High School Magazine*, July 1904.

36. *Letters*, p. 491; LHB, p. 79.

37. LHB, p. 40.

38. Ibid., p. 79.

39. Lawrence to Dick Knowles, July 14, 1927, Bod Res MSS, d56.

40. *Mint*, p. 154.

41. Report from Councillor Hutchins, May 11, 1902, Bod Res MSS, c52.

42. Interview with Theo Chaundy, August 26, 1964.

43. Interview with E. F. Hall, December 16, 1965.

44. Ibid.

45. Interview with Janet Laurie Hallsmith, March 25, 1965.

46. Interview with E. F. Hall, December 16, 1965.

47. LHB, p. 24.

48. Ibid., p. 51.

49. *Mint*, p. 132.

50. Knightley and Simpson treat the episode as entirely factual and offer the additional details that Lawrence bicycled to St. Just in Roseland in Cornwall and enlisted as a private in the Royal Artillery and that his father went to Cornwall and bought him out (*Secret Lives*, p. 16). But this information comes, I believe, from one of Lawrence's RAF pals, who was speculating about the episode from fragmentary knowledge, and when I questioned him about it myself, he was quite unsure about the whole matter (several discussions with A. E. "Jock" Chambers, 1965–1972).

51. *Friends*, p. 26.

52. Personal communication from Arnold Lawrence, March 24, 1974.

53. Interview with C. F. C. Beeson, March 22, 1965.

54. Hilda Chaundy to the author, June 18, 1966.

### 3. LAWRENCE AND HIS FAMILY: THE BURDEN OF ILLEGITIMACY

1. About 1922 or 1923 Lawrence told his brother Arnold of his parents' legal inability to marry. Arnold laughed and T.E. told him that his parents did not regard it at all as a laughing matter and thought he was "practically a pervert" for taking it lightly (Arnold Lawrence to the author, March 23, 1972).
2. Lawrence to Charlotte Shaw, April 14, 1927, BM Add MSS, 45903.
3. Interview with Arnold Lawrence, July 15, 1968.
4. Interviews with Arnold Lawrence, March 16, 1965, and July 15, 1968.
5. Richard Aldington, *Lawrence of Arabia*, p. 42.
6. Interview with Christine Longford, March 18, 1965.
7. Lawrence to Charlotte Shaw, April 14, 1927, BM Add MSS, 45903.
8. The fact that Lawrence's parents were unmarried was known by Lord Stamfordham, King George's secretary, in 1927. He wrote about it — including some speculation about its traumatic meaning — to one of Lawrence's former chiefs, so presumably the information was widespread at this time (Stamfordham to Reginald Wingate, March 15, 1927 in *Sunday Times* papers, Imperial War Museum, London; the original is in the School of Oriental Studies, University of Durham).
9. Interview with Arnold and Barbara Lawrence, March 16, 1965.
10. Interviews with Elsie Newcombe, August 27, 1964, and August 20, 1972.
11. Lawrence to Lord Winterton, October 27, 1923, Bod Res MSS, d44.
12. Lawrence to Lionel Curtis, March 8, 1926, Bod Res MSS, d51.
13. Lawrence to A. E. Chambers, August 8, 1924, Bod Res MSS, d51.
14. Lawrence to Sir Fred Kenyon, June 1, 1927, Bod Res MSS, d43.
15. Lawrence to F. N. Doubleday, August 25, 1927, Bod Res MSS, d52.
16. Lawrence to Lionel Curtis, November 27, 1927, Bod Res MSS, d51.
17. *Letters*, pp. 50, 301, 382, 721.
18. Interview with Arnold Lawrence, March 16, 1965.
19. LHB, p. 78.
20. "My mother is an enraged housewife," he wrote to Mrs. Hardy on October 24, 1930, when Mrs. Lawrence was "remorselessly" cleaning his cottage (Bod Res MSS, d55).
21. Lawrence to Charlotte Shaw, April 14, 1927, BM Add MSS, 45903.
22. Lawrence to Charlotte Shaw, May 8, 1928, BM Add MSS, 45904.
23. Lawrence to Charlotte Shaw, August 18, 1927, BM Add MSS, 45903.
24. Interview with Robert Lawrence, August 24, 1965.
25. Interview with Hilda Chaundy, March 24, 1965, and Arnold Lawrence, December 8, 1965.
26. Interview with Arnold Lawrence, December 8, 1965.
27. Vyvyan Richards to Helen J. Cash, March 4, 1965, in the *Sunday Times* research materials, Imperial War Museum, London.
28. Interviews with Theo and Hilda Chaundy, August 26, 1964.
29. *Home Letters*, p. 81.
30. Especially in passages that were omitted by Bob in the published version (*Home Letters*). The originals are in Bod Res MSS, c13.
31. Arnold Lawrence to Robert Graves, June 15, 1927, Bod Res MSS, c52.
32. Interview with Hilda Chaundy, August 26, 1964.
33. Lawrence to Charlotte Shaw, May 30, 1928, BM Add MSS, 45904.
34. Interview with Arnold Lawrence, July 21, 1968.
35. The same quality of being overwhelmed is suggested in a comment Lawrence wrote to Mrs. Shaw referring to the way he was given medicine as a boy: "They dosed me sometimes, when I was a child, too weak to kick against them; but I take no medicine now for many years" (Lawrence to Charlotte Shaw, December 8, 1927, BM Add MSS, 45903).
36. Interview with Arnold Lawrence, July 21, 1968.
37. Letter of April 11, 1911, *Home Letters*, pp. 147–148.
38. Letter of May 19, 1911, ibid., p. 160.

### INTRODUCTION TO PART II

1. *Oriental Assembly*, p. 143.
2. *Seven Pillars*, p. 661.
3. LHB, p. 80.
4. T. E. Lawrence, *Crusader Castles*, II, 5.
5. Bod Res MSS, b55.

6. Leonard Woolley, *Dead Towns and Living Men*, pp. 94–95.

7. RGB, p. 81.

8. *Friends*, p. 92.

4. LITERARY INFLUENCES

1. Interview with Arnold Lawrence, August 24, 1964.

2. *Friends*, p. 586.

3. RGB, p. 48.

4. LHB, p. 50.

5. J. G. Edwards, "T. E. Lawrence," *Jesus College Magazine*, IV (1935), 343–345.

6. F. S. Shears, "The Chivalry of France," *Chivalry: A Series of Studies to Illustrate Its Historical Significance and Civilizing Influence*, p. 22.

7. *Letters*, p. 87.

8. *Friends*, p. 53.

9. Will Lawrence to the Lawrence family, July 14, 1914, *Home Letters*, p. 555.

10. *Home Letters*, p. 34.

11. J. W. Thompson and E. N. Johnson, *An Introduction to Medieval Europe, 300–1500*, p. 322.

12. Eileen Powell, "The Position of Women," Chap. 7, *The Legacy of the Middle Ages*, edited by C. G. Crump and E. F. Jacob, pp. 401–430.

13. Shears, "The Chivalry of France," p. 67.

14. Thompson and Johnson, p. 322. See also, C. S. Lewis, *The Allegory of Love* (1972).

15. Henry Adams, *Mont-Saint-Michel and Chartres* (1904), p. 213.

16. As Eileen Powell pointed out, the elevation of women in the chivalric ideal "was at least better than placing them, as the Fathers of the Church had inclined to do, in the bottomless pit" (in Crump and Jacob, *The Legacy of the Middle Ages*, p. 406).

17. Steven Runciman, *A History of the Crusades*, III, 480.

18. T. E. Lawrence, *Crusader Castles*, foreword by Arnold Lawrence. It must be pointed out, however, that these special theses were required to be no longer than twelve hundred words and that the student was obliged to keep his discussion within the limits of his subject.

19. Lawrence to his family, August 11, 1907, *Home Letters*, p. 55.

20. Runciman, III, 53.

21. LHB, pp. 31, 80.

22. Lawrence to his family, August 6, 1908, *Home Letters*, p. 67.

23. Thompson and Johnson, p. 322.

24. E. Lévi-Provençal, *Islam d'occident: Etudes d'histoire médiévale*.

25. Lawrence to his family, June 2, 1912, *Home Letters*, p. 210.

26. *Friends*, p. 586.

5. CRUSADER CASTLES

1. *Friends*, p. 54.

2. RGB, p. 60.

3. There is a curious comment, omitted by his older brother from the published *Home Letters*, that Lawrence was in Wales "at last discovering where I got my large mouth from; it's a national peculiarity" (letter to Mrs. Lawrence, April 1907, Bod Res MSS, c13). The comment implies, or at least conveys to the mother that Lawrence considered himself, at eighteen and a half, to have some Welsh parentage or ancestry. This conflicts to a degree with his later claims that he knew his parents' situation "before I was ten." Whether he was playing along with the family fiction, showing consideration for his mother's sensibilities, or confused then in his own mind about his ancestral origins, is not clear.

4. *Friends*, p. 54.

5. Interview with the author, March 22, 1965.

6. Ibid.

7. Jean Beraud Villars, *T. E. Lawrence or the Search for the Absolute*, p. 20.

8. Lawrence to his mother, August 31, 1906, Bod Res MSS, c13. This letter was omitted from *Home Letters*.

9. Lawrence to his mother, August 26, *Home Letters*, p. 35.

10. Letter of August 17, 1906, ibid., p. 20.

11. Letter of August 9, 1908, ibid., p. 70.

12. Lawrence to his mother, August 6, 1908, ibid., p. 68.

13. Handwritten by Shaw on the flyleaf of a copy of T.E.'s *A Letter to His Mother*. This copy is in Houghton Library, Harvard University.

14. Bod Res MSS, c13.

15. Lawrence to his mother, August 24, 1906, Bod Res MSS, c13.

16. Ibid.

17. Ibid.

18. Lawrence to Arnie, August 14, 1906, *Home Letters*, p. 19.

19. Lawrence to Arnie, August 31, 1906, ibid., p. 45. Lawrence loved to play with images of worms when writing his small brother, calling him "worm" frequently. He seemed to enjoy the use of nonsense or gently degrading animal nicknames when addressing a younger boy or man toward whom he had a fond fatherly or big brotherly feeling. In a letter of June 23, 1909 (Bod Res MSS, c13), he closed with a drawing depicting members of the family as "worms" of varying size:

(The drawing is reproduced through the courtesy of the Bodleian Library, Oxford.)

20. Lawrence to Beeson, August 9, 1908, *Letters*, p. 57.

21. T. E. Lawrence, *Crusader Castles*, I, 3.

22. Ibid., I, 29.

23. Letter of August 2, 1908, *Home Letters*, p. 66.

24. In connection with Lawrence's challenge of Oman's views, Richard Aldington says of Lawrence, "He tried to pretend that Oman was a relic of the past and not worth wasting time on, since he was a charlatan, an imbecile and a smatterer" (*Lawrence of Arabia*, p. 68). In the two references Aldington provides to support his assertion that Lawrence damned Oman in this way there is nothing of the sort to be found. In one, from *Crusader Castles*, Lawrence does challenge Oman's theory, but says nothing accusatory. The other is a letter of June 8, 1911, to his brother Will, in which he is encouraging the younger boy to think and see for himself concerning the study of the Crusades and to question traditional authorities. "Oman," he writes, "is a monument: and one doesn't need to look at such things over long" (*Letters*, p. 110). There is nothing about charlatanism, imbecility or smattering. This sort of denigration is characteristic of Aldington's assault.

25. *Crusader Castles*, I, 29.

26. *Friends*, p. 47.

27. Lawrence to his mother, August 28, 1908, *Home Letters*, p. 79.

28. Lawrence to his mother, August 14, 1906, Bod Res MSS, c13. The passage was omitted by Robert Lawrence from the published collection.

29. Lawrence to C. F. C. Beeson, August 16, 1908, *Letters*, p. 61.

30. Lawrence to his family, February 18, 1911, *Home Letters*, p. 134.

31. *Crusader Castles*, I, 56.

32. Ibid., I, 15.

33. L. C. Jane to Robert Graves, 1927 (undated), Bod Res MSS, c52.

34. LHB, p. 52. After Lawrence's death, Arnold Lawrence had the manuscript prepared for publication under the title *Crusader Castles*. A limited edition of one thousand copies was printed. In the foreword, Arnold explained that the many photographs and extensive sketches and illustrations made it too expensive for the university press to publish.

35. Lawrence to a Mr. Field, April 26, 1929, Bod Res MSS, d43.

36. *Friends*, p. 62.

37. See, for example, discussions in T. S. R. Boase, *Castles and Churches of the Crusading Kingdom* (1967); Robin Fedden, *Crusader Castles* (1950); W. Mueller-Wiener, *Castles of the Crusaders* (1966).

38. LHB, p. 87; RGB, p. 49.

39. *Home Letters*, p. 69.

40. RGB, p. 61.

## 6. LAWRENCE AT JESUS COLLEGE, 1907–1910

1. J. N. L. Baker, *Jesus College, Oxford, 1571–1971*, p. 111.

2. J. G. Edwards, "T. E. Lawrence," *Jesus College Magazine* 4 (1935): 343–345.

3. LHB, p. 41.

4. Jesus College had a large number of students from Wales. As it could be said that there would be no place for the Westcountrymen to go if Exeter College were abolished, "Jesus would say the same about itself and the Welsh" (Dacre Balsdon, *Oxford Life*, p. 190).

5. Interview with W. O. Ault, September 22, 1972.

6. Baker, p. 108.

7. *Friends*, p. 28.

8. Ibid., pp. 67–68.

9. Baker, p. 108.

10. Ibid., pp. 108–109.

11. *Friends,* p. 28.

12. Interviews with Sir Basil Blackwell, March 21, 1965, and Sir Goronwy Edwards, July 12, 1968.

13. *Friends,* p. 47.

14. Ibid.

15. Ibid.

16. H. D. Littler, as quoted in Edwards, p. 344.

17. *Friends,* p. 29; LHB, p. 72.

18. Biographical material about Hogarth was obtained from the memoirs of his sister Janet Courtney: *An Oxford Portrait Gallery* (1931), pp. 3–50, and "David George Hogarth: In Memoriam Fratris," *Fortnightly Review* 129 (1928): 23–33. Also from the following sources: C. R. L. Fletcher, "David George Hogarth," *The Geographical Journal* 71 (1928): 321–344; F. G. Kenyon's biographical essay in the *Dictionary of National Biography;* James H. Breasted, "David George Hogarth," *Geographical Review* 18 (1928): 159–161; Hogarth Papers, St. Antony's College, Oxford; interviews with Arnold and Barbara Lawrence; interview with Hogarth's son, William, March 18, 1965.

19. Lawrence to Charlotte Shaw, March 20, 1924, BM Add MSS, 45903.

20. Interview with William Hogarth, March 18, 1965.

21. Ibid.

22. Lawrence to Edward Garnett, December 1, 1927, *Letters,* p. 551; and to Lionel Curtis, December 22, 1927, ibid., p. 557.

23. Lawrence to P. C. Rothenstein, April 14, 1928, *Letters,* p. 583.

24. C. F. Bell to Lawrence, November 11, 1927, Bod Res MSS, d60.

25. V. W. Richards, *Portrait of T. E. Lawrence,* pp. 19–49.

26. *Secret Lives,* p. 29.

27. Richards, p. 24.

28. Ibid., p. 41.

29. Interview with W. O. Ault, September 22, 1972.

30. Ibid.

31. LHB, p. 96.

32. *Friends,* p. 28.

33. Ibid. Another story has it that Lawrence and the poet A. G. Prys-Jones were both tutored by Jane, who agreed to take them at a weekly single session for the price of one (letter from D. W. T. Jenkins to Richard Brinkley of Aberystwyth College, Wales, February 12, 1973).

34. RGB, p. 50.

35. Lawrence to his family, February 20, 1912, *Home Letters,* p. 193.

36. Lawrence to William Lawrence, May 11, 1912, ibid., p. 208.

37. Graves, *Lawrence and the Arabs,* pp. 16–17.

38. L. C. Jane to Robert Graves [1927] Bod Res MSS, d60.

39. Lawrence to his family, January 11, 1911, *Home Letters,* p. 126.

40. This information and other facts about Jane come from a letter of February 12, 1973, from D. W. T. Jenkins, professor emeritus of education in University College, Bangor, who was a former student of Jane's at Aberystwyth, to Richard Brinkley, a specialist in English history there. The correspondence grew out of my inquiries to Aberystwyth concernng Lawrence's relationship with Jane.

41. The relationship between Janet and Will deepened: he wrote poems which he gave her, and despite Mrs. Lawrence's opposition (ostensibly on the ground that Will — nearly twenty-five when the war began — was young for his age), intended to marry her. Without his parents' knowledge, Will left private instructions with T.E. that in the event of his death T.E. should arrange to have any money he might leave given to Janet (personal communication from Arnold Lawrence, August 26, 1972). When Will was killed he left little of his own except some insurance and his army pay.

In 1914, at the death of a cousin in Ireland, Mr. Lawrence inherited a considerable amount of capital from the estate, along with the baronetcy. In March 1916, realizing perhaps that he was not in good health, Mr. Lawrence gave some of this money to his three surviving sons, but with a stipulation "that if our Will should prove to be alive [Will was then officially only missing, although presumed dead] . . . you and Bob and Arnie should each return me what I would ask for of your capital, so that Will may have the same capital as you others" (Mr. Lawrence to T.E., March 8, 1916, Bod Res MSS, d60). But by early May Mr. Lawrence had received news leaving no doubt about Will's death and he wrote T.E. again: "Poor Will, as you know, left everything he had to you and made you sole executor" (letter of May 11, 1916, Bod Res MSS, d60).

In a letter written in 1923 to David

Hogarth, T.E. referred to his share of his father's bequest as "my father's £5,000," and implied he had fulfilled Will's desire to leave money to Janet by giving £3,000 of his own share to her on Will's behalf. Lawrence wrote to Hogarth, "(I don't want my mother or other brothers to know about it; they think I still have it). One of those killed left a tangle behind, and it took £3,000 to straighten it. Two thousand was no good to me: so I put £1,000 into Epping [perhaps given to his friend Richards, with whom he shared his plot at Epping] and £1,000 into that book of mine; pictures mostly" (Lawrence to Hogarth, June 27, 1923, Bod Res MSS, d35). Lawrence signed the letter:

### · E ·

After Will was killed Janet Laurie had a long row over Will with Mrs. Lawrence. When the war began he had written to his sweetheart for advice on whether he should return from India to join the army. Unable to decide how or what to reply, she had written, finally, after much deliberation, that it might trouble him later if he did not return. When he was killed, Mrs. Lawrence learned of Janet's letter to Will and accused her of being responsible for his death. The two women were estranged in their grief and remained separated for seventeen years. In 1932 Mrs. Lawrence visited the place where Janet Laurie (now Mrs. Hallsmith) was living and they saw each other. When Mrs. Lawrence missed her train home, she stayed with Mrs. Hallsmith overnight. The mood was cordial and the younger woman felt forgiven, to her great relief and perhaps to Mrs. Lawrence's as well (interview with Mrs. Hallsmith, March 25, 1965).

42. Interview with the Reverend E. F. Hall and his wife, December 16, 1965.

43. Baker, p. 111.

### 7. THE FIRST TRIP TO THE MIDDLE EAST, 1909

1. Letter of August 2, 1909, Bod Res, MSS, c13.
2. *Letters*, p. 81.
3. RGB, p. 63.
4. *Letters to TEL*, p. 37.

5. Lawrence to C. M. Doughty, February 8, 1909 (unpublished; courtesy of Arnold Lawrence).
6. Foreword to Bertram Thomas's *Arabia Felix* (1932), p. xvii.
7. *Friends*, p. 73.
8. Ibid., pp. 29–30; LHB, p. 82.
9. *Home Letters*, p. 100.
10. Lawrence to his mother, September 7, 1909, Bod Res MSS, c13.
11. Lawrence to his mother, September 22, 1909, *Home Letters*, p. 107.
12. LHB, p. 52.
13. *Letters*, p. 81.
14. LHB, p. 53; *Friends*, p. 29.
15. RGB, p. 48.
16. *Home Letters*, p. 84.
17. Ibid., p. 103.
18. *Letters*, p. 72.
19. Lawrence to his mother, August 2, 1909, Bod Res MSS, c13.
20. *Letters*, p. 74.
21. Ibid., p. 66.
22. Lawrence to his mother, August 2, 1909, Bod Res MSS, c13.
23. Lawrence to his family, August 13, 1909, Bod Res MSS, c13.
24. *Home Letters*, p. 105.
25. *Letters*, p. 79.
26. *Friends*, pp. 76–77.
27. *Letters*, p. 81.
28. RGB, pp. 61–62.
29. Ibid., p. 62.
30. *Letters*, p. 82.
31. *Home Letters*, p. 108.
32. *Friends*, p. 74.
33. September 22, 1909, *Home Letters*, p. 108.
34. *Friends*, p. 76.
35. *Home Letters*, p. 81.
36. *Letters*, p. 81.
37. *Friends*, p. 61.
38. *Letters*, p. 83.
39. *Home Letters*, p. 105.
40. D. G. Hogarth, *The Life of Charles Doughty*, p. 174.
41. Ibid., p. 175.

### 8. LAWRENCE AT CARCHEMISH

1. Lady Florence Bell, *The Letters of Gertrude Bell*, I, 305–306.
2. Lawrence to E. T. Leeds, November 2, 1910, Bod Res MSS, d57.
3. C. L. Woolley, T. E. Lawrence, D. G. Hogarth, *Carchemish: Report on the Excavations at Djerabis on Behalf of the British Museum*, Vol. I.

4. Lawrence to Leeds, November 2, 1910, Bod Res MSS, d57.

5. Lawrence to his family, January 24, 1911, *Home Letters*, p. 130. This project (to be distinguished from the *Seven Pillars* of the Revolt) was to be downgraded and disparaged in a letter to Robert Graves in 1927: "Wrote travel book (later destroyed in Ms.) called 'The Seven Pillars of Wisdom,' about Cairo, Smyrna, Constantinople, Beirut, Aleppo, Damascus and Medina" (RGB, p. 49).

6. *Letters*, p. 89.

7. Lawrence to his family, December 16, 1910, *Home Letters*, p. 121.

8. Either she means 1910, or she has condensed the first meeting in the summer of 1909 with this second one in December 1910.

9. Actually, he was twenty-two at the time of the Christmas visit.

10. Fareedah el Akle to the author, June 20, 1969. Written from Brummana, Lebanon, upon receiving an article about Lawrence from him.

11. Fareedah el Akle to Helen Cash, June 12, 1969.

12. Lawrence to his family, January 31, 1912, *Home Letters*, p. 190.

13. Lawrence to Florence Messham, June 13, 1911, *Letters*, p. 112.

14. RGB, p. 50.

15. Letter of March 20, 1911, *Home Letters*, p. 141.

16. Letter of April 29, 1911, ibid., p. 151.

17. Letter of March 31, 1911, ibid., p. 143.

18. Ibid., p. 144.

19. *Oriental Assembly*, p. 2.

20. Lawrence to E. T. Leeds, April 1912, Bod Res MSS, d57.

21. Letter of March 20, 1912, *Home Letters*, p. 198.

22. *Friends*, p. 115.

23. Ibid., p. 84.

24. Ibid., p. 91.

25. Lawrence to E. T. Leeds, April 1912, Bod Res MSS, d57.

26. *Friends*, p. 91.

27. Letter of May 9, 1911, *Home Letters*, p. 159.

28. Letter of June 13, 1911, ibid., p. 169.

29. Letter of June 23, 1912, ibid., p. 216.

30. Lawrence to James Elroy Flecker, February 18, 1914, Houghton Library, Harvard University.

31. C. L. Woolley, *Dead Towns and Living Men*, p. 176.

32. Letter of June 2, 1912, Bod Res MSS, c13.

33. Lawrence to V. W. Richards, December 10, 1913, *Letters*, p. 161.

34. *Friends*, p. 84.

35. Letter of July 28, 1912, *Letters*, p. 145.

36. Lawrence to his family, February 22, 1913, Bod Res MSS, c13.

37. Will Lawrence to the family, September 16, 1913, *Home Letters*, p. 442.

38. Will Lawrence to the family, September 27, 1913, ibid., p. 447.

39. *Friends*, p. 91.

40. Luther Fowle, prologue to Lowell Thomas's "The Soul of the Arabian Revolution," *Asia* 20 (1920): 257.

41. *Friends*, p. 90.

42. Ibid., p. 87.

43. Ibid., p. 69. Volume III of *Carchemish*, which reported the findings of the archeologists in excavating the inner town and the interpretations of the Hittite inscriptions, was not published by the British Museum until 1952 because of various delays and destruction to the objects themselves caused by World War I. In this volume Woolley and R. D. Barnett, although disputed in regard to certain details by other archeologists, were able to establish the sequence of the Hittite dynasties spanning the tenth to the eight centuries B.C. References: H. G. Güterbock, "Carchemish," *Journal of Near Eastern Studies* 13: (1954): 102–114; J. D. Hawkins, "Building Inscriptions of Carchemish," *Anatolian Studies* 22 (1972): 87–114; M. E. L. Mallowan, "Carchemish: Reflections on the Chronology of the Sculpture," *Anatolian Studies* 22 (1972): 63–85; P. Meriggi, "La Ricostruzione di Kargamis," *Rivista degli Studi Orientali*, 29 (1954): 1–16; D. Ussishkin, "Observations on Some Monuments from Carchemish," *Journal of Near Eastern Studies* 26: (1967): 87–92; and "On the Dating of Some Groups of Reliefs from Carchemish and Til Barsib," *Anatolian Studies* 17 (1967): 181–192. One of these scholars praised the work in these terms: "This rich and beautiful volume fills a long-felt gap and lets Carchemish, and especially the city of Katuwas [a late king] emerge in all its greatness" (Güterbock, p. 114). In 1969 Barnett wrote: "That Carchemish . . . was a first class Hittite imperial site has re-

cently been demonstrated by the discovery of letters in Hittite cuneiform script in the French excavations at Ras Shamra, showing that in the fourteenth–thirteenth centuries B.C. it was the seat of the Hittite Viceroy of North Syria. Hogarth's prescience has thus been fully vindicated" (letter to *The Times Literary Supplement*, October 16, 1969).

44. Lawrence to his family, April 11, 1911, Bod Res MSS, c13. Robert Lawrence apparently thought the passage too damaging to include in the published version.

45. *Friends*, pp. 89, 90.

46. Lawrence to E. T. Leeds, February 25, 1912, Bod Res MSS, d57, which contains all the letters to Leeds cited in the next five notes.

47. Letter of June 16, 1913.

48. Letter written at the end of February 1913.

49. Letter of June 1, 1913.

50. Letter of January 24, 1914.

51. Letter to Leeds, July 14, 1912.

52. Lawrence to his family, April 26, 1913, *Home Letters*, p. 254.

53. *Letters*, p. 156.

54. Interview with Janet Laurie Hallsmith, March 25, 1965.

55. Letter of August 29, 1913, *Home Letters*, p. 262.

56. *Friends*, p. 97.

57. Ibid., p. 96.

58. Ibid., pp. 98–99.

59. Ibid., p. 96.

60. Ibid., p. 88.

61. Ibid., p. 87.

62. Hubert Young, *The Independent Arab*, p. 18.

63. Luther R. Fowle, "Prologue," *Asia* 20 (1920): 257.

64. Ibid., p. 258.

65. Lawrence to his family, May 23, 1911, *Home Letters*, p. 163.

66. Letter of June 24, 1911, *Letters*, pp. 113–114.

67. *Friends*, p. 92.

68. Young, p. 20.

69. Woolley, *Dead Towns and Living Men*, pp. 107–108.

70. Letter of June 18, 1911, *Home Letters*, p. 170.

71. Lawrence to Mrs. Rieder, June 14, 1913, *Letters*, p. 155.

72. Lawrence to E. T. Leeds, September 9, 1913, Bod Res MSS, d57.

73. Will Lawrence to the family, November 13, 1913, *Home Letters*, p. 467.

74. Fowle, p. 257.

75. Lawrence to Eddie Marsh, June 10, 1927, *Letters*, p. 521.

76. Letter of June 24, 1911, *Home Letters*, p. 174.

77. *Friends*, p. 106.

78. Letter of April 23, 1914, *Home Letters*, p. 295.

79. LHB, p. 85.

80. Winifred Fontana to Robert Graves, December 5, 1927, Bod Res MSS, c52.

81. *Friends*, p. 593.

82. Letter of March 28, 1913, Bod Res MSS, c13.

83. Letter of March 1, 1911, Bod Res MSS, c13.

84. Lawrence to E. T. Leeds, April 1912, Bod Res MSS, d57.

85. *Friends*, pp. 92–93.

86. *Home Letters*, p. 142.

87. Lawrence to Leeds, May 6, 1914, Bod Res MSS, d57.

88. Lawrence to Doughty, November 24, 1911, courtesy of Arnold Lawrence.

89. Letter of May 11, 1912, *Home Letters*, p. 207.

90. *Friends*, p. 591.

91. RGB, p. 5.

92. See *An Essay on Flecker* (1925), a copy of which is in Houghton Library, Harvard University.

93. Personal communication from Arabella Rivington in 1967, following her visit with Miss Akle.

94. Richard Aldington, *Lawrence of Arabia*, p. 104. Aldington's snide criticism of Lawrence's use of archaic "schoolboy phrases" in this letter is absurd, as these are a deliberately self-conscious part of the humor.

95. Lawrence to Mrs. Von Heidenstam, August 29, 1912, Bod Res MSS, c52.

96. *Friends*, p. 84.

97. Woolley, *Dead Towns and Living Men*, p. 142.

98. Dahoum's name is discussed convincingly in Jeremy M. Wilson's introduction to Lawrence's *Minorities*, p. 29.

99. Woolley, p. 142.

100. Lawrence to Fareedah el Akle, June 26, 1911 (a copy was shown to the author by Arabella Rivington).

101. *Oriental Assembly*, p. 26.

102. Lawrence to his family, September 12, 1912, *Home Letters*, p. 229.

103. *Friends*, p. 89.

104. Interviews with Arnold Lawrence, September 13, 1969.

105. Interviews with Arnold Lawrence. In *Secret Lives,* Knightley and Simpson claim on the evidence of Thomas Beaumont, a gunner who was with Lawrence during the war, that Dahoum worked for Lawrence during the campaigns as a spy, moving back and forth through the Turkish lines. But this is highly improbable. As Arnold Lawrence indicated in a note to me (September 1969), the difficulties a North Syrian of military age would have experienced in traveling to and through the vague Turkish lines would have made it virtually impossible.

106. Lawrence to Fareedah el Akle, January 3, 1921 (a copy was shown to the author by Arabella Rivington); interview with Arnold Lawrence, September 13, 1969. The matter is discussed by J. M. Wilson in his introduction to Lawrence's *Minorities,* pp. 29–30.

107. Lawrence to "Dear Poppet" (probably R. M. Guy), December 25, 1923, Houghton Library, Harvard University.

108. Penciled note on the back flyleaf of Vansittart's *The Singing Caravan,* Bod Res MSS, d230. "Written between Paris and Lyons in Handley Page" is penciled at the bottom of the page.

9. THE EPIC DREAM AND THE
FACT OF WAR

1. *Letters,* p. 85.
2. Letter of April 11, 1911, *Home Letters,* pp. 147–148. See page 34 for a longer quotation from this letter.
3. Fareedah el Akle to Lawrence, March 30, 1920, Bod Res MSS, d60.
4. Entry of August 3, 1911, in "Diary of a Journey Across the Euphrates," *Oriental Assembly,* p. 51.
5. Lawrence to his family, March 20, 1912, *Home Letters,* p. 198.
6. Ibid., p. 193.
7. Quoted in Violet Bonham Carter's *Winston Churchill: An Intimate Portrait,* p. 313.
8. *Secret Lives,* pp. 35 ff.
9. Elizabeth Monroe, review of Knightley and Simpson's *Secret Lives,* in *The Times Literary Supplement,* October 2, 1969.
10. Interview with William Hogarth, March 18, 1965.
11. Lawrence to Hogarth, June 24, 1911, *Letters,* p. 114.

12. Lawrence to Mrs. Rieder, May 20, 1912, ibid., p. 139.
13. Lawrence to Leeds, end of February 1913, Bod Res MSS, d57.
14. Hubert Young, *The Independent Arab,* p. 16.
15. Letter in Ashmolean Museum, Oxford, undated, but the reference to a trip to Abu Galgal places it most likely in late June or July of 1913, after Lawrence's trip to Abu Galgal in Mesopotamia.
16. Quoted in *Secret Lives,* p. 41.
17. Letter to *The Times Literary Supplement,* October 16, 1969.
18. The matter is discussed by George Kirk in *A Short History of the Middle East,* pp. 308–309.
19. Lawrence to his family, January 2, 1912, *Home Letters,* p. 182.
20. Lawrence to Leeds, February 25, 1912, Bod Res MSS, d57.
21. Lawrence to his family, November 4 and 12, 1912, *Home Letters,* pp. 241, 242.
22. Letter of March 28, 1913, ibid., p. 252.
23. Lawrence to Mrs. Rieder, *Letters,* p. 152.
24. Letter of January 4, 1914, *Home Letters,* p. 288.
25. Interview with William Yale, August 10, 1966.
26. C. L. Woolley, "The Desert of the Wanderings," *Palestine Expedition Fund Quarterly Statement* (1914).
27. Letter of June 26, 1912, *Letters,* p. 142.
28. Letter of June 11, 1913, *Home Letters,* p. 256.
29. Letter of October 16, 1913, ibid., p. 269.
30. C.J.G. [Lawrence], "The Kaer of Ibn Wardani," *Jesus College Magazine* (1912–1913), p. 39.
31. Lawrence to V. W. Richards, December 10, 1913, *Letters,* p. 161.
32. February 18, 1914, *Friends,* p. 104.

10. THE BACKGROUND OF THE
ARAB REVOLT

1. P. J. Vatikiotis, *Conflict in the Middle East,* pp. 15–16.
2. George Antonius, *The Arab Awakening,* p. 18.
3. Ibid., p. 32.
4. Manfred Halpern, "Four Contrasting Repertories of Human Relations in Islam," paper presented to a conference

on psychology and Near Eastern studies at Princeton, New Jersey, May 8, 1973.

5. The suppressed introductory chapter for *Seven Pillars of Wisdom*, in *Oriental Assembly*, p. 143. This chapter was not published until after Lawrence's death.

6. George Kirk, *A Short History of the Middle East*, p. 34.

7. Zeine N. Zeine, *The Emergence of Arab Nationalism*, p. 25.

8. Ibid., p. 68.

9. Ibid., p. 92.

10. John E. Mack, "The Young Turk Revolution of 1908 and Its Consequences, 1908–1914," unpublished term paper, Oberlin College, 1951, p. 9.

11. Ahmad Qadri, *Mudhakkirati 'an al-Thawra al-'Arabiyah al-Kubra* [My Memoirs of the Great Arab Revolt], pp. 40–47.

12. Kirk, p. 95.

13. G. P. Gooch, and H. W. V. Temperley, *British Documents on the Origin of the War, 1898–1914*, Vol. IX, quoted in Zeine, *The Emergence*, p. 119.

14. Zeine, *The Emergence*, p. 114.

15. Elizabeth Monroe, *Britain's Moment in the Middle East, 1914–1956*, p. 3.

16. D. G. Hogarth, "Mecca's Revolt Against the Turk," *Century Magazine* 100 (1920): 403.

17. E. C. Dawn, "The Amir of Mecca Al-Husayn Ibn-Ali and the Origin of the Arab Revolt," *Proceedings of the American Philosophical Society* 104 (1960): 11–34.

18. Ronald Storrs, *Orientations*, p. 143.

19. Foreign Office, "Summary of Documents from the Outbreak of War between Great Britain and Turkey, 1914, to the Outbreak of the Revolt of the Sherif of Mecca in June, 1916" (January 1921), PRO/FO 371/6237; also quoted in Storrs, p. 173.

20. Storrs, pp. 175–176.

21. PRO/FO 371/6237; also quoted in Storrs, p. 176.

22. PRO/FO 882/6 (December 1916); also quoted in T. E. Lawrence, *Secret Dispatches from Arabia*, p. 52.

23. Antonius, p. 133.

24. Zeine, *The Emergence*, p. 126.

25. *Seven Pillars*, p. 50; see also Zeine, *The Emergence*, p. 27.

26. Antonius, pp. 152–156.

27. Faisal's contacts with the secret societies in Syria during 1915 and 1916

had an important impact on the development of his commitment to Arab nationalistic aspirations. His relationship to these societies is discussed in Ahmad Qadri's memoirs. Faisal's frustration with the fact that other members of his family did not share his interest in the Arab national movement in Syria is reflected in a letter written by Colonel Joyce during the war: "Faisal still considers that his father and brothers are taking no interest in the Syrian movement and it takes a lot of talk to prevent him getting very depressed on the subject" (Pierce Joyce to Sir Gilbert Clayton, September 17, 1917, in Joyce's "Akaba" Papers, King's College, London).

28. *Seven Pillars*, p. 47.

29. Suleiman Mousa, "The Role of Syrians and Iraqis in the Arab Revolt," *Middle East Forum* 43 (1967): 5–17.

30. Antonius, p. 158.

31. Kirk, pp. 313–314.

32. Hogarth, "Mecca's Revolt," p. 405.

33. Elie Kedourie, *England and the Middle East*, p. 30.

34. This issue is discussed in Zeine N. Zeine, *The Struggle for Arab Independence*, p. 10; Kedourie, p. 281; and Monroe, pp. 9–10.

35. PRO/FO 371/6237; also quoted in Antonius, pp. 414–415. The Foreign Office translations of these documents and those by Antonius differ considerably.

36. A. L. Tibawi, "Syria in the McMahon Correspondence," *Middle East Forum* 40 (1966): 20–21; PRO/FO 371/6237; Monroe, *Britain's Moment*, p. 36.

37. Sir Ronald Wingate, *Wingate of the Sudan*, p. 181.

38. Antonius, p. 176.

39. Kirk, p. 316.

40. Dawn, p. 27.

41. Hogarth, p. 408.

42. LHB, p. 60.

43. Monroe, p. 35.

44. McMahon to Husayn, Cairo, December 13, 1915, and Husayn to McMahon, January 1, 1916, PRO/FO 371/6237; see also, Antonius, pp. 423–425.

45. PRO/CAB 27/36.

46. Hogarth, p. 406.

47. *Arab Bulletin* #42, February 15, 1917, II, 79; quoted in *Letters*, p. 219.

48. Jemal Pasha, *Memories of a Turkish Statesman, 1913–1919*, pp. 214–221.

49. Dawn, p. 27.

50. Ibid.

51. *Seven Pillars*, pp. 52–53.

52. Ibid., p. 53.

53. *Arab Bulletin* #3, June 14, 1916, I, 30–31.

54. Storrs, p. 180.

55. Ibid., pp. 180–188.

56. Ibid., p. 181.

57. Antonius, p. 195.

58. PRO/FO 882/25.

59. Zeine, *The Struggle*, p. 4.

60. Hogarth, p. 411.

11. TWO YEARS IN CAIRO, 1914–1916

1. The poem continues:

*And caught our youth, and wakened us*
*from sleeping.*
*With hand made sure, clear eye, and*
*sharpened power,*
*To turn, as swimmers into cleanness leap-*
*ing,*
*Glad from a world grown old and cold*
*and weary,*
*Leave the sick hearts that honour could*
*not move,*
*And half-men, and their dirty songs and*
*dreary,*
*And all the little emptiness of love!*

From *The Collected Poems of Rupert Brooke* (London: Sidgwick and Jackson, 1918).

2. Arnold Lawrence to the author, November 1, 1968.

3. Lawrence to James Elroy Flecker, December 3, 1914, Houghton Library, Harvard University.

4. Lawrence to John Buchan, June 20, 1927, Bod Res MSS, b55.

5. Sir Coote Hedley to Liddell Hart, November 23, 1933, quoted in LHB, p. 196.

6. Ibid., p. 193.

7. Ibid., p. 91.

8. 'Abd al-Rahman Shahbandar, "al-Colonel Lawrence," *al-Muqtataf* 78 (March 1931): 269–270.

9. *Friends*, p. 136.

10. Pierce Joyce, BBC broadcast of July 14, 1941 (typescript), King's College, London.

11. Ronald Storrs, *Orientations*, pp. 218–219.

12. *Friends*, p. 177.

13. Storrs, pp. 219–220.

14. *Friends*, pp. 137–142.

15. Lawrence to Leeds, December 7, 1914, Bod Res MSS, d57.

16. Lawrence to Leeds, December 24, 1914, Bod Res MSS, d57.

17. *Home Letters*, p. 303.

18. Lawrence to Hogarth, March 22, 1915, pp. 195–196.

19. Lawrence to Hogarth, April 15, 1915, ibid., p. 196.

20. Lawrence to Leeds, April 18, 1915, Bod Res MSS, d57.

21. Ibid.

22. Letter of June 1915 (undated), *Home Letters*, p. 304.

23. Letter of October 19, 1915, ibid., p. 310.

24. Lawrence to Leeds, November 16, 1915, Bod Res MSS, d57.

25. Letter of December 25, 1915, *Home Letters*, p. 311.

26. Lawrence to Mrs. Hasluck, February 28, 1916, Bod Res MSS, c52.

27. Dispatch of November 8, 1915, to "Foreign, Simla (India)," Houghton Library, Harvard University.

28. Note of Lawrence's on the manuscript of Robert Graves's biography, quoted in RGB, p. 82.

29. Telegram from the War Office, London, #14895, March 29, 1916, Houghton Library, Harvard University.

30. Sir Percy Cox, report of April 7, 1916, Houghton Library, Harvard University.

31. McMahon to Cox, March 20, 1916, Houghton Library, Harvard University.

32. LHB, pp. 61–62.

33. Telegram from the War Office, London, to the commanding general, Basra, April 28, 1916, Houghton Library, Harvard University.

34. Suleiman Mousa has provided an account of a meeting between Lawrence and Sulayman Faydi, one of the Mesopotamian deputies in the Ottoman Chamber of Deputies. Lawrence tried to persuade Faydi to participate in leading the revolt of Iraqi Arabs and said that he had been commissioned to offer British support for such a rebellion. Faydi is said to have surprised Lawrence by refusing, on the grounds of insufficient power on his own part and lack of interest in vengeance against the Turks. "They are your enemies, not ours," Faydi states that he told Lawrence ("The Role of Syrians and Iraqis in the Arab Revolt," *Middle East Forum* 43 [1967]: 15–17; this portion of the article is based on Faydi's memoirs).

35. LHB, p. 18.

36. Townshend to Army Headquarters, April 27, 1916, Houghton Library, Harvard University.

37. Aubrey Herbert, *Mons, Kut and Anzac*, pp. 204–244.

38. W. F. Stirling, "Tales of Lawrence of Arabia," *Cornhill Magazine* 74 (1933): 494–510.

39. PRO/FO 882/15, April 8, 1916; PRO/FO 882/18, May 5, 1916; *Arab Bulletin* #3, June 16, 1916, I, 23, published in *Letters*, pp. 208–209 (not *Arab Bulletin* #23 as indicated there).

40. PRO/FO 882/15, April 8, 1916.

41. Ibid.

42. PRO/FO 882/15, March 26, 1916.

43. *Arab Bulletin* #3, June 16, 1916, I, 24; published in *Letters*, p. 209.

44. Hubert Young, *The Independent Arab*, p. 72.

45. *Home Letters*, pp. 317–327.

46. Letter of July 1, 1916, ibid., p. 327.

47. Descriptive material on *The Arab Bulletin*, Bod Res MSS, b55. Lawrence's personal copy is in Houghton Library, Harvard University, and his penciled notes in it have clarified the authorship of some of the unsigned entries. The majority of the later issues were signed by Kinahan Cornwallis, director of the Arab Bureau.

48. John Brophy, an English novelist, wrote of *The Arab Bulletin*, "These reports are obviously the raw material from which the full book [*Seven Pillars of Wisdom*] was made, and apart from historical considerations are useful literary evidence. They give the lie to those who have urged that Lawrence after the event, created his own past as a myth. That he was a self-conscious writer cannot be denied, but the self-consciousness was an integral part of his personality" (*John's Weekly*, London, November 17, 1939).

49. *Home Letters*, p. 329.

50. *Arab Bulletin* #20, September 14, 1916, I, 241–243.

51. PRO/FO 371/6237, p. 72.

52. Telegram from the War Office, London, to the commander-in-chief, September 17, 1916, PRO/FO 371/6237, p. 72. The arguments and controversy in Allied policy during the fall of 1916 regarding the support to be offered to the Arab effort are presented concisely by Philip Graves in *Memoirs of King Abdullah of Transjordan*, pp. 165–166.

53. *Seven Pillars*, p. 62.

54. Letter of July 22, 1916, *Home Letters*, p. 328.

55. "The Sayings and the Doings of T.E. as heard and experienced by the Sims Family" (unpublished manuscript).

56. Sir Gilbert Clayton, *An Arabian Diary*, p. 67.

57. LHB, p. 92.

58. *Seven Pillars*, p. 63.

59. Storrs, p. 199.

60. Ibid., pp. 199–200.

61. Lawrence to Leeds, January 18, 1916, Bod Res MSS, d57.

62. Lady Florence Bell, *The Letters of Gertrude Bell*, II, 372.

63. *Friends*, p. 123.

64. Hogarth, "Mecca's Revolt Against the Turk," *Century Magazine* 100 (1920): 409.

65. *Letters*, pp. 193–196.

66. Ibid., p. 196.

67. "The Conquest of Syria, If Complete" (1916), PRO/FO 882/16.

68. Ibid.

69. "The Politics of Mecca" (late January 1916), PRO/FO 371/2771 and PRO/FO 141/461 (not 414/461 as noted in *Secret Lives*), quoted in *Secret Lives*, pp. 52–53, 62–63.

70. LHB, p. 17.

71. G. C. Arthur, *General Sir John Maxwell*, p. 153.

72. RGB, p. 80.

73. D. G. Hogarth, entry on Lawrence in the *Encyclopaedia Britannica*, 14th ed.

## 12. THE COURSE OF THE ARAB REVOLT

1. Lawrence to Mr. Evans-Wentz, October 12, 1916, California private collection.

2. *Arab Bulletin* #24, October 5, 1916, I, 323–324.

3. *Seven Pillars*, p. 91.

4. Ibid., p. 111.

5. Lord Hankey, *The Supreme Command, 1914–1918*, II, 500–501.

6. Janet E. Courtney, *An Oxford Portrait*, p. 43.

7. PRO/FO 882/6, December, 1916.

8. *Arab Bulletin* #18, September 5, 1916, I, 210.

9. "The Evolution of a Revolt," first published in *The Army Quarterly*, October 1920; reprinted in *Oriental Assembly*, pp. 103–134, and in *Evolution of a Revolt: Early Postwar Writings of T. E. Lawrence*, pp. 100–119.

10. *Oriental Assembly,* p. 119.

11. *Seven Pillars,* p. 160.

12. Ibid., p. 167.

13. "Report of a Journey of Lawrence through Arabia on Military Intelligence," January 17–25, 1917, Houghton Library, Harvard University.

14. Lawrence to Newcombe, January 17, 1917. I first saw the letter in photocopy. Haig Nicholson, the former chief of Reuter's Middle East bureau in Cairo, had gotten the original from a Turkish colonel, who took it from Newcombe's saddlebag when Newcombe was captured in Beersheba.

15. Letter of January 31, 1917, *Home Letters,* p. 334.

16. Letter of February 12, 1917, ibid., pp. 334–335.

17. See Edouard Brémond, *Le Hedjaz dans la guerre mondiale* (1931).

18. Letters of February 25 and 28, 1917, *Home Letters,* p. 337.

19. PRO/FO 882/6, February 16, 1917.

20. *Seven Pillars,* p. 174.

21. Lawrence to Clayton, July 10, 1917, *Letters,* pp. 225–226.

22. Wingate to Mark Sykes in London, July 1917, in Wingate Papers, Durham University, England. Actually, Lawrence was not eligible for the V.C. (Victoria Cross) because one of the prerequisites of award was the presence of another British officer who had witnessed the meritorious act. Instead, Lawrence was awarded the C.B. (Companion of the Bath).

23. Letter to H. S. Ede, September 1, 1927, *Shaw-Ede: T. E. Lawrence's Letters to H. S. Ede, 1927–1935,* p. 10.

24. Entry of July 11, 1917, in "Diary of Captain Orlo C. Williams, June 29–December 27, 1917," Imperial War Museum, London.

25. George Lloyd to Wingate, August 17, 1917, Wingate Papers, Durham University, England.

26. *Seven Pillars,* p. 324.

27. Lawrence to his family, August 12, 1917, *Home Letters,* p. 338.

28. *The Times,* May 20, 1935; quoted in Brian Gardner, *Allenby of Arabia: Lawrence's General,* p. 210.

29. For one of the political consequences of placing the leadership of the Revolt under Allenby, see Sir Ronald Wingate, *Wingate of the Sudan,* pp. 194–197.

30. Lawrence to Charlotte Shaw, April 3, 1927, BM Add MSS, 45903.

31. Lawrence to Alan Dawnay, April 14, 1927, Bod Res MSS, d43. Flinders Petrie was the famous Egyptologist.

32. Letter of August 27, 1917, *Home Letters,* p. 339.

33. Ibid.

34. Lawrence to W. F. Stirling, September 24, 1917; copy loaned to author by Jeremy Wilson.

35. Letter to "A Friend" (actually Leeds), September 25, 1917, *Letters,* p. 238.

36. Letter of September 24, 1917, *Home Letters,* p. 341.

37. Hogarth to his wife, October 17, 1917, Hogarth Papers, St. Antony's College, Oxford.

38. C. Falls and A. F. Becke, eds., *History of the Great War,* II, 51.

39. *Arab Bulletin #72,* December 5, 1917, II, 490–504.

40. Letters of November 7, 11, and 26, 1917, Hogarth Papers, St. Antony's College, Oxford.

41. *Seven Pillars,* p. 439.

42. "Pocket Diary for 1917," BM Add MSS, 45983.

43. Hogarth Papers, St. Antony's College, Oxford.

44. Letter of December 14, 1917, *Home Letters,* p. 345. According to Arnold Lawrence, T.E. kept of his decorations only the Croix de Guerre, "which he sent around the streets of Oxford on the neck of Hogarth's dog" (*Friends,* p. 301). T.E. himself wrote that he returned the decoration to Brémond in November of 1918 (LHB, p. 157).

45. Hogarth to his wife, December 16, 1917, Hogarth Papers, St. Antony's College, Oxford.

46. *Seven Pillars,* p. 453.

47. Letter of December 14, 1917, *Home Letters,* p. 343.

48. Ibid., p. 344.

49. Lawrence to Leeds, December 13, 1917, Bod Res MSS, d57.

50. Hogarth to his son, William, December 16, 1917, Hogarth Papers, St. Antony's College, Oxford.

51. Hogarth to his wife, December 23, 1917, Hogarth Papers, St. Antony's College, Oxford.

52. After the publication of Richard Aldington's biography of Lawrence in 1955, Gilman wrote specifically of his objections to Aldington's failure to obtain

information regarding these operations "when there were several British officers present to see Lawrence at work in the field and to bear testimony to his courage and ability. Why? The impression one gets from reading this part of the book is that Lawrence was anywhere but in Arabia" (from Gilman's manuscript found in the Storrs Papers). Gilman then goes on to provide his recollection of these operations and Lawrence's active part in them, concluding his account as follows: "The next day was spent mostly in completing the havoc that we had made of the railway, and there is one incident worth recording which illustrates Lawrence's utter disregard for his own safety. We had driven the Turks from Ramleh station and they took to the nearby hills from which they kept up an annoying fire. Dawnay and Lawrence had set their hearts on blowing up this station, and, accordingly, we loaded some explosives on an armoured car and proceeded towards the station. Unfortunately the ground was so strewn with boulders that the car was held up some little distance from the station. Nothing daunted, Dawnay and Lawrence seized a box of explosives and, under fire, staggered across the open to the station and blew it up."

53. J. B. Glubb, *Britain and the Arabs*, p. 85.

54. Falls and Becke, II, 404.

55. Letter of March 8, 1918, *Home Letters*, p. 348.

56. *Seven Pillars*, p. 502.

57. *Arab Bulletin* #80, February 26, 1918, III, 60.

58. *Seven Pillars*, p. 503.

59. Letter of March 8, 1918, *Home Letters*, p. 349. Lawrence later expressed regret about his bodyguard to Mrs. Shaw: "Yes, I was very sorry, then and now, for the body guard. They were worked too hard and too constantly hurt. And I was a spasmodic inconsiderate chief, too busied over my own difficulties to spare any kindness to them. So they didn't love me!" (May 20, 1926, BM Add MSS, 45903).

60. Hogarth to his son, William, February 25, 1918, Hogarth Papers, St. Antony's College, Oxford.

61. William Yale to Leland Harrison, U.S. Department of State, March 11, 1918, Middle East Centre, St. Antony's College, Oxford.

62. Falls and Becke, II, 408.

63. *Seven Pillars*, p. 534.

64. C. H. C. Pirie-Gordon, ed. *A Brief Record of the Advance of the Egyptian Expeditionary Force, July 1917 to October 1918* (London: His Majesty's Stationery Office, 1919), text opposite plate 53.

65. PRO/FO 371/3381.

66. See Basil Liddell Hart, *"T. E. Lawrence": In Arabia and After*, pp. 317–318.

67. PRO/FO 371/3381.

68. Ibid.

69. Pierce Joyce, BBC broadcast of July 14, 1941 (typescript), in King's College, London.

70. Lord Winterton, diary entry for August 26, 1918, in A. H. Brodrick, *Near to Greatness: A Life of Lord Winterton*, p. 178.

71. R. D. Blumenfeld, *All in a Lifetime*, p. 136.

72. LHB, p. 154.

73. Hubert Young, *The Independent Arab*, p. 209.

74. Ibid., p. 198.

75. Ibid., p. 218.

76. Ibid., pp. 219–220.

77. Ibid., p. 243.

78. C. S. Jarvis, *Arab Command: The Biography of Lieutenant-Colonel F. G. Peake Pasha*, p. 46.

79. Glubb, p. 88.

80. *Seven Pillars*, p. 635.

81. George Barrow, *The Fire of Life*, p. 210.

82. Alec Kirkbride, *An Awakening*, p. 85.

83. Lord Birdwood, *Nuri As-Said: A Study in Arab Leadership*, p. 85.

84. Barrow, p. 211.

85. Birdwood, p. 86.

86. Ibid., p. 86.

87. *Seven Pillars*, pp. 635–636.

88. Barrow, p. 211.

89. Young, p. 252.

## 13. THE CAPTURE OF DAMASCUS

1. Gertrude Bell, *The Desert and the Sown*, p. 134.

2. W. T. Massey, *Allenby's Final Triumph*, p. 240.

3. Lawrence to the General Staff, G.H.Q., October 1, 1918, quoted in Massey, p. 343; "The Destruction of the Fourth Army," *Arab Bulletin* #106, October 22, 1918, III, 343–350; quoted in *Letters*, pp. 247–257.

4. See discussions in Elie Kedourie, *England and the Middle East*, pp. 113–117; George Antonius, *The Arab Awakening*, pp. 270–274, 433n.

5. Elie Kedourie, *The Chatham House Version and Other Middle Eastern Studies*, pp. 33–51; *Seven Pillars*, p. 643.

6. Massey, p. 343.

7. Lawrence to the General Staff, G.H.Q., quoted in Massey, p. 343; the original is in the Public Record Office, London.

8. *Seven Pillars*, p. 645.

9. Lawrence to W. F. Stirling, October 15, 1924; copy loaned to the author by Jeremy Wilson.

10. Elie Kedourie, "The Capture of Damascus, October, 1918," *Middle Eastern Studies* (1964–1965), p. 71; the article is reprinted in Kedourie's *Chatham House*, pp. 33–51. *Seven Pillars* had been read by only a few people in 1926 and thus could have had no effect on the political outcome in Syria.

11. Ibid., p. 73. General Barrow argued wisely in connection with the capture of Der'a that no "peculiar merit attaches to troops who are the first to occupy a town or locality of historic interest in enemy territory. . . . When the place is unoccupied or weakly defended, there is no glory in being the first to enter" (*Fire of Life*, p. 210). But in the case of Damascus the matter had considerable political significance.

12. Henry Chauvel, letter of January 1, 1936, to the director of the Australian War Memorial, Allenby Papers, St. Antony's College, Oxford.

13. C. Falls and A. F. Becke, eds., *History of the Great War*, II, 591.

14. Ahmad Qadri, *Mudhakkirati 'an al-'Arabiyah al-Kubra* [My Memoirs of the Great Arab Revolt], p. 74. The Jaza'iri brothers were grandsons of an Algerian national hero.

15. Chauvel, letter of January 1, 1936.

16. Alec Kirkbride, *An Awakening*, pp. 94–95. Massey has provided a colorful firsthand account of the rejoicing in Damascus and the dramatic outpouring of enthusiasm with which the townspeople greeted Lawrence upon his entry into the city: "The rejoicings lasted all day. They reached an extraordinary height when sections of the Arab army came into the city. The Emir Feisal had had his agents in Damascus and they had sown good seed. Colonel Lawrence had

come in with a small following, and the people recognized the small brave English scholar who had turned soldier to influence Arabs to fight to throw off the Turkish yoke. Colonel Lawrence wore the head-dress, robes, and sword of an Arab chief of high degree, but this was not a complete disguise, and if the Damascenes had not been told they were to expect him they certainly very readily identified this gallant gentleman, who, more than any one else had striven through good times and bad to put Arab pressure on the Turkish garrisons at Medina and Maan, and to spread Arab disaffection throughout the Turkish Empire. The good report of Colonel Lawrence's work had filtered through the land. The Turks had great fear of him, a personal fear as well as dread of his influence, for they knew he had led scores of raids and had marshalled the Arabs for battle. On the head of this heroic figure they had placed a price of £50,000 [sic] but no Arab desired to gain such a reward. There was a scene of remarkable enthusiasm when Colonel Lawrence rode into the city. The Arabs came in at a fast trot, and in the narrow winding streets, badly paved and neglected so that the tramway rails were in places nearly a foot above the level of the road, there was not sufficient room for demonstration. But as the party rode towards the city, firing at the heavens, as Arabs will in their moments of rejoicing, the people received them delightedly, throwing sweetmeats in Colonel Lawrence's path and showering upon him the perfumes of Araby" (*Allenby*, pp. 249–250).

17. *Letters*, p. 257.

18. Massey, pp. 262–263; Kirkbride, *A Crackle of Thorns*, p. 9, and *Awakening*, pp. 95–96; Chauvel, letter of January 1, 1936.

19. Kedourie, "The Capture," p. 75.

20. Chauvel, letter of January 1, 1936.

21. General Allenby to his wife, October 3, 1918, Allenby Papers, St. Antony's College, Oxford; quoted in Brian Gardner, *Allenby of Arabia*, p. 190.

22. W. F. Stirling, "Tales of Lawrence of Arabia," *Cornhill Magazine* 74 (1933): 509.

23. Archibald Wavell, *Allenby: A Study in Greatness*, p. 285.

24. Lawrence to William Yale, October 22, 1929.

25. Chauvel, letter of January 1, 1936.

26. Kirkbride, *Awakening*, pp. 96–98.

27. Ibid., p. 97.

28. Interview with William Yale, August 10, 1966. Notes made by Yale in response to Lawrence's 1929 letter to him found among the Lawrence papers in Oxford substantiate this account: "My official notes record my interview with General Clayton. An Australian officer, quartermaster, asked me to do something about the hospital. *He said he had received orders from General Chauvel not to provision the hospital, and that he could not do so without risking court-martial* [italics added]. The Italian attaché and I visited the hospital twice and I then went to see Clayton who said that there were barely enough food supplies to provision the troops and consequently nothing could be done about the hospital. This was in contradiction to what the Australian officer told me who said he had enough food to supply the hospital" (Bod Res MSS, d44).

29. Chauvel, letter of January 1, 1936.

30. Chauvel reports of October 22, 1929, and October 3, 1935, Allenby Papers, St. Antony's College, Oxford; Allenby's report to the War Office, October 6, 1918, PRO/CAB 27/34.

31. Chauvel report of October 22, 1929.

32. Chauvel reports of October 22, 1929, and October 31, 1935.

33. Shukri Pasha was soon replaced by Ali Ridah al-Riqabi.

34. Chauvel report of October 22, 1929.

35. Bod Res MSS, d44.

36. Lawrence to Yale, October 22, 1929, *Letters*, p. 670 (see p. 313).

37. Interview with Robert Lawrence, March 24, 1965.

38. W. F. Stirling, *Safety Last*, p. 94.

39. Massey, p. 343.

40. LHB, p. 165.


14. THE ACHIEVEMENTS OF "AURENS"

1. Brian Gardner, *Allenby of Arabia*, p. 210; Field Marshal Alexander Wavell in *Friends*, p. 149.

2. J. B. Glubb, *Britain and the Arabs*, p. 89.

3. Letter to the editor, *The Times Literary Supplement*, November 3, 1961, p. 789.

4. C. Falls and A. F. Becke, eds., *History of the Great War*, II, 409.

5. RGB, p. 104.

6. W. F. Stirling, *Safety Last*, p. 248.

7. Suleiman Mousa, *T. E. Lawrence*, p. 66.

8. Jean B. Villars, *T. E. Lawrence*, p. 151.

9. Correspondence of Theodora Duncan, in a California private collection.

10. *The Times*, May 20, 1935.

11. Massey, *Allenby's Final Triumph*, p. 272.

12. *Friends*, p. 149. Colonel Pierce Joyce, Lawrence's immediate superior during most of the campaign, never questioned that Lawrence was the moving force of the Revolt, and Stirling wrote of Lawrence: "By his daring courage, his strategy, his novel tactics," he welded the turbulent Arab tribes into a fighting machine of such value that he was able "to immobilise two Turkish divisions and provide a flank force for Lord Allenby's final advance through Palestine and Syria, the value of which that great general has acknowledged again and again" (*Friends*, p. 154; *Safety Last*, pp. 245–246). Ramsey, a medical officer who served in the Revolt, reflected on Lawrence's predominant role in a letter to him in 1919: "I will always cherish tender memories of the Hedjaz campaign, although as you know from the British point of view I will always look upon it as a one-man show, the rest of us attempting to do our bit with perhaps only moderate success" (August 28, 1919, Bod Res MSS, d60).

13. Captain L. H. Gilman, unpublished notes in Storrs Papers, 1955.

14. Captain Gilman to the author, May 17, 1973. As of 1975, Gilman is one of the few surviving officers of the desert campaigns.

15. C. S. Jarvis, *Three Deserts* (1936). "One fact, however, stands out," Jarvis wrote (pp. 295–303), "and that is but for some very useful spade-work by Colonel S. F. Newcombe, 'Skinface Newcombe,' the whole credit for the Arab campaign must be given to Lawrence and no one else, for anyone cognizant of the hopeless waterless country in which he operated and the still more hopeless people with whom he had to deal, must realize that no ordinary man could have made anything approaching a success of the revolution. Lawrence is criticized by some for abrogating to himself the duties of Commander-in-Chief, leader of demolition parties, transport officer, liaison offi-

cer, etc., and the criticism seems sound on the face of it if one is unacquainted with the race with which he was dealing. The fact is that Lawrence's many-sided activities were forced upon him, not because he was deficient of capable British assistants — as an actual fact he had many — but because the Arab, being a man of one idea, had no faith in anybody but the queer forceful character that had caught their fancy — 'El Aurens.'

"In the Arab campaigns it had to be Lawrence and no one else — if the Billi tribe were disgruntled Lawrence had to travel some 300 miles to smooth them down; if the Beni Sakhr failed in their demolition work Lawrence had to go and conduct the raid personally; if the Howeitat were weakening in their allegiance it was Lawrence who must go to pull things together. . . .

"There is no questioning the fact that Lawrence was a great man and that he will go down to posterity as the finest guerrilla commander that has ever existed; for, in his campaign, whilst avoiding anything in the nature of a general engagement, except on one occasion, he kept the Turks in a state of anxiety as to his intentions — and caused them to tie up on the Hedjaz line troops that were urgently required elsewhere. He enticed them to strike out blindly against forces that did not exist and by using ju-jitsu methods compelled the enemy to expend his strength on an empty desert. In action they [the Bedouin] were entirely without discipline, and the first hint of loot meant that the greater part of the attacking force broke off the engagement before it was completed to rifle the enemy's baggage.

"Most famous guerrilla leaders have had the advantage of leading insurrectionists amongst whom there has been definite cohesion, and who have been fighting for some national object or aim, but this was entirely lacking in Lawrence's campaign. . . .

"It is only when one studies the campaign from this standpoint that one realizes the magnitude of the task that Lawrence undertook and it is no exaggeration to say that only a superman could have achieved what he did."

16. See H. St. John Philby, *Forty Years in the Wilderness,* Chap. V ("T. E. Lawrence and his Critics"), pp. 82–109.

17. Franz von Papen, *Memoirs,* pp. 80–81.

18. L. Farago, "No Nazi Revolt in the Desert," *Asia* 40 (April 1940): 175–178.

19. Interviewing across cultures is, as one might suspect, full of traps, and the possibility of bias and distortion is compounded by the presence of an interpreter. The interviewee, and sometimes the interpreter, wish to please the interviewer, "to tell him what he wants to hear" (especially true of many Bedouin, I have been told), or to persuade him of a point of view; and the interviewer may unintentionally distort what he records and interprets. The interviewer can only keep these pitfalls in mind and try to overcome them. In my interviews of Arabs, I introduced such safeguards as obtaining more than one account of a particular event and more than one viewpoint on its interpretation. I tape-recorded the interviews whenever I could and submitted the tapes to translators with different backgrounds and points of view.

20. Philip Graves, ed., *Memoirs of King Abdullah of Transjordan,* p. 170.

21. Talk with Andrawes Barghout, April 14, 1967.

22. Interview on April 14, 1967, in Jordan with Howeitat shaykhs who had been young teen-agers during World War I and did not take direct part in the campaigns, although their respective fathers and other relatives did.

23. Interview with Shaykh 'Ayd Ibn Awad al-Zalabani, April 28, 1967, translated by Antoine Hallac and Basim Musallam.

24. Anis Sayigh, *al-Hashimiyun Wa al-Thawrah al-'Arabiyah al-Kubra* [The Hashemites and the Great Arabic Revolution].

25. 'Abd al-Rahman Shahbandar, "al-Colonel Lawrence," *al-Muqtataf* 78 (March 1, 1931): 275.

26. Suleiman Mousa, *T. E. Lawrence: An Arab View.*

27. *Letters,* pp. 225–231.

28. Mousa, pp. 74–79.

29. Ibid., p. 287.

30. Subhi al-'Umari, *Lawrence Kama 'Araftuhu* [Lawrence As I Knew Him] (1969).

31. Sayigh, *al-Hashimiyun.*

32. David G. Hogarth to Sir Gilbert F. Clayton, July 20, 1917, Hogarth Papers, St. Antony's College, Oxford.

33. Jeremy M. Wilson, *Minorities,* p.

33; letter of Lilith Friedman to the author, September 3, 1973, concerning BM Add MSS, 45915.

34. *Secret Lives*, p. 81 (from BM Add MSS, 45915, not 49515 as printed).

35. Interview with Shaykh Salim Ibn Nasir, April 16, 1967.

36. Interview with S. 'Ayd, April 28, 1967.

37. James D. Lunt, "An Unsolicited Tribute," *Blackwood's Magazine* 277 (1955): 294.

38. Ibid., p. 296.

39. Arnold W. Lawrence, ed., *Letters to TEL*, p. 141.

40. *Friends*, p. 409.

41. Carl R. Raswan, *Black Tents of Arabia*, p. viii.

42. al-'Umari, *Lawrence*.

43. Ali Jawdat, *Dhikrayat* [Memoirs], 1900–1958.

44. Mousa, p. 199.

45. See Birdwood's biography, *Nuri As-Said*.

46. Nuri al-Sa'id, in the Baghdad *Times*, March 24, 1927. Peter Kimber, an Australian, interviewed Nuri not long before Nuri's death in 1958, and wrote to Arnold Lawrence of the meeting: "I have not yet read the biography of Nuri by Birdwood, but it would have warmed your heart if you had heard what he had to say about T.E., when he talked to me about him for two hours in the garden of the Semiramis Hotel by the river in Baghdad. I wish now I had had a tape-recorder" (letter of June 14, 1966).

47. George Antonius, *The Arab Awakening*, p. 217.

48. 'Abd al-Rahman Shahbandar, "Lawrence fi al-Mizan" [Lawrence in the Balance], *al-Muqtataf* 79 (July 1, 1931): 38. There are many other Arab descriptions of Lawrence that reflect particular points of view. Zuhdi al-Fatih's *Lawrence al-'Arab: 'ala Khuta Hartzal: Taqarir Lawrence al-Sirriyah* [Lawrence of Arabia: In the Steps of Hertzel and the Secret Reports of Lawrence] links Lawrence to the Crusaders of the Middle Ages out to crush the Muslims, and is perhaps typical of the anti-Zionist propaganda that utilizes Lawrence's name for political, anti-Western purposes. On the other hand, Shakir Khalil Nassar's *Lawrence Wa al-'Arab* [Lawrence and the Arabs] is a characteristically hero-worshipping account of the sort that is not unfamiliar to Western readers.

49. RGB, p. 117.

50. Introduction to the 1922 (Oxford) edition of *Seven Pillars of Wisdom*.

15. THE QUESTION OF MOTIVATION

1. RGB, p. 137.

2. Lawrence to Alan Dawnay, April 14, 1927, Bod Res MSS, d43.

3. Lawrence to a Foreign Office staff member, probably November 1919, Bod Res MSS, b55.

4. Epilogue to the 1922 (Oxford) edition, *Seven Pillars of Wisdom*, p. 285.

5. "To S.A.," *Seven Pillars*, p. 5.

6. Interview with Arnold Lawrence, September 13, 1969.

7. *Friends*, p. 593.

8. Ibid., p. 258.

9. *Seven Pillars*, pp. 42, 195.

10. *Seven Pillars* (Oxford edition, 1922), p. 1.

11. *Seven Pillars*, pp. 562–563.

12. Ibid., p. 563.

13. Ibid., p. 564.

14. Ibid., p. 563.

15. Anis Sayigh, "Ra'y 'Arabi fi Lawrence," [An Arabic Opinion on Lawrence], *Hiwar* 5 (July–August 1963): 15–23.

16. Ibid., p. 18.

17. Ibid., p. 20.

18. Arnold Lawrence has suggested that Robert may have been guessing how T.E. felt and that T.E., usually very reticent about his feelings, did not convey them directly (letter to the author, March 23, 1974).

19. Elie Kedourie, *England and the Middle East*, p. 105.

20. *Seven Pillars*, p. 634. The idealistic union with the mother in the lives of men who became great has been described by Helene Deutsch. Such children are born and reared *ad maiorem Dei gloriam* ("Some Clinical Considerations of the Ego Ideal," *Journal of the American Psychoanalytic Association* 12 (1964): 512–516). Out of the ascetic union with the mother, for whom the child is destined to fulfill his special mission, will come great and glorious deeds. If, as in Lawrence's case, a major element in the mother's psychology is *her* sense of sin, then the mission and the great deeds will naturally contain strong elements of renunciation, asceticism and redemption. The fallen self-regard that is the product of this union of selves be-

tween the mother and the son needs to be elevated by such great deeds, and its associated pain converted into glorious fulfillment (interview with Helene Deutsch, 1966).

21. *Seven Pillars*, p. 39.
22. Ibid., p. 41.
23. Ibid., p. 544.
24. Ibid., p. 44.
25. Ibid., pp. 551–552.
26. Ibid., p. 565.

### 16. LAWRENCE THE ENABLER

1. Letter of October 18, 1927, BM Add MSS, 45093.
2. *Seven Pillars*, p. 31.
3. Lawrence to V. W. Richards, July 15, 1918, *Letters*, p. 246.
4. The leader of the Arab Legion, F. G. Peake ("Peake Pasha"), provided his friend and biographer, C. S. Jarvis, with examples "of the many occasions when Lawrence saw things clearly from the enemy's point-of-view, and this uncanny gift, which savoured almost of second sight or a sixth sense, was able to foresee the course of a battle with the various contingencies he would have to guard against before the operation started" (C. S. Jarvis, *Arab Command: The Biography of Lieutenant-Colonel F. G. Peake Pasha*, pp. 35–36).
5. LHB, p. 182.
6. W. F. Stirling, "Tales of Lawrence," *Cornhill Magazine* 74 (1933): 497; also reprinted in Stirling's *Safety Last*, p. 83, and in *Friends*, p. 155.
7. Pierce Joyce, transcript of BBC broadcast of July 14, 1941, in "Akaba" Papers, King's College, London. A copy was provided the author through the courtesy of Arnold Lawrence.
8. Pierce Joyce, transcript of BBC broadcast of April 30, 1939, in "Akaba" Papers, King's College, London.
9. *Seven Pillars*, p. 91.
10. *Arab Bulletin* #1, June 6, 1916, I, 7.
11. *Arab Bulletin* #26, October 16, 1916 (not by Lawrence), I, 387; and #32, November 26, 1916 (by Lawrence), I, 482. The latter was printed in *Secret Dispatches*, pp. 37–38.
12. Letter of January 17, 1917, in a private collection in California. See Chap. 12, n. 14.
13. See, for example, Richard Aldington's documentation for his inaccurate

assertion that "neither of the two heroes in fact thought very highly of each other" (*Lawrence of Arabia*, pp. 163–164).
14. Interview with Liddell Hart, March 27, 1965.
15. From official dispatches, *Seven Pillars of Wisdom*, army diaries, conversations with Liddell Hart (further details of which are revealed in a talk I had with him in 1965), and letters to his family and to Mrs. Shaw.
16. *Secret Dispatches*, pp. 17–18.
17. Ibid., pp. 37–38 (from *Arab Bulletin* #32, November 26, 1916, I, 482).
18. Ronald Wingate, *Wingate of the Sudan*, p. 197.
19. *Seven Pillars*, p. 97.
20. Ibid., p. 98.
21. Letter of January 16, 1917, *Home Letters*, p. 333.
22. Philip Graves, *Memoirs of King Abdullah*, p. 170.
23. Ronald Storrs, *Orientations*, p. 520.
24. Arnold W. Lawrence, ed., *Letters to TEL*, pp. 56–57.
25. Mrs. Stuart Erskine, *King Faisal of Iraq*, p. 51.
26. Lawrence to Husayn, June 1918, in the *Sunday Times* research materials, Imperial War Museum, London.
27. RGB, p. 51.
28. F. G. Peake, notes in Bodleian Library, Oxford, May 26, 1963.
29. A. F. Nayton to Arnold Lawrence, January 9, 1946, Bod Res MSS, c52.
30. *Arab Bulletin* #66, October 21, 1917, II, 413; reprinted in *Secret Dispatches*, p. 138.
31. *Oriental Assembly*, p. 131.
32. Compare with Suleiman Mousa, *T. E. Lawrence*, pp. 65–72 and 132–142. Mousa minimizes Lawrence's role in both the Aqaba and the Tafila enterprises.
33. Interviews with Howeitat tribesmen, April 1967.
34. Interview with Shaykh Salim Ibn Nasir, April 16, 1967.
35. *Seven Pillars*, p. 157.
36. Interview with Shaykh 'Ayd Ibn Awad, April 28, 1967. Translation by Antoine Hallac and Basim Musallam.
37. Ibid. Making the presentation of gifts and rewards vivid and concrete evidently appealed to the Arab tribesmen and was employed by Lawrence on other occasions. Lawrence wrote, for example, to Edward Garnett after the war: "When an Arab did something individual and intelligent during the war I would call

him to me, and opening a bag of sovereigns would say, 'Put in your hand,' and this was thought the very height of splendour. Yet it was never more than £120: but the exercise of spreading and burying your fingers in the gold made it feel better than a cold-blooded counting out of two or three hundred pounds" (letter of June 20, 1927, *Letters*, p. 520).

38. Interview of April 28, 1967.

39. Samir Khalaf, remarks made at a conference on psychology and the Near East, May 8, 1973, Princeton University.

40. *Seven Pillars*, p. 219.

41. Lawrence to V. W. Richards, July 15, 1918, *Letters*, p. 244.

42. Anis Sayigh, *al-Hashimiyun Wa al-Thawrah al-'Arabiyah al-Kubra* [The Hashemites and the Great Arab Revolution] and "Ra'y 'Arabi fi Lawrence" [An Arabic Opinion of Lawrence].

### 17. THE CONFLICT OF RESPONSIBILITY

1. General Harry Chauvel to Mr. Bean, editor of the *Official History of the War in Egypt and Palestine*, October 8, 1929, Allenby Papers, St. Antony's College, Oxford.

2. Letter of August 12, 1917, *Home Letters*, p. 338.

3. *Seven Pillars*, p. 542.

4. Ibid., p. 192.

5. *Oriental Assembly*, pp. 117–118; see also a similar statement in *Seven Pillars*, p. 195.

6. From the suppressed introductory chapter, 1922 (Oxford) edition, *Seven Pillars*.

7. *Seven Pillars*, p. 163.

8. Ibid., p. 191.

9. Ibid., p. 548.

10. Ibid., pp. 253, 257.

11. Ibid., p. 517.

12. F. G. Peake to Arnold Lawrence, May 26, 1963.

13. *Seven Pillars*, p. 378.

14. Ibid., p. 467.

15. Ibid., pp. 181–182.

16. *Friends*, p. 246.

17. *Seven Pillars*, p. 544.

18. LHB, p. 126; *Seven Pillars*, pp. 275–276.

19. *Seven Pillars*, p. 386.

20. Jeremy M. Wilson, introduction to *Minorities*, p. 33; the original is in BM Add MSS, 45915.

21. Elie Kedourie, *England and the Middle East*, pp. 96–97; *Seven Pillars*, p. 275.

22. *Seven Pillars*, p. 275.

23. Ibid., p. 276.

24. Ibid., p. 277.

25. Ibid., p. 555.

26. Ibid., p. 550.

### 18. THE HEROIC LEGEND AND THE HERO

1. James Notopoulos, "The Tragic and the Epic in T. E. Lawrence," *Yale Review* (Spring 1965), pp. 331–345.

2. Statement of Guillaume, a member of the Arab Bureau, as conveyed to the author by Arabella Rivington.

3. Irving Howe, *A World More Attractive*, Chap. 1, p. 20. The quotation "a man with a load on his mind" is from Herbert Read's review of *Seven Pillars*, in *The Bibliophile's Almanack for 1928*, p. 39.

4. Howe, p. 36.

5. Ibid., p. 39.

6. Read, review of *Seven Pillars*, pp. 38–39.

7. Lawrence to Edward Garnett, December 1, 1927, *Letters*, pp. 549–550.

8. In his classic work, *The Myth of the Birth of the Hero*, Otto Rank examined the ways in which the elements of the hero-fantasy, with its many variations, have found expression in the hero-myths of Western and Middle Eastern civilization (pp. 1–96).

9. Arnold Lawrence to the author, July 23, 1973.

10. Arnold Lawrence still receives letters from people — sometimes persons suffering from the torments of self-hate — who tell him how they resolved conflicts or "found peace" through their familiarity with his brother's life and writings.

11. See, for example, James T. Shotwell, *At the Paris Peace Conference*, p. 131; or Winston Churchill, *Great Contemporaries*, p. 157.

12. *Friends*, p. 242.

13. Lawrence to Charlotte Shaw, April 14, 1927, BM Add MSS, 45903.

14. *Seven Pillars*, p. 327.

15. Notes, undated, Bod Res MSS, c52.

16. *Seven Pillars*, p. 91.

17. Ibid., p. 322.

18. Ibid., p. 323.

19. *Friends*, pp. 226, 228.

20. LHB, p. 169.

21. Richard Goodwin, *The New Yorker*, May 25, 1968, p. 93.

22. RGB, pp. 84–90.

23. Lawrence to Graves, July 22, 1927, RGB, p. 90. The italics are Lawrence's.

### 19. THE SHATTERING OF THE DREAM

1. *Friends*, p. 245.

2. The original is in the Humanities Research Center, University of Texas.

3. This copy of *Seven Pillars* is in the Arents Collection, New York Public Library.

4. Report to GHQ, Cairo, June 28, 1919, Humanities Research Center, University of Texas.

5. In the Bodleian Library.

6. Manuscript of *Seven Pillars of Wisdom*, Bodleian Library.

7. *Seven Pillars*, p. 443.

8. Ibid., p. 444.

9. Ibid., pp. 444–445.

10. Ibid., p. 445.

11. Ibid., p. 446.

12. Ibid., p. 447.

13. Ibid.

14. According to his pocket diary he arrived in Azraq on November 22 and in Aqaba on the 26th.

15. Manuscript of *Seven Pillars*. This paragraph was omitted from the subscribers' edition.

16. Arnold Lawrence to the author, December 22, 1968.

17. Joyce's "Akaba" Papers, King's College, London. An Englishman who had served in the desert campaigns told me that he learned from Turkish prisoners that it was common practice for their officers, even those who had been most active heterosexually during peacetime, to take younger soldiers as sexual partners. Some of the younger soldiers volunteered; others were forced to submit. The soldiers also sought young boys for sexual partners and sometimes had sexual relations, or took part in mutual masturbation, with each other.

18. William Langer, discussion of J. E. Mack, "T. E. Lawrence: A Study of Heroism and Conflict," *Journal of the American Psychiatric Association* 125 (1969): 1092.

19. Richard Meinertzhagen, *Middle East Diary*, p. 32.

20. Interview with Basil Liddell Hart, March 27, 1965. T. W. Beaumont, a young gunner who served with Lawrence in the desert campaigns, told me that he spoke with the medical officer, Captain Ramsey, at Aqaba after Lawrence came back from Der'a. He learned from Ramsey that Lawrence had badly swollen testes, for which he required a suspensory bandage, and whipmarks on his thighs. Beaumont claims Lawrence told him, "When I kneed the Bey in the groin these chaps hided me" (interview with the author, September 11, 1969). But Beaumont was only nineteen at the time of the Der'a episode, and his reliability as a witness after more than half a century may be questioned.

21. Gilman was referring here only to my being a psychiatrist. He did not know that I happened, in fact, to have written a book about nightmares.

22. Captain L. H. Gilman to the author, May 17, 1973.

23. Lawrence to Charlotte Shaw, March 26, 1924, BM Add MSS, 45903.

24. Alan Watts, the late student of Eastern philosophies and religions, made an investigation of persons who had undergone torture. He found that for most sufferers the worst time was the beginning, when the agony was experienced as totally destructive, tearing the person apart. During this period the torture was terrifying. But in some instances if the individual surrendered to the experience, "cooperated" with it, it changed into a drunken masochistic giving in. A point would then come when the pain was no longer negative, but became converted into ecstasy, with the disappearance of all terror and meaning (lecture, taped, WBUR radio broadcast, Boston, January 20, 1974). This finding of Watts's corresponds closely to Lawrence's description of his experience and suggests that his response to the torture was not unusual. What was unique to his personality, however, was the lasting shame and intolerance, the refusal to forgive himself. It is not known how many victims of such violations suffer from subsequent disorders of the sort that Lawrence did.

25. RGB, p. 92.

26. *Friends*, p. 272.

27. "Book VI was written first of all the 7 Pillars: and has only been twice rewritten: except the Deraa chapter, which is in about its ninth revise" (letters to Charlotte Shaw, July 30, 1925, BM Add MSS, 45903).

28. Lawrence to Charlotte Shaw, December 26, 1925, BM Add MSS, 45903.

29. Lawrence to Edward Garnett, August 22, 1922, *Letters*, p. 358.

30. *Seven Pillars*, p. 13.

31. Interviews with A. E. "Jock" Chambers; Lawrence to Captain Snagge, June 29, 1927, Bod Res MSS, d44; Lawrence to Charlotte Shaw, July 30, 1930.

32. Toronto *Telegram*, January 31, 1963.

33. Information which casts doubt on Staples's claims of being a witness to these events, or of knowing Lawrence, is contained in a letter of March 28, 1974, from Christopher Dowling of the staff of the Imperial War Museum to Arnold Lawrence.

34. *Arab Bulletin* #106, October 22, 1918, III, 343–350; published in *Letters*, pp. 247–257.

35. *Letters*, pp. 253–254.

36. Ibid., p. 256.

37. Arnold Lawrence believes that the context indicates this could only have been said to his bodyguard (unpublished manuscript, "The Aftermath of Tafas," Bod Res MSS, b56).

38. In the original manuscript "first" is crossed out and replaced by "only."

39. *Seven Pillars*, pp. 632–633.

40. Ibid., p. 633.

41. Brian Gardner, *Allenby of Arabia*, p. 190.

42. See al-'Umari's *Lawrence Kama 'Araftuhu* [Lawrence As I Knew Him].

43. Suleiman Mousa, *T. E. Lawrence*, p. 199.

44. Lord Winterton ["W."], "Arabian Nights and Days," *Blackwood's Magazine* 207 (June 1920): 761.

45. Hubert Young. *The Independent Arab*, p. 251.

46. Unpublished notes of May 26, 1963, and 1965 (no month and day), of which a copy was loaned to the author by Arnold Lawrence.

47. F. G. Peake, notes of May 26, 1963.

48. Ibid.

49. *The Observer*, December 16, 1962.

50. "The Aftermath of Tafas," probably written in 1965 or 1966, Bod Res MSS, b56.

51. Alec Kirkbride, *An Awakening*, pp. 81–82.

52. Alec Kirkbride, *A Crackle of Thorns*, pp. 8, 9.

53. Kirkbride to Basil Liddell Hart, December 8, 1962, Bod Res MSS, b56.

54. Arnold Lawrence wrote me that he guessed "that T.E. reacted as an Arab to the sight of the Tafas villagers" (letter of August 20, 1973).

55. Arnold Lawrence to the author, August 20, 1973.

56. Richard Aldington seized upon the Tafas episode ("the spectacle of a British officer encouraging a mass slaughter of prisoners is deplorable") to attack Lawrence (*Lawrence of Arabia*, p. 237), and his account omits any discussion of the complexities of Lawrence's position. Although Aldington is perhaps unique in his venom, he shares with other denigrators a readiness to accept as factual any of Lawrence's statements about himself that discredit him, while devoting extraordinary effort to disproving those which do a service to his memory. The adulators have done the reverse.

57. Lawrence to Mrs. Hardy, January 15, 1928, *Letters*, p. 564.

58. *Seven Pillars*, p. 661.

59. Ibid., p. 659.

60. *Secret Lives*, pp. 217–219. I would not place the emphasis that Knightley and Simpson do upon the role of medical illness in the personality changes that resulted from Lawrence's war experiences. Although these illnesses were exhausting and at times incapacitating, I do not know of evidence indicating that they would lead to lasting changes of this sort.

61. Lawrence to Herbert Samuel, December 14, 1927, made available through the courtesy of Arnold Lawrence.

INTRODUCTION TO PART IV

1. LHB, p. 73.

2. Arnold Toynbee, *Aquaintances*, p. 192.

3. Hannah Arendt, "The Imperialistic Character," *Review of Politics* 12 (July 1950): 316.

4. Letter to James Hanley, July 2, 1931, *Letters*, p. 729.

5. Elie Kedourie, *England and the Middle East*, p. 88.

20. ARAB SELF-DETERMINATION AND ARAB UNITY

1. Lawrence to Charlotte Shaw, October 18, 1927, BM Add MSS, 45903.

2. This was confirmed for me by several of the Bedouin tribesmen in Jordan whom I interviewed. Lawrence helped them during the war, they said, but then he went away and "signed a treaty" which differed from what he had assured them during the campaigns.

3. *Oriental Assembly*, pp. 144–145.

4. Irving Howe, *A World More Attractive*, p. 27.

5. *Letters*, p. 291.

6. *Oriental Assembly*, pp. 94–95. See also Jon Kimche, *The Second Arab Awakening*, pp. 12–14.

7. *Oriental Assembly*, p. 94.

8. *Letters*, p. 577.

9. *Oriental Assembly*, pp. 95–97.

10. Ibid., pp. 82–83.

11. *Letters*, p. 577.

12. Lawrence to Charlotte Shaw, April 26, 1928, BM Add MSS, 45903.

13. LHB, p. 101.

14. *Oriental Assembly*, p. 88.

15. Ibid., pp. 88–89.

16. Ibid., pp. 92–93.

17. I am speaking of Syria here as Greater Syria, comprising what would now be Syria, Lebanon, Jordan and Israel (see J. P. Spagnolo, "French Influence in Syria Prior to World War I: The Functional Weakness of Imperialism." p. 47).

18. "Syrian Cross Currents," in *Secret Dispatches from Arabia*, p. 159.

19. *Oriental Assembly*, p. 85; George Kirk, *A Short History of the Middle East*, pp. 140–141.

20. David Lloyd George, *Memoirs*, II, 672.

21. Suleiman Mousa, *T. E. Lawrence*, p. 215.

22. See ibid. and "The Role of Syrians and Iraqis in the Arab Revolt"; and Anis Sayigh, *al-Hashimiyun Wa al-Thawrah al-'Arabiyah al-Kubra* [The Hashemites and the Great Arabic Revolution].

23. From "Syria: The Raw Material," *Secret Dispatches*, p. 77.

24. 'Abd al-Rahman Shahbandar, "Lawrence fi al-Mizan" [Lawrence in the Balance], *al-Muqtataf* 79 (July 1, 1931): 38.

25. Woolley summarized the question of Lawrence's attitude toward the French concisely: "He liked France and often talked of the pleasant times he had had there, and I think he was even fond of the French people. But especially after a long stay in the Lebanon, he felt a profound jealousy of the part they played or wished to play in Syria. That French politicians should aim at a control of the country he had come to love infuriated him. He hated the Turks because they were masters of Syria and treated the Arabs as inferiors; that their place should be taken by another non-Arab power was monstrous. Long before the Sykes-Picot Agreement drove him into a deliberate policy of frustration Lawrence was an enemy of France in the Levant, and that sentiment was the key to many of his later acts" (*Friends*, pp. 93–94).

## 21. LEAVING DAMASCUS BEHIND

1. LHB, p. 156.

2. C. H. Pirie-Gordon, ed., *A Brief Record of the Advance of the Egyptian Expeditionary Force*, Plate 56.

3. J. Nevakivi, *Britain, France and the Arab Middle East*, pp. 71–73; *Letters*, p. 670.

4. *Letters*, p. 258.

5. *Secret Lives*, p. 99.

6. RGB, p. 94.

7. See, for example, RGB, pp. 93–94; *Friends*, p. 162.

8. PRO/CAB 27/24.

9. Interview with Robert Lawrence, August 24, 1964.

10. The portrait hangs in the Junior Common Room, Jesus College, Oxford.

11. Harold Nicolson, *Curzon: The Last Phase*, p. 4.

12. Meeting of October 29, 1918, PRO/CAB 27/24.

13. *Letters*, pp. 265–269.

14. Ibid., p. 270.

15. *Letters to TEL*, p. 187.

16. Quoted in *Letters to TEL*, p. 186.

17. Ibid., p. 187.

18. Lord Birdwood, *Nuri As-Said*, p. 102.

19. Meeting of November 21, 1918, PRO/CAB 27/24.

20. Ahmad Qadri, *Mudhakkirati*, pp. 91–95.

21. Edouard Brémond, *Le Hedjaz dans la guerre mondiale*, p. 311.

22. LHB, p. 157.

23. Birdwood, p. 103.

24. Qadri, pp. 91–95.

25. LHB, p. 168. See also a detailed account of this incident in Jean Beraud Villars, *T. E. Lawrence*, pp. 255–257.

26. *The Times*, November 26, 1918. The three articles were reprinted by the

New York *Times* as a single piece in the magazine *Current History* (February 1919, pp. 348–357), "written by a correspondent of the London *Times* who was in touch with the Arabs throughout their campaign against the Turks."

27. Sir Evelyn Wrench, "Recollections," Bod Res MSS, b55; see also Wrench's *Struggle: 1914–1920*, pp. 362–366.

28. For example: "It took him months to obtain the suffrages of all the tribes, and the expenditure of as much tact and diplomacy as would suffice for years of ordinary life. What he achieved, however, is a little short of wonderful. From time immemorial the desert has been a confused and changing mass of blood-feuds among the Arabs from Damascus to Mecca; for the first time in the history of Arabia since the seventh century there is peace along all the pilgrim road" (*The Times*, November 27, 1918; reprinted in Stanley and Rodelle Weintraub, *The Evolution of a Revolt: Early Postwar Writings of T. E. Lawrence*, p. 41).

29. Lawrence to Dawson, November ("Sunday," probably November 24) 1928, Bod Res MSS, b55.

30. Ibid. Lawrence also wrote that when "things got bad in the early days of the rising," McMahon was fired "largely" because he had brought the sharif into the war.

31. "The French made very heavy weather over Faisal, which added to the trouble [for the Arab cause], and made him a fortnight late," Lawrence wrote to Dawson (December 11).

32. Brémond, p. 317.

33. Leonard Stein, *The Balfour Declaration*, p. 638.

34. See the discussion in Jon Kimche, *The Second Arab Awakening*, pp. 178–183. According to the account of a Palestinian historian, Aref al-Aref, Lawrence had conversations with Palestinian nationalists, in which he is said to have expressed his preference for Jewish or Hashemite dominance in Palestine over rule by Syrian or Palestinian Arabs.

35. *Jewish Chronicle*, December 13, 1918.

36. Ibid.

37. Esco Foundation for Palestine, *A Study of Jewish, Arab and British Policies*, I, 139.

38. Chaim Weizmann, *Trial and Error*, p. 235.

39. See George Antonius, *The Arab Awakening*, pp. 437–439.

40. Ibid., p. 439.

41. Christopher Sykes, *Crossroads to Israel*, pp. 45–49.

42. George Kirk, *A Short History of the Middle East*, pp. 152–157; Zeine N. Zeine, *The Struggle for Arab Independence*, pp. 62–64.

43. Qadri, pp. 96–97.

44. Letter of December 25, 1918, *Letters*, p. 271.

45. LHB, p. 157.

46. Lawrence to Eddie Marsh, January 7, 1919, *Letters*, p. 272.

47. Rudyard Kipling to Lawrence, January 7, 1919, *Letter to TEL*, pp. 120–121.

48. Lawrence to B. E. Leeson, January 8, 1919, *Letters*, p. 272.

22. AT THE PARIS PEACE CONFERENCE

1. Quoted in Ella Winter and Granville Hicks, eds., *The Letters of Lincoln Steffens* (New York: Harcourt, Brace, 1938), pp. 465–466.

2. Jon Kimche, *The Second Arab Awakening*, p. 10.

3. Lloyd George, *Memoirs*, II, 673.

4. PRO/FO 608/92.

5. Lawrence to Ernest Thurtle, April 26, 1929, *Letters*, p. 653.

6. Gertrude Bell to Lady Florence Bell, March 16, 1919, in Lady Florence Bell, *The Letters of Gertrude Bell*, II, 468.

7. H. N. Howard, *The Partition of Turkey*, p. 231.

8. Laurence Evans, *United States Policy and the Partition of Turkey, 1914–1924*, p. 121.

9. Winston Churchill, *Great Contemporaries*, p. 158.

10. David Hunter Miller, *My Diary at the Peace Conference*, I, 74.

11. By Lionel Curtis, in *Friends*, p. 259.

12. Miller, I, 74–75.

13. James T. Shotwell, diary entry of January 15, 1919, in *At the Paris Peace Conference*, p. 121.

14. Diary entry of January 20, 1919, Ibid., pp. 129–131.

15. Interview of William Yale, August 10, 1966. Yale, seventy-nine at the time, was a soured man.

16. *Letters*, pp. 273–274.

17. Jukka Nevakivi, *Britain, France and the Arab Middle East*, pp. 134–135.

18. Letter of January 30, 1919, *Home Letters*, p. 352. Elsie Newcombe, Colonel Newcombe's widow, with whom he was engaged to be married at the time of the Paris Conference, gave me a warm and amusing picture of Lawrence in Paris. Before she met Lawrence, Newcombe said to her: "If you meet a very rude young Englishman, pay no attention. It will be Lawrence." (Lawrence's friends seem, as far as I could discover, never to have been offended by his "rudeness," and did not feel that his humor was of a hurting kind or at their expense.) Colonel Newcombe and his fiancée were at a dinner attended by nineteen other men, and Elsie had no opportunity to meet Lawrence then; but at the end of the evening Lawrence sent the butler with a message that he wished to meet her. A dinner was duly arranged, he arrived, and when she asked him to sit next to her Lawrence said, "No, I am not worthy." Later, he apparently changed his mind because he did sit down beside her, looking sad and soulful and eating a banana. After dinner was over they all went outside. Lawrence was on the sidewalk and the future Mrs. Newcombe was standing in the street. "Now I'm taller than you," he said. She shoved him into the gutter and stood on the sidewalk and replied, "Now I'm taller than you." Colonel Newcombe came along and interrupted this horseplay, saying, "Come with me. Soon you'll want to marry him instead of me." She replied, "Oh no, you're better looking and much nicer." Lawrence laughed, but Newcombe blushed and was silent. (Elsie Newcombe, interview with the author, August 27, 1964; compare the incident with Lawrence's relationship with Janet Laurie, Chap. 6, especially p. 65.)

19. Evans, p. 117.

20. Ibid.; Miller, IV, 297, and XIV, 226 ff.

21. "Territorial Claims of the Government of the Hedjaz" (memorandum of January 29, 1919), PRO/FO 608/92.

22. Lloyd George, II, 673; Arnold Toynbee, *Acquaintances*, p. 182; LHB, p. 157.

23. Toynbee, pp. 182–183. Aldington based his account of this meeting on the memoirs of Lloyd George, who happened to make no mention of Lawrence's role as an interpreter or translator. Lawrence's assertion that he interpreted for Faisal before the Council of Ten (LHB, p. 157) was therefore assumed by Aldington to be "an elaborately built up story" of Lawrence's own devising. Toynbee's account substantiates Lawrence's version of the event, and describes Lawrence's remarkable performance, which, to my knowledge, Lawrence himself never referred to. In the speech Faisal focused upon his memorandum of January 29 and spoke of the Allied promises of independence, of Arab contributions and sacrifices during the war, of the desire for unity for the Arab-speaking peoples, and of the wish of the Syrians to choose their own mandate (Miller, XIV, 226 ff., and Lloyd George, pp. 673–678). Faisal expressed gratitude for the work of the French military contingent during the war, and made no reference to the growing hostility in Syria toward France. Because Lloyd George was busy "building up the German Treaty" he did not give the matter of Syria much attention and left it with Lord Milner, who had become colonial secretary.

24. See discussions by Lloyd George (II, 678–699), Evans (pp. 125–144), Howard (pp. 225–234), Nevakivi (pp. 126–147), and Zeine N. Zeine (*The Struggle for Arab Independence*, pp. 85–96).

25. Lloyd George, II, 695.

26. Elizabeth Monroe, *Britain's Moment in the Middle East, 1914–1956*, p. 63.

27. Harold Nicolson, *Peace Making — 1919*, p. 142.

28. Alexander Michailovitj, *När Jag Var Storfurste Av Ryssland* [When I Was Grand Duke of Russia], pp. 314–315. The English translation of this passage is by Gunilla Jainchill.

29. Lincoln Steffens, "Armenians Are Impossible: An Interview with Lawrence of Arabia," *Outlook and Independent*, October 14, 1931, pp. 203, 223.

30. E. M. House and C. S. Seymour, *What Really Happened at Paris*, pp. 178, 179.

31. See Esco Foundation, *Palestine*, I, 159–177, for the sequence of events leading up to the approval by the League of Nations in 1922 of the British mandate for Palestine.

32. Ibid., p. 161.

33. Ibid., p. 142.

34. Some contemporary Arab nationalists reject the idea that Faisal could ever have had a letter expressing such sentiment sent with his agreement. Suleiman Mousa states categorically: "The letter that the Zionists claimed Feisal had written on March 3, 1919, to Mr. Felix Frankfurter, then a member of the American Zionist Delegation, is certainly a forgery" (*T. E. Lawrence: An Arab View*, p. 229). Mousa quotes extensively from interviews with 'Awni 'Abd al-Hadi, a member of Faisal's delegation in Paris, who suggested that the letter was sent by Lawrence without Faisal's knowledge. Mr. Frankfurter, however, reprinted the letter in the October 1930 issue of the *Atlantic Monthly*, vouched for its authenticity, and discussed there the circumstances of its framing. "Prince Feisal's letter was a document prepared under the most responsible conditions," Frankfurter wrote. "It received important publicity at the time. It has ever since been treated as one of the basic documents affecting Palestinian affairs and Arab-Jewish relations" (p. 50). Although Faisal objected to those interpretations of his letter which understood it to convey his consent to Zionist policy, he did not disavow its authorship. See also discussions in the Esco Foundation's *Palestine* (I, 142–143) regarding the meeting and the letter; in Leonard Stein, *The Balfour Declaration*, p. 643; and in R. Meinertzhagen, *Middle East Diary*, pp. 14–15.

Hadi, who later became a Palestinian leader, resented what he called "Lawrence's Zionist propensities," indicated to Mousa that whatever Faisal's personal feelings were about the possibility of Arab-Jewish cooperation in Palestine, his support for British Zionist policy was contingent upon obtaining the independence of Syria, and that Faisal's attitude toward Zionism changed when he lost British support for Syria. Hadi, who also served at one time as Faisal's private secretary, claimed to Mousa that Faisal's confidence in Lawrence was lost in 1919 because of the latter's pro-Zionist attitude (Mousa, *T. E. Lawrence*, p. 230), but unpublished letters from Faisal to Lawrence in 1921, seeking his help after he became king of Iraq, are filled with expressions of warmth and affection and suggest no diminution of confidence in his English friend (copies of these letters are in the British Museum).

35. Evans, p. 137.

36. H. Wickham Steed, *Through Thirty Years*, II, 300; see also, Jukka Nevakivi, *Britain, France and the Arab Middle East*, pp. 137–138.

37. Letter of March 26, 1919, in Elizabeth Burgoyne, *Gertrude Bell*, II, 110.

38. Zeine, *The Struggle*, p. 81. The information was obtained by Zeine from al-Husri, *Yawn Maisalun*. Sati al-Husri was Faisal's advisor and future minister of education in the government of Damascus (from Nevakivi, p. 141).

39. Nevakivi, p. 143.

40. Faisal to Clemenceau, April 20, 1919, in E. S. Woodward and R. Butler, eds., *Documents on British Foreign Policy, 1918–1939*, Ser. 1, IV, 252.

41. Interview with Robert Lawrence, March 24, 1965.

42. Interview with Arnold Lawrence, March 16, 1965, and on other occasions. There is a curious entry dated "April 8th, 1919," concerning Lawrence in the published diary of Richard Meinertzhagen, an eccentric ornithologist and Zionist who was at the Peace Conference. Although purporting to be made from contemporary notes, and reporting "we lunched together" (presumably that day), the diary, first published in 1959, makes no mention of Lawrence's having received a telegram from home about his father's illness, or his having just returned from England or being about to go. Perhaps Meinertzhagen is off on his date by a few days or is describing events that occurred a little earlier.

The entry is of considerable potential interest as it provides the only account of Lawrence's troubled state in the early stages of writing his narrative of the Revolt. But I also question whether Meinertzhagen did not draw upon memories from later periods, and from various readings, in reconstructing his diary. He seems to have been much influenced by Aldington. Yet Lawrence's admission of embroidering "dull little incidents" into "hair-breadth escapes" seems a valid observation, and the confession of self-hatred for having "overdone it" is believable. But the statements that describe a kind of pathetic despair and relate it to terror lest he be "found out and deflated" are suggestive of Aldington, as is the statement "he excuses himself by saying that none of his exaggerations can be checked or verified" (p. 31). This is not only untrue but is inconsistent with Lawrence's later comment on the manuscript of Graves's biography: that the documents of the Arab Revolt in the archives of the Foreign Office would corroborate his account. These documents have now become available, and Lawrence's statement to Graves has been largely borne out. The validity of portions of Meinertzhagen's diary as a contemporary record must accordingly be questioned. It must be added that assessing Meinertzhagen's work is not made any easier by his condescending tone ("I cannot help liking the little man"), and his claim to be the only person to understand Lawrence (*Middle East Diary*, p. 30).

43. James Rennell Rodd, *Social and Diplomatic Memories*, Ser. 3, p. 383.

44. Interview with David Garnett, October 29, 1964; see also *Letters*, p. 276.

45. Francis Lord Rennell of Rodd to the author, November 17, 1965.

46. Rodd, *Memories*, p. 383.

47. *Friends*, p. 162.

48. RGB, p. 55.

49. LHB, p. 129; "History of Seven Pillars," Bod Res MSS, d230.

50. *Oriental Assembly*, pp. 142–143.

51. H. St. John Philby, *Forty Years in the Wilderness*, p. 88.

52. Ibid., p. 92.

53. *Secret Dispatches*, pp. 145–147. There is a curious entry in the minutes of March 19, 1919, of the American Commissioners in Paris: "Memorandum No. 168 was read in which General Churchill submitted a proposal that Captain William Yale accept an invitation tendered to him by Colonel Lawrence to accompany the British Forces on an expedition which they are planning for the month of May against the tribes of the Nejd. The Commissioners did not approve of this proposal and suggested that in any reply that should be made to Colonel Lawrence, it be stated that the American Commission to Negotiate Peace cannot take cognizance of any expedition which the British Forces are proposing to make against certain Arabian tribes" (*Papers Relating to the Foreign Relations of the United States*, IX (*The Paris Peace Conference, 1919*), 123. There is no further information on whether the British government actually planned to send Lawrence on such a mission, presumably against Ibn Saud, or whether Lawrence's ill-fated trip to Egypt was related to such

a plan. A note by Lawrence on a Foreign Office telegram of April 18, 1919, suggests that some sort of British mission against Ibn Saud may have been contemplated (PRO/FO 608/80, quoted in part in *Secret Lives*, p. 151):

"If he [Ibn Saud] abandons the Wahabi creed, we will not do too badly. If he remains Wahabi, we will send the Moslem part of the Indian Army to recover Mecca, and break the Wahabi movement. This was done early in the 19th century when the present state of things existed by Ibrahim Pasha of Egypt. It took him three years, and cost him 80,000 men. The Indian Army is better than Ibrahim's, and will do it quicker and cheaper.

TEL

I offered at Christmas 1918 to do it with ten tanks!"

54. Toynbee, *Acquaintances*, p. 184.

55. Lawrence to Charlotte Shaw, December 11, 1928, BM Add MSS, 45904.

56. Essay by Wavell, *Friends*, p. 148. Lawrence found time in Cairo to send a check for £10 to A. C. Frederick J. Daw, who had helped him after the crash in Rome. The check was accompanied by a note: "Will you buy yourself some trifle to remind you of our rather rough landing at Rome? I was not at all comfortable hanging up in the wreck, and felt very grateful to you for digging me out —" (Lawrence to Daw, July 5, 1919, Bod Res MSS, b55).

57. Woodward and Butler, IV, 314.

58. Curzon to Balfour, July 17, 1919, ibid., from PRO/FO 608/92. Two more entries from Meinertzhagen's diary cover these weeks of July 1919, but they are of limited value as contemporary documents (he quotes, for example, from *Seven Pillars of Wisdom*, giving 1918 as the year of its writing). One note dated July 20, 1919, is filled with bits and pieces of the most personal revelations about Lawrence's parents' relationship, his illegitimacy, and the assault at Der'a, which it is highly doubtful Lawrence would have shared with Meinertzhagen (he wrote critically of him in *Seven Pillars of Wisdom*).

What does seem to be substantiated — both Lawrence and Meinertzhagen telling the same story independently — is that Lawrence, who had moved to the Arab delegation headquarters in Paris, had a room above Meinertzhagen's, where he continued to work on his book. Lawrence would lower the book by a string from his balcony ("Romeo and Juliet act") for Meinertzhagen to read (entry of July 17, 1919, *Middle East Diary*, p. 31; LHB, p. 129).

59. PRO/FO 608/92.

### 23. RETURN TO ENGLAND: LONDON AND ALL SOULS

1. I had my own "adventure with Lowell Thomas" as a result of my interest in Lawrence. It happened that the day we had arranged in New York to talk about my work (November 9, 1965) was the day of the power failure that blacked out a large section of the northeastern United States, including New York City. Mr. Thomas, not to be kept from giving his nightly broadcast, took me and members of his staff across the darkened city to an auxiliary studio on Tenth Avenue, which had its own electric power, where we helped him with the broadcast. After that, Mr. Thomas took me to dinner at the Marco Polo Club at the Waldorf Astoria (a private club for journalists, of which he was president) and we talked in the candle-lit dining room for several hours about his experiences with Lawrence and the Lawrence legend. The experiences must have evoked memories of this critical turning point in his career because the next night, in the broadcast in which he described the blackout, he reported: "A young doctor from Boston had flown down to talk to me about Lawrence of Arabia, a psychiatrist who plans to do a book on Lawrence, attempting to explain why he was the way he was — one of the most unusual men of modern times, who finally wound up as an enlisted man in the R.A.F. — searching for escape" (Lowell Thomas, November 10, 1965). Thomas made it clear to me that if he had done much to expand the public image of Lawrence, so too his experience in reporting Lawrence's campaigns "changed the whole direction of my own life — toward the world in general, films, writing and speaking."

2. Interview with Lowell Thomas, November 9, 1965. See also accounts in *Friends*, pp. 205–215, and Brian Gardner, *Allenby of Arabia*, pp. XI–XXVI, for Thomas's familiar story of his meetings with Allenby and Lawrence in Palestine and the Hijaz and his shows in America and England.

3. Interview with Lowell Thomas, November 9, 1965.

4. The British newspaper publisher, Lord Beaverbrook, launched a campaign in 1917 to bring home to Americans Britain's part in the war. Beaverbrook arranged for British lecturers to visit the United States and for American newspapermen to come to London and the Western Front. One of the latter was Lowell Thomas, who came to Europe looking for a dramatic story. When he could not find what he was looking for on the Western Front he appealed to John Buchan, who had played a major part in Beaverbrook's campaign. Buchan arranged for transport to Allenby's headquarters in the Middle East, where Thomas met Lawrence (Janet Adam Smith, *John Buchan*, p. 212).

5. Lawrence to Archibald Murray, January 10, 1920, Houghton Library, Harvard University.

6. Lawrence to H. R. Hadley, September 2, 1920, *Letters*, p. 319.

7. Lowell Thomas, *With Lawrence in Arabia*, p. ix.

8. Interview with Lowell Thomas, November 9, 1965; *Friends*, p. 209.

9. Percy Burton (as told to Lowell Thomas), *Adventures Among Immortals*, p. 207.

10. Interview with Lowell Thomas, November 9, 1965.

11. Lawrence to G. Wren Howard, December 17, 1933, *Letters*, p. 783.

12. Interview with Lowell Thomas, November 9, 1965.

13. Lawrence to Archibald Murray, January 10, 1920, Houghton Library, Harvard University.

14. *Letters*, p. 301.

15. Lawrence to Greenhill, March 20, 1920, Humanities Research Center, University of Texas.

16. Lawrence to Ralph Isham, August 10, 1927, Bod Res MSS, d55.

17. Dawson to Lawrence, January 31, 1919, Bod Res MSS, d60.

18. Dawson to "Mr. Warden," February 12, 1919, Bod Res MSS, b55.

19. Francis W. Pember, warden of All Souls, to Lawrence, June 18, 1919, Bod Res MSS, d60.

20. See especially discussions by Jukka Nevakivi, *Britain, France and the Arab Middle East*, pp. 148–196, and Zeine N. Zeine, *The Struggle for Arab Independence*, pp. 85–119, for analyses of the

shifts in the Allied policies toward Syria during the summer of 1919.

21. E. L. Woodward and R. Butler, eds., *Documents on British Foreign Policy, 1918–1939*, Ser. 1, IV, 289–292, 311–313.

22. H. C. Howard, *The King-Crane Commission*, p. 78.

23. Woodward and Butler, IV, 340–349.

24. Memorandum by Pierce Joyce, July 1919, in Joyce's "Akaba" Papers, King's College, London.

25. Interview with Arnold Lawrence, March 16, 1965.

26. *Letters*, p. 280.

27. *The Times*, September 11, 1919, in *Letters*, pp. 281–282; reprinted in Stanley and Rodelle Weintraub, *The Evolution of a Revolt*, pp. 63–65.

28. *Letters*, p. 284.

29. *The Times*, September 11, 1919.

30. See discussions in Zeine, *The Struggle*, pp. 107–111; Nevakivi, pp. 186–194; and *Letters*, pp. 283–285, for the negotiations that led to this agreement and its terms.

31. Letter of September 3, 1919, in Woodward and Butler, IV, 370–371. The following are some excerpts from the Foreign Office files of September 11 (PRO/FO 371/4182), the day Lawrence's letter was published by *The Times*.

"It is most emphatically not the case, as Col. Lawrence implies, that the area known as O.E.T.A. [Occupied Enemy Territory Administration] (Dasmascus-Aleppo) was liberated by the 'military action' of the Arabs. Although the Arabs were allowed to make a spectacular try into these places, their fall was the direct result of General Allenby's advance."

\* \* \*

"Colonel Lawrence's letter is a carefully calculated indiscretion, written with the object of presenting the Arab case, and of guarding against the risk of the whole subject being discussed purely from the Franco-British point-of-view. He hits us as hard as the French, and if the letter had been written by an Arab, no possible exception could be taken to it. It is quite clear that, contrary to the opinion expressed in the Times leader [the accompanying editorial], his motive is solely to justify himself in the eyes of the people who helped to overthrow the Turks through his influence, and as a

result of the confidence placed in him personally. And his attitude is quite understandable. But it is perhaps open to question whether, as an employee of the F.O. [actually Lawrence had been demobilized by September 1], his action is justifiable."

\* \* \*

"From the official point of view Col. Lawrence's publication of this letter is quite unpardonable. His claim to be a freelance is definitely disposed by Mr. Balfour's insistence that he is an official member of the Delegation in Paris. [The reference here is to a dispatch from Lord Balfour to Curzon sent in August about the time Lawrence was returning to England. It stated that "Lawrence could still be regarded as technical advisor to this Delegation as his services here are likely to be required when the question of Syria comes to be discussed with the French and possibly with Feisal on the latter's return to Paris" (Woodward and Butler, IV, 315).]

\* \* \*

"But from the practical point-of-view I believe his 'indiscretion' may be productive of good. It remains to be seen how the French Govt. and the French Press take it. If they accept Col. Lawrence's statement that he is a free-lance and has access to these documents through Faisal [Lawrence did not actually say that he obtained the documents "through" Faisal. What he wrote was, "When on Prince Faisal's staff I had access to the documents in question"] all may be well, but if they realize his official position and imagine that he has been put up to publishing his letter by H.M.G. there may be a row. Faisal, for instance, has, so far as we know, never been given a copy of the Sykes-Picot Agreement and Lawrence's claim that he had access to it through him is obviously untrue. The truth is far more likely to have been the other way about."

32. Zeine, *The Struggle*, pp. 108–109, and Lloyd George, *Memoirs*, II, 699.

33. Zeine, *The Struggle*, pp. 112–114. According to Zeine (p. 287), the originals of Faisal's letter are published in Arabic in Hafiz Wahbah, *Jazirat al-'Arab fi al-Qarn al-'Ishrin* (Cairo, 1935).

34. *Letters*, pp. 288–293.

35. PRO/FO 371/4183, with a date of late September 1919.

36. Lawrence to Curzon, September 27, 1919, *Letters*, p. 292.

37. Ibid., p. 291.

38. Bodleian Library; the complete letter is quoted in *Secret Lives*, pp. 119–120 and 129–130.

39. *Letters*, pp. 283–287.

40. Zeine, *The Struggle*, p. 119.

41. Letter of October 8, 1919, *Letters to TEL*, p. 122.

42. Lawrence to F. N. Doubleday, August 25, 1927, Bod Res MSS, d52.

43. "History of Seven Pillars," reprinted in *Texas Quarterly* 5 (Autumn 1962); the original is in Humanities Research Center, University of Texas.

44. Elizabeth Burgoyne, *Gertrude Bell*, II, 108–111.

45. D. G. Hogarth, "Lawrence of Arabia: The Story of His Book," *The Times*, December 13, 1926.

46. Lawrence to Charlotte Shaw, June 11, 1926, BM Add MSS, 45903. The diary is now in the British Museum.

47. Lawrence to Miss Doughty, November 3, 1919, shown to me through the courtesy of Arnold Lawrence.

48. Doughty to Lawrence, November 4, 1919, *Letters to TEL*, pp. 38–39.

49. Lawrence to Doughty, November 25, 1919, *Letters to TEL*, p. 296.

50. Lawrence to Frederic Manning, May 15, 1930, *Letters*, p. 693.

51. LHB, p. 145; also *Letters*, p. 693.

52. LHB, p. 145; Joyce Knowles to Theodora Duncan, November 29, 1964, in a California private collection.

53. LHB, p. 145; *Letters to TEL*, p. 39.

54. *Oriental Assembly*, p. 139.

55. Notes in the manuscript of *Seven Pillars of Wisdom*, Bodleian Library, Oxford; RGB, p. 51; *Seven Pillars* (1926 edn.), p. 21.

56. Robert Graves, *Goodbye to All That*, p. 300.

57. Lawrence to Richards, February 27, 1920, *Letters*, p. 300.

58. Lawrence to Newcombe, February 16, 1920, *Letters*, p. 299.

59. Lawrence to Pound, late April 1920, Bod Res MSS, c52.

60. *Friends*, p. 249. The reference to "airmen's clothes" concerns the fact that Lawrence continued to work on the text of *Seven Pillars* after he had joined the RAF in August 1922.

61. Lawrence to Frederick Manning, May 15, 1930, *Letters*, pp. 691–692.

62. Robert Graves, *Lawrence and the Arabs*, p. 406; LHB, p. 45. See also *Seven Pillars*, p. 21, where Lawrence states that in writing the second version he did "many thousand words at a time, in long sittings."

63. *Seven Pillars*, p. 21.

64. *Letters*, p. 300.

65. *Seven Pillars*, p. 21.

66. Lawrence to Murray, January 10, 1920, Houghton Library, Harvard University.

67. LHB, p. 146.

68. F. N. Doubleday, "The Strange Character of Colonel T. E. Lawrence," in *A Few Indiscreet Recollections*, p. 83.

69. Interview with Dermot Morrah, December 11, 1965.

70. Manuscript of *Seven Pillars of Wisdom*, Bodleian Library, Oxford.

71. Lawrence to Doubleday, July 22, 1920, Bod Res MSS, d52.

72. *Letters*, p. 318.

73. Doubleday to Lawrence, October 7, 1920, Bod Res MSS, d60.

74. *Letters*, pp. 304–306.

75. RGB, p. 5. Lawrence came to know Augustus John in Paris. According to John, Lawrence sat frequently for him there and later in England; he enjoyed being painted "and always seemed tickled by the results" (*Chiaroscuro*, p. 238). A friendship developed and Lawrence wrote comments about John's paintings which the artist found amusing, although he often did not agree with them. Once Lawrence wrote: "A friend of mine went to the Alpine Club [where John had a show] and said my larger one was a conscious effort by you to show how long contact with camels had affected my face! But I explained that it wasn't my face which had been in contact with camels" (*Chiaroscuro*, p. 246, from a letter, undated, but of 1920). Christine Longford, who settled later in County Westmeath near the Chapman estate, once spied Lawrence staring long and fixedly at John's portrait of him at the Alpine Club Gallery. Friends came in, and Lawrence would converse with them, but from time to time gazed back over his shoulder, as if he were checking to see that the painting was still there (interview with Christine Longford, March 18, 1965).

76. *Minorities*, p. 40; RGB, p. 21.

The anthology was not published until 1971. Jeremy M. Wilson was the editor.

77. Lawrence to Charlotte Shaw, November 17, 1927, BM Add MSS, 45903; *Minorities*, p. 18.

78. Interview with Dermot Morrah, December 11, 1965.

79. *Friends*, pp. 295 and 298. Morrah also said that Lawrence rarely ate in the common room, choosing instead to "cook up an ungodly scruffy dish of rice on a chafing dish in his room."

80. Ibid., p. 250.

81. Ibid., p. 294.

82. Interview with Arnold Lawrence, March 16, 1965.

83. Letter of March 20, 1920, addressee unknown, in a private collection in California.

84. Excerpt of a letter of February 27, 1920, addressee unknown, printed in a 1951 auction catalogue; the catalogue is in a private collection in California.

85. *Letters*, pp. 298–299.

86. Interview with Elsie Newcombe, August 27, 1964.

87. Lawrence to Greenhill, March 20, 1920, Humanities Research Center, University of Texas.

88. Lawrence to Frederick C. Stern, May 14, 1920, in a California private collection.

89. See accounts by Zeine N. Zeine, *The Struggle for Arab Independence*, pp. 151–188; George Antonius, *The Arab Awakening*, pp. 302–309; and Jukka Nevakivi, *Britain, France and the Middle East*, pp. 216–220.

90. P. Guy to Lawrence, March 19, 1920, Bod Res MSS, d60.

91. "Creation of a New Department for Middle Eastern Administration," document in the Middle East Library, St. Antony's College, Oxford.

92. Lawrence to Philby, May 21, 1920, St. Antony's College Library.

93. It was probably at about this time that Hogarth wrote the following perceptive portrait of his friend: "He is not so young as he looks and he is hardly anything that he is popularly supposed to be — not Daredevil for example, nor Knight-Errant nor Visionary nor Romantick. The things he wants not to be are quite numerous; but things he could be, if he wanted, are more numerous still. He is not fond of being anything, and official categories do not fit him. He can do most things and does some; but to expect him to do a particular thing is rash. Besides being anti-official, he dislikes fighting and Arab clothes, Arab ways, and social functions, civilized or uncivilized. He takes a good deal of trouble about all things but quite a great deal about repelling the people whom he attracts, including all sorts and conditions of men and some sorts and conditions of women; but he is beginning to be discouraged by consistent failure, which now and then he does not regret. He has as much interest as faith in himself: but those that share the last are not asked to share the first. He makes fun of others or kings of them, but if anyone tries to make either one or the other of him he runs away. Pushing (not himself) he finds more congenial than leading and he loves to push the unsuspecting body: but if it does not get on as fast as he thinks it should he pushes it into the gutter and steps to the front. What he thinks is his Law. To think as fast or as far as he thinks is not easy, and still less easy is it to follow up with such swift action. He can be as persuasive as positive; and the tale of those he has hocussed into doing something they never meant to do and are not aware that they are doing, is long. It is better to be his partner than his opponent, for when he is not bluffing, he has a way of holding the aces: and he can be ruthless, caring little what eggs he breaks to make his omelettes and ignoring responsibility either for the shells or for the disgestion of the mess. Altogether a force felt by many but not yet fully gauged either by others or by himself. He should go far; but it may be in driving lonely furrows where at present few expect him to plow" ("Thomas Edward Lawrence," in William Rothenstein, *Twenty-four Portraits*, text opposite the portrait of Lawrence).

94. *Daily Express*, May 28, 1920; reprinted in Weintraub and Weintraub, *Evolution*, pp. 66–69.

95. *Daily Express*, May 29, 1920; reprinted in Weintraub and Weintraub, *Evolution*, pp. 70–71.

96. *Sunday Times*, May 30, 1920; reprinted in Weintraub and Weintraub, *Evolution*, pp. 76–77.

97. John to Lawrence, "Thursday, 1920," *Letters to TEL*, p. 118.

98. P. W. Ireland, *Iraq*, p. 239.

99. Ibid., pp. 239–265; George Kirk,

*A Short History of the Middle East,* pp. 141–143.

100. Quoted in Ireland, p. 263.

101. *The Times,* July 22, 1920; *The Observer,* August 8, 1920; *Sunday Times,* August 22, 1920. All three articles were published in *Letters,* pp. 306–317, and reprinted in Weintraub and Weintraub, *Evolution,* pp. 78–80, 92–99.

102. *Letters,* p. 314.

103. Ibid., p. 308.

104. Ibid., p. 312.

105. Ibid., pp. 315–317.

106. *Letters to TEL,* p. 12.

107. Burgoyne, *Gertrude Bell,* II, 162–163.

108. Ibid., II, 164–165.

109. *Letters to TEL,* p. 15. Lawrence visited Blunt, who was eighty then, at his home in Sussex in the summer of 1920 and has left this impression of the visit: "An Arab mare [Blunt bred Arabian horses] drew Blunt's visitors deep within a Sussex wood to his quarried house, stone-flagged and hung with Morris tapestries. There in a great chair he sat, prepared for me like a careless work of art in well-worn Arab robes, his chiselled face framed in silvered, curling hair. Doughty's voice was a caress, his nature sweetness. Blunt was a fire yet flickering over the ashes of old fury" (preface to Bertram Thomas, *Arabia Felix,* p. xvii).

110. *Letters to TEL,* p. 124.

111. Lawrence to Robert Cunninghame-Graham (addressed "Dear Don Roberto"), August 10, 1920, in a California private collection.

112. Lawrence to Charlotte Shaw, October 18, 1927, BM Add MSS, 45903.

113. *Oriental Assembly,* pp. 103–134. The piece appeared in the October issue.

114. Ibid., p. 117.

115. *Letters to TEL,* p. 194.

116. LHB, p. 145.

117. Charles Doughty, *Travels in Arabia Deserta,* p. 18.

118. Ibid., pp. 24–25.

119. In his preface Doughty paid a tribute to his friend in his archaic style: "These volumes, published originally by the Cambridge University Press, have been some time out of print. A re-print has been called for; and is reproduced thus, at the suggestion chiefly of my distinguished friend, Colonel T. E. Lawrence, leader with Feysal, Meccan Prince, of the nomad tribesmen; whom they, as might none other at that time marching from Jidda, the port of Mecca, were able (composing, as they went, the tribes' long-standing blood feuds and old enmities), to unite with them in Victorious arms, against the corrupt Turkish sovereignty in those parts; and who greatly thus serving his Country's cause and her Allies, from the Eastward, amidst the Great War; has in that imperishable enterprise, traversed the same wide region of Desert Arabia" (*Arabian Deserta,* p. 33).

120. See *Arabian Days* by Philby (who was serving then in Baghdad) for a detailed account of these months in Iraq (pp. 186–195).

121. Lawrence to the *Sunday Times,* August 22, 1920, *Letters,* p. 315; Philip Graves, *The Life of Sir Percy Cox,* p. 275.

122. *Friends,* p. 263.

123. *Friends,* pp. 264–265. It is interesting to compare Kennington's verbal portrait of Lawrence with that of another sculptor, Kathleen Scott (later Lady Kennet). During 1921 Lawrence sat for a statuette, which she cast in pewter and terra-cotta. She wrote of the figure: "In sitting for the portrait . . . he submitted himself, consciously for judgment; and the statuette shows first of all with what completeness he could assume an oriental immobility. Yet it brings to light two incongruities. One is in the countenance, where the actor lets himself be seen, as it were, commenting on his own make-up. The duality of the personage is emphasized, as when a mask is lifted. Again, those strong feet are not an easterner's. They indicate the extraordinary physical vigour which the small slender body did not otherwise suggest . . . for so strong a leadership, infinite patience was needed. If the statuette expresses one thing more than another, it is the power in a swift creature to wait" (Kathleen Scott [Lady Kennet], *Homage,* text facing photograph of the statuette).

## 24. LAWRENCE AND CHURCHILL

1. Lawrence to Buxton, February 16, 1927, Jesus College Library, Oxford; RGB, p. 54.

2. *Letters,* p. 324.

3. *Friends,* pp. 263–264.

4. LHB, p. 143.

5. *Letters,* p. 324.

6. *Friends,* p. 197; Winston Churchill, *Great Contemporaries,* p. 159.

7. Churchill, p. 260.

8. RGB, p. 113.

9. LHB, p. 144.

10. Discussions in Samuel Hoare, *Empire of the Air,* pp. 46–48.

11. See discussions in *Secret Lives,* pp. 138–140.

12. *Letters,* p. 302. But in 1934 Lawrence claimed that the concept of RAF control had grown out of his own experience during the desert campaigns. "The war showed me," he wrote on Liddell Hart's typescript, "that a combination of armoured cars and aircraft could rule the desert: but that they must be under non-army control, and without infantry support. You rightly trace the origin of the R.A.F. control in Irak, Aden and Palestine to this experience. As soon as I was able to have my own way in the Middle East [this is confusing, for in March and April 1920, when Lawrence was first discussing the scheme with Trenchard, he did not yet by any means have his "own way" in the Middle East] I approached Trenchard on the point, converted Winston easily [actually Churchill had invited Trenchard *before* his meetings with Lawrence to prepare a scheme of RAF control — see *Secret Lives,* pp. 138–139], persuaded the cabinet swiftly into approving (against the wiles of Henry Wilson [of the India Office]) — and it has worked very well." In this passage Lawrence has credited himself with the principal role in conceiving and masterminding a valuable and successful plan that he had an important role in developing, but which appears to have been a collaborative effort of Churchill, Trenchard and himself.

13. PRO/CAB 27/24; *Letters,* p. 270.

14. Memorandum of April 22, 1919, PRO/FO 608/92.

15. Arnold Wilson, *Loyalties: Mesopotamia,* II, 30.

16. *The Times,* August 11, 1920; published in Stanley and Roselle Weintraub, *The Evolution of a Revolt,* p. 91.

17. P. W. Ireland, *Iraq: A Study in Political Developments,* p. 309.

18. Lord Winterton, *Orders of the Day,* pp. 101–102.

19. *Friends,* p. 230.

20. Aaron Klieman's monograph *Foundations of British Policy in the Arab World: The Cairo Conference of 1921* (1970) makes use of Public Record Office documents to examine the historical place of the Cairo Conference, and the events leading up to and following it. It is an essential source for the study of this period of British relations in the Middle East. Chapters XXI and XXII of Philip Graves's *The Life of Sir Percy Cox* contain an objective and useful account of the Cairo Conference and the events leading to the crowning of Faisal as king of Iraq on August 23, 1921. Philby, who was a personal advisor and friend to the murderous Sayyid Talib, minister of the interior in the Provisional Government in Baghdad, opposed Faisal's candidacy, favored a republic, believed in the assurances Cox had given him that Faisal's kingship would not be imposed on Iraq, and resigned his position in June 1921 over a disagreement with Cox regarding his (Philby's) role in Faisal's reception and the "rigging" of his election (*Arabian Days,* p. 204). Philby's colorful account of these events in his autobiography must be read with these facts in mind. Although he lost out in the struggle with Cox, Gertrude Bell, Lawrence and others who backed the candidacy of Faisal, Philby never questioned that Lawrence was "an uncompromising champion of Arab independence," but he saw Lawrence as "trammelled by the obsession that the future of Arabia must be worked out under the shadow of Sharifian Hegemony" (*Arabian Days,* p. 208; see also Churchill, *Great Contemporaries,* pp. 159–160, and Ireland, pp. 315–316).

21. *Letters,* p. 325.

22. *Home Letters,* pp. 352–353.

23. W. H. Thompson, *Assignment Churchill* (1955).

24. Ibid., p. 29.

25. Ibid., p. 30.

26. Ibid., p. 31.

27. Philip Graves, *The Life of Sir Percy Cox,* pp. 279–280.

28. Ibid., p. 281.

29. Lawrence to Charlotte Shaw, October 13, 1927, BM Add MSS, 45903.

30. See discussions by P. Graves, *Cox,* pp. 287–304; Ireland, pp. 319–337; Elie Kedourie, *England and the Middle East,* pp. 208–214; *Secret Lives,* pp. 141–142; Philby, *Arabian Days,* pp. 186–205; and Bell, *Letters of Gertrude Bell.*

31. *Parliamentary Debates,* quoted in Ireland, p. 326.

32. P. Graves, *Cox,* p. 296.

33. Ibid., p. 301.

34. Ireland, p. 336.

35. Faisal to Lawrence, undated (probably November 1921), British Museum (copy in English).

36. Ibid.

37. Lawrence to Charlotte Shaw, October 18, 1927, BM Add MSS, 45903.

38. F. G. Peake, *A History and Tribes of Jordan,* p. 105.

39. Abdullah, *Memoirs,* p. 200.

40. *Secret Lives,* pp. 143–146; Ireland, pp. 310–311; LHB, p. 131.

41. Abdullah, pp. 203–204.

42. Ireland, p. 310.

43. *Home Letters,* p. 353.

44. *Friends,* p. 267.

45. Herbert Samuel, *Memoirs,* p. 174.

46. Klieman, *Foundations,* pp. 152–153, 210–213; Lawrence to Graves, May 21, 1921, RGB, p. 13.

47. Letter of May 21, 1921, RGB, p. 14. The articles appeared in *World's Work* (July–October 1921) and are reprinted in Weintraub and Weintraub, pp. 120–171.

48. Lawrence to Graves, May 21, 1921, RGB, p. 15.

49. Interview with Arnold Lawrence, July 21, 1968.

50. Lawrence to "Looker-on," August 11, 1927, Bod Res MSS, d43.

51. *Friends,* pp. 373–374.

52. Doughty to Lawrence, June 14, 1921, *Letters to TEL,* p. 44.

53. PRO/FO 686/93.

54. *Secret Lives,* p. 148.

55. Lawrence to Curzon, August 4, 1921, PRO/FO 686/93.

56. Lawrence to Kennington, August 25, 1921, Bod Res MSS, b56; *Oriental Assembly,* pp. 151–154.

57. From the introduction to the catalogue of drawings.

58. The Lawrence collection in Houghton Library, Harvard University, contains Lawrence's Colonial Office Time Account and his Travelling Allowances Account for the period July 8–December 20, 1921, which makes it possible to trace accurately on a daily basis his movements during this five-month period.

59. Lawrence, Jidda, to Prodrome, London, September 7, 1921, PRO/FO 686/93.

60. Ibid. Faisal, now king of Iraq, was evidently sympathetic to Lawrence's struggles with his father and wrote to him on October 6, 1921: "I am extremely sorry for the obstacles which I see you met in this your last journey to Jeddah, but I know well that you are yourself and that the people who sent you belong to a nation which is patient in the face of obstacles which it meets especially when they result from a friend." A copy of the letter is in the British Musum.

61. LHB, p. 159.

62. Lawrence, Jidda, to Prodrome, London, September 22, 1921, PRO/FO 686/93.

63. Uriel Dann, "T. E. Lawrence in Amman, 1921" (report of a conversation with Kirkbride), paper read to the 28th International Congress of Orientalists, Canberra, Australia, January 11, 1971.

64. Klieman, pp. 221–222.

65. Ibid., p. 219.

66. *Letters,* p. 334.

67. Klieman, p. 224.

68. C. S. Jarvis, *Arab Command: The Biography of Lieutenant Colonel F. G. Peake Pasha,* pp. 84–85.

69. Ibid., p. 84.

70. "Colonel Lawrence's Report of Trans-Jordan, October 24, 1921," Bod Res MSS, d230; *Letters,* p. 335.

71. Ibid.

72. Dann, "T. E. Lawrence in Amman"; Jarvis, p. 84; Philby, *Forty Years in the Wilderness,* pp. 100–101.

73. Lawrence to Newcombe, November 8, 1921, *Letters,* p. 336.

74. Philby, *Forty Years,* pp. 92–93.

75. Abdullah, pp. 225–226.

76. Philby, diary entry of November 29, 1921, *Forty Years,* p. 97; the original diary is in St. Antony's College, Oxford.

77. Ibid., p. 107.

78. Ibid., p. 97; Dann, "T. E. Lawrence in Amman."

79. Colonial Office Time Account, Houghton Library, Harvard University; Philby, *Forty Years,* p. 108.

80. Philby, *Forty Years,* p. 108.

81. RGB, p. 15.

82. Notes for a TV interview on the Jack Paar Show, recorded September 1963 and shown in the U.S. on January 24, 1964, Bod Res MSS, b56.

83. LHB, pp. 73, 159.

84. Personal communication, Philip Townshend Somerville, November 8, 1973.

85. Lawrence to Isham, August 10, 1927, Bod Res MSS, d55.
86. RGB, pp. 16, 17.
87. Letter of March 3, 1922; made available through the courtesy of Arnold Lawrence.
88. *Letters*, p. 338.
89. *Letters to TEL*, p. 45.
90. Ibid., p. 47; Viola Meynell, ed., *Friends of a Lifetime: Letters to Sydney Carlyle Cockerell*, p. 247.
91. Notes in the manuscript of *Seven Pillars of Wisdom*.
92. *Friends*, p. 273.
93. Lawrence to Paul Nash, August 3, 1922, in a California private collection.
94. Quoted in LHB, p. 129.
95. Lawrence to Shuckburgh, July 4, 1922, *Letters*, p. 344.
96. A. Boyle, *Trenchard*, p. 429.
97. Trenchard to Lawrence, August 20, 1922, *Letters to TEL*, p. 195.
98. *Letters*, p. 424.
99. *Friends*, p. 593.
100. Speech of May 23, 1939, quoted in *The Jewish National Home in Palestine*, p. 474.
101. See the discussion of an Arab view by Antonius, *Awakening*, pp. 319–324.
102. Zeine, *The Struggle*, p. 36.
103. *Letters*, p. 670.
104. *Letters to TEL*, p. 12.
105. Lawrence to Trenchard, June 30, 1927, *Letters*, p. 525.
106. Lawrence to Captain Snagge, June 29, 1927, Bod Res MSS, d44.
107. *Seven Pillars*, p. 276; *Letters*, pp. 345–346.
108. Lawrence to "Looker-on," August 11, 1927, Bod Res MSS, d43.
109. Lawrence to Charlotte Shaw, October 18, 1927, BM Add MSS, 45903; also *Letters*, p. 671.
110. *Letters*, p. 853.
111. Draft preface to an abridgment of *Seven Pillars of Wisdom*, November 18, 1922; *Letters*, pp. 345–346.
112. Lawrence to Captain Snagge, June 29, 1927, Bod Res MSS, d44.
113. Lawrence to "Looker-on," August 11, 1927, Bod Res MSS, d43.
114. Lawrence to Snagge, June 29, 1927, Bod Res MSS, d44.
115. Ibid.; confirmed by his hut neighbor at Farnborough, A. E. Chambers, in interviews in 1965.
116. *Friends*, p. 593.
117. Ibid.

25. THE SERVICE YEARS: AN OVERVIEW

1. Air Ministry personnel file, May 22, 1935, Bod Res MSS, d48.
2. Letter of August 6, 1934, *Letters*, p. 813.
3. *The Mint* is a basic source for Lawrence's two months at the RAF training station at Uxbridge. Stanley Weintraub's *Private Shaw and Public Shaw* contains valuable information about Lawrence during his years in the ranks, and Claire Sydney Smith's *The Golden Reign* is indispensable for the period after Lawrence's return from India in 1929. Jeremy Wilson's introductory biographical essay accompanying the publication of Lawrence's private anthology of poetry, *Minorities*, provides additional insights.
4. Lawrence to Baker, November 6, 1928, Bod Res MSS, d49.
5. Lawrence to a pilot who had flown with him to Egypt in 1919, April 17, 1931, *Letters*, p. 719.
6. Arnold Lawrence to the author, October 8, 1973.
7. Andrew Boyle, *Trenchard*, p. 384.
8. Ibid., p. 427; quoted also in *Secret Lives*, pp. 166–167.
9. LHB, p. 73.
10. Ibid.
11. Lawrence to Allanson, January 18, 1927, in a California private collection.
12. Lawrence to H. G. Andrews, March 15, 1934, Bod Res MSS, d43.
13. Lawrence to H. S. Ede, June 30, 1928, *Letters*, p. 615.
14. RGB, p. 23.
15. Lawrence to E. M. Forster, February 20, 1924, *Letters*, pp. 456–457.
16. Lawrence to Ernest Dowson, fall of 1924, Bod Res MSS, d52.
17. Lawrence to Charlotte Shaw, September 28, 1925, BM Add MSS, 45903.
18. Lawrence to Edward Garnett, September 22, 1927, *Letters*, p. 540.
19. Lawrence to Ralph Isham, November 22, 1927, ibid., p. 546.
20. Lawrence to George Bernard Shaw, December 20, 1923, ibid., p. 447.
21. Lawrence to G.B.S., July 19, 1928, ibid., p. 618.
22. RGB, pp. 169–170; also in *Letters*, p. 759.
23. *Letters*, p. 559.
24. Lawrence to Charlotte Shaw, June 17, 1926, BM Add MSS, 45903.
25. Interview with A. E. Chambers, July 23, 1968.

26. Lawrence to Charlotte Shaw, August 31, 1924, BM Add MSS, 45903.
27. *Friends,* p. 244.
28. *Letters,* p. 554.
29. Ibid., p. 594.
30. Lawrence to Charlotte Shaw, January 9, 1932, BM Add MSS, 45903.
31. Lawrence to Ernest Thurtle, July 29, 1929, *Letters,* p. 669.
32. Lawrence to Hugh Trenchard, December 21, 1928, Bod Res MSS, d46.
33. Lawrence to Herbert Baker, October 29, 1928, Bod Res MSS, d49.
34. Lawrence to Edward Garnett, April 23, 1928, *Letters,* p. 597.
35. Letter of May 2, 1930, ibid., pp. 689–690.
36. Lawrence to Trenchard, April 16, 1929, Bod Res MSS, d46.
37. Reginald Sims, "The Sayings and the Doings of T.E. as heard and experienced by the Sims family" (1937); the manuscript is in a private collection.
38. Lawrence to Trenchard, June 20, 1929, Bod Res MSS, d46.
39. LHB, p. 30; also quoted in *Letters,* p. 665.
40. "In Pocket Diary for 1933," Bod Res MSS, d230; Arnold Lawrence showed me the original diary in 1965.
41. Forster to Lawrence, July 5, 1928, Bod Res MSS, d60.
42. *Letters to TEL,* p. 70.
43. Charlotte Shaw to Lawrence, December 31, 1922, quoted in full in Janet Dunbar, *Mrs. G.B.S.: A Portrait,* pp. 237–238, and in *Secret Lives,* pp. 248–249.
44. Charlotte Shaw to Lawrence, May 17, 1927, quoted in Dunbar, p. 251.
45. Lawrence to Charlotte Shaw, undated but June or July of 1928, BM Add MSS, 45904.
46. Blanche Patch, *Thirty Years with G.B.S.,* p. 85.
47. Lawrence to Charlotte Shaw, July 10, 1929, BM Add MSS, 45904.
48. *Letters,* p. 661.
49. *Friends,* p. 448.
50. Lawrence to Lord Wavell, July 23, 1929, Bod Res MSS, d59.
51. *Letters,* p. 760.
52. Letter of September 25, 1933, *Shaw-Ede: T. E. Lawrence's Letters to H. S. Ede, 1927–1935,* pp. 56–57.
53. David Garnett, *The Familiar Faces,* p. 109.
54. *Letters,* p. 725.
55. "Confession of Faith," 1933, Bod Res MSS, d230.

56. Lawrence to Graves, February 4, 1935, *Letters,* pp. 851–852.

26. ROSS: THE FIRST RAF ENLISTMENT

1. *Letters,* p. 353.
2. Trenchard to Oliver Swann, August 17, 1922, Bod Res MSS, d48.
3. Bod Res MSS, c52.
4. *Mint,* p. 19.
5. W. E. Johns, *Sunday Times,* April 8, 1951.
6. *Mint,* pp. 11–12; RAF medical record, copy made available to me through the courtesy of Arnold Lawrence.
7. *Sunday Times,* April 8, 1951; RAF medical record; *Mint,* p. 20. Lawrence's body was evidently well covered with scars of one sort or another. Mrs. Clare Sydney Smith, wife of Lawrence's commander at Mount Batten in 1929–1931, has written "Sydney [Wing Commander Sydney Smith, her husband] pointed out to me all the scars on Tes's [a pet name she used] fair skin. There was hardly a place on his body that wasn't marked in this way" (*The Golden Reign*), p. 102.
8. *Sunday Times,* April 8, 1951.
9. Lawrence to Swann, September 1, 1922, *Letters,* p. 364.
10. *Mint,* pp. 38–39.
11. Personal communication, March 24, 1974.
12. *Mint,* p. 73.
13. Ibid., p. 86.
14. Ibid., p. 107.
15. Ibid., p. 152.
16. Ibid., p. 154.
17. Ibid., p. 163.
18. Ibid., p. 159.
19. Ibid.
20. Ibid., p. 164.
21. Ibid., p. 163.
22. Lawrence to Group Captain Robinson, May 26, 1933, Humanities Research Center, University of Texas.
23. E. G. Metcalfe, "An Erk's Eye View of Lawrence," Manchester *Guardian,* February 17, 1955.
24. Ibid.
25. Ibid.
26. Ibid.
27. *Friends,* p. 275.
28. Lawrence to Edward Garnett, August 26, 1922, *Letters,* p. 360.
29. Paul Nash to Gordon Bottomley, September 12, 1922; quoted in Anthony Bertram, *Paul Nash,* p. 112.

30. Lawrence to Edward Garnett, September 7, 1922, *Letters,* p. 366.
31. Lawrence to Edward Garnett, October 23, 1922, ibid., p. 371.
32. Edward Garnett to Lawrence, September, 1922, *Letters to TEL,* p. 88.
33. The letters to Roberts are in a California private collection.
34. Lawrence to Edward Garnett, November 8, 1922, Humanities Research Center, University of Texas.
35. Lawrence to J. M. Keynes, September 18, 1922.
36. The note is in the Humanities Research Center, University of Texas.
37. Interview with A. E. Chambers, March 17, 1965; see also *Friends,* pp. 339–340.
38. "I'm awkward anyway at rifle drill," Lawrence wrote at the time to Swann (*Letters,* p. 377).
39. Unpublished notes of A. E. Chambers's furnished to the author in 1965.
40. Lawrence to F. L. Lucas, March 26, 1929, Bod Res MSS, d58.
41. Lawrence to Edward Garnett, November 12, 1922, *Letters,* p. 380.
42. Shaw to Lawrence, December 1, 1922, *Letters to TEL,* pp. 161–162.
43. Ibid., p. 163.
44. Janet Dunbar, *Mrs. G.B.S.,* p. 237.
45. Lawrence to Charlotte Shaw, January 8, 1923, BM Add MSS, 45903; quoted in Dunbar, p. 238.
46. *Letters,* pp. 393–397.
47. Lawrence to R. D. Blumenfeld, November 11, 1922, Bod Res MSS, d43.
48. Lawrence to William Roberts, October 27, 1922, in a California private collection.
49. Charles Findlay, "The Amazing AC2," *The Listener,* June 5, 1958, pp. 937–938.
50. Chambers's notes.
51. *Letters,* p. 398.
52. Findlay, "The Amazing AC2," p. 938.
53. *Letters,* p. 426; 'Samuel Hoare, *Empire of the Air,* p. 255.
54. Stanley Weintraub, *Private Shaw and Public Shaw,* pp. 12–17; *Letters,* p. 363.
55. Guilfoyle to Trenchard, December 16, 1922, Bod Res MSS, d48.
56. *Letters to TEL,* p. 166.
57. Chambers's notes.
58. George Bernard Shaw to Law-

rence, December 17, 1922, *Letters to TEL,* p. 166.
59. R. D. Blumenfeld, editor, of the *Daily Express* — one of the newspapers that revealed Lawrence's enlistment in the RAF — has taken upon himself some of the responsibility for giving away his secret. "He asked me to guard his secret," Blumenfeld wrote in his memoirs. "I got ill and was away for some months. In the interval someone in the office learned the story which could not of course be a secret long, and 'the beans were spilled'" (*R.D.B.'s Procession,* p. 116).
60. January 4, 1923, *Letters to TEL,* pp. 168–169.
61. *Letters,* p. 393.
62. Lawrence to Graves, January 18, 1923, RGB, p. 24.

27. THE YEARS IN THE TANKS

1. *Letters,* p. 425.
2. Lawrence to T. B. Marson, January 28, 1923, ibid., p. 395.
3. Leopold Amery to Lawrence, February 2, 1923, Bod Res MSS, c52.
4. Notes in the margin of George Bernard Shaw's appeal to the Prime Minister, May 31, 1923, Bod Res MSS, c52.
5. Lawrence to William Rothenstein, February 5, 1923, Bod Res MSS, c52.
6. Lawrence to William Roberts, February 7, 1923, in a California private collection.
7. Lawrence to B. E. Leeson, February 16, 1923, Bod Res MSS, d58.
8. See the discussion in Andrew Boyle, *Trenchard,* pp. 459–460.
9. Ibid., p. 460.
10. RGB, p. 53; the question of Lawrence's assumption of the name Shaw is discussed by Stanley and Roselle Weintraub, in *Private Shaw and Public Shaw,* pp. 31–35.
11. Lawrence to Lionel Curtis, March 19, 1923, *Letters,* p. 411.
12. Lawrence to R. M. Guy, March 30, 1923, Houghton Library, Harvard University.
13. Lawrence to Jonathan Cape, April 10, 1923, *Letters,* p. 408.
14. Lawrence to Edward Garnett, April 12, 1923, *Letters,* p. 409.
15. "A Sea Trip Essay" by Pvt. T. E. Shaw, April 18, 1923, Bod Res MSS, d230.
16. Lawrence to George Bernard Shaw,

May 3, 1923, and Shaw to Lawrence, May 13, 1923. Copies of these letters were made available to the author through the courtesy of Jeremy Wilson.

17. Lawrence to Lionel Curtis, May 14, 1923, *Letters*, pp. 415-417.

18. Lawrence to Curtis, May 3, 1923, pp. 417-419.

19. *Letters*, p. 446.

20. "I was able to understand his determination to make no money by the Seven Pillars, much as it could place within his grasp," Shaw wrote later. "This was not a refusal to coin his blood in drachmas; for he had shed none he could not spare. But the gesture led to a belief that he would not accept payment for his services on any terms.

"I knew better. He was quite willing as a baptized and enlisted soldier and servant to be pensioned as such by his country. I asked him how much would suffice. He replied, with a promptitude which shewed he had fully considered the matter, £300 a year.

"I went to Stanley Baldwin, then prime minister, and demanded £800. Baldwin, pipe in mouth, and always agreeable, approved of all I said, but feared that parliament might object. I, instructed in parliamentary procedure by Lord Olivier, explained how it could be done without raising any question. He very kindly left me under the impression that the pension would be granted.

"It never was. That was Baldwin's way, and the secret of his promotion. He could always be depended on to smoke amiably and do nothing." (Handwritten note by G.B.S. on the flyleaves of Charlotte Shaw's copy of *Seven Pillars* (subscribers' edition), Arents Collection, New York Public Library; quoted in part in Weintraub, *Private Shaw*, p. 62.)

21. Florence Hardy to Sydney Cockerell, April 11, 1924, in Viola Meynell, ed., *Friends of a Lifetime*, p. 311.

22. Lawrence to Graves, September 8, 1923, *Letters*, pp. 429-431; also RGB, p. 26.

23. Lawrence to David Hogarth, June 27, 1923, *Letters*, p. 426.

24. Lawrence to Curtis, June 27, 1923, ibid., pp. 419-420.

25. Ibid., p. 420.

26. *Friends*, pp. 361-365.

27. Ibid., pp. 277-278.

28. Alec Dixon to the author, June 25, 1967.

29. Alec Dixon, *Tinned Soldier*, pp. 295-296.

30. Ibid., p. 297.

31. *Friends*, p. 363.

32. Dixon, p. 294.

33. Ibid., p. 301.

34. Ibid., pp. 301-302.

35. *Friends*, p. 371.

36. Alec Dixon to the author, June 25, 1967.

37. Letter of December 19, 1923, *Home Letters*, p. 357.

38. *Friends*, p. 362.

39. Lawrence to Florence Hardy, August 15, 1923, *Letters*, p. 427.

40. Lawrence to D. G. Hogarth, August 23, 1923, *Letters*, p. 429.

41. Ibid.

42. Notes in a California private collection.

43. Lawrence to his mother, May 18, 1924, Bod Res MSS, c13.

44. *Letters*, p. 435.

45. Ibid., pp. 528, 594. Lawrence went to great lengths to preserve the peace and beauty of his cottage. In 1925 he pleaded with the chief engineer of the district to have removed some recently erected and ugly telephone poles, "festooned with wires," that blocked his view. When the engineer refused to act, Lawrence appealed successfully to the postmaster general of England and the poles and wires were taken down (Reginald Sims, "The Sayings and the Doings of T.E. as heard and experienced by the Sims family" (1937); the manuscript is in a private collection).

46. *Letters*, p. 654.

47. E. M. Forster, "Clouds Hill," *Listener* (September 1, 1938), pp. 426-427.

48. *Friends*, p. 375.

49. *Letters*, p. 436.

50. Forster, "Clouds Hill," p. 426. See p. 66 for a fuller discussion of the meaning of this motto for Lawrence.

51. *Letters*, p. 746.

52. *Letters to TEL*, p. 154.

53. Lawrence to Hogarth, December 9, 1923, Bod Res MSS, d55.

54. Lawrence to Shaw, December 13, 1923, Bod Res MSS, d44.

55. *Letters*, pp. 444-446.

56. Lawrence to Winterton, October 27, 1923, Bod Res MSS, d44.

57. Lawrence to Cockerell, December 25, 1923, in a California private collection.

58. Lawrence to Lionel Curtis, August 25, 1924, *Letters*, p. 465.

59. Apparently Lawrence had threatened to go AWOL or do something to get himself expelled from the Tank Corps, for Trenchard had written him on December 6, "you must not be a defaulter or you will get kicked out. Do not be an ass! If you start being a defaulter it will be impossible for me to help you or for you to help yourself" (*Letters to TEL*, December 6, 1923, pp. 197–198).

60. Lawrence to Guy, December 25, 1923, Houghton Library, Harvard University.

61. *Letters to TEL*, p. 172.

62. *Letters*, p. 452.

63. Ibid.

64. Lawrence to Forster, February 20, 1924, ibid., p. 455.

65. *Letters to TEL*, p. 64.

66. Lawrence to James Hanley, December 28, 1931, *Letters*, p. 738. For an analysis of Lawrence's literary relationship with E. M. Forster see Jeffrey Meyers's "E. M. Forster and T. E. Lawrence: A Friendship," *South Atlantic Quarterly* LXIX (Spring 1970): 205–216.

67. Lawrence to F. N. Doubleday, April 8, 1924, Bod Res MSS, d52.

68. Doubleday, "The Strange Character of T. E. Lawrence" (1928), Houghton Library, Harvard University.

69. The actual contract is in a California private collection, where I examined it.

70. William Matheson, chief of the Rare Book Division, Library of Congress, to the author, October 16, 1973.

71. George Doran, *Chronicles of Barabbas*, pp. 395–397.

72. Ibid., p. 397.

73. Lawrence to Doughty, April 30, 1924, *Letters*, p. 459. Three years later, Lawrence wrote to Hogarth: "I'm afraid *The Seven Pillars* was rather a bitter pill for C.M.D. to swallow. The tone of it must have shocked him. I did not send it, till he had twice written to me asking for it" (letter of May 19, 1927, *Letters*, p. 517).

74. Doughty to Lawrence, May 16, 1924, *Letters to TEL*, p. 54.

75. David Hogarth, *The Life of Charles Doughty*, p. 204.

76. Lawrence to Charlotte Shaw, February 8, 1926, BM Add MSS, 45903.

77. Lawrence to Hogarth, May 9, 1924, *Letters*, p. 460.

78. Michael S. Howard, *Jonathan Cape, Publisher*, pp. 86, 87.

79. Of Lawrence's letters to Buxton, more than ninety are in the library of Jesus College, Oxford.

80. Lawrence to his family, August 18, 1924, *Home Letters*, p. 359.

81. Lawrence to "Dear Sir," August 21, 1924; copy lent to the author by Jeremy Wilson.

82. In his letter Shaw gave teasing examples of properly punctuated passages: "Thus Luruns said nothing; but he thought the more. Luruns could not speak: he was drunk. Luruns, like Napoleon, was out of place and a failure as a subaltern; yet when he could exasperate his officers by being a faultless private he could behave himself as such. Luruns, like Napoleon, could see a hostile city not only as a military objective but as a stage for a coup de theatre: he was a born actor" (Shaw to Lawrence, October 7, 1924; a copy was lent the author by Jeremy Wilson).

83. Charlotte Shaw's copy of *Seven Pillars* is in the Arents Collection, New York Public Library.

84. Ibid.

85. Lawrence to Stirling, October 15, 1924.

86. Lawrence to Trenchard, February 6, 1925, Bod Res MSS, d46.

87. Lawrence to Buxton, May 16, 1925, Jesus College, Oxford.

88. *Letters*, p. 476.

89. Letter of June 1, 1925, Humanities Research Center, University of Texas.

90. Lawrence to Edward Garnett, June 13, 1925, *Letters*, p. 477.

91. Janet Adam Smith, *John Buchan*, p. 242.

92. *Letters*, p. 477.

93. Ibid., p. 485.

94. Boyle, *Trenchard*, p. 516.

95. Letter of July 5, 1925, *Letters*, p. 478.

## 28. CRANWELL

1. Lawrence to John Buchan, August 27, 1925, *Letters*, p. 483.

2. Lawrence to Marsh, November 21, 1925, Bod Res MSS, d58.

3. Lawrence to Charlotte Shaw, November 27, 1928, BM Add MSS, 45904.

4. *Mint*, p. 170.

5. Robert Graves, *Lawrence and the Arabs*, p. 429 (Sergeant Pugh to Graves).

6. *Mint*, p. 206.

7. Ibid., p. 171; Graves, *Lawrence and the Arabs*, p. 434.

8. Graves, *Lawrence and the Arabs*, pp. 428–429.

9. Ibid., p. 428.

10. Ibid., pp. 435–436.

11. Ibid.

12. Ibid., p. 434.

13. *Mint*, pp. 195–196.

14. Lawrence to Charlotte Shaw, September 28, 1925, BM Add MSS, 45903.

15. Ibid.

16. *Letters*, p. 487.

17. Lawrence to Charlotte Shaw, December 26, 1925, BM Add MSS, 45903.

18. Lawrence to Raymond Savage, December 30, 1925, Bod Res MSS, d59.

19. Lawrence to his mother, December 28, 1925, Bod Res MSS, c13.

20. Lawrence to Charlotte Shaw January 15, 1926, BM Add MSS, 45903.

21. Lawrence to Francis Rodd, January 28, 1926, *Letters*, p. 493.

22. Ibid.

23. Lawrence to Charlotte Shaw, February 22, 1926, BM Add MSS, 45903.

24. Lawrence to F. L. Lucas, March 14, 1926, Bod Res MSS, d58; see also *Seven Pillars*, p. 23.

25. Lawrence to Lucas, March 14, 1926, Bod Res MSS, d58.

26. Michael S. Howard, *Jonathan Cape, Publisher*, p. 91.

27. Lawrence to Charlotte Shaw, March 18, and April 6, 1926, BM Add MSS, 45903. This episode, described in detail to Robert Graves by Sergeant Pugh, who observed it at first hand, was typical of the stoically heroic conduct that characterized Lawrence all his life. After Lawrence had taken care of a pedestrian who was injured in the accident he got someone to start his Brough "and with his arm dangling and changing gear with his foot S. [Shaw] got his bus home and parked without a word to a soul of the pain he was suffering" (Graves, *Lawrence and the Arabs*, p. 431). Because the medical officer was away the arm could not be set until the next day. When he reported sick the next morning he told the medical officer

he had an impacted Colles fracture involving both bones of the wrist. At first the doctor did not believe him, but when he saw the X-ray films showing the fractures, he ordered Lawrence into the hospital for an operation. Lawrence refused both the hospitalization and the operation, had the wrist bound up by a doctor off the base and returned to work (Sims document, 1937, pp. 10–11). According to Sergeant Pugh this was the only time he ever saw a man refuse to go into the hospital with a broken arm.

28. *Letters*, p. 518.

29. Howard, p. 90.

30. Lawrence to Edward Garnett, September 22, 1927, *Letters*, p. 542. For a further discussion of these and other textual changes and differences among the various versions and editions of *Seven Pillars of Wisdom*, see the study of Jeffrey Meyers, *The Wounded Spirit: A Study of Seven Pillars of Wisdom*, especially Chap. 3, pp. 45–73.

31. Lawrence to David Garnett, April 6, 1926, *Letters*, p. 494.

32. Howard, p. 90.

33. Lawrence to Charlotte Shaw, June 17, 1926, BM Add MSS, 45903.

34. Lawrence to his mother, July 6, 1926, Bod Res MSS, c13.

35. Will dated August 28, 1926, Bod Res MSS, d230.

36. Lawrence to Mrs. Friedlow, October 14, 1926, Houghton Library, Harvard University.

37. Lawrence to Geoffrey Dawson, March 16, 1927, Bod Res MSS, b55.

38. Lawrence to Francis Rodd, December 3, 1926. Loaned to the author by Rodd.

39. Lawrence to Dick Knowles, December 3, 1926, in a California private collection.

40. Lawrence to Sergeant Pugh, December 16, 1926, Arts Catalogue, Bodleian Library.

41. "Leaves in the Wind," *Letters*, pp. 502–503.

42. Ibid., p. 612.

43. Interviews with Elsie Newcombe, March 18, 1965, and S. L. ("Jimmy") Newcombe, March 20, 1965.

## 29. INDIA

1. Lawrence to Charlotte Shaw, January 28, 1927, BM Add MSS, 45903.

2. *Friends*, pp. 415, 418.

516 Notes for Pages 362–371

3. *Friends*, pp. 401, 402; Lawrence to Trenchard, December 22, 1927, Bod Res MSS, d46.
4. *Friends*, p. 403.
5. Ibid., p. 405.
6. Ibid., p. 409.
7. Ibid., p. 417.
8. *Letters*, p. 505.
9. Lawrence to Fareedah el Akle, January 28, 1927.
10. Lawrence to Charlotte Shaw, August 28, 1928, BM Add MSS, 45904.
11. *Letters*, p. 504.
12. Lawrence to Captain Hollings, January 11, 1927, Bodleian Library, Arts Catalogue.
13. Lawrence to his mother, February 24, 1927, Bod Res MSS, c13.
14. Letter of January 11, 1927, Bod Res MSS, c13.
15. Lawrence to Robin Buxton, March 4, 1927, Jesus College, Oxford.
16. George Bernard Shaw, *The Spectator*, March 12, 1927.
17. Lawrence to Charlotte Shaw, April 14, 1927, BM Add MSS, 45903.
18. Letter to H. H. Banbury, April 20, 1927, *Letters*, p. 514.
19. Lawrence to Trenchard, June 30, 1927, Bod Res MSS, d46.
20. *Letters*, p. 412.
21. George Bernard Shaw to Cockerell, July 14, 1944, in Viola Meynell, ed., *The Best of Friends: Letters to Sydney Cockerell*, p. 123.
22. *Home Letters*, p. 368.
23. Lawrence to Hogarth, June 1, 1927, Bod Res MSS, d55.
24. Michael S. Howard, *Jonathan Cape, Publisher*.
25. Lawrence to Buxton, March 25, 1927, library of Jesus College, Oxford.
26. Lawrence to Alan Dawnay, April 14, 1927, Bod Res MSS, d43.
27. Lawrence to Charlotte Shaw, March 29, 1927, BM Add MSS, 45903.
28. Lawrence to Charlotte Shaw, May 12, 1927, BM Add MSS, 45903.
29. Lawrence to Fareedah el Akle, April 27, 1927.
30. Lawrence to his family, June 16, 1927, Bod Res MSS, c13, omitted from the printed letter, which is in *Home Letters*, pp. 366–367.
31. Ibid.
32. Howard, p. 96.
33. Lawrence to Dick Knowles, June 30, 1927, in a California private collection.
34. RGB, pp. 48–95.

35. Lawrence to Curtis, July 14, 1927, *Letters*, p. 530.
36. Lawrence to Buchan, June 20, 1927, Bod Res MSS, b55.
37. Lawrence to "Dear Hugh" (Trenchard), June 30, 1927, Bod Res MSS, d46.
38. Lawrence to Garnett, July 7, 1927, *Letters*, p. 526.
39. Lawrence to Charlotte Shaw, August 3, 1927, BM Add MSS, 45903.
40. Lawrence to Charlotte Shaw, August 12, 1927, BM Add MSS, 45903.
41. Ibid.
42. Letter of November 11, 1927, BM Add MSS, 45903.
43. Mrs. Hogarth to Lawrence, December 18, 1927, Bod Res MSS, d60.
44. Lawrence to Charlotte Shaw, November 17, 1927, BM Add MSS, 45903; quoted in *Minorities*, p. 19.
45. Lawrence to H. S. Ede, December 1, 1927, *Shaw-Ede: T. E. Lawrence's Letters to H. S. Ede, 1927–1935*, p. 12.
46. Lawrence to Charlotte Shaw, December 21, 1927, BM Add MSS, 45903.
47. Lawrence to Trenchard, December 22, 1927, Bod Res MSS, d46.
48. Lawrence to Edward Garnett, December 25, 1927, Bod Res MSS, d54.
49. Letter of December 24, 1927, RGB, p. 143.
50. *Letters*, p. 561.
51. Forster to Lawrence, December 16, 1927, Bod Res MSS, d60.
52. Lawrence to Charlotte Shaw, December 27, 1927, BM Add MSS, 45903.
53. Letter of August 1, 1927, *Letters*, p. 532.
54. Letter of November 12, 1928, *Shaw-Ede*, pp. 22–23. Wyndham Lewis has suggested that Lawrence's reading of Buddhist or other Eastern philosophies while living in the dusty barrenness of the Drigh Road barracks may have stimulated him to turn once again to his Uxbridge notes, in a further act of self-purging ("Perspectives of Lawrence," *Hudson Review* [Winter, 1956]). This seems far-fetched, though there is no evidence on the point.
55. *Mint*, p. 167.
56. Lawrence to Charlotte Shaw, January 2, 1928, BM Add MSS, 45916. Blanche Patch, secretary for many years to the Shaws, has provided additional details of the unexplained but rather characteristic mystery with which Lawrence surrounded the mailing of the manuscript of *The Mint*: "He posted it

to Charlotte direct, asking her, when G.B.S. and she had read it, to send it on, within ten days, to Edward Garnett, reader to Jonathan Cape the publisher, in a plain wrapper, and with no indication of who was forwarding it to him. By the same post he wrote to Edward Garnett announcing that the manuscript had gone 'by an official by-pass for safety', and asking him to let him know what he had to pay on the parcel 'if the first receiver does not put on stamps', which will indicate Lawrence's views upon the unreliability of womankind. Charlotte did keep the manuscript for a few days longer than his stipulated ten; but she played her part in the conspiratorial affair. She was in North Wales at the time, and the postmark might have given a clue to the sender, so she tied *The Mint* up in a plain parcel, with a second wrapping addressed to me in London, and I posted it on to Edward Garnett (correctly stamped), when I had got back from a holiday I was having" (*Thirty Years with G.B.S.*, p. 80).

57. Lawrence to Charlotte Shaw, March 20, 1928, BM Add MSS, 45903.

58. *Letters,* p. 579.

59. Lawrence to Trenchard, March 17, 1928, Bod Res MSS, d46; personal communication from Arnold Lawrence, March 24, 1974.

60. Letter of April 10, 1928, *Letters to TEL,* pp. 200–201.

61. Letter of April 12, 1928, ibid., pp. 174–175.

62. Letter of April 22, 1928, ibid., p. 97.

63. Letter of May 3, 1928, ibid., p. 99.

64. Lawrence to Trenchard, May 1, 1928, Bod Res MSS, d46.

65. Ibid.; this part of the letter was printed in *Letters,* pp. 598–599.

66. Letter of May 7, 1928, *Letters,* p. 604.

67. Lawrence to Edward Garnett, August 28, 1928, Bod Res MSS, d54.

68. Edward Garnett to Lawrence, May 3, 1928, *Letters to TEL,* p. 99.

69. Personal communication from Arnold Lawrence, March 24, 1974. At that time piracy would have been possible under U.S. copyright law.

70. *Letters to TEL,* p. 67.

71. Ibid., pp. 21–22.

72. R. P. Blackmur, "The Everlasting Effort: A Citation of T. E. Lawrence," in *The Expense of Greatness,* pp. 1–37.

73. *Letters,* pp. 564–565.

74. Florence Hardy to Lawrence, March 5, 1928, Bod Res MSS, d60.

75. From Introduction by Bruce Rogers to *Letters from T. E. Shaw to Bruce Rogers* (unpaged).

76. Lawrence to Isham, February 1, 1928, ibid.

77. Lawrence to Bruce Rogers, April 16, 1928, *Letters,* pp. 586–590.

78. Letter of April 26, 1928, *Home Letters,* p. 374.

79. Lawrence to Francis Yeats-Brown, May 1928, Bod Res MSS, d59.

80. Ibid.

81. Lawrence to Joyce, June 14, 1928, Bod Res MSS, d43; and to H. S. Ede, June 30, 1928, *Letters,* p. 615.

82. Lawrence to Trenchard, September 11, 1928, Bod Res MSS, d46.

83. *Letters,* p. 615.

84. Ibid., p. 625.

85. I. E. Brodie, "Lawrence Was My Orderly," *Naafi Review* (Summer 1963).

86. Ibid.

87. *Letters to TEL,* Trenchard to Lawrence, July 5, 1928, pp. 212–214.

88. Lawrence to Cape, July 10, 1928, Bod Res MSS, d50. Having promised Cape his next book, he offered *The Mint* to him but asked for a £1,000,000 advance in order to make sure that the book would be refused (*Letters,* p. 613).

89. Tomlinson to Lawrence, December 12, 1928, *Letters to TEL,* pp. 189–192.

90. Lawrence to H. S. Ede, August 30, 1928, *Shaw-Ede,* p. 18.

91. Lawrence to Baker, July 17, 1928, and November 6, 1928, Bod Res MSS, c52 and d54.

92. Lawrence to Charlotte Shaw, August 15, 1928, BM Add MSS, 45904.

93. Lawrence to Edward Garnett, August 8, 1928, Bod Res MSS, d54.

94. Lawrence to Alan Dawnay, December 25, 1928, Bod Res MSS, d43.

95. Lawrence to Charlotte Shaw, November 27, 1928, BM Add MSS, 45904.

96. Lawrence to Emery Walker, December 25, 1928, Bod Res MSS, d59.

97. Lawrence to Trenchard, December 27, 1928, Bod Res MSS, d46.

### 30. MOUNT BATTEN

1. *Friends,* p. 351.

2. *Empire News,* London, December 16, 1928; quoted in *Secret Lives,* p. 233.

3. See Clare Sydney Smith, *The Golden Reign,* pp. 20–24.

4. Lawrence to Trenchard, February 5, 1929, Bod Res MSS, d46.

5. Lawrence to F. N. Doubleday, April 1, 1929, Bod Res MSS, d52.

6. Lawrence to H. S. Ede, March 28, 1929, *Shaw-Ede,* p. 30.

7. *Friends,* p. 580.

8. Interview (taped) of Arabella Rivington with Tommy Jordan, former NCO at Mount Batten, March 1965.

9. Lawrence to Bruce Rogers, May 24 and December 12, 1929, *Letters from T. E. Shaw to Bruce Rogers* (unpaged).

10. *Letters,* p. 660.

11. *Letters,* p. 673; RGB, p. 164.

12. RGB, p. 165.

13. *Golden Reign,* p. 71.

14. Lawrence to Charlotte Shaw, late September 1929, BM Add MSS, 45904.

15. Letter of December 15, 1929, BM Add MSS, 45904.

16. Letter of November 23, 1929, BM Add MSS, 45904.

17. Lawrence to Brooks, December 30, 1929, *Letters,* p. 674.

18. Lawrence to Charlotte Shaw, December 5, 1930, BM Add MSS, 45904.

19. Lawrence to H. G. Hayter, January 8, 1930, Humanities Research Center, University of Texas.

20. Lawrence to Charlotte Shaw, January 4, 1930, BM Add MSS, 45904.

21. Letter of February 12, 1930, *Letters . . . to Bruce Rogers.*

22. Letter of August 3, 1930, ibid.

23. Letter of January 25, 1931, ibid.

24. David Garnett, *The Familiar Faces,* p. 104.

25. *Letters,* p. 708.

26. Letter of December 2, 1930, *Letters . . . to Bruce Rogers.*

27. *Letters,* p. 705.

28. *Shaw-Ede,* p. 41.

29. Letter of February 8, 1930, *Shaw-Ede,* p. 42. Ede had been writing a study of the relationship between the French sculptor Henry Gaudier and an unusual Polish woman, Sophie Brzeska.

30. Lawrence to Charlotte Shaw, July 3, 1930, BM Add MSS, 45904.

31. Letter of July 15, 1930, *Shaw-Ede,* p. 43.

32. Smith, *Golden Reign,* pp. 94–95.

33. Lawrence to Charlotte Shaw, February 6, 1930, BM Add MSS, 45904.

34. *Letters,* pp. 682–683; Manning, *Her Privates We;* also L. T. Hergenhan,

ed., "Some Unpublished Letters from T. E. Lawrence to Frederic Manning," 23 *Southerly* (1963): 242–252.

35. Letter of May 15, 1930, *Letters,* pp. 692–693.

36. Lawrence to Manning, August 7, 1930, Hergenhan, p. 246.

37. Letters of July 25, 1934, and January 2, 1932, Hergenhan, pp. 250, 248.

38. Lawrence to Manning, September 1, 1931, ibid., p. 247.

39. Lawrence to Graves, January 24, 1933, *Letters,* p. 760.

40. Janet Adam Smith, *John Buchan,* p. 327.

41. Reginald Sims, "The Sayings and the Doings of T.E. as heard and experienced by the Sims family (1937); the manuscript is in a private collection.

42. Lawrence to Buchan, March 21, 1930, *Letters,* p. 685.

43. Ibid., p. 686.

44. Sims, "The Sayings and the Doings . . ."

45. Ibid.

46. *Letters,* pp. 694–695, also LHB, p. 41.

47. *Letters,* p. 705.

48. Smith, *Golden Reign,* pp. 124–125.

49. *Letters,* p. 707.

50. Smith, *Golden Reign,* pp. 124–125.

51. Ibid., pp. 133–139.

52. Shaw to Lawrence, February 8, 1931, *Letters to TEL,* p. 180.

53. *Letters,* pp. 713–714.

54. Lawrence to Rogers, January 31, 1931, *Letters,* p. 710. Lawrence particularly found unsupportable the idea, accepted by most translators, that expert archers of the time shot through the holes in a row of hollow axes, and wrote a long letter to Rogers arguing the point (Lawrence to Rogers, February 25, 1931, *Letters,* pp. 710–712).

55. Lawrence to Charlotte Shaw, March 26, 1931, BM Add MSS, 45904.

## 31. "BOATS, BOATS, BOATS"

1. He wrote Liddell Hart on April 13, 1931: "My two year war with the Air Ministry over the type of motor boats suited to attend seaplanes is bearing results now, and experimental boats are being offered by contractors. I've become a marine expert, and test the things for

them, acquiring incidentally and by de- grees quite a knowledge of the S.W. coast of England" (*Letters,* p. 718).

2. Letter of June 5, 1934, *More Letters from T. E. Shaw to Bruce Rogers* (unpaged).

3. Lawrence to Curtis, May 11, 1931, All Souls College, Oxford.

4. Clare Sydney Smith, *The Golden Reign,* p. 143.

5. *Friends,* p. 578.

6. The original manuscript of this treatise is in a California private collection.

7. RGB, pp. 168–169.

8. Lawrence to T. W. Beaumont, June 10, 1931. A copy of the letter was loaned to the author by Beaumont.

9. Lawrence to Hanley, August 21, 1931, *Letters,* p. 735.

10. Letter of July 2, 1931, ibid., p. 729.

11. Lawrence to C. F. Greenwood, July 17, 1931, ibid., p. 730.

12. Smith, *Golden Reign,* p. 155.

13. Ibid., p. 157.

14. Bod Res MSS, d59.

15. T. E. Shaw, *The Odyssey of Homer,* translator's note.

16. Ibid.

17. Ibid.

18. Smith, *Golden Reign,* p. 160.

19. Ibid., p. 161.

20. Lawrence to "Poppet" (R. M. Guy), September 30, 1931, Houghton Library, Harvard University.

21. Smith, *Golden Reign,* p. 169.

22. Lawrence to Trenchard, July 12 and 29, 1929, *Letters,* pp. 662–663, 666.

23. Lawrence to Edward Marsh, March 10, 1931, *Letters,* p. 715.

24. Bertram Thomas, *Arabia Felix,* p. xviii.

25. Lawrence to Charlotte Shaw, November 21, 1931, BM Add MSS, 45904.

26. Smith, *Golden Reign,* p. 177.

27. Quoted in Stanley and Roselle Weintraub, *Private Shaw and Public Shaw,* p. 217.

28. Lawrence to Charlotte Shaw, June 26, 1931, quoted in Weintraub, pp. 209–210.

29. Lawrence to Charlotte Shaw, January 9, 1932, BM Add MSS, 45904; quoted in part in Weintraub, p. 215.

30. Weintraub, p. 216.

31. Lawrence to Charlotte Shaw, January 27, 1932, BM Add MSS, 45904; quoted in Weintraub, pp. 218–219.

32. Smith, *Golden Reign,* p. 182.

33. A letter to his old friend Geoffrey Dawson, editor of *The Times,* conveys Lawrence's behind-the-scenes approach to such political matters: "Today it struck me that as editor you might be interested in the new type of motor boat that we have been producing lately for the R.A.F. I'm partly the guilty cause of them — after a big crash a year ago in Plymouth Sound, which showed me convincingly that we had nothing in the Service fit to help marine aircraft in difficulties. Nor could the Navy supply even an idea of the type of craft we needed. The Navy is rather Nelsonic in its motor boats. I suppose it knows something about steam. . . . "So the R.A.F. (partly, as I confessed above, at my prompting) went into the science of it, and have had produced for them, by the Power Boat works at Hythe here, an entirely new type of seaplane tender. They are 37 ft. boats, twin engined, doing 30 m.p.h. in all weathers, handy, safe, and very cheap. Many of their features are unique. They cost less than any boats we have ever bought before.

"All this has been done through the admiralty, in the teeth of its protests and traditions. Now the boats are finished, the sailors are beginning to take notice, and wonder if there isn't something in it" (letter of March 22, 1932, Bod Res MSS, b55).

34. Lawrence to Childs, June 14, 1932, in a California private collection.

35. Lawrence to Ede, September 5, 1932, *Shaw-Ede,* p. 52.

36. Lawrence to Ede, October 18, 1932, ibid., p. 54.

37. Weintraub, *Private Shaw and Public Shaw,* p. 227.

38. Letters of September 26, 1932, *Letters to TEL,* p. 213.

39. Letter of September 5, 1932, *Shaw-Ede,* p. 52.

40. *Letters,* p. 754.

41. Lawrence to G. W. M. Dunn, November 9, 1932, *Letters,* pp. 752–753.

42. C. M. Bowra considered Lawrence's translation to be the best rendering of the *Odyssey* into English up to that time. Preferring prose to verse translations of the work generally, Bowra agreed with Lawrence's view of the *Odyssey* as primarily a story and felt that his work gave the *Odyssey* a new freshness and light (*The New Statesman and Nation,* April 8, 1933). Henry Hazlitt

regarded the translation as among the half dozen most eminent and found the total effect one of great dignity and beauty, "more delightful in itself" than any prose translation he had read. He thought the preface was mannered and affected, "even smart alecky" (*The Nation*, December 12, 1932). Louis Lord, a classical scholar, gave examples in his review of how Lawrence had been too free with the Greek. He thought the translation lacked a consistent tonal quality and also contained awkward English sentences. He felt, however, the gripping power of the translation, especially in the scenes of action (*Classical Journal*, April 1933). A. T. Murray, a classicist and an *Odyssey* translator himself, felt that Lawrence had been "unduly free" in his choice of words (*Classical Philology*, July 1933). Bruce Rogers's printing was admired by those reviewers who chose to comment.

Robert Fitzgerald, who has published a verse translation, wrote me that he had thought Lawrence's translation generally very unlike Homer (March 25, 1974), but as E. E. Kellett pointed out in 1935, every age or even every man, will want his own translation of Homer "as his experience widens and his moods change" (*The Spectator*, August 10, 1935).

43. Lawrence to Harley Granville-Barker, December 23, 1932, Houghton Library, Harvard University.

44. Letter of February 17, 1933, *More Letters to Bruce Rogers*.

45. Lawrence to Maurice Baring, December 5, 1932, Humanities Research Center, University of Texas.

46. Lawrence to Robin Buxton, April 7, 1933, Jesus College, Oxford.

47. Letter of February 9, 1933, in the possession of Francis Rodd; name of addressee withheld.

48. Smith, *Golden Reign*, p. 204.

49. Letter of March 23, 1933, *Letters*, p. 765.

50. Letter of March 30, 1933, *Letters*, p. 765.

51. Lawrence to Thurtle, May 23, 1933, Bod Res MSS, d59.

52. Lawrence to Charlotte Shaw, June 29, 1933, BM Add MSS, 45904.

53. Lawrence to G. Wren Howard, December 17, 1933, *Letters*, p. 783.

54. *Home Letters*, pp. 383–384.

55. Lawrence to Buxton, August 12, 1933, Jesus College, Oxford.

56. Lawrence to A. E. Chambers, October 5, 1933, Bod Res MSS (no box no.).

57. Lawrence to Buxton, August 12, 1933, Jesus College, Oxford.

58. Ibid.

59. *Letters*, p. 780.

60. *British Legion Journal* (November 1933), pp. 160, 161, 169.

61. Lawrence to K. W. Marshall, November 12, 1933, Bod Res MSS, d58.

62. David Garnett, *The Familiar Faces*, p. 106.

63. A copy is in the Bodleian Library (Res MSS, d230). "Something happened to me last night, when I lay awake to 5," he wrote to Mrs. Shaw on December 9. "You know I've been moody or broody for years, wondering what I was at in the RAF, but unable to let go — well, last night I suddenly understood that it was to write a book called 'Confession of Faith,' beginning in the Cloaca of Covent Garden, and embodying *The Mint,* and much that has happened to me before and since as regards the air. Not the conquest of the air, but our entry into the reserved element, 'as lords that are expected, yet with a silent joy in our arrival.' It would include a word on Miranshah and Karachi, and the meaning of speed, on land and water and air. I see the plan of it. It will take a long time to do. Clouds Hill, I think — In this next and last R.A.F. year I can collect feelings for it. The thread of the book will come because it spins through my head; there cannot be any objective continuity — but I think I can make it whole enough to do. *The Mint,* you know, was meant as notes for something (smaller) of the sort. I wonder if it will come off. The purpose of my generation, that's really it" (BM Add MSS, 45904).

64. Letter of February 2, 1934, *Home Letters*, p. 386.

65. Lawrence to S. C. Rolls, December 21, 1933, Bod Res MSS, d44.

66. Lawrence to H. S. Ede, December 31, 1933, *Shaw-Ede*, p. 57.

67. Lawrence to Charlotte Shaw, December 31, 1933, BM Add MSS, 45904.

68. Lawrence to Lady Astor, December 31, 1933, *Letters*, p. 788.

69. February 2, 1934, *Home Letters*, p. 386.

70. Lawrence to Charlotte Shaw, February 2, 1934, BM Add MSS, 45904.

71. *Home Letters*, p. 385.

72. Lawrence to "Poppet" (R. M. Guy),

February 18, 1934, Houghton Library, Harvard University.

73. *Letters*, p. 792.

74. Lawrence to Curtis, March 19, 1934, *Letters*, pp. 792–794.

75. Lawrence to Mrs. Peck, May 4, 1934, Bod Res MSS, d44.

76. Kirstein to Lawrence, December 14, 1933, Bod Res MSS, d60.

77. Lawrence to Kirstein, April 12, 1934, *Letters*, p. 797.

78. Kirstein to Lawrence, April 27, 1934, Bod Res MSS, d60.

79. Lawrence to Kirstein, May 11, 1934, Bod Res MSS, d43.

80. Letter to the author, March 12, 1969.

81. For example, in LHB, May 17, 1934, p. 216.

82. Lawrence to Liddell Hart, June 14, 1934, *Letters*, p. 810.

83. Smith, *Golden Reign*, p. 233.

84. LHB, p. 219.

85. Ibid., p. 222.

86. Lawrence to Kennington, August 6, 1934, *Letters*, pp. 813–814.

87. Lawrence to Liddell Hart, October 19, 1934, LHB, p. 225.

88. Smith, *Golden Reign*, p. 239.

89. *Letters*, pp. 819–824.

90. Lawrence to Liddell Hart, October 19, 1934, LHB, p. 225.

91. Lawrence to T. B. Marson, November 23, 1934, Bod Res MSS, d46.

92. Lawrence to Charlotte Shaw, November 16, 1934, BM Add MSS, 45904.

93. Reginald Sims, "The Sayings and the Doings of T.E. as heard and experienced by the Sims family" (1937); the manuscript is in a private collection.

94. Ibid.

95. *Friends*, p. 547.

96. Sims, "The Sayings and the Doings . . ."

97. Francis Rodd, unpublished notes, probably written in 1954 or 1955, sent to the author with an accompanying letter dated November 17, 1965.

98. Ibid.

99. *Letters*, p. 830.

100. Lawrence to Jimmy Newcombe, December 20, 1934, *Letters*, p. 838.

101. *Letters*, p. 844.

102. Lawrence to Baring, end of 1934, Humanities Research Center, University of Texas.

103. Lawrence to Charlotte Shaw, end of 1934 or early 1935, BM Add MSS, 45904.

104. *Shaw-Ede*, p. 58.

105. Letter of January 18, 1935, in Smith, *Golden Reign*, p. 241.

106. *Letters*, p. 845.

107. Lawrence to Charlotte Shaw, January 26, 1935, BM Add MSS, 45904.

108. Sims, "The Sayings and the Doings . . ."

109. *Letters*, p. 864.

110. Ibid., p. 849.

111. Lawrence to Graves, February 4, 1935, ibid., p. 853.

112. *Friends*, p. 561.

113. Lawrence to Lorna Norrington, February 24, 1935, *Letters*, p. 857.

114. Lawrence to T. W. Beaumont, February 25, 1935; lent to the author by Mr. Beaumont.

115. *Friends*, p. 435.

### 32. RETIREMENT AND DEATH

1. RAF discharge documents (the originals), in a California private collection.

2. Lawrence to Sergeant Robinson, February 26, 1935, in a California private collection.

3. Interview with Arnold Lawrence, July 15, 1968.

4. Lawrence to Rodd, March 6, 1935.

5. Lawrence to Sydney Cockerell, March 6, 1935, in Viola Meynell, ed., *Friends of a Lifetime*, p. 373.

6. Lawrence to Davies, February 28, 1935, *Letters*, p. 859.

7. BBC broadcast, December 3, 1958, notes in a California private collection.

8. Excerpt from a letter to L. H. Ingham, March 6, 1935, Bod Res MSS, b55, and to Alec Dixon, March 6, 1935, in a California private collection.

9. *Letters*, p. 865.

10. Ibid., p. 863.

11. LHB, p. 230.

12. *Friends*, p. 306.

13. Foreword by Liddell Hart in the 2d Edition of *Letters*, p. 29.

14. *Friends*, p. 254.

15. Ibid., p. 595.

16. *Shaw-Ede*, p. 60.

17. Lawrence to "Walter," April 5, 1935, in a California private collection; and to T. B. Marson, April 6, 1935, Bod Res MSS, d46.

18. Lawrence to Flight Lieutenant Norrington, April 20, 1935, *Letters*, p. 868.

19. Lawrence to Lieutenant Robin White, April 13, 1935, Bod Res MSS, d44.

20. *Friends,* pp. 571–572.
21. Lawrence to Lady Nancy Astor, May 5, 1935, Bod Res MSS, d49.
22. Lawrence to the Honorable Stephen Tennant, May 5, 1935, Bod Res MSS, d49.
23. *More Letters to Bruce Rogers* (unpaged).
24. Letter of May 6, 1935, *Letters,* p. 871.
25. Letter of May 8, 1935, ibid., p. 872.
26. Lawrence to Sir Karl Parker, keeper of the Department of Western Art, Ashmolean Museum, May 12, 1935, Bod Res MSS, b55.
27. Interview with Henry Williamson, by a chance meeting on a train from Exeter to London, December 17, 1965.
28. *Secret Lives,* p. 270.
29. The speed was Corporal Catchpole's estimate at the inquest (Bod Res MSS, b56). Knightley and Simpson suggest that 38 mph was the maximum possible speed, as the Brough, they state, was jammed in second gear (*Secret Lives,* p. 274).
30. The Inquest Report, May 21, 1935, Bod Res MSS, b56.
31. LHB, p. 233.
32. Clare Sydney Smith to Charlotte Shaw, May 20, 1935, BM Add MSS, 45922.
33. New York *Times,* May 20, 1935.
34. Service Record, May 22, 1935, Bod Res MSS, d48.
35. Newcombe to Beaumont, undated (lent by Beaumont to the author).
36. See, for example, Colin Graham, "The Crash That Killed Lawrence of Arabia," *Dorset — The Country Magazine* (Summer 1968).
37. *Friends,* p. 595.
38. Churchill, *Great Contemporaries,* p. 167.
39. Smith, *Golden Reign,* p. 144.

33. INTIMACY, SEXUALITY AND PENANCE

1. Letter to the author, November 28, 1969.
2. Edmund Gosse, *Fathers and Sons,* p. 306.
3. I believe Lawrence is using the "me" and "they" to indicate his relationships with men during the campaigns, but that he also means the passage to express his more general feelings and attitudes.
4. *Seven Pillars,* pp. 563–564.
5. Lawrence to Charlotte Shaw, March 26, 1924, BM Add MSS, 45903.
6. Lawrence to Charlotte Shaw, May 8, 1928, and August 18, 1928, BM Add MSS, 45904.
7. There also is no factual support for the view suggested by some that the Der'a beatings rendered Lawrence sexually impotent on a physical basis.
8. Lawrence to Charlotte Shaw, September 28, 1925, BM Add MSS, 45903.
9. *Seven Pillars,* p. 348.
10. *Mint,* p. 109.
11. Lucas to Lawrence, March 9, 1929, Bod Res MSS, d60.
12. Lawrence to Lucas, March 26, 1929, Bod Res MSS, d58.
13. Lawrence to Graves, November 6, 1928, Houghton Library, Harvard University.
14. *Letters,* p. 395.
15. *Mint,* p. 161.
16. Arnold Lawrence to Miss Early, Bod Res MSS, b96.
17. *Letters,* p. 458.
18. Lawrence to B. E. Leeson, April 18, 1929, Bod Res MSS, d58.
19. Lawrence to Charlotte Shaw, June 10, 1924, BM Add MSS, 45903.
20. Lawrence to Cockerell, June 13, 1924, *Letters,* p. 450.
21. Lawrence to Hanley Granville-Barker, December 5, 1924, Houghton Library, Harvard University.
22. *Letters,* p. 728.
23. Ibid., p. 649.
24. Ibid., p. 652.
25. Arnold Lawrence to Miss Early, December 17, 1963, Bod Res MSS, b56.
26. Lawrence to Charlotte Shaw, November 6, 1928, Bod Res MSS, 45904.
27. Interview with A. E. Chambers, March 17, 1965.
28. Bod Res MSS, c52.
29. E. M. Forster, *Abinger Harvest,* p. 136.
30. Letter of March 25, 1930, *Letters,* p. 687.
31. Letter of March 27, 1923, ibid., p. 414.
32. *Friends,* p. 592.
33. Interview with A. W. Lawrence, December 8, 1965.
34. Letter to the author, July 23, 1973.
35. David Garnett, *The Familiar Faces,* p. 110.
36. The passage appears both in the manuscript of *Seven Pillars* in the Bodleian Library and (with minor changes of

wording and punctuation) in the 1922 (Oxford) edition. It was omitted from the subscribers' edition.

37. In the manuscript of his *Essay on Flecker,* Lawrence referred to conversations he had with Flecker before World War I about whipping, and it is possible that Flecker had a problem of this sort.

38. *Journal of the American Medical Association,* Supplement to Vol. 227 (February 18, 1974), p. 834.

39. G. R. Scott, *The History of Corporal Punishment,* p. 125.

40. Quoted in H. Salt, *The Flogging Craze,* p. 88.

41. Scott, p. 196.

42. *Friends,* p. 592. The information that follows is, though detailed, admittedly incomplete. It was obtained with considerable difficulty and with the full cooperation of the Lawrence family, without whose wish to set this aspect of T.E.'s life in an appropriate perspective, this account could not have been provided. Some of the raw facts were presented in the third of the four articles which appeared in the *Sunday Times* in June 1968, and which were written by Colin Simpson and Phillip Knightley, the *Times* "Insight team" (June 9, 16, 23 and 30). A substantially revised and corrected version appears in their book, *The Secret Lives of Lawrence of Arabia.* Most of Knightley and Simpson's account is based on what was told them by John Bruce. I have sought to include as much independent information as possible, and to place Bruce's role in psychological and historical perspective. It is my hope that the reader will look upon this material with empathy and understanding, and be sensitive to the pathetic suffering that Lawrence underwent in serving the demands of a distorted internal sense of psychic justice. Since the discovery of such an unusual aspect of the personal history of a family member cannot help but have a significant impact on other relatives, and because of its highly sensitive personal nature, on the biographer as well, I have approached this dimension of Lawrence's history from a somewhat different direction. Instead of describing the sequence of events solely from the standpoint of Lawrence's history, I have relied more upon the perspectives of its discovery — by the family and subsequent investigation by myself. This approach will, I hope, lead to greater understanding of a part of Lawrence's life that he ashamedly felt the need to keep to himself, and will reveal some of the methodological problems to be met by the biographer engaged in this type of study.

43. From notes written by Arnold Lawrence in 1967 or 1968 and furnished in 1968.

44. From notes, "My Knowledge of Bruce," prepared by Arnold Lawrence in 1970.

45. Ibid.

46. Notes prepared for the author by Arnold Lawrence, received May 8, 1968.

47. Letter of February 8, 1969.

48. John Bruce, "I Knew Lawrence," *The Scottish Field* (August 1938), pp. 20–21.

49. Clach Mackenny, "Gaveloc Gossip," *Helensburgh Advertiser* (February 1963).

50. These efforts on the part of members of the Lawrence family to prevent Bruce's publication of his "story" should not be interpreted as an effort on their part to suppress the truth. Rather, they wished to avoid an account based exclusively on Bruce's material. After publication of the four *Sunday Times* articles and the Knightley and Simpson book, Arnold Lawrence wrote a letter to the newspaper on October 6, 1969. In publishing the letter (on November 22), the *Sunday Times* omitted several portions, among them the following statement: "I had given similar information to Dr. John Mack, of the Harvard Medical School, before Bruce approached the *Sunday Times* (and so frustrated my hope that a psychiatrist would be the first to describe the association with my brother, in whom Dr. Mack had long been interested)."

51. My own involvement with this aspect of Lawrence's history began at a luncheon meeting with my editor in November 1966. He told me that another Little, Brown author, William Sargent, an English psychiatrist and a friend of Robert Graves, had been told at one time by Graves that he was aware of certain facts concerning Lawrence's sexuality which were not generally known. Dr. Sargent put me in touch with Graves, whom I visited in Majorca during the summer of 1967. Graves told me that Lawrence had "become a flagellant" in the ranks after the war, that he had become impotent as a result of the Der'a experience

(not literally true). Not wanting to write Arnold Lawrence "out of the blue" about this matter, I asked Captain Liddell Hart for further information about the flagellation as Graves had indicated that Liddell Hart had also known about it. (Eric Kennington and his wife learned after T.E.'s death of Arnold Lawrence's conclusions regarding his brother's regimen of penance and purification, but letters they wrote to Graves at the time reflect some misunderstanding of its significance [California private collection].) Liddell Hart, however — he must have known that Arnold Lawrence would not take offense — referred my letter to him. Lawrence replied cordially, acknowledged that there was "a basis of fact" regarding the flagellation disorder. He wrote further: "To write a statement not liable to be misunderstood would take more time than I can spare at present, whereas you would quickly get everything aright in conversation" (Arnold Lawrence to the author, August 10, 1967). It is worth pointing out that this offer to discuss the matter occurred ten months before the *Sunday Times* made Bruce's story public and some months before Arnold Lawrence had knowledge that Bruce had been successful in selling his story to a newspaper.

52. Arnold Lawrence to the author, March 21, 1968.

53. *Sunday Times*, June 23, 1968.

54. Interview with John Bruce, July 22, 1968.

55. Letter of Colonel Toby Farnell Watson to Liddell Hart, April 1, 1969. Although the document which came to the Lawrence solicitors in 1967 and which was sold to the *Sunday Times* early in 1968 contains elaborate descriptions of meetings between Bruce and Lawrence in 1922 around the time of Lawrence's enlistment in the RAF, this part of Bruce's account, much of which has been relayed in the *Sunday Times* article of June 23, 1968, and more cautiously in the Knightley and Simpson book published in the following year, has not been substantiated. Other documentation provided by Bruce indicated that the relationship actually began when he met Lawrence in the Tank Corps in 1923. In the 1937 letter to Storrs, Bruce wrote that he was Lawrence's friend for the last twelve years of Lawrence's life, that is, from 1923. The *Helensburgh Adver-*

*tiser* article of 1963 states that Bruce and Lawrence met in 1923, and Bruce also told me in our meeting that he had known Lawrence for twelve years.

56. Arnold Lawrence to the author, January 1970.

57. In addition to Bruce I have been able to establish only a few others who were involved in the beatings in any way — one witness and one or two other men who administered floggings on rare occasions when Bruce was not available.

58. A letter from Lawrence to F. N. Doubleday, written September 18, 1930, contains a long, highly detailed, poetically written account of a trip on leave to a bleak cottage on the north coast of Scotland, where he was joined by John Bruce and one of Bruce's relatives. This was one of the instances in which Lawrence, according to Bruce, had himself beaten (interview with Phillip Knightley, July 23, 1968). There is nothing in Lawrence's description of the stark coastline, the fishing and swimming late in September in the North Sea (!), the sad, cold "disembodied voices" of the gulls, or the matter-of-fact comments on books to suggest that he was involved in any unusual, conflictual or disturbing activity. In fact, another thoughtful letter written later to Doubleday again gives the impression that this trip was, for Lawrence, nothing but a health visit to a spa. "You have liked my letter from Scotland," he wrote, "but that was for what lay behind the words: my care for you and thinking about you as I was there on happy holiday. The health I have is rather a selfish and wonderful thing. It does not feel quite right to keep it all to myself. I would have liked to transfuse you a few quarts of it, out of fairness" (Lawrence to Doubleday, January 27, 1931, Bod Res MSS, d52). This is surely another instance of Lawrence's unusual ability to compartmentalize various aspects of his life, to separate them from one another, when he thought it necessary.

59. Arnold Lawrence is of the opinion that had T.E. been allowed to remain in the RAF in 1923, he probably would not have succumbed to the residuum of the Der'a experience (letter to the author, July 8, 1974).

60. Lawrence to Curtis, March 19, 1923, *Letters*, p. 411.

61. Lawrence to Curtis, March 27, 1923, ibid., p. 413.

62. Lawrence to Curtis, May 14, 1923, ibid., p. 416.

63. Arnold Lawrence to the author, June 4, 1968.

64. Arnold Lawrence to the author, July 23, 1973.

65. Bruce's document sent to the *Sunday Times* in 1968.

66. Draft of a letter to a riding and hunting establishment, July or August 1933.

67. *Seven Pillars*, p. 445.

68. On this point Arnold Lawrence wrote me (on July 23, 1973): "From my slight experience of psychological warfare (of which T.E. had plenty) an elaborate fiction is more plausible the nearer it comes to fact, although the fact is unknowable to the audience; hence he gives his lies a garbled foundation of fact about inheritance and estate and a true foundation about illegitimacy. He cannot possibly have felt any grievance about inheritance because the money had actually come to his father, and why should he regret Bob's exclusion from the landed estate (but he did once remark how funny it would be if Bob had been able to become Sir Montague)."

69. Observation by Arnold Lawrence, July 23, 1973.

70. *Friends*, p. 592.

71. Arnold Lawrence to the author, July 23, 1973.

### 34. LAWRENCE ASSAYED

1. Arnold Lawrence on the Jack Paar television show, January 24, 1964.

2. Personal observation to the author, August 29, 1972.

3. *Seven Pillars*, p. 157.

4. Lawrence to Dick Knowles, July 14, 1927, Bod Res MSS, d56.

5. Lawrence to Charlotte Shaw, April 17, 1925, BM Add MSS, 45903.

6. Lawrence to Allanson, June 18, 1927, in a California private collection.

7. *Letters*, p. 494.

8. Actually Lawrence's father took the name Lawrence before T.E. was born and the child was registered at birth as Thomas Edward Lawrence.

9. Lawrence to Granville-Barker, May 9, 1924, Houghton Library, Harvard University.

10. *Friends*, p. 332.

11. Lawrence to Charlotte Shaw, July 19, 1934, BM Add MSS, 45904.

12. She wrote: "Then T.E. came up to see me: he sat on a hard stool leaning forward and gripping it with his hands; he fixed his eyes on me and began, 'Of course you must be feeling very miserable, you feel you have failed in your job, and it's about the most important job in the world; . . . you must be feeling you are utterly no good and nothing can ever be worth while . . .' On and on he went, describing me to myself, clarifying all the nightmare fears by defining them, and doing it all from the woman's point of view, not the man's. He seemed to know everything that miscarriage could mean [his mother had lost three infants at birth or in utero], even down to the shame of being laughed at for it, and as he talked warmth began to come into me, instead of flooding out of me, for besides putting things as they were, he brought a power to remake them all afresh" (*Friends*, pp. 311–312).

13. RGB, p. 186.

14. *Letters*, p. 618.

15. Lawrence to Charlotte Shaw, March 18, 1927, BM Add MSS, 45903.

16. Lady Pansy Lamb to the author, December 19, 1964.

17. Lawrence to Joyce, March 19, 1929, Bod Res MSS, b55.

18. *Letters*, p. 744.

19. Lawrence to Edward Garnett, August 10, 1933, ibid., p. 775.

20. Lawrence to Lady Astor, February 15, 1934, ibid., p. 790.

21. Lawrence to Graves, August 27, 1928, RGB, p. 153.

22. *Letters*, p. 510.

23. *Friends*, p. 261.

24. LHB, p. 210.

25. He could also forgive wrongs of various sorts, even those committed against himself, if the injured party were strong enough not to suffer unduly. Bertram Rota, the London bookseller, told me of an incident involving himself. A young man brought to him two documents written by and belonging to Lawrence, the preface to Doughty's *Arabia Deserta* and a shorter preface to *Revolt in the Desert*. Rota sold these to a wealthy collector. Soon thereafter the publisher, Jonathan Cape, "descended" on Rota with the information that the documents had been stolen from Cape by a disaffected young employee of the publishing firm who had gotten into financial difficulty. It would have been difficult for

Rota to recover the documents and an impasse arose. Lawrence provided the solution by suggesting to Cape that Rota merely give over the profit he had made in the transaction to the RAF Benevolent Fund and he would consider the matter closed (interview in March 1965).

26. Florence Hardy to Graves, June 13, 1927, Bod Res MSS, c52.

27. *Letters*, p. 537.

28. Lawrence to Sergeant Pugh, June 30, 1927, Arts Catalogue, Bodleian Library.

29. Lawrence to Elsie Falcon, November 28 (no year given), in a California private collection.

30. *Letters*, pp. 606, 813.

31. Lawrence to Charlotte Shaw, May 22, 1929, BM Add MSS, 45904.

32. Lawrence to Ernest Altounyan, December 28, 1933, Bod Res MSS, d49.

33. RGB, p. 138.

34. *Letters*, p. 691.

35. *Friends*, p. 559.

36. Interview with William Hogarth, March 18, 1965.

37. *Friends*, p. 537.

38. LHB, p. 208.

39. Interview on March 20, 1965.

40. *Letters*, p. 607.

41. Letter of April 1, 1929, ibid., p. 649.

42. Robert Graves, *Lawrence and the Arabs*, p. 429.

43. *Friends*, p. 565.

44. A. H. R. Reiffer, letter of April 1970, Imperial War Museum, London.

45. RGB, p. 121. The quote is actually Lawrence's editing of a passage of Graves's, made to seem like a quotation from a letter by him to Graves.

46. LHB, p. 160.

47. Lawrence to Edward Garnett, April 24, 1923, *Letters*, p. 410.

48. *Mint*, pp. 199–202.

49. Lawrence to Charlotte Shaw, August 24, 1926, BM Add MSS, 45903.

50. *Letters*, p. 501.

51. *Mint*, p. 202.

52. Lawrence to Curtis, May 14, 1923, *Letters*, pp. 416–417.

53. A. E. Chambers, BBC broadcast, December 3, 1958.

54. Lawrence to Charlotte Shaw, June 6, 1924, BM Add MSS, 45903.

55. Edward Mack, unpublished notes on Lawrence as a literary critic, March 29, 1965.

56. *Friends*, p. 465.

57. Lawrence to C. Day Lewis, December 20, 1934, *Letters*, p. 839.

58. Lawrence to Charlotte Shaw, October 15, 1924, BM Add MSS, 45903.

59. Letter of May 12, 1927, BM Add MSS, 45903.

60. *Friends*, p. 449.

61. Ibid., p. 307.

62. Lawrence to A. Dawnay, April 14, 1927, Bod Res MSS, d43.

63. Lawrence to Charlotte Shaw, March 26, 1931, BM Add MSS, 45904.

64. The following is a typical excerpt from Muggeridge: "What could be more extraordinary than the survival of his cult, which flourishes the more as his lies and attitudinizing are made manifest? . . . He is superlatively a case of everything being true except the facts. Who more fitting to be a Hero of Our Time than this, our English Genêt, our Sodomite Saint, with Lowell Thomas for his Sartre and Alec Guinness to say Amen?" (review of Ronald Blythe's *The Age of Illusion* in *New York Times Book Review*, Sunday May 10, 1964).

65. Lucas to Lawrence, January 2, 1928, Bod Res MSS, d60.

66. Interview of October 29, 1964.

67. John Buchan, *Memory Hold-the-Door*, p. 229.

# BIBLIOGRAPHY

## Unpublished Sources

British Museum. Department of Western Manuscripts. Among the "Additional Manuscripts" are Lawrence's correspondence with Charlotte Shaw (Mrs. George Bernard Shaw) and his war diaries, all of which she bequeathed to the museum. (Only a few of her letters to Lawrence are in the collection: he destroyed many of them at her request.) The materials from the Additional Manuscripts are referred to in the notes as BM Add MSS.

Durham University. Library of the School of Oriental Studies. The Wingate Papers contain documentary material concerning the war in the Middle East, 1916–1918.

Harvard University. Houghton Library. A large collection of Lawrence material: letters; manuscripts and books, including one of the copies of the 1922 (Oxford) edition of *Seven Pillars of Wisdom*; Lawrence's own copy of *The Arab Bulletin* with his handwritten annotations; and a copy of his *Letter to His Mother* (privately printed by Lord Carlow at the Corvinus Press), which contains handwritten comments by George Bernard Shaw; and a copy of *An Essay on Flecker*.

Imperial War Museum, London. In the library are the research materials obtained by staff members of the *Sunday Times* and used by Phillip Knightley and Colin Simpson in preparing their book, *The Secret Lives of Lawrence of Arabia*. There is also a small collection of documentary material related to Lawrence's activities during and after the war.

King's College, London. The library contains the "Akaba" Papers of Colonel Pierce Joyce, an important source on the Arab Revolt.

New York Public Library. Arents Collection. Mrs. George Bernard (Charlotte) Shaw's copy of the subscribers' (1926) edition of *Seven Pillars of Wisdom* with a four-page handwritten essay by G.B.S. on the front flyleaves.

Oxford University. Library of All Souls College. Letters of Lawrence to Lionel Curtis.

———. Library of the Ashmolean Museum. A few of Lawrence's letters from the Carchemish period.

———. Bodleian Library. Among the Reserve Manuscripts is a very large collection of Lawrence's private papers, including thousands of his letters, mostly in typescript copies, and various other documents and photographs. The material has been embargoed until the year 2000 and may be seen only with the permission of Lawrence's executors. The manuscript of *Seven Pillars of Wisdom*, given to the library in 1923, and a small collection of original letters are held separately by the library and may be seen by qualified scholars without special permission. Materials in the Reserve Manuscripts are referred to in the notes as Bod Res MSS.

————. Library of Jesus College. Letters of Lawrence to Robin Buxton.

————. St. Antony's College. Middle East Centre. The Private Papers Collection contains some of Hogarth's letters, the Allenby Papers, and other manuscript material.

Public Record Office, London. Documents from Foreign Office papers and cabinet papers. Referred to in the notes as PRO/FO and PRO/CAB respectively.

University of Texas, Austin. Humanities Research Center. The Lawrence Collection is large and contains hundreds of Lawrence's letters and other original manuscript materials relating to him.


PUBLISHED SOURCES


*Lawrence's Principal Writings*

*Arab Bulletin, The.* Papers of the Arab Bureau, 1916–1918, of which Lawrence was one of the authors. Eighteen copies were printed and bound after the war. Lawrence's own copy, with his annotations, is in Houghton Library, Harvard University. His contributions to the *Bulletin* were published separately by Arnold Lawrence under the title *Secret Dispatches from Arabia* (see below).

*Crusader Castles.* 2 vols. London: Golden Cockerell Press, 1936. Lawrence's thesis for his Oxford degree, which Arnold Lawrence had published after his death.

*Essay on Flecker, An* (1925). New York: Doubleday, Doran, 1937. A copy is in the Houghton Library, Harvard University.

*Evolution of a Revolt: Early Postwar Writings of T. E. Lawrence.* Edited by Stanley and Roselle Weintraub. University Park: Pennsylvania State University Press, 1968.

*Home Letters of T. E. Lawrence and His Brothers, The.* Edited by M. Robert Lawrence. Oxford: Blackwell, 1954.

*Letters of T. E. Lawrence, The.* Edited by David Garnett. London: Cape, 1938. Referred to in the notes as *Letters.*

*Minorities.* Edited by Jeremy M. Wilson. London: Cape, 1971. The first publication of Lawrence's anthology of favorite poems in a "minor key." It includes a valuable introductory biographical essay by the editor.

*Mint, The.* London: Cape, 1973. Lawrence's description of life in the barracks of the RAF. He finished the manuscript in 1928 and made revisions later, but except for a few copies privately printed shortly after his death, the work remained unpublished until 1955. Two versions appeared: an expurgated edition (names were changed) for the general public; and an unexpurgated text in a limited edition. Not until 1973 was a corrected, unexpurgated edition published without limitation. Referred to in the notes as *Mint.*

*Oriental Assembly.* Edited by Arnold W. Lawrence. London: Williams and Norgate, 1939. An important collection of Lawrence's essays and other writings.

*Revolt in the Desert.* New York: Doran, 1927. An abridgment of *Seven Pillars of Wisdom* which Lawrence made in 1926.

*Secret Dispatches from Arabia.* Edited by Arnold W. Lawrence. London: Golden Cockerell Press, 1939. Lawrence's contributions to *The Arab Bulletin.* Referred to in the notes as *Secret Dispatches.*

*Seven Pillars of Wisdom: A Triumph.* New York: Doubleday, 1935. Lawrence's account of the Arab Revolt was first printed in 1922 by the Oxford *Times.* Eight copies were made, of which five, or possibly six, remain. One of them is in Houghton Library, Harvard University, and is the one from which Edward Garnett made his abridgment (never published). The manuscript of this "Oxford edition" is in the Bodleian Library at Oxford University. The 1926 "subscribers'" or "Cranwell" edition was the result of Lawrence's extensive revision and abridgment of the Oxford edition from 1923 to 1926. Over two hundred copies were elaborately printed by Lawrence, of which he sold 128 for thirty guineas each to the subscribers. The remainder — he was secretive about how many there were — were given away to friends and to those he knew could not afford the price of a copy. The copy belonging to George Bernard Shaw's wife, Charlotte, is in the Arents Collection of the New York Public Library and contains a four-page handwritten essay by G.B.S. on the front flyleaves. No edition of *Seven Pillars of Wisdom* was issued for the general public until after Lawrence's death in 1935. The trade editions published by Cape in England and Doubleday, Doran in the United States in 1935 and reprinted thereafter are identical with the subscribers' edition. *Revolt in the Desert,* first published in 1927 by Cape in England and by George Doran in the United States, is a popular abridgment of *Seven Pillars* — about half its length — which Lawrence made in 1926 in order to pay off the debts he had incurred in publishing the subscribers' edition. *Seven Pillars of Wisdom* is referred to in the notes as *Seven Pillars.*

As T. E. SHAW

*Letters from T. E. Shaw to Bruce Rogers.* Privately printed by Bruce Rogers at the Printing House of William Edwin Rudge, 1933.
*More Letters from T. E. Shaw to Bruce Rogers.* Privately printed by Bruce Rogers at the Printing House of William Edwin Rudge, 1936.
*Odyssey of Homer, The* (translation). New York: Oxford University Press, 1932. Lawrence completed the translation in 1931.
*Shaw-Ede: T. E. Lawrence's Letters to H. S. Ede, 1927–1935.* London: Golden Cockerell Press, 1942.

Lawrence was a co-author of the reports on the archeological work at Carchemish, Anatolia, undertaken before World War I, and on the survey of the eastern Sinai Peninsula that he and others made in 1914:

Woolley, C. Leonard; Lawrence, T. E.; Hogarth, D. G.; and Guy, P. L. O. *Carchemish: Report on the Excavations at Djerabis.* 3 vols. London: British Museum, 1914, 1921, 1952.
Woolley, C. Leonard, and Lawrence, T. E. *The Wilderness of Zin.* London: Palestine Exploration Fund Annual, 1915.

## Other Sources

Adams, Henry. *Mont-Saint-Michel and Chartres* (1904). Boston: Houghton Mifflin, 1927.
Aldington, Richard. *Lawrence of Arabia: A Biographical Enquiry.* London: Collins, 1955.
Antonius, George. *The Arab Awakening.* London: Hamish Hamilton, 1938.
Arendt, Hannah. "The Imperialistic Character." *The Review of Politics* 12 (July 1950): 303–320.
Arthur, G. C. *General Sir John Maxwell.* London: Murray,, 1932.
Baker, J. N. L. *Jesus College, Oxford, 1571–1971.* Oxford: Oxonian Press, 1971.
Balsdon, Dacre. *Oxford Life.* London: Eyre & Spottiswoode, 1957.
Barrow, George. *The Fire of Life.* London: Hutchinson, 1943.
Bell, Gertrude. *The Desert and the Sown.* London: Heinemann, 1907.
Bell, Lady Francis. *The Letters of Gertrude Bell.* 2 vols. New York: Boni and Liveright, 1927.
Benson, G. M. P., and Glover, Edward. *Corporal Punishment: An Indictment.* London: Howard League for Penal Reform, 1931.
Berlin, Isaiah. *Historical Inevitability.* London: Oxford University Press, 1954.
Bertram, Anthony. *Paul Nash: The Portrait of an Artist.* London: Faber and Faber, 1955.
Birdwood, Lord. *Nuri as-Said: A Study in Arab Leadership.* London: Cassell, 1959.
Blackmur, Richard P. "The Everlasting Effort: A Citation of T. E. Lawrence." In *The Expense of Greatness.* New York: Arrow Editions, 1940.
Blumenfeld, R. D. *All in a Lifetime.* London: Ernest Benn, 1931.
———. *R.D.B.'s Procession.* London: Ivor Nicholson, 1935.
Boase, T. S. R. *Castles and Churches of the Crusading Kingdom.* London: Oxford University Press, 1967.
Bowra, C. M. "Two Translations." *The New Statesman and Nation,* April 8, 1933, p. 449.

Boyle, Andrew. *Trenchard*. London: Collins, 1962.
Breasted, James H. "David George Hogarth." *Geographical Review*, 18 (1928): 321–344.
Brémond, Edouard. *Le Hedjaz dans la guerre mondiale*. Paris: Payot, 1931.
Brodie, I. E. "Lawrence Was My Orderly." *Naafi Review* (Summer 1963), pp. 6–7.
Broderick, A. H. *Near to Greatness: A Life of Lord Winterton*. London: Hutchinson, 1965.
Brooke, Rupert. *The Collected Poems of Rupert Brooke*. London: Sidgwick and Jackson, 1918.
Buchan, John. *Pilgrim's Way*. Boston: Houghton Mifflin, 1940. (American ed. of *Memory Hold-the-Door*)
Burgoyne, Elizabeth. *Gertrude Bell*. 2 vols. London: Ernest Benn, 1961.
Burton, Percy (as told to Lowell Thomas). *Adventures Among Immortals*. London: Hutchinson, 1938.
Churchill, Winston. *Great Contemporaries*. London: Butterworth, 1937.
Clayton, Sir Gilbert. *An Arabian Diary*. Berkeley and Los Angeles: University of California Press, 1969.
Courtney, Janet E. *An Oxford Portrait Gallery*. London: Chapman and Hall, 1931.
Crump, C. G., and Jacob, E. F., eds. *The Legacy of the Middle Ages*. Oxford: Clarendon Press, 1926.
Dawn, C. E. "The Amir of Mecca Al-Husayn Ibn- 'Ali and the Origin of the Arab Revolt." *Proceedings of the American Philosophical Society* 104 (1960): 11–34.
————. *From Ottomanism to Arabism: Essays on the Origins of Arab Nationalism*. Urbana: University of Illinois Press, 1973.
Denomy, Alexander. *The Heresy of Courtly Love*. New York: Declan X. McMullen, 1947.
Deutsch, Helene. "Some Clinical Considerations of the Ego Ideal." *Journal of the American Psychoanalytic Association* 12 (1964): 512–516.
Dixon, Alec. *Tinned Soldier: A Personal Record, 1919–1926*. London: Jonathan Cape, 1941.
Djemal Pasha. *Memories of a Turkish Statesman — 1913–1919*. New York: Doran, 1922.
Doran, George. *Chronicles of Barabbas*. New York: Harcourt, Brace, 1935.
Doubleday, F. N. "The Strange Character of Colonel T. E. Lawrence," in *A Few Indiscreet Recollections*, pp. 77–78. Privately printed, December 1928. One of the edition of 57 copies is in Houghton Library, Harvard University.
Doughty, Charles M. *Travels in Arabia Deserta* (1888), with an Introduction by T. E. Lawrence. London: Medici Society and Cape, 1921.
Dunbar, J. *Mrs. G.B.S.: A Portrait*. New York: Harper and Row, 1963.
Edwards, J. G. "T. E. Lawrence." *Jesus College Magazine* 4 (1935): 343–345.
Erikson, Erik. *Gandhi's Truth: On the Origins of Militant Nonviolence*. New York: Norton, 1969.
Erskine, Mrs. Stuart. *King Faisal of Iraq*. London: Hutchinson, 1933.
Esco Foundation for Palestine. *Palestine: A Study of Jewish, Arab and British Policies*. 2 vols. New Haven: Yale University Press, 1947.
Evans, Laurence. *United States Policy and the Partition of Turkey, 1914–1924*. Baltimore: Johns Hopkins Press, 1965.
Falls, Cyril, and Becke, A. F., eds. *Military Operations in Egypt and Palestine*, Vol. II. *History of the Great War*, London: His Majesty's Stationery Office, 1930.
Farago, Ladislas. "No Nazi Revolt in the Desert." *Asia* 40 (April 1940): 175–178.
Fatih, Zuhdi, al-. *Lurins al- 'Arab: 'ala Khuta Hartzal: Taqarir Lurins al-Sirriya* [Lawrence of Arabia in the steps of Herzl: Lawrence's Secret Reports]. Beirut: Dar al-Nafa'is, 1971.
Fedden, Robin. *Crusader Castles*. London: Art and Technics, 1950.
Findlay, Charles. "The Amazing AC 2." *The Listener*, June 5, 1958, pp. 937–938.
Fletcher, C. R. L. "David George Hogarth." *The Geographical Journal* 71 (1928): 321–344.
Forster, E. M. *Abinger Harvest*. London: Edward Arnold, 1936.
Fowle, L. R. "Prologue." *Asia* 20 (April 1920): 257–258.

Frankfurter, Felix. Correspondence in "The Contributor's Column." *Atlantic Monthly* 146 (October 1930): 49, 50, 52, and 54.

Freud, Sigmund. "Psychopathic Characters on the Stage" (1905 or 1906). In Vol. VII of *Standard Edition of the Complete Psychological Works of Sigmund Freud*, pp. 305–310. London: Hogarth, 1952.

Gardner, Brian. *Allenby of Arabia*. New York: Coward-McCann, 1966.

Glubb, J. B. *Britain and the Arabs*. London: Hodder and Stoughton, 1959.

Graham, Colin. "The Crash That Killed Lawrence of Arabia." *Dorset: The Country Magazine* (Summer 1968).

Graves, Philip. *The Life of Sir Percy Cox*. London: Hutchinson, 1941.

————, ed. *Memoirs of King Abdullah of Transjordan*. London: Cape, 1950.

Graves, Robert. *Goodbye to All That*. 1929. Garden City, N.Y.: Doubleday Anchor Books, 1957.

————. *Lawrence and the Arabs*. London: Cape, 1927. (American edition: *Lawrence and the Arabian Adventure*. New York: Doubleday, Doran, 1928.) The material for the book that Graves obtained from Lawrence in interviews and correspondence, and Lawrence's notes on the manuscript, are in *T. E. Lawrence to His Biographer Robert Graves* below.

————. *T. E. Lawrence to His Biographer Robert Graves*. 1938. Reprinted: Garden City, N.Y.: Doubleday, 1963. This work and its counterpart by Basil Liddell Hart were published originally by Faber and Faber as companion volumes. They contain the source materials that Graves and Liddell Hart obtained from their interviews and correspondence with Lawrence as well as Lawrence's notes on their manuscripts. Only five hundred or perhaps a thousand copies of each volume were printed. In 1963 Doubleday reprinted them in a single volume. The Graves work is referred to in the notes as RGB.

Güterbock, H. G. "Carchemish." *Journal of Near Eastern Studies* 13 (1954): 102–114.

Hankey, Lord. *The Supreme Command, 1914–1918*. 2 vols. London: Allen and Unwin, 1961.

Hawkins, J. D. "Building Inscriptions of Carchemish." *Anatolian Studies* 22 (1972): 87–114.

Hazlitt, Henry. "On Translating Homer." *The Nation* 135 (December 21, 1932): 620–621.

Herbert, Aubrey. *Mons, Kut and Anzac*. London: Edward Arnold, 1919.

Herodotus. *The Histories*. Book Six. Baltimore: Penguin, 1961.

Hewlett, Maurice. *Richard Yea-and-Nay*. London: Macmillan, 1900.

Hoare, Samuel. *Empire of the Air*. London: Collins, 1957.

Hogarth, David G. *The Life of Charles Doughty*. New York: Doubleday, Doran, 1929.

————. "Mecca's Revolt Against the Turk." *Century Magazine* 100 (1920): 403–409.

————. *The Penetration of Arabia*. New York: Frederick A. Stokes, 1904.

House, E. M., and Seymour, C. S. *What Really Happened at Paris*. New York: Scribner's, 1921.

Howard, Harry N. *The King-Crane Commission*. Beirut: Khayats, 1963.

————. *The Partition of Turkey: A Diplomatic History*. Norman: University of Oklahoma Press, 1931.

Howard, Michael S. *Jonathan Cape, Publisher*. London: Cape, 1971.

————. "The Reluctant Money-Spinner." *The Times Saturday Review*, January 9, 1971.

Howe, Irving. *A World More Attractive*. New York: Horizon, 1963.

Ireland, Philip W. *Iraq: A Study in Political Development*. London: Cape, 1937.

Jarvis, C. S. *Arab Command: The Biography of Lieutenant-Colonel F. G. Peake Pasha*. London: Hutchinson, 1942.

————. *Three Deserts*. London: Murray, 1936.

Jawdat, Ali. *Dhikrayat* [Memoirs], *1900–1958*. Beirut: al-Wafa, 1967.

Jaza'iri, Amir Saʻid ʻAbd al-Qadir, al-. *Jihad Nusf Qarn* [Struggle of Half a Century]. Edited by Anwar al-Rifai. Damascus, n.d.

Jemal Pasha. *See* Djemal Pasha

*Jewish National Home in Palestine, The*. New York: KTAV, 1970.

John, Augustus, *Chiaroscuro: Fragments of an Autobiography*. London: Cape, 1952.

Kedourie, Elie. "The Capture of Damascus, October, 1918." *Middle Eastern Studies* (1964–1965), pp. 66–83.

———. *England and the Middle East.* London: Bowes and Bowes, 1956.

Kellett, E. E. "The Man of Many Devils." *The Spectator* 155 (August 16, 1935): 264.

Kennet, Kathleen, Lady Kennet. *See* Scott, Kathleen

Kimche, Jon. *The Second Arab Awakening.* New York: Holt, Rinehart and Winston, 1970.

Kirk, George. *A Short History of the Middle East.* New York: Praeger, 1964.

Kirkbride, Alec. *An Awakening.* London: University Press of Arabia, 1971.

———. *A Crackle of Thorns.* London: Murray, 1956.

Klieman, Aaron. *Foundations of British Policy in the Arab World: The Cairo Conference of 1921.* Baltimore: Johns Hopkins Press, 1970.

Knightley, Phillip, and Simpson, Colin. *The Secret Lives of Lawrence of Arabia.* London: Nelson, 1969. Referred to in the notes as *Secret Lives.*

Lawrence, Arnold W. "The Fiction and the Fact." *The Observer,* December 16, 1962.

———, ed. *Letters to T. E. Lawrence.* London: Cape, 1962. A valuable companion volume to *Letters of T. E. Lawrence,* edited by David Garnett. Referred to in the notes as *Letters to TEL.*

———, ed. *T. E. Lawrence by His Friends.* London: Cape, 1937. Essays by Lawrence's friends, family and associates that concern each period of his life. The book was prepared soon after his death and is an invaluable biographical source. Referred to in the notes as *Friends.*

Lay, F. C. "Dr. Montague Robert Lawrence." *Jesus College Record* (1971), pp. 23–28.

Lévi-Provençal, E. *Islam d'Occident: Etudes d'histoire médiévale.* Islam d'hier et d'aujourd'hui, Vol. VII. Paris: Maisonneuve, 1948.

Lewis, C. S. *The Allegory of Love.* London: Oxford University Press, 1972.

Liddell Hart, Basil H. *'T. E. Lawrence': In Arabia and After.* London: Cape, 1934. (American edition: *Colonel Lawrence: The Man Behind the Legend.* New York: Dodd, Mead, 1934.) The material for the book that Liddell Hart obtained from Lawrence in interviews and correspondence, and Lawrence's notes on the manuscript, are in *T. E. Lawrence to His Biographer Liddell Hart* below.

———. *T. E. Lawrence to His Biographer Liddell Hart.* 1938. Reprinted: Garden City, N.Y.: Doubleday, 1963. This work and its counterpart by Robert Graves were published originally by Faber and Faber as companion volumes. They contain the source materials that Graves and Liddell Hart obtained from their interviews and correspondence with Lawrence as well as Lawrence's notes on their manuscripts. Only five hundred or perhaps a thousand copies of each volume were printed. In 1963 Doubleday reprinted them in a single volume. The Liddell Hart work is referred to in the notes as *LHB.*

Lloyd George, David. *Memoirs of the Peace Conference.* 2 vols. New Haven: Yale University Press, 1939.

Lord, L. E. "T. E. Shaw, The Odyssey of Homer" (review of Lawrence's translation). *Classical Journal* 28 (April 1933): 533–536.

Lunt, J. D. "An Unsolicited Tribute." *Blackwood's Magazine* 277 (1955): 289–296.

Mack, John E. "Psychoanalysis and Historical Biography." *Journal of the American Psychoanalytic Association* 19 (January 1971): 143–179.

MacMunn, George, and Falls, Cyril, eds. *Military Operations in Egypt and Palestine,* Vol. I. *History of the Great War.* London: His Majesty's Stationery Office, 1928.

Mallowan, M. E. L. "Carchemish: Reflections on the Chronology of the Sculpture." *Anatolian Studies* 22 (1972): 63–85.

Massey, W. T. *Allenby's Final Triumph.* London: Constable, 1920.

Meinhertzhagen, Richard. *Middle East Diary: 1917–1956.* London: Cresset Press, 1959.

Meyers, Jeffrey. "E. M. Forster and T. E. Lawrence: A Friendship." *South Atlantic Quarterly* 69 (Spring 1970): 205–216.

———. *The Wounded Spirit: A Study of Seven Pillars of Wisdom.* London: Martin Brian and O'Keefe, 1973.

Meynell, Viola, ed. *The Best of Friends: Further Letters to Sydney Cockerell.* London: Rupert Hart-Davis, 1956.

————. *Friends of a Lifetime: Letters to Sydney Carlyle Cockerell.* London: Cape, 1940.

Michailovitj, Alexander. *När Jag Var Storfurste Av Ryssland* [When I Was Grand Duke of Russia]. Helsingfors: Söderström, 1933.

Miller, David Hunter. *My Diary at the Conference of Paris.* 21 vols. New York: Appeal Printing, 1924.

Monroe, Elizabeth. *Britain's Moment in the Middle East, 1914–1956.* Baltimore: Johns Hopkins Press, 1956.

Mousa, Suleiman. "The Role of Syrians and Iraqis in the Arab Revolt." *Middle East Forum* 43 (1967): 15–17.

————. *T. E. Lawrence: An Arab View.* Translated by Albert Butros. New York: Oxford University Press, 1966.

Mueller-Wiener, Wolfgang. *Castles of the Crusaders.* London: Thames and Hudson, 1966.

Murray, A. T. "The 'Odyssey' of Homer Newly Translated into English Prose, by T. E. Shaw." *Classical Philology* 28 (July 1933): 275–277.

Nassar, Shakir Khalil. *Lawrence Wa al- 'Arab* [Lawrence and the Arabs]. Beirut: American Press, 1930.

Nevakivi, Jukka. *Britain, France and the Arab Middle East.* London: Athlone. 1969.

Nicolson, Harold. *Curzon: The Last Phase.* London: Constable, 1934.

————. *Peace Making — 1919.* London: Constable, 1933.

Notopoulos, James. "The Tragic and the Epic in T. E. Lawrence." *Yale Review* (Spring 1965), pp. 331–345.

Ocampo, Victoria. *338171 T. E. [Lawrence of Arabia].* New York: Dutton, 1963.

Papen, Franz von. *Memoirs.* New York: Dutton, 1953.

Patch, Blanche, *Thirty Years with G.B.S.* London: Gollancz, 1951.

Peake, Frederick G. *A History and Tribes of Jordan.* Coral Gables, Fla.: University of Miami Press, 1958.

Philby. H. St. John. *Arabian Days.* London: Robert Hale, 1948.

————. *Forty Years in the Wilderness.* London: Robert Hale, 1957.

Pirie-Gordon, C. H. C., ed. *A Brief Record of the Advance of the Egyptian Expeditionary Force: July 1917 to October 1918.* London: His Majesty's Stationery Office, 1919.

Powell, Eileen. "The Position of Women." In C. G. Crump and E. F. Jacob, eds., *The Legacy of the Middle Ages.* Oxford: Clarendon, 1926.

Qadri, Ahmad. *Mudhakkirati 'an al-Thawra al- 'Arabiyah al-Kubra* [My Memoirs of the Great Arab Revolt]. Damascus: Ibn Zaydoun, 1956.

Rank, Otto. *The Myth of the Birth of the Hero* (1914). Edited by P. Freund. New York: Knopf, 1939.

Raswan, Carl. *Black Tents of Arabia* (1935). New York: Creative Age, 1947.

Read, Herbert. "*The Seven Pillars of Wisdom*" (review). In *The Bibliophile's Almanack for 1928.* London: The Fleuron, 1928.

Reynolds, J. S. *Canon Christopher of St. Aldates, Oxford.* Abingdon, Eng.: Abbey Press, 1967.

Richards, Vyvyan W. *Portrait of T. E. Lawrence.* London: Cape, 1936.

Rodd, James Rennell. *Social and Diplomatic Memories.* 3d ser. (1902–1919). London: Edward Arnold, 1925.

Rothenstein, William. "Thomas Edward Lawrence." In *Twenty-Four Portraits.* London: Allen and Unwin, 1920.

Runciman, Steven. *The Kingdom of Acre.* Vol. III of *A History of the Crusades.* Cambridge: Cambridge University Press, 1954.

Sachar, Howard. *The Emergence of the Middle East, 1914–1924.* New York: Knopf, 1969.

Salt, Henry. *The Flogging Craze.* London: Allen and Unwin, 1916.

Sayigh, Anis. *al-Hashimiyun Wa al-Thawrah al- 'Arabiyah al-Kubra* [The Hashemites and the Great Arabic Revolution]. Beirut: Dar al-Tali'ah, 1966.

————. "Ra'y 'Arabi fi Lawrence" [An Arabic Opinion of Lawrence]. *Hiwar* 5 (July-August 1963): 15–23.

Scott, G. R. *The History of Corporal Punishment.* London: T. Werner Laurie, 1938.

Scott, Kathleen [Lady Kennet]. *Homage*. London: Geoffrey Bles, 1938.

Shahbandar, 'Abd al-Rahman. "al-Colonel Lawrence." *al-Muqtataf* 78 (March 1, 1931): 269–276.

———. "al-Colonel Lawrence: Safahat Matwiyah Min al-Thawram al- 'Arabiyah" [Pages Turned Over from the Arab Revolt]. *al-Muqtataf* 78 (April 1, 1931): 426–434.

———. "Lawrence fi al-Mizan" [Lawrence Weighed in the Balance]. *al-Muqtataf* 78 (June 1, 1931): 655–663.

———. "Lawrence fi al-Mizan" [Lawrence Weighed in the Balance]. *al-Muqtataf* 79 (July 1, 1931): 35–44.

Shears, F. S. "The Chivalry of France." *Chivalry: A Series of Studies to Illustrate Its Historical Significance and Civilizing Influence*. Edited by Edgar Prestage. London: Kegan Paul, French, Trubner, 1928.

Shotwell, James T. *At the Peace Conference*. New York: Macmillan, 1937.

Smith, Clare Sydney. *The Golden Reign*. London: Cassell, 1940.

Smith, Janet Adam. *John Buchan*. London: Hart-Davis, 1965.

Spagnolo, J. P. "French Influence in Syria Prior to World War I: The Functional Weakness of Imperialism." *Middle East Journal* 23 (1969): 44–62.

Steed, H. Wickham. *Through Thirty Years*. 2 vols. London: Heinemann, 1924.

Steffens, Lincoln. "Armenians Are Impossible: An Interview with Lawrence of Arabia." *Outlook and Independent* (October 14, 1931), pp. 203–205, 222–223.

———. *The Letters of Lincoln Steffens*. Edited by Ella Winters and Granville Hicks. New York: Harcourt, Brace, 1938.

Stein, Leonard. *The Balfour Declaration*. New York: Simon and Schuster, 1961.

Stirling, W. F. *Safety Last*. London: Hollis and Carter, 1953.

———. "Tales of Lawrence of Arabia." *Cornhill Magazine* 74 (1933): 494–510.

Storrs, Ronald. *Orientations*. London: Nicholson and Watson, 1937.

Sykes, Christopher. *Crossroads to Israel*. London: Collins, 1965.

Taylor, H. O. *The Mediaeval Mind*. 2 vols. Cambridge: Harvard University Press, 1914.

Temperley, H. W. V., ed. *A History of the Peace Conference of Paris*. London: Oxford University Press, 1924.

Thomas, Bertram. *Arabia Felix*. New York: Scribner's, 1932.

Thomas, Lowell. *With Lawrence in Arabia*. New York: Century, 1924.

Thompson, J. W., and Johnson, E. N. *An Introduction to Medieval Europe, 300–1500*. New York: Norton, 1937.

Thompson, Walter H. *Assignment: Churchill*. New York: Farrar, Straus and Young, 1955.

Tibawi, A. L. "Syria in the McMahon Correspondence." *Middle East Forum* 42 (1966): 20–21.

Toynbee, Arnold. *Acquaintances*. London: Oxford University Press, 1967.

'Umari, Subhi al-. *Lawrence Kama 'Araftuhu [Lawrence As I Knew Him]*. Beirut: al-Nahar, 1969.

Ussishkin, David. "Observations on Some Monuments from Carchemish." *Journal of Near Eastern Studies* 26 (1967): 87–92.

———. "On the Dating of Some Groups of Reliefs from Carchemish and Til Barsib." *Anatolian Studies* 17 (1967): 181–192.

Vatikiotis, P. J. *Conflict in the Middle East*. London: Allen and Unwin, 1971.

Villars, Jean Beraud. *T. E. Lawrence or the Search for the Absolute*. New York: Duell, Sloan and Pearce, 1955.

Wavell, Archibald. *Allenby: A Study in Greatness*. New York: Oxford University Press, 1941.

Weintraub, Stanley. *Private Shaw and Public Shaw*. New York: Braziller, 1958.

Weizmann, Chaim. *Trial and Error*. New York: Harper, 1949.

Williamson, Henry. *Genius of Friendship: T. E. Lawrence*. London: Faber and Faber, 1941.

Wilson, A. T. *Loyalties: Mesopotamia*. 2 vols. London. Oxford University Press, 1931.

Wilson, Jeremy M., ed. *Minorities*. London: Cape, 1971.

Wingate, Sir Ronald. *Wingate of the Sudan*. London: Murray, 1955.

Winterton, Lord ["W."]. "Arabian Nights and Days." *Blackwood's Magazine* 207 (May and June 1920).

Wolff, Robert L., and Hazard, Harry E., eds. *The Later Crusades, 1189–1311*. Vol. II of *A History of the Crusades*. K. M. Sutton, general ed. 2 vols. Madison: University of Wisconsin Press, 1969.

Woodward, E. L., and Butler, R., eds. *Documents on British Foreign Policy, 1918– 1939*. Ser. 1, vol. IV. London: Her Majesty's Stationery Office, 1952.

Woolley, C. Leonard. *Dead Towns and Living Men*. London: Humphrey Milford, 1920.

———. "The Desert of the Wanderings." In *Palestine Expedition Fund, Quarterly Statement*, 1914.

Wrench, Evelyn. *Struggle: 1914–1920*. London: Nicholson and Watson, 1935.

Young, Hubert. *The Independent Arab*. London: Murray, 1933.

Zeine, Zeine N. *The Emergence of Arab Nationalism*. 1958. Reprinted: Beirut: Khayats, 1966.

———. *The Struggle for Arab Independence*. Beirut: Khayats, 1960.

# Copyright Acknowledgments

# INDEX

## A

'Abd al-Qadir. *See* Jaza'iri, 'Abd al-Qadir al-

'Abdarrahman ibn Sa'id. *See* ibn Sa'id, 'Abdarrahman

Abd el Kadir. *See* Jaza'iri, 'Abd al-Qadir al-

Abdul Hamid II (sultan of Turkey), 116, 117

Abdullah (son of Husayn), 119–120, 148, 304; and Arab Revolt, 121, 123, 128, 142, 147, 160, 202, 272; assassinated, 309; defeated by Ibn Saud, 272; proposed by TEL as ruler of Lower Mesopotamia, 298; TEL's negotiations with, 308–309; views on TEL, 180, 204; as amir of Trans-Jordan, 303, 307

Abu el Jurdhan, Jordan, 160

Abu Tayi (tribe), 152

abu-Tayyi, 'Awdah, 167, 202, 223, 421; and plan for capture of Aqaba, 152, 177; at Tafas, 235, 236, 239

Adams, Henry, 44

Afghanistan, 377

'Ahd, al- (Arab secret society), 121, 122, 137

Ahmed, Salim. *See* Dahoum

Air Ministry, 378, 398

Akaba, Jordan. *See* Aqaba

Akle, Fareedah el. *See* el Akle, Fareedah al-. *For names beginning* al-, *see under first letter of name following* al-.

Aldington, Richard, 175, 176, 178, 459, 483 n.94; on TEL and Arab Revolt, 488 n.52; on TEL and Der'a incident, 229, 420; on TEL's knowledge of his illegitimacy, 27; on TEL's challenge of Oman's views, 479 n.24; on TEL at Paris Peace Conference, 500 n.23; on TEL's precocity, 19–20, 475 n.17; on TEL and *Seven Pillars*, 501–502 n.42; on TEL and Tafas incident, 497 n.56; his *Lawrence of Arabia: A Biographical Enquiry*, 3, 10–11

Aleppo, Syria, 82–83, 280

Alexandretta (Iskenderun), Turkey, 135, 145

Ali (son of Husayn), 127, 305, 306–307; and Arab Revolt, 128, 160, 202

Allenby, Edmund, 156, 157, 160, 163, 169, 176, 211, 272; and Arab government in Beirut, 255; and capture of Damascus, 167, 168, 170, 171; and capture of Der'a, 164; on capture of Tafas, 236; meeting with Faisal in Damascus, 172–173; first meeting with TEL, 223; on TEL in Arab Revolt, 177; gives TEL permission to leave Damascus, 174; working relationship with TEL, 153–154; and Lowell Thomas, 274, 275; reaction to *Seven Pillars*, 366

All Souls College, Oxford University: TEL's fellowship at, 249, 277, 285–287

Altounyan, Ernest, 40, 81, 86, 89, 95, 384
Amanullah (emir of Afghanistan), 377
Amery, Leopold, 340, 341
Amin, 'Ata, 410
Anglo-French declaration on Arab nationalism, 253, 279, 290
Anglo-Hijaz Treaty, 309
Anglo-Iranian Oil Company, 118
"Antiquarian and a Geologist in Hants, An" (TEL), 22
Antonius, George, 114, 115, 125, 147n, 181, 184
Aqaba, Jordan, 152, 177; capture of, 152–153, 206, 223
Arab, defined, 114
*Arab Bulletin*, 141, 158–159, 205, 487 n.47; Faisal described in, 202–203; TEL's reports to, on capture of Damascus, 167, 169; and *Seven Pillars*, 487 n.48
Arab Bureau, 142–143, 146
Arabia, 119
*Arabia Deserta*. See *Travels in Arabia Deserta*
*Arabia Felix* (B. Thomas): TEL's foreword to, 391
Arab nationalism, 114, 119; Anglo-French declaration on, 253, 279, 290; and Arab Revolt, 129, 176, 290; and colonialism, 116, 117; Husayn and, 119; TEL and, 184, 194–195; TEL quoted on, 250–251; in Mesopotamia (Iraq), 137, 290–291; in Syria, 126, 127, 253
Arab Revolt, 147–153, 147n; and Arab nationalism, 129, 176, 290; background of, 113–129; beginning of, 128; ends in the Hijaz, 153; Great Britain and, 122, 123, 141–142, 150, 153; military importance of, 175–176; *see also* Lawrence, Thomas Edward, and the Arab Revolt; World War I, desert campaigns
Arabs: and the desert campaigns, 160, 162, 163, 164; and Great Britain, 139–140, 144–145, 160; of the Hijaz, 119; and TEL, 200, 202, 206–209, 300, 304, 494 n.37; TEL's postwar interest in, 249–254, 256, 279, 280–281; view of TEL's accomplishments, 179–184, 206–208, 303, 313, 314, 493 n.48; attitude toward Ottoman Empire, 138; and Zionist movement, 159, 256, 260–261; *see also* Bedouin

Arab secret societies, 121–122, 485 n.27
Aref, Aref al-, 499 n.34
Arendt, Hannah: on TEL and postwar politics, 245–246
Armenia, 268
*Army Quarterly*, 293, 380
'Askari, Ja'far Pasha al-, 158, 162, 183
Astor, Nancy Witcher, vicountess, 325, 380, 385, 386, 403, 408; letters of TEL to, 397, 446
*Atlantic Monthly*, 501 n.34
Auda Abu Tayi. See abu-Tayyi, 'Awdah
Ault, W. O.: on TEL at Jesus College, 61–62
'Awdah abu-Tayyi. See abu-Tayyi, 'Awdah
'Ayd, Shaykh, 208
Ayyubi, Shukri al-, 168, 169, 173, 174, 313, 491 n.33
Aziz, Abd el-. See Ibn Saud

B

Baalbek, Lebanon, 152
Baghdad Railway, 80, 83, 103, 104, 118
Baghdad *Times*, 184
Baker, Herbert, 286, 376, 402, 407; letters of TEL to, 320, 325; on writing of *Seven Pillars*, 283–284
Baker, J. N. L., 67
Bakri, Nasib al-, 181
Balbo, Italo, 380
Baldwin, Stanley, 344, 349, 354, 355, 384, 513 n.20
Balfour, Andrew, 9
Balfour, Arthur James, 259, 268, 273, 278, 504 n.31
Balfour Declaration, 259n, 268
Bani Sakhr (tribe), 160, 492 n.15
Baring, Maurice, 403
Barker, Ernest, 54, 75
Barnett, R. D., 103, 482 n.43
Barrow, George, 164–165, 236, 490 n.11
Bassam, al- (friend of Doughty), 94
Beauforte-Greenwood, W. E. G., 388, 389, 408
Beaumont, Thomas W., 96, 484 n.105, 496 n.20
Beaverbrook, W. M. A., first baron, 503 n.4
Bedouin: in Arab Revolt, 148, 158
Beersheba, Israel, 156

Beeson, C. F. C. ("Scroggs"), 21–22, 25; letters of TEL to, 52, 53; travels in France with TEL, 48, 49, 50

Beirut, Lebanon, 173–174, 255

Bell, C. F., 87

Bell, Gertrude, 76, 166, 303, 312, 313, 508 n.20; at Cairo Conference, 301; and TEL, 282; quoted, on TEL, 143, 264, 269; reaction to TEL's articles on British Mesopotamian policy, 292–293

Beni Sakhr (tribe). *See* Bani Sakhr

Billi (tribe), 492 n.15

Birdwood, William Riddell Birdwood, first baron, 147n, 164, 237

*Biscuit* (speedboat), 379–380, 381

"Black Diaries" (Casement), 370

Blackmur, R. P., 373

Blackwell, Basil, 58; on the Lawrence family, 12–13

Bliss, Howard S., 266

"Blue Mist" (car), 201–202

Blumenfeld, R. D., 512 n.59

Blunden, Edmund, 286

Blunt, Wilfred Scawen, 293, 507 n.109

Bolshevik Revolution, 249, 290

Bouchier, Lieutenant-Colonel, 170

Bovington Camp: TEL stationed at, 341–354

Bowra, C. M., 519 n.42

*Boy* (Hanley), 389, 404

Boyle, Andrew, 341

Bradbury, W., 379; on TEL at Southampton, 388–389

Brémond, Edouard, 148, 151, 177, 258, 259, 488 n.44

Bridlington, England: TEL stationed in, 330, 400–405

Brinkley, Richard, 480 n.40

Britain. *See* Great Britain

*British Legion Journal:* prints last three chapters of *The Mint*, 396–397

British Museum, 482 n.43; excavations at Carchemish, 76, 82, 83, 87–88; publishes *The Wilderness of Zin*, 105

Brodie, I. E., 374

Brook, W. H., 381

Brooke, Rupert, 102

Brophy, John, 487 n.48

Brough, George, 450, 451

Bruce, John, 234, 428–433, 439, 441, 523 n.42, 524 nn.57 & 58; and TEL, 430–433, 436, 437, 524 n.55; sells story to

*Sunday Times,* 429, 430, 523 n.50, 524 n.51

Bruce, Mrs. John, 431

Buchan, John, 286, 325, 327, 360, 384, 454, 503 n.4; letters of TEL to, 4, 367, 384; to TEL, on *The Mint,* 372; helps TEL return to the RAF, 353–354; quoted, on TEL, 459–460

Bullitt, William, 265

Burton, Percy, 274, 276

Buxton, Robin, 352, 367, 368; letters of TEL to, 364, 366, 396, 449

Byblos, Lebanon. *See* Jebail

C

Cairo, Egypt: Intelligence Office in, 136n; TEL in intelligence service in, 131–146

Cairo Conference, 299–301, 508 n.20

Campbell-Thompson, R., 79, 81, 90, 93

Cape, Jonathan (publisher), 367, 525–526 n.25; and *The Mint,* 374, 396, 517 n.88; and *Revolt in the Desert,* 358, 365

Capitulations (Ottoman laws), 83–84, 122

Carchemish (Karkamis), Turkey: excavations at, 39, 79–80, 87–88, 482 n.43; TEL at, 39–40, 79–80, 81–97, 102–105

Carlow, Lord, 51, 409

Casement, Roger, 369, 370, 403

Cattewater Air Station. *See* Mount Batten Air Station

Chaignon family, 48, 49–50, 52

Chambers, A. E. ("Jock"), 324, 338, 339, 347, 407, 424; letters of TEL to, 29, 348; quoted, on TEL, 336–337, 442

Chapman, Lady Edith, 4, 5, 472 n.6 (ch. 1)

Chapman, Sarah (TEL's mother). *See* Lawrence, Sarah Junner

Chapman, Thomas Robert Tighe (TEL's father). *See* Lawrence, Thomas

Chase, Harry, 275

Chauvel, Henry, 168, 210, 237; on capture of Damascus, 169–170; and Faisal-Allenby meeting, Damascus, 172–173; and Turkish military hospital, Damascus, 171, 172, 491 n.28

Chingford, TEL's property at. *See* Pole Hill

Christopher, Alfred M. W., 13

Churchill, Winston, 102, 246, 257, 312, 314, 325, 353, 508 n.12; meeting with Abdullah, 303; at Cairo Conference, 299–301; TEL as advisor to, 297–312; relationship with TEL, 297–298; view of TEL, 313, 459; heads Middle East Department, 295; and Paris Peace Conference, 264, 502 n.53

Clayton, Gilbert, 152, 157, 259, 491 n.28; at Arab Bureau, 143; and Arab Revolt, 123; heads Intelligence Office, Cairo, 131, 142

Clemenceau, Georges, 270, 280, 288; and Lloyd George, 263–264, 278, 279; at Paris Peace Conference, 267, 269

Clemenceau-Lloyd agreement, 281

Clouds Hill, 66, 329, 407, 431, 513 n.46; improvements to, 394, 396; TEL obtains, 330; TEL's retirement at, 408; use of, by TEL's friends, 327, 347–348, 399

Cockerell, Sydney, 338, 351, 365; letters of TEL to, 349, 423

Colonial Office, Middle East Department, 295, 297, 298, 304; TEL employed by, 297–310, 312

Committee of Union and Progress (CUP), 116–117; *see also* Young Turks

"Confessions of Faith" (unwritten TEL autobiography), 425

Constantinople (Istanbul), Turkey, 116

Cornwallis, Kinahan, 128, 173, 280, 299, 487 n.47

Council of Ten, 267, 268, 500 n.23

Coward, Noel, 327

Cox, Percy, 138, 139, 295, 301, 508 n.20

Crane, Charles, 278

Cranwell, England: TEL stationed in, 329, 355–360

Cromer, Evelyn Baring, first earl, 123, 291

*Crusader Castles* (TEL's thesis), 45, 52, 54–55, 478 n.18 (ch. 4), 479 nn.24 & 34

Ctesiphon, Iraq, 138

Curtis, Lionel, 26, 102, 189, 249, 265, 288, 293, 347, 398; quoted, on TEL, 447
    LETTERS OF TEL TO, 188, 365, 367, 388: on his illegitimacy, 29; on his motorcycle, 451; on sex, 426; on the Tank Corps, 342–344, 345, 432

Curtis, Mrs. Lionel, 342

Curzon of Kedleston, G. N. Curzan, first marquess, 69, 123, 256, 273, 280, 288, 290, 291, 299

Cyrenaica, Libya, 119

### D

Dahoum, 88, 89, 93, 106, 241; TEL and, 96–97, 98, 192, 224, 310; as a "spy" for TEL, 484 n.105

*Daily Express*, 289

*Daily Telegraph*, 359

Damascus, Syria, 163, 280; capture of, 166–174, 190–191, 240–241, 490 nn.11 & 16; TEL's mission to, 152; Turkish military hospital in, 170–172, 491 n.28

Dardanelles operation: TEL and, 146

Da'ud (friend of TEL), 195

Davenport, W. A., 148

Davies, Peter, 383, 384, 406; TEL to, on his longing for death, 407

Daw, Frederick J., 502 n.56

*Dawn in Britain* (Doughty), 311

Dawnay, Alan, 158, 275, 280, 285, 489 n.52

Dawnay, Guy, 293

Dawson, Geoffrey, 259, 277, 279n, 392; TEL to, on motorboats, 519 n.33

"Declaration to the Seven," 167, 254

Deheer, Ian, 405

Der'a, Syria: Arab atrocities in, 164; capture of, 164–165, 490 n.11; TEL's mission to, 156; TEL's plan for attack on, 162

Der'a incident, 227, 229–234, 496 n.20; effects of, on TEL, 233, 234, 241–242, 419–420, 438, 522 n.7; TEL's accounts of, 229–232, 233–234

Der'a railroad, 156, 163

*Derbyshire* (troopship): TEL's trip to India aboard, 360–361

Deutsch, Helene, 493 n.20

Dixon, Alec, 345, 346, 348

Djemal Pasha. *See* Jemal Pasha

Doran, George, 350, 351, 367

Doubleday, F. N., 261, 285, 350, 385; letters of TEL to, 29, 277, 328, 524 n.58

Doughty, Charles M., 72, 80, 293, 305, 365; his *Dawn in Britain*, 311; death of, 351; and TEL, 47, 69, 75, 94–95, 246, 282, 311; letters of TEL to, 75,

261; TEL quoted on, 294–295; quoted, on TEL, 507 n.119; and *Seven Pillars*, 283, 351; his *Travels in Arabia Deserta*, 246, 285, 294–295, 350

Doughty, Mrs. Charles M., 311, 351

Dowson, Ernest, 132, 133–134, 143

Duncan, Theodora, 177

Dunn, G. W. M., 394, 408

### E

East Cowes, Isle of Wight: TEL stationed in, 395

Ede, H. S., 370, 407, 518 n.29

  LETTERS OF TEL TO, 393, 397: on Hogarth's death, 368–369; on *The Mint*, 370; on the prospect of retirement, 403; on applying for RAF discharge, 395

Egypt, 116, 118, 253; *see also* Cairo; Port Said

Egyptian Expeditionary Forces, 166

*Egypt Since Cromer* (Lloyd), 400

el Akle, Fareedah, 73, 84, 363; letters of TEL to, 96, 363, 366; relationship with TEL, 77–78, 95, 100; quoted, on TEL, 74, 78

el 'Askari, Jaafar Pasha. *See* 'Askari, Ja'far Pasha al-

el-Aziz, Abd. *See* Ibn Saud

Elgar, Edward, 327

el Harith, Ali. *See* Harith, Ali el

el Kadir, Abd. *See* Jaza'iri, 'Abd al-Qadir al-

Empty Quarter (Rub' al Khali), 391, 393

Enver Pasha, 127–128

Erikson, Erik, 459

Erskine, Mrs. Stuart, 204

Erzurum, Turkey, 138, 146

es-Salt, Jordan, 160, 232

*Essay on Flecker* (TEL), 523 n.37

Evans, Arthur, 58

"Evolution of a Revolt, The" (TEL), 148, 150, 293–294

### F

Faisal (son of Husayn), 150, 162, 184, 206, 213, 251, 257, 272–273, 280, 304, 306, 309, 313, 371, 490 n.16, 504 n.31; becomes commander under Allenby, 153; meets with Allenby in Damascus, 172–173; and plan for capture of Aqaba, 177; *Arab Bulletin* quoted on, 202–203; and Arab nationalism, 485 n.27; negotiates possible separate settlement of Arab Revolt, 160–161; urges delay in Arab revolution, 123; and Arab secret societies, 121, 122, 485 n.27; proclaims independence of Arabs from Ottoman rule, 128; in England, 259–261, 281, 357; in France, 258, 281; French intention to impose advisors on, 256; audience with George V, 261; complains of lack of military support from Great Britain, 141; tribes of the Hijaz join, 151; obtains assurance of loyalty from Howeitat, 152; placed on throne of Iraq, 298–299, 300–301, 508 n.20; TEL and, 148, 154, 170, 200, 203–204, 210, 253, 265–266, 301–303, 509 n.60; TEL's articles supporting, 258–259, 290, 291, 298–299; first meeting with TEL, 147, 223; TEL's postwar plans for, 256; TEL sponsors as delegate to Paris Peace Conference, 257–258; professes loyalty to Ottoman Empire, 122, 127; review of Ottoman troops, 127–128; at Paris Peace Conference, 264, 265–267, 269–270, 500 n.23; quoted, on Arab-Jewish understanding, 260; driven out of Syria, 281, 288; establishes Syrian government, 278; proclaimed king of Syria, 288; agreement with Weizmann on Arab-Jewish cooperation, 260–261; meeting with Weizmann, 259–260; and Zionist movement, 259–260, 260–261, 269, 501 n.34

Fareedah el Akle. *See* el Akle, Fareedah

Farnborough, England: TEL stationed in, 336–339

Farraj (friend of TEL), 195, 212

Faruqi, al- (Arab nationalist), 125

Fatat, al- (Arab secret society), 117, 121, 122

Faydi, Sulayman, 486 n.34

Feisal. *See* Faisal

Felixtowe, England: TEL stationed in, 395

Fielden, T. P., 57

Findlay, Charles, 338, 339

Fitzgerald, Robert, 520 n.42

Flecker, James Elroy, 95, 96, 130, 337, 523 n.37

Fontana (consul in Aleppo), 84

Fontana, Winifred, 81, 84, 92, 95, 96, 419

Foreign Office, 272, 288, 289, 290; TEL and, 273, 279–280, 287, 305, 307, 504 n.31

*Forest Giant, The. See Gigantesque, Le*

Forster, E. M., 217, 327, 369, 372, 375, 384, 408; letters of TEL to, 324, 447; on TEL's heroic dream, 38; on TEL at Clouds Hill, 348; and *Seven Pillars,* 349–350, 425

Fourth British Cavalry Division, 164

Fourteen Points, 263

Fowle, Luther, 85, 90, 91

France: Anglo-French declaration on Arab nationalism, 253, 290; objects to proposed British landing at Alexandretta, 122; and Faisal, 258, 499 n.31; struggle with Great Britain over Syria, 267, 269, 278, 307; and King-Crane Commission, 278; TEL's attitude toward, 135, 143, 254, 498 n.25 (ch. 20); mandate for Lebanon, 288; and McMahon-Husayn correspondence, 126; prewar presence in Middle East, 117–118; and Paris Peace Conference, 267, 269–270; and Sykes-Picot negotiations, 125; mandate for Syria, 280, 288; occupation of Syria, 281, 287–288; position on Syria, 151, 254, 269–270; Syrian rebellion against, 307, 315

Frankfurter, Felix, 269, 501 n.34

Freud, Sigmund, 416; his "Psychopathic Characters on the Stage," 472 n.1 (intro)


G

Gallipoli, 122, 129, 135, 146

Garland, H., 148

Garnett, David, 74, 86, 279, 311, 372, 375, 382–383, 393, 426n, 458, 472 n.6 (ch. 1); letters of TEL to, 359, 382

  QUOTED, 327: on Sarah Lawrence, 10; on TEL, 396–397, 459; on TEL's plane crash, 270; on TEL in the RAF, 330; on TEL's sexual conflict, 426–427

Garnett, Edward, 332, 335, 338, 375, 517 n.56; his abridgment of *Seven Pillars,* 336, 359; on TEL as critic, 451; on *The Mint,* 372

  LETTERS OF TEL TO, 446, 447: on the Arabs, 494 n.37; on Der'a incident, 234; on being a hero, 218–219; on Hogarth's death, 369; on marriage, 422; on plans after RAF discharge, 367; on service life, 337, 342; on *The Mint,* 370, 371; threatening suicide, 353

Gasim (straggler retrieved by TEL), 212

George V (king of Great Britain), 257, 261, 360, 409

Germany: and construction of Baghdad Railway, 80, 83, 90, 103, 118; Haldane's peace mission to, 104, 104n; prewar presence in Middle East, 118; mission to Yenbo, 128

*Gigantesque, Le (The Forest Giant):* TEL's translation of, 332

Gilman, L. H., 158, 178, 233, 488 n.52, 491 n.14, 496 n.21

Glasgow University, 384

Glubb, J. B., 176

*Golden Reign, The* (Smith), 378, 379, 411

Goodwin, Richard, 224

Gordon, Charles, 337

Gosse, Edmund, 417

Granville-Barker, Harley, 423, 445

Graves, Robert, 15, 62–63, 72, 73, 181, 225n, 286, 287, 296, 322, 344, 360, 381, 422, 523–524 n.51; his *I Claudius,* 384; his *Lawrence and the Arabs,* 3, 62, 92, 224–225, 276, 367, 368; his and Riding's *No Decency Left,* 389; quoted, on TEL, 95, 446, 475 n.17; and "To S.A.," 310–311

  LETTERS OF TEL TO, 55, 146, 297, 304, 314, 339, 369: on taking alias "Shaw," 341; on his accounts of Arab Revolt, 185; on his motivation in Arab Revolt, 187; on Der'a incident, 233; on his trips to France, 48; on Husayn, 205; on L. Cecil Jane, 62; on his interest in the Middle Ages, 41; on his RAF service, 322–323, 330, 404–405; on his self-denial, 447; on *Seven Pillars,* 482 n.5; on writing of *Seven Pillars,* 283, 284; on the sex act, 422; on his love of speed, 450

Great Britain: Anglo-French declaration on Arab nationalism, 253, 290; collaboration with Arab forces, 160; attitude toward Arab independence, 137–138, 139–140; encouragement of Arab rebellion, 122, 123; and Arab Revolt,

141–142, 150, 153; policy on liberated Arab territory, 161; Balfour Declaration, 259n; and Cairo Conference, 299, 301; "Declaration to the Seven," 167, 254; and Faisal, 273, 298, 299, 301; struggle with France over Syria, 267, 269, 278, 307; defeat at Gallipoli, 122, 129, 135; and Husayn, 120–121, 126, 127, 272, 289, 305; Husayn-McMahon understandings, 123–125; and Ibn Saud's invasion of the Hijaz, 272; support of Ibn Saud, 272, 289, 305; mandate for Iraq, 288; policy on Iraq, 295, 298, 299, 301; and rebellion in Iraq, 291; and King-Crane Commission, 278; in Mesopotamia (Iraq), 129, 290, 293; prewar presence in Middle East, 117–118; policy on Ottoman Empire, 117, 118; position at Paris Peace Conference, 267, 269; mandate for Palestine, 288, 500 n.31; and Sykes-Picot Agreement, 123–125; withdraws from Syria, 280, 287–288; declares war on Turkey, 120

Greenhill (commander in desert campaigns), 277

Gregori (Cypriot headman at Carchemish), 78–79

Grey of Fallodon, Edward Grey, first viscount, 102, 118, 145

Guest, Lord, 312

Guilfoyle, W., 339

Guy, R. M., 323–324; letters of TEL to, 342, 349

H

Hachim, 182

Hadi, 'Awni 'Abd al-, 501 n.34

Hajim Bay, 230, 232

Hajj Wahid. *See* Wahid

Haldane, Richard, 104, 104n

Halim (companion of TEL), 231

Hall, E. F. ("Midge"), 15–16, 53, 58; on TEL and Janet Laurie, 65–66

Hallsmith, Guthrie, 65

Hallsmith, Janet (Mrs. Guthrie). *See* Laurie, Janet

Halpern, Manfred, 115

Hama, Syria, 280

Hamilton, Edith Sarah. *See* Chapman, Lady Edith

Hamoudi (foreman at Carchemish), 88, 89, 94, 97

Handley-Page squadron, 320, 342

Hankey, M. P. A. Hankey, first baron, 148, 407

Hanley, James, 424; his *Boy*, 389, 404

Hardy, Florence (Mrs. Thomas), 10, 327, 344, 373, 447; TEL to, on *Seven Pillars*, 347

Hardy, Thomas, 286, 327, 344; death of, 373

Harith, Ali el, 259

Harlech, Lord, 299

Hart, Basil Liddell. *See* Liddell Hart, Basil

Hashemite family, 119, 123, 180, 253, 313; *see also* Husayn Ibn Ali

Hashimi, Husayn al-. *See* Husayn Ibn Ali

Hassan (killed at Tafas), 236, 238, 239

*Hassan* (Flecker), 337

Hazlitt, Henry, 519 n.42

Hedjaz, Saudi Arabia. *See* Hijaz

Hedley, Coote, 130–131

Hejaz, Saudi Arabia, *See* Hijaz

*Helensburgh Advertiser*, 524 n.55

Henderson, T., 271

Herbert, Aubrey, 131, 135, 139

*Her Privates We* (Manning), 383

Hewlett, Maurice: his *Richard Yea and Nay*, 101

Hijaz, Saudi Arabia, 119, 121, 153; invaded by Ibn Saud, 272; tribes of, join Faisal's army, 150, 151

Hijaz railroad, 119–120, 144, 150, 158–159, 160

Hitler, Adolf, 409

Hoare, Samuel, 339, 340, 341, 349, 353, 354

Hogarth, David G., 26, 58–59, 74, 75, 76, 86, 123, 126, 130, 145, 182, 275, 282, 288, 351, 472 n.5 (ch. 1); and *Arab Bulletin*, 141; and Arab Bureau, 143; and beginning of Arab Revolt, 128; at Carchemish, 79, 85, 94, 102–103, 104; death of, 368–369; obtains Magdalen demyship for TEL, 77; becomes TEL's literary executor, 348

LETTERS OF TEL TO, 135, 349, 365: on his inheritance, 481 n.41; on the Tank Corps, 345

QUOTED, 181: on Arab Revolt, 129, 148, 158–159; on British pro-Arab policies, 118–119; on TEL, 143, 146, 506

Hogarth, David G.
QUOTED (continued)
n.93; on TEL's Arab dress, 159; on TEL during Arab Revolt, 155–156, 157–158; on TEL in the RAF, 340
Hogarth, Laura (Mrs. David G.), 368
Hogarth, William, 59, 102
Holdich, Thomas, 142
Holmes, Miss, 73, 77, 78, 94, 95
Home Letters of T. E. Lawrence and His Brothers, 48, 66; omissions from, 51, 73, 107
Homs, Syria, 280
Hornby, Captain, 148
House, Edward, 269
Howard, Michael, 359
"How Lawrence of Arabia Cracked Up" (article in Sunday Times), 430
Howe, Irving, 249, 459; his "T. E. Lawrence: The Problem of Heroism," 218
Howeitat (tribe), 152, 152n, 156, 180, 206n, 492 n.15
Hudd, Walter, 393
Hurley, W. M. M., 183
Husayn Ibn Ali, 113, 119–121, 143, 160, 162, 253, 258, 259, 292, 313; and Arab Revolt, 128–129, 140, 147; and Arab secret societies, 121, 122; postwar British support of, 272, 289; and Great Britain, 120–121, 122, 126; and the Hijaz railroad, 119–120; and Ibn Saud's invasion of the Hijaz, 272; proclaims himself king, 153; TEL's negotiations with, 305–307, 309; TEL quoted on, 144, 205; TEL designs postage stamps for, 142; correspondence with McMahon, 123–125, 126–127; and the Ottoman government, 120, 121, 122, 126, 127; meets Picot and Sykes, 213; knowledge of Sykes-Picot Agreement, 126, 214
Husayn-McMahon understandings, 123–125
Husayn I (king of Jordan), 309
Husri, Sati al-, 501 n.38
Hussein. See Husayn Ibn Ali

I

Ibn Ali, Husayn. See Husayn Ibn Ali
Ibn Husayn. See Abdullah; Ali; Faisal; Zayd

Ibn Murshid, 182
Ibn al-Najdawi, 232
ibn Sa'id, Abdarrahman, 272
Ibn Saud, 183, 292, 309, 313, 371, 502 n.53; British support of, 289, 305; invasion of the Hijaz, 272; TEL quoted on, 295
Ibrahim Pasha, 116, 502 n.53
I Claudius (Graves), 384
Idrisi, al- (territorial ruler in Yemen), 119, 143
India: and Arab Revolt, 128; TEL stationed in, 329, 330, 362–376
India Office, 272, 288, 289, 292; and Arab Revolt, 141
Irak. See Iraq
Iran. See Persia
Iraq (formerly Mesopotamia), 119; Arab nationalism in, 290–291; British mandate for, 288; British policy on, 295, 298, 299, 301; Faisal becomes king of, 299; TEL quoted on, 302, 303; rebellions in, 253, 291; see also Kut-el-Amara; Mesopotamia
Iraq Committee, 341
Irish Academy of Letters, 393, 446
Isham, Ralph, 286–287, 373, 407, 441; TEL to, on his poverty, 310
Iskenderun, Turkey. See Alexandretta
Istanbul, Turkey. See Constantinople
Italy: prewar presence in Middle East, 118

J

Ja'far al-'Askari. See 'Askari, Ja'far Pasha al-
Jane, L. Cecil, 8, 62–64, 480 n.33
Jarvis, C. S., 179, 491 n.15, 494 n.4
Jawdat, Ali, 183, 237
Jaza'iri, 'Abd al-Qadir al-, 168, 169, 229, 490 n.14; betrayal of TEL, 230, 241
Jaza'iri, Muhammad Sa'id al-, 168–169, 229, 490 n.14
Jebail (Byblos), Lebanon: mission school in, 77, 88
Jemal Pasha, 122, 127, 128, 160, 168, 235
Jenkins, D. W. T., 480 n.40
Jenner, Sarah. See Lawrence, Sarah Junner
Jerdun, Jordan. See Abu el Jurdhan
Jerusalem, Palestine, 157

Jesus College, Oxford University, 56, 479
n.4; Lawrence family scholarship to,
67; TEL at, 56–63
*Jewish Chronicle,* 260
Jidda, Saudi Arabia, 141
John, Augustus, 277, 286, 290, 505 n.75
Jordan. *See* Trans-Jordan
Jordan, Tommy, 379, 518 n.8
Joyce, Pierce, 148, 163, 177, 184, 275,
485 n.27, 491 n.12; letters of TEL to,
374, 446; quoted, on TEL, 132, 161,
201–202
Jubail, Lebanon. *See* Jebail
Junner, Elizabeth, 9
Junner, John, 9
Junner, Sarah. *See* Lawrence, Sarah
Junner

### K

Kadir, Abd el. *See* Jaza'iri, 'Abd al-Qadir
al-
Karachi, India: TEL stationed in, 362–
373
Karkamis, Turkey. *See* Carchemish
Kedourie, Elie, 167–168, 169, 195, 214,
246
Kellett, E. E., 520 n.42
Kennet, Lady. *See* Scott, Kathleen
Kennington, Eric, 286, 297, 310, 335,
345, 368, 406, 524 n.51; letters of TEL
to, 306, 307, 320, 400, 408; efforts to
persuade TEL to publish *Seven Pillars,*
311–312; quoted, on TEL, 233, 295–
296, 304
Kennington, Mrs. Eric, 345, 445, 524
n.51, 525 n.12
Kenyon, Fred, 29
Kerr, Philip, 398
Kerry, A. S., 383
Killua Castle, 4
Kimber, Peter, 493 n.46
Kimche, Jon, 263
King-Crane Commission, 278
Kipling, Rudyard, 261, 281–282, 312
Kirk, George, 115, 116
Kirkbride, Alec, 164, 169, 170, 171, 239
Kirstein, Lincoln, 399
Kitchener, H. H. Kitchener, earl, 105,
118–119, 120, 121, 122, 126, 145
Knightley, Phillip, 103, 176, 182, 409,
497 n.60, 523 n.50, 524 n.55; on Da-

houm as a "spy," 484 n.105; on Der'a
incident, 229, 232; on TEL's fatal accident, 522 n.29 (ch. 32); on TEL's
purported espionage activities at Carchemish, 102, 103; on TEL's flagellation problem, 523 n.42; on TEL's early
military service, 476 n.50; on TEL's
precocity, 475 n.17; on TEL and Vyvyan Richards, 60; his and Simpson's
*Secret Lives of Lawrence of Arabia,*
475 n.5, 523 n.42; his and Simpson's
*Sunday Times* articles, 430, 523 n.42
Knowles, Dick, 360, 443
Knowles, Pat, 403
Korda, Alexander, 404
Kut-el-Amara, Iraq, 137, 138, 139, 211

### L

*Lady Chatterley's Lover* (D. H. Lawrence), 424, 425
Lamb, Pansy, 446
Langley Lodge, 20
Laurie, Andrew, 7
Laurie, Janet, 20–21, 67, 88, 101, 418–
419; and TEL, 64–66; and Will Lawrence, 480 n.41, 481 n.41
Lawrence, Arnold Walter (Arnie)
(brother), 16–17, 72, 155, 181, 238n,
270, 287, 333, 342, 371, 382, 458,
473 n.35, 475 n.86, 493 n.18, 495 n.10
(ch. 18), 497 n.37, 524 nn.51 & 59; birth
of, 6; and John Bruce, 428–430; view
of his father, 13, 440; his inheritance,
480 n.41; TEL and, 15, 16, 17, 84, 93,
152, 155, 479 n.19; letters of TEL to,
52, 84, 93, 157; last meeting with TEL,
406; and publication of TEL's thesis
(*Crusader Castles*), 479 n.34; mentioned in TEL's will, 360; relationship
with his mother, 32, 474 n.50; view of
his mother, 10, 196; and his parents'
situation, 477 n.1 (ch. 3); his letter to
the *Sunday Times,* 523 n.50
    QUOTED, 8, 10, 415, 525 n.68: on
Der'a incident, 232; on TEL, 441, 442;
on TEL's interest in aircraft, 320; on
TEL's choice of alias, 332; on reasons
for TEL's death, 410; on TEL's decorations, 488 n.44; on TEL's enlistment,
310; on TEL's flagellation disorder, 428,

Lawrence, Arnold Walter
QUOTED (continued)
432; on TEL and his friends, 95; on
TEL's friendships with men, 93; on
TEL's audience with George V, 257; on
TEL's negotiations with Husayn, 305;
on TEL and the possibility of marriage,
426; on TEL's medievalism, 41; on
TEL's loss of interest in the Middle
East, 312; on TEL and the Middle
East settlement, 315; on TEL and his
mother, 33; on TEL's patriotism, 192;
on TEL's view of sex, 424; on his parents' religious views, 474 n.70; on identity of "S.A.," 97; on Tafas incident,
238, 239–240, 497 n.54; on start of
World War I, 130
Lawrence, Barbara (Mrs. Arnold), 342,
426
Lawrence, D. H.: his Lady Chatterley's
Lover, 424, 425–426
Lawrence, Frank Helier (brother), 10, 19,
32, 33, 130n; birth of, 6; death of, 136;
TEL and, 16, 93
Lawrence, Montague Robert (Bob)
(brother), 14–15, 20, 25, 33–34, 53, 64,
65, 137, 256, 360, 366, 391, 431, 473
n.35, 474 n.51, 493 n.18; birth of, 5;
attitude toward his family background,
11, 18; omissions from Home Letters,
51, 73, 477 n.30; his inheritance, 480
n.41; TEL to, 364; and memorial to
TEL at Jesus College, 67; quoted, 7,
18; TEL quoted on, 14; relationship
with his mother, 10, 14, 32–33
Lawrence, Sarah Junner (mother), 5–6,
8–12, 12–14, 15, 20, 48, 51, 69, 88, 97,
283, 360, 366, 391, 431, 440, 473 n.35;
Arnold and, 32, 474 n.50; and her
children, 10, 19, 32, 196, 220, 418,
440; family background of, 473 n.35,
474 n.57; view of her family life, 18;
her introduction to The Golden Reign,
379; and Janet Laurie, 65, 480 n.41,
481 n.41; relationship with Thomas
Lawrence, 8, 11; letters of TEL to, 52,
53, 75, 136, 359, 364, 398; relationship
with TEL, 11, 15, 30–32, 33, 99–100,
278, 357–358, 381, 418, 420, 440, 455;
childhood beatings of TEL, 33, 419,
420; attempt to arrange marriage for
TEL, 426; and TEL's memorial service,

410; TEL quoted on, 12, 14, 27–28,
31–32, 33; personality of, 474 n.50;
physical appearance of, 8–9; quoted,
on TEL, 19, 25, 57; religious views of,
10, 11, 12, 13–14, 32, 474 n.70; and
Robert, 10, 14, 32–33; and Will, 16
Lawrence, Thomas (Thomas Robert
Tighe Chapman) (father), 4, 5–8, 9, 11,
12–14, 27–28, 106, 347n, 440; inherits
baronetcy, 480 n.41; and his children,
7; death of, 270; relationship with
TEL, 6–7, 33, 48–49, 270; letters of
TEL to, 52, 70; TEL quoted on, 6–7,
12; TEL's view of, 30–31, 100, 418;
takes name "Lawrence," 525 n.8; religious views of, 474 n.70

Lawrence, Thomas Edward: adolescence,
21, 25, 476 n.23; aliases, 29, 277, 283,
319, 332, 341, 368, 390, 396, 398, 407,
445, 473 n.30, 512 n.10; ancestry, see
family background below; archeological work, see "at Carchemish" below;
fellowship at All Souls College, Oxford, 277, 285–287; awards and decorations, 156–157, 158, 257, 393, 488
nn.22 & 44; declines post of secretary
at Bank of England, 402; childhood
beatings, 33, 419, 420; birth, 5, 18,
525 n.8; at Carchemish, 39–40, 76–98,
102–105; childhood, 7, 14, 15, 18–24,
418; and Clouds Hill, 329, 330, 347–
348, 394, 396, 399, 400, 408, 513 n.46;
studies of Crusader castles, 48–55, 68,
70, 72, 75, 77, 80; personal crusade
(epic dream), 37–38, 99–100; and Dahoum, 96–98, 192, 484 n.105; death,
409–411; education, 22, 23–24, 56–63;
purported espionage activity, 102–105;
family background and his attitude to
it, 3–6, 478 n.3 (ch. 5); family situation, 12–14; efforts to make a film of
his life, 404; bicycle tours of France,
48–52; friendships, 95–96, 327, 396,
398–399; conflicts with Germans on
Baghdad Railway, 91, 104; health, 55,
72, 74–75, 80, 83, 89, 96, 310, 333,
351, 497 n.60; refuses honorary de-
grees, 384; his illegitimacy, 26–30, 477
n.8; impersonator of, 399; inheritance
from his father, 480 n.41; as an Irishman, 393, 446; at Jesus College, Ox-

ford, 56–67; love for Janet Laurie, 64–66; literary influences on, 38, 41–47, 100–102; obtains Magdalen demyship, 77; and possibility of marriage, 426; memorials to, 67; preference for the companionship of men, 93, 419, 424–425, 440, 479 n.19; travels in the Middle East, 53, 68–75, 76, 77, 78–79, 80–81; changes name legally to Shaw, 368; at City of Oxford High School, 23–24; in Oxford Officers' Training Corps, 58; and his parents' situation, 417, 418, 477 n.1 (ch. 3); pension proposed for, 344, 349, 513 n.20; physical appearance, 61, 81, 132, 256, 296, 333, 401, 511 n.7; physical endurance, 38, 200–201, 455; portraits of, 256, 498 n.10, 505 n.75, 507 n.123; efforts to prepare and perfect himself, 24, 37–38, 40, 58, 86, 443, 454; and religion, 13–14, 32–33, 94; retirement, 406–409; use of the name John Hume Ross, 332; and Schneider Cup Trophy Race incident, 380–381; survey of eastern Sinai (1914), 105; threatens suicide, 353, 354; prepares his will, 360; relationships with women, 25, 39, 46, 64, 67, 418–419, 422–423, 440; debate with himself on being a writer, 375

AND THE ARAB REVOLT, 113, 139–140, 143, 147–174, 201–202, 454
accuracy of his accounts of, 184–185; achievements in, 175, 176–186, 491 nn.12, 15; capture of Aqaba, 152–153, 177; hopes for an Arab uprising, 143; mission to Baalbek and Damascus, 152; strategy for British support of, 148–150; capture of Damascus, 166–174, 240–241, 490 n.16; departure from Damascus, 174; mission to Der'a, 156; capture of Der'a, 164–165; Der'a incident and its effects, 227, 229–234, 241–242, 419–420, 438, 496 n.20, 522 n.7; attempts to cut Der'a railroad, 156, 163, 489 n.52; first meeting with Faisal, 147, 223; meets with Faydi on revolt of Iraqi Arabs, 486 n.34; designs postage stamps for Husayn, 142;

mission to ransom garrison at Kut, 138–140; motivation for participation in, 189–197; assumption of responsibility for, 210–215; role in, 113, 148, 194–195, 213–215; stories of, 286, 310; journey into Syria (June 1917), 181–182; accounts of Tafas incident and its effects, 227, 234–240, 241–242, 439; battle of Tafila, 158; reward for offered by Turks, 161, 490 n.16; views on partition of Ottoman Empire, 143–144

AND THE ARABS
adaptation to Arab culture, 68–69; use of Arab dress, 83, 159, 202; knowledge and study of Arabic, 70, 75, 77–78, 83, 89; vision of Arab future, 185–186, 192, 193, 208–209, 249–254, 256; and postwar Arab-British politics, 288–293; intervention in Arab tribal disputes, 212–213; Arab views of his accomplishments, 179–184, 206–208, 303, 313, 314, 493 n.48; at Carchemish, 88–89, 90–91; his role as their "enabler," 198–207; identification with, 68–69, 75, 88–89, 91–92, 106, 195, 196–197, 198–199, 206–207, 239; relationship with, 200, 201, 202, 205–209, 212–213, 214–215, 300, 304, 313–316, 494–495 n.37; his view of his relationship with the Arabs, 192–193, 196–197, 198, 454–455, 455–456

CHARACTER AND PERSONALITY, 40, 133–134, 199–200, 270
contradictions in, 457–458; craze for speed, 161, 202, 450; creativity, 448; depression and despondency, 279, 286, 410; doubts of worth and need to prove himself, 49, 193, 342–344, 439, 447–448, 455–456, 459; need to dramatize and expose himself, 222, 228; capacity for empathy, 445; ability to feel and ability to love, 448, 451; feeling for children, 427, 448–449; feminine side of, 445; flagel-

Lawrence, Thomas Edward

CHARACTER AND PERSONALITY (cont.)

lation disorder, 234, 242, 415, 420, 427–428, 430–441, 524 n.57; ability to forgive, 525 n.25; generosity and kindness to others, 217–218, 323, 365, 382–383, 396, 398–399, 443–444, 447, 456–457; guilt feelings, 321, 439; hatred of the Turks, 498 n.25 (ch. 20); hostility toward the French, 135, 143, 254, 255, 498 n.25 (ch. 20); sense of humor, 85, 92, 134, 189, 287; sense of identity, 199, 444–445, 446; immature behavior, 131; ability to influence others, 131, 188, 458–459, 459–460, 495 n.10 (ch. 18); intellectual abilities, 20; introspection, 242, 456; inventiveness, 363; leadership ability, 106; nihilism, 89, 364, 368, 407, 457; powers of observation, 22; pessimism, 451; fear of physical intimacy, 419, 424; precocity, 19–20, 475 n.17; exaggerated sense of responsibility, 456; self-denial, 447; sexuality, 67, 415–416, 420–426; stoicism, 515 n.27; thrift, 50; vegetarianism, 57

FAMILY RELATIONSHIPS

with Arnold, 15, 16, 84, 93, 152, 479 n.19; with his brothers, 14, 15, 16, 93; with his father, 6–7, 270, 418; with Frank, 16, 93; with his mother, 15, 31–32, 33, 99–100; 278, 357–358, 418, 420, 440, 455; with his parents, 27–28, 29, 30–33, 33–34, 220–221, 454; with Will, 15, 16, 192

INTERESTS AND ABILITIES

aircraft, 320, 330–331; archeology, 22 (see Carchemish); brass rubbing, 61; during childhood, 21–22; craftsmanship, 8, 329; the Crusades, 38, 55; literature, 328–329, 389, 394, 404, 451; mechanical, 379–380; medieval armor, 61; the Middle Ages, 38, 41–42, 45–47, 49, 50, 100–101, 329; motorboats, 379–380, 388, 396, 398, 401–402, 519 n.33; motorcycling, 340, 342, 343, 345, 346, 356, 357, 400, 405, 409, 450–451, 515 n.27; music, 329; photography, 48–49, 334; pottery making, 398; printing, 60, 86, 100, 106–107, 279, 283, 310, 403

LEGEND OF, 74, 221–225, 264, 265, 274–275, 321–322, 458
his attitude toward, 276; his part in creation of, 222–225

LETTERS OF. See names of recipients

MILITARY SERVICE

transferred to Arab Bureau, 142–143; awarded C.B., 488 n.22; in intelligence service in Cairo, 131–146; awarded Croix de Guerre, 156–157, 488 n.44; awarded D.S.O., 158; early (1906), 24–25, 476 n.50; transferred to Egyptian Expeditionary Force, 153; promoted to lieutenant-colonel, 158; nonmilitary aspect of, 132–133; attitude toward his military rank, 255–256; in the RAF, 312, 319–331, 332, 333–339, 354, 355–405; commissioned second lieutenant, 130; in Army Tank Corps, 329–330, 341–354; see also AND THE ARAB REVOLT, above; IN THE ROYAL AIR FORCE, below

THE POSTWAR YEARS (1918–1922)

attacks on British Mesopotamian policy, 291–292; at Cairo Conference, 299–301; as advisor to Churchill, 297–312; meets with Eastern Committee of War Cabinet, 256; sponsors Faisal as delegate to Paris Peace Conference, 257–258; flight with Handley-Page squadron, 270–271, 502 n.56; work for Middle East Department of Colonial Office, 297–310, 312; at Paris Peace Conference, 264–270, 500 nn.18, 23; in Trans-Jordan, 303–304; attack on Treaty of Sèvres, 289–290; see also AND THE ARABS, above

QUOTED

on the Acropolis, 77; on aging, 375, 397; on Aleppo, 83; on his relationship with Allenby, 154; on his ambition, 194; on his Arab dress, 162; on Arab nationalism and a plan for the Arab future, 250–251, 251–252; on Arab Revolt, 121, 140–141, 142, 154–155; on planning campaigns of Arab Revolt, 200; on effects of Arab Revolt, 242; on his motive for activity in Arab Revolt, 187; on his role in Arab Revolt, 153, 214; on aims of Arab secret societies, 122; on the Arabs, 92; on the Arabs at Carchemish, 91; on his feelings for the Arabs, 75, 306; on the Arabs and a "new imperialism," 250; on his postwar aid to the Arabs, 248; on working with the Arabs, 205, 463–467; on awards, 158; on boats, 519 n.33; on the British and the Arab Revolt, 150–151; on the British in India, 363–364; on his popularity at Carchemish, 82; on time spent at Carchemish, 79–80, 81–82; on his childhood, 477 n.35; on China, 366; on Clouds Hill, 348; on his personal crusade, 37; on the Crusades, 45; on Crusader castles, 53–54; on capture of Damascus, 169, 190–191, 240–241; on Der'a incident, 233–234, 419–420, 496 n.27; on Faisal, 204; on his family background, 3, 4–5; on his family relations, 14; on his family situation, 12; on his father, 6–7; on Flecker, 95; on Frank's death, 136; on the French in the Middle East, 281; on Thomas Hardy, 344; on being a hero, 218–219; on views of history, 157; on Hogarth, 59; on Husayn, 153; on his illegitimacy, 27–28, 29; on his inheritance, 481 n.41; on his tutor L. Cecil Jane, 62, 64; on capture of Jerusalem, 157; on his legend, 321–322; on Liddell Hart's biography, 395, 399; on love, 397; on his interest in the Middle Ages, 41; on his first trip to the Middle East, 70;

on his return to the Middle East, 304–305; on creation of Middle East Department, 288, 290; on his early military service, 24; on *The Mint*, 370–371, 374–375, 520 n.63; on missionaries, 366–367; on his mother, 12, 14, 27–28, 31–32; on his resemblance to his mother, 33; on his name, 29; on his *Odyssey* translation, 381, 382, 394; on his parents, 27–28, 477 n.35; on Paris Peace Conference, 261–262, 266; on his precocity, 20, 475 n.17; on his retirement, 367, 398, 400–401, 407; on reviews of *Revolt in the Desert*, 365; on his RAF enlistment, 336; on his need to stay in the RAF, 322–323; on his return to the RAF, 355; on his schooldays, 23; on service life, 324, 336, 337, 392, 404–405; on *Seven Pillars*, 284, 285, 351, 352, 358–359, 360, 366, 382; on Sykes-Picot Agreement, 126; on his service in the Tank Corps, 342–344; on his thesis, 54; on situation in Trans-Jordan, 308–309; on Turkish military hospital, Damascus, 171; on emotional effects of his war experiences, 382, 383; on Will's death, 136–137; on women, 423, 424; on himself as a writer, 423; on the Zionist movement, 252–253

IN THE ROYAL AIR FORCE, 319–331

promoted from AC/2 to AC/1, 368; accused of involvement in Afghan rebellion, 377; stationed in Bridlington, 400–405; at Cadet College, Cranwell, 355–360; applies for discharge, 395; fear of discharge, 391, 403; first discharge, 339, 340; second discharge, 405; stationed in East Cowes, 395; first enlistment, 312, 332, 333–339; motivation for enlistment, 320–322; second enlistment, 354, 355–405; efforts to return for second enlistment, 349, 353–354; granted extension of service, 376; stationed in Felixtowe, 395; his identity discovered, 338–339; journey to In-

Lawrence, Thomas Edward

IN THE ROYAL AIR FORCE (*continued*)
   dia, 360–361; prepares for transfer
   to India, 360; requests transfer to
   India, 359; continuing influence
   on men and bases, 326–327, 334–
   335; stationed in Karachi, India,
   362–373; requests transfer from
   Karachi, 373; relationship with
   men in the ranks, 323–324, 334,
   346, 356, 363, 379, 381; stationed
   in Miranshah, India, 373–376;
   work with motorboats, 388–389,
   396, 398, 519 n.33; at Mount Batten Air Station, Plymouth, 378–
   387, 389–391, 393–395; initial rejection, 332–333; at School of Photography, Farnborough, 336–339;
   at Scott Paine yards, Southampton, 388–389, 391–393; seaplane
   rescue operations, 385, 386, 394;
   presses for service reform, 325–
   326, 378, 380, 386, 392–393; stationed in Uxbridge, 329, 333–336;
   stationed in Wolverhampton, 398

WRITINGS, 23, 106, 246, 293–294, 319,
   328
   "An Antiquarian and a Geologist in
   Hants," 22; for *Arab Bulletin*, 167,
   169, 202–203, 205; foreword to
   *Arabia Felix*, 391; articles on British Middle East policy, 289–290;
   articles supporting Faisal, 258–
   259, 290, 291, 298–299; article in
   *Round Table* on Arab future, 249–
   250; projected biography of Roger
   Casement, 369–370, 403; "Confessions of Faith" (unwritten autobiography), 425; *Crusader Castles*
   (thesis), 52, 54–55, 479 nn.24, 34;
   critique of *Egypt Since Cromer*,
   400; *Essay on Flecker*, 523 n.37;
   "Evolution of a Revolt," 148, 150,
   293–294; translation of *Le Gigantesque (The Forest Giant)*, 332;
   letters of, 319–320; "Minorities,"
   286, 328, 368, 510 n.3; essay for
   *No Decency Left*, 389; "Politics
   of Mecca," 144–145; projected
   work on the RAF, 397, 520 n.63;
   *Revolt in the Desert*, 319, 358,
   365; "Service Life" (last 3 chapters of *The Mint*), 396; "Seven
   Pillars of Wisdom" (unwritten
   work), 77, 482 n.5; technical reports for the RAF, 389, 392; introduction to *Travels in Arabia
   Deserta*, 294–295, 350; "Twenty-
   seven Articles," 205, 206, 463–
   467; *The Wilderness of Zin*, 105;
   see also *Mint, The; Odyssey, The,*
   TEL's translation of; *Seven Pillars
   of Wisdom*
Lawrence, William George (Will)
   (brother), 5, 10, 15–16, 18, 30, 32, 62,
   479 n.24; birth of, 6; visits Carchemish,
   84; death of, 136, 480 n.41, 481 n.41;
   and Janet Laurie, 65, 480 n.41; TEL
   and, 15, 16, 192; TEL's letters to, from
   France, 52; his poem on TEL, 95, 107;
   quoted, on TEL at Carchemish, 91
*Lawrence and the Arabs* (Graves), 62–63,
   367, 368; preparation of, 224–225, 276,
   367
*Lawrence of Arabia* (film), 176, 237, 429;
   Tafas incident depicted in, 234, 238,
   240
*Lawrence of Arabia: A Biographical En-
   quiry* (Aldington), 3, 10–11; see also
   Aldington, Richard
Lawrence Brothers Memorial Scholarship,
   67
League of Nations, 500 n.31
Lebanon, 280, 288; *see also* Beirut
Leeds, E. T., 76, 86
   LETTERS OF TEL TO, 86–87, 94, 104:
   on the Arab Revolt, 155; on the Bagh-
   dad Railway, 103; on his work in Cairo,
   134–135, 143; on Carchemish, 77, 81–
   82; on the capture of Jerusalem, 157;
   on the Turkish Army and the British
   Indian government, 135–136; on Will's
   death, 136–137; on Woolley, 93
*Letters of T. E. Lawrence, The*, 74, 270
Lévi-Provençal, E., 47
Lewis, Wyndham, 516 n.54
Libya, 118; *see also* Cyrenaica
Liddell Hart, Basil, 72, 126, 147n, 181,
   232–233, 255, 258, 307, 325, 327, 399,
   400, 407, 524 n.51; his biography of
   TEL, 276, 395, 399; LETTERS OF TEL
   TO, 14, 37, 41, 45, 70, 145, 146, 310,
   447: on his Arab dress, 162; on plan-
   ning campaigns of Arab Revolt, 200; on
   air bombing, 385; on his departure from

Damascus, 174; on his family background, 3, 4, 40; on his early military service, 24; on his mother, 9; on "S.A.," 224; on his schooldays, 23; on *Seven Pillars*, 282–283, 284, 285; on his love of speed, 450: and TEL, 380; quoted, on TEL's achievement in Arab Revolt, 176

Lloyd, George, 131, 135, 153; his *Egypt Since Cromer*, 400

Lloyd George, David, 264n, 267, 274–275, 288, 293, 500 n.23; and Clemenceau, 263–264, 278, 279; agreement with Clemenceau, 280

Lodge, Henry Cabot, 261

Longford, Christine, 505 n.75

Lord, Louis, 520 n.42

Lucas, F. L., 422; TEL to, on *Seven Pillars*, 358–359

Lunt, James D., 183

M

Ma'an, Jordan, 153, 154, 160

McBey, James, 256

McMahon, Henry, 126, 138, 143, 259, 499 n.30; correspondence with Husayn, 123–125, 126–127, 128; pledges to Husayn, 213, 214

McMahon-Husayn correspondence, 144, 279

Maden, Sarah. *See* Lawrence, Sarah Junner

Malory, Thomas: his *Morte d'Arthur*, 42

Manning, Frederic, 327, 383–384; death of, 406–407; his *Her Privates We*, 383

Marsh, Edward, 372, 391, 424; letters of TEL to, 355, 424

Massey, W. T., 166, 169, 177–178, 490 n.16

Maxwell, John, 122, 145

Mecca, Saudi Arabia, 119, 128, 141

Medina, Saudi Arabia, 119, 141, 147, 148, 160

Mediterranean Expeditionary Force, 136n

Meinertzhagen, Richard, 232, 285: diary of, 501 n.42, 502 n.58

Mesopotamia (later Iraq), 255, 288; Arab independence movements in, 137; British in, 129, 137, 290, 291–292, 293; TEL's postwar view of, 251–252, 280–281; *see also* Iraq

Messham, Florence, 19, 20

Metcalfe, E. B.: on TEL's influence at Uxbridge, 334–335

Michailovitj, Alexander: on TEL at the Paris Peace Conference, 267–268

Middle East Department. *See* Colonial Office, Middle East Department

Miller, David Hunter, 265

Milner, Alfred Milner, viscount, 500 n.23

*Mint, The* (TEL), 188, 228, 328, 335, 372–373, 378, 510 n.3, 516 n.56; last three chapters appear in *British Legion Journal*, 396; TEL considers publishing, 384, 517 n.88; TEL's refusal to publish, 374–375; TEL's view of, 370–371, 375, 520 n.63; reactions to, from TEL's friends, 371–372; RAF men's attitude toward, 335; writing of, 319, 329, 370

"Minorities" (TEL's collection of poetry), 286, 328, 368, 510 n.3

Miranshah, India: TEL stationed in, 373–376

Misri, 'Aziz Ali al-, 120, 137

*Mongolia* (steamship), 68

Monroe, Elizabeth, 126, 267

Morocco, 118

Morrah, Dermot, 285, 286

Morris, William, 42, 60, 106, 360; his *Sigurd the Volsung*, 101

*Morte d'Arthur* (Malory), 42

Mosley, Oswald, 409

Mount Batten Air Station, Plymouth: TEL stationed at, 330, 378–387, 389–391, 393–395

Mousa, Suleiman, 138, 147n, 177, 182, 253, 486 n.34, 494 n.32, 501 n.34; his biography of TEL, 181; and Turkish atrocities at Tafas, 183, 237

Moyne, Lord, 299

Mudawara, Jordan, 158, 160

Muggeridge, Malcolm, 175, 459, 526 n.64

Muhammad, Shaykh, 180

Muhammad Ali, 116

Murray, A. T., 520 n.42

Murray, Archibald, 139, 142, 150, 153, 176; letters of TEL to, 276, 285

N

Najdawi, Ibn al-. *See* Ibn al-Najdawi

Namier, L. B., 224

Nash, Paul, 312, 335

Nasir (sharif of Medina), 152, 167, 168, 202, 259

Nayton, A. F., 206

Newcombe, Elsie (Mrs. Stewart F.), 9, 10, 17, 29, 287, 361, 383, 473 n.35, 500 n.18

Newcombe, Stewart F., 29, 134, 148, 177, 184, 266, 275, 287, 361, 383, 409, 473 n.35, 488 n.14, 491 n.15, 500 n.18; in intelligence service in Cairo, 131; LETTERS OF TEL TO: on Arab Revolt, 150; on Faisal, 203; on assuming new name, 283; on situation in Trans-Jordan, 308–309. QUOTED, on TEL, 92, 103; and survey of eastern Sinai, 105

Newcombe, Stewart Lawrence (Jimmy), 383, 402–403; TEL and, 287, 449; letters of TEL to, 364, 402–403, 445

Newspaper Proprietors' Association, 407

New York Globe, 274

New York Times, 269, 410

Nicholas II (czar of Russia), 138, 146

Nicholson, Haig, 488 n.14

No Decency Left (Graves and Riding), 389

Norman, Montague, 402

Norrington, Flight Lieutenant, 408

Northcliffe, A. C. W. Harmsworth, first viscount, 276, 279n

Northern Arab Army, 169

Notopoulos, James: his "Tragic and the Epic in T. E. Lawrence," 217

Nuri Shaalan. See Sha'lan, Nuri


O

O'Campo, Victoria: her 338171 T. E.: Lawrence of Arabia, 9

O'Casey, Sean, 446

Observer, The, 291

Odyssey, The (Homer): TEL's translation of, 319, 328, 330, 373, 390n, 396; TEL quoted on, 380, 381–382, 386; published in U.S., 394; reviews of, 519 n.42; work on, 376, 380, 381, 382, 389–390

Olden, Major, 168

Oman, C. W. C., 53, 54, 479 n.24

Ormsby-Gore, W. G. A., fourth baron Llarlech, 261

Osler, William, 14

O'Toole, Peter, 234

Ottoman Empire, 103–104, 115–116, 121, 129; Arab enmity toward, 138; British policy on, 117, 118; Great Powers' interest in partition of, 123; Husayn and, 120, 121, 122, 126; TEL's views on partition of, 144; and sharifs of Mecca, 119

Oxford, England, 56

Oxford Book of English Verse, The, 286

Oxford High School, City of, 22–23; TEL at, 23–24, 56

Oxford Officers' Training Corps, 58

Oxford Times, 311, 332

Oxford University, 476 n.30; see also All Souls College: Jesus College


P

Palestine, 125, 288, 500 n.31

Palestine campaigns. See World War I, desert campaigns

Palestine Exploration Fund, 105

Pan-Turanianism, 116–117, 118

Papen, Franz von, 179

Paris Peace Conference, 254, 263; TEL at, 264–270, 500 n.18, 500 n.23

Parsons, Mrs., 402

Patch, Blanche, 328, 516 n.56

Peake F. G., 177, 179, 239, 240, 308, 494 n.4; on TEL and the Arabs, 205–206; on Tafas incident, 237–238

Persia (Iran), 118

Petrie, Flinders, 68, 81, 488 n.31

Philby, H. St. John, 179, 272, 293, 313, 393, 508 n.20; TEL to, on creation of Middle East Department, 288; in Trans-Jordan, 308, 309, 310

Picot, Georges, 213, 256

Pierce, Sergeant Major, 337

Pike (printer), 365

Pirie-Gordon, C. H. C., 69, 74

Plymouth, England: TEL stationed in, 330, 378–387, 389–391, 393–395

Pole Hill, Chingford: TEL's property at, 310, 352, 360

"Politics of Mecca" (TEL), 144–145

Poole, Reginald Lane, 61–62, 63

Port Said, Egypt, 70

Pound, Ezra, 283

Powell, Eileen, 478 n.16 (ch. 4)

Private Shaw and Public Shaw (Weintraub), 391

Prys-Jones, A. G., 480 n.33
"Psychopathic Characters on the Stage" (Freud), 472 n.1 (intro)
Pugh, Sergeant, 356, 449, 515 n.27; letters of TEL to, 360, 447–448

### Q

Qadir, 'Abd al-. *See* Jaza'iri, 'Abd al Qadir al-
Qadri, Ahmad, 258; on capture of Damascus, 168–169

### R

RAF. *See* Royal Air Force
*Rajputana* (ship), 377
Raleigh, Walter, 4, 5
Ramleh, Israel, 158, 489 n.52
Ramsey, Captain, 491 n.12, 496 n.20
Rank, Otto, 495 n.8 (ch. 18)
Raswan, Carl R., 183
Read, Herbert, 218, 219
Rennell of Rodd. *See* Rodd
*Revolt in the Desert* (TEL), 319, 350, 365; TEL's preparation of, 358; published, 350–351, 364; reviews of, 184, 222, 365; serialization of, 359
Rey, E. G., 53, 54
Rhys, John, 72, 73, 75; TEL to, on his first trip to the Middle East, 74
*Richard Yea and Nay* (Hewlett), 101
Richards, Vyvyan W., 60, 68, 86, 279, 360, 481 n.41; his and TEL's printing plan, 106–107, 310; letters of TEL to, 199, 208, 283, 284, 285
Riding, Laura, 448; her and Graves' *No Decency Left*, 389
Rieder, Mrs., 77, 475 n.17
Riqabi, Ali Ridah al-, 181, 313, 491 n.33
Rivington, Mrs. Charles, 320
Roberts, William, 327, 336, 338, 340, 399
Rodd, Francis Rennell, second baron Rennell, 402; on TEL's plane crash, 270–271
Rodd, James Rennell, first baron Rennell, 271
Rogers, Bruce, 373, 386, 520 n.42; letters of TEL to, 381, 382, 386, 388, 394, 408
Ross, John Hume. *See* Lawrence, Thomas Edward

Rota, Bertram, 525–526 n.25
Rotherstein, William, 286
Rothschild, Lionel Walter Rothschild, second baron, 260
*Round Table:* TEL's articles for, 249–250, 293
Royal Air Force, 298, 299, 346n, 385; TEL's influence on, 458; initial rejection of TEL, 332–333; TEL's service in, 312, 319–331, 333–339, 340, 355–405
Royal Air Force Cadet College, Cranwell, 354; TEL stationed at, 329, 355–360
Royal Air Force School of Photography, Farnborough: TEL stationed at, 336–339
Rub' al Khali. *See* Empty Quarter
Runciman, Steven, 44
Russia: prewar presence in Middle East, 117–118, 123; and Sykes-Picot negotiations, 125
Ruwallah (tribes), 160, 164

### S

"S.A.," identity of, 97, 189, 310–311
*Safety Last* (Stirling), 177
Sa'id, Abdarrahman ibn. *See* ibn Sa'id, Abdarrahman
Sa'id, Muhammad. *See* Jaza'iri, Muhammad Sa'id
Sa'id, Nuri al-, 164, 167, 183–184, 258, 493 n.46
Sa'id Abd el-Kadir. *See* Jaza'iri, 'Abd al-Qadir al-
St. Andrews University, 384
*Saint Joan* (Shaw), 419
Salmond, Geoffrey, 373, 395, 396
Salmond, John, 395
Salt, Jordan. *See* es-Salt
Samuel, Herbert, 303, 304, 307; TEL to, on effects of Arab Revolt, 242
Sargent, William, 523 n.51
Sassoon, Siegfried, 286, 348, 359
Savage, Raymond, 350
Sayigh, Anis, 180, 181, 253; on TEL's motivation in Arab Revolt, 194–195; on TEL and the Arabs, 208–209
Schneider Cup Trophy Race, 380
Scott, Kathleen (Lady Kennet), 299, 507 n.123

Scott, Robert, 426

Scott, Mrs. Robert, 426

*Scottish Field, The,* 429

Scott Paine boatyards, Southampton: TEL's service at, 330, 388–389, 391–393

"Secret Life of Lawrence of Arabia, The" (series in *Sunday Times*), 430, 523 n.42

*Secret Lives of Lawrence of Arabia* (Knightley and Simpson), 475 n.5, 523 n.42; *see also* Knightley, Phillip; Simpson, Colin

Secret societies. *See* Arab secret societies

"Service Life" (TEL), 396

"Seven Pillars of Wisdom, The" (projected TEL work), 77, 482 n.5

*Seven Pillars of Wisdom: A Triumph* (TEL), 177, 181, 188, 196–197, 199, 213, 218, 223, 239, 378, 390, 421, 447, 490 n.10; Garnett's abridgment of, 336, 359; TEL's abridgment of, *see Revolt in the Desert;* accuracy questioned by Antonius, 184; *Arab Bulletin* as a source for, 487 n.48; dedicatory poem ("To S.A."), 97, 189, 310; distortions in, 177, 222–224; introduction to, 185, 271–272, 283, 485 n.5; first manuscript and its loss, 282–283; second manuscript and its destruction, 283–284, 310; third manuscript, 282, 285, 311, 321; *see also* OXFORD EDITION (1922) *below;* meaning of, for men in RAF, 335; possible piracy of, in U.S., 350; American rights sold, 350; sexual frankness of, 425; significance of the subtitle, 227; TEL's conflicts and feelings about himself revealed in, 210, 213, 222, 223–224, 228, 456; TEL's view of, 322, 335, 347, 352, 353, 382; value as a contemporary epic, 222; writing of, 59, 246, 282–285, 310, 311, 357, 505 n.60

OXFORD EDITION (1922), 276, 311, 327, 332, 349–350, 351, 352

SUBSCRIBERS' EDITION (1926): design and production, 351–352, 360; final corrections, 357, 358; financing, 352; illustrations, 335; publication, 319, 347, 348–349; reviews of, 218, 365, 425

Seven Syrians ("Syrian Seven"), 180, 254, 279

Shahbandar, 'Abd al-Rahman, 254; on TEL's accomplishments, 180–181, 184; on TEL in Cairo, 131–132

Sha'lan, Nuri, 160, 167

Shaw, Charlotte (Mrs. George Bernard), 282, 330, 338, 371, 378, 386–387, 391, 393, 396, 430, 517 n.56; friendship with TEL, 12, 327–328; LETTERS OF TEL TO, 30, 319, 381, 387, 391, 398, 445: on Allenby, 154; on his postwar interest in the Arabs, 251, 293; on his relationship with the Arabs, 198; on continuing effects of Arab Revolt, 382; on his fortieth birthday, 375; on his bodyguard, 489 n.59; on the British in India, 363–364; on the Cairo Conference, 301; on Roger Casement, 369–370; on his childhood, 477 n.35; on Der'a incident, 229, 233–234, 419–420, 438; on Doughty's death, 351; on Faisal, 302–303; on his family background and situation, 4–5, 12, 221; on Graves' biography, 368; on Hogarth, 59, 369; on homosexuality, 424; on his illegitimacy, 27–28; on being Irish, 446; on Liddell Hart, 395; on his problems with love, 397; on Frederic Manning, 383; on marriage and children, 423; on his part in the Middle East settlement, 314; on "Minorities," 286; on *The Mint,* 370–371; on his mother, 12, 14, 31–32, 33, 418; on his motorcycle, 450–451; on his name, 445; on his parents, 27–28, 477 n.35; on facing retirement, 410; on reviews of *Revolt in the Desert,* 365; on being in the RAF, 322, 323, 324, 356–357, 358, 359, 362, 366, 376; on a projected book on the RAF, 520 n.63; on his schooldays, 23; on his self-dramatizing, 222; on *Seven Pillars,* 233–234, 357; on his sexual inhibitions, 421

Shaw, George Bernard, 221, 303, 312, 323, 325, 327, 329, 332, 370, 375, 378, 386–387; letters of TEL to, 322, 342, 348–349, 448; on *The Mint,* 371–372; plans pension for TEL, 344, 349, 513 n.20; quoted, on TEL, 21, 213, 228, 229, 324; TEL quoted on, 384; attitude toward TEL's RAF service, 322, 339; on TEL's description of Chartres, 51; and TEL's return to the RAF, 354; his review of *Revolt in the Desert,*

365; his *Saint Joan*, 419; his corrections of *Seven Pillars* proof, 352, 514 n.83; his *Too True to Be Good*, 386, 391–392, 393

Shaw, T. E., *See* Lawrence, Thomas Edward

Sherif Bey, 235

Shotwell, James: on TEL at the Paris Peace Conference, 265–266

Shukri Pasha. *See* Ayyubi, Shukri al-

Siggett, Allen H., 263

*Sigurd the Volsung* (Morris), 101

Simpson, Colin, 103, 176, 182, 409, 497 n.60, 523 n.50, 524 n.55; on Dahoum as a "spy," 484 n.105; on Der'a incident, 229, 232; on TEL's fatal accident, 522 n.29 (ch. 32); on TEL's purported espionage activity at Carchemish, 102, 103; on TEL's flagellation problem, 525 n.42; on TEL's early military service, 476 n.50; on TEL's precocity, 475 n.17; on TEL and Vyvyan Richards, 60; his and Knightley's *Secret Lives of Lawrence of Arabia*, 475 n.5, 523 n.42; his and Knightley's *Sunday Times* articles, 430, 523 n.42

Sims, Reginald, 384, 401, 449

Sinai Peninsula, 105

Sirhan, Wadi, 152

Smith, Clare Sydney (Mrs. Sydney), 330, 378, 380, 385, 386, 390–391, 394; her *Golden Reign*, 378, 379, 411; letters of TEL to, 390, 391, 392, 400, 403; on TEL's death, 409–410; on TEL at Mount Batten, 381, 383; on TEL's scars, 511 n.7

Smith, "Squeak," 381

Smith, Sydney, 330, 378–379, 380, 386, 388, 390–391; letters of TEL to, 390, 391, 392, 400, 403

Southampton, England: TEL stationed in, 330, 388–389, 391–393, 395

South Hill, 4, 347

Stamfordham, Lord, 477 n.8

Standard Oil Company, 105

Staples, George: on TEL and Tafas incident, 234–235, 497 n.33

Steed, Wickham, 269, 279

Steffens, Lincoln, 263, 268, 316

Stern, Frederick, 287

Stirling, W. F., 147n, 174, 177, 275; letters of TEL to, 154, 167, 352; quoted, on TEL, 170, 200–201, 491 n.12; his *Safety Last*, 177

Storrs, Ronald, 120, 123, 143, 161, 259, 429, 473 n.35; and beginning of Arab Revolt, 128, 142, 147; on Faisal, 204; on TEL in Cairo, 132–133

Stotzingen, Baron von, 128

Suez Canal, 121

*Sunday Times*, 432, 524 n.55; Bruce sells story to, 429, 430; Knightley-Simpson articles in, 430, 523 n.42; TEL's articles in, 289, 291

Supreme Council of the Allies, 280, 288

Survey of Egypt, 132, 133

Swann, Oliver, 332, 333, 337

Sykes, Mark, 126, 213, 261

Sykes-Picot Agreement, 123–125, 126, 167, 254, 257, 264n, 278, 279; Faisal informed of, 172–173; TEL's knowledge of, 213, 214, 504 n.31; negotiations for, 125, 144

Syria, 122, 125, 126, 128, 151, 255, 498 n.17 (ch. 20); Arab nationalism in, 250, 253; British withdrawal from, 280, 287–288; French demands for new colony in, 254; opposition to French mandate for, 278; French occupation of, 280, 281, 287–288; rebellion against French in, 315; King-Crane Commission visits, 278; TEL's postwar view of, 252, 256; question of, at Paris Peace Conference, 267, 269–270, 501 n.34; *see also* Aleppo; Damascus; Der'a; Tafas

"Syrian Seven." *See* Seven Syrians

**T**

"T. E. Lawrence: The Problem of Heroism" (Howe), 218

*T. E. Lawrence by His Friends*, 23, 74

*T. E. Lawrence to His Biographer, Robert Graves*, 225

Tafas, Syria, 156; Turkish atrocities at, 163–164, 183

Tafas incident, 227, 234–240, 497 n.56; effects of, on TEL, 241–242

Tafila, Jordan, 158, 206

Talal (shaykh of Tafas), 156, 235, 236

Talib, Sayyid, 137, 300, 301, 508 n.20

Tank Corps, 346n; TEL's service in, 329–330, 341–354

Tell Shahm, Jordan, 158

Thomas, Bertram, 393; his *Arabia Felix*, 391

Thomas, Lowell, 178, 265, 347, 503 n.1, 503 n.4; and TEL, 275–276; his publicizing of TEL, 221, 274–275; his *With Lawrence in Arabia*, 275, 276, 347n

Thomas, Mrs. Lowell, 276

Thompson, Walter Henry: on TEL in Cairo, 299–300

Thomson, Christopher Birdwood, first baron, 380, 381, 385

*338171 T. E.: Lawrence of Arabia* (O'-Campo), 9

Thurtle, Ernest, 325, 378, 380; letters of TEL to, 325, 385, 395, 424, 449

*Times, The*, 279, 279n, 291, 392, 504 n.31; TEL's articles in, 258, 291, 298–299

*Times Literary Supplement, The*, 103

"To S.A." (TEL), 97, 192, 224, 310

"To T.E.L." (W. G. Lawrence), 95, 107

Tomlinson, H. M., 294, 375

*Too True to Be Good* (Shaw), 338, 386, 393; TEL's critique of, 391–392

Townshend, Charles, 137, 138, 139

Toynbee, Arnold, 245, 265, 272, 288; on TEL at Paris Peace Conference, 267, 500 n.23

"Tragic and the Epic in T. E. Lawrence, The" (Notopoulos), 217

Trans-Jordan, 303, 307; becomes independent, 309; TEL on, 308–309

*Travels in Arabia Deserta* (Doughty), 247, 285, 294, 350; TEL's introduction to, 294–295, 306, 350

Treaty of Sèvres, 288, 289

Trenchard, Hugh, 6–7, 339, 349, 360, 384, 391; and Iraq Committee, 341; letters of TEL to, 6–7, 313, 353, 362, 369, 367, 374, 376, 378; relationship with TEL, 325–326; offers TEL commission in the RAF, 340; and TEL's entry into the RAF, 312, 320, 332; grants TEL extension of RAF service, 376; and TEL's efforts to return to the RAF, 353, 354, 514 n.60; and *The Mint*, 333, 371, 372, 374, 396; quoted, on TEL, 410; and RAF control of Mesopotamia, 298, 508 n.12

Tumah, Salim, 80

Turkey, 118, 121; signs armistice, 255; Great Britain declares war on, 120; *see also* Alexandretta; Carchemish; Erzurum; Ottoman Empire

Turks, 492 n.15, 496 n.17; massacre of Armenians, 128; offer reward for TEL's capture, 161, 490 n.16; TEL's hatred of, 498 n.25 (ch. 20); atrocities at Tafas, 163, 164

"Twenty-seven Articles" (TEL), 205, 206, 463–467

## U

'Umari, Subhi al-, 181, 182, 183, 237

Unionists. See Young Turks

Union Jack Club, 356, 398

United States, 264, 265; and King-Crane Commission, 278; position of, at Paris Peace Conference, 267, 268

Uxbridge, England: TEL stationed in, 329, 333–336

## V

Valentino, Rudolph, 274

Vatikiotis, P. J., 114

Versailles Treaty, 315

Vickery, Kate, 19

Villars, Jean Beraud, 49, 102, 177

## W

Wadi Sirhan. See Sirhan, Wadi

Wahhabi (tribe), 116, 272, 295, 502 n.53

Wahib (Ottoman representative in Mecca), 119

Wahid (guard at Carchemish), 80, 80n, 90, 97, 104

War Cabinet, 159; Eastern Committee of, 256, 258

War Office, 130, 181, 289; and Arab Revolt, 141

Warren, Aircraftsman, 337

Watts, Alan, 496

Wavell, Archibald P. Wavell, first earl, 170, 176, 178; TEL to, on *The Mint*, 329

Webb, Sidney, 22

Weintraub, Stanley, 392, 393; his *Private Shaw and Public Shaw*, 391

Weizmann, Chaim: agreement with Faisal on Arab-Jewish cooperation, 260–261; meeting with Faisal, 259–260; at Paris Peace Conference, 268–269

Wejh, Saudi Arabia, 150

Wemyss, Rosslyn Erskine, baron Wester Wemyss, 132, 150

Westermann, William, 268

Wigram, Clive, 173

Wilde, Oscar, 32

*Wilderness of Zin, The* (TEL), 105

Williams, A. T. P., 57

Williams, Orlo, 153

Williamson, Henry, 327, 408–409; TEL to, on *Lady Chatterley's Lover*, 425–426

Wilson, Arnold, 291, 295, 298

Wilson, C. E., 141

Wilson, Henry, 508 n.12

Wilson, Woodrow, 264, 271, 278, 281; TEL quoted on, 261; at Paris Peace Conference, 263, 266, 267, 269

Wingate, Reginald, 123, 132, 141, 150, 182, 255; on Faisal and TEL, 203–204; on TEL's mission to Baalbek and Damascus, 152

Winterton, Edward Winterton, sixth earl, 163, 177, 258–259, 298, 299, 357; letters of TEL to, 29, 349; quoted, on Turkish atrocities at Tafas, 237

*With Lawrence in Arabia* (L. Thomas), 276

Wolverhampton, England: TEL's service in, 398

Woolley, Leonard, 89, 96, 97, 428 n.43; in intelligence service in Cairo, 131, 135; and Carchemish, 39, 81, 83, 85, 87, 92, 93, 94; and TEL, 84, 85, 90, 91, 93–94; as "secret agent," 103; on TEL's attitude toward the French and the Turks, 498 n.25 (ch. 20); survey of eastern Sinai, 105, 118

World War I, 130, 250–251; desert campaigns, 147n, 156, 157, 158, 160, 162–163, 164–165, 166–174, 255, 489 n.52

Wrench, Evelyn, 259

Wuld Ali (tribe), 231

## Y

Yale, William, 105, 266, 281, 499 n.15, 502 n.53; on Arab seizure of Beirut, 173–174; TEL to, on capture of Damascus, 171; on TEL and the Arabs, 159–160; and Turkish military hospital, Damascus, 172, 491 n.28

Yarmuk River railroad bridge, 156

Yeats, W. B., 393, 446

Yemen, 119

Yenbo, Saudi Arabia, 148

Young, Hubert, 140, 143, 147n, 177; on capture of Der'a, 165; on TEL, 140, 143; on TEL at Carchemish, 90; on TEL as "secret agent," 103; on TEL in Arab Revolt, 162–163; on Tafas incident, 237

Young Turks (Unionists), 116–117, 119, 121, 128, 253

## Z

Zayd (son of Husayn), 298, 305–306, 306–307; and Arab Revolt, 128, 158, 159

Zeid. *See* Zayd

Zeine, Zeine N., 116, 123, 129, 313

Zionist movement, 159; Arabs and, 256, 260–261; Faisal and, 259–260, 260–261, 269, 501 n.34; TEL's view of, 252–253; and Paris Peace Conference, 268–269

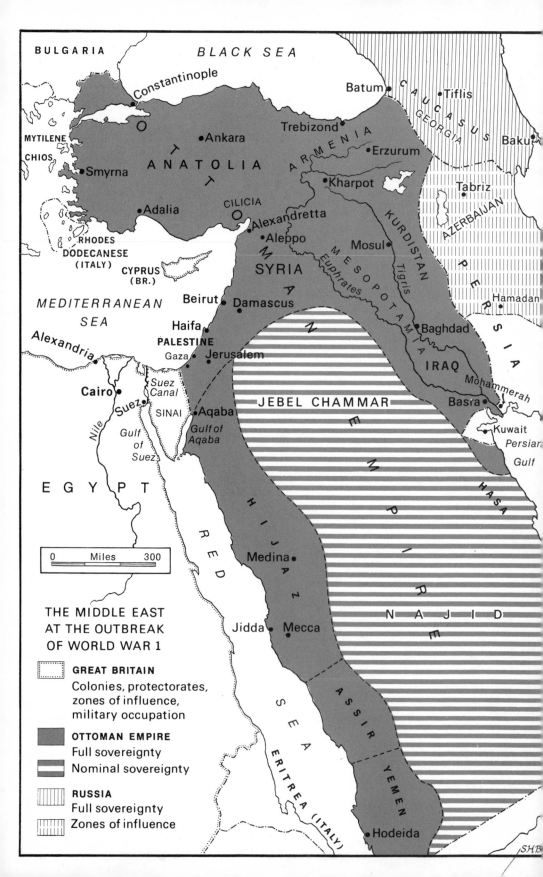

THE MIDDLE EAST
AT THE OUTBREAK
OF WORLD WAR 1